The Women of Warner Brothers

The Women of Warner Brothers

The Lives and Careers of 15 Leading Ladies, with Filmographies for Each

by DANIEL BUBBEO

McFarland & Company, Inc., Publishers
Jefferson, North Carolina, and London

Library of Congress Cataloguing-in-Publication Data

Bubbeo, Daniel, 1958–
The women of Warner Brothers : the lives and careers
of 15 leading ladies, with filmographies for each / by Daniel Bubbeo
p. cm.
Includes bibliographical references and index.
Contents: Joan Blondell — Nancy Coleman — Bette Davis —
Olivia de Havilland — Glenda Farrell — Kay Francis — Ruby Keeler —
Andrea King — Priscilla Lane — Joan Leslie — Ida Lupino —
Eleanor Parker — Ann Sheridan — Alexis Smith — Jane Wyman.
ISBN 0-7864-1137-6 (softcover : 50# alkaline paper) ∞

1. Motion picture actors and actresses — United States — Biography.
2. Actresses — United States — Biography.
3. Warner Bros. I. Title
PN1998.2.B82 2002   791.43'028'0820973 — dc21 [B]   2002044513

British Library cataloguing data are available

©2002 Daniel Bubbeo. All rights reserved

*No part of this book may be reproduced or transmitted in any form
or by any means, electronic or mechanical, including photocopying
or recording, or by any information storage and retrieval system,
without permission in writing from the publisher.*

Manufactured in the United States of America

On the cover: Glenda Farrell in a publicity photo from *Stolen Heaven* (Paramount 1938)

*McFarland & Company, Inc., Publishers
Box 611, Jefferson, North Carolina 28640
www.mcfarlandpub.com*

To my wife, Kathy, the leading lady in my life

Acknowledgments

I will forever be indebted to the many people who helped in the preparation of this book. First and foremost, I must thank my dear wife, Kathy, and my son, Philip, for their support and patience with me, especially in the last few months as my deadline seemed to stretch further and further.

I am also grateful to Dan Van Neste for his help with my research on Glenda Farrell, as well as our long telephone conversations on our mutual love of Warner Bros. movies. Michael Cohen likewise was of tremendous assistance in supplying me with numerous articles about and interviews with Ruby Keeler. Susan Caputo was also a great help in providing me with access to her vast collection of early Kay Francis films.

Several organizations were instrumental in completing this book. Most helpful was the Actors Fund Retirement Home in Englewood Cliffs, New Jersey — in particular, Rose Aster, who arranged my meetings with Nancy Coleman. And Howard and Ron Mandelbaum of Photofest for their assistance in selecting portraits shots of each actress and John A. Johns for donating snapshots from Ann Sheridan's USO tour.

Naturally, this book would have been impossible without the gracious cooperation of the following people who agreed to be interviewed or responded to my queries: Henry Beckman, Rand Brooks, Ken Easdon, Tommy Farrell, Sally Forrest, Coleen Gray, Joseph Howard, Kim Hunter, Sybil Jason, Anne Jeffreys, John A. Johns, Evelyn Keyes, Jimmy Lydon, Karl Malden, Nancy Marlow-Trump, Bob Neese, Robert Osborne, Paul Picerni, Mala Powers, Frances Rafferty, Vincent Sherman, Stephen Talbot, Audrey Totter, Lieutenant James M. White, Robert Wise and Jane Withers.

Finally, there are six special people who will always have a warm place in my heart: Jane Wyman for her critical feedback and clarification of key points in her life; Olivia de Havilland for the extensive notes she provided and for answering my questions and clearing up many incidents that had previously been reported incorrectly; Andrea King and Joan Leslie, who both consented to lengthy interviews on their lives and careers; Craig Stevens, who shared many wonderful memories of his courtship and marriage to lovely Alexis Smith; and Nancy Coleman, with whom I spent many delightful hours in rapt discussion. My one regret with this project is that both she and Craig Stevens did not live long enough to see its completion, but their spirit is found throughout its pages.

Contents

Acknowledgments	vii
Introduction	1
Joan Blondell: "A Studio Dame"	3
Nancy Coleman: "The Fragile Heroine"	19
Bette Davis: "The Fourth Warner Brother"	31
Olivia de Havilland: "The Perfect Lady"	54
Glenda Farrell: "The Gimme Girl"	74
Kay Francis: "Trouble in Paradise"	86
Ruby Keeler: "Those Dancing Feet"	102
Andrea King: "The Femme Fatale"	116
Priscilla Lane: "Warners' Blonde Sweetheart"	130
Joan Leslie: "The Girl Next Door"	141
Ida Lupino: "Mum"	155
Eleanor Parker: "Woman of a Thousand Faces"	175
Ann Sheridan: "The Oomph Girl"	191
Alexis Smith: "The Ice Princess"	211
Jane Wyman: "The Late Bloomer"	228
Bibliography	247
Index	249

Introduction

In the two years that I spent researching and writing this book, there was always one question that everyone immediately asked me: "Why are you writing about the women of Warner Brothers?"

My flippant response was almost always, "Why not?" It seemed better than going into a long-winded diatribe explaining how Warner Bros. movies of the 1930s and 1940s were just so much better than those of the other Hollywood studios. Gritty stories and fast-moving direction gave Warners' films a crisp air of believability that made a greater impression than the lush spectacles of the polished floor variety from rival studios.

Much of the continued appeal of Warners' films comes from the lively performances of the Warners stock company, the most versatile group of actors any studio had under contract. Warners was essentially a male-driven studio, where Edward G. Robinson, Humphrey Bogart, Errol Flynn and James Cagney reigned as the kings of the lot. On the distaff side, there was really only one queen — Bette Davis.

As a result, except for Davis (and possibly Olivia de Havilland), most of the women of Warner Bros. have never been given their proper due by film historians. Books have been written about "The RKO Gals" and "The Paramount Pretties," as well as the glamour queens of MGM, but up to now no one has done a collective set of profiles on those Warners women. And if ever a group of women deserved to be paid tribute, it's the Warners women, who regularly had to fight the studio system for better parts and more money. In Davis' case, taking on her bosses in a highly publicized lawsuit led to better roles. The strategy also worked for Olivia de Havilland; only her best work ended up being away from Warners. Not everyone was so fortunate. Other stars, such as Kay Francis and Joan Leslie, found it difficult to revive their careers after piquing the ire of Jack Warner.

And then there were the ones who never complained, such as Joan Blondell and Glenda Farrell, regardless of the fact that they often made two or three films at the same time. Yet their performances were always bright and energetic, even if they were sometimes so tired they asked to be checked into a hospital out of exhaustion.

Despite the hard work and long hours at Warners, there was a sense of family that formed a bond among all the performers. While some of the people interviewed for this book may not always have had kind words for Jack Warner, they enjoyed working with the casts and crews assembled at Warners. Likewise, social gatherings were also family affairs. If a Warners star had a party at their home, chances are that everyone on the lot was invited. That family feeling seemed to reach out to the audience as well. Unlike glamour queens such as Hedy Lamarr or Marlene Dietrich, the Warners women seemed like people everyone could identify with. Though attractive, Bette Davis wasn't so beautiful that women were intimidated by her; whereas they could also marvel at the elegance of Kay Francis, Alexis Smith or Andrea King. Eleanor Parker, Priscilla Lane and Joan Leslie were the girls that every GI dreamed of coming home to. Down-to-earth types like Ann Sheridan, Glenda Farrell and

Joan Blondell were ones with whom women could envision going out on a shopping trip, or with whom men could imagine having a cold beer.

One of the most difficult aspects of writing this book was selecting the women that should be covered. Obviously, any book about the women of Warner Bros. had to include a chapter on Bette Davis to have any ounce of credibility. Other choices were equally obvious— Ann Sheridan, Ida Lupino, Jane Wyman, Olivia de Havilland. By establishing a cutoff of 1945, I was able to narrow the list to those other actresses who were most identified with the studio up to that point, including Joan Blondell, Glenda Farrell, Kay Francis, Ruby Keeler, Joan Leslie, Eleanor Parker and Alexis Smith.

Perhaps the greatest pleasure was in putting the spotlight on some of the lesser-known Warners women, the ones that deserved to be bigger stars, such as Nancy Coleman, Andrea King and Priscilla Lane, who either didn't get the breaks or became victims of the studio system's sometimes unpleasant brand of politics. All had compelling stories, some of which turned out more happily than others.

There were many other Warners women from that era — Faye Emerson, Geraldine Fitzgerald, Margaret Lindsay, Anita Louise, Aline MacMahon — that I wish I had both the time and the resources to cover. Likewise, the women who worked at the studio from 1945 and beyond, such as Lauren Bacall, Joan Crawford, Doris Day, Dorothy Malone, Virginia Mayo and Janis Paige, also deserve attention. Covering so many women in one book would have made it impossible to do justice to each one. I hope a positive response to this volume might result in a sequel in which those other ladies can also be profiled.

The pages that follow are meant to be a loving tribute to 15 talented women who brought enjoyment to audiences of a bygone era and still continue to entertain new generations today. I hope I have succeeded in covering the lives of each actress, as well as providing insights on their careers and their films. If this book inspires even one person to discover the films of Joan Blondell, Nancy Coleman, Alexis Smith or any of the other women being profiled, then my purpose in writing it will have been accomplished.

Joan Blondell: "A Studio Dame"

Joan Blondell was the dream employee of Warner Bros. She took any part she was handed, never went on suspension, worked tirelessly on as many as four films at once and never engaged in a salary dispute. Oh yeah, she could always be relied upon to give a lively performance.

While Joan was certainly an asset for Warners, her complacency didn't always work to her advantage. Though most of her Warners films were pleasant, easygoing fluff, few are revered by film buffs, with the notable exceptions of the films she made with Busby Berkeley. What is cherished is Joan's flip delivery of even the dullest lines, her youthful exuberance, and her expressive face and popped-out eyes that made even the most brazen gold diggers seem likable. She never became a huge star, but her presence was always an added plus to any movie.

Rose Joan Blondell seemed destined for a life in show business from the time she was born on August 30, 1909. Joan's father, Ed Blondell, had been one of the original Katzenjammer Kids, and remained on the stage, becoming a popular vaudeville comic. When he married Kathryn Cain, his act became a double called Ed Blondell and Company, which toured the country performing comedy sketches interspersed with song and dance routines.

Joan's first appearance on stage was at three months old as a carry-on in *The Greatest Love*. She officially joined her parents' act three years later during a tour in Sydney, Australia. For the next two years the three Blondells performed in Europe and China before returning to the United States in 1914. One of Joan's numbers in the act was something called "In a Rosebud Garden of Girls," which earned her the nickname of Rosebud, which she detested.

Joan grew up in theatrical boarding houses, train stations and dressing rooms. Every once in a while Ed would take a stab at something "respectable," such as the tea room he set up when the family was holed up in Denton, Texas, for a season. When Ed realized he wasn't cut out for the tea and crumpets set, Ed Blondell and Company, which at that point also included Joan's younger brother, Edward, and her sister, Gloria, was back on the road.

By 1926, motion pictures had supplanted vaudeville as the chief form of entertainment, and theatrical palaces were being turned into movie houses. Joan, then seventeen, had developed into a shapely blonde with a Kewpie doll face. She decided to use her physical attributes to good advantage and entered a beauty contest in Dallas, for which the first prize was $2,000. Joan won and used the money to help support her family as Ed Blondell and Company faced lean times.

The Blondells by this point moved to New York where they lived in a small, crowded flat. To help with expenses, Joan took odd jobs at Macy's Department Store and a circulating library. At night she performed for free at the Provincetown Theater in Greenwich Village, a renowned acting troupe where another future Warners star, Bette Davis, got her start. Joan's success with the Provincetown troupe led to a

No one worked harder than Joan Blondell, and no one made it look so easy.

scholarship with the prestigious John Murray Anderson Drama School. Though Joan was honored, she had to turn it down because the scholarship only covered her tuition; plus her family needed her regular income from her day jobs. "My ambition at that time was to make a buck so we could get the act together again and go again," Joan told *Films in Review* in 1972.

Realizing that the death of vaudeville also meant the end of Ed Blondell and Company, Joan struck out on her own. She landed a small part in *Tarnish* in 1927, which led to a featured role in the Chicago production of *The Trial of Mary Dugan*, with Ann Harding. She spent most of the next two years traveling the subway circuit in *My Girl Friday* and *This Thing Called Love*.

Joan's big break came in October of 1929 when she won a showy role in the serio-comedy *Maggie the Magnificent*, written and directed by George Kelly. Joan was the brassy, gum-chewing wife of a bootlegger, played by an up-and-comer named James Cagney. Although both Joan and Cagney earned excellent reviews, they were victims of bad timing. *Maggie the Magnificent* opened during the week of the stock market crash and closed three weeks later.

Both performers made enough of an impression that they were quickly reteamed in a new show, *Penny Arcade*, a strong drama about the seamy side of Coney Island. Cagney played an underworld thug, and Joan was a photographer's sassy assistant. Once again the two performers were singled out by critics, and once again the show closed in three weeks. They found a savior in Al Jolson, who purchased the rights and sold them to Warner Bros. He also suggested to Jack Warner that he hire Joan and Cagney to repeat their stage roles for the film.

In typical Hollywood fashion, Warners changed the title to the more lurid *Sinners Holiday* (1930), which Cagney said "had as much to do with the picture as Winnie-the-Pooh." Warners also decided Joan and Cagney weren't marquee names, and they were replaced by Grant Withers and Evelyn Knapp. The two newcomers were relegated to supporting roles.

By the second day of shooting, Warners brass were so impressed with the snappy delivery of Joan and Cagney that they were offered five-year contracts. For Joan, the deal came with one condition: "They wanted to change my name to, hold everything ... Inez Holmes."

Joan refused, and after much debate, the studio backed off, to her relief. "I was scared almost out of my wits they wouldn't give me that five-year contract," she said.

Even though *Sinners Holiday* was the first feature Joan filmed, her second movie, *The Office Wife* (1930), was the one in which audiences got their first glimpse of her. Dorothy Mackaill was top billed, and she and Joan played sisters who work in the same office and dally with their married employer (Lewis Stone).

In 1931 Warners certainly got their money's worth — which wasn't a lot — out of Joan by tossing her into ten films. Most of these had pithy titles such as *Illicit*, *Millie* (on loan to RKO), *My Past*, *God's Gift to Women*, *Other Men's Women*, *Big Business Girl*, *Night Nurse* and *The Reckless Hour*. In all of these she had supporting roles, usually playing the best friend to stars like Barbara Stanwyck, Helen Twelvetrees and Loretta Young. Joan's best roles that year were in two more with Cagney: the gangster epic *Public Enemy,* and the snappy comedy *Blonde Crazy.*

"I just sailed through things, took the scripts I was given, did what I was told. I couldn't afford to go on suspension — my family needed what I could make. For five people you gotta make money, even though it's small money. I was most grateful to be making it," she said in *Films in Review.*

Joan cranked out ten more films in 1932, although at least she was now beginning to get more lead assignments. Her first effort that year, *Union Depot,* traced the stories of a myriad of characters at a railroad terminal à la MGM's *Grand Hotel* (1932). Joan gave her usual peppy performance as a chorus girl who becomes involved with a thief (Douglas Fairbanks, Jr.).

On loan to Samuel Goldwyn, Joan had one of her best early roles, as Schatze, the gold digger with a heart of gold in *The Greeks Had a Word for Them* (1932). The plot about three party girls (Madge Evans and Ina Claire were the others) seeking rich husbands was hardly novel, but it benefited from a smart screenplay by Sidney Howard, who adapted Zoe Akins' play.

During production of *The Greeks Had a Word for Them,* Joan began a romance with the film's cinematographer, George Barnes, who was sixteen years older than she and had been thrice-married. Joan became wife number four on August 5, 1933, but due to legal entanglements concerning Barnes' previous divorce, they had a second ceremony on January 4, 1934.

Considering how busy Warners kept Joan, it was amazing that she found time to date anyone. She was excellent once again sparring with Cagney in *The Crowd Roars* (1932), an exciting auto racing yarn directed by Howard Hawks. In *The Famous Ferguson Case* (1932) she played a newspaper sob sister covering a murder. She was delightful as a silent screen actress in *Make Me a Star* (1932) for Paramount, which also featured Stuart Erwin, ZaSu Pitts and Ben Turpin. *Miss Pinkerton* (1932) found Joan as a nurse investigating a murder, and in *Big City Blues* (1932) she helped country bumpkin Eric Linden clear himself of a murder.

In general, most of Joan's films of this period were in the sixty- to seventy-minute range, filmed in the Warners assembly-line style. Whatever the films may have lacked in production values, they made up for in crisp, fast-paced direction, sharp screenplays and the rapid-fire delivery of the Warners stock company, which included Glenda Farrell, Frank McHugh, Ruth Donnelly, Allen Jenkins, Hugh Herbert and Guy Kibbee. Joan fit right in.

"I knew everybody in the cast. It was like working with your brother or sister," she said.

That camaraderie extended to the directors and technicians that also worked on these films. "Guys like Lloyd Bacon, John Adolfi and Ray Enright were terrific directors, even though their budgets didn't let them do things they wanted to do," said Joan in *Films in Review.* "Even though they were saddled with us, just as we actors were saddled with them, the all-important compulsion was to finish on schedule and under budget."

Three on a Match (1932), for director Mervyn LeRoy, is a prime example of the Warners programmer done at top efficiency. LeRoy and screenwriter Lucien Hubbard managed to cram as much drama, sex and corruption as possible into sixty-three minutes, and the result was far more memorable than many bigger budget films that ran twice as long. Joan, Ann Dvorak and Bette Davis played former classmates whose paths cross again as adults. Filmed two years before the Production Code was established, *Three on a Match* is fascinating for its graphic depiction of Dvorak's downward spiral from rich bitch to guttersnipe and cocaine addict. Joan had a less flamboyant role than Dvorak, but was still interesting as Mary, who rises from ex-con to become the new wife to Dvorak's ex-husband (Warren William).

Only Davis seemed to fare poorly in the underwritten and almost nonexistent role of Ruth. Throughout filming of *Three on a Match,* LeRoy went out of his way to tell Joan what a bright future he saw for her, whereas he pointedly ignored Davis. Joan, however, became good friends with her co-star and respected her for standing up to the Warners brass to get better parts.

"I guess I was what they call a studio dame. The *brilliant* thing — making the front office aware that *you're* the one in front of the camera, *you're* the one who makes what people pay to see — I didn't think that way," she said in 1972. "I never fought for better roles, and became known as 'one-take Blondell.' But I admire Bette Davis for fighting. She fought every inch of the way."

Joan finished out 1932 in two more zippy Warners films: *Central Park*, in which she and Wallace Ford played a hungry couple who get mixed up with gangsters and an escaped lion; and *Lawyer Man*, where she was outstanding as the faithful secretary of an honest attorney (William Powell) who discovers he can be more successful by breaking a few laws.

At one point the dizzying pace was so bad that Joan checked into the hospital, suffering from exhaustion, and slept for forty-eight hours. After her hospital stay, Joan took on a lighter workload — in 1933 she only made seven pictures. *Broadway Bad* (1933) at Fox lived up to its title; but she was in good form, and tougher than usual, as a gangster in *Blondie Johnson* (1933).

As a reward for her hard work, Joan headlined the big budget *Gold Diggers of 1933* (1933), which came on the heels of Warners' smash *42nd Street* (1933). Like its predecessor, *Gold Diggers of 1933* benefited from dance director Busby Berkeley's eye-popping production numbers and featured musical sweethearts Dick Powell and Ruby Keeler. Joan, Warren William, Aline MacMahon, Ginger Rogers, Guy Kibbee and Ned Sparks delivered the zippy one-liners when the music wasn't playing. Joan played a chorus girl out to fleece stuffy businessman William, who thinks all showgirls are "cheap and vulgar." Instead, she falls for him.

The high point was the stirring "Remember My Forgotten Man," Berkeley's paean to unemployed World War veterans now fighting the war of poverty. Though Joan was not a trained singer, Berkeley knew she could give the number the heartfelt delivery it needed. Joan, as a streetwalker, talks through the song as she stands beneath a streetlight. The number gets more intense as one hundred and fifty extras, dressed as soldiers, are shown marching in a huge half-wheel contraption, followed by a cutaway to those same soldiers receiving food at a breadline. At the end, Joan is heard again (her singing dubbed by Etta Moen) delivering her torchy plea to "Remember My Forgotten Man." Gritty and honest, the number was a well-conceived blending of Berkeley's genius for staging musical entertainment and an important social commentary.

Joan and William were reteamed for *Goodbye Again* (1933), a comedy directed by Michael Curtiz about a novelist (William) who becomes the amorous target of several women during a book tour but remains oblivious to his adoring secretary (Joan). In a 1969 interview with Leonard Maltin, Joan remembered Curtiz as "a cruel man, sadistic with animals and actors, and he swung that whip around pretty good. He overworked everyone. But he was amusing, and he turned out some good pictures."

Footlight Parade (1933), which followed, had Joan back with Cagney and director Lloyd Bacon in the best of the Busby Berkeley–staged Warners musicals. The film was essentially a showcase for Cagney, who played a theatrical producer whose ideas are being stolen by a competitor. Joan was his lovesick secretary, whom he only thinks of as a good friend.

Havana Widows (1933) was an amusing if conventional comedy that was important as the first of many pairings with Joan and Glenda Farrell, Warners' favorite wise-cracking tootsie. The plot wasn't very different from the other films they'd go on to make: They played gold diggers on the prowl, out to fleece a rich sugar daddy (Guy Kibbee). The film's chief asset was the sassy interplay between Joan and Glenda, who became lifelong friends. Both spent many hours socializing at each other's homes or engaging in their favorite pastime — shopping.

"The thing I remember most about Joan Blondell was that she used to love to laugh," said Tommy Farrell, Glenda's son. "She had a great sense of humor and she would just laugh at everything. We always had a great time with her."

Warners decided Joan's fun-loving attitude would be perfect for *Convention City* (1933), a risqué comedy about executives from a rubber factory who go in for some frolicking during a convention in Atlantic City. Joan was once again a gold digger and Kibbee her prime target.

Variety called *Convention City* "one of the few comedies that can truthfully be called positive entertainment." Unfortunately, the film has since become high on cinephiles' list of lost movies. Interest in the film has been piqued by its supposedly racy content, which inspired Jack Warner to compose the following memo: "I just saw '*Convention City*.' You've got to cover up those ... [breasts] of Joan Blondell, or they're going to shut us down every place we play."

Joan whiled away in *I've Got Your Number* (1934), *He Was Her Man* (1934) and *Smarty* (1934) before getting the spotlight role in *Dames* (1934), another Busby Berkeley spectacular. As a showgirl who blackmails prudish Guy Kibbee into backing a show featuring his daughter (Ruby Keeler), Joan sparkled. She was at her best in the novelty number "The Girl at the Ironing Board," in which she played a laundress singing the praises of the men's undies she washes. Joan's playfulness prompted *Photoplay* to cite that she gave *Dames* "the snap it needs."

Kansas City Princess (1934), which followed, was one of the funniest of the Blondell-Farrell pairings; in it they play manicurists out to snare rich husbands. Critic Lionel Collier noted of their pairing that it was "something of a stroke of genius, and the pictures they have made together always reach a level of infectious mirth that it is impossible to resist."

Joan then took some time off when her son Norman Scott Barnes was born in November of 1934—not that impending motherhood had slowed down her work pace. She made seven films during her pregnancy and continued working until her seventh month, which prompted her directors to be creative about hiding her condition. "They kept shooting me higher and higher. They had me in back of everything—desks, barrels, anything," Joan said.

Joan's maternity leave was short, but she was now making only five movies per year. Her 1935 output included *The Traveling Saleslady*, an amusing effort with Farrell; *Broadway Gondolier*, with Dick Powell; and *We're in the Money* and *Miss Pacific Fleet*, both with Farrell.

Just a few months after Norman's birth, Joan divorced Barnes on grounds of mental cruelty. She claimed that he would read books and newspapers while she had guests in the house "and otherwise humiliated her."

It wasn't long after her divorce when she began dating Dick Powell, and their romance intensified while they made *Colleen* (1936), although Ruby Keeler was the object of his affections on screen. Joan played a blonde cutie out to charm millionaire Hugh Herbert.

Sons o' Guns (1936) was a poor Joe E. Brown comedy set in World War I France, with Joan miscast as the mademoiselle of his affections. *The New York Times* commented that Joan was "guilty, it might be said in passing, of one of the most atrocious French accents that has been encountered since we left high school." She was better as the runner of a numbers game in *Bullets or Ballots* (1936), a tough crime drama with Edward G. Robinson and Humphrey Bogart.

Shortly after the release of *Bullets or Ballots*, Joan and Powell were married on September 19, 1936, in a shipboard ceremony on the Santa Paula in the harbor at San Pedro, California. Actor Regis Toomey was Powell's best man, and Joan's sister Gloria served as maid of honor. For their honeymoon, the couple traveled through the Panama Canal.

The timing was perfect as far as Warners was concerned, since their marriage gave *Stage Struck* (1936) a much-needed box-office lift. In this takeoff on *42nd Street*, Joan gave one of her best performances as a temperamental star who makes life hell for her producer (Powell).

She was even better in *Three Men on a Horse* (1936), an enjoyable film version of the hit play by John Cecil Holm and George Abbott about a writer (Frank McHugh) of greeting card verses who's better at picking winners at the racetrack.

Joan and Dick worked together for the first time as husband and wife in *Gold Diggers of 1937* (1936), a weak entry in the series, which was highlighted by "All is Fair in Love and War." The Berkeley spectacle had Dick and Joan leading opposing armies in the battle of the sexes.

The Powells shared a large bungalow on the Warners lot. Visitors had no problem figuring out which half was Dick's—corresponding clothes and shoes, shaving materials and toiletries were all neatly stored. Joan, by contrast, had shoes and undergarments scattered over chairs and on the floor, and cigarette butts thrown into the most readily accessible receptacle.

Joan made only three films at Warners in 1937: *The King and the Chorus Girl* (1937), an entertaining comedy in which she charmingly played a member of the Folies Bergere who catches the attention of a royal (Fernand Gravet); *Back in Circulation* (1937), a newspaper yarn with George Brent; and *The Perfect Specimen* (1937), a comedy with Errol Flynn in the title role.

"Oh, I loved Errol," Joan told Leonard Maltin in 1971. "He was a dear friend of mine and quite unlike his publicity.... He most of all was just a guy who liked to tell stories, have fun, have some drinks and be with his friends."

Producer Walter Wanger then borrowed Joan for *The Stand-In* (1937), his witty satire on the movie industry, with Leslie Howard as a numbers cruncher who takes over a Hollywood studio. Joan was excellent as the secretary who helps him learn the business. Also in the cast was Humphrey Bogart, on loan from Warners, and surprisingly funny as a director.

Joan ranked *The Stand-In* among her favorite films, and cited Tay Garnett as one of the best directors she worked with. "I love Tay. He knows what he wants and he lets you go," Joan told Maltin.

Unfortunately, neither Joan nor Howard were strong box-office names, and *The Stand-In* faced a rough time at the box office. In several cities it was shown with a live vaudeville show and was never reviewed. Only in Boston, on a double bill with *Navy Blue and Gold* (1937), a football yarn starring James Stewart and Robert Young, did *The Stand-In* play to full houses.

Joan fared better with *There's Always a Woman* (1938), opposite Melvyn Douglas, for Columbia. One of the best of the many *Thin Man* imitations the studios turned out in the '30s, it had Joan as a dizzy version of Nora Charles, who takes over her husband's dismal detective agency when he decides to go back to work for the District Attorney's office.

Joan and Douglas had a breezy, sexy rapport, and the film was a winner for Columbia. The studio immediately announced a sequel, *There's That Woman Again* (1939), but because Joan was pregnant, her part was taken over by Virginia Bruce.

Dick had adopted Norman shortly after he and Joan were married. With the arrival of their second child, Ellen, on June 30, 1938, Joan, more than ever, wanted to spend more time with her family. She made the low-budget *Off the Record* (1939) at Warners, and then went to Universal for *East Side of Heaven* (1939) with Bing Crosby, whom she remembered as aloof.

Her nine years at Warners wrapped up with the poor boxing comedy *The Kid from Kokomo* (1939), with Pat O'Brien and Wayne Morris. Dick's contract was about to terminate, "So," recalled Joan, "when he said 'Let's leave, we'll do better,' I agreed immediately." As a farewell gesture, Joan and Dick treated everyone on the Warners lot to lunch in the commissary.

Anxious to duplicate the success of *There's Always a Woman*, Columbia reteamed Joan and Melvyn Douglas in the enjoyable *Good Girls Go to Paris* (1939), about a waitress who'll do anything to get a trip to Paris. The film was originally called *Good Girls Go to Paris, Too*, but censors objected to the implications of the last word.

Following *The Amazing Mr. Williams* (1939), another amusing entry with Douglas, Joan made *Two Girls on Broadway* (1940), a mediocre reworking of *The Broadway Melody* (1929), with Joan and Lana Turner as sisters in love with a dancer (George Murphy).

In general, her films of this period seemed no more or less distinguished than her Warners entries, but Joan didn't seem to mind. "I wasn't that ambitious," Joan admitted to Maltin. "I enjoyed a home life more than a theatrical career. I just took what they gave me because I wanted to get home quickly."

Joan lived for Sunday, her day off. She and Dick rarely ventured out of the house, and instead spent the day reading the newspaper, playing with their children and grilling hamburgers. "That's the way we live, like any other family," Joan told a *New York Times* reporter. "You'd be surprised how easy it is in Hollywood. It's nothing like as complicated a place as people say."

It seemed ironic that after Joan's description of the Powells home life that the couple should choose *I Want a Divorce* (1940) as their next co-starring venture. Soon after doing that film, Joan agreed to star in an already popular radio program, also called *I Want a Divorce*, which bore no resemblance to the film. *I Want a Divorce* was an anthology series in which Joan played a different heroine each week, one whose problems were resolved by the end of the half hour.

Joan admitted that many of the scripts for the radio show were "corny," such as one in which she was newly married to a man whose grown-up son hated her. In the midst of this family crisis, a flood swept through their town and everyone had to swim out of the house.

Joan had to breathe heavily into the microphone to make it sound as if she was drowning.

Despite the frequently ridiculous plots, the show was a hit, and Joan felt energized by the challenge of radio acting. "You forget all about real acting in pictures. You have to concentrate for one minute and then you have perhaps a couple of hours' rest. You have no worries about timing or anything else, for the directors, the cameramen do it all for you," she told *The New York Times*. "But on the radio you have got to be alert; you have to prepare as well as execute whatever evolutions the script calls for."

Joan took time off from her radio venture to shoot *Topper Returns* (1941), the spirited second sequel to *Topper* (1937), in which she played a sexy ghost who enlists the help of staid banker Cosmo Topper (Roland Young) to find her murderer. She also joined Dick for *Model Wife* (1941) at Universal, a bright comedy about newlyweds trying to keep their marriage a secret.

The Powells worked that summer on *Miss Pinkerton Inc.*, a detective series that ran on NBC radio. Joan played Mary Vance, a law school graduate who inherits her uncle's detective agency and finds herself pitted against seemingly tough New York police sergeant Dennis Murray (Dick). Joan was her usual sexy, wise-cracking self, and was delightful in the series.

After two more undistinguished Bs — *Three Girls About Town* (1941) at Columbia and *Lady for a Night* (1942) at lowly Republic — Joan left Dick and the children in California to spend six months in 1942 visiting nearly 7,000 U.S. army camps with a six-a-day USO vaudeville unit.

She then spent the next three months touring the frigid North Atlantic with a solo fifteen-minute song-and-dance act she put together. The first half was all jokes and GI patter, but it was the second part, a rather tame striptease, that garnered attention. For the strip, Joan wore a sexy costume with strapless shoulders. She shed various portions of the outfit while cavorting onstage to a tune which related how she always wanted to be air-conditioned. The running gag was that all of her zippers got stuck, and she would invite some of the GIs onstage to help her out. No matter how hard they tugged, the zippers never unzipped. The act was a sensation at every camp.

Joan went beyond the call of duty during her army visits. She ate with the boys, talked with them, danced with them, wrote their letters and even let them cut off locks of her hair to send back home. She fired their guns, rode in their planes and once even made a parachute jump.

Even after she returned to Hollywood in early 1943, Joan received thousands of letters from soldiers she visited during her tour. She also made about 1,500 phone calls to families of the soldiers she met, especially those who had written too few letters back home.

Joan returned to the screen in *Cry Havoc* (1943), a first-rate war drama about a group of stranded females on the island of Bataan who volunteer as army nurses; it seemed made to order. In a top-flight cast that included Margaret Sullavan, Ann Sothern, Fay Bainter and Marsha Hunt, Joan was the standout. As a burlesque queen drafted into duty, Joan offered a glimmer of her USO act by doing a mock striptease to boost the morale of her fellow nurses during enemy fire. The film served as the beginning of Joan's transition from leading lady to character player.

One admirer who was bowled over by Joan's burlesque routine in *Cry Havoc* was Broadway producer Mike Todd, who wanted her to play Ethel Merman's role in the national company of *Something for the Boys*. Joan headed east to test for the part, but her inability to belt out a tune in Merman's flashy style cost her the role. Instead, Todd developed a show especially for her: *The Naked Genius*, a comedy about a burlesque stripper who fancies herself as an author. The play was written by Gypsy Rose Lee and staged by George S. Kaufman.

Production on the show got off to a rough start. Leading man Philip Ober, fed up with his lines, disappeared one day and never returned. He was replaced by Millard Mitchell. All during rehearsals, Kaufman sat in the front row grinning whenever an actor read his lines. His "grin" was actually a nervous muscular reaction to the awkward dialogue and some of the performers.

The Naked Genius opened in Boston on September 27 to scathing reviews. Kaufman and Lee begged Todd to close the show before it hit Broadway. Since Todd had invested

$60,000 of his own savings in the production, he refused.

Prior to its Baltimore tryout, *The Naked Genius* underwent extensive changes. The first act was almost entirely rewritten, and Joan's main costume was changed from a long, thick bathrobe to a sheer, slinky negligee. A mock striptease and several burlesque routines were also added, but the show was still bashed by critics. By then, Joan had developed a case of the shakes.

After the Pittsburgh premiere on October 11, a frustrated Lee began bad-mouthing the show to the press. She knocked the revisions, which she felt destroyed her plot and her dramatic cohesion. "Every time I see that show, I get a new fever blister on my upper lip," she said.

The Naked Genius opened at the Plymouth Theater on October 21 to critical pans. "No bumps, no grinds, no cries of 'take 'em off'— not even, to be blunt about it, a play that can hold the interest," said Lewis Nichols of *The New York Times*. "Joan Blondell, as the leading player, is okay for figure, manner and accent, and she seems to be having fun — all of which is proper."

Todd tried to outfox the critics by publicly stating *The Naked Genius* was "guaranteed not to win the Pulitzer Prize" and "It ain't Shakespeare but it's laffs." His ploy failed and the show closed after thirty-six performances. Todd wisely sold the rights to the play for $350,000 to 20th Century–Fox before it even went into rehearsal. It was eventually adapted as a pleasant, but minor, screen musical, *Doll Face* (1945), with Vivian Blaine in Joan's role.

Joan's attraction to Todd was one of several elements that led to the end of her marriage. Dick was seeing actress June Allyson, whom he met while filming *Meet the People* (1944). His preoccupation with his many business ventures was also a source of contention with Joan.

On July 14, 1944, Joan was granted a divorce from Dick based on her testimony that he had been guilty of numerous acts of cruelty, including a demand that she "get the hell out of the house." Joan further stated that Dick insisted on using their home for his office, and that two telephones were ringing nearly all the time, which made it impossible for her to get any rest or privacy. Dick, who didn't attend the proceedings, had told Joan that he didn't care whether she got a divorce or not. Their eight-year marriage was dissolved in four minutes.

Around the time of the divorce, Joan began work on what would be the finest film of her career, the wonderful film adaptation of Betty Smith's novel *A Tree Grows in Brooklyn* (1945). This affecting coming-of-age story focused on thirteen-year-old Francie Nolan (Peggy Ann Garner), a dreamy-eyed girl growing up in turn-of-the-century Brooklyn. The heart of the film is the tender relationship between Francie and her father Johnny (James Dunn), a smooth-talker whose penchant for alcohol and aversion to work have turned his wife, Katie (Dorothy McGuire), into a cold-hearted woman forced to scrub floors to support her family. Joan played Aunt Sissy, Katie's much-married sister, whose good humor is a welcome presence in the Nolan household.

A Tree Grows in Brooklyn was the feature-film directorial debut of Elia Kazan, who did an outstanding job of recreating the teeming streets of 1910 Brooklyn. Although Kazan regretted that he wasn't allowed to film on location, the 20th Century–Fox lot proved to be an excellent stand-in for the Council of Churches.

Adding to the movie's realism were the flawless performances of the cast. Garner won a special Juvenile Oscar for her extraordinary performance, while Dunn won a richly deserved Supporting Actor Oscar. As Katie, McGuire gave the character far more warmth than originally depicted in the novel. As for Joan, she was never better, and she often cited Sissy as her favorite role. "Before that there was a pattern," she said in a 1971 *Life* interview. "I was the fizz on the soda: I just showed my big boobs and tiny waist and acted glib and flirty. Once you do something like that, it's hard for you to come out of that trap. Then *Tree* came along and let me have a moment or two of tenderness, of maturity that nobody had ever given me before."

Joan also praised Kazan, whom she called the best director she ever worked with. "There were no big meetings, or going into closets to figure out what your mood was. You just did it. He chose you because you were the right one for that role and then let you go," she said to Maltin.

A Tree Grows in Brooklyn made most critics' Ten Best list for the year. *The New York Times*' Bosley Crowther cheered that, "Joan

Blondell's performance of Aunt Sissy, the family's 'problem,' is obviously hedged by the script's abbreviations and the usual 'Hays Office' restraints, but a sketchy conception of a warm character is plumply expanded by her."

Although Joan's performance seemed like a shoo-in for a Supporting Actress Oscar nomination, she didn't make the cut, one of the great Oscar gaffes of all time. Even sadder is that she didn't capitalize on her fine notices. Rather than hold out for another good character part, she did a piece of fluff called *Don Juan Quilligan* (1945), as the wife of bigamist William Bendix.

Nor was she better served by *Adventure* (1945), an oddball romance between a rowdy sailor (Clark Gable) and a ladylike librarian (Greer Garson), which was Gable's first film since his return from army service. Billed with the catchphrase, "Gable's back and Garson's got him!" the movie was anything but an adventure, and was sabotaged by the lack of chemistry between the two stars. As Garson's good-time girl roommate, Joan handily walked off with the movie.

Joan's willingness to accept any part was one reason she wasn't seen to better advantage after *A Tree Grows in Brooklyn*. Another was her turbulent relationship with Todd, even though gossip maven Louella Parsons reported on several occasions that they were washed up. Joan and Todd fooled her and other naysayers when they got married in Las Vegas on July 5, 1947.

Joan continued to act, and occasionally found a choice role among the dross. A case in point: Sandwiched between the dire comedies *The Corpse Came C.O.D.* (1947) and *Christmas Eve* (both with George Brent), Joan was in excellent form as a blowzy carnival performer in *Nightmare Alley* (1947), director Edmund Goulding's seamy film noir that provided Tyrone Power with his best role, as Stan Carlyle, an opportunistic carnival barker. Joan played Zeena, the middle-aged fortune teller he seduces so that she'll teach him a secret code for a mind reading act.

Nightmare Alley was adapted by Jules Furthman from William Lindsay's pulp novel, and the result is one of the most mesmerizing films of the 1940s, with its sordid images of burnt-out derelicts and sideshow geeks. With the exception of Molly (Coleen Gray), the innocent girl whom Stan marries, none of the characters are sympathetic, yet all are fascinating. Power shed his glamour boy image and demonstrated a dramatic talent that had long been wasted by Fox.

As Zeena, who has "a heart like an artichoke—a leaf for everyone," Joan equaled his performance. Gray, who was still a newcomer, remembers observing Joan and taking note of her acting technique. "She had self-confidence. She was very professional, always knew her lines. She had a way of using her body that I thought was fascinating. She was just exquisite the way she delivered that line about having a heart like an artichoke. It was a wonderful example of a sexy blonde who was past her prime."

Reviewers were split on *Nightmare Alley*. *Time* called it "a hair-raising carnival show," while *The New York Times* slammed the picture as it "traverses distasteful dramatic ground." The *Times* did say that Joan "as the duped mind reader, gives a good, earthy characterization."

The film's worst critic was Fox chief Darryl F. Zanuck, who was talked into doing the movie by Power, who welcomed the chance to at last play a heel. Zanuck agreed only on the condition that Power also do the dull swashbuckler *Captain from Castile* (1947). With Zanuck distanced from *Nightmare Alley*, it was given little push by the studio's publicity department. As Zanuck also predicted, the grim storyline and Power's uncharacteristic portrayal were box office poison. By contrast, his fans lined up for the tedious *Captain from Castile*. Lack of support for *Nightmare Alley* ostensibly hurt both Power's and Joan's chances to be recognized at Oscar time.

Since then, *Nightmare Alley* has developed a tremendous cult following and has become recognized as a minor masterpiece. Gray was in attendance for an April 1999 revival at the Egyptian Theater in Los Angeles, where the film played to packed houses.

After *Nightmare Alley* Joan was off the screen for three years. She and Todd moved to New York, settling into an estate in Irvington-on-the-Hudson, where Averill Harriman was their next-door neighbor. In Mike's typical grand style, their estate had a staff of servants as well as several guards who were on hand to protect Mike Todd, Jr., his son from a previous marriage.

The lavish home and trimmings seemed to be strictly for appearances, since Mike at the time was going through a lean period. Much of the financial burden seems to have fallen on Joan, who even loaned her husband $80,000, which was never repaid. To help with expenses, Joan appeared in summer stock and with the road company of *Something for the Boys*. In 1949 she returned to Broadway in her husband's short-lived production of *Happy Birthday*.

Joan and Todd argued frequently, which prompted her to ask Powell to let Norman and Ellen live with him and his new wife, June Allyson, until the situation was ironed out. She got a divorce in Las Vegas on June 8, 1950, charging Mike with cruelty. She never married again.

Even though Joan once described living alone as "a miserable kind of life," none of her marriages gave her the fulfillment she expected. "Barnes provided my first real home," she said in *Films in Review*. "Powell was my security man and Todd was my passion. Each was totally different. If you could take a part of each one of them and put them into one man, you'd have one helluva husband."

Anxious to resume her film career, Joan moved back to California. Her return film was *For Heaven's Sake* (1950), a forced attempt at fantasy, with Clifton Webb and Edmund Gwenn as angels sent to help prospective parents Joan Bennett and Robert Cummings. *Variety* gave Joan a warm welcome: "Blondell is so good, you realize she's been absent from the screen far too long."

Joan lived up to that assessment in *The Blue Veil* (1951), a tearjerker in which she played a Broadway star who's so preoccupied with her theatrical career that she neglects her daughter (Natalie Wood). Jane Wyman had the leading role as the governess who helps the actress get her priorities straight. Joan had some good dramatic moments, plus she got to belt out "Hey Daddy" and "There'll Be Some Changes Made." Joan received a long-overdue Oscar nomination in the Supporting Actress category, but she lost to Kim Hunter for *A Streetcar Named Desire* (1951).

The Oscar nomination made little impression on Joan, who began focusing on other media. She made her television debut on *Naish Airflyte Theater* in the January 18, 1951, episode entitled "Pot of Gold." Throughout the 1950s she made twelve more television appearances in such popular shows as *Lux Video Theater*, *The U.S. Steel Hour*, *Playhouse 90* and *Studio One*.

More of Joan's output in the 1950s was on the stage. She appeared in the touring companies of *Come Back Little Sheba*, the musical production of *A Tree Grows in Brooklyn*, *Call Me Madam*, *The Time of the Cuckoo* and *The Dark at the Top of the Stairs*.

Joan didn't return to the screen until *The Opposite Sex* (1956), a musical remake of *The Women* (1939), which starred June Allyson, of all people. Joan had a small but amusing role as the member of the catty clique of Park Avenue females who seems to be chronically pregnant.

Joan had her most productive moviemaking year in a long time in 1957, starting with *Lizzie*, a preposterous warm-up to *The Three Faces of Eve* (1957). *This Could Be the Night* (1957) for director Robert Wise was somewhat better; but *Desk Set* (1957), with Spencer Tracy and Katharine Hepburn, was one of the real highlights of Joan's career. Walter Lang helmed this clever comedy about workers in a television network's research department who fear their jobs are about to be taken over by a computer. Much of the fun came from the sparring between the department's head (Hepburn) and the developer of the electronic brain (Tracy). Joan was a delight as Hepburn's co-worker and best friend.

Joan ranked *Desk Set* as one of her favorite films to make, even though she was briefly hospitalized during production. Joan had much admiration for Hepburn, who graciously cared for Joan's dog during that time and saw to it that Lang shot around Joan's scenes until her recovery.

Joan finished the year in *Will Success Spoil Rock Hunter?* (1957), director Frank Tashlin's bright spoof of Madison Avenue and television. Though the movie was a showcase for Fox's latest Marilyn Monroe wannabe, Jayne Mansfield (repeating her stage role), Joan made the most of her role as Mansfield's secretary, and was delightful in her scenes with huckster Henry Jones.

A return to the stage in *Copper and Brass*, with Nancy Walker, was set for late 1957, but as Joan's role kept getting reduced, she withdrew from the show. Later that year she turned up in

The Rope Dancers, with Art Carney and Siobbhan McKenna, which *The New York Times* called "small, but it's gold." Joan liked the writing but considered it an "awfully depressing" play to do.

More enjoyable was *Crazy October*, a comedy that teamed Joan with stage legend Tallulah Bankhead in 1958. Joan admitted that she was initially put off by Bankhead, whom she considered unprofessional because she would often take pills or drink to calm her nerves during rehearsal. As time went on, Joan revised her opinion.

"Her sarcasm, drunkenness and misbehavior in public were all something she put on so as to be talked about," Joan said in *Films in Review*. "She was a sensitive, lonely woman and I think she wanted to die. I was sorry she died before she had one more crack at something glamorous and got to be the toast of Broadway once again." Sadly for both women, *Crazy October* never hit Broadway.

In 1961 Joan guest-starred on *The Untouchables* in "The Underground Court" episode. Working with Joan brought back fond memories for one of the show's regulars, Paul Picerni.

"In 1942 I was a cadet at an Air Force base which was close to the Arrowhead Springs Hotel," recalled Picerni. "On one weekend pass, I went up to the hotel and went to the pool. I was the only one there, and then all of a sudden this very lovely woman, who looked familiar, and was with a young boy, showed up. The boy dove into the pool and, since we were the only two there, we became acquainted. The boy turned out to be Norman Powell and the woman was Joan Blondell. She then invited me to go to the coffee shop with them and have an ice cream soda. We got to talking and then she asked me what I was going to do next. When I said I was thinking of going horseback riding, she asked Norman if he wanted to go with me, and we spent the rest of the day together. Later, when I worked with her, I never brought up the incident, and she didn't seem to remember, but it was a memorable afternoon for me."

Picerni noted little difference between the Joan Blondell he shared an ice cream soda with and the actress. "She was very good in that *Untouchables* episode. And even though it had been thirty years since I first saw her on the screen with Dick Powell, she still had that sex appeal about her. She always retained that."

The Untouchables was just one of about thirty guest appearances Joan made on television in the 1960s. *Bonanza*, *Burke's Law*, *The Twilight Zone*, *Petticoat Junction*, *That Girl*, *The Man from U.N.C.L.E.*, *The Virginian*, *Family Affair* and *The Lucy Show* all featured Joan at one point or another.

Joan occasionally found film work in the 1960s, but most of the pictures—*Angel Baby* (1961), *Advance to the Rear* (1964), *Ride Beyond Vengeance* (1966), *Waterhole No. 3* (1967), *Kona Coast* (1968) and *Stay Away, Joe* (1968)—she remembered with little affection.

"It takes all the talent you've got in your guts to play unimportant roles," she told *Life*. "It's not degrading, just tough to do. It's fine to start out as a curvy biz-whiz, but, unfortunately, when you can't do those roles anymore, people think you're finished. I accept change. I say, 'It's all right, it's a new generation growing up.' So you support the young kids, and you have great respect for them because that's the way you were at one time."

Her one notable film of the 1960s was *The Cincinnati Kid* (1965), director Norman Jewison's taut drama about gamblers vying for supremacy in a poker game. Joan had only a few scenes as a reformed poker addict, but she was memorable in every one of them.

In 1968 Joan made the plunge into series television as Lottie, a saloon owner, in *Here Come the Brides*, an hour-long drama based loosely on *Seven Brides for Seven Brothers* (1954). Joan played the part with rowdy charm and was a welcome contrast to the dewy-eyed brides. She received her only Emmy nomination for her work on the series.

When ABC divorced itself from *Here Come the Brides* in 1970, Joan had no regrets. "It was an uphill thing, that series. You turn into an absolute phony. You have to keep saying how much you love everybody. It's just as well it's over; I think in another few months I'd have turned into an amateur myself!"

Joan didn't socialize much with her co-stars from the show, although she was friendly with veteran actor Henry Beckman, who played Cap'n Clancey. Beckman remembered Joan as a total professional who never exhibited any signs of temperament or questioned the show's directors.

"I had seen her in a few motion pictures and thought of her as a ditzy blonde, but she was very gracious, courteous and down to earth," he said.

Beckman recalled visiting Joan at her home, and most especially how Joan doted on her dogs. The two animals had been loving companions to Joan, and when they both died, at 19 and 17, in 1970, Joan grieved as if she lost two of her children.

"Hell, they were with me so long, you know," she said. "On New Year's Eve I took about as many sleeping pills as I could safely take. I just wanted to have that year over and done with."

Another reason Joan may have wanted to forget 1970 was because of a bizarre film she made called *The Phynx*, which also wasted the talents of Dorothy Lamour, Louis Hayward, Ruby Keeler, Maureen O'Sullivan and many other stars from vintage Hollywood. The absurd plot had a rock group trying to save film and stage stars from a mythical country behind the Iron Curtain. The movie thankfully had limited showings before it was withdrawn from release.

Support Your Local Gunfighter (1971) was a fair sequel to the western satire *Support Your Local Sheriff!* (1969), but Joan gave it some much-needed vitality as a saloon keeper.

Joan returned to the stage for a three-month run as the demented Beatrice in Paul Zindel's *The Effect of Gamma Rays on Man-in-the-Moon Marigolds*. Joan was upfront in stating that she had no idea what the play was about, but that she just did her best with it. "My whole day is spent trying to make the character of the mother explicable, so I guess inside I'm quite a serious actress. At least I want audiences to get their money's worth," she said.

Joan despised the rampant sex and explicit language that had become the norm in modern movies and refused all of the film projects offered to her. Instead, she wrote a novel, *Center Door Fancy*, which borrowed heavily from her own experiences. The book followed a heroine named Nora from her days as a child star in vaudeville to her adult years as a Hollywood actress. Though the book wasn't a darling of the critics, it sold well, and Joan was proud of it.

She was even prouder of her children. Ellen, who ran three stereo shops, took after her father when it came to business. Norman entered show business as a television and film producer.

Joan took another stab at series television in 1972 with *Banyon*, a detective drama set in 1930s Los Angeles. Robert Forster had the title role, and Joan played the owner of a secretarial school in the same building as Banyon's office, a plot device which meant he could employ a new sexy receptionist each week. Low ratings meant *Banyon* only got to solve thirteen cases.

Even though Joan was now in her mid-sixties, she was fortunate to continue getting television roles, even if they were sometimes on things like *The Love Boat* and *Fantasy Island*. She also scored a hit playing the heroine's mother in a tour of Neil Simon's *Barefoot in the Park*.

Following a few forgettable made-for-television films, Joan returned to the big screen, most notably as Vi, the motherly waitress in *Grease* (1978), and as a wealthy race horse owner in Franco Zefferelli's remake of *The Champ* (1979). But by now she looked and seemed tired.

In 1979 Joan was diagnosed with leukemia and by the fall needed to be hospitalized. She died on December 25, 1979, with her two children and her sister, Gloria, at her bedside.

Joan's last film was released posthumously, and, even worse, it was one of the poorest she ever appeared in—a piece of Canadian bacon called *The Woman Inside* (1981), in which she played the aunt of a Vietnam vet (Gloria Manon) who decides to have a sex change operation.

Like the character she played in *Nightmare Alley*, Joan herself also seemed to have a heart like an artichoke. And each of her joyous performances could be representative of its leaves, which she gave generously to audiences one at a time.

FILMOGRAPHY

The Office Wife (Warner Bros., 1930) Directed by Lloyd Bacon. *Cast:* Dorothy Mackaill, Lewis Stone, Joan Blondell, Hobart Bosworth, Blanche Frederici, Natalie Moorehead, Brooke Benedict.

Sinners Holiday (Warner Bros., 1930) Directed by John Adolfi. *Cast:* Grant Withers, Evelyn Knapp, James Cagney, Joan Blondell, Lucille La Verne, Noel Madison, Warren Hymer.

Illicit (Warner Bros., 1931) Directed by Archie Mayo. *Cast:* Barbara Stanwyck, James Rennie, Charles Butterworth, Joan Blondell, Natalie Moorehead, Ricardo Cortez, Claude Gillingwater.

Millie (RKO Pathé, 1931) Directed by John Francis Dillon. *Cast:* Helen Twelvetrees, Lilyan Tashman, Robert Ames, Joan Blondell, John Halliday, James Hall, Anita Louise, Frank McHugh.

My Past (Warner Bros., 1931) Directed by Roy Del Ruth. *Cast:* Bebe Daniels, Ben Lyon, Lewis Stone, Joan Blondell, Natalie Moorehead, Albert Gran, Virginia Sale, Saisy Belmore.

God's Gift to Women (Warner Bros., 1931) Directed by Michael Curtiz. *Cast:* Frank Fay, Laura La Plante, Joan Blondell, Charles Winninger, Arthur Edmund Carewe, Louise Brooks.

Other Men's Women (Warner Bros., 1931) Directed by William A. Wellman. *Cast:* Grant Withers, Regis Toomey, Mary Astor, James Cagney, Joan Blondell, Fred Kohler, Lillian Worth.

Public Enemy (Warner Bros., 1931) Directed by William A. Wellman. *Cast:* James Cagney, Eddie Woods, Jean Harlow, Beryl Mercer, Donald Cook, Joan Blondell, Mae Clarke.

Big Business Girl (Warner Bros., 1931) Directed by William A. Seiter. *Cast:* Loretta Young, Ricardo Cortez, Joan Blondell, Frank Albertson, Frank Darion, Dorothy Christy, Mickey Bennett.

Night Nurse (Warner Bros., 1931) Directed by William A. Wellman. *Cast:* Barbara Stanwyck, Ben Lyon, Charles Winninger, Joan Blondell, Charlotte Merriam, Edward Nugent, Clark Gable.

The Reckless Hour (Warner Bros., 1931) Directed by John Francis Dillon. *Cast:* Dorothy Mackaill, Conrad Nagel, H.B. Warner, Joan Blondell, Walter Byron, Helen Ware, Joe Donahue.

Blonde Crazy (Warner Bros., 1931) Directed by Roy Del Ruth. *Cast:* James Cagney, Joan Blondell, Louis Calhern, Noel Francis, Guy Kibbee, Raymond Milland, Polly Walters.

Union Depot (Warner Bros., 1932) Directed by Alfred E. Green. *Cast:* Douglas Fairbanks, Jr., Joan Blondell, Guy Kibbee, Alan Hale, George Rosener, Dickie Moore, Ruth Hall, Mae Madison.

The Greeks Had a Word for Them (Goldwyn-United Artists, 1932) Directed by Lowell Sherman. *Cast:* Madge Evans, Joan Blondell, Ina Claire, David Manners, Lowell Sherman, Phillips Smalley.

The Crowd Roars (Warner Bros., 1932) Directed by Howard Hawks. *Cast:* James Cagney, Ann Dvorak, Eric Linden, Joan Blondell, Guy Kibbee, Frank McHugh, William Arnold.

The Famous Ferguson Case (Warner Bros., 1932) Directed by Lloyd Bacon. *Cast:* Joan Blondell, Tom Brown, Adrienne Dore, Walter Miller, Leslie Fenton, Vivienne Osborne.

Make Me a Star (Paramount, 1932) Directed by William Beaudine. *Cast:* Stuart Erwin, Joan Blondell, Zasu Pitts, Ben Turpin, Charles Sellon, Florence Roberts, Helen Jerome Eddy.

Miss Pinkerton (Warner Bros., 1932) Directed by Lloyd Bacon. *Cast:* George Brent, Joan Blondell, Mae Madison, John Wray, Ruth Hall, Allan Lane, C. Henry Gordon.

Big City Blues (Warner Bros., 1932) Directed by Mervyn LeRoy. *Cast:* Eric Linden, Joan Blondell, Inez Courtney, Evalyn Knapp, Guy Kibbee, Lyle Talbot, Gloria Shea, Walter Catlett.

Three on a Match (Warner Bros., 1932) Directed by Mervyn LeRoy. *Cast:* Joan Blondell, Ann Dvorak, Bette Davis, Warren William, Lyle Talbot, Humphrey Bogart, Edward Arnold.

Central Park (Warner Bros., 1932) Directed by John Adolfi. *Cast:* Joan Blondell, Wallace Ford, Guy Kibbee, Henry B. Walthall, Patricia Ellis, Charles Sellon, Spencer Charters, John Wray.

Lawyer Man (Warner Bros., 1932) Directed by William Dieterle. *Cast:* William Powell, Joan Blondell, Helen Vinson, Alan Dinehart, Allen Jenkins, David Landau, Claire Dodd, Sheila Terry.

Broadway Bad (Fox Film, 1933) Directed by Sidney Lanfield. *Cast:* Joan Blondell, Ricardo Cortez, Ginger Rogers, Adrienne Ames, Allen Vincent, Victor Jory, Phillip Tead.

Blondie Johnson (Warner Bros., 1933) Directed by Ray Enright. *Cast:* Joan Blondell, Chester Morris, Allen Jenkins, Claire Dodd, Earle Foxe, Mae Busch, Joe Cawthorne, Sterling Holloway.

Gold Diggers of 1933 (Warner Bros., 1933) Directed by Mervyn LeRoy. *Cast:* Joan Blondell, Warren William, Dick Powell, Ruby Keeler, Aline MacMahon, Ginger Rogers, Guy Kibbee.

Goodbye Again (Warner Bros., 1933) Directed by Michael Curtiz. *Cast:* Warren William, Joan Blondell, Genevieve Tobin, Wallace Ford, Helen Chandler, Ruth Donnelly, Hugh Herbert.

Footlight Parade (Warner Bros., 1933) Directed by Lloyd Bacon. *Cast:* James Cagney, Joan Blondell, Dick Powell, Ruby Keeler, Guy Kibbee, Frank McHugh, Hugh Herbert, Ruth Donnelly.

Havana Widows (Warner Bros., 1933) Directed by Ray Enright. *Cast:* Joan Blondell, Glenda Farrell, Lyle Talbot, Allen Jenkins, Guy Kibbee, Ruth Donnelly, Mayo Methot, Frank McHugh.

Convention City (Warner Bros., 1933) Directed by Archie Mayo. *Cast:* Dick Powell, Joan Blondell, Adolphe Menjou, Mary Astor, Guy Kibbee, Frank McHugh, Patricia Ellis.

I've Got Your Number (Warner Bros., 1934) Directed by Ray Enright. *Cast:* Joan Blondell, Pat O'Brien, Glenda Farrell, Allen Jenkins, Eugene Pallette, Gordon Westcott, Henry O'Neill.

He Was Her Man (Warner Bros., 1934) Directed by Lloyd Bacon. *Cast:* James Cagney, Joan Blondell, Victor Jory, Frank Craven, Harold Huber, Russell Hopton, Rolf Harolde, Sarah Padden.

Smarty (Warner Bros., 1934) Directed by Robert Florey. *Cast:* Joan Blondell, Warren William, Frank McHugh, Edward Everett Horton, Claire Dodd, Joan Wheeler, Virginia Sale.

Dames (Warner Bros., 1934) Directed by Ray Enright. *Cast:* Joan Blondell, Ruby Keeler, Dick Powell, Guy Kibbee, Hugh Herbert, Zasu Pitts, Arthur Vinton, Lela Bennett, Berton Churchill.

Kansas City Princess (Warner Bros., 1934) Directed by William Keighley. *Cast:* Joan Blondell, Glenda Farrell, Robert Armstrong, Hugh Herbert, Osgood Perkins, Hobart Cavanaugh.

Traveling Saleslady (Warner Bros., 1935) Directed by Ray Enright. *Cast:* Joan Blondell, Glenda Farrell, William Gargan, Hugh Herbert, Grant Mitchell, Al Shean, Ruth Donnelly.

Broadway Gondolier (Warner Bros., 1935) Directed by Lloyd Bacon. *Cast:* Dick Powell, Joan Blondell, Louise Fazenda, William Gargan, The Mills Bros., Grant Mitchell, Hobart Cavanaugh.

We're in the Money (Warner Bros., 1935) Directed by Lloyd Bacon. *Cast:* Joan Blondell, Glenda Farrell, Hugh Herbert, Ross Alexander, Hobart Cavanaugh, Phil Regan, Henry O'Neill.

Miss Pacific Fleet (Warner Bros., 1935) Directed by Ray Enright. *Cast:* Joan Blondell, Glenda Farrell, Hugh Herbert, Allen Jenkins, Minna Gombell, Warren Hull, Marie Wilson, Mary Treen.

Colleen (Warner Bros., 1936) Directed by Alfred E. Green. *Cast:* Joan Blondell, Dick Powell, Ruby Keeler, Jack Oakie, Hugh Herbert, Louise Fazenda, Paul Draper, Marie Wilson.

Sons o' Guns (Warner Bros., 1936) Directed by Lloyd Bacon. *Cast:* Joe E. Brown, Joan Blondell, Winifred Shaw, Eric Blore, Robert Barratt, Beverly Roberts, Craig Reynolds.

Bullets or Ballots (Warner Bros., 1936) Directed by William Keighley. *Cast:* Edward G. Robinson, Joan Blondell, Humphrey Bogart, Barton MacLane, Frank McHugh, Joseph King.

Stage Struck (Warner Bros., 1936) Directed by Busby Berkeley. *Cast:* Dick Powell, Joan Blondell, Warren William, Frank McHugh, Jeanne Madden, Carol Hughes, Craig Reynolds.

Three Men on a Horse (Warner Bros., 1936) Directed by Mervyn LeRoy. *Cast:* Frank McHugh, Joan Blondell, Guy Kibbee, Carol Hughes, Allen Jenkins, Sam Levene, Edgar Kennedy.

Gold Diggers of 1937 (Warner Bros., 1936) Directed by Lloyd Bacon. *Cast:* Dick Powell, Joan Blondell, Victor Moore, Glenda Farrell, Lee Dixon, Osgood Perkins, Rosalind Marquis, Charles D. Brown.

The King and the Chorus Girl (Warner Bros., 1937) Directed by Mervyn LeRoy. *Cast:* Joan Blondell, Fernand Gravet, Edward Everett Horton, Jane Wyman, Alan Mowbray, Mary Nash.

Back in Circulation (Warner Bros., 1937) Directed by Ra Enright. *Cast:* Joan Blondell, Pat O'Brien, Margaret Lindsay, John Litel, Eddie Acuff, Craig Reynolds, George E. Stone.

The Perfect Specimen (Warner Bros., 1937) Directed by Michael Curtiz. *Cast:* Errol Flynn, Joan Blondell, Hugh Herbert, Edward Everett Horton, Dick Foran, Beverly Roberts.

The Stand-In (Wanger-United Artists, 1937) Directed by Tay Garnett. *Cast:* Leslie Howard, Joan Blondell, Humphrey Bogart, Alan Mowbray, Marla Shelton, C. Henry Gordon, Jack Carson.

There's Always a Woman (Columbia, 1938) Directed by Alexander Hall. *Cast:* Joan Blondell, Melvyn Douglas, Mary Astor, Frances Drake, Jerome Cowan, Robert Paige, Thurston Hall.

Off the Record (Warner Bros., 1939) Directed by James Flood. *Cast:* Joan Blondell, Pat O'Brien, Bobby Jordan, Alan Baxter, William Davidson, Morgan Conway, Clay Clement.

East Side of Heaven (Universal, 1939) Directed by David Butler. *Cast:* Bing Crosby, Joan Blondell, Mischa Auer, Irene Hervey, C. Aubrey Smith, Jerome Cowan, Baby Sandy.

The Kid from Kokomo (Warner Bros., 1939) Directed by Lewis Seiler. *Cast:* Pat O'Brien, Joan Blondell, Wayne Morris, May Robson, Jane Wyman, Stanley Fields, Maxie Rosenbloom.

Good Girls Go to Paris (Columbia, 1939) Directed by Alexander Hall. *Cast:* Joan Blondell,

Melvyn Douglas, Walter Connolly, Alan Curtis, Joan Perry, Isabel Jeans, Alexander D'Arcy.

The Amazing Mr. Williams (Columbia, 1939) Directed by Alexander Hall. Cast: Joan Blondell, Melvyn Douglas, Clarence Kolb, Ruth Donnelly, Edward Brophy, Donald MacBride.

Two Girls on Broadway (MGM, 1940) Directed by S. Sylvan Simon. Cast: Joan Blondell, Lana Turner, George Murphy, Kent Taylor, Richard Lane, Wallace Ford, Otto Hahn.

I Want a Divorce (Paramount, 1940) Directed by Ralph Murphy. Cast: Dick Powell, Joan Blondell, Gloria Dickson, Frank Fay, Jessie Ralph, Harry Davenport, Conrad Nagel.

Topper Returns (Hal Roach-United Artists, 1941) Directed by Roy Del Ruth. Cast: Joan Blondell, Carole Landis, Roland Young, Billie Burke, Dennis O'Keefe, Patsy Kelly, H.B. Warner.

Model Wife (Universal, 1941) Directed by Leigh Jason. Cast: Dick Powell, Joan Blondell, Charles Ruggles, Lee Bowman, Lucile Watson, Ruth Donnelly, Billy Gilbert, John Qualen.

Three Girls About Town (Columbia, 1941) Directed by Leigh Jason. Cast: Joan Blondell, Binnie Barnes, Janet Blair, John Howard, Robert Benchley, Eric Blore, Una O'Connor.

Lady for a Night (Republic, 1942) Directed by Leigh Jason. Cast: Joan Blondell, John Wayne, Ray Middleton, Philip Merivale, Blanche Yurka, Edith Barrett, Leonid Kinskey.

Cry Havoc (MGM, 1943) Directed by Richard Thorpe. Cast: Margaret Sullavan, Ann Sothern, Fay Bainter, Joan Blondell, Marsha Hunt, Ella Raines, Frances Gifford, Diana Lewis.

A Tree Grows in Brooklyn (20th Century–Fox, 1945) Directed by Elia Kazan. Cast: Dorothy McGuire, James Dunn, Joan Blondell, Peggy Ann Garner, Lloyd Nolan, Ted Donaldson.

Don Juan Quilligan (20th Century–Fox, 1945) Directed by Frank Tuttle. Cast: William Bendix, Joan Blondell, Phil Silvers, Anne Revere, B.S. Pully, Mary Treen, John Russell.

Adventure (MGM, 1945) Directed by Victor Fleming. Cast: Clark Gable, Greer Garson, Joan Blondell, Thomas Mitchell, Tom Tully, John Qualen, Richard Haydn, Lina Romay.

The Corpse Came C.O.D. (Columbia, 1947) Directed by Henry Levin. Cast: Joan Blondell, George Brent, Adele Jergens, Jim Bannon, Leslie Brooks, John Berkes, Fred Sears.

Nightmare Alley (20th Century–Fox, 1947) Directed by Edmund Goulding. Cast: Tyrone Power, Joan Blondell, Coleen Gray, Helen Walker, Taylor Holmes, Mike Mazurki, Ian Keith.

Christmas Eve (United Artists, 1947) Directed by Edwin L. Marin. Cast: George Raft, George Brent, Randolph Scott, Ann Harding, Joan Blondell, Virginia Field, Dolores Moran.

For Heaven's Sake (20th Century–Fox, 1950) Directed by George Seaton. Cast: Clifton Webb, Edmund Gwenn, Robert Cummings, Joan Bennett, Joan Blondell, Gigi Perreau, Harry Von Zell.

The Blue Veil (RKO Radio, 1951) Directed by Curtis Bernhardt. Cast: Jane Wyman, Charles Laughton, Richard Carlson, Joan Blondell, Agnes Moorehead, Don Taylor, Audrey Totter.

The Opposite Sex (MGM, 1956) Directed by David Miller. Cast: June Allyson, Ann Sheridan, Joan Collins, Dolores Gray, Ann Miller, Leslie Nielsen, Agnes Moorehead, Joan Blondell.

Lizzie (MGM, 1957) Directed by Hugo Haas. Cast: Eleanor Parker, Richard Boone, Joan Blondell, Hugo Haas, Ric Roman, Johnny Mathis, Dorothy Arnold, Marion Ross.

This Could Be the Night (MGM, 1957) Directed by Robert Wise. Cast: Jean Simmons, Anthony Franciosa, Paul Douglas, Joan Blondell, Julie Wilson, Nelle Adams, J. Carrol Naish.

Desk Set (20th Century–Fox, 1957) Directed by Walter Lang. Cast: Spencer Tracy, Katharine Hepburn, Gig Young, Joan Blondell, Dina Merrill, Sue Randall, Neva Patterson, Harry Ellerbe.

Will Success Spoil Rock Hunter? (20th Century–Fox, 1957) Directed by Frank Tashlin. Cast: Tony Randall, Jayne Mansfield, Betsy Drake, Joan Blondell, John Williams, Henry Jones.

Angel Baby (Allied Artists, 1961) Directed by Paul Wendkos. Cast: Salome Jens, George Hamilton, Mercedes McCambridge, Joan Blondell, Henry Jones, Burt Reynolds.

Advance to the Rear (MGM, 1964) Directed by George Marshall. Cast: Glenn Ford, Stella Stevens, Melvyn Douglas, Jim Backus, Joan Blondell, Andrew Prine, Jesse Pearson.

The Cincinnati Kid (MGM, 1965) Directed by Norman Jewison. Cast: Steve McQueen, Edward G. Robinson, Ann-Margret, Karl Malden, Tuesday Weld, Rip Torn, Joan Blondell.

Ride Beyond Vengeance (Columbia, 1966) Directed by Bernard McEveety. Cast: Chuck Connors, Michael Rennie, Kathryn Hays, Joan Blondell, Gloria Grahame, Gary Merrill, Paul Fix.

Waterhole No. 3 (Paramount, 1967) Directed by William Graham. Cast: James Coburn, Carroll O'Connor, Margaret Blye, Claude Akins, Timothy Carey, James Whitmore, Harry Davis.

Kona Coast (Warner Bros., 1968) Directed by Lamont Johnson. Cast: Richard Boone, Vera Miles, Joan Blondell, Steve Ihnat, Chips Rafferty, Kent Smith, Sam Kapir, Jr., Gina Villines.

Stay Away, Joe (MGM, 1968) Directed by Peter Tewksbury. Cast: Elvis Presley, Burgess Meredith, Joan Blondell, Katy Jurado, Thomas

Gomez, Henry Jones, L.Q. Jones, Anne Seymour.

The Phynx (Warner Bros., 1970) Directed by Lee H. Katzin. *Cast:* A. Michael Miller, Ray Chippeway, Dennis Larden, Lonny Stevens, Lou Antonio, Mike Kjellin, Joan Blondell.

Support Your Local Gunfighter (United Artists, 1971) Directed by Burt Kennedy. *Cast:* James Garner, Suzanne Pleshette, Jack Elam, Harry Morgan, Joan Blondell, Marie Windsor.

Won Ton Ton, the Dog Who Saved Hollywood (Paramount, 1976) Directed by Michael Winner. *Cast:* Madeline Kahn, Art Carney, Bruce Dern, Ron Leibman, Teri Garr.

The Baron (Paragon, 1977) Directed by Philip Fenty. *Cast:* Calvin Lockhart, Raymond St. Jacques, Joan Blondell, Marlene Clark, Richard Lynch, Charles McGregor, Gail Strickland.

The Glove (PRO International, 1978) Directed by Ross Hagen. *Cast:* John Saxon, Roosevelt Grier, Joanna Cassidy, Joan Blondell, Jack Carter, Aldo Ray, Keenan Wynn, Howard Honig.

Opening Night (Faces Distribution, 1978) Directed by John Cassavetes. *Cast:* Gena Rowlands, Ben Gazzara, John Cassavetes, Joan Blondell, Paul Stewart, Zohra Lampert, Laura Johnson.

Grease (Paramount, 1978) Directed by Randal Kleiser. *Cast:* John Travolta, Olivia Newton-John, Stockard Channing, Jeff Conaway, Eve Arden, Frankie Avalon, Joan Blondell, Sid Caesar.

The Champ (MGM, 1979) Directed by Franco Zeffirelli. *Cast:* Jon Voight, Ricky Schroeder, Faye Dunaway, Jack Warden, Arthur Hill, Strother Martin, Joan Blondell, Elisha Cook.

The Woman Inside (20th Century–Fox, 1981) Directed by Joseph Van Winkle. *Cast:* Gloria Manon, Michael Champion, Joan Blondell, Dane Clark, Marlene Tracy, Davison Clark.

TELEVISION FILM CREDITS

The Dead Don't Die (1975) *Cast:* George Hamilton, Ray Milland, Joan Blondell.

Winner Take All (1975) *Cast:* Shirley Jones, Laurence Luckinbill, Sam Groom, Joan Blondell.

Death at Love House (1976) *Cast:* Robert Wagner, Kate Jackson, Sylvia Sidney, Joan Blondell.

Battered (1979) *Cast:* Mike Farrell, Karen Grassle, LeVar Burton, Joan Blondell.

The Rebels (1979) *Cast:* Andrew Stevens, Kevin Tighes, Kim Cattrall, Joan Blondell.

Nancy Coleman: "The Fragile Heroine"

If ever an actress seemed to have all the tools for stardom, it was Nancy Coleman. Her stage training, natural beauty and sincerity should have fortified her position as a top Warner Bros. star. During her brief period at Warners she proved herself a formidable dramatic actress whether playing the fragile, spurned girlfriend of Ronald Reagan in *King's Row*, the high-strung mistress of commandant Helmut Dantine in *Edge of Darkness* or the most ingenuous of *The Gay Sisters*.

Unlike her often neurotic screen incarnations, the real Nancy Coleman was a self-assured and strong-willed professional who gained the respect of both directors and her fellow actors. And while she never attained peak status, the studio's belief in Nancy was evident by the fact that she was only cast in "A" pictures. At the height of her popularity she opted to marry Whitney Bolton, Warners' head of publicity. It was a decision that brought her much personal happiness, but professional antagonism from the top brass at Warners. She was released from her contract, and though she continued to work, her screen career never regained its momentum.

Ironically, Nancy originally had no interest in becoming a film star. Her first love was the stage, and achieving success on Broadway was her original ambition. Nancy's interest in the arts can be traced back to her parents, both of whom had careers in writing and music. Her father, Charles Coleman, worked for *The Everett Daily Herald*, a highly respected publication. He began as a reporter but eventually took over as editor of the newspaper. It was during his early days as a reporter that he met Grace Sharplass, a handsome young woman who covered the paper's society beat. Grace had originally started out as a violinist, but abandoned her musical career for journalism. After a reasonable courtship, the two married.

On December 30, 1912, the couple welcomed their first child, Nancy. Even as a girl, Nancy displayed a spirited streak and was determined in her plans. A second daughter, Barbara, was born in April, 1916. Both sisters got along well despite their different personalities. Barbara had a sweet disposition but lacked Nancy's assertiveness and could therefore be easily manipulated by her parents, a character flaw which would later cause her much unhappiness.

From an early age, Nancy showed an interest in learning and became an avid reader, a passion that she enjoyed for the rest of her life. Her love of reading also helped her get her first taste of being in the spotlight. "In third grade I was the little girl who read the story on a Friday afternoon to the class," she said.

Nancy's love of storytelling eventually took a natural turn to a fascination with the theater. As a perk of his job, Charles would often receive free theater tickets. Although he had no interest in attending any of the performances, Grace would often take the passes, asking Nancy to accompany her. Nancy was enthralled by the plays she saw and the rich performances of such acting troupes as the distinguished Moroni Olsen Players. "Seeing them was my theater

Nancy Coleman's fragile screen portrayals were a sharp contrast to her strong-willed offscreen persona.

education," Nancy recalled. "They did good plays—a lot of J.M. Barrie. I remember *Dear Brutus*. That made a great impression on me." The memories of those performances took on a deeper meaning when Nancy and Olsen became friends while working together in *Dangerously They Live* at Warners.

From that point on, Nancy became intent on pursuing a career in the theater. In 1930 attended the University of Washington in Seattle. Though the school had an excellent reputation, its one drawback was that students were not allowed to major in drama. Instead, Nancy sought a degree in English literature while including several drama classes in her curriculum. The drama department was headed by Glenn Hughes, who later wrote several scholarly books about the theater.

An apt pupil, Nancy landed important roles in several of the school's productions while continuing to hone her craft. One of her fellow classmates was Frances Farmer, a talented actress who was a year younger than Nancy. "She was very beautiful and I was jealous because she got the parts I wanted," recalled Nancy. Today Farmer is primarily remembered for her struggle with mental illness, which was chronicled quite graphically in the 1982 film *Frances*.

College proved to be a happy and memorable period for Nancy. In addition to her theatrical ventures, she became a sorority member of Kappa Alpha Theta. By the time she graduated, Nancy had developed into a talented actress as well as a striking young woman. A titian-haired beauty, Nancy was also quite statuesque at five feet, seven inches. Although she felt both her height and her hair color could be barriers to landing ingenue roles, she was secure in her abilities. "I had a great belief in myself. I thought I was good and I still do. I had a very youthful face, but ingenues were not supposed to be tall in the theater. I developed into a character ingenue in the beginning, not a straight ingenue," she said.

The Depression was still in full swing in 1934 when Nancy graduated from college. Her family was naturally concerned that during such difficult times, landing work as an actress would be a struggle. Nancy half-heartedly agreed to a back-up plan of attending teacher's college—provided she could go to New York. With her parents' approval, she headed east upon her acceptance to Columbia University's graduate school.

"My father was against my being an actress," Nancy explained. "He thought it was a hard life for a woman. So I went to teacher's college and studied to be a liberal arts teacher. I was getting my master's, but I realized I wasn't going to be a teacher."

While at Columbia, Nancy met a handsome young man, and within a matter of weeks they were engaged. After some careful soul-searching, Nancy realized that she didn't really love him and instead looked upon him as an escape from her present arrangement. There was no question that she was also still determined to pursue her theatrical ambitions, and marriage at this time was out of the question. She broke the engagement and instead made plans to move to San Francisco, a mecca for aspiring actors seeking work in radio programs. Nancy set a lofty goal for herself: She would spend two years in San Francisco and land a radio job that would provide her with both a reasonable income and solid experience before returning to New York.

Nancy made the lengthy trip from New York to California with her mother and sister. At the time, Barbara was engaged, but Nancy's mother disapproved and forced her younger daughter to move to San Francisco. "My mother was wrong for doing that," criticized Nancy. "My sister couldn't say no to my mother, and this decision ruined her life. She ended up marrying a man who was all wrong for her. He was a good businessman, but he wasn't a nice person."

The Coleman women arrived in San Francisco in the spring of 1935. Nancy has vivid memories of her first glimpse of the Bay City. "It was a lovely San Francisco day. The fog was rolling in. We drove into the middle of San Francisco and went to a realtor's office. Mother said 'I'll see what I can find for us.' The realtor took us to this place which had a huge living room, a nice alcove, a dining room and a kitchen. The rent was something we could afford. As soon as we settled in and started exploring, we realized we were in the red light district."

Although they stuck it out in the apartment for a while, within months they moved to a more respectable neighborhood in nearby Berkeley. Barbara began going to business college. With both her mother and sister living with her, Nancy knew she'd need to find any kind of work until she got an acting job She applied for a sales position at the Emporium, a major department store on Market Street, but was hired as an elevator operator for $11 a week. "It wasn't electric, but manual. They taught me how to run it, but I was not a very good elevator operator," she said.

The grueling job kept Nancy on her feet all day, and she often looked forward to even the slightest chance to rest. Using her own cunning, Nancy devised ways of taking breaks. "I discovered that if you left the elevator on the upper floor, you'd lock it and you couldn't go. So I'd ring a bell and say I'm stuck and I'd get to rest a while."

One of the accessories Nancy always wore to dress up her elevator operator's outfit — her Kappa Alpha Theta sorority pin — proved to be a lucky charm. "A woman came on the elevator one day and asked me, 'What are you doing here? Are you going to stay here?' I told her I wanted to be an actress. She then said, 'I have a friend who's a casting director at NBC. I think I can get you an audition. The rest is up to you.'

I later found out that the woman took an interest in me because I was wearing my sorority pin. She saw I was a Kappa Alpha Theta and asked me about it. That's how that started. I got the audition very quickly."

Her audition was a success and she was hired for a radio soap opera. She continued to work regularly at the station, which was owned by NBC, for the next two years. She was able to afford a nicely furnished apartment on Nob Hill, which she shared with her mother.

By the time her two-year limit was up, Nancy had managed to save $1,000, which would easily pay for her passage back to New York. She would also have enough money left over to support herself for a few months while looking for work.

For her trip back east, Nancy's adventurous spirit got the better of her. Rather than traveling by bus or train, she bought a first-class ticket on the Panama Pacific and literally came to New York by way of the Panama Canal. The cruise also included a stopover in Acapulco, where Nancy enjoyed the lush beaches.

When she arrived in New York, Nancy headed to the home of the Sinceheimer family, who were friends of her mother's. She stayed with the Sinceheimers for a short time before moving into the Barbizon Plaza on West 57th St. The fringe benefit to living at the Barbizon was a free continental breakfast delivered to every tenant each morning.

Nancy only stayed at the Barbizon for three months. A letter of introduction that she had received from a friend in San Francisco eventually became Nancy's passport to the famed Rehearsal Club, a theatrical boarding house for aspiring actresses, dancers and singers that was the inspiration for the Footlights Club depicted in the play and film *Stage Door*. Nancy showed the letter to an actress whom the writer of the letter was acquainted with, and she arranged for Nancy to move into the club. For $11 a week Nancy shared a spacious room, private bathroom and large closet with two other boarders. The rent also included lunch and dinner. Occupants had to abide by two ironclad rules: They couldn't stay out past 1 a.m., and no men were allowed beyond the parlor. Breaking either meant immediate eviction.

Staying at the Rehearsal Club proved to be a fun-filled and educational experience for

Nancy. "I learned how to dress and how to apply for work," she recalled. "In the beginning, I'd apply for a job at 9:00 in the morning. I soon realized that it was 11:00 before anyone showed up. I'd try to see agents and producers. If you knew them, you would try to see the better ones. If you didn't, you'd try to make up some lie to get in to see them."

Nancy remembered going on lots of auditions, often without success. Her tall, slender figure led to some modeling jobs, which paid her expenses until an acting offer came along.

Nancy's breakthrough role came through her friend Nancy Kelly. Kelly had been appearing at the Plymouth Theater in *Susan and God* as the shy, neglected daughter of a shallow socialite played by Gertrude Lawrence. Kelly's performance in the Rachel Crothers' play was spotted by a 20th Century–Fox talent scout. When Kelly announced that she had accepted an offer from Fox and would be leaving the play, pandemonium ensued.

"They had to look for a replacement and they had great trouble finding someone that Ms. Lawrence approved of, that Ms. Crothers approved of, that [the producer] John Golden approved of and that all the people in charge approved of," Nancy said.

Convinced that she had the necessary qualities the role called for, Nancy was determined to get it. "I remember the agent who saw me. His name was Richard Pittney. I didn't know how you went about getting the part, but I knew I could do it. I walked into his office one rainy day and read the lines. I guess he liked it," she said.

The reading for Pittney was only the first of many auditions for Nancy. She then had to play the scenes over for Lawrence, Crothers and Golden. All were pleased with Nancy's audition and she was asked to be ready in one week.

Crothers worked with Nancy nonstop for the entire week, and by the following Saturday, when she made her debut, she was letter perfect. Nancy's salary at the time was a meager $40 per week. She stayed with the play during its New York run, commuting between the Rehearsal Club on 52nd St. and the Plymouth Theater on 45th St.

Lawrence, who could sometimes be difficult and thought nothing of upstaging her costars, was quite taken with Nancy. When both women appeared together on a radio broadcast during the run of the play, Lawrence introduced her young co-star as "Nancy Coleman, who plays my daughter in *Susan and God*. One of these days she will be one of our most important actresses in the theater."

When *Susan and God* ended its Broadway run, Nancy went on tour with the play. At the end of the tour she returned to New York, where once again finding acting jobs proved difficult. Things took an upward turn when CBS agreed to become Nancy's agent. Sarah Lauritz of CBS took an interest in Nancy. She thought that Nancy's red hair, wholesome look and sincere acting ability could be parlayed into a successful motion picture career. Lauritz arranged several tests for Nancy, including one for David O. Selznick's production company and another at Astoria on Long Island for Paramount. The latter test turned out to be a disaster.

"It wasn't even an acting test," complained Nancy. "They just photographed me and I wasn't photographed well. I decided very quickly that if I was going to do any more tests, they would not be in New York. So I refused several for New York."

According to Nancy, Lauritz noticed that her agreement with CBS was "one of the weirdest contracts ever promulgated." It essentially allowed Nancy to go out to Hollywood and collect a salary for doing tests. Nancy headed to the West Coast and tested for several roles, including two at Warner Bros.—the female lead in *They Died with Their Boots On* (1941), an epic on the life of General George Custer, starring Errol Flynn; and a smaller but meatier role as the mentally unstable daughter of an unscrupulous doctor in *King's Row* (1942). Of the two, Nancy was far more interested in the latter, which she felt would provide her with strong scenes that would make an impression on audiences.

"I was not necessarily interested in star parts. I really wanted just to work and to work in really good things. I liked what Warners was doing at that time," she said.

Although all of Nancy's acting experience had been either on stage or radio, she was undaunted by the camera and gave a poised and polished performance in her *King's Row* test. "I was a little more intelligent than some of the other girls who came out for parts. I seemed to know what to do. I had instincts for how to do things like walk or turn in front of the camera. I got the *King's Row* role. The only thing I had to do was fix my two front teeth, which were large. I didn't get them capped at that point, but just had things pasted on the front of them."

Her acceptance for the role of Louise Gordon in *King's Row* led to a seven-year contract with Warner Bros., which also set up a stylish apartment in Los Angeles for Nancy and her mother.

King's Row was being earmarked as Warners' most prestigious production of 1941, and the studio was pulling out all the stops. It boasted a superlative cast, headed by Robert Cummings, Ann Sheridan, and Claude Rains, and was being helmed by esteemed director Sam Wood. Erich Wolfgang Korngold composed a haunting score that evoked the desperation and desires of the townspeople. Celebrated cinematographer James Wong Howe brilliantly photographed each scene, and screenwriter Casey Robinson penned a tight screenplay that compressed the dramatic elements of Henry Bellamann's sprawling bestseller.

King's Row, which could be viewed as a precursor to *Peyton Place*, was a searing look at the underbelly of turn-of-the-century Middle America, behind whose doors lurked sadism, madness and despair. The center of the story is Parris Mitchell (Cummings), who grows from innocent youth to idealistic doctor over the course of the film's 127 minutes. The characters he encounters all have an influence on his life: his best friend, roguish Drake McHugh (Ronald Reagan); Drake's girlfriend and eventual wife, Randy (Sheridan); his devoted grandmother (Maria Ouspenskaya); his mentor, Dr. Tower (Rains); Cassie Tower, the doctor's mentally unbalanced daughter (Betty Field); Dr. Gordon (Charles Coburn), who willfully performs operations without the use of chloroform; and his daughter Louise, who rejects Drake because her parents disapprove of him. A climactic scene involves Gordon's unnecessary amputation of Drake's legs after he has a mining accident. The moment when Drake wakes up after surgery and discovers what has happened gave Reagan the chance to mutter the immortal line "Where's the rest of me?"

As Louise, whose knowledge of her father's butchering methods leads to her confinement and mental collapse, Nancy had several highly emotional screen moments, which she performed with relish. In a pivotal scene in which Louise threatens to reveal her father's secret about his botched operation on Drake, Coburn was required to slap Nancy. Though the scene lasted only a few moments on screen, it was a long and painful one to film.

"I was a wreck from it," recalled Nancy. [Coburn] couldn't remember my character's name in the movie. He knew it began with an L. He was quite elderly then and he was also finishing up a movie at Universal at the same time, so he had a hard time remembering lines. He would get to the line and say, 'And I tell you Laraine' or 'And I tell you Lucille,' and the slap always came with the name. If we played that scene once, I think we played it forty times. It wasn't a full slap, but it came with a sting. My face was swollen at the end of that scene. After that, he never forgot me. He always sent me little presents and cards and notes. He felt so sorry about that. He was a wonderful man."

Despite the trouble filming the scene, the end result pleased Jack Warner. In a memo dated August 20, 1941, Warner wrote the following to associate producer David Lewis: "Dailies last night of Nancy Coleman and Charles Coburn were excellent. This is a great scene."

In his 1965 examination of *King's Row* for *Screen Facts*, John Cosgrove also cited Nancy's contribution to this scene. "Another rewarding virtue was the gifted, never gauche performance of Nancy Coleman, as Louise Gordon. When goaded beyond endurance, by the wreckage of her love affair with Drake, the sinister dominance of her sadistic father, and the knowledge that he has unnecessarily amputated her lover's legs, she confronts him in a blood-stained dress with the accusation, 'You butcher! You monster!'"

Although *King's Row* was completed in 1941, the studio held up its release for a year, fearful that wartime audiences would be put off by its somber tone. Instead, film audiences first got a look at Nancy in the minor spy thriller *Dangerously They Live* (1941), directed by Robert Florey. In the film, a young doctor (John Garfield) is puzzled by his latest case, a mysterious girl named Jane who claims to be a British secret agent on the run from German spies. Although the doctor doesn't believe her at first, he eventually discovers that she's telling the truth and then helps her escape so she can alert authorities about a secret German U-boat fleet waiting off the U.S. coast. Despite the absurd plot, Florey kept the action moving at a crisp pace.

Still, neither Nancy nor Garfield held the film in high regard. Garfield's sole reason for making it was money. He had already been on suspension for refusing two other roles, and at this point needed a steady paycheck. However, he enjoyed working with Nancy, even though he had to stand on a box during many of their scenes, since she was a few inches taller. As was his custom when making a film, ladykiller Garfield did his best to seduce his leading lady.

"He'd call me up on Sunday to try and get me to come over to his house. And I'd always tell him I wasn't interested. He couldn't get me to do things that the average girl would do," she said.

In general, the critics were kind to the film and the actors. *Variety* labeled it "a good action film," and the usually tough Bosley Crowther of *The New York Times* wrote "*Dangerously They Live* is purest pretense, but it manages to hide its shoddy rather well." He also singled out Nancy's performance: "Nancy Coleman, an engaging newcomer, provides much interest as the distraught British girl."

A couple of months later Warners at last released *King's Row* (1942). "The town they talk of in whispers!" was how Warners touted the movie. Crowther was unmoved by the film, which he called "gloomy and ponderous ... one of the bulkiest blunders to come out of Hollywood in some time."

James Agee only partially agreed with Crowther, calling *King's Row* "half masterpiece and half junk."

Most other critics, though, gave the film glowing reviews. *Redbook* called it "a beautiful and moving film," while *The New Yorker* raved, "*King's Row* will give you that rare glow which comes from seeing a job done crisply, competently and with confidence. It has such distinction that it is plainly too good for the shoddy fellowship of the ten best pictures of the year."

Apparently not, since *King's Row* landed on *Film Daily*'s Ten Best List and even earned an Academy Award nomination for Best Picture (*Mrs. Miniver* took the honor). Despite the acclaim, the film only did modest business at the box office.

Nancy's next picture was *The Gay Sisters* (1942), one of her favorite assignments. Directed by Irving Rapper, the film dealt with the loves and legal battles of the Gaylord sisters: proud Fiona (Barbara Stanwyck), lusty Evelyn (Geraldine Fitzgerald) and romantic Susanna (Nancy). Soap opera of the highest class, the drama followed the women as they sorted out their financial misfortunes and romantic entanglements. Years of legal hassles between Fiona and her estranged husband Charles Barclay (George Brent), an enterprising businessman who wants to take possession of the Gaylord estate, are further complicated when Barclay learns that a child (Larry Simms) was produced on his wedding night, just before Fiona ran out on him. Fiona isn't the only one with a complicated love life: Susanna is desperately in love with a budding artist (Gig Young), but she fears that Evelyn will try to steal him away from her. All problems were handily resolved by screenwriter Lenore Coffee.

Though Nancy was sixth-billed, she had more screen time than third-billed Fitzgerald. The rapport between Nancy and Stanwyck was evident throughout the entire film, and their joint scenes are among the best moments in *The Gay Sisters*. "There's one scene of Barbara and I in the cellar drinking up all that was left of the family wine," Nancy recalls. "I had never played a drunk. How I did it, I don't know. I still think that may be the best piece of acting I ever did."

Nancy adored Stanwyck, and the two became close friends off the set. Stanwyck proved to be a humorous and supportive companion whose only bad influence was that she got Nancy hooked on cigarettes, a habit that took her decades to break.

Critics, in general, were less entranced than Nancy with *The Gay Sisters*. "Another pointlessly caustic inquiry into the lives of the eccentric offspring of a once grand family," is how *The New York Times* summed up the film.

The Gay Sisters failed to click at the box office. Stanwyck, in fact, never even listed it among her film credits. "She never liked it," Nancy said. "She never even mentioned it. I think she resented the title. Maybe it did keep the picture from being as popular as it might have been." Today the movie is most notable as the first featured role of Byron Barr, whom Warners rechristened Gig Young, the name of his screen character.

Nancy's next two ventures, *Desperate Journey* (1942) and *Edge of Darkness* (1943), both starred Warners' top adventure star, Errol Flynn. The former, which *The New York Times* described as "an action melodrama of the wildest stripe," dealt with American fliers trapped in Germany during World War II. Nancy was the sole female in this testosterone-charged epic that struck a responsive chord with wartime audiences eager for pure thrills.

Edge of Darkness was far sturdier material, and it impressed both critics and theatergoers. Based on William Woods' novel, *Edge of Darkness* was a flag-waving drama of Norwegian freedom fighters who oppose the Nazis after they invade their quiet fishing village. At the time, resistance dramas were a staple of each studio (Fox's *The Moon Is Down*, MGM's *The Cross of Lorraine* and RKO's *This Land Is Mine* are but three examples), but *Edge of Darkness* had a grittier look as a result of on-location shooting in Carmel, California. It also benefited from strong direction by Lewis Milestone and an exceptional cast, headed by Flynn, Ann Sheridan, Judith Anderson, Ruth Gordon, Walter Huston and Helmut Dantine.

Flynn played the leader of an underground army made up of several locals, including his girlfriend Karen (Sheridan) and a partisan (Anderson) who's in love with a German soldier. Nancy had the emotional role of Dantine's Polish mistress, which afforded her several scenery-chewing moments, including her first onscreen death scene when she's murdered.

Nancy may have welcomed being killed off, since it meant she no longer had to play any more scenes with Dantine. "Helmut was a frantic actor," she recalled. "He couldn't just say things, he had to do everything physically as well. He always grabbed me by my arms, so that I was black and blue. By the end of the day, the makeup people had to cover me with thick body paint to hide the bruises. Finally, I had to talk to Helmut and in effect give him an acting lesson. I said, 'Helmut you don't have to hold me so tight. You can do that with your fingers without grabbing me the way you're doing.' And he'd say 'That's right, that's right.' But he never did do it, so I was a wreck."

Variety called the film "a dramatic, tense, emotion-stirring story." *The Motion Picture Herald* was equally moved, and wrote, "It is not a tea party. It is an icy shower turned loose on audiences in the hope of driving home what this war is about."

Seen today, *Edge of Darkness* pales in comparison to Milestone's superior anti-war masterpiece *All Quiet on the Western Front*. Although the performances in *Edge of Darkness* were uniformly good, even wartime audiences had a hard time believing Flynn and Sheridan as Norwegian citizens, particularly since neither made an attempt at affecting an accent. Still, there are some powerful scenes, including one in which Nancy lashes into a hysterical outburst when the Nazis are besieged.

Realism seemed to be amazingly absent from Nancy's next film, *Devotion* (1946), purported to chronicle the lives and loves of the Brontë sisters in Victorian England. Whatever resemblance to actual history the picture possessed occurred was purely coincidental.

Directed in fanciful fashion by Curtis Bernhardt, *Devotion* starred Ida Lupino as Emily Bronte, Olivia de Havilland as sister Charlotte and Nancy as Anne, the least remembered of the trio. Rounding out the cast were Arthur Kennedy as their composer brother Branwell, who was consumed by a love of alcohol; Sydney Greenstreet as William Makepeace Thackeray; and Paul Henreid as Reverend Arthur Nichols. Anyone hoping for an insightful look at the literary aspirations of the three sisters, or how they were inspired to pen *Wuthering Heights* and *Jane Eyre*, were in for a major disappointment.

"It tells ALL about those Brontë sisters! ... They didn't dare call it love — they tried to call it Devotion," was the girls-dormitory style ad campaign Warners used. Behind the titillating tagline was a maudlin love triangle involving Emily, Charlotte and Nichols. As Anne, poor Nancy only appeared fleetingly.

In spite of the numerous inaccuracies, *Devotion* did have some virtues. All three leading ladies gave convincing performances, and Kennedy was outstanding as the tortured Branwell. Most memorable was the final shot of a dying Emily, who envisions Death as a black-hooded figure on horseback taking her with him.

Unfortunately, the film's liabilities outweighed those high points. Henreid seemed lost in his role as the reverend; and the stilted dialogue, which contained the classic exchange, "Good morning, Mr. Thackeray." "Good morning, Mr. Dickens," didn't help matters.

Although the film was made in 1943, it wasn't released until 1946. Primary cause for the delay was the lawsuit that de Havilland initiated against Warner Bros. in 1943. She took the studio to court because it wanted to add her suspension time onto the seven years of her contract. The case took three years to settle, with de Havilland scoring an important victory that took a swipe at the crumbling studio system.

When *Devotion* was finally released, the critics were less than kind. *The New York Times*' Crowther called the whole endeavor "a ridiculous tax upon reason and an insult to plain intelligence." One snide critic commented: "They should have called it *Distortion*."

Nancy agreed: "I knew most of it was made up. The nearest part that had any truth to it was that of the brother, Branwell. He did drink himself to death. And he was extremely talented. I always thought that was a silly movie, but I got to wear beautiful clothes."

Almost as silly were some of the off-camera escapades. Lupino and de Havilland had many differences while making the film, but their mutual British heritage led to some peaceful moments between the two. "Olivia was conscious of her British background, what there was of it. She and Ida would have tea served at 4:00 just for them," Nancy remembered. "I was never invited and it really didn't bother me. I thought it was kind of funny, but it bothered the extras. They knew what was going on and they resented what they were doing to me. So [the extras] started serving tea at 4:00 and inviting me. It eventually stopped because it got to be a nuisance, but I loved them for it."

The extras weren't the only ones on the Warners lot who were enamored of Nancy. By this time, Nancy had begun dating Whitney Bolton, the studio's head of publicity. The handsome Bolton was a tall, distinguished looking gentleman who sported a droopy mustache. He was also 18 years older than Nancy. His roots as a newspaperman, like Nancy's father, was an immediate bond the two shared.

Bolton was born on July 23, 1900, in Spartanburg, South Carolina, and had a deep-rooted southern upbringing, which included being educated at the famous Staunton Military Institute and later the University of Virginia. In 1925 he headed to New York, where he began work as a reporter for *The New York Herald Tribune*. Bolton's star rose considerably as a result of his coverage of the Snyder-Gray execution in Sing Sing and Rudolph Valentino's funeral in 1926.

He eventually began writing theater articles for *The Herald Tribune*, which caught the eye of Gene Fowler, managing editor of *The Morning Telegraph*. Bolton switched over to that publication and became its Broadway columnist and, by 1932, its drama critic. During this period Bolton was a regular at the Manhattan night spots and also formed a friendship with "Queen of the Night Clubs" Texas Guinan.

Not long after, he moved to the West Coast, where he wrote several screenplays, including *42nd Street*. He then switched to publicity and worked for Selznick, RKO and Columbia before joining Warners in the early '40s. Bolton was known for being outspoken and, as such, was not always popular on the Warners lot. It was no surprise that the studio opposed the relationship between one of its rising stars and the older and garrulous Bolton.

When Nancy and Bolton got engaged in 1943, both were summoned to Jack Warner's office, where they were told bluntly that they couldn't be married. "They said if we were married, Whitney couldn't give me the proper publicity," Nancy said. "Either he would be accused of giving me too much or too little because he was my husband. This made no sense then and it still doesn't."

Both Nancy and Bolton were iron-willed and would not relent to the studio's strongarm tactics. Their wedding preparations continued, which led to a second meeting with the Warners brass. "They told me, 'You know Miss Coleman, you'll never work again.' And Charlie Einfield, who was a great friend of Jack Warner's, said to Whitney right in front of me, 'What do you want to marry her for. You can have an affair with her.' I was insulted. Whitney was appalled."

Nancy and Whitney were married on September 16, 1943. Despite their differences with the studio, the Boltons received some lovely presents from Warner Bros. Unfortunately, a good script was not among them. At the time, Nancy was anxious to play Mrs. Mark Twain in *The Adventures of Mark Twain* (1944), but she lost the role to Alexis Smith.

Nancy's last Warners film, *In Our Time* (1944), directed by Vincent Sherman, was an uninvolving romance set in Poland on the brink of World War II. The story opens in London, where Jennifer (Ida Lupino) is with her employer (Mary Boland) to buy antiques. While there, she meets Count Stephen Orvid (Paul Henreid), a charming Polish nobleman. In no time at all the couple gets engaged and heads to Poland to be married and live and work on the Orvid family farm. But Stephen's family, which includes his old-fashioned mother (Alla Nazimova) and anti-social sister Janina (Nancy), take an instant dislike to Jennifer. The young couple then attempts to modernize the farm, but their plans are put on hold after the Nazis invade Poland.

Sherman was impressed with Nancy's talent, and the two became good friends. He also felt Nancy's true gifts were never fully exploited by the studio. "Nancy was a talented actress. She had an unusual look. Unfortunately, she was not well used at Warner Bros. That goes on much too often in this town," he said.

Nancy was also fascinated by the flamboyant Nazimova, and the two became quite close. The eccentric actress was invited to Nancy's wedding, but she sent a kind refusal which stated that she would not attend because she didn't believe in marriage. She wished Nancy much happiness and gave her a handsome pewter and copper fruit bowl as a present.

It was not long after the completion of *In Our Time* that Nancy's association with Warners came to an abrupt end. Still smarting from Nancy's disobedience in marrying Bolton, the studio handed her one dreadful script after another, all of which she refused. Nancy was also anxious to start a family and soon after her wedding became pregnant. She kept her condition a secret for as long as possible before it would be noticeable on camera.

"They used that against me. They put me constantly on suspension, which they shouldn't have. My pictures were still running and all doing well," Nancy said.

In 1944 CBS approached Nancy about appearing in a radio version of *Intermezzo*, which had been a big-screen hit for Ingrid Bergman in Sweden in 1936 and for her American film debut in 1939. Nancy was thrilled at the chance to star in the tale of illicit love between a beautiful pianist and a married violinist. Warners refused permission for her to do it.

"I had three pictures out at that time," Nancy recalled. "CBS said this would give me publicity and would only do the pictures good. So I went to my agent, Lew Wasserman [of MCA]. I said 'I'm a pregnant woman who's not allowed to earn her living. I'm constantly on suspension.' He said 'They've got no right, but they can do it.' And Whitney agreed. I didn't care at that point. I was ready to fight. They kept sending me bad scripts and I stayed on suspension. That was the last part of my career at Warners."

It wasn't long after that Nancy finally went to Warner's office one last time. "I said, 'I guess you're not interested in me. I think we'd better call it a day.' I remember I had a check for $1,500 from Warners for the last week or so that I wasn't on suspension. I put it in my desk. I almost tore it up, but I didn't. I also had on my desk a contract for MCA. I then called MCA and said, 'Our time is up.'"

Most of Nancy's time was spent caring for her twin daughters Grania and Charla, born in July, 1944. Whitney also had a son, Whitney French Bolton, from a previous marriage.

In 1946, after a two-year absence, Nancy returned to the screen. Warners, frustrated with both Nancy and de Havilland, finally released *Devotion*, but with little fanfare. Nancy then showed up in *Her Sister's Secret* (1946), one of the more ambitious efforts of low-budget Producers Releasing Corporation. In that one she played a young woman who has a baby out of wedlock, which she gives to her sister (Margaret Lindsay) to raise. The secret mentioned in the title was that the married sister's husband does not know the truth about the child.

The following year she starred in *Violence* (1947), a cheaply made social drama at Monogram about war veterans who become involved with an activist group. While these two Poverty Row enterprises lacked the polish and production values of Nancy's Warners efforts, she did get top billing and, for those studios, above-average scripts.

When RKO announced plans to film *Mourning Becomes Electra* (1947), Nancy campaigned for the role of Hazel Niles, which she saw as her chance to revitalize her career. The ambitious filming of Eugene O'Neill's tragedy featured a srong cast, including Rosalind

Russell, Michael Redgrave, Raymond Massey, Katina Paxinou, Kirk Douglas and Leo Genn. The drama, which was patterned after Sophocles' tale of Agamemnon, dealt with murder and infidelity in post–Civil War New England. Director Dudley Nichols adapted the screenplay for Theater Guild Productions in only three weeks. The Production Code necessitated that he delete any of the play's incestuous references, a crucial element, which greatly weakened the screen adaptation.

The tale centered on the dysfunctional Mannon family, which includes hard-hearted Lavinia (Russell); her weak brother Oren (Redgrave), a Civil War soldier who returns home with deep emotional scars; Ezra (Massey), their cruel patriarch; and his wife Christine (Paxinou), who enters into an adulterous relationship with the sailor (Genn) with whom Lavinia is also in love. Rounding out the cast were Douglas as Peter Niles, Lavinia's fiancée; Nancy as his sister Hazel, who's engaged to Oren; and Henry Hull as the caretaker and one-man Greek chorus.

Clearly it was an artistic venture with little commercial appeal, but it offered choice roles for the entire cast. Nancy was delighted when she won the role, though she nearly didn't get it. "Boy did I work for that," she recalled. "That's the only time I ever got my hair bleached. I wanted to test and they said, 'Nancy, you're too dark and it's going to be a black and white picture. We want a blonde for the part.' So I had my hair lightened. It was still red, but it looked like hair that had been dyed. It was done well. I let it grow out and then had it dyed back to the original color."

Despite the efforts of everyone involved, *Mourning Becomes Electra* emerged as a lugubriously photographed stage play. Bosley Crowther's review in *The New York Times* did little to stir up interest. "There's no escaping that *Mourning Becomes Electra* is far from electric entertainment — it is a static and tiresome show, in fact."

Mourning Becomes Electra was initially released on a reservations-only basis but failed to emerge as the cinematic event distributors hoped for. The film originally ran 159 minutes but was later cut by nearly one hour and put into general release, a decision that both made the film incomprehensible and whittled Nancy's role down to little more than a walk-on. Even after it was edited, audiences stayed away. RKO's total loss on the film was $2.31 million.

Following the disappointment of *Mourning Becomes Electra*, Nancy put her film career on hold. Whitney had been asked to return to his old job as columnist and drama critic with *The Morning Telegraph*. He accepted and, in 1949, the Boltons moved to New York.

"That was a low point. We essentially had to start all over again," Nancy said. "Whitney had one fault — he couldn't save money. He never invested it, he spent it."

The first few years back in New York were a struggle for the Boltons as they managed, minus Nancy's salary, with Whitney's smaller income. Within a few years their situation improved. In addition to his newspaper work, Whitney did two daily newscasts for the Mutual Broadcasting System. Nancy, meanwhile, concentrated on caring for their two children.

In 1950 she made her first film in three years, a Spanish-made thriller called *That Man from Tangier*. The film was made as a tax shelter for its producers who had money in Spain that they needed to spend. Nancy considered it forgettable, and it had few bookings in the United States. "The only good thing I got from that was some beautiful clothes," she said.

In February, 1955, Nancy made an impressive return to the stage in *The Desperate Hours*, a grim drama about a middle-class family held hostage in their home by gunmen. Paul Newman played the gang leader, with Karl Malden and Nancy as the terrified couple trying to protect themselves and their children. The play, staged by Robert Montgomery, ran for 212 performances. Brooks Atkinson of *The New York Times* said Malden and Nancy were "admirable."

Nancy spent the remainder of the '50s doing work on television, including a regular role on the soap opera *Valiant Lady* and guest appearances on such programs as *The U.S. Steel Hour*. In the '60s she again popped up in a daytime serial, *The Edge of Night*.

In 1961 Nancy was chosen to go on a European tour for the State Department and the Theater Guild. The group traveled throughout the continent, except for the British Isles and the Iron Curtain countries.

Far more controversial was a second tour Nancy made in 1964. She agreed to appear with a South African repertory company for a tour, despite warnings from friends and colleagues that it looked as if she was showing support for apartheid. "I was criticized greatly for taking employment with South Africa," she recalled. "I told everyone 'I don't approve of apartheid, but how do I know it until I experience it?'"

While in South Africa, Nancy lived in Johannesburg, Capetown and Pretoria. She became friendly with some of the British citizens, who acquainted her with South African history, including the Dutch takeover of the area and their ban on apartheid. The tour was cut short for Nancy when Grania announced that she planned to be married in London immediately.

In 1969 Nancy made her first film in nearly 20 years, a pre–Civil War drama called *Slaves*, directed by Herbert Biberman, who had been blacklisted in the '50s. Ossie Davis played a slave who leads a revolt of the other slaves against their plantation owner (Stephen Boyd). Although Nancy liked being before the camera again, she wasn't happy with the final print.

Later that year Nancy was dealt a tragic blow when her beloved Whitney died from cancer on November 4. With her daughters now married and starting families of their own, Nancy had to deal with being alone in New York.

She found some solace a few years later when she began seeing Dr. Henry Ross, a prominent New York surgeon who was also the widower of actress Glenda Farrell. The two enjoyed attending various events together in New York, including plays and concerts.

Nancy continued to find occasional work on television, most notably her appearance as Abigail Adams in public television's *The Adams Chronicles*, and on stage, including a role in Paul Osborn's comedy *Morning's at Seven* at the Theater of the Performing Arts in Miami Beach in February 1981. Sylvia Sidney, Dana Andrews and Patricia O'Connell were her co-stars.

In 1987 Nancy had a brief run portraying a nun on *Ryan's Hope*, an ABC daytime serial. By this point Nancy had occasional difficulty remembering lines. After only a few months she was let go. "I guess they decided they didn't want to bother dealing with me," she said.

Nancy spent her last few years living in Manhattan, where she indulged in her favorite pastimes—reading and spending time with her daughters and grandchildren. In 1998 she moved into the Actors Fund Retirement Home in Englewood, New Jersey, and the next year she relocated to another retirement home in Brockport, New York. Though she had gotten frail in her last few years, she still had vivid memories of her career and was as feisty as ever right up to the end of her life. Nancy died on January 18, 2000, after a bout with pneumonia.

Although she may have graced just a handful of Warners movies, Nancy still received a tremendous amount of mail from her many fans up until the time she died. "I find the reactions to my so-called career very interesting," she said in 1999. "I get a lot of fan mail from Europe, especially from Germany and some from Spain. I also get a lot from Scotland. It doesn't do me any good, but it makes me realize that I made an impression."

FILMOGRAPHY

Dangerously They Live (Warner Bros., 1941) Directed by Robert Florey. *Cast:* John Garfield, Nancy Coleman, Raymond Massey, Lee Patrick, Moroni Olsen, Esther Dale, John Ridgeley.

King's Row (Warner Bros., 1942) Directed by Sam Wood. *Cast:* Ann Sheridan, Robert Cummings, Ronald Reagan, Betty Field, Charles Coburn, Claude Rains, Judith Anderson, Nancy Coleman, Kaaren Verne, Maria Ouspensakaya.

The Gay Sisters (Warner Bros., 1942) Directed by Irving Rapper. *Cast:* Barbara Stanwyck, George Brent, Geraldine Fitzgerald, Donald Crisp, Gig Young, Nancy Coleman, Gene Lockhart.

Desperate Journey (Warner Bros., 1942) Directed by Raoul Walsh. *Cast:* Errol Flynn, Ronald Reagan, Nancy Coleman, Raymond Massey, Alan Hale, Arthur Kennedy, Albert Basserman.

Edge Of Darkness (Warner Bros., 1943) Directed

by Lewis Milestone. *Cast:* Errol Flynn, Ann Sheridan, Walter Huston, Nancy Coleman, Helmut Dantine, Judith Anderson, Ruth Gordon.

In Our Time (Warner Bros., 1944) Directed by Vincent Sherman. *Cast:* Ida Lupino, Paul Henreid, Nancy Coleman, Mary Boland, Victor Francen, Alla Nazimova, Michael Chekhov.

Devotion (Warner Bros., 1946) Directed by Curtis Bernhardt. *Cast:* Ida Lupino, Paul Henreid, Olivia de Havilland, Sydney Greenstreet, Nancy Coleman, Arthur Kennedy, Dame May Whitty.

Her Sister's Secret (PRC, 1946) Directed by Edgar G. Ulmer. *Cast:* Nancy Coleman, Margaret Lindsay, Philip Reed, Felix Bressart, Regis Toomey, Henry Stephenson, Fritz Feld.

Unusual Occupations (1947) Documentary short narrated by Ken Carpenter and featuring appearances by Candice Bergen, Nancy Coleman, Brian Donlevy, Nora Eddington, Kay Kyser, Alan Ladd, Dorothy Lamour, Maureen O'Sullivan, Gail Patrick, Ann Rutherford.

Violence (Monogram, 1947) Directed by Jack Bernhard. *Cast:* Nancy Coleman, Michael O'Shea, Emory Parnell, Sheldon Leonard, Peter Whitney, Richard Irving, Frank Reicher.

Mourning Becomes Electra (RKO Radio, 1947) Directed by Dudley Nichols. *Cast:* Rosalind Russell, Michael Redgrave, Raymond Massey, Katina Paxinou, Leo Genn, Kirk Douglas, Nancy Coleman.

That Man from Tangier (Elemsee–United Artists, 1950) Directed by Luis María Delgado and Robert Elwyn. *Cast:* Fernando Aguirre, Nils Asther, Julia Caba Alba, Nancy Coleman, Gary Land, Sara Montiel.

Slaves (Slaves Company/Theatre Guild/Walter Reade, 1969) Directed by Herbert J. Biberman. *Cast:* Stephen Boyd, Dionne Warwick, Marilyn Clark, Nancy Coleman, Ossie Davis.

Bette Davis: "The Fourth Warner Brother"

Olivia de Havilland called Bette Davis "a basically benevolent volcano." Jack Warner described her as "an explosive little girl with a sharp left." As for what Joan Crawford or Miriam Hopkins may have called her, it was probably nothing that would be fit to print in *The New York Times*.

Bette may have ruffled a few feathers, but in looking at her career, any trouble she caused was usually for the betterment of her films rather than from merely playing the prima donna. Offscreen, her life was filled with as much drama as any role she played, having weathered a broken home, four failed marriages, literary revenge brought forth by her daughter and frail health in her later years.

"She could be a controlling person, but at the same time, she wouldn't enter a room and go off on this entire bitch display. People have this image of her as Margo Channing, but she wasn't anything like that," said her friend Robert Osborne.

Still, Ruth Elizabeth Davis did enter the world rather dramatically on April 5, 1908, during an electrical storm in Lowell, Massachusetts, an industrial area outside of Boston. Her staid father, Harlow Morrell Davis, was a patent attorney of Welsh-English stock, a sharp contrast to his wife, Ruth Favor, who was of French Huguenot descent and had a zest for life and adventure.

Bette had little affection for Harlow, who so detached himself from Bette and her younger sister, Barbara, affectionately called Bobbie, that he even ate at a separate table from them. One of Bette's few memories of Harlow was his promise to pay her a dollar if she learned to laugh like a lady. She never collected.

Whereas the girls referred to Harlow as Daddy, their mother was always called Ruthie. She was protective of her girls and filled them, especially Bette, with her own theatrical dreams.

Another influence in Bette's early years was her uncle, Dr. Paul Favor, an Episcopalian minister who saw to it Bette and Bobbie regularly attended church and Sunday school. "We were reared in the strict New England manner, with one eye always toward God," Bette said.

In 1915 the Davises divorced. Ruthie and the girls moved to Newton, Massachusetts, but soon after Ruthie took a job as a governess in New York to pay the steep tuition for both girls at Crestalban, a farm school in the Berkshires. It was there that Bette first learned the power of attracting an audience when her Santa Claus costume caught fire during a Christmas pageant.

At the end of the girls' third year at Crestalban, Ruthie lost her job, and she and the girls moved into a small Manhattan flat. The musketeers, as they called themselves, had to manage on the $200 a month they got from Harlow, a feat made more difficult by the steep tuition Ruthie paid to study at the Clarence White School of Photography. Another difficult adjustment for her daughters was attending P.S. 186, which was a far cry from the Crestalban, which only had thirteen students. It was during this time that a friend of Ruthie's suggested that Ruth Elizabeth shorten her

Forceful yet feminine, Bette Davis earned her place as queen of the Warners lot.

name to Betty but use the more distinctive spelling of Honore Balzac's Cousin Bette.

The next year Ruthie set up a photography studio in East Orange, New Jersey, and Bette attended East Orange High School. After Ruthie suffered some health problems that year and collapsed at one point, the musketeers moved back to Newton, near Ruthie's family.

By the end of Bette's sophomore year at Newton High, Ruthie was able to transfer the girls to Cushing Academy, a private co-educational school in Ashburnham, Massachusetts. To help pay for her tuition, Bette waited on tables. At Cushing, Bette wangled a part in *Seventeen* by Booth Tarkington. Also in the play was a shy musician named Harmon O.

Nelson. Good-looking, lanky and unassuming, Bette fell for him immediately, and they were soon engaged to be engaged.

During a summer vacation in Peterboro, New Hampshire, Bette studied at Mariarden, a school that specialized in dance and drama. Her mentor at Mariarden was Roshanara, an Anglo-Italian dancer who gave free dance classes. Those studies led to Bette's stage debut on July 23, 1925, as a dancing fairy in Frank Conroy's production of *A Midsummer Night's Dream*. Conroy's words of encouragement spurred Ruthie to arrange a meeting for Bette with Eva Le Gallienne, who ran a dramatic school at New York's Civic Repertory Theatre. When the French diva asked Bette to read the part of a seventy-year-old Dutch woman, Bette responded, "That is why I want to come to your school, to learn how to play a part like this." The unimpressed La Gallienne replied, "I'm sorry. You're a frivolous little girl and you'll never make an actress."

This setback didn't deter Ruthie, who enrolled Bette in John Murray Anderson's drama school in New York. To pay the pricey tuition, Ruthie took a job as a housemother in a private school, a position that also provided room and board for Bobbie. With Bette's focus on her career, she and Ham decided to wait a while before marrying. Bette studied under such notables as Martha Graham, who taught Bette how to use her body on a stage. Bette became the school's star pupil and won a $500 scholarship after playing the lead role in *The Famous Mrs. Fair*.

Bette left the school to star in *The Earth Between* at the Provincetown Playhouse in Greenwich Village, but the show was postponed. Through Conroy, she met George Cukor, who ran a stock company in Rochester, New York, and gave her a small role in *Broadway*. Then, on opening night the female star sprained her ankle and Bette went on in her place.

Cukor was impressed with Bette's performance and signed her as an ingenue for the next fall. That summer Bette worked with the Cape Playhouse in Dennis, Massachusetts—as an usher. The company was performing *Mr. Pim Passes By*, starring Laura Hope Crews. When the management couldn't find an ingenue to play an English girl, Bette won the part thanks to her piano playing and her rendition of "I Passed by Your Window." She got an ovation on opening night, and at the end of its run was asked to return the next summer as the company ingenue.

Back with Cukor's troupe, Bette was Louis Calhern's mistress in *Yellow*. When the actor griped that she looked more like his daughter, he had Cukor fire her. Luckily, The Provincetown Playhouse was at last ready to launch *The Earth Between*, and Bette signed a run of the play contract at $35 a week. She then toured in *The Wild Duck* and played Boletta in *The Lady from the Sea*.

Bette's real break came playing henpecked Donald Meek's rebellious daughter in *Broken Dishes*, a domestic comedy which opened at Broadway's Ritz Theater on November 5, 1929. Bette adored Meek, and was also well-paid—$75 a week, which was doubled after three months.

During the run of *Broken Dishes*, Bette tested for the female lead in *Raffles* (1930) for Samuel Goldwyn. Upon viewing her test, Goldwyn reportedly said, "Where did you find that horrible-looking creature?" The more glamorous Kay Francis got the part instead.

Following a three-week run in *Solid South*, Bette made a successful test for Universal's *Strictly Dishonorable* (1931). When the studio suggested changing her name to Bettina Dawes, Bette's Yankee temper flared up. "Oh no you don't," she snapped. "I'm not going through life being known as 'Between the Drawers.'"

Bette and Ruthie arrived in Hollywood on December 13, 1930. A studio representative was supposed to meet them at the train station, but after waiting for an hour, the two women took a cab to their hotel. When Bette phoned Universal to find out why no one met her, she was told, "We sent a man to the station, but he said he didn't see anyone who looked like an actress."

When studio boss Carl Laemmle, Jr., saw Bette, he pulled her out of *Strictly Dishonorable*. Instead, she was humiliated by appearing in two screen tests—one using only her legs, and another in which she lay on a couch while 15 men in succession embraced her passionately.

Bette's inauspicious debut was *The Bad Sister* (1931), in which she was the good sister of small town coquette Sidney Fox, who falls for a city slicker (Conrad Nagel). In one scene,

Bette had to bathe a naked infant. As a prank, Nagel saw to it that Bette had a male infant to wash. As the scene was shot, Nagel was found snickering off the set, while Bette's face turned crimson.

In a 1974 television interview, Bette summed up her film debut: "Talk about disaster movies—this was the first!" Bette later asked for a print of *The Bad Sister*, which she used to show discouraged young actresses how hopeless she was in her first film.

Universal was not surprised by the response to Bette's debut, which was none. Her relationship with Laemmle worsened when he began calling her "The Little Brown Wren" and "Slim," the latter referring to his comment that she had as much sex appeal as sour-pussed character actor Slim Summerville.

Bette had been set for the female lead in *Frankenstein* (1931), but Laemmle instead cast Mae Clarke. After a few more lackluster films, Universal loaned Bette to RKO for *Way Back Home* (1932), a rural drama about feuding farmers. Though it was another bland ingenue role, Bette considered this the first film in which she was well-photographed (by J. Roy Hunt).

She was farmed out to Columbia for *The Menace* (1932), in which she claimed all she did was pull corpses out of closets, but it was a fortuitous assignment. One day she heard an electrician shout "Get that broad out of the way!" Angered by his crudeness, she yelled, "He can't talk to me that way!" Bette learned that "broad" is a technical term for a specific kind of light. She felt ridiculous, but her co-star, Murray Kinnell, was sympathetic and they became acquaintances.

When Universal dropped Bette, the only offer she got was a Poverty Row quickie called *Hell's House* (1932), which she claimed took five minutes to make but seemed endless. Bette was all set to return to New York, but a call from George Arliss altered her plans. Kinnell had told the esteemed actor about Bette, whom he thought could play Arliss' love interest in *The Man Who Played God* (1932). Arliss asked Bette to meet him that afternoon to discuss the role.

At sixty-four and with a craggy, ungainly face that hardly screamed of matinee idol looks, Arliss was an unlikely choice to star in *The Man Who Played God*, a romantic tale about a concert pianist who is slowly losing his hearing. Instead of being defeated by his handicap, he learns to read lips and uses that ability to help others less fortunate than himself. Bette was his loyal girlfriend torn between her devotion to him and her love for a younger man (Donald Cook).

As far as Bette was concerned, Arliss lived up to the film's title. He saw to it that "The Little Brown Wren" became an elegant swan by making sure she was photographed well, given appropriate makeup and a stylish wardrobe. Bette, now a blonde, was also given a stylish bob.

Bette scored a hit and was signed to a long-term Warners contract. Her follow-up role as an artist in the Edna Ferber warhorse *So Big* (1932) was small, but she fared better as Ruth Chatterton's friend in *The Rich Are Always with Us* (1932). Chatterton was one of Bette's idols, and Bette was understandably jittery about shooting her first scene with the star. Afterwards Bette admitted, "I'm so damned scared of you I'm speechless!" Chatterton went out of her way to help her young co-star, a kindness Bette tried to emulate later on when she worked with a newcomer.

Bette's only other 1932 appearance of any note was in *Cabin in the Cotton* as the sexy slattern who teases Richard Barthelmess with her favorite screen line: "Ah'd love to kiss ya, but ah just washed mah hair." Director Michael Curtiz reputedly called Bette that "God-damned-nothing-no-good-sexless-son-of-a-bitch," but she was quite seductive, especially with her cooing of "Minnie the Moocher," one of the overheated melodrama's few lively moments.

With her career getting on track, Bette was ready to contemplate marriage. On August 18, 1932, Bette and Ham ran off to Yuma, Arizona, and were wed. The next day Bette reported to the studio with Ham in tow for a photo shoot. Their "honeymoon" was a fourteen-city tour to promote *42nd Street* (1933). Bette told an interviewer shortly after eloping that "domesticity is all right, if it is not carried too far."

Their domesticity wasn't helped by Bette bringing her studio troubles home. She had no gripes about *20,000 Years in Sing Sing* (1933), a powerful prison flick, but despised *Parachute Jumper* (1933), a B about narcotics smuggling. Bette insisted scenes from the latter be used in 1962's *Whatever Happened to Baby Jane?* to show the poor quality of the grown-up Jane's films.

Bette had her last ingenue role opposite Arliss in *The Working Man* (1933) and then made *Ex-Lady* (1933), in which she played a liberated woman who shocks her boyfriend (Gene Raymond) by suggesting they live together. The risque material was at odds with Bette's Puritan ethic; small wonder that she called it "a piece of junk. My shame was only exceeded by my fury."

She had plenty to be furious about in *Bureau of Missing Persons* (1933). Bette didn't even show up until the midpoint of the seventy-three minute film, and then had little to do.

After making *Bureau of Missing Persons*, Bette learned she was pregnant, but she was the only one happy about the news. Ruthie feared a child would jeopardize Bette's career, and Ham wanted to establish his own success before they had a child, so that he could pay the family's medical bills. Bette reluctantly consented to an abortion, a decision she forever regretted.

She also regretted making *Fashions of 1934* (1934), in which she and William Powell played con artists scooping the fashion industry by stealing original designs. A witty screenplay and Busby Berkeley's lavish "Spin a Little Web of Dreams," which featured dozens of chorines as human harps, were poor compensation to Bette for the "glamour" treatment she was given to fit in with the Paris fashion world. With her heavily lacquered hair and thickly lined eyes, Bette described herself as "the worst imitation of Miss Garbo that you've ever seen."

She was also not pleased with *The Big Shakedown* (1934), *Jimmy the Gent* (1934), *Fog Over Frisco* (1934) or *Housewife* (1934). *Variety* called the last one "satisfactory entertainment." Bette was more to the point: "Dear God, what a horror!"

In *Bordertown* (1935) Bette had a fine role as Marie, a schemer who murders her boorish husband (Eugene Pallette) so she can run off with a slick Mexican lawyer (Paul Muni). When her paramour gets engaged to a socialite (Margaret Lindsay), Marie names him in her crime. Guilt overtakes her and she breaks down at the trial. Bette and director Archie Mayo argued over how she should play her mad scene. He begrudgingly bowed to Bette, whose instincts were perfect.

It was Bette's former adversary, Michael Curtiz, who saved her from forever playing corpses and dull girlfriends. Curtiz ran *Cabin in the Cotton* for director John Cromwell, who was planning *Of Human Bondage* (1934) at RKO. Cromwell was then convinced that no one else but Bette could play Mildred, the shrewish Cockney waitress in W. Somerset Maugham's tale. Bette was delighted, until Jack Warner told her she couldn't do it. "My employers believed I would hang myself playing such an unpleasant heroine. I think they identified me with the character and felt we deserved one another!" Bette rationalized.

A determined Bette badgered Warner every day for six months. Finally, the mogul couldn't take it any more. "Okay. Do it," he agreed. "Just don't come in and pester me any more."

Always the perfectionist, Bette hired a British wardrobe mistress from Warners to live at her home so she could study her Cockney accent. Bette also telephoned every man she knew and asked, "Did you ever know a girl like Mildred? Tell me what she was like." Her diligence was evident from her first scene in *Of Human Bondage*. Her Mildred is a repugnant soul who delights in her skewering of the club-footed medical student (Leslie Howard) who is obsessed with her. Throughout the whole film Bette towers over Howard with her fire-breathing performance, which culminates in a wonderful scene in which she destroys all of the etchings in his flat.

Critics hailed Bette's performance (*Life* called it "probably the best performance ever recorded on the screen by a U.S. actress"), but Depression-era audiences were indifferent. One sneak previewer wrote on his questionnaire, "This is a sordid and dirty picture."

Though *Of Human Bondage* was a box-office flop, Bette seemed certain of an Oscar nomination. When she didn't get one, the Academy was flooded with angry telegrams and agreed to add a write-in slot on the ballot. All the hoopla seemed futile. When the awards were presented on February 27, 1935, Claudette Colbert won for *It Happened One Night*. Bette claimed that Warner instructed every eligible voter at the studio to mark their ballot for anyone but her.

The insulting script Bette was next given, *The Case of the Howling Dog* (1934), lends credence to her claim. She refused to do it and went on her first of many suspensions.

She reluctantly returned to work for *The Girl from Tenth Avenue* (1935), *Front Page Woman* (1935) and *Special Agent* (1935), all of which Bette called "stinkers." She initially held no higher opinion of *Dangerous* (1935). "It was maudlin and mawkish with a pretense at quality which in scripts, as in home furnishings, is often worse than junk," Bette wrote in her autobiography. "But it had just enough material in it to build into something if I approached it properly."

The self-destructive Joyce Heath in *Dangerous* was patterned after the late actress Jeanne Eagels. Joyce's past exploits had her branded as a jinx, which caused her to turn to the bottle. Don (Franchot Tone), an architect, finds the impoverished Joyce in a bar and brings her to his farm. He arranges for her comeback, but not without succumbing to her charms first. Their romance is jeopardized when he learns she has a husband (John Eldredge).

The Laird Doyle screenplay is never entirely believable, with its soap opera machinations and predictable resolutions. The allure of *Dangerous* is all generated by Bette, who brings more spark to her role than the screenplay warrants. *The New York Times* noted: "Best under taut restraint, Miss Davis is least satisfactory when lines lead her to be sputtery and even tearful."

Thanks to a massive publicity campaign, Bette won the Best Actress Oscar, but she admitted, "It's common knowledge that I got this first Oscar as a delayed reward for *Of Human Bondage*."

Bette's Oscar victory was some consolation for her personal difficulties. In early 1935 her estranged father Harlow Davis died. "He was too bright to enjoy being alive," was Bette's unfeeling reaction. Bette, in effect, was now the head of her family, or as Bobbie called her, "the golden goose" who spoiled Ruthie with diamonds, furs and a house that was three times the size of Bette's. "She became my daughter, a spoiled, enchanting little girl," Bette said.

Bette's star ascended even further with *The Petrified Forest* (1936), the film adaptation of Robert E. Sherwood's drama. Her distinguished co-stars, both of whom were in the original Broadway production, were Leslie Howard as the poet Alan Squier and Humphrey Bogart as vicious gangster Duke Mantee, who holds an assorted group of restaurant patrons hostage. Bette played Gabby, a starry-eyed waitress who quotes Francois Villon and dreams of visiting Paris.

Bette recalled Howard's playfulness during the pivotal shootout. "Leslie bit me. This was a sample of his humor. He was trying to make me laugh in one of the most serious moments of the film. I managed to hold back the giggles, but I emerged from the scene with nibble marks on my arms and shoulders which I found difficult to explain for days to come," she wrote in a 1955 *Colliers* article.

The Petrified Forest should have given Bette more leveraging power at Warners, but instead, her career went south with *The Golden Arrow* (1936), a feeble attempt to duplicate *It Happened One Night* (1934). The low point was *Satan Met a Lady* (1936), a botched reworking of *The Maltese Falcon*, which inspired Bosley Crowther of *The New York Times* to plead, "A Bette Davis Reclamation Project to prevent the waste of this gifted lady's talent would not be a too-drastic addition to our various programs for the conservation of natural resources."

Since joining Warners, Bette had been on seven suspensions. An especially bitter pill was not being allowed to test for Queen Elizabeth in *Mary of Scotland* (1936) at RKO. The final insult was *God's Country and the Woman* (1937), which conjured up the ludicrous vision of Bette as a lumberjack's sweetheart. After reading the script, Bette stormed off the lot and headed home, where she sat idly for three months. She made a final plea to Warner, who said if she made *God's Country and the Woman*, he'd star her in a film based on a book the studio had optioned.

"I want you to play the lead, a woman named Scarlett O'Hara. The book is *Gone with the Wind*," he said.

"What's that?" Bette asked, leaving before she got an answer. A year later, she found out.

A disgruntled Bette then accepted producer Ludovico Toeplitz's offer of $50,000 to make two films in England. Soon after reaching London, Bette was served with an injunction barring her from working for anyone besides Warners. Bette secured the services of Sir William Jowitt, who accepted her case even though Bette couldn't pay him the $10,000 advance he requested.

Bette's legal imbroglio was made even more arduous when Ham picked that moment to head back to the United States to look for work. Alone and vulnerable, Bette was also reduced to living in the cheapest inside-court room she could find at the Savoy Hotel.

The showdown between Bette and her home studio was a muddy affair from day one when Warners' attorney painted Bette as a "naughty young lady who simply wants more money."

Sir William's cross-examination of Warner supported Bette's claims that she was little more than an indentured servant, and she seemed confident of a victory. Instead, the court granted Warners an injunction "for three years or for the duration of the contract, whichever is shorter." Bette felt defeated personally and financially: Not only did she have to pay her own court costs, but also those of Warner Bros. Her total costs were a staggering $103,000.

It was her old friend Arliss who advised her to return to Hollywood, say nothing and do her work. "I somehow don't think you'll have to do anything you don't want to do," he said.

Arliss was right. Bette was given a warm welcome back at Warners. Not only did the studio agree to pay its own trial expenses, but half of Sir William's retainer. Bette also liked the script for *Marked Woman* (1937), a brutal drama about dance hostesses who assist a headstrong District Attorney (Humphrey Bogart) in convicting their mob boss (Eduardo Ciannelli) of murder.

Director Lloyd Bacon pulled no punches in depicting the violence in *Marked Woman*. The most shocking scene involved Mary Dwight (Bette) being roughed up by several of the mobster's henchmen while her friends listen in the adjoining room. The horror of the beating is reflected in the terrified faces of the women as they listen to the sounds of solid punches, accented by Mary's painful shrieks.

When Bette arrived to shoot the following scene set at the hospital, she was shocked to find that her makeup consisted of some extra eye shadow and a head bandage that looked like a nun's headdress. Bette stormed off the lot and headed to her physician's office for some more expert makeup. Her doctor had a field day putting plugs in her nose and stuffing her cheeks with cotton wadding. For the crowning touch, he bandaged her entire head in true hospital fashion. When Bette arrived at the studio gate, the guard thought she had been in an accident.

Marked Woman was a triumph, and *The New York Times* remarked that Bette "turned in her best performance since she cut Leslie Howard to the quick in *Of Human Bondage*."

Bette followed *Marked Woman* with *Kid Galahad* (1937), a steel-jawed boxing tale with Edward G. Robinson. The ringside drama followed the problems a crooked promoter (Robinson) encounters when he turns a naive bellhop (Wayne Morris) into a fighter. As Robinson's mistress, Fluff, a seemingly tough cookie who softens when she falls for the boxer, Bette was touching.

She finished out 1937 in *That Certain Woman*, a sudsy remake of *The Trespasser* (1929), and *It's Love I'm After* (1937), with Bette and Leslie Howard as bickering Shakespearean actors.

During Bette's litigation, Warners dropped its option on *Gone with the Wind*. As a consolation prize, Bette was given *Jezebel* (1938), a tasty bit of southern corn pone based on a Broadway flop that had starred Miriam Hopkins. Bette played Julie, an antebellum vixen who toys with the affections of her decent but dull fiancée, Preston Dillard (Henry Fonda), and Rhett Butler wannabe Buck Cantrell (George Brent). Julie was one of Bette's three favorite screen roles (Judith Traherne in *Dark Victory* and Margo Channing in *All About Eve* were the others), which she played with a honey-dripping sweetness that seemed to sugarcoat the brains of everyone else.

Bette's new stature at Warners was evident by the fact that the studio's top technicians were assembled for *Jezebel*. Orry-Kelly designed Bette's sumptuous period gowns, Max Steiner composed the stirring score and Ernest Haller photographed her. Melding them together was William Wyler, a tough and exacting director who proved to be the perfect match for Bette.

At first Bette was not keen on Wyler, who had turned her down for a bit in *A House Divided* (1931) at Universal. She came to admire his craftsmanship and credited him with helping her realize her full potential. Not that their relationship was all honeysuckle and roses. In her autobiography, Bette said, "That handsomely homely dynamo Wyler could make your life hell."

Because of the obvious comparisons between *Jezebel* and *Gone with the Wind*, Warners was anxious to get its film to theaters first. The fastidious Wyler, however, did as many as forty-five takes on some scenes to get a precise line or gesture. He also taught Bette to moderate her excesses. Bette found the role physically draining, and her frequent illnesses contributed to *Jezebel*'s long schedule, which caused it to go over budget. An impatient Warner threatened to have Wyler removed from the picture until Bette stated that she refused to work for anyone else.

By the time *Jezebel* wrapped, Bette and Ham were living on opposite coasts. Bette's loneliness, coupled with her admiration for Wyler, blossomed into her first extramarital affair. "He was the only man strong enough to control me. I adored him," Bette said.

When *Jezebel* was released, critics were generous with their accolades. Pauline Kael singled out Bette as the driving force behind *Jezebel*: "Without the zing Davis gave it, it would have been very mousy indeed." Bette received an Oscar for *Jezebel*, and in her acceptance speech she credited Wyler for her performance and insisted that he take a bow.

Even after winning her second Academy Award, Bette was still being handed dross like *Comet Over Broadway* (1938) and again was on suspension. Bette claimed she was ill when she received the script for it, but more likely she didn't become ill until after she read it.

She did report for *The Sisters* (1938), a sturdy drama about the marital woes of three siblings (Bette, Anita Louise and Jane Bryan) in 1906 San Francisco. Bette plunged into an affair with the film's director, Anatole Litvak, and soon after became involved with billionaire Howard Hughes. These affairs were detrimental to her fragile marriage, and she and Ham were finally divorced in December of 1938.

Wyler was also still in the picture, but as much as Bette loved him, she also feared him and was reluctant to make a commitment. Fed up with her indecisiveness, Wyler married starlet Margaret Tallichet in October 1938. Bette never recovered from losing the love of her life.

If 1938 ended on a bitter note for Bette, her four box-office giants of 1939 were some compensation. Bette had to beg Jack Warner to buy the rights to the first of these, *Dark Victory*. "Who's going to want to see a picture about a girl who dies?" he argued.

Bette played Judith Traherne, a carefree heiress with a malignant brain tumor. Her condition is helped by the bedside manner of the surgeon (George Brent) who performs a seemingly successful operation on her. He later discovers that Judith only has six months to live. Complicating his decision to tell Judith the bad news is that he has fallen in love with her. Judith accidentally discovers the truth from his nurse, and fears that her doctor made love to her out of pity. After much soul-searching, she realizes his love is genuine and they marry. They enjoy an idyllic life in Vermont, all the time trying not to think about the day when Judith will die.

Bette responded well to the sensitive direction of Edmund Goulding. Unlike Wyler, Goulding mapped out scenes before filming. Whereas Wyler needed twenty or thirty takes per scene, Goulding could get the desired effect in one or two takes. The result was what *The New Yorker* called "a gooey collection of clichés, but Davis slams through them in her nerviest style."

Dark Victory opened in April 1939, and industry pundits suggested Bette had a lock on the Best Actress Oscar. Once *Gone with the Wind* opened in December, the Oscar race became a dead heat between Bette and Vivien Leigh. In the end, Leigh won by a slight margin.

Bette also became involved in a romance with Brent, and there was talk of marriage, but she resisted out of fear that Brent might try to run her career. They continued to remain friends.

The Story of Maximilian and Carlotta had long been planned for Bette, but by the time it was given a green light, Emperor Maximilian (Brian Aherne) and Empress Carlotta (Bette) of Mexico had been demoted to supporting roles. The focus was now on revolutionary leader Benito Pablo Juarez (Paul Muni), and the film renamed *Juarez* (1939). Bette claimed Muni had much of her footage excised to have his role padded. In fact, director William Dieterle shot Bette's and Aherne's scenes before Muni was even attached to the film.

The *Dark Victory* triumvirate of Bette, Brent and Goulding were reunited for *The Old Maid* (1939), a well-mounted tearjerker with

Bette as Charlotte, an unwed mother whose lover (Brent) was killed in battle during the Civil War. Charlotte and her infant daughter Tina move in with Charlotte's wealthy cousin Delia (Miriam Hopkins), who ultimately steals Tina's love from Charlotte and legally adopts the child. Seeing Delia become mother to Tina turns Charlotte into a bitter woman whose constant scolding makes the now-grown Tina (Jane Bryan) resent her.

Bette's performance in *The Old Maid* is among her most satisfying, and her subtlety is remarkable considering the histrionics that took place behind the camera. "The only real feud I ever had was with Miriam Hopkins—and that was a beauty," said Bette in 1955.

Hopkins was furious about Bette's affair with her husband, Anatole Litvak, and she went out of her way to make Bette pay for her mistake. On the first day of production Hopkins arrived to shoot her first scene in an exact replica of the gown Bette wore in *Jezebel*. It was an obvious snipe at Bette for what Hopkins considered an inferior replication of her stage role. Hopkins made a sweeping entrance, one which Bette suspected had taken weeks of painstaking care to master. In the end, Bette got the last laugh when the scene wound up on the cutting room floor.

That incident was just the tip of the iceberg. On another occasion when Bette was delivering a difficult speech, Hopkins broke in with, "Oh, I'm so sorry. One of my buttons came unbuttoned."

One cast member who got caught in their crossfire was Rand Brooks, who played Hopkins' grown son. "On *The Old Maid*, they both directed me. One would tell me one thing, then the other would say something else. They were both so anxious to look good and be better than the other. Edmund Goulding just stood by and was amused by the whole thing," Brooks said.

Bette at last got to play England's Queen Elizabeth I in the screen version of Maxwell Anderson's play *Elizabeth the Queen*. Errol Flynn, who was cast as Lord Essex, was put off by the title, which indicated that it was to be Bette's film. Warners came up with the lame *The Knight and the Lady* before settling on *The Private Lives of Elizabeth and Essex* (1939).

For Elizabeth, Bette had her hairline shaved to mesh with the tightly coiled wig she wore. She arrived early for her makeup and to be fitted into her unwieldy costumes. The result was a fiery performance, in which she nicely captured the dominance and loneliness of the aging ruler.

The love shared between Bette and Flynn onscreen didn't extend to their off-camera lives. In his autobiography, Flynn said that one time when Bette gave him a rather heavy-handed stage slap, he retaliated later by giving her an equally vigorous smack on her royal behind.

Bette also continued to lead an active social life. According to a 1939 *Life* profile, she loved the Palomar dance hall and was fond of swimming. She had a houseful of Scotties, Dobermans, Pekingese and Sealyhams, and was president of the Southern California Tailwaggers Foundation. The article also described her as "a constant talker, she curses ably, but usually does it quietly."

By contrast she was reasonably subdued in *All This and Heaven, Too* (1940), based on a Rachel Field novel set in nineteenth-century France. Bette played Henriette Desportes, a French governess whose love for her employer (Charles Boyer), a respected member of French nobility, leads to a vicious scandal fueled by his unstable wife (Barbara O'Neill). It was another smash.

The Letter (1940), which followed, was one of the real high points of Bette's career. W. Somerset Maugham's tale of a crime of passion had Bette playing Leslie Crosbie, the sexually frustrated wife of a Malaysian plantation owner (Herbert Marshall), who shoots an intruder in self-defense. Her innocence seems certain until her lawyer (James Stephenson) receives an incriminating letter written by Leslie which indicates that she and her victim were lovers.

Bette was thrilled to have Wyler direct the film, despite some skirmishes. They fought bitterly over how Bette should deliver Leslie's confession to her husband, "With all my heart, I still love the man I killed!" At one point, Bette stomped off the set, but then return and played it Wyler's way. As she stated in her autobiography, "I lost a battle, but I lost it to a genius."

The Letter was hailed by critics as one of the year's best films. Pauline Kael called Bette's performance "the best study of female sexual hypocrisy in film history." Bette again was Oscar-nominated, but did little campaigning and lost to Ginger Rogers for RKO's *Kitty Foyle* (1940).

After *The Letter*, Bette took a much-needed vacation to peaceful Sugar Hill, New Hampshire, where she met Arthur Farnsworth, assistant manager of Puckett's Inn, where she was staying. Bette and Farnsworth discovered they had much in common, not the least of which was their Yankee background. Within a few months, Bette bought a new home there, which she called Butternut, and acquired a new husband, whom she married on New Year's Day, 1941, at the ranch of Jane Bryan Dart in Rimrock, Arizona. After the marriage, Farney, a former flyer, went to work for the Minneapolis Honeywell Company, in charge of Disney training films for the Air Force.

The new bride returned to work in *The Great Lie* (1941), a silly triangle notable for Mary Astor's Oscar-winning performance. Bette was set to make *Affectionately Yours* (1941) but was replaced by Merle Oberon. The unbalanced Cassie in *King's Row* (1942) was a part Bette eyed, but the studio didn't deem it large enough. Instead, she made *The Bride Came C.O.D.* (1941), a late entry in the *It Happened One Night* pool. Bette said she "reached bottom with this one."

When producer Samuel Goldwyn bought the rights to *The Little Foxes* (1941), Lillian Hellman's drama of a money-grubbing Southern family, he asked to borrow Bette from Warners for marquee value to what might otherwise be a prestigious flop. Warners in return borrowed Gary Cooper for *Sergeant York* (1941). Bette also benefited — to the tune of $385,000.

The powerful drama centered on the scheming and thieving among vixenish Regina Giddens and her greedy brothers as they attempt to invest in a new steel mill. In between their double-dealing, a number of complicated relationships are explored, including the strained marriage of Regina and her weak husband Horace (Herbert Marshall), and her cool relationship with her naive daughter Alexandra (Teresa Wright).

The Little Foxes was Bette's stormiest collaboration with director William Wyler. Their first altercation occurred when he told Bette to see Tallulah Bankhead in the play. Fearful that Bankhead's interpretation would influence her own, Bette at first refused, but gave in. As she expected, she saw no other way to play Regina than the way Bankhead did it.

Despite Bette's reservations, she is mesmerizing as Regina, especially in the celebrated scene when she coldly watches as her dying husband attempts to climb the stairs to get his medicine. With the camera on her the whole time, Bette commands attention without saying a word.

In 1941 Bette served briefly as president of the Academy of Motion Picture Arts and Sciences. The Japanese bombing of Pearl Harbor made nightly blackouts the norm, which meant the usual Hollywood glitz was out for that year's Oscars. When Bette proposed opening the ceremony to the public at $25 per ticket and giving the proceeds to British War Relief, former Academy president Walter Wanger replied, "What have you got against the Academy, Bette?" She resigned on Janaury 30, 1942, despite threats that she'd be blacklisted in Hollywood.

The incident hurt her chances of winning the Best Actress Oscar that year for *The Little Foxes*. Joan Fontaine took home the prize for *Suspicion* (1941).

In early 1942 Bette and John Garfield set up the Hollywood Canteen, a haven for visiting servicemen. The founders recruited dozens of stars to entertain, socialize and even wash dishes. Bette worked tirelessly to obtain funds for the Canteen, and spent most of her evenings there.

Bette worked just as hard onscreen during the war years, starting with *The Man Who Came to Dinner* (1942), an enjoyable version of the George Kaufman-Moss Hart comedy, in which she agreed to play the loyal secretary to overbearing Sheridan Whiteside, with the promise that John Barrymore would play Whiteside. Warners tested Barrymore, but years of self-abuse had taken their toll and he proved unsuitable. Prior to production, Bette's dog accidentally bit her on the nose, which forced her to be away from the studio. Warners took that opportunity to inform Barrymore that he had not gotten the role, and then hired Monty Woolley to recreate his signature stage role. Bette was furious and regretted missing her chance to work with Barrymore.

Bette was her old flamboyant self in *In This Our Life* (1942), director John Huston's overblown version of Ellen Glasgow's Pulitzer Prize–winning novel. As a southern menace named Stanley, Bette caused harm to everyone, including her fiancée (George Brent), her demure sister Roy (Olivia de Havilland), Roy's suicidal husband Peter (Dennis Morgan) and a black law student (Ernest Anderson) whom Stanley implicates in a hit-and-run accident with which she was involved.

In This Our Life is unique for several reasons, not the least of which are its Faulknerian elements, including its flamboyant Dixie heroine and its implicit sexual themes. Charles Coburn, as Bette's uncle, plays the role with more than a dash of incestuous intimation. In one telling scene, his invitation to Stanley to come live with him comes across more like a marriage proposal.

The movie also struck a minor blow for its radical non-stereotypical portrayal of African-Americans. Though Hattie McDaniel is once again relegated to playing a servant, her son (Anderson) is depicted as a hard-working, intelligent student with a bright future.

Bette's next film, *Now Voyager* (1942), is probably her most cherished work among fans, despite the ludicrous elements of the Casey Robinson screenplay. Bette played Charlotte Vale, a neurotic spinster whose lack of self-esteem is the handiwork of her domineering mother (Gladys Cooper). It takes the help of Dr. Jaquith (Claude Rains), a psychiatrist who transforms the shattered woman into a beautiful swan, and the love of Jerry Durrence (Paul Henreid), a charming married man whom she meets on an ocean voyage, to help her discover her independent and romantic nature.

Bette proved to be a miracle worker in making the implausible situations and contrived plot coincidences of *Now Voyager* seem credible. Once again, Bette went to great pains to deglamorize herself in the early part of the film. Bushy eyebrows, a grandmotherly hair style, dowdy print dresses with high starched colors, studious wire-rimmed glasses and black button shoes created the illusion to make the thirtyish Charlotte look more like a middle-aged hausfrau. Bette neatly captures Charlotte's repression and is marvelous when she finally breaks down after being taunted by her niece (Bonita Granville).

Her romantic scenes with Henreid were equally impressive, with her eyes all aglow as he lights up two cigarettes in his mouth and then gives one to Charlotte. *Now Voyager* only drifts out to sea in the sugary final portion, which deals with Charlotte's relationship with Jerry's annoying daughter Tina.

Bette was nominated for a Best Actress Oscar for the fifth consecutive year, a feat that was accomplished only one other time, by Greer Garson from 1939 to 1944. Ironically, it was Garson to whom she lost that year for the sentimental favorite *Mrs. Miniver* (1942).

Bette followed up *Now, Voyager* in the secondary role as the wife of an underground freedom fighter in *Watch on the Rhine* (1943), a verbose filming of the Lillian Hellman play. More fun was her cameo in *Thank Your Lucky Stars* (1943), Warners' all-star patriotic musical. Her froggy-voiced rendition of "They're Either Too Young or Too Old," and her raucous jitterbug with a professional dance champion, made the number the high point of the movie.

She had mixed feelings over *Old Acquaintance* (1943), John Van Druten's story of two college friends who weather rivalries in both work and love. Bette hoped to get Norma Shearer as her co-star, but when the former MGM queen opted for a well-earned retirement, Bette's nemesis, Miriam Hopkins, was cast. Bette warned the film's director, Vincent Sherman, "She'll do just what she did in *The Old Maid*. As my character gets older, hers will get younger! You'll see."

Sure enough, in the latter part of the film, in which the two actresses are supposed to be in their forties, Bette went all out by getting her hair tinted with a silver streak and wearing horn-rimmed glasses. Hopkins, however, looked as youthful and glamorous as she had in the earlier half of the film.

Hopkins at one point employed a long cigarette holder as a prop to show her character's superficiality. Sherman considered it harmless, until Hopkins began waving it about frantically during Bette's scenes. Hopkins would also straighten pictures or arrange flowers to divert attention away from Bette, until Sherman finally had to demand that she stand still.

Bette, however, was waiting for her revenge. The film's most famous scene called for Bette to literally shake some sense into Hopkins. The studio was abuzz with anticipation as the big showdown was about to be shot. Hopkins was not one to be easily outfoxed. When Sherman yelled "Action!," Hopkins went as limp as an empty sack. After a seemingly endless number of takes, Sherman finally got the scene, but it was a grueling task for everyone except Hopkins.

By the time *Old Acquaintance* was finished, Bette was infatuated with Sherman and invited him to meet her in Mexico. At Farney's urging, Sherman didn't go.

A few weeks later Farney fell unconscious on a Los Angeles sidewalk. It was determined that he had suffered a brain hemorrhage, and he died in the hospital two days later without ever regaining consciousness. Doctors told Bette that he had suffered previous damage from a fall at Butternut one month earlier.

Those recent cirumstances caused Bette to be moody and temperamental thoughtout *Mr. Skeffington* (1944), an opulent soap opera directed by Sherman. Unlike their harmonious relationship on *Old Acquaintance*, this time Bette questioned every piece of direction Sherman gave her. In the film, Bette played Fanny Trellis, a vain socialite who opts for a marriage of convenience to her embezzling brother's employer, Job Skeffington (Claude Rains), to keep her sibling out of jail. Fanny remains indifferent to Job until the last scene: Elderly and alone, Fanny finally feels compassion for Job, now blind, after he returns from a German concentration camp.

Against Sherman's objections, Bette insisted on playing Fanny with a high-pitched, little girl voice that was more irritating than flirtatious. Sherman also disapproved of her garish makeup and coiled wig as the older Fanny, which gave the effect that she was about to be embalmed.

After much battling, Bette finally spoke to Sherman and explained the roots of her unruly behavior. She was wracked with guilt over her treatment toward him and Farney. On the morning Bette was to leave for Mexico, she and Farney, who had been drinking, argued. He insisted on driving Bette to the train station and helped her get aboard. As the train was pulling out, he informed her of his talk with Sherman. Bette begged him to get off the train, but he kept on making bitter remarks. Finally, Bette pushed him toward the platform. Farney took the last few steps before jumping off, but by then the train was moving too fast. As the train rode off, Bette noticed Farney had fallen and was holding his head.

Sherman tried to comfort the distraught Bette. He took her to dinner and drove her home. Their evening ended, as Bette had hoped, in her bedroom. Mrs. Sherman was very philosophical in dealing with their relationship: "Well, that's one way to handle her," she told her husband.

Bette completed *Mr. Skeffington* without a hitch, except for one freakish incident. She innocently filled an eyecup with eyewash, but after pressing the cup to her eye, she felt a stinging sensation and screamed in pain. Quick-thinking Perc Westmore, Bette's makeup man, ran for a bottle of castor oil which he used to flush out her eye. She later discovered that someone had accidentally filled her eyewash bottle with acetone, a corrosive liquid used to dissolve adhesives.

Mr. Skeffington was another Davis hit and garnered her another Oscar nomination. She lost to Ingrid Bergman for *Gaslight*.

Bette next appeared as herself in *Hollywood Canteen* (1944), Warners' star-studded tribute to the Canteen, and then had her last choice role at Warners in *The Corn Is Green* (1945). The Emlyn Williams play had been a success for sixty-one-year-old Ethel Barrymore in 1940. Bette was only thirty-six when she undertook the role of Miss Moffat, a spinster schoolteacher who becomes interested in helping a Welsh coal miner (John Dall) win an Oxford scholarship.

To affect a stodgy look, Bette used little makeup and wore her hair in a high pompadour capped by a matronly bun. Her dresses were all very prim, with high collars and ankle-length hems.

While the relationship between Moffat and her protégée is at the heart of the film, director Irving Rapper tried to play up Moffat's drive to improve the Welsh community. "We did make her a woman more interested in the youth of the village rather than in one boy," he said. "That seemed important in the picture. The play showed her devoting herself to one gifted boy."

Bette was superb, imbuing Miss Moffat with a maternal touch that deepens her relationship with Morgan. Sadly, *The Corn Is Green* marked the end of her reign at Warners.

It also ushered in the beginning of a turbulent period in Bette's personal life. During production of *The Corn is Green*, Bette met William Grant Sherry at a cocktail party in Laguna Beach. The hulking Sherry was an ex–Marine who was now a landscape artist. Their courtship lasted only a few months before they were married. The anger and violence that was to be a regular element of their marriage began on their honeymoon when Sherry threw a trunk at Bette. They quarreled frequently, mostly about the fact that Bette was the primary support of her family, and Sherry's bluntness with Ruthie. "I was unhappy from almost the first day," Bette said.

Around this time, Bette renegotiated her contract with Warners, and for the first time was producing as well as acting. The challenge of playing twins attracted Bette to *A Stolen Life* (1946), but Catherine Turney's screenplay defied logic at every turn. Bette played virginal Kate and evil Pat, both of whom are out to land Bill, a handsome lighthouse inspector (Glenn Ford). When Pat wins, Kate finds solace with a moody artist (Dane Clark). After Pat drowns in a boating accident, Kate assumes her sister's identity. She finds that Pat made Bill's life unbearable by forcing him to take a dull office job and dallying with a married man (Bruce Bennett). Kate's deception is finally revealed, but the vapid Bill forgives her with no questions asked.

The accident sequence, which was filmed in a studio tank, was perilous to shoot, and Bette came close to drowning when she got caught in one of the wires connecting the tank to a boat. Divers rescued her in time, and Bette, always the trouper, went back to work soon afterward.

Despite the plot shortcomings, *A Stolen Life* was popular. Bette's B.D. Productions was supposed to make four more films for Warners, but after this one Bette lost interest in producing. "I simply meddled as usual. If that was producing, I had been a mogul for years," she said.

Deception (1946) marked a reunion of Bette with her *Now, Voyager* alumni — co-stars Paul Henreid and Claude Rains, and director Irving Rapper. Unfortunately, the magic of that first film was missing in this remake of *Jealousy* (1929), in which Bette, as the mistress of a flamboyant symphony conductor (Rains), tries to hide the relationship from her new husband (Henreid). She comes up with the only solution to keep her benefactor from revealing her secret — murder.

Rapper expressed little affection for *Deception* and was unhappy with the ending: Rather than having Bette murder Rains and going to prison, Rapper said he preferred "a gay, light, natural, 'So what?' ending." When Bette insisted on a dramatic conclusion, he gave in.

Bette was absent from the screen for several months to give birth to her daughter. Barbara Davis Sherry, who was nicknamed B.D., was born on May 1, 1947, and as Bette said in a 1971 television interview, "I got a beautiful daughter from one of those awful marriages."

Another of her marriages, the one to Warners, was crumbling as quickly as the one to Sherry. *Winter Meeting* (1948) and *June Bride* (1948) fared poorly, but were screen caviar compared to *Beyond the Forest* (1949), a King Vidor potboiler that ranks as the Camp Champ of all time. Bette balked at playing Rosa Moline, a Latin-blooded slattern who sported a frightful yard-long Morticia Addams-style wig and low-cut peasant blouses. She begged Jack Warner not to make the movie, but he convinced her that Rosa would be as strong a role as Mildred Rogers.

The outlandish train wreck of a movie looked as if *Of Human Bondage* had collided with *Duel in the Sun*, David O. Selznick's 1946 western that wallowed in an excess of vapid kitsch. The overbaked plot of *Beyond the Forest* had trashy Rosa leaving her dreary husband (a woefully miscast Joseph Cotten) to follow her true love (David Brian) to Chicago. When he rejects her, Rosa goes back home but spices things up a bit by committing a murder. As with all bad girls of the '40s, she must meet her bad end, which she does in a way that would make Anna Karenina proud.

Bette's eccentric performance and the laughable dialogue, which includes her immortal line "What a dump!" (in reference to the boring town where she lives), made *Beyond the Forest* a yardstick by which bad taste and bad acting would forever be measured. Yet, the whole thing is so incredibly bad it's good in a perverse way. It's impossible not to savor the moment when Rosa utters, "I've got to get out of here," as she stares from her porch at the soot and smoke belching from a nearby factory. Bette took the line to heart and got her release from Warners.

Bette described her departure to reporter Thomas Brady: "After a certain age, when you find yourself doing something you don't believe in, you know it is basically your own fault.

You become a towering fiend of impotence in your anger at yourself, but you release the anger on the people around you. I finally left Warners because of the lack of material suitable for me there."

Though offers were slow coming in, she finally got a good one from RKO for *Payment on Demand* (1951), an honest look at the deterioration of a marriage. Bette's friend Curtis Bernhardt co-wrote the screenplay, originally called *The Story of a Divorce*, with Bruce Manning. Bette liked the role of social-climbing Joyce Ramsey, whom she called "a woman who behaves badly, but naturally." Although the film was completed in 1949, it wasn't released until shortly after *All About Eve* (1950), which helped make *Payment on Demand* a modest success.

The fact that Bette made *Payment on Demand* as her own marriage came apart seemed more than a tad ironic. Sherry discovered that Bette was having an affair with Barry Sullivan, her husband in the film, and created an unpleasant scene at the picture's wrap party. Bette was granted a divorce in 1950 and, in an oddly feminist twist, was ordered to pay Sherry alimony.

Bette reached the apex of her career with *All About Eve* (1950), Joseph L. Manckiewicz's biting look at the theater. His witty screenplay centered on Margo Channing, a fortyish Broadway star in the Tallulah Bankhead vein, whose life is complicated by Eve Harrington (Anne Baxter), a seemingly innocent fan who worms her way into the star's confidence. Margo invites Eve to move into her apartment and hires Eve as her secretary. Everyone, including Margo's best friends, Lloyd (Hugh Marlowe) and Karen (Celeste Holm), thinks Eve is wonderful. Only Margo's maid, Birdie (Thelma Ritter), is suspicious of Eve's motives. Eve reveals her true nature when she tries to steal Margo's fiancée, Bill Sampson (Gary Merrill), and the lead in Margo's next play. Eve's one error is conspiring with muckraking columnist Addison DeWitt (George Sanders). In the end, Eve wrecks Lloyd's and Karen's marriage, gets the role she covets and finds herself enslaved to Addison.

All About Eve is arguably the most brilliantly scripted film to ever come out of Hollywood. Every line is a gem, from Birdie's reaction to Eve's sob story of her life ("Everything but the dogs nippin' at her rear end") to Margo's icy warning to her party guests ("Fasten your seats—it's going to be bumpy night"), and each one is delivered with gusto by the fine cast.

Bette's larger-than-life performance caught the ire of Tallulah Bankhead, who accused Bette of doing an imitation of her. While Bette may have been using Bankhead as a model for Margo, her performance is devoid of impersonation. Bette's histrionic moments, such as her emotional scene when she learns that Eve is her understudy, are delicious fun, but she's equally memorable in quieter moments, such as when Margo explains to Karen what it means to be a woman.

All About Eve won unanimous raves and racked up a record fourteen Oscar nominations, including one for Bette, but she lost to Judy Holliday for *Born Yesterday* (1950). Instead, she won the heart of her leading man, Gary Merrill, whom she married on July 28, 1950. Bette later said, "Gary fell in love with Margo Channing and I fell in love with Bill Sampson."

While honeymooning in England, the Merrills made *Another Man's Poison* (1952), which should have been grounds for divorce, with director Irving Rapper cited as co-respondent. In Hollywood they appeared together in *Phone Call from a Stranger* (1952), an episodic film that starred Gary as the lone survivor of a plane crash who relays the news of the deaths of three of his fellow passengers to their families. Bette had the small but choice role of the bedridden widow of a practical joking salesman (Keenan Wynn), and critics singled out her moving performance.

The Star (1952), for producer Bert Friedlob, saw Bette as Margaret Elliott, a former Oscar winner who can no longer find work. The most memorable scene is the dreadful screen test she makes for her "comeback" role. After viewing the poor test, Margaret forgets any illusions about her career and opts for happiness with a boat builder (Sterling Hayden).

The Star seemed to be a late ride on the wave of *Sunset Boulevard*'s success, though Margaret seems closer in spirit to the self-destructive Joyce Heath of *Dangerous* than *Sunset*'s delusional Norma Desmond Bosley. Crowther noted: "If ever humiliation and cold, clammy, cantankerous chagrin have been thoroughly acted in a movie, it is done by Miss Davis here."

Bette earned her ninth Best Actress Oscar nomination for *The Star*, but odds-on favorite Shirley Booth walked off with the award for *Come Back, Little Sheba* (1952).

Bette complained of fatigue while filming *The Star*, but that didn't prevent her from accepting *Two's Company*, a musical revue for director Jules Dassin, with musical numbers by Vernon Duke and Ogden Nash, and staging by Jerome Robbins. The demanding numbers took their toll on Bette. On opening night in Detroit she fainted during her first song. She later staggered back to the stage and joked to the audience, "You can't say I didn't fall for you."

Two's Company was not well-received, and Bette's former drama coach, John Murray Anderson, was asked to do some doctoring. Bette also received her fair share of doctoring. As the show progressed, she developed swollen glands and lost her voice periodically. Penicillin became part of her daily diet, and after the show hit New York she was treated with dexedrine, a potent stimulant. Reporters erroneously stated that Bette was neurotic and her ills were psychosomatic.

The show's Broadway opening on December 15, 1952, was greeted with mediocre reviews. Walter Kerr of *The New York Herald-Tribune* described Bette as "thoroughly workmanlike" and "magnificently willing."

The show did fair business thanks to Bette, but her health continued to be a problem. She was taken off antibiotics, which caused an excruciating toothache. Dentists then found the root of Bette's medical problems—a bone disease called osteomyelitis, which required surgery on her jaw. Bette left the show, which soon after closed. Columnist Walter Winchell mistakenly reported that Bette had cancer of the jaw. A furious Bette demanded that he print a retraction, which he did.

Bette then took on a new role as a full-time housewife. She and Gary bought a huge house just outside of Portland, Maine, which they called Witch Way. They settled into family life with B.D. and their two adopted children, Margot, then two, and Michael, who was a year younger. In a 1955 *Colliers* article, Bette described the Merrills attending PTA meetings, coaching an amateur ice hockey team, roasting chestnuts during the games and collecting money for charities.

But life at Witch Way was far from idyllic. Most heartbreaking for Bette was the discovery that Margot had been born with brain damage. As an infant, Margot cried incessantly. By the time she was four, she had become destructive and cruel to Michael. She was also slow to learn basics, such as dressing herself. Though it was difficult, Bette and Gary placed Margot in the Lochland School in Geneva, New York, a home for children of similar mental capacities.

The situation with Margot was one of many problems. If Bette thought her marriage to Sherry was, as she once said, "the worst mistake of my life," life with Gary proved even more tempestuous. His violent temper and heavy drinking led to verbal and physical abuse toward Bette. Often Bette provoked his anger by belittling him until he would finally snap and strike her.

Gary would often disappear for days, leaving Bette frantic and thinking that he had been injured or was dead. He would eventually return, but after more battling with Bette the cycle would begin again.

Bette was also feeling creatively and financially starved. Gary had been dropped by 20th Century–Fox, and with Margot in Lochland, plus the expenses on the new home Bette bought for Ruthie, money was scarce. Bette was relieved when producer Charles Brackett contacted her to recreate her role as Queen Elizabeth I in *The Virgin Queen* (1955). Although she was nervous about performing before the cameras for the first time in three years, her anxieties gradually subsided as she began filming. Bette even insisted on shaving her head for the role. Several critics felt Bette surpassed her original turn as Queen Bess sixteen years earlier.

She followed with *Storm Center* (1956), a well-meaning but melodramatic look at Communism and free speech with Bette as a small-town librarian who refuses to remove a scathing pro–Communist book from library shelves and is branded a Communist.

Screenwriter Daniel Taradash managed to get Columbia to release the film on the condition that he bring it in on an extremely tight budget. To keep costs down, the film was shot on location in Santa Rosa, California. Likewise, everyone in the cast, which also included Brian Keith, Kim Hunter and Paul Kelly, agreed to work for less than their usual salaries.

To save a director's fee, Taradash took on that duty, even though he had never directed a film before. "Bette was absolutely marvelous, helping him where and when she could," recollected Hunter. "She didn't take over the direction, but would offer suggestions, give him clues, ideas, when he was confused. It was clear he was grateful for her every thought, and they got on superbly."

Bette and Hunter often socialized together on their evenings and days off, whether it was having dinner together or "just nattering," Hunter recalled. "She became a good friend for that short period of our lives. A delightful human being, no question."

Storm Center wasn't released until after *The Catered Affair* (1956). Paddy Chayefsky's story of a poor Bronx housewife (Bette) who wants to throw an elaborate wedding for her daughter (Debbie Reynolds) had originally been presented as a teleplay with Thelma Ritter in Bette's part. Although Ritter won raves for her performance, she was not a big enough name to carry the film. Bette, unfortunately, was miscast, despite her best efforts to affect a Bronx accent.

At the end of 1956 Bette and Gary closed Witch Way and rented a home in Malibu, California, since they both began doing more work in television. Bette became a frequent guest star on such series as *Alfred Hitchcock Presents*, *Wagon Train* and *Gunsmoke*. In general, Bette was not excited about the new medium, but she needed the work. "I've done many TV shows I didn't want to do just to keep busy. Any of us would be delighted to make movies again, if there were any to do. Unfortunately, this is the age of mediocrity in show business," she complained.

At the same time, she praised the medium for renewing interest in her career. "Thank God for television," she told columnist Eugene Archer. "Warners was the first to release their oldies in the fifties, and there I was, everything I ever did, over and over. They couldn't forget me if they tried."

People might have tried to forget her next two films: *John Paul Jones* (1959), a long and ponderous biography of the naval hero (Robert Stack), in which she had a three-minute cameo as Catherine the Great; and *The Scapegoat* (1959), in which Bette played the morphine-addicted, cigar-smoking mother of a French count (Alec Guinness). Bette and Guinness fought throughout *The Scapegoat*, and she blamed him for having her scenes chopped considerably.

Bette and Gary worked together one last time in *The World of Carl Sandburg*, which wove Sandburg's poems, stories, songs and jokes into what *Life* called a "breezy, poetic vaudeville which shows off Sandburg at his best." The tour was a hit, but they realized they could no longer work or live together, and Gary left the show in San Francisco. On July 6, 1960, Bette was granted a divorce based on her claims that Gary was guilty of "cruel and abusive treatment."

The World of Carl Sandburg hit Broadway in September with Leif Erickson in Gary's place. The show was panned and closed after twenty-nine performances. A despondent Bette spent the winter in New York, dividing her time between her children and writing her autobiography.

She headed to the West Coast for *A Pocketful of Miracles* (1961), Frank Capra's weak remake of his *Lady for a Day* (1933). Bette was poorly cast as Apple Annie, a Bowery-based apple seller who is given a makeover by an assortment of Damon Runyon characters to impress her visiting daughter (Ann-Margret), her fiancée and his family.

Shortly before the release of *A Pocketful of Miracles*, Ruthie died. Bette always claimed she "would have been nothing" without Ruthie's spirit and determination. Bette and her sister had Ruthie's tombstone inscribed: "Ruthie — You will always be in the front row."

In the fall of 1961 Bette's autobiography *The Lonely Life* was released and quickly became a best-seller. Later that year she took another stab at Broadway as Maxine, the blowsy hotel owner in Tennessee Williams' *Night of the Iguana*. But the drama that ensued behind the scenes eclipsed the one that audiences saw. Bette was told that her part, which was much smaller than those of her co-stars Patrick O'Neal and Margaret Leighton, would be built up, but it wasn't. Bette couldn't acclimate herself to the Method actors she was working with, and her style didn't mesh well with theirs. The play was a disaster during its tryouts and was not helped by Bette's attempts to play Maxine as a sexpot with flaming red hair and wearing a denim shirt open to the navel. In New York Bette's fans greeted her warmly, but it was Leighton who won the ovation.

Walter Kerr of *The New York Times* had only faint praise for Bette's acting: "In the coarse and blowsy effrontery of her flat-footed walk ... there is some tattered and forlorn splendor." Bette gladly left *Night of the Iguana* after four months and was replaced by Shelley Winters.

Bette was apprehensive when producer-director Robert Aldrich approached her about a horror film he was planning called *Whatever Happened to Baby Jane?* (1962). Horror films had not been her stock in trade, and she loathed the idea of working with Joan Crawford, who owned the property. Two things won her over: She loved the script and she needed the money.

Baby Jane was a Grand Guignolish tale about two sisters: Blanche Hudson, a former Hollywood movie queen whose career was cut short by a crippling automobile accident; and Jane Hudson, a once-popular child star in vaudeville who was blamed for Blanche's accident. Both women have since become mere shells of their former selves. The invalid Blanche is treated like a prisoner in her Hollywood home and is tortured by Jane, whose cruelties including serving Blanche rats for dinner. Jane, who has been forced to care for her sister, has become an ugly, aged alcoholic, whose bitterness is equaled by her periods of delusion, which includes her belief that she can rekindle her long-dead career. When Jane learns that Blanche has been plotting to sell the sisters' home, Jane plans her revenge, which leads to murder and her own descent into madness.

Bette, in grotesque makeup and a beat-up blonde wig, resembled a pickled version of Fanny Skeffington. Crawford, who was appalled at the lengths to which Bette went to look ugly, remained as attractive as possible throughout the movie, much to Bette's annoyance. Bette complained to Aldrich about Crawford wearing padded bras when her character was supposed to be withering away. Worst of all, she couldn't tolerate Crawford's drinking on the set.

As filming progressed, tempers flared. In one scene when Jane cruelly punts her sister across the floor, Bette's foot allegedly made contact with Crawford's head. Crawford got even, though. During a pivotal scene in which Jane was supposed to drag Blanche, Crawford rigged weights under her robe, which resulted in Bette hurting her back.

At night Bette would call Aldrich at home and spend an hour rehashing the day's events and complaining about everything Crawford did wrong. As soon as he was done talking to Bette, Aldrich would get a call from Crawford, bitching about everything Bette did to annoy her.

In spite of everything, *Baby Jane* was a riveting mix of macabre suspense and morbid humor. Bette created her most electrifying screen portrait since Margo Channing, and her gooey rendition of "I've Written a Letter to Daddy," Baby Jane's signature song, became a camp standard for many a female impersonator. It was less a case of brilliant acting than of capturing all of the excesses of one character and molding them into a memorable amalgam of eccentricity.

Aldrich confounded skeptics who expected a film with two women regarded as has-beens to be a bust. Instead, the movie earned back its production costs after the first week of its release.

In September of 1962, prior to *Baby Jane*'s release, Bette spent $500 on an ad in the trade papers as a publicity gimmick. Although some in the industry took it as a sign of desperation, others saw it as an example of Bette's humor. The offers she turned down included a Las Vegas production of *Bye, Bye Birdie* and a role as a madam in *Four for Texas* (1963).

Anyone who doubted Bette's stature in the industry was soon convinced she was back on top when she earned a Best Actress Oscar nomination for her work in *Baby Jane*.

Bette's follow-up to *Baby Jane* was *Dead Ringer* (1964), a throwback to her Warners vehicles of the '40s, and for the second time she played good and bad twins. Then, as if to undo all of the good that *Baby Jane* had done for her, Bette appeared in a disastrous Italian import called *The Empty Canvas* (1964). As the mother of artist Horst Buchholz, who is involved in an affair with a seductive model (Catherine Spaak), Bette's artifical performance was further sabotaged by a dreadful Dutch boy wig, layers of makeup and a honey-sweet southern accent.

When asked why she made *The Empty Canvas*, Bette replied: "There just aren't that many good women's roles around any more — most of the top parts now are being written for men. But we'll be back when the cycle is completed."

More dismal, though more successful commercially, was *Where Love Has Gone* (1964), Harold Robbins' piece of pulp inspired by the 1958 scandal involving Lana Turner and her daughter Cheryl Crane in the murder of mobster Johny Stompanato. Bette's reason for doing this one was more succinct: "It paid for my daughter's wedding." On January 4, 1964, sixteen-year-old B.D. married Jeremy Hyman, a twenty-nine-year-old executive with Seven-Arts.

Hush ... Hush Sweet Charlotte (1964) was an attempt to duplicate the success of *Baby Jane* by reuniting Bette with Crawford, but the latter left during pre-production and was replaced, at Bette's urging, by Olivia de Havilland. The genteel de Havilland serves as a nice counterpoint to Bette's Charlotte, a tempestuous wrecking ball whose outbursts are frequent and frenzied.

Hush ... Hush Sweet Charlotte was nearly as successful as *Baby Jane*, although Bette began to get locked into one thriller after another. She went to England for *The Nanny* (1965), an interesting suspense flick in which she played an English governess suspected of murdering one of her charges. Clearly no Mary Poppins, Bette gave a thoughtful, relaxed performance.

Bette hoped to play Martha in *Who's Afraid of Virginia Woolf?* (1966) or get the Beryl Reid role in *The Killing of Sister George* (1970). Instead, she got saddled with this sorry lot: *The Anniversary* (1968), a disastrous black comedy made in England, in which she sported an assortment of fashionable eye patches; *Connecting Rooms* (1970), another British import, in which she played a cellist who takes an interest in a fellow roomer; and *Bunny O'Hare* (1971), in which she and Ernest Borgnine reached their nadirs as over-the-hill Bonnie and Clyde–types disguised as hippies.

In 1973 Bette began work on Joshua Logan's musical reworking of *The Corn Is Green*, which moved the story from Wales to the American South. Unfortunately, *Miss Moffat*, as the show was called, was fraught with problems, including Bette's difficulty with the songs and her insecurity about her stage techniques. Although her performance seemed to improve by the time the show hit Philadelphia, and initial audience reaction was positive, Bette was exhausted and pulled out of the show. Without Bette, Logan had to close *Miss Moffat* before it reached New York.

Bette had a more enjoyable experience in 1975 taking her show, *An Informal Evening with Bette Davis*, to Australia and the United Kingdom. She loved discussing her career and answering questions from audience members about her years in Hollywood, her co-stars and even her husbands. Though Bette was apprehensive about doing the show at first, her fears subsided as soon as she heard the applause. "I always walk out and say 'What a dump!' and that brings down the house. They know it's not going to be a pompous evening; it's going to be a ball," Bette said.

Bette hated the horrific *Burnt Offerings* (1976), but was seen to good advantage as the mother of evangelist Aimee Semple McPherson (Faye Dunaway) in *The Disappearance of Aimee* (1976) on television. The movie was a ratings winner, and both actresses were praised by critics; but Bette didn't get along with Dunaway, whom she resented for showing up late and unprepared.

In 1977 Bette's career enjoyed a further resurgence when she became the first actress to be honored by the American Film Institute. Olivia de Havilland, Celeste Holm, Ann-Margret, Paul Henreid and many others offered their tributes to Bette, which were interspersed with film clips.

As a result of the tribute she landed roles in the all-star *Death on the Nile* (1978), a follow-up to the successful *Murder on the Orient Express* (1974); *The Dark Secret of Harvest Home* (1978), based on Tom Tryon's best-seller; *Strangers: The Story of a Mother and a Daughter* (1979), for which she won an Emmy as Gena Rowlands' domineering mother; and the Disney thrillers *Return to Witch Mountain* (1978) and *Watcher in the Woods* (1980).

When Bette agreed to play a school teacher traveling cross country to see her relatives in *Family Reunion* (1980), an NBC mini-series, she arranged to have B.D.'s son Ashley play the young student who accompanies her. Bette thought that the money he earned on the film would help pay for his college education, an expense his parents could ill afford. Though the youngster had never acted professionally before, Bette coached him and he gave a sincere performance.

"She loved to work and she spent a lot of money on her family," said Robert Osborne. "She felt it was her duty to take care of her family and she never complained about that."

Bette was equally loyal to friends such as Osborne, who never forgot her generosity when he began his broadcasting career. "When I got my first important job as a CBS entertainment reporter, Bette called and volunteered to have me do a live interview with her. She didn't have to do that. It meant getting a new dress, getting made up and being ready early in the morning. She was willing to do that for a friend because she knew it would help me get established," he said.

In her later years Bette also developed friendships with such unlikely types as Lana Turner and Alice Faye, whom she didn't get a chance to know during their heyday. "She was friends with people you would not expect to be her friends," Osborne said. "I went with Bette one time to Italy where she was getting an award. While there I introduced her to June Allyson. I figured these two would never get along, but Bette adored June. Bette went on about the movies June made and how good she was in certain scenes. June almost fainted."

Another new friend she made at this time was Kathryn Sermak, who became her personal assistant and closest companion for the remainder of her life. Sermak organized Bette's finances as well as her personal affairs, and served as a good friend to the lonely Bette.

Bette continued to work primarily in television dramas such as *Skyward* (1980); *White Mama* (1980); *Little Gloria, Happy at Last* (1982), and *A Piano for Mrs. Cimino* (1982), which featured one of her loveliest performances as an elderly woman whose children fear she can no longer handle her personal affairs. She also was excellent in *Right of Way* (1980), with James Stewart.

Bette also became introduced to a new generation in 1981 when she was immortalized in Kim Carnes' hit record "Bette Davis Eyes." Bette contacted Carnes to tell her how much she liked the song and how it helped her grandson gain new respect for her. As a thank you gesture, Carnes gave Bette a gold record of the song, which Bette immediately hung up on her wall.

In 1983 producer Aaron Spelling asked Bette to appear in *Hotel*, his series based on Arthur Hailey's bestseller, as the owner of the hotel who barks orders at star James Brolin. His generous offer was seven episodes per season at $100,000 for each. Prior to shooting her third appearance, Bette detected a lump in her left breast. Doctors wasted no time in performing a mastectomy. The operation was a success, but nine days later she had a mild stroke. Doctors held little hope but, true to her fighting spirit, Bette made a recovery. Spelling told Bette she would be welcome to return to *Hotel* anytime, but she refused.

Bette's mental well-being took a hit as well in 1985 when B.D. published *My Mother's Keeper*, a *Mommie Dearest*–type memoir. The malicious book, which painted Bette as a ruthless egomaniac who ran everyone's lives, caused a hurt in Bette from which she never recovered.

"It was only in the last three years of her life that she became difficult," Osborne said. "She had a lot of anger from the betrayal by her daughter. Much of what her daughter said in her book was true, but the other side was not told, how she helped them out financially and how her family drained her of her money. That's why she had to keep working."

Not to be upstaged, Bette wrote *This 'n That*, which, unlike B.D.'s book, dealt with the more pleasant memories mother and daughter shared. Bette also spent much time discussing her friendship with Sermak. Despite its rambling nature, the book did well.

Since Bette's health scare a few years earlier, she found it difficult to find work. Frail, with a wizened look and weighing a skeletal ninety pounds, production companies were reluctant to hire Bette, out of fear that no one would insure her. She did get one last worthwhile project with *The Whales of August* (1987), a quiet tale of two elderly sisters in New England. Lillian Gish played the patient sister forced to care for her cantankerous, blind sibling (Bette), who is on the verge of senility. With a cast of pros, including Vincent Price, Harry Carey, Jr., and Ann Sothern, *The Whales of August* was a class production that *Daily Variety* called "lovely on all counts."

Bette's final appearance was in a supposed comedy about witchcraft called *Wicked Stepmother* (1989). Amazingly, the part called for Bette to play a glamorous vamp who seduces an elderly widower (Lionel Stander) with her sorcery. Wearing a 1920s red wig, heavily made up and dressed in slinky gowns, Bette looked ludicrous and was horrified when she saw the rushes.

She only filmed a few early scenes before her doctor called the director to say Bette wouldn't return to work on the film since her weight had dropped to seventy-five pounds. The script was revamped so that it looked like Bette's character had turned herself into a feline. After sixty-eight years in films, how sad that Bette's last role should be completed by a mechanical cat.

Bette's health continued to deteriorate, and in April 1989 she developed the cancer that would continue to spread throughout her body over the next six months. Still, she refused to let it slow her down and attended many tributes all over the world, accompanied by her loyal companion Sermak. Bette finally succumbed to cancer in Paris on October 6, 1989.

Almost to the day she died, Bette never stopped working. Work was her life and her passion, and she embraced it like no other actress before or since. In 1972 Bette said, "I'll never make the mistake of saying I'm retired. You do that and you're finished. You just have to make sure you play older and older parts. Hell, I could do a million of those character roles. But I'm stubborn about playing the lead. I'd like to go out with my name above the title."

She kept her word.

FILMOGRAPHY

The Bad Sister (Universal, 1931) Directed by Hobart Henley. *Cast:* Conrad Nagel, Sidney Fox, Bette Davis, Zasu Pitts, Slim Summerville, Charles Winninger, Emma Dunn, Humphrey Bogart.

Seed (Universal, 1931) Directed by John M. Stahl. *Cast:* John Boles, Frances Dade, Bette Davis, Raymond Hackett, Zasu Pitts, Genevieve Tobin, Richard Tucke, Jack Willis, Lois Wilson.

Waterloo Bridge (Universal, 1931) Directed by James Whale. *Cast:* Mae Clarke, Douglass Montgomery, Doris Lloyd, Frederick Kerr, Enid Bennett, Bette Davis, Ethel Griffies.

Way Back Home (RKO Radio, 1932) Directed by William A. Seiter. *Cast:* Phillips Lord, Effie Palmer, Mrs. Phillips Lord, Bennett Kilpack, Raymond Hunter, Frank Albertson, Bette Davis.

The Menace (Columbia, 1932) Directed by Roy William Neill. *Cast:* H.B. Warner, Walter Byron, Bette Davis, Natalie Moorehead, Halliwell Hobbes.

Hell's House (State Rights, 1932) Directed by Howard Higgin. *Cast:* Junior Durkin, Frank Coghlan, Jr., Pat O'Brien, Bette Davis, Emma Dunn, Charley Grapewin, Morgan Wallace, Hooper Atchley.

The Man Who Played God (Warner Bros., 1932) Directed by John G. Adolfi. *Cast:* George Arliss, Violet Heming, Bette Davis, André Luguet, Louise Closser Hale, Donald Cook.

So Big (Warner Bros., 1932) Directed by William A. Wellman. *Cast:* Barbara Stanwyck, George Brent, Dickie Moore, Bette Davis, Mae Madison, Hardie Albright, Alan Hale, Earle Foxe.

The Rich Are Always with Us (Warner Bros., 1932) Directed by Alfred E. Green. *Cast:* Ruth Chatterton, George Brent, Bette Davis, John Miljan, Adrienne Dore, John Wray.

The Dark Horse (Warner Bros., 1932) Directed by Alfred E. Green. *Cast:* Warren William, Bette Davis, Guy Kibbee, Vivienne Osborne, Frank McHugh, Sam Hardy, Harry Holman.

Cabin in the Cotton (Warner Bros., 1932) Directed by Michael Curtiz. *Cast:* Richard Barthelmess, Dorothy Jordan, Bette Davis, Hardie Albright, David Landau, Berton Churchill.

Three on a Match (Warner Bros., 1932) Directed by Mervyn LeRoy. *Cast:* Joan Blondell, Ann Dvorak, Bette Davis, Warren William, Lyle Talbot, Humphrey Bogart, Edward Arnold.

20,000 Years in Sing Sing (Warner Bros., 1933) Directed by Michael Curtiz. *Cast:* Spencer Tracy, Bette Davis, Arthur Byron, Lyle Talbot, Warren Hymer, Louis Calhern.

Parachute Jumper (Warner Bros., 1933) Directed by Alfred E. Green. *Cast:* Douglas Fairbanks, Jr., Bette Davis, Frank McHugh, Claire Dodd, Leo Carrillo, Harold Huber, Thomas E. Jackson.

The Working Man (Warner Bros., 1933) Directed by John G Adolfi. *Cast:* George Arliss, Bette Davis, Theodore Newton, Hardie Albright, Gordon Westcott, J. Farrell MacDonald.

Ex-Lady (Warner Bros., 1933) Directed by Robert Florey. *Cast:* Bette Davis, Gene Raymond, Frank McHugh, Claire Dodd, Monroe Owsley.

Bureau of Missing Persons (Warner Bros., 1933) Directed by Roy Del Ruth. Cast: Lewis Stone, Pat O'Brien, Glenda Farrell, Bette Davis, Allen Jenkins, Ruth Donnelly, Hugh Herbert.

Fashions of 1934 (Warner Bros., 1934) Directed by William Dieterle. Cast: William Powell, Bette Davis, Frank McHugh, Verree Teasdale, Reginald Owen, Henry O'Neill, Hugh Herbert.

The Big Shakedown (Warner Bros., 1934) Directed by John Francis Dillon. Cast: Charles Farrell, Bette Davis, Ricardo Cortez, Glenda Farrell, Allen Jenkins, Henry O'Neill.

Jimmy the Gent (Warner Bros., 1934) Directed by Michael Curtiz. Cast: James Cagney, Bette Davis, Alice White, Allen Jenkins, Arthur Hohl, Alan Dinehart, Philip Reed, Hobart Cavanaugh.

Fog Over Frisco (Warner Bros., 1934) Directed by William Dieterle. Cast: Bette Davis, Donald Woods, Margaret Lindsay, Lyle Talbot, Arthur Byron, Hugh Herbert, Douglas Dumbrille.

Of Human Bondage (RKO Radio, 1934) Directed by John Cromwell. Cast: Leslie Howard, Bette Davis, Frances Dee, Kay Johnson, Reginald Denny, Alan Hale, Reginald Owen.

Housewife (Warner Bros., 1934) Directed by Alfred E. Green. Cast: George Brent, Ann Dvorak, Bette Davis, John Halliday, Ruth Donnelly, Hobart Cavanaugh, Robert Barrat.

Bordertown (Warner Bros., 1935) Directed by Archie Mayo. Cast: Paul Muni, Bette Davis, Margaret Lindsay, Gavin Gordon, Arthur Stone, Robert Barrat, Eugene Pallette.

The Girl from Tenth Avenue (Warner Bros., 1935) Directed by Alfred E. Green. Cast: Bette Davis, Ian Hunter, Colin Clive, Alison Skipworth, John Eldredge, Katharine Alexander.

Front Page Woman (Warner Bros., 1935) Directed by Michael Curtiz. Cast: Bette Davis, George Brent, June Martel, Dorothy Dare, Joseph Crehan, Winifred Shaw, Roscoe Karns.

Special Agent (Warner Bros., 1935) Directed by William Keighley. Cast: Bette Davis, George Brent, Ricardo Cortez, Jack LaRue, Joseph Crehan, J. Carrol Naish, Joseph Sawyer.

Dangerous (Warner Bros., 1935) Directed by Alfred E. Green. Cast: Bette Davis, Franchot Tone, Margaret Lindsay, Alison Skipworth, John Eldredge, Dick Foran.

The Petrified Forest (Warner Bros., 1936) Directed by Archie Mayo. Cast: Leslie Howard, Bette Davis, Genevieve Tobin, Dick Foran, Humphrey Bogart, Joseph Sawyer, Porter Hall.

The Golden Arrow (Warner Bros., 1936) Directed by Alfred E. Green. Cast: Bette Davis, George Brent, Eugene Pallette, Dick Foran, Carol Hughes, Craig Reynolds, Ivan Lebedeff.

Satan Met a Lady (Warner Bros., 1936) Directed by William Dieterle. Cast: Warren William, Bette Davis, Alison Skipworth, Arthur Treacher, Winifred Shaw, Marie Wilson, Porter Hall.

Marked Woman (Warner Bros., 1937) Directed by Lloyd Bacon. Cast: Bette Davis, Humphrey Bogart, Eduardo Ciannelli, Jane Bryan, Lola Lane, Mayo Methot, Isabel Jewell.

Kid Galahad (Warner Bros., 1937) Directed by Michael Curtiz. Cast: Edward G. Robinson, Bette Davis, Humphrey Bogart, Wayne Morris, William Haade, Jane Bryan, Harry Carey.

That Certain Woman (Warner Bros., 1937) Directed by Edmund Goulding. Cast: Bette Davis, Henry Fonda, Ian Hunter, Anita Louise, Donald Crisp, Katherine Alexander, Mary Phillips.

It's Love I'm After (Warner Bros., 1937) Directed by Archie Mayo. Cast: Leslie Howard, Bette Davis, Olivia de Havilland, Patric Knowles, Eric Blore, George Barbier, Bonita Granville.

Jezebel (Warner Bros., 1938) Directed by William Wyler. Cast: Bette Davis, Henry Fonda, George Brent, Donald Crisp, Fay Bainter, Margaret Lindsay, Henry O'Neill, John Litel.

The Sisters (Warner Bros., 1938) Directed by Anatole Litvak. Cast: Errol Flynn, Bette Davis, Anita Louise, Ian Hunter, Donald Crisp, Beulah Bondi, Jane Bryan, Alan Hale, Henry Travers.

Dark Victory (Warner Bros., 1939) Directed by Edmund Goulding. Cast: Bette Davis, George Brent, Geraldine Fitzgerald, Humphrey Bogart, Ronald Reagan, Henry Travers, Dorothy Peterson.

Juarez (Warner Bros., 1939) Directed by William Dieterle. Cast: Paul Muni, Bette Davis, Brian Aherne, Claude Rains, John Garfield, Donald Crisp, Joseph Calleia, Gale Sondergaard.

The Old Maid (Warner Bros., 1939) Directed by Edmund Goulding. Cast: Bette Davis, Miriam Hopkins, George Brent, Donald Crisp, Jane Bryan, Louise Fazenda, Jerome Cowan.

The Private Lives of Elizabeth and Essex (Warner Bros., 1939) Directed by Michael Curtiz. Cast: Bette Davis, Errol Flynn, Olivia de Havilland, Donald Crisp, Vincent Price, Alan Hale.

All This and Heaven, Too (Warner Bros., 1940) Directed by Anatole Litvak. Cast: Bette Davis, Charles Boyer, Jeffrey Lynn, Barbara O'Neill, Virginia Weidler, Helen Westley.

The Letter (Warner Bros., 1940) Directed by William Wyler. Cast: Bette Davis, Herbert Marshall, James Stephenson, Frieda Inescourt, Gale Sondergaard, Bruce Lester, Elizabeth Inglis.

The Great Lie (Warner Bros., 1941) Directed by Edmund Goulding. Cast: Bette Davis, George Brent, Mary Astor, Lucile Watson, Hattie McDaniel, Grant Mitchell, Jerome Cowan.

The Bride Came C.O.D. (Warner Bros., 1941) Directed by William Keighley. Cast: James Cagney, Bette Davis, Stuart Erwin, Eugene Pallette, Jack Carson, Harry Davenport.

The Little Foxes (Goldwyn-RKO Radio, 1941) Directed by William Wyler. *Cast:* Bette Davis, Herbert Marshall, Teresa Wright, Richard Carlson, Dan Duryea, Patricia Collinge, Charles Dingle.

The Man Who Came to Dinner (Warner Bros., 1942) Directed by William Keighley. *Cast:* Bette Davis, Ann Sheridan, Monty Woolley, Richard Travis, Jimmy Durante, Reginald Gardiner.

In This Our Life (Warner Bros., 1942) Directed by John Huston. *Cast:* Bette Davis, Olivia de Havilland, George Brent, Dennis Morgan, Charles Coburn, Frank Craven, Billie Burke.

Now, Voyager (Warner Bros., 1942) Directed by Irving Rapper. *Cast:* Bette Davis, Paul Henreid, Claude Rains, Gladys Cooper, Bonita Granville, Ilka Chase, John Loder, Lee Patrick.

Watch on the Rhine (Warner Bros., 1943) Directed by Herman Shumlin. *Cast:* Bette Davis, Paul Lukas, Geraldine Fitzgerald, Lucile Watson, Beulah Bondi, George Couloris.

Thank Your Lucky Stars (Warner Bros., 1943) Directed by David Butler. *Cast:* Dennis Morgan, Joan Leslie. Guest stars: Humphrey Bogart, Eddie Cantor, Bette Davis, Olivia de Havilland, Errol Flynn, John Garfield, Alan Hale, Ida Lupino, Ann Sheridan, Alexis Smith.

Old Acquaintance (Warner Bros., 1943) Directed by Vincent Sherman. *Cast:* Bette Davis, Miriam Hopkins, Gig Young, John Loder, Dolores Moran, Philip Reed, Roscoe Karns.

Mr. Skeffington (Warner Bros., 1944) Directed by Vincent Sherman. *Cast:* Bette Davis, Claude Rains, Walter Abel, Richard Waring, George Couloris, Jerome Cowan.

Hollywood Canteen (Warner Bros., 1944) Directed by Delmer Daves. *Cast:* Joan Leslie, Robert Hutton. Guest stars: Jack Benny, Joe E. Brown, Eddie Cantor, Joan Crawford, Bette Davis, John Garfield, Ida Lupino, Eleanor Parker, Alexis Smith, Barbara Stanwyck, Jane Wyman.

The Corn Is Green (Warner Bros., 1945) Directed by Irving Rapper. *Cast:* Bette Davis, John Dall, Joan Lorring, Nigel Bruce, Rhys Williams, Rosalind Ivan, Mildred Dunnock, Arthur Shields.

A Stolen Life (Warner Bros., 1946) Directed by Curtis Bernhardt. *Cast:* Bette Davis, Glenn Ford, Dane Clark, Walter Brennan, Charles Ruggles, Bruce Bennett, Peggy Knudsen.

Deception (Warner Bros., 1946) Directed by Irving Rapper. *Cast:* Bette Davis, Paul Henreid, Claude Rains, John Abbott, Benson Fong, Richard Walsh, Richard Erdman, Russell Arms.

Winter Meeting (Warner Bros., 1948) Directed by Bretaigne Windust. *Cast:* Bette Davis, Jim Davis, Janis Paige, John Hoyt, Florence Bates, Walter Baldwin, Ransom Sherman.

June Bride (Warner Bros., 1948) Directed by Bretaigne Windust. *Cast:* Bette Davis, Robert Montgomery, Fay Bainter, Betty Lynn, Tom Tully, Barbara Bates, Jerome Cowan, Mary Wickes, Marjorie Bennett.

Beyond the Forest (Warner Bros., 1949) Directed by King Vidor. *Cast:* Bette Davis, Joseph Cotten, David Brian, Ruth Roman, Minor Watson, Dona Drake, Regis Toomey.

All About Eve (20th Century–Fox, 1950) Directed by Joseph L. Manckiewicz. *Cast:* Bette Davis, Anne Baxter, George Sanders, Celeste Holm, Gary Merrill, Hugh Marlowe, Thelma Ritter.

Payment on Demand (RKO Radio, 1951) Directed by Curtis Bernhardt. *Cast:* Bette Davis, Barry Sullivan, Jane Cowl, Kent Taylor, Betty Lynn, John Sutton, Frances Dee, Peggie Castle.

Another Man's Poison (United Artists 1952) Directed by Irving Rapper. *Cast:* Bette Davis, Gary Merrill, Emlyn Williams, Anthony Steel, Barbara Murray, Reginald Beckwith, Edna Morris.

Phone Call from a Stranger (20th Century-Fox, 1952) Directed by Jean Negulesco. *Cast:* Bette Davis, Gary Merrill, Shelley Winters, Michael Rennie, Keenan Wynn, Craig Stevens. (Bette's segment was used in a Fox TV drama entitled **Crack-Up** in 1957.)

The Star (20th Century-Fox, 1952) Directed by Stuart Heisler. *Cast:* Bette Davis, Sterling Hayden, Natalie Wood, Warner Anderson, Minor Watson, June Travis, Katharine Warren.

The Virgin Queen (20th Century-Fox, 1955) Directed by Henry Koster. *Cast:* Bette Davis, Richard Todd, Joan Collins, Jay Robinson, Herbert Marshall, Dan O'Herlihy, Robert Douglas.

Storm Center (Columbia, 1956) Directed by Daniel Taradash. *Cast:* Bette Davis, Brian Keith, Kim Hunter, Paul Kelly, Kevin Coughlin, Joe Mantell, Kathryn Grant, Edward Platt.

The Catered Affair (MGM, 1956) Directed by Richard Brooks. *Cast:* Bette Davis, Ernest Borgnine, Debbie Reynolds, Barry Fitzgerald, Rod Taylor, Robert F. Simon, Madge Kennedy.

John Paul Jones (Warner Bros., 1959) Directed by John Farrow. *Cast:* Robert Stack, Marisa Pavan, Charles Coburn, Erin O'Brien, Bruce Cabot, Basil Sydney, Thomas Gomez, Bette Davis, David Farrar.

The Scapegoat (MGM, 1959) Directed by Robert Hamer. *Cast:* Alec Guinness, Bette Davis, Nicole Maurey, Irene Worth, Pamela Brown, Annabel Bartlett, Geoffrey Keen, Peter Bull.

A Pocketful of Miracles (United Artists, 1961) Directed by Frank Capra. *Cast:* Bette Davis, Glenn Ford, Hope Lange, Arthur O'Connell, Peter Falk, Thomas Mitchell, Ann-Margret.

Whatever Happened to Baby Jane? (Warner Bros., 1962) Directed by Robert Aldrich. *Cast:* Bette Davis, Joan Crawford, Victor Buono, Marjorie Bennett, Maidie Norman, Anna Lee.

Dead Ringer (Warner Bros., 1964) Directed by Paul Henreid. *Cast:* Bette Davis, Karl Malden, Peter Lawford, Phillip Carey, Jean Hagen, George Macready, Estelle Winwood.

The Empty Canvas (*La Noia*) (Embassy, 1964) Directed by Damiano Damiani. *Cast:* Horst Buccholz, Catherine Spaak, Bette Davis, Daniela Rocca, Lea Padovani, Isa Miranda.

Where Love Has Gone (Paramount, 1964) Directed by Edward Dmytryk. *Cast:* Susan Hayward, Michael Connors, Bette Davis, Joey Heatherton, Jane Greer, DeForest Kelly.

Hush ... Hush, Sweet Charlotte (20th Century–Fox, 1964) Directed by Robert Aldrich. *Cast:* Bette Davis, Olivia de Havilland, Joseph Cotten, Agnes Moorehead, Cecil Kellaway, Mary Astor, Victor Buono.

The Nanny (20th Century–Fox, 1965) Directed by Seth Holt. *Cast:* Bette Davis, Wendy Craig, Jill Bennett, James Villiers, William Dix, Pamela Franklin, Jack Watling, Maurice Denham.

The Anniversary (20th Century–Fox, 1968) Directed by Roy Ward Baker. *Cast:* Bette Davis, Sheila Hancock, Jack Hedley, James Cossins, Christian Roberts, Elaine Taylor.

Connecting Rooms (LSD, 1971) Directed by Franklin Gollings. *Cast:* Bette Davis, Michael Redgrave, Alexis Kanner, Kay Walsh, Gabrielle Drake, Olga Georges-Picot, Leo Genn.

Bunny O'Hare (American-International, 1971) Directed by Gerd Oswald. *Cast:* Bette Davis, Ernest Borgnine, Jack Cassidy, Joan Delaney, Jay Robinson, John Astin, Reva Rose.

The Scientific Cardplayer (*Lo Scopone Scientifico*) (CIC, 1972) Directed by Luigi Comencini. *Cast:* Bette Davis, Alberto Sordi, Silvana Mangano, Joseph Cotten, Domenico Modugno.

Burnt Offerings (United Artists, 1976) Directed by Dan Curtis. *Cast:* Oliver Reed, Karen Black, Bette Davis, Lee Montgomery, Burgess Meredith, Eileen Heckart, Dub Taylor.

Return from Witch Mountain (Disney, 1978) Directed by John Hough. *Cast:* Bette Davis, Christopher Lee, Ike Eisenmann, Kim Richards, Jack Soo, Denver Pyle, Brad Savage.

Death on the Nile (Paramount, 1978) Directed by John Guillermin. *Cast:* Peter Ustinov, Bette Davis, Mia Farrow, Angela Lansbury, Jane Birkin, David Niven, George Kennedy, Maggie Smith.

The Watcher in the Woods (Disney, 1980) Directed by John Hough (and Vincent McEveety). *Cast:* Bette Davis, Carroll Baker, David McCallum, Lynn-Holly Johnston, Kyle Richards.

The Whales of August (Circle/Nelson, 1987) Directed by Lindsay Anderson. *Cast:* Lillian Gish, Bette Davis, Ann Sothern, Vincent Price, Harry Carey, Jr., Mary Steenburgen, Tisha Sterling.

Wicked Stepmother (MGM, 1989) Directed by Larry Cohen. *Cast:* Bette Davis, Colleen Camp, Lionel Stander, David Rasche, Tom Bosley, Barbara Carrera, Richard Moll, Evelyn Keyes.

TELEVISION MOVIE CREDITS

Madame Sin (1972) *Cast:* Bette Davis, Robert Wagner.

The Judge and Jake Wyler (1972) *Cast:* Bette Davis, Doug McClure, Eric Braeden.

Scream Pretty Peggy (1973) *Cast:* Bette Davis, Ted Bessell, Sian Barbara Allen.

The Disappearance of Aimee (1976) *Cast:* Faye Dunaway, Bette Davis, James Sloyan.

The Dark Secret of Harvest Home (1978) *Cast:* Bette Davis, David Ackroyd.

Strangers: The Story of a Mother and Daughter (1979) *Cast:* Bette Davis, Gena Rowlands.

White Mama (1980) *Cast:* Bette Davis, Ernest Harden, Eileen Heckart.

Skyward (1980) *Cast:* Bette Davis, Suzy Gilstrap, Howard Hessemann.

Family Reunion (1981) *Cast:* Bette Davis, J. Ashley Hyman.

A Piano for Mrs. Cimino (1982) *Cast:* Bette Davis, Penny Fuller, Keenan Wynn, Alexa Kenin.

Little Gloria ... Happy at Last (1982) *Cast:* Bette Davis, Angela Lansbury, Martin Balsam.

Right of Way (1983) *Cast:* James Stewart, Bette Davis, Melinda Dillon.

Agatha Christie's Murder with Mirrors (1985) *Cast:* Helen Hayes, Bette Davis, John Mills.

As Summers Die (1986) *Cast:* Scott Glenn, Jamie Lee Curtis, Bette Davis, John Randolph.

Olivia de Havilland: "The Perfect Lady"

With two Academy Awards and a roster of memorable characterizations to her credit, including one in what may be the most famous American film of all time, Olivia de Havilland has earned a place in the hearts of film buffs as one of the screen's finest dramatic actresses. Yet one would be hard-pressed to find evidence of her dramatic skills from the mediocre roles she was given while under contract to Warner Bros. Her fragile beauty and velvety voice almost locked her forever into playing the poor damsel in distress to heroic leading men such as Errol Flynn.

While the off-camera Olivia was just as refined as the heroines she played, on several occasions the lady also proved to be a tiger, such as when she took on her Warners bosses and scored a landmark legal victory. Her independence from Warners at last brought her the freedom to tackle flesh and blood roles. And for an all-too-brief period, Olivia was the reigning actress of the screen with a quartet of exceptional performances (*To Each His Own, The Dark Mirror, The Snake Pit* and *The Heiress*) that reinforced the fact of how ill-used she had been at Warners.

Unlike Bette Davis, though, Olivia was less driven. At the peak of her stardom she bid farewell to Hollywood and instead took on a more fulfilling role as a Parisian wife and mother. While her career never again reached the apex of her Oscar years, it continued to flourish as Olivia channeled her talents in different directions, including the stage and writing, as well as making occasional film appearances.

"She's about as well-adjusted and level-headed a person as I've ever met who's become a superstar," said long-time friend Robert Osborne. She's very interested in the world, politics and her family. She has a great handle on life. In the '40s she was known as the Bachelor Girl of Hollywood. Men like Jimmy Stewart, Burgess Meredith and John Huston were all in love with her, and who could blame them. She was—and is still—very attractive, very feminine."

Olivia Mary de Havilland was born on July 1, 1916, in Tokyo, Japan, to British parents. Her mother, Lilian Ruse, had been an accomplished student of music and voice who had won a pair of three-year scholarships to Reading Musical College in England. In the summer of 1907 Lilian was offered a position in Tokyo as a teacher of choral singing. She was also reunited with her brother, Ernest Percy Ruse, one of two non–Asiatic professors at the city's celebrated Waseda University. It was also in Tokyo, at an embassy tea, where Lilian met Walter de Havilland, a suave Englishman who ran a successful firm of patent attorneys. The two had a whirlwind courtship, and within a few days Walter proposed.

However, marriage was not foremost on Lilian's mind. According to Olivia, Lilian's performance of a solo, most likely during Sunday mass at St. Andrew's Anglican Church, impressed one of the women in attendance, and she offered to write a musical play for Lilian. As such, Lilian decided to return to England in December of 1911 to study acting at Sir Beerbohm

Tree's Academy, now known as the Royal Academy of Dramatic Arts.

Walter was persistent and in 1914 caught up with Lilian again. He returned to England to enlist with the British Army after the First World War began. Despite being an accomplished marksman, Walter, then forty-two, was rejected because of his age. At the same time, he looked up Lilian and again asked her to marry him. She tossed a crown to help her make a decision. They were married soon after. That precarious beginning was a harbinger of the difficulties that lay ahead. In later years Lilian described her husband as a tall, handsome but terrifying man who "spoke like God, but behaved like the Devil."

Their relationship grew even more strained after the birth of Olivia and her sister Joan the following year. In early 1919 Walter and Lilian bundled up their daughters and set sail for the United States, arriving in San Francisco on March 1. Eight days later Walter headed back to Japan. Shortly after their arrival the girls were taken to see Dr. Langley Porter, a noted child specialist. He looked at Olivia's tonsils and insisted they be removed immediately. The prognosis was worse for Joan, who soon after developed pneumonia. Porter insisted the climate in Saratoga, in the foothills of the Santa Cruz mountains, would do a world of good for Joan.

Following his advice, Lilian and the girls left San Francisco and first settled into the Vendome Hotel in the Santa Clara valley. According to Olivia, it was during their stay at the Vendome when Lilian met George M. Fontaine at the hotel's annual New Year's Eve ball. Fontaine was both pleasant-looking and a successful businessman, who was part owner and general manager of Hale Brothers, a renowned department store in San Jose. He was immediately smitten with Lilian, and the two of them soon began seeing a lot of each other.

The family stayed at the Vendome for several months before moving to Saratoga when Olivia was four. Joan by this time had become anemic and spent a great deal of time in bed. Not surprisingly, she became resentful that Olivia had more fun than she did. In one instance, Olivia got to play the lead in a local theater production of *Alice in Wonderland*, a part Joan had envisioned for herself. Such instances led to the phrase "Olivia can, Joan can't," a common expression in the de Havilland home and a catalyst for the sisters' reputed "feud."

In October 1924 Lilian, who had now decided to take up permanent residence in California, left her daughters in the care of a nurse and embarked for Tokyo to file suit for divorce from Walter. By this time Olivia's father had sold the family's Tokyo home to the Swedish Legation and was living in bachelor's quarters, which were tended to by a young Japanese woman who was a descendant of a Samurai family.

The divorce was granted in February 1925, and Lilian and Fontaine were married two months later. Two years afterward, Walter also took a new spouse—his Japanese housemaid, Yoki-san, whose devotion to her husband was "extraordinary," Olivia said.

The girls had a hard time dealing with their stepfather's rigid brand of discipline. He imposed a strict 8:15 curfew, which meant that Olivia often had to do her homework in bed with a flashlight beneath the covers. He also forbade the girls to engage in extra-curricular activities, although on the sly, Olivia joined the hockey club and the debate team. She also was a member of the Student Council at Los Gatos Union High School, and served as class secretary in her freshman year, and secretary of the student body in her sophomore year. By that point Joan returned to Japan to live with Walter and Yoki-san.

The well-versed Lilian taught her daughters diction and voice control at an early age, as well as exposing them to great works of literature. As such, Olivia developed an interest in the arts and joined the school's drama club. Olivia was thrilled in her junior year when she was chosen to play Violet in *Mrs. Bumpstead-Leigh*, but her elation was replaced by disbelief when Fontaine issued her an ultimatum: either she withdraw from the play or permanently leave the house. Olivia refused to let down her fellow castmates or the prospective audience, so she temporarily moved in with friends. Lilian related the incident to her bridge club, who were so moved that they raised $200 to help Olivia, a debt she repaid during her first year in films. With the money, Olivia was eventually able to rent a room in the residence of a former nurse. Even after the play was finished, Olivia did not move back home. She did not make her peace with Fontaine for many years afterward, and even then she did so only to please her mother.

Olivia graduated among the top of her

Olivia de Havilland achieved her greatest screen successes away from Warner Bros.

class in 1934. She won a scholarship to Mills College in Oakland, which was noted for its drama and speech arts course, and planned to attend the school in the fall. Although Olivia was still uncertain as to her eventual career path, drama was becoming a growing interest. She had recently appeared as Puck in the Saratoga Community Players production of *A Midsummer Night's Dream*, and made the acquaintance of an assistant to producer Max Reinhardt who attended the performance. When she learned that Reinhardt was going to produce *A Midsummer Night's Dream* at the Hollywood Bowl that summer, she asked the maestro's assistant for permission to watch rehearsals. Instead, she was told by another of Reinhardt's assistants that she could understudy the role of Hermia.

When Olivia arrived in Los Angeles four weeks later, she discovered that she was actually the second understudy to Gloria Stuart, cast as Hermia. Jean Rouverol, daughter of playwright Aurania Rouverol, was first understudy, but she soon dropped out because of a film commitment. Stuart, likewise, was unable to attend more than three rehearsals, since she was filming at Warner Bros., and Olivia took her place during much of the preparatory period. Five days before opening night the company learned that Stuart's film was running over schedule. Reinhardt then told Olivia, "You will play the part." After that success, she repeated the role at the San Francisco Opera House, and in the Faculty Glade and Greek Theater of the University of California at Berkeley.

During rehearsals, Henry Blanke, a producer at Warner Bros. who was preparing a film version of the Shakespearean romp (which Reinhardt and William Dieterle were to direct), noticed Olivia and asked Reinhardt to introduce him "to the girl with the ethereal face." By the end of his visit he offered her the screen role of Hermia, but she turned him down.

Prior to going on a national tour with the play and immediately after a screen test at Warner Bros., Olivia was persuaded by Blanke, Reinhardt and Dieterle to not only sign for *A Midsummer Night's Dream*, but also for a five-year contract to go into effect when the film was completed. Olivia wanted it written into her contract that she could accept play offers in between film assignments. Warners refused and, after considerable arguing, Olivia left the office. Reinhardt immediately dragged her back in, shouting at her in German. She reluctantly signed the contract.

A Midsummer Night's Dream (1935) was an honest effort by Warners to try something artistic. For box-office insurance, the studio cast James Cagney as Bottom, Joe E. Brown as Flute and Dick Powell as Lysander. Shakespeare's comedy about the mixed-up relationships of four lovers, as well as other residents of an Athenian forest, was, if nothing else, visually stunning (thanks to Hal Mohr's gorgeous cinematography) and a treat for the ears (courtesy of Felix Mendelssohn's pulsating music). *A Midsummer Night's Dream* was a studio's worst nightmare — an expensive prestige picture that bombed at the box office.

As Hermia, Olivia gave an impressive performance. Playwright Zoe Akins found her so charming that she asked for Olivia to play the ingenue in *The Old Maid*, but Warners refused. Olivia was heartbroken, and it was her last theatrical offer while under contract to the studio.

Warners held back the premiere of *A Midsummer Night's Dream* until October 1935, by which time Olivia had appeared in two artistically inferior but commercially more successful releases. First up was *Alibi Ike* (1935), the funniest of Joe E. Brown's films, with the rubber-mouthed comic as an ace baseball player with an excuse for everything. During the movie's seventy-minute running time, Brown runs afoul of fast balls and gangsters, and also romances, breaks up with and eventually marries sweet Dolly Stevens (Olivia). While the movie was an excellent showcase for Brown, it did little for Olivia, except pigeonhole her into playing dull ingenues.

Likewise, *The Irish in Us* (1935) was an amusing bit of blarney with Olivia as the girl loved by brothers James Cagney and Pat O'Brien. It was little more than a variation of her *Alibi Ike* role, and she played it with sincerity but little enthusiasm.

It was Olivia's next film that served as the springboard for her future at Warner Bros. Rafael Sabatini's swashbuckler *Captain Blood* had been intended as a vehicle for Robert Donat, fresh from his success in *The Count of Monte Cristo* (1934). A miscommunication involving Donat's salary led to a lawsuit and his withdrawal from the project. As a replacement, the studio decided to gamble on dashing newcomer Errol Flynn, who had appeared in a few programmers. Flynn's virility and athletic prowess seemed ideal for the role of Peter Blood, a doctor who is unjustly sentenced to serve on a slave ship after he treats a criminal. When the slaves revolt over their cruel treatment, Blood becomes the ship's captain, leading a pack of buccaneers. With her British heritage and cultured manners, Olivia was the obvious choice to play Arabella Bishop, the beautiful niece of a Jamaica plantation owner who is swept away by the renegade Blood.

The combination of dashing swordplay and storybook romance made *Captain Blood* one of Warners' top films of the year. Key to its success were the amorous sparks between Flynn and Olivia. But despite the many intimate moments between Olivia and Flynn on the set, not to mention Flynn's weakness for the opposite sex, no actual romance ever developed between them. Not that both parties didn't have feelings for each other. In his memoirs, Flynn remembered Olivia as "a young woman of extraordinary charm" with warm brown eyes and a soft manner.

Olivia was equally enamored of her leading man. "I had such a crush on him all through *Captain Blood*, and years later I learned he had a crush on me during *The Charge of the Light Brigade*. What a shame neither one of us let on," Olivia told a London audience in 1971. She then quipped, "No it isn't, he would have ruined my life."

After the popularity of *Captain Blood*, Olivia was locked in a series of damsel in distress roles, such as Angela in Warners' opulent production of *Anthony Adverse* (1936), based on Hervey Allen's bestseller. Fredric March played the illegitimate Anthony, an eighteenth-century adventurer who travels the world and does much soul searching before returning to Europe and his true love (Olivia), who is now mistress to Napoleon. Though *Anthony Adverse* suffered from a verbose script, and Olivia's role was poorly written, it captured the fancy of moviegoers.

Olivia finished the year back with Flynn in *The Charge of the Light Brigade*, a rousing yarn inspired by the famous poem by Lord Alfred Tennyson. Olivia appeared sparingly as the charming lass engaged to Flynn but in love with his brother (Patric Knowles), both of whom are officers of the Royal Lancers. Their triangle was secondary to the pageantry of the action scenes, especially the thrilling reenactment of the brigade's legendary charge. While the film may have been a questionable history lesson, it was glorious bravado that translated into box-office gold.

Since Olivia had few scenes, she was often bored during production. At one point she became so envious of her fellow castmates cavorting about on horseback that she mounted one of the horses and began galloping about. A nervous assistant director ordered her to dismount for fear that she might suffer an injury.

Flynn's attempt to liven things up during a location shoot in Sherwood Lake, California, proved even worse. As a joke, Flynn hid a dead snake in the pantalettes Olivia was to wear in her next scene. Needless to say, he found the incident far more amusing than she did.

Despite his childish pranks, Olivia had great respect for her co-star, and also much sympathy. Prior to shooting *Captain Blood*, Olivia and Flynn found themselves alone on the set one day waiting for the dialogue director, script girl and a few other personnel to begin rehearsal. During that time they sat on the stage's ramp and became involved in the lengthiest conversation they ever had. Olivia recalled: "I asked him 'What do you want out of life?' and he said 'Success.' And yet in the end he had success and that wasn't enough."

Olivia was seen sans Flynn in her trio of 1937 releases. *Call It a Day* (1937) was an amiable film based on Dodie Smith's play about the romantic exploits of a middle class English family within a twenty-four hour period, and marked the first time Olivia was top billed.

The Great Garrick (1937) was a whimsical farce set in eighteenth-century Europe about a troupe of French actors who take over a country inn to plot their revenge on British stage great David Garrick (Brian Aherne) after he maligns the French style of acting. Garrick catches on and plots his retaliation. Unfortunately, one of his victims is the elegant Germaine Dupont (Olivia), a countess who is unaware of the shenanigans taking place. Following much confusion, director James Whale leads to the fade-out with Garrick and Germaine living happily ever after.

It's Love I'm After (1937) also involved actors—in this case, Leslie Howard and Bette Davis as a madcap version of Alfred Lunt and Lynn Fontanne. Olivia was amusing as a dewy-eyed heiress with a crush on Howard.

Following such urbane fare, it was a surprise to see Olivia in the rustic *Gold Is Where You Find It* (1938) opposite George Brent and Claude Rains. The film was basically a variation on the sheep rancher versus cattle rancher theme, but director Michael Curtiz kept the action fast-paced, and Olivia looked stunning in her first Technicolor film.

Olivia looked even more ravishing opposite Flynn in their signature film, *The Adventures of Robin Hood* (1938). Flynn donned tights for this spin on the legend of Robin of Locksley, a spirited rebel whose quest is to restore King Richard (Ian Hunter) to the throne of England after he is unseated by his villainous brother Prince John (Claude Rains). Besides the many duelers he encounters, Robin finds a worthy sparring partner in the lovely Maid Marian (Olivia), who is loyal to John. The Norman Marian at first finds the Saxon Robin both politically and socially distasteful, but she later succumbs to his charms and helps in his endeavor to rescue King Richard. With its simple message that good triumphs over evil, and such memorable moments as Robin's humorous log duel with Little John, the archery contest and the climactic duel between Robin and Sir Guy of Gisbourne (Basil Rathbone), *The Adventures of Robin Hood* was exceptional fare.

Warners accorded the film a $1.6 million budget, making it the studio's most expensive production to date. By the time it was finished, the cost had spiraled to $2 million, but the expense was justified. Cinematographers Sol Polito and Tony Gaudio captured the richness and beauty of Sherwood Forest in gorgeous three-strip Technicolor. Erich Wolfgang Korngold delivered a stirring score which earned him an Academy Award. In addition to Flynn's vibrant performance, the brilliant cast of character actors, which also included Alan Hale as Little John, Eugene Pallette as Friar Tuck and Una O'Connor as Marian's servant, lent outstanding support.

As Marian, Olivia was every schoolboy's fantasy. Lavishly costumed and angelically framed in Technicolor, she never looked more fetching. Her Marian is a thoroughbred, fiercely independent and spirited in her early scenes when she is held hostage by Robin; warm and desirable in their love scenes. It was by far her finest role in her films with Flynn.

The New York Times raved, "*The Adventures of Robin Hood* is payment in full for many dull hours of picture going," and that, "Maid Marian has the grace to suit Olivia de Havilland."

Olivia never saw *The Adventures of Robin Hood* until twenty years after its release, and the film proved to be quite a revelation. "I went to see *Robin Hood* on the Champs Elysees and I was quite impressed with it. I even wrote Errol a letter saying how much I enjoyed his performance, but I hesitated about mailing it. A few days later he was dead," Olivia sadly related in her 1971 London appearance.

Spurred on by the success of *Robin Hood*, Warners decided to see if the pair could be as effective in modern dress as they were in period garb. Though screwball comedy was not the forte of either Flynn or Olivia, they did their best in *Four's a Crowd* (1938), a frenetic farce about publicists and newspaper reporters whose paths cross both in business and romance. Olivia played Lorri Dillingwell, a typically dizzy heiress who was a stock character in '30s comedies. The film's best gag had PR man Flynn, in swimming trunks, being chased by a pack of yapping Great Danes set on him by Lorri's grandfather.

Following *Hard to Get* (1938) and *Wings of the Navy* (1939), Olivia and Flynn were transported to the wild west of *Dodge City* (1939), an above-average oater directed by Michael Curtiz. Although with their British accents the stars seemed better suited to Oxford than the prairie, Flynn proved himself capable in chaps and with a six-shooter. As the editor of the town newspaper, Olivia had little to do but appear feisty. As with the previous Flynn-de Havilland pairings, *Dodge City* was hugely profitable.

By the late 1930s the United States was caught up in the hype surrounding the filming of Margaret Mitchell's sprawling novel *Gone with the Wind*. The Civil War epic became an instant bestseller, and shortly afterward became the prize in a bidding war among film producers for the movie rights. David O. Selznick was the lucky winner, and he began a wave of publicity like Hollywood had never seen before. Most of the attention focused on the nationwide search to find an actress to play Scarlett O'Hara, the vixenish, strong-willed heroine of the novel. Olivia was probably the only actress in Hollywood who had no desire to test for the role.

"I knew that I was going to have to earn my own living and be self-reliant and independent and self-supporting," said Olivia. "And when I made *Gone with the Wind*, that's exactly what I was. So was Scarlett. Since I was myself leading that life, the role didn't interest me at all."

Olivia's sister, Joan Fontaine, was one of hundreds who tried out for Scarlett. Ironically, it was her audition that opened the door for Olivia to play Melanie, Scarlett's kind-hearted cousin. When director George Cukor asked Joan to read for Melanie instead, she declined and said, 'If it is a Melanie you are looking for, why don't you try my sister."

Cukor took her advice and contacted

Olivia, who agreed to an audition. Olivia read one of the scenes, much to Cukor's pleasure. He then asked her to commit the scene to memory and to meet him at Selznick's home the following Sunday to perform it again before the producer.

Olivia arrived that Sunday for what she called (in a 1967 article she wrote for *Look*) "one of the most richly significant moments of my life." According to Olivia, the scene that took place was pure comedy. "It was George's role to play opposite me. He was at that time portly, his hair was black, curly and closely cropped, and his spectacles were large and thickly rimmed. To this day, I have claimed that it was his passionate portrayal of Scarlett clutching the portieres that convinced David that afternoon he had finally found his Melanie."

Standing in her way was Jack Warner, who refused to loan her because he feared she'd then be difficult to handle. Olivia found an ally in Ann Warner, Jack's wife, who convinced her husband to let Olivia play Melanie. Not that Warner's intentions were at all altruistic. In exchange, he secured the services of James Stewart from MGM, which was releasing *Gone with the Wind*, for one film.

By now the saga of *Gone with the Wind* has become part of American folklore. Set against the backdrop of the Civil War, the sprawling tale follows the exploits of Scarlett (Vivien Leigh), a spoiled Southern belle who loves the supercilious Ashley Wilkes (Leslie Howard), who's engaged to her gentle cousin Melanie Hamilton. Hoping to steal Scarlett's affections is dashing adventurer Rhett Butler (Clark Gable).

The sweet as molasses role of Melanie seemed almost impossible for any actress, but Olivia managed to dig beneath Melanie's candy-coated veneer and bring her rich inner strength to the surface. Melanie, in effect, serves as a beacon by which the frailties of the seemingly stronger Scarlett are reflected. Olivia admired Melanie's humility and gentleness, and, through the nurturing direction of Cukor, made Melanie likable without being cloying.

Cukor, who was known as the ultimate "woman's" director in Hollywood, lived up to his reputation. Olivia and Leigh received great encouragement from Cukor, who discussed each role in great detail with both actresses.

Both were disheartened when Selznick fired Cukor early on at the urging of Gable, who was perturbed by the attention Cukor was giving both actresses. Gable requested that Selznick then hire the actor's favorite director — and hunting pal — Victor Fleming.

Olivia and Leigh spent three hours begging Selznick to change his mind, but to no avail. That evening, a despondent Olivia dined with her then-beau, eccentric billionaire Howard Hughes, who offered her unexpected encouragement. "Everything is going to be all right — with George and Victor, it is the same talent, only Victor's is strained through a coarser sieve," he said.

Though Olivia credited Fleming with helping her discover Melanie's sincerity, she missed Cukor's nurturing and began to drop by his house for tea and black-market direction. Olivia felt guilty about seeing Cukor behind Leigh's back, until she learned that Leigh did the same thing.

The pressure of filming became too much for Fleming, who at one point suffered a nervous breakdown and had to be replaced by Sam Wood. By the time Fleming returned, production was several weeks behind schedule. To make up for lost time, Selznick advised the entire cast, sans Gable, that they would have to shoot scenes with both directors. For Leigh and Olivia, that meant working on one scene with Wood in the morning, then working with Fleming in the afternoon on another part of the film that took place many years later in the screenplay.

Gone with the Wind wrapped in July 1938, much to Olivia's sadness. Her welcome back present when she returned to Warner Bros. was playing lady in waiting to Queen Elizabeth in the costume drama *The Private Lives of Elizabeth and Essex* (1939). Olivia was clearly not happy about being third-billed after stars Bette Davis and Errol Flynn, and not even getting Flynn in the end. "I did it, and didn't say a word, to show I wasn't being difficult," Olivia recalled.

She was also unhappy about next making *Raffles* (1940), a remake of the 1930 Ronald Colman hit, for producer Samuel Goldwyn, but again she kept quiet. It wasn't until Warner refused to let her attend the premiere of *Gone with the Wind* in Atlanta that she defied him.

Olivia was thrilled by the enthusiastic

crowd that braved near-freezing temperatures to gather at the Loew's Theater on Peachtree Street on December 15, 1939. She was also happy to be reunited with Gable, Leigh and Selznick, as well as finally meeting Margaret Mitchell. They were all anxious as they awaited the audience response to the film.

"Oh, how you wanted the Southerners to accept it," Olivia enthused upon the film's sixtieth anniversary. "Because it was about their city and their ancestors."

Their fears were for naught: *Gone with the Wind* was a wow with critics and audiences in every city. "For by any and all standards, Mr. Selznick's film is a handsome, scrupulous and unstinting version of the 1,037-page novel," praised Bosley Crowther of *The New York Times*. He added: "Olivia de Havilland's Melanie is a gracious, dignified, tender gem of characterization."

The only one not charmed with Olivia was Jack Warner, even after her Supporting Actress Oscar nomination as Melanie. In late 1939 she had refused to do a remake of *Saturday's Children* (1940) and was replaced by Anne Shirley. Then in early 1940 she rejected *Flight Angels* (1940), a leaden comedy about stewardesses. Warner's response was, "Ah-ha! I knew she'd be difficult! She *did* get difficult. You can't trust actors." She wound up being put on suspension.

Olivia reluctantly returned for *My Love Came Back* (1940), a sweet confection that had been turned down by Priscilla Lane. Director Kurt Bernhardt's sprightly film cast Olivia as a talented classical violinist who can no longer afford her music lessons at the academy she attends. One of the school's benefactors (Charles Winninger) is impressed with her talent and agrees to subsidize her lessons. His good intentions are misconstrued by his young business associate (Jeffrey Lynn), who thinks the old man is keeping a younger woman on the sly from his wife (Spring Byington). The situation gets stickier when the two young people fall for each other.

"Light, fluffy, musical and human," was how *Variety* described *My Love Came Back*.

Olivia was saddled with another lackluster role in *Santa Fe Trail* (1940), her seventh — and least interesting — pairing with Flynn. As her dissatisfaction with Warners grew, she had to use her wiles to find a good script. In the case of *The Strawberry Blonde* (1941), she sneaked the script out of the makeup department. As Amy, the free-thinking nurse who wins the heart of rough-hewn dentist Biff Grimes (James Cagney), Olivia gave a charming performance.

The popularity of *The Strawberry Blonde* did little to soften Olivia's tense relationship with Jack Warner, something that would be put to the test once again. Screenwriter Charles Brackett penned the role of schoolteacher Emmy Brown in *Hold Back the Dawn* (1941) specifically for Olivia, but getting her was another matter. Paramount, which was producing the film, had to loan Fred MacMurray to Warners for *Dive Bomber* in exchange for Olivia's services.

Based on a semi-autobiographical story by Ketti Frings, *Hold Back the Dawn* dealt with Roumanian immigrant Georges Iscuvesco (Charles Boyer), who is being detained at the Mexican border from entering the United States. An old flame (Paulette Goddard) convinces him that he could speed up his entry into the States by marrying an American. He finds a willing victim in Emmy Brown (Olivia), a retiring American schoolteacher. In a matter of days he woos her and marries her, even though he finds her at first unappealing. During their impromptu honeymoon, Georges begins to develop genuine affection for Emmy. When Emmy learns about Georges' deception, she heads back to California, and along the way is involved in a car crash. Georges risks being arrested by immigration officials to be near her, now realizing that he does love her.

Like Cukor, Mitchell Leisen, director of *Hold Back the Dawn*, had an affinity for actresses, and he and Olivia had an excellent relationship. He helped her make Emmy more than just a stereotypical mousy schoolteacher. In one seductive shot, a dimly lit Olivia is shown with her hair draped across her shoulders and wearing a low-cut nightgown while sprawled across the bed on her wedding night. Olivia does a wonderful job of capturing Emmy's yearning and disappointment when Georges cannot consummate the marriage because of a feigned injury.

Equally memorable is the key scene when the couple stops along the beach to pour water into the radiator of their overheated car. While Georges fills the radiator, Emmy is shown from a distance joyously frolicking in the water with all of her clothes removed. For the first time, Emmy arouses Georges' passion, and after she comes out he forgets about his fake injury.

Olivia received her best notices to date for *Hold Back the Dawn*. *The New York Times'* Bosley Crowther raved, "Olivia de Havilland plays the schoolteacher with romantic fancies whose honesty and pride are her own — and the film's — chief support. Incidentally, she is excellent."

Olivia's performance was a popular one when voting time came for The New York Film Critics Award. She ultimately lost the award to her sister for her fine performance in *Suspicion* (1941), but both were neck-and-neck contenders until the sixth and final ballot.

On the west coast RKO decided to show *Suspicion* at Hollywood's Pantages Theater for just one day — January 11, the final day of eligibility for the 1941 Academy Awards. It was no surprise a few weeks later when both sisters were announced as Best Actress Oscar nominees. On Oscar night Olivia and Joan sat at a table with David and Irene Selznick. When the previous winner, Ginger Rogers, announced that Joan had won, Joan remained frozen until Olivia whispered to her "Get up there!" When Joan returned to her table, Olivia seized her hand and exclaimed, "We've got it!"

Later, a reporter from *Life* overheard Olivia. "If *Suspicion* had been delayed just a little, it wouldn't have gotten in under the wire for this year's award and I might have won. I think that voters are inclined to remember with the highest favor the pictures they have seen most recently. By the time they saw *Suspicion*, they had almost forgotten *Hold Back the Dawn*."

Although *Hold Back the Dawn* had added plenty of cash to Paramount's coffers, Jack Warner still refused to acknowledge Olivia's star power, and she was back to playing the demure damsel. *They Died with Their Boots On* (1941) was her last teaming with Flynn, a rousing account of the life of General George Armstrong Custer. The film's primary enjoyment came from Flynn's devil-may-care performance as Custer and Raoul Walsh's marvelous recreation of Custer's fatal showdown at Little Big Horn. As Libby Bacon, who later becomes Mrs. Custer, Olivia looked smashing, but the role was hardly a worthy follow-up to *Hold Back the Dawn*.

She was surprisingly stiff as college professor Henry Fonda's wife in *The Male Animal* (1942), but then had a good role opposite Bette Davis in *In This Our Life* (1942). John Huston directed the tempestuous drama based on Ellen Glasgow's Pulitzer Prize–winning novel about a lying southern vixen (Davis) who jeopardizes the lives of everyone she comes in contact with.

While Davis damn near chewed up the scenery with her mannered performance, Olivia shone as her much-put-upon sister. Olivia was nervous about working with Davis on *In This Our Life* after hearing about Davis' stormy collaborations with Miriam Hopkins on the sets of *The Old Maid* (1939) and *Old Acquaintance* (1943), which she was then also filming. Olivia made it clear to Davis that she didn't want to compete with her.

"Our first scene together was a very difficult one for her and easy for me, since she had to lie in bed and go through a lot of dialogue while I just sat and listened. I was hoping she'd get it right on the first take, and wondering if she could possibly. She did it perfectly, and I think she realized then that I was with her all the way," Olivia said in London in 1971.

Davis also respected Olivia's appreciation for hard work and her perfectionism. "Olivia was serious about her craft, not frivolous. These were traits Bette liked," noted Robert Osborne.

At the time, Olivia was dating Huston, who worked closely with her to perfect her characterization in *In This Our Life*. Their romance came shortly after the end of Olivia's highly publicized relationship with James Stewart. Following their breakup, Olivia began to frequent nightclubs, which she had rarely done in the past. Her escorts included Clifford Odets and Franchot Tone. At the time she met Huston, he and his wife were still living in the same house, though he told Olivia they were estranged from one another. Huston asked his wife for a divorce in the spring of 1942, but she soon afterward suffered a nervous breakdown. "It was only in 1945 that the divorce finally took place. By that time the strain of the war years, long separations and misunderstandings had taken their toll, and our relationship, as far as I was concerned, was at an end," Olivia said.

In 1946 Huston wed Evelyn Keyes, though that didn't deter him from making further overtures to Olivia.

Olivia's film output continued to be as active as her love life. Warners loaned her to RKO for *Government Girl* (1943), an overripe comedy about the housing shortage in Washington, D.C., which contains what may be Olivia's poorest performance, in which she relied heavily on mugging. Critics loathed the film, but as with most wartime fare, it made a bundle.

Olivia was far more humorous in the enchanting *Princess O'Rourke* (1943), one of her favorites. Directed by Norman Krasna (who also penned the Oscar-winning screenplay), *Princess O'Rourke* is a fluffier version of *Roman Holiday*, lacking that film's splendor or its more serious (and comprehensible) ending. Olivia stars as Princess Maria, a European royal in exile in New York faced with the prospect of marriage to a dull suitor. She longs for some fun before settling down, which she finds with a handsome pilot (Robert Cummings). A romance develops, although he is unaware of her true identity. After getting his draft acceptance to the Air Force, he proposes, thus forcing Maria to reveal her royal origins. Will he renounce his American citizenship to marry her? A plot contrivance involving Franklin D. Roosevelt ensures that love will conquer all.

Despite its overly cute ending, *Princess O'Rourke* is the best of Olivia's solo starring efforts at Warners, and, as Crowther put it, "a film which is in the best tradition of American screen comedy." He also found Olivia "charming as the princess—so modest, yet so eagerly thrilled."

Olivia's last Warners film was *Devotion* (1946), which reduced the lives of the Brontë sisters to a cardboard romance. Olivia played Charlotte Brontë, with Ida Lupino as Emily and Nancy Coleman as Anne, but all were done in by the phony screenplay.

Olivia and Lupino took a break during *Devotion* to appear in Warners' wartime musical *Thank Your Lucky Stars* (1943), with George Tobias in a boisterous jitterbug version of "The Dreamer." Gaudily costumed with huge bows in their hair, striped jumpers, puffy-sleeved blouses and heavily curled wigs, the actresses looked as far removed from Victorian England as possible.

The completion of *Devotion* meant Olivia's release from "Jack the warden," as she referred to her boss. The studio, however, told her that she had six months left on her contract to make up for the time she had spent on suspension. Through attorney Martin Gang, Olivia discovered a California law which stated that "no employer shall hold an employee to a contract longer than seven years," which she interpreted as calendar years and not accumulated work time. At the risk of committing career suicide, she filed suit against Warner Bros. She asked the Supreme Court for declaratory relief, an interpretation of the law as it applied to an actor's contract.

Warners' lawyers did their best to intimidate Olivia in the courtroom so that she'd appear temperamental and ungrateful. Their ploy failed and the court ruled in favor of Olivia. Warners' lawyers wasted no time filing an appeal. Jack Warner went one step further by attempting to get every studio in Hollywood to join forces with him. As a result, Olivia was blacklisted from every studio and remained offscreen for three years. Warners even shelved the release of *Devotion*.

Olivia kept busy with episodes of *Lux Radio Theater*, which her lawyer felt would be safe to do since Warner failed to enjoin the broadcasting medium in his work stoppage against Olivia. One positive aspect of Olivia's layoff was that she was able to appear at a bond rally in Madison Square Garden, and to visit servicemen in army and navy hospitals in the United States, Alaska and the South Pacific.

"I loved doing the tours because it was a way I could serve my country and contribute to the war effort," Olivia said. "These were endeavors which I might not have been able to engage in had I not been on suspension by Warner Bros. and enjoined by them from working at any studio whatsoever."

Meanwhile, the case dragged on until December 1944 when the appellate court voted unanimously in favor of Olivia. In February 1945 the State Supreme Court of California decided not to even review the case, since the other two courts had already ruled in her favor. The landmark judgment became known as the de Havilland Decision in law books. Bette Davis served as a spokesperson for the entire industry years later when she commented, "Every actor in the business owes a debt of gratitude to Olivia de Havilland for taking us out of bondage."

Anxious to return to work, Olivia signed a three-picture deal with Paramount, but the initial offering, *The Well-Groomed Bride* (1946) with Ray Milland, was poorly received. Olivia admitted that the flat farce about the search for a magnum of champagne in San Francisco was a mistake, and she made it at the insistence of her agent, whom she sued after it was made.

Warners then released the long-delayed *Devotion*, but as far as critics and the public were concerned, the project could just as easily have stayed forgotten.

Olivia had finally reached the point where she was fully in charge of her career, selecting only those roles that she felt would challenge her and enable her to grow as an actress. Certainly the multi-faceted role of unwed mother Jody Norris in Paramount's *To Each His Own* (1946) was unlike anything she was ever offered at Warners.

"The script by Charley Brackett was one of the most perfect I'd ever read. The dialogue was tight and forceful, and the character of Jody Norris romantic and sentimental. I'm that way myself, and I felt I could play the part as I had played no other," Olivia told Lloyd Shearer.

The story, told in flashback, opens in London during World War II, where lonely, middle-aged Jody Norris (a convincingly made-up Olivia) is spending New Year's Eve fire watching with a crusty and equally lonely man (Roland Culver). They make a hasty date, which is cut short when Jody learns that a train carrying American soldier Jody Piersen (John Lund) is arriving that evening. As Jody waits for the train, she recalls her brief romance during the first World War with a flier (also played by Lund) who was killed, the circumstances which caused her illegitimate son to be adopted by another couple and her bitterness over her failed attempts to get him back. The movie then returns to the present where Jody meets the soldier, who is actually her son. He remains oblivious to the truth even as she scrambles to prepare an instant wedding for him and his fiancée. It is only at the misty-eyed finale that he at last realizes Jody is his mother.

Credit for the film's poignancy belongs almost entirely to Olivia, whose complex performance takes Jody from dreamy-eyed maiden to stern businesswoman to lonely spinster. Best of all is her adoring expression in the film's finale as her icy heart melts in motherly love.

Leisen also deserves praise for presenting Olivia in a new light to audiences. Olivia had enjoyed working with Leisen so much on *Hold Back the Dawn* that she asked him to direct *To Each His Own*, even though he originally had no interest in the project. "The first couple of weeks on the set Mitch was charming, helpful, a real professional about the whole thing, but his heart wasn't in it," Olivia said in 1971. "Then suddenly he began to realize he had here one of the best pictures of his whole career, and his whole being lit up, which was a wonderful relief for me, since I had insisted on him, and it all would have been my fault had it not worked out."

Leisen insisted that the film be shot in continuity, which was hard for Olivia, who had to age more than twenty years throughout the film. Olivia had been ill prior to filming and had lost seventeen pounds, which made it difficult for her to adopt the matronly appearance needed in the opening portion of the film. "We started when she was thin, and with as attractive a makeup as we could get on her, flattering her as much as we could," Leisen told Leonard Maltin in 1971. "As the picture progressed, I fed her up every day and she gained back the seventeen pounds, and she wound up wearing a Frankly Forty foundation garment. They wanted her to have gray hair. I said, 'She's only forty, she doesn't have gray hair!' And we used a more unflattering lighting."

Leisen was so pleased with Olivia's performance that on the final day of production he and Brackett presented her with a live special Oscar—a bald man in a gold body stocking.

Olivia took on an even greater challenge in her next film, playing good/bad twin sisters in *The Dark Mirror* (1946), an intriguing thriller which came in the wake of Alfred Hitchcock's surreal psychodrama *Spellbound* (1945).

Olivia played Ruth and Terry Collins, the prime suspects in the murder of a doctor they were each linked with romantically. Because none of the witnesses can positively identify which one was at the scene of the crime, the police lack sufficient evidence to charge either one. A determined detective (Thomas Mitchell) enlists the aid of a psychiatrist (Lew Ayres) to help him trap the real killer. The good doctor soon finds himself falling for the sweet-natured Ruth, which causes the psychotic Terry's jealous nature to surface. Terry then hatches a plan to slowly drive her sister insane and ultimately contemplate suicide.

"*The Dark Mirror* was a film I very much wanted to do because of the two characterizations which it required," Olivia said. "The technical problems were difficult, but not insurmountable, and though she was a character who to this day appalls and disturbs me, Terry nonetheless was an immense challenge, which is, after all, what I wanted."

In light of her statement, it's no surprise that Olivia is marvelous as Ruth but seems more uncomfortable as the vile Terry. However, her best moment is when Terry affects a look of unadulterated hate at the climax and then throws an object at Ruth.

As a mystery, the thinness of *The Dark Mirror* is apparent. Its premise is intriguing, but there is little doubt as to its outcome. Technically, however, it is an amazing achievement — in particular, the astonishing moment when one twin comforts the other in her arms.

Olivia spent the summer of 1946 appearing in James M. Barrie's *What Every Woman Knows* at the famed Westport Country Playhouse in Connecticut. During a visit to New York with Phyllis Loughton, the play's director, Olivia was reacquainted with Marcus Goodrich, a strapping and well-spoken former Naval officer who had written the 1941 bestseller, *Delilah*. Olivia knew Goodrich slightly, having met him five years earlier at the home of Arthur Hornblow and Myrna Loy, and again in Washington in May 1942. Although Goodrich was eighteen years older than Olivia and had been married four times before, she was charmed by him and they had a brisk courtship before marrying on August 26 at the Weston, Connecticut, estate of Armina and Lawrence Langner, who operated the Westport Country Playhouse.

The day after the wedding Olivia's agent telephoned Joan Fontaine to ask her if she knew anything about her new brother-in-law. Joan quipped, "All I know about him is that he has had four wives and written one book. Too bad it's not the other way around." Her comment was printed in several publications, and Olivia was understandably offended.

As expected, Olivia received an Oscar nomination for her performance in *To Each His Own*. Two weeks before the ceremony, Joan's press agent Henry Rogers asked Olivia if she would have photos taken with Joan if Olivia won the award. Olivia agreed, but only if Joan apologized for her remark about Marcus. Olivia warned Rogers that if her condition was not met, she would turn away from her sister after accepting the award.

The night of March 13, 1947, should have been one of the most jubilant of Olivia's life. She won the Best Actress Award and looked, as *Time Magazine* put it, "as gauzy and misty-eyed as a Walt Disney angel." After accepting her award, Olivia walked to the wings en route to the press room. As she turned toward the corridor leading to the press area, she saw Joan, who had just presented the Best Actor Oscar to Fredric March, flanked by no less than 15 photographers.

"I could not comprehend this insensitivity and I did indeed turn away, saying 'I do not understand how she can do this when she knows how I feel.' I then walked round the stage curtain and down the steps, into the theater to take my seat again," Olivia said.

The incident was caught by photographers who splashed the photo of Olivia snubbing Joan across newspapers everywhere.

The Oscar victory did give Olivia a wealth of projects to choose from. The most intriguing was *The Snake Pit* (1948), an uncompromising look at the horrors of life in a mental institution. As in Mary Jane Ward's novel, the focus was on Virginia (Olivia), a fragile young bride who is brought to Juniper Hill Hospital by her loving husband (Mark Stevens) after she suffers a nervous breakdown. She's treated by Dr. Kik (Leo Genn), a compassionate therapist anxious to find the root of Virginia's illness. He learns that Virginia believes she caused the deaths of both her father and her fiancée (Leif Erickson). Even though she was not responsible for either's demise, she now believes she is incapable of loving anyone. Complicating her recovery is her fixation on Dr. Kik.

The Snake Pit was not an easy project to bring to the screen. Anatole Litvak had first read the galley proofs of Ward's novel in 1945 when he was in the U.S. Army making films for the War Department. He purchased the rights for $75,000, and then spent more than a year shopping the project to the major studios. "They all thought I was as crazy as the girl in the book," Litvak quipped. Finally, 20th Century–Fox chief Darryl F. Zanuck, who championed bringing social issues to the screen, bought the rights from Litvak for $175,000 and let him direct.

To give the film a realistic look, Litvak and his cast and crew visited several U.S. mental institutions. On one of these visits Olivia confronted a schizophrenic patient who had developed a relationship with her doctor which was similar to the one between Virginia and Dr. Kik. "If I had not seen that ... I would have perhaps missed the key to the whole characterization," Olivia said.

The director also fought to keep the actresses in the film as unglamorous as possible. Hairdressers were on hand to make sure that the performers' straggly coiffures matched from one camera set-up to the next. The actresses were even told not to wear girdles or brassieres. Olivia lost considerable weight and sported dark circles under her eyes to achieve Virginia's haggard appearance. Such touches added layers of conviction to her performance.

Considering the somber subject matter, *The Snake Pit* is peppered with several amusing sequences, such as the game that's played by Virginia's tablemates when she sits down for lunch. Each person passes a bowl of stew to the next one with the warning to "leave some for Virginia." Naturally, by the time it reaches Virginia there's nothing left.

The Snake Pit also benefits from the brilliant cinematography of Leo Tover. The celebrated "snake pit" shot in which the camera slowly moves above Virginia so that she envisions herself as the sane member of the ward where she's been placed, is visually stunning.

But the film's chief asset is the electrifying performance of its leading lady. Olivia explored the complexity of Virginia's mind and stitched together the many remnants of the character's personality into a tightly-woven tapestry of emotions. She brilliantly balanced Virginia's childlike nature, displayed in such simple moments as getting a dish of ice cream, with her tormented side, especially in the flashback when she recoils from her husband's touch and suffers her breakdown.

The reviews for Olivia's performance were the sort that every actress dreams of receiving. "Miss de Havilland gives one of those unglamorized and true performances generally associated with only the more distinguished foreign films," gushed *The Saturday Review*.

Critical raves and strong word of mouth helped make *The Snake Pit* a huge success. Olivia expressed great pride in the film and was glad that mental illness was finally being presented in an honest manner. "This picture is going to do so much good," she told *Time*. "When I visited the institutions for the mentally ill, I felt a great surge of compassion for the people. We are all victims of life, you see, and these people are the ones who have been hardest pressed."

Olivia's performance was the overwhelming choice of the New York Film Critics that year, and she was chosen Best Actress at the Venice Film Festival. Olivia was also in Oscar contention, but she was unable to attend the ceremony because of a more important production — the birth of her son, Benjamin. Olivia was listening on the radio when it was announced that Jane Wyman was the winner for *Johnny Belinda*. Olivia was not bitter about the loss. "Jane really deserved it," she said, "plus I had just made *The Heiress*."

The Heiress (1949), based on Henry James' novella *Washington Square*, saw Olivia in the plum role of Catherine Sloper, an ugly duckling whose gaucherie has left her feeling unloved for her entire life. As far as Catherine's cruel father (Ralph Richardson) is concerned, she has only two assets: her talent for embroidery and the huge inheritance she will receive upon his death. Catherine is resigned to her ordinary existence until she meets the charming Morris Townshend (Montgomery Clift). Catherine is immediately smitten, but her father suspects Morris is a fortune hunter and threatens to disinherit Catherine if she marries him. Undeterred, she makes plans to elope with Morris. In the most heartbreaking scene, Catherine waits all night for Morris, pleading to her aunt (Miriam Hopkins), "Morris must love me for all those that haven't." When morning arrives the jilted Catherine realizes her father was right about Morris. The sweet, retiring heiress becomes embittered and feels no remorse when her father dies. Several years later, when Morris returns and once more proposes, Catherine again accepts. The final harrowing scene shows a satisfied Catherine ascending the stairs as Morris bangs at her locked door, calling her name.

Director William Wyler elicited a stunning performance from Olivia in *The Heiress*. From her early scenes, in which she awkwardly tries to appear clever at her cousin's engagement party, to the moment when she justifies her cruelty to her aunt by saying, "I have been taught by masters," Olivia never misses a single beat.

The Heiress earned Olivia her second Best Actress Oscar. In her acceptance speech, written by her husband, Olivia said, "Your award for *To Each His Own* I took as an incentive to venture forward. Thank you for this very generous assurance that I have not failed to do so."

Later, Olivia seemed quite subdued when she was interviewed by reporters: "When I won the first award in 1946, I was terribly thrilled. But this time I felt solemn, very serious and … shocked. Yes, shocked! It's a great responsibility to win the award twice."

The Heiress represented the apex of Olivia's screen career. It was the last real showcase role she was given onscreen and marked the end of her glory years in Hollywood. Sadly, despite the plaudits handed to the film and Olivia's performance, *The Heiress* was not a popular success at the time, although it has since become regarded as a classic.

Shortly after giving birth to Benjamin, Olivia was offered the role of Blanche Du Bois in Warners' screen version of *A Streetcar Named Desire* (1951). Though she loved the screenplay, she turned it down. "The role of Blanche Du Bois, challenging though it was, did not and could not appeal to me at that time," Olivia said. "Motherhood is a profound experience, especially with one's first child. A year later, when the financial responsibility involved in parenthood became quite clear to me, I had second thoughts about playing Blanche, but by this time [Elia] Kazan was considering Vivien Leigh and eventually signed her for the part. I have no regrets about this, as I think her work was superb."

Instead, Olivia in 1951 appeared in a Broadway-bound production of *Romeo and Juliet*. Back when she was appearing on stage in *A Midsummer Night's Dream*, Max Reinhardt had made Olivia promise that one day she would play Juliet, so she kept her word. On the opening night in Detroit, Katherine Cornell, whom Olivia remembered vividly as Juliet many years earlier, sent Olivia a good-luck telegram which said, "Hie to high fortune!"—Juliet's line to her nurse just before the girl rushes off to meet Romeo.

The drama played to sell-out crowds in Detroit, Cleveland and Boston prior to its New York run. "Miss de Havilland is amazingly youthful in appearance and manner. It is a softly spoken, carefully studied interpretation of the great role, offering contrast to the more robust performances of her associates," said *The Daily Mirror*.

Brooks Atkinson of *The New York Times* thought Olivia "a lovely Juliet worth any Romeo's attention."

Hefty production costs led to the play's closing after one hundred performances between its out-of-town and Broadway runs.

Olivia then signed on for an eleven-week summer stock season in George Bernard Shaw's *Candida*, which played to sell-out crowds. Producer Thomas Hammond proposed taking the show on a transcontinental tour, which would conclude with a four-week limited engagement in New York in early 1952. Despite a successful national run, the show closed in New York after its four-week engagement. Walter Kerr of *The New York Herald-Tribune* described Olivia's performance as "all method and no magic."

It wasn't long after the closing of *Candida* that Olivia and Goodrich were divorced. From the start, Goodrich had put his writing endeavors on hold to focus on all aspects of Olivia's career, which resulted in his reputation as a Svengali figure. He presided over Olivia's business affairs, her social engagements and even saw to it that she got enough sleep and didn't overwork. On the witness stand, Olivia cited that Goodrich beat her in such violent rages she feared for her life. Olivia waived alimony and child support, and undertook full responsibility for Benjamin.

Olivia returned to the screen in *My Cousin Rachel* (1952), a handsome and evocative adaptation of Daphne du Maurier's novel, co-starring Richard Burton in his American film debut. As the mysterious and alluring Rachel, who may or may not be a murderess, Olivia was at her most ravishing. Olivia again received good reviews for her work, including one from George Cukor, who was originally set to direct the film but was replaced by Henry Koster.

"One of the compliments I treasure most came from George Cukor who, long ago, phoned me after seeing the film and, to my gratified surprise, said he thought my work as Rachel 'brilliant.' Wasn't that wonderful?" Olivia recalled.

In 1953 Olivia, for the first time, agreed to

attend the Cannes Film Festival with Benjamin in tow. Her first stop, though, was Paris, which was enjoying a post-war Renaissance that enraptured Olivia. It was here that she also met Pierre Galante, associate secretary general of *Paris Match*. He joined Olivia at Cannes and later followed her to London and the United States.

In October 1953 Olivia and Benjamin returned to Paris at Pierre's urging. It then became their new adopted home. "Hollywood was becoming a frightening place," said Robert Osborne. "TV was dominating the entertainment industry. It was a town which had gone as far as it could go, and the industry had gone as far as it could go. She had a new son with her husband Marcus Goodrich. It was not the kind of situation or place to raise a son. Paris was the total opposite of Hollywood. It was building itself back up after the war. Everyone had a future and a goal."

Olivia took French lessons three times a week with a professor, and then practiced her vocabulary on cab drivers. Although it took some time, she became fluent in the language.

Olivia at last returned to the screen in 1955 for *That Lady*, a costume epic filmed in England and Spain. As Ana de Mendoza, a Spanish princess in love with both King Philip II (Paul Scofield) and his advisor, Antonio Perez (Gilbert Roland), Olivia sported an eyepatch. The film was not a success, and its director, Terence Young, admitted, "I made a mess of it."

As if playing a Spaniard wasn't enough of a stretch, Olivia affected a Swedish accent and blonde hair to play a noble nurse in *Not as a Stranger* (1955), a sudsy medical drama made in Hollywood that was Stanley Kramer's directorial debut. The film's focal point was opportunistic intern Robert Mitchum, who marries "the Swedish nightingale" for her knowledge of operating room procedure and the small fortune that pays for his medical education. He later dallies with sultry neighbor Gloria Grahame, a liaison that nearly destroys his marriage. Critics tore the film to shreds, but it was a sturdy grosser.

Soon after completing *Not as a Stranger*, Olivia and Pierre were married on April 2, 1955, by the local mayor, publishing magnate Jean Prouvost, in Yvoy le Marron, a rustic area noted for pheasant shooting, near the Loire River. The next year, the couple had their first child, Gisele.

"Olivia was too smart to only have a career as a goal," observed Osborne. "After her second Oscar, she had reached her career goal. She had other goals. She had a daughter and she wrote."

Prior to the birth of Gisele, Olivia made *The Ambassador's Daughter* (1956), a frothy comedy written, directed and produced by her friend Norman Krasna, and filmed in Paris.

Olivia made two other '50s films: *The Proud Rebel* (1958), a family drama set during the Civil War, with Olivia as a Yankee farmer who befriends a southerner (Alan Ladd) seeking a doctor for his mute son (played by Ladd's son, David); and *Libel* (1959), a courtroom drama with Dirk Bogarde. Of the two, the former was the better film, with a moving performance by Olivia.

Olivia had her best screen role in years in the charming *Light in the Piazza* (1962), which was tastefully directed by Guy Green. She played Meg Johnson, an American visiting Florence with her teenage daughter Clara (Yvette Mimieux). Their vacation takes an unexpected turn when a handsome local (George Hamilton) woos Clara, whose mentality is at the level of an eight-year-old child. Meg's concerns deepen when Clara's suitor proposes, which leads to a conflict between Meg and her cold-hearted husband (Barry Sullivan). Eventually Meg realizes that Clara's happiness lies in letting her daughter begin a new life, and she allows the couple to wed.

Light in the Piazza was designed as a vehicle for MGM to show off its young contract players Mimieux and Hamilton as a new screen couple, but since Meg grapples with the key decisions that will affect her daughter, Olivia is really at the film's center. Olivia's lovely performance is reminiscent of her work in *To Each His Own*, especially at the film's finale: As she watches her newly married daughter leaving the church, the camera is on Olivia, who mutters, "I did the right thing, I know I did." Sadly, MGM did little to promote the movie and it fared poorly.

Olivia returned to Broadway in *A Gift of Time* (1962) by Garson Kanin, a heartfelt drama based on Lael Tucker Wertenbaker's book *Death of a Man*. Olivia played Lael and Henry Fonda was her cancer-stricken husband, Charles. The play dealt with the couple's dilemma as they cope with the prospect of his imminent death.

Despite its sober subject matter, *A Gift of Time* was well-received by audiences and critics. *The New York World Telegram and Sun* was unsparing in its praise for Olivia: "For all the virtuosity of Fonda's performance, it is Miss de Havilland who gives the play its unbroken continuity. This distinguished actress reveals Lael as a special and admirable woman."

It was also around this time that Olivia's book, *Every Frenchman Has One* (a liver, that is), was published. *Life* called it a "happy, Jean Kerr-ish account of Olivia de Havilland's seven-year stint as Madame Pierre Galante, a sharp-eyed, Franco-U.S. housewife, and what she found out about French husbands." Among Olivia's observations: "The average one prefers to be faithful to his wife"; and French fashion is unsexy because "in France, it's assumed that if you're a woman, you're sexy already." The book demonstrated Olivia's wit and was a best-seller.

Oddly, it was also in 1962, after Olivia wrote of her joyful life in Paris, that she and Galante announced they were separating, although they continued to live in the same house. The two remained friends, and Olivia even promoted his book, *The Berlin Wall*, in 1965.

Olivia returned to Hollywood in 1964 in the nightmarish *Lady in a Cage* (1964), as a domineering matron who gets trapped in the private elevator in her home when the electricity goes out on a sweltering July 4 weekend. Her cries for help instead attract the attention of a wino (Jeff Corey), an over-the-hill prostitute (Ann Sothern) and a trio of hoodlums (a young James Caan, Jennifer Billingsley and Rafael Campos) who take delight in torturing the three older folks.

Initial critical reaction to *Lady in a Cage* was mostly negative. It was banned in England until 1967, at which time it was well-reviewed by *The Manchester Guardian*. Later that year Olivia received the British Films and Filming Award for her performance.

"Perhaps it was two or three years ahead of its time. I think someday it will be recognized as a depiction of the aimless violence of our era," she said. To some extent she was correct, since the film has since attracted a cult following.

Her next film also had its gory moments. *Hush ... Hush, Sweet Charlotte* (1964) was designed as a follow-up to *Whatever Happened to Baby Jane?* (1962), with Bette Davis and Joan Crawford. Several weeks into production Crawford claimed she was ill and was hospitalized. Given Crawford's stormy relationship with Davis, industry buzz was that she was faking her illness to get out of the film, which she did. A new co-star was needed for Davis. Vivien Leigh and Loretta Young were mentioned, but the only one Davis considered was Olivia.

As in *The Dark Mirror*, the role of Miriam called for Olivia to exhibit a dual personality: honey-dripping sweet in the first half of the film, and a scheming blackmailer bent on driving Charlotte insane in the second portion. Originally the part was written to emphasize Miriam's wicked nature. Playing Terry in *The Dark Mirror* had been distressful for Olivia, and, as originally written, Miriam seemed as dark and unredeeming a character. Olivia refused the role.

"When I hit upon the idea of giving Miriam perfect manners, I saw that in bestowing upon her this extra dimension, not only would she become theatrically more interesting, but the objective would then be to keep the audience ignorant of her true character until the last possible moment—a fascinating game," Olivia said. "And so, in the end, I accepted."

The eerie tale opens in the Deep South in the 1920s with the grisly ax murder of John Mayhew (Bruce Dern) on the night of his engagement party to wealthy Charlotte Hollis (Bette Davis). When Charlotte arrives at the party with blood splattered on her dress, everyone assumes she killed him. The film then moves to the present, where the once-decadent Hollis estate is about to be torn down to make way for a new highway. Charlotte is now a bitter and eccentric recluse whose only visitors are her slovenly housekeeper and the neighborhood children who taunt her. When Charlotte is served with an eviction notice by the sheriff, she writes to her cousin Miriam (Olivia) to help save the estate. When Miriam arrives, Charlotte is taken aback when she learns that Miriam has come with the intention of assisting with the packing. It soon becomes clear that, as the next-in-line to the Hollis estate, Miriam is anxious to get what's left of the family fortune. She enlists the aid of unsavory Dr.

Drew (Joseph Cotten) in her plan to drive Charlotte insane.

Hush ... Hush, Sweet Charlotte was a demanding project. Because of the problems caused by Crawford's "illness," the shooting schedule went from thirty-two days to fifty-nine. Still, none of the problems were evident onscreen. As Miriam, Olivia does a nice job of bringing her character's oily demeanor to the surface, particularly during the dinner scene where she has her first head-on confrontation with Charlotte. Olivia's nastiest moment occurs when she brutally slaps Charlotte as they try to dispose of the body of Dr. Drew.

No one was more elated with Olivia's performance than director Robert Aldrich. "No matter how great Crawford might have been, we're better off with de Havilland," he said.

The bulk of Olivia's work over the next few years was on television. She looked radiant on *The Hollywood Palace* with Davis, and won kudos for her performance as the embittered wife of a dairy farmer in *Noon Wine*, based on the Katharine Anne Porter novella. Also noteworthy was *The Screaming Woman* (1971), which starred Olivia as a wealthy widow recovering from a nervous breakdown who discovers a woman buried alive, but no one will believe her.

Olivia returned to the big screen for a cameo in *The Adventurers* (1970), a Harold Robbins trashfest. As Deborah Hadley, a married American tourist who dallies with gigolo Bekim Fehmiu, Olivia lent the film its sole shred of dignity.

Olivia garnered far more attention when she appeared in London in August of 1971 for a lecture at the National Film Theater. The program, which was sponsored by the John Player Cigarette Company, was a sellout, thanks largely to the press reports of a "date" between Olivia and then Prime Minister Edward Heath. Olivia became friendly with Heath in December 1961 when they met on board the Queen Elizabeth at a reception he was giving. She was sailing to New York to begin work on *A Gift of Time*, and he was bound for Ottawa to attend a conference on the common market.

When Olivia arrived in London in 1971, Heath invited her to a friendly dinner at Chequers, the traditional country house of the Prime Minister. The next day the headline "Olivia's Date with Ted" was the talk of the town. When Olivia arrived at the theater that afternoon, she was mobbed by onlookers. Still, she looked radiant as she arrived onstage to thunderous applause. The program consisted of a clipfest followed by questions from the audience, which Olivia answered with her customary wit and charm.

Olivia was in London earlier in 1971 to work on *Pope Joan* (1972) for director Michael Anderson. Olivia played an abbess in ninth-century England who is crucified by pillaging Saxons.

For the next few years Olivia devoted most of her energies to her family. She suffered a bitter loss when her mother died in February 1975 after a long illness. Lilian Fontaine's death, in effect, also brought an end to the relationship between Olivia and her sister. Olivia was in California with Lilian when she died, but Joan was touring in *Dial M for Murder*. Claire Loftus, a close friend of Lilian's and executrix of her estate, felt that the memorial service should take place within a month of Lilian's death and while Olivia was still in the United States. Joan wanted it to be delayed until the following August, when she would be in California, but Claire refused. Claire agreed to postpone the service until March 27, the beginning of Joan's Easter vacation. Still, Joan was upset that she had not been consulted regarding any of the arrangements. She and Olivia didn't speak at all that day — and they haven't since.

Olivia only made three film appearances for the remainder of the '70s. She first had a cameo in the disaster epic, *Airport '77* (1977), the third entry in the *Airport* series (and the repetition was clearly showing), and then made *The Swarm* (1978), Irwin Allen's stingingly bad flick about African killer bees, which pretty much put an end to the disaster movie genre.

Olivia's final theatrical venture was *The Fifth Musketeer* (1979), another spin on Alexander Dumas' *The Three Musketeers*. As the mother of Queen Anne of England, Olivia looked every bit as regal as she had forty years earlier as Maid Marian.

Since then, Olivia has made occasional television appearances, most notably in *Roots II: The Next Generation* (1979), *Agatha Christie's Murder Is Easy* (1982), as the Queen Mother in *The Royal Romance of Charles and Diana* (1982) and in *North and South Book II* (1986).

Olivia gave a breathtaking performance as

Dowager Empress Maria in the outstanding miniseries *Anastasia: The Mystery of Anna* (1986), with Amy Irving in the title role. The role earned Olivia a Golden Globe as Best Supporting Actress in a Mini Series or Movie for Television, as well as an Emmy nomination.

Olivia last appeared as Aunt Bessie in the telefilm *The Woman He Loved* (1988), about the romance of the Prince of Wales (Anthony Andrews) and Wallis Simpson (Jane Seymour).

It was around that time that Olivia also began work on her memoirs, an ambitious project which has been slowed down by personal difficulties. Saddest of these was the death of her beloved son Benjamin in 1991. "People think he died of cancer," she said. "He conquered cancer." The direct cause of his death was heart damage due to poorly administered radiation treatments.

In February 1998, when Olivia learned that her ex-husband Galante was ill, she graciously let him stay at her home where she and Gisele could care for him. Pierre stayed in the master bedroom, while Olivia moved into an adjoining room. Olivia even prepared special meals for him and did her best to make him as comfortable as possible.

Many people, particularly reporters, wondered why she would go to so much trouble for a man she had divorced nineteen years earlier. "She knew how much he meant to her daughter." said Osborne. "She also said to me, 'Even though we're no longer married and I'm not in love with him anymore, I did make a commitment to love, honor and cherish him. I like to keep my commitments.' That's just the way Olivia is."

Because of that commitment, Olivia turned down an invitation to appear at the 70th Academy Awards ceremony in which former Oscar winners were asked to appear for a reunion. Olivia continued to care for Galante until he died in the fall of 1998.

Olivia made several appearances in 1998 to promote the sixtieth anniversary and rerelease of *Gone with the Wind*. The warmth and vibrance she exhibited when the film first came out were still there six decades later. So were the de Havilland beauty and the radiant smile, even if they were now capped by a becoming head of silver tresses. Her youthful appearance is a reflection on her continued zest for living.

"Olivia has had a great third act. She now has a rich life in Paris," said Osborne.

For Olivia, the third act has only just begun. In 1998 she said: "I want to be there for the 70th anniversary [of *Gone with the Wind*'s release], and I'd like to make the 80th."

FILMOGRAPHY

Alibi Ike (Warner Bros., 1935) Directed by Ray Enright. *Cast:* Joe E. Brown, Olivia de Havilland, Ruth Donnelly, Roscoe Karns, William Frawley, Paul Harvey.

The Irish in Us (Warner Bros., 1935) Directed by Lloyd Bacon. *Cast:* James Cagney, Pat O'Brien, Olivia de Havilland, Frank McHugh, Allen Jenkins, J. Farrell MacDonald, Mary Gordon.

A Midsummer Night's Dream (Warner Bros., 1935) Directed by Max Reinhardt and William Dieterle. *Cast:* James Cagney, Dick Powell, Joe E. Brown, Olivia de Havilland, Mickey Rooney.

Captain Blood (Warner Bros., 1935) Directed by Michael Curtiz. *Cast:* Errol Flynn, Olivia de Havilland, Lionel Atwill, Basil Rathbone, Ross Alexander, Guy Kibbee, Henry Stephenson.

Anthony Adverse (Warner Bros., 1936) Directed by Mervyn LeRoy. *Cast:* Fredric March, Olivia de Havilland, Claude Rains, Edmund Gwenn, Gale Sondergaard, Anita Louise, Louis Hayward.

The Charge of the Light Brigade (Warner Bros., 1936) Directed by Michael Curtiz. *Cast:* Errol Flynn, Olivia de Havilland, Patric Knowles, Henry Stephenson, Nigel Bruce, David Niven.

Call It a Day (Warner Bros., 1937) Directed by Archie Mayo. *Cast:* Ian Hunter, Olivia de Havilland, Anita Louise, Alice Brady, Roland Young, Frieda Inescort, Walter Woolf King.

The Great Garrick (Warner Bros., 1937) Directed by Mervyn LeRoy. *Cast:* Brian Aherne, Olivia de Havilland, Edward Everett Horton, Melville Cooper, Lionel Atwill, Henry O'Neill.

It's Love I'm After (Warner Bros., 1937) Directed

by Archie Mayo. *Cast:* Leslie Howard, Bette Davis, Olivia de Havilland, Patric Knowles, Eric Blore, George Barbier, Spring Byington, Bonita Granville.

Gold Is Where You Find It (Warner Bros., 1938) Directed by Michael Curtiz. *Cast:* George Brent, Olivia de Havilland, Claude Rains, Margaret Lindsay, John Litel, Barton MacLane.

The Adventures of Robin Hood (Warner Bros., 1938) Directed by Michael Curtiz and William Keighley. *Cast:* Errol Flynn, Olivia de Havilland, Basil Rathbone, Claude Rains, Patric Knowles, Alan Hale, Ian Hunter.

Four's a Crowd (Warner Bros., 1938) Directed by Michael Curtiz. *Cast:* Errol Flynn, Rosalind Russell, Olivia de Havilland, Patric Knowles, Walter Connolly, Hugh Herbert, Melville Cooper.

Hard to Get (Warner Bros., 1938) Directed by Ray Enright. *Cast:* Dick Powell, Olivia de Havilland, Charles Winninger, Allen Jenkins, Bonita Granville, Melville Cooper, Isabel Jeans.

Wings of the Navy (Warner Bros., 1939) Directed by Lloyd Bacon. *Cast:* George Brent, Olivia de Havilland, John Payne, Frank McHugh, John Litel, Victor Jory, Henry O'Neill, John Ridgeley.

Dodge City (Warner Bros., 1939) Directed by Michael Curtiz. *Cast:* Errol Flynn, Olivia de Havilland, Ann Sheridan, Bruce Cabot, Frank McHugh, Alan Hale, John Litel, Henry Travers.

Gone with the Wind (MGM-Selznick, 1939) Directed by Victor Fleming. *Cast:* Clark Gable, Vivien Leigh, Leslie Howard, Olivia de Havilland, Hattie McDaniel, Thomas Mitchell.

The Private Lives of Elizabeth and Essex (Warner Bros., 1939) Directed by Michael Curtiz. *Cast:* Bette Davis, Errol Flynn, Olivia de Havilland, Donald Crisp, Vincent Price, Alan Hale.

Raffles (Goldwyn-United Artists, 1940) Directed by Sam Wood. *Cast:* David Niven, Olivia de Havilland, Dame May Whitty, Dudley Digges, Douglas Walton, Lionel Pape, E.E. Clive.

My Love Came Back (Warner Bros., 1940) Directed by Kurt (Curtis) Bernhardt. *Cast:* Olivia de Havilland, Jeffrey Lynn, Charles Winninger, Eddie Albert, Spring Byington, Jane Wyman.

Santa Fe Trail (Warner Bros., 1940) Directed by Michael Curtiz. *Cast:* Errol Flynn, Olivia de Havilland, Raymond Massey, Ronald Reagan, Alan Hale, Van Heflin, William Lundigan.

The Strawberry Blonde (Warner Bros., 1941) Directed by Raoul Walsh. *Cast:* James Cagney, Olivia de Havilland, Rita Hayworth, Jack Carson, Alan Hale, George Tobias, Una O'Connor.

Hold Back the Dawn (Paramount, 1941) Directed by Mitchell Leisen. *Cast:* Charles Boyer, Olivia de Havilland, Paulette Goddard, Victor Francen, Walter Abel, Rosemary De Camp.

They Died with Their Boots On (Warner Bros., 1941) Directed by Raoul Walsh. *Cast:* Errol Flynn, Olivia de Havilland, Arthur Kennedy, Sydney Greenstreet, Walter Hampden.

The Male Animal (Warner Bros., 1942) Directed by Elliott Nugent. *Cast:* Henry Fonda, Olivia de Havilland, Jack Carson, Joan Leslie, Eugene Pallette, Herbert Anderson, Don De Fore.

In This Our Life (Warner Bros., 1942) Directed by John Huston. *Cast:* Bette Davis, Olivia de Havilland, George Brent, Dennis Morgan, Charles Coburn, Frank Craven, Billie Burke.

Government Girl (RKO Radio, 1943) Directed by Dudley Nichols. *Cast:* Olivia de Havilland, Sonny Tufts, Anne Shirley, James Dunn, Paul Stewart, Agnes Moorehead, Harry Davenport.

Thank Your Lucky Stars (Warner Bros., 1943) Directed by David Butler. *Cast:* Dennis Morgan, Joan Leslie, Edward Everett Horton, S.Z. Sakall. Guest stars: Humphrey Bogart, Eddie Cantor, Jack Carson, Bette Davis, Olivia de Havilland, Errol Flynn, John Garfield, Alan Hale, Spike Jones and his orchestra, Ida Lupino, Hattie McDaniel, Ann Sheridan, Alexis Smith.

Princess O'Rourke (Warner Bros., 1943) Directed by Norman Krasna. *Cast:* Olivia de Havilland, Robert Cummings, Charles Coburn, Jack Carson, Jane Wyman, Harry Davenport.

The Well-Groomed Bride (Paramount, 1946) Directed by Sidney Lanfield. *Cast:* Ray Milland, Olivia de Havilland, Sonny Tufts, James Gleason, Percy Kilbride, Constance Dowling.

Devotion (Warner Bros., 1946) Directed by Curtis Bernhardt. *Cast:* Ida Lupino, Paul Henreid, Olivia de Havilland, Sydney Greenstreet, Nancy Coleman, Arthur Kennedy, Dame May Whitty.

To Each His Own (Paramount, 1946) Directed by Mitchell Leisen. *Cast:* Olivia de Havilland, John Lund, Mary Anderson, Roland Culver, Philip Terry, Bill Goodwin, Virginia Welles.

The Dark Mirror (Universal, 1946) Directed by Robert Siodmak. *Cast:* Olivia de Havilland, Lew Ayres, Thomas Mitchell, Richard Long, Charles Evans, Garry Owen, Lester Allen.

The Snake Pit (20th Century–Fox, 1948) Directed by Anatole Litvak. *Cast:* Olivia de Havilland, Mark Stevens, Leo Genn, Celeste Holm, Glenn Langan, Helen Craig, Leif Erickson.

The Heiress (Paramount, 1949) Directed by William Wyler. *Cast:* Olivia de Havilland, Montgomery Clift, Ralph Richardson, Miriam Hopkins, Vanessa Brown, Mona Freeman.

My Cousin Rachel (20th Century–Fox, 1952) Directed by Henry Koster. *Cast:* Olivia de Havilland, Richard Burton, Audrey Dalton, Ronald Squire, George Dolenz, John Sutton.

That Lady (20th Century–Fox, 1955) Directed by Terence Young. *Cast:* Olivia de Havilland, Gilbert Roland, Paul Scofield, Francoise Rosay,

Dennis Price, Anthony Dawson, Christopher Lee.

Not as a Stranger (United Artists, 1955) Directed by Stanley Kramer. *Cast:* Robert Mitchum, Olivia de Havilland, Frank Sinatra, Gloria Grahame, Broderick Crawford, Charles Bickford.

The Ambassador's Daughter (United Artists, 1956) Directed by Norman Krasna. *Cast:* Olivia de Havilland, John Forsythe, Myrna Loy, Adolphe Menjou, Francis Lederer, Edward Arnold

The Proud Rebel (MGM, 1958) Directed by Michael Curtiz. *Cast:* Alan Ladd, Olivia de Havilland, Dean Jagger, David Ladd, Cecil Kellaway, Dean Stanton, Henry Hull, John Carradine.

Libel (MGM, 1959) Directed by Anthony Asquith. *Cast:* Dirk Bogarde, Olivia de Havilland, Paul Massie, Robert Morley, Wilfrid Hyde-White, Anthony Dawson, Richard Wattis.

Light in the Piazza (MGM, 1962) Directed by Guy Green. *Cast:* Olivia de Havilland, Rossano Brazzi, Yvette Mimieux, George Hamilton, Barry Sullivan, Isabel Dean.

Lady in a Cage (Paramount, 1964) Directed by Walter Grauman. *Cast:* Olivia de Havilland, James Caan, Ann Sothern, Jeff Corey, Jennifer Billingsley, Rafael Campos, Scatman Crothers.

Hush ... Hush, Sweet Charlotte (20th Century–Fox, 1964) Directed by Robert Aldrich. *Cast:* Bette Davis, Olivia de Havilland, Joseph Cotten, Agnes Moorehead, Cecil Kellaway, Mary Astor, Victor Buono.

The Adventurers (Paramount, 1970) Directed by Lewis Gilbert. *Cast:* Bekim Fehmiu, Candice Bergen, Charles Aznavour, Alan Badel, Thommy Berggren, Ernest Borgnine, Olivia de Havilland.

Pope Joan (Columbia, 1972) Directed by Michael Anderson. *Cast:* Liv Ullmann, Maximilian Schell, Franco Nero, Trevor Howard, Olivia de Havilland, Lesley-Ann Down, Jeremy Kemp.

Airport '77 (Universal, 1977) Directed by Jerry Jameson. *Cast:* Jack Lemmon, Lee Grant, Brenda Vaccaro, Darren McGavin, Olivia de Havilland, Tom Sullivan, James Stewart.

The Swarm (Warner Bros., 1978) Directed by Irwin Allen. *Cast:* Michael Caine, Katharine Ross, Richard Widmark, Olivia de Havilland, Henry Fonda, Fred MacMurray, Ben Johnson.

The Fifth Musketeer (Columbia, 1979) Directed by Ken Annakin. *Cast:* Beau Bridges, Sylvia Kristel, Ursula Andress, Rex Harrison, Cornel Wilde, Lloyd Bridges, Olivia de Havilland.

TELEVISION FILM CREDITS

The Screaming Woman (1971) *Cast:* Olivia de Havilland, Joseph Cotten, Walter Pidgeon.

Roots: The Next Generation (1979) *Cast:* Marlon Brando, Georg Stanford Brown, Ruby Dee, Olivia de Havilland, Henry Fonda, James Earl Jones, Harry Morgan, Della Reese.

Agatha Christie's Murder Is Easy (1979) *Cast:* Bill Bixby, Helen Hayes, Olivia de Havilland.

Royal Romance of Charles and Diana (1982) *Cast:* Christopher Baines, Catherine Oxenberg, Dana Wynter, Olivia de Havilland.

Anastasia: The Mystery of Anna (1986) *Cast:* Amy Irving, Olivia de Havilland, Omar Sharif.

The Woman He Loved (1988) *Cast:* Anthony Andrews, Jane Seymour, Olivia de Havilland.

Glenda Farrell: "The Gimme Girl"

The wisecracking dame was a staple of films of the '30s and '40s, and no one played the part better than smart and sassy Glenda Farrell. Unlike most stars in the Warners stable, Glenda never complained about any role she was given, though she had plenty to gripe about after being stereotyped as either the smart-assed reporter or the gold digger out to seduce rich sugar daddy Guy Kibbee or Hugh Herbert.

But Glenda's Warners films, especially those with her good friend Joan Blondell, were never meant to be more than pleasant diversions. That they still continue to entertain is a testament to the comedic skills of both women. Eventually Glenda returned to her first love, the Broadway stage, and moved into television where she finally broke out of her wisecracking mold and showed what a versatile and gifted character actress she was.

Glenda was born on June 30, 1904, in Enid, in the Oklahoma territory. Her father, Charles Farrell, was a horse trader of Irish and Cherokee Indian descent, who was known as "Unky" to family and friends. Glenda's mother, Wilhemina, was the driving force behind her daughter's theatrical career, as well as the show business aspirations of Glenda's brothers, Dick and Gene. "Minnie," as Mrs. Farrell was affectionately known, encouraged her daughter to pursue all aspects of the arts. By the time Glenda was seven, she had made her stage debut playing Little Eva in a production of *Uncle Tom's Cabin* in Wichita, Kansas, where her family had relocated. During this time Glenda received a formal education at the Mount Carmel Catholic Academy in Wichita. She remained a devout Catholic her entire life.

A few years later the Farrells headed to San Diego, where Glenda again appeared in local productions. At thirteen Glenda joined The Virginia Brissac Players, where she was usually cast in ingenue roles, including Meg in *Little Women*. At sixteen, Glenda played Rebecca of Sunnybrook Farm, a sharp contrast to the hard-as-nails image she created at Warner Bros.

In 1920, at a Navy benefit ball in San Diego where she was performing, Glenda met handsome nineteen-year-old Thomas Richards, who had recently been awarded the Distinguished Service Medal for his heroic naval duty in the First World War. Richards was everything a young girl could ask for — tall, with blue eyes and curly jet black hair — and, as Glenda put it, "it was violent love at first sight." Minnie, however, objected to Richards being penniless and without a job, and always chased him away from the house.

Minnie's disapproval forced Glenda to meet Richards on the sly at a local candy store. After six weeks of their secret courtship, the couple ran off to Los Angeles and were married. They put together a vaudeville dance act which they took on the road, but landing bookings was a full-time job in itself. When they did find work, it was usually for starvation wages. "We danced so beautifully together," Glenda recalled in a 1969 *New York Times* interview. "The towns we played were pretty drab, the theaters — terrible. But at night when we were alone, we seemed to be shut into some vast dream world of our own that was all beauty and happiness."

In early 1921 Glenda learned that she was pregnant. Since they were barely making enough money to support themselves, the newlyweds knew their only recourse was to move in with Glenda's parents. The situation was a strain for both families, but Minnie was a tremendous help following the birth of Glenda's son Tommy on October 7, 1921. From the beginning there was a strong bond between Glenda and Tommy which would last throughout Glenda's life. Tommy still regards his mother as the best friend he ever had.

Unfortunately, the Richards' financial situation had worsened. "We were so poor that I was forced to make my baby's diapers out of old flour sacks Dad brought home from the store.... But I hemmed them all by hand tenderly as if they had been of the finest materials, for my Tommy was the most welcome and looked-forward-to baby in the world," Glenda told the *Times*.

Family responsibilities, financial woes and difficulty in obtaining a job caused Richards to drink heavily. When the intoxicated Richards would come home, he was dangerous. More often, he would drink and then disappear for weeks and sometimes months. Not surprisingly, Glenda ended up filing for divorce in 1929. Three years later Tommy asked Glenda to have his last name legally changed to Farrell.

One year before the divorce, Glenda asked Minnie to take care of Tommy so that she could head to New York and finally try to begin

Glenda Farrell often worked on four films at one time and managed it effortlessly.

her stage career. Minnie's words provided just the encouragement Glenda needed: "Don't give up the stage until your name is in lights. When your name gets on a marquee, my work will be done." Within two weeks of her arrival in New York, Glenda was signed to replace Erin O'Brien Moore in *Skidding*, a domestic drama that later served as the inspiration for the Andy Hardy films. The following year Glenda landed roles in John Van Druten's *The Third Day*, and *Divided*

Honors, a mystery. Later that year she played the ingenue in *Love, Honor and Betray*, a comedy which also featured two other promising newcomers—Clark Gable and George Brent.

In 1930 Glenda had a small role opposite Melvyn Douglas in *Recaptured*, giving a delightful performance which *The New York Times* described as "funny, abrupt, slangy and very cute." Later that year she made a strong impression in *On the Spot*, a searing drama by Edgar Wallace, in which she played a gangster's moll. She continued with the show when it went on tour.

It was during the run of *On the Spot* when Glenda learned that Minnie had died. Tommy was sent east to be reunited with Glenda. She enrolled him in the St. John's Military Academy, where he stayed for most of the school year, spending his vacations with Glenda.

In between her stage roles Glenda made her inauspicious film debut with a bit part in *Lucky Boy* (1929) for Tiffany. In 1930 she had her first featured screen role in the granddaddy of all gangster epics, *Little Caesar*. The landmark film starred Edward G. Robinson as Rico Bandello, a two-bit hoodlum who rises to become a notorious gang leader. Douglas Fairbanks, Jr., played Tony Massara, Rico's best friend who wants to break his gang ties and continue his dance act with his girlfriend Olga (Glenda). Robinson's towering performance dominated the film, but Glenda also attracted attention. "Glenda Farrell is excellently authentic as Massara's moll," wrote *The New York Times* reviewer.

Little Caesar was a box-office bonanza and did much to boost Glenda's career. It was also a good learning experience for Glenda on the fine art of film acting. "She was a fast study and had an amazing mind," said her son Tommy. "She was very observant. She watched the other actors while she made *Little Caesar*. Edward G. Robinson, in particular, was very helpful."

Following *Little Caesar*, Glenda joined the Players at the Westchester Theater in Mount Vernon, New York. During the troupe's 1931 season, Glenda was in *Strictly Dishonorable*, opposite Cesar Romero, and in *Cobra* with Romero, Ralph Morgan and Judith Anderson.

Glenda's breakthrough role came in March 1932 when she opened in *Life Begins*, an episodic drama set entirely in the maternity ward of a hospital. Glenda had the flashy role of Florette Darien, a brassy showgirl whose heart melts after giving birth to her child. "I played a hard-boiled, wisecracking dame who drank gin out of a hot water bottle, and I really didn't know how to do the part," Glenda said. "Arthur Hopkins [then a top Broadway producer] told me to make it very theatrical, and I got great laughs and great notices." *The New York Times*' Brooks Atkinson found Glenda "amusing as the professionally sullen chorus girl."

Glenda's superb performance was also noticed by producer Mervyn LeRoy, who had bought the screen rights to *Life Begins* for Warner Bros. She was asked to repeat her role on screen, and again earned raves. Warners then signed her to a seven-year contract.

After small roles in *Three on a Match* (1932) at her home lot and *Scandal for Sale* (1932) at Universal, Warners gave Glenda a plum role in *I Am a Fugitive from a Chain Gang* (1932), a scathing indictment of life on a Southern chain gang, based on Robert E. Burns' autobiography. Paul Muni starred as Jim Allen, a World War I veteran who is wrongly accused of a crime and put on a chain gang to do hard labor. He eventually escapes and becomes a respected leader in the community. A scheming landlady (Glenda, in one of her rare unsympathetic roles) blackmails the ex-convict into marrying her when she threatens to reveal the truth about his past to the police. Eventually Jim is sent back to work on the chain gang, where he suffers even greater indignities. Although Muni had a reputation as a scene stealer, Glenda held her own beautifully, creating an excellent portrait for the Bad Girls Hall of Fame. *Chain Gang* became one of Warners' biggest hits of 1932 and even led to some investigations of the penal system.

Hard-working Glenda seemed to be the perfect fit for the sweatshop mentality that prevailed at Warners. It wasn't unusual for Glenda to be working on four films at one time. Juggling scripts as she traveled from one set to another became part of Glenda's daily routine.

"When I went out there to do *Little Caesar* in 1930, the talkies were still new," Glenda recalled in 1969. "Not many actors could talk, so they shoved the ones who came from Broadway into everything. It all went so fast. I used to ask myself, 'What set am I on today? What script am I supposed to be doing—this one or that one?' Up at five every morning, start work at a quarter of six, work till seven or eight at night. By the time you got home it was nine. Then you had to study your lines, have your dinner and bath, and go to bed. You worked till midnight on Saturday. All I ever really wanted was a day off. Our contracts gave us six weeks' vacation each year, but they got around that by loaning us to other studios. I could have gone on suspension, but I had responsibilities—my father to support and my son in military school, all that."

Small wonder that Glenda became one of the hardest working actresses on the Warners lot, appearing in eleven films in 1933 alone. Her first film that year, *Mystery of the Wax Museum*, was an important assignment and proved to be instrumental in molding the Farrell image. In this horror classic Glenda had her first crack at playing a reporter, a role she'd repeat many more times. In this case she was investigating the disappearance of bodies from the city morgue, which were being used in the creation of wax figures at a new museum devoted to famous murders.

Mystery of the Wax Museum was shot in two-strip Technicolor, and director Michael Curtiz did an excellent job of creating the proper aura of suspense. In the pressbook written for the film's release, Curtiz wrote of deliberately invoking German expressionism to represent unease, mystery and horror, and he succeeded in evoking a macabre atmosphere. He was ably abetted by Lionel Atwill, deliciously sinister as the deranged museum owner, and Glenda, whose snappy performance provided comic relief. Although billed third below Atwill and nominal leading lady Fay Wray, Glenda had more screen time and was clearly the film's protagonist.

Glenda's son Tommy, who was then eleven, has vivid memories of visiting the *Wax Museum* set—in particular, one moment that seemed more horrific than anything occurring onscreen. "I got out of the car and went through the double doors to the sound stage," he recalled. "There was a little cubicle I had to enter first, though. In the cubicle I saw this horrible man with this ugly face. It turned out to be Lionel Atwill in his hideous mask that he wore in the movie. I let out a holler that they must have heard in Chicago. Lionel then started to laugh and said, 'It's me Tommy.' My mom then came over to see what was wrong, and we all had a good laugh.'"

Mystery of the Wax Museum fared poorly at the box office during its initial run and was soon forgotten. The film had been lost for nearly twenty-five years until an original thirty-five millimeter color print was found in Jack Warner's private vault in 1968. A restored print was screened at the New York Film Festival in September 1970, where it was well-received. Since then, *Mystery of the Wax Museum* has become a cult favorite.

Following her next assignments, *Grand Slam* (1933), *The Keyhole* (1933) and *Central Airport* (1933), Glenda was given her first starring role—in a B movie called *Girl Missing* (1933), which co-starred her good friend Mary Brian. The film's wild story of gold diggers in Palm Beach who become involved in a murder contained enough holes to make a Swiss cheese manufacturer envious, but Glenda's tart performance made it diverting.

Warners then loaned Glenda out for her next two projects. At Paramount she appeared in the forgotten *Gambling Ship* (1933). Her second loanout, this time to Columbia, was far more prestigious. At the time, Glenda was dating screenwriter Robert Riskin, and through her association with him she got the part of nightclub hostess Mississippi Martin in Frank Capra's *Lady for a Day* (1933). The Runyonesque comedy revolves around Apple Annie (May Robson), a poor apple seller in New York who has told her daughter (Jean Parker), who's living in Europe, that she's a married socialite. When her daughter writes that she's headed to New York with her fiancé and his parents, Annie enlists the help of Dave the Dude (Warren William) and other colorful characters to help her masquerade as a Park Avenue dowager. The showy role of Mississippi not only provided several hilarious scenes for Glenda, but she even got to sing. The film could easily pass for a Warners film, with fellow contract players William, Guy Kibbee and Ned Sparks rounding out the cast. *Lady for a Day* became one of the year's biggest hits and scored several Oscar nominations, including one for Robson as Best Actress. The film was one of Glenda's favorites, as shown by her vibrant performance. Surely, if supporting players had been honored at Academy Awards time in 1933, Glenda would have been nominated.

Unfortunately, back at Warners, Glenda was again relegated to supplying the comic relief in *Mary Stevens, M.D.* (1933) and *Bureau of Missing Persons* (1933). Her next film, *Havana Widows* (1933), served mainly as a springboard for the teaming of Glenda and Joan Blondell, both of whom were humorous as gold diggers on the prowl in Havana. "Hasn't been a picture in weeks with the same content of rapid-fire laughs, all legitimately gained and inescapable," noted *Variety*.

More importantly, *Havana Widows* marked the beginning of a lifelong friendship between both women that lasted until Glenda's death. "Joan Blondell and Mary Brian were her two best friends," said Tommy Farrell. "At lunch time they would jump in the studio car and go off shopping. Then the director would say, 'Where are the girls?' He'd have to go chasing them."

Glenda's last film that year was Columbia's *A Man's Castle* (1933), directed by Frank Borzage. This time she played a vamp out to lure Spencer Tracy away from loyal wife Loretta Young. Of this performance, Mordaunt Hall of *The New York Times* noted, "Glenda Farrell in her impersonation of Fay LaRue, an actress, imitates Mae West both in speech and walk."

Glenda was one of many stars in the Warners stable who boarded the train for the rigorous cross-country publicity tour to promote *42nd Street* (1933), which resurrected the movie musical thanks to the dazzling production numbers choreographed by Busby Berkeley. Bette Davis, Lyle Talbot, Toby Wing and Joe E. Brown were among Glenda's fellow travelers on the jaunt from Los Angeles to New York. During stopovers in such places as Denver and Cleveland the stars would come out and meet the locals, and then appear in a parade. Glenda also performed in a live stage show prior to a screening of *42nd Street*, singing songs from the film.

It was in Chicago that Lyle Talbot discovered just how far removed Glenda was from her brassy screen image. Stephen Talbot, Lyle's son, recalled that his father was visited at the Warners lot by a bootlegger named Spike O'Donnell, who complimented the actor on his realistic performance as a bank robber in *Ladies They Talk About* (1933). When O'Donnell learned that the *42nd Street* tour would be stopping in Chicago, he showed up at Talbot's hotel room with two hulking bodyguards named Dingy and Babe. The gangster welcomed Lyle and informed him that Dingy would be his escort during his stay in Chicago. "My dad really didn't want an escort, but he was hardly in a position to say 'No,'" laughed Stephen Talbot.

In his journal, Lyle Talbot described the events of the evening as follows: "Glenda Farrell, who had played all sorts of tough dames in gangster movies, joined me in the studio car that night, along with Dingy. She took one look at Dingy and the gun that he had in his pocket and she nearly peed in her pants. The car then took us to O'Donnell's gambling joint, which was made to look like the New York Stock Exchange."

As a going-away present, Lyle Talbot discovered a burlap bag containing twenty-four pints of bootleg whiskey mixed in with his baggage, his son said.

It was also during the middle of the tour that all of the actors on board were notified that Warners had to slash their salaries. Despite those cutbacks, Warners was as demanding as ever. In 1934 Glenda made eight films, starting with *The Big Shakedown* (1934) with Bette Davis.

In *Hi Nellie!* (1934), opposite Paul Muni, Glenda was again a reporter, but she still considered it one of her most challenging roles. "The character was always sitting at a typewriter with a cigarette dangling from her mouth, and I can't type and I don't smoke," she said.

She finished out the year playing supporting roles in a series of Bs: *I've Got Your Number* (again with Blondell), *Dark Hazard*, *Heat Lightning*, *Merry Wives of Reno* (doing more gold digging with Blondell), *The Personality Kid* and *Kansas City Princess*. The last film, which Andre Sennwald of *The New York Times* described as "fast and lively, even when it isn't funny," got its heartiest laughs from Glenda's and Blondell's outlandish impersonation of a pair of Girl Scouts.

The new year began with Glenda as Warren William's secretary accused of murder in *The Secret Bride* (1935), a minor mystery. Then, for a change, Glenda was featured in an 'A' film, *Gold Diggers of 1935* (1935), one of the last of Busby Berkeley's Warners extravaganzas. Although the film is remembered today for the brilliant "Lullaby of Broadway" number, Glenda's performance is delicious fun. As a scheming stenographer out to trap millionaire Hugh Herbert in a breach of promise suit, Glenda had the films' best lines, which she tossed off with her appropriate acerbic delivery. When Herbert claims she won't have a leg to stand on in a courtroom, Glenda snaps back, "My dear Mosley, you've given me more legs to stand on than a centipede."

After *The Traveling Saleslady* (1935), another pairing with Blondell, Glenda played Al Jolson's manager sister in *Go Into Your Dance* (1935), the only screen pairing of Jolson and his wife Ruby Keeler. Glenda gave a good performance, although even she couldn't steal the film from Jolson, who dominated nearly every frame.

Her remaining 1935 films — *In Caliente, We're in the Money, Little Big Shot* and *Miss Pacific Fleet* — made little impression on anyone. Unlike many of the Warners stars who rebelled at being thrown into one film after another, Glenda was grateful to be steadily working, even if the roles often had a sameness to them. "Warners typed you," she said. "but you'd get a starring part in one picture and a small part in another. They built their people fast and it was like a family. All the actors were so loyal, it was our home and we adored it."

Still, it's hard to imagine she could have been pleased with her first crop of films in 1936: *Snowed Under, The Law in Her Hands, Nobody's Fool* (at Universal) and *High Tension* (about a cable layer in Hawaii for Fox). Her next role, in *Gold Diggers of 1937* (1936), was essentially a reprise of the gold digger she portrayed in the previous entry in that series. This time she was out to fleece "dying" millionaire Victor Moore, and she was again a delight tossing off such lines as, "It's so hard to be good under the capitalistic system!"

For *Smart Blonde* (1937) Glenda was back to playing a troublemaking reporter. This time, though, Warners gave her the starring role of fast-talking Torchy Blane, who spends more time romancing her police inspector boyfriend Steve McBride (Barton MacLane) and interfering in his attempts to solve a murder than she does behind a typewriter. It was neither better nor worse than any other Warners B, but Glenda's smooth portrayal of Torchy made it a popular second feature — and thus a new movie series was born.

Glenda tried to make Torchy believable, compared to some of the other newspaperwomen she played. "They were caricatures of newspaperwomen as I knew them. So before I undertook to do the first Torchy, I determined to create a real human being — and not an exaggerated comedy type. I met those [newswomen] who visited Hollywood, and watched them work on visits to New York City. They were generally young, intelligent, refined and attractive. By making Torchy true to life, I tried to create a character practically unique in movies," Glenda explained in her 1969 *Times* interview.

Obviously Glenda succeeded, since she received a huge amount of fan mail for the Torchy Blane films. Her expert playing gave the series distinction, and it's doubtful that many other actresses could have matched Glenda's feat of delivering a four-hundred word speech in forty seconds in *Torchy Gets Her Man* (1938). In all, Glenda appeared in seven Torchy films, with Lola Lane and Jane Wyman as her replacements for two installments.

The greatest honor Glenda received for her performance as Torchy came from Joe Shuster and Jerry Siegel, the creators of Superman. In a letter to *Time* magazine in 1988, Siegel related that Glenda's performance as Torchy served as the inspiration for Lois Lane. "My wife Joanne was Joe's original art model for Superman's girlfriend Lois Lane back in the 1930s," Siegel wrote. "Our heroine was, of course, a working girl whose priority was grabbing scoops. What inspired me in the creation was Glenda Farrell, the movie star who portrayed Torchy Blane in a series of exciting motion pictures. Because the name of the actress Lola Lane (who also played Torchy) appealed to me, I called my character Lois Lane."

In between the Torchy films Glenda made several other Bs for Warners, and was the one bright spot in Busby Berkeley's otherwise dull *Hollywood Hotel* (1938). Glenda balanced her film appearances with several radio stints, including *Vanity and Some Sable*s with Tyrone Power on *Hollywood Playhouse* in 1937, and *Manhattan Latin* with Humphrey Bogart in January 1938.

The oddest turn of her career was her election to the post of honorary mayor of North Hollywood. Glenda handily beat her competition, Bing Crosby and Lewis Stone, by a three-to-one margin. Although Glenda's political "career" may have begun as a publicity stunt, she took her job very seriously. "Let me tell you, politics just don't mix with acting," she mused. "My being mayor started as partly a publicity idea, but it turned into a hard job. There were functions, presentations, ceremonies.... I never knew there were so many Rotarians, Kiwanians and Lions!"

During Glenda's one-year term, the North Hollywood Chamber of Commerce announced that it wanted to put sewers along Ventura Highway, and Glenda was put in charge of the project. "I remember people coming to our house," related her son Tommy, "and saying, 'We're here for the sewer meeting.' Pat O'Brien and Hugh Herbert were also very much involved. She couldn't get out of it, but once she started it, she jumped in it with both feet. They did get the sewers in shortly after her term, but she started the groundwork."

In 1939 Glenda made two final films for Warners — *Torchy Blane in Chinatown* and, ironically, *Torchy Runs for Mayor*. Although Warners wanted to renew her contract, she was ready to make a break. After seven years of working at a breakneck pace, Glenda needed a rest. She was also anxious to return to her first love — the New York stage. The fact that Jack Warner at the time reneged on a promised raise made her decision even easier.

"Her relationship with Jack Warner was like all the other actors' relationships with Mr. Warner. I think I was fifteen years old before I found out that 'that son of a bitch Jack Warner' wasn't all one word," joked Tommy Farrell.

Still, Glenda cherished her tenure at Warner Bros., especially for the many friends and colleagues she loved working with at the studio. "So you weren't Kay Francis. You were still well paid, and you didn't get a star complex. We were a very close group — Cagney, Kibbee, Hugh Herbert, Aline MacMahon, Dick Powell and Joan Blondell. Of course, Bette [Davis] was always an outsider," Glenda said in 1969.

As a free agent, Glenda was determined to find more versatile roles than she was offered at Warners. "I want to show that I can do more than talk out of the corner of my mouth," Glenda told *Movies* magazine.

Her first venture was about as far removed from her screen image as she could get. She kicked off the ninth season of the Westport Country Playhouse in July 1939 in the lead role of *Anna Christie*, a role made famous onscreen by Greta Garbo. The idea of Glenda playing Eugene O'Neill's tragic prostitute seemed like a stretch, but she received excellent notices. She followed that with a summer stock production of S.N. Behrman's *Brief Moment* at the Cape Playhouse in Dennis, Massachusetts.

Glenda's next project would prove to be both a fortuitous boon to her career and to her personal life. In March 1940 Glenda was featured in *Separate Rooms*, a drawing room comedy which opened in Seattle as *Thanks for My Wife*. The play eventually made it to Broadway's Plymouth Theater for a successful 613-performance run. Co-starring with Glenda were Alan Dinehart and her Warners buddy Lyle Talbot.

On several occasions the action backstage was livelier than the show itself. On August 30, 1940, after the performance, the doorman at the Plymouth was wounded by a gunman. Cast members and technicians took up a collection to help with his medical expenses.

On another (less traumatic) occasion, Glenda was the injured party in an incident that resembled the backstage plot of an old Warners musical. In between scenes of a performance, Glenda sprained her ankle, said Tommy Farrell. In typical theatrical fashion, a stagehand went out onstage and inquired if there was a doctor in the house. Dr. Henry Ross, a staff surgeon at New York's Polyclinic Hospital, came to the rescue. Both doctor and patient took to each other immediately, and after a few follow-up visits to his office, they began dating.

Glenda and Dr. Ross were married in a quiet ceremony on January 19, 1941, at the home of the groom's friends, Dr. and Mrs. Irving H. Saxe, in Passaic, New Jersey. Mary Brian was the maid of honor. After the ceremony the couple returned to Glenda's apartment at the Essex House in Manhattan, and then Glenda the trouper went onstage in *Separate Rooms* that evening.

Tommy was attending college during Glenda's run in *Separate Rooms*, but he always joined her in New York during the summer. He loved watching Glenda perform onstage, and inevitably began to long for a career as an entertainer. Tommy, who was a trained drummer, made his first foray into show business in the summer of 1939 when he competed in a drum contest held by Gene Krupa and his band at the New York World's Fair. He did so well that band member Buddy Rich asked him to sit in with the band. Glenda was totally supportive of her son's career.

One year later, playwrights Howard Lindsay and Russell Crouse were looking for an actor who could also play drums for a new show they were preparing. "They asked me to read for it, and then they asked my mom, 'We know he can play the drums, but can he act?' She said, 'He's my son, isn't he?' I got the job and never went back to college," Tommy said.

Tommy ultimately developed into a successful nightclub entertainer and later landed roles in many films, including *Singin' in the Rain* (1952).

Glenda left *Separate Rooms* in July 1941 and headed back to Hollywood for a supporting role in *Johnny Eager* (1942), with Robert Taylor and Lana Turner, at MGM. She then co-starred with George Brent and Joan Bennett in the marital farce *Twin Beds* (1942), and joined Cary Grant, Jean Arthur and Ronald Colman in George Stevens' social comedy *Talk of the Town* (1942). Although her roles in all three films were small, she made the most of her screen time.

In April 1942 Glenda returned to Broadway in a short-lived comedy, *The Life of Reilly*. She and her husband then officially made the East Coast their home. They settled into an apartment on Park Avenue and also bought a fifty-acre estate in Brewster, New York. She sold her San Fernando Valley home to screen cowboy Gabby Hayes.

The fact that Glenda had bought two homes in New York by no means indicated that she was abandoning her film career. In 1942 she made a quickie for PRC called *A Night for Crime*, and then did three films for Columbia: *Klondike Kate* (1943), *City Without Men* (1943) and *Ever Since Venus* (1944). Columbia boss Harry Cohn had a reputation for being profane and extremely hard on actors, but Glenda had no problem with him. "Harry could be a bugger if you were under contract to him, but she wasn't," Tommy said. "Because of that, she never had to argue about money with Harry and they got along fine."

While in California, Glenda stayed with Tommy at his home, and also spent many happy hours visiting with her brothers Gene, a special effects cameraman at Warners, and Dick, a film editor at Paramount, and her cousins—director Jerry Hopper and Paramount projectionist Karny Ballard. "At home she wasn't the funny one, she was always the audience. She loved to laugh and they could always make her laugh," recalled Tommy.

In 1945 Glenda was back on Broadway in *The Overtons*, a comedy starring Arlene Francis and Jack Whiting, which settled in for a lengthy run. Glenda returned to Hollywood in 1947, but the films—Eagle-Lion's *Heading for Heaven* and then *I Love Trouble* (1947) and *Lulu Belle* (1948), a pair of Bs for Columbia—attracted little attention. *Lulu Belle*, starring Dorothy Lamour and George Montgomery, was Glenda's first western, and its premise about a saloon singer who toys with the affections of many men sounded promising. Unfortunately, the film suffered in the casting of its two leads, both of whom had lost their box-office luster, and a story that had been sanitized to a squeaky-clean veneer.

Following the brief run of *Mrs. Gibbons' Boys* in New York and some summer stock in 1949, Glenda made her television debut in February 1950 in "Gaudy Lady" on *Silver Theater*. She soon became a frequent guest on countless television shows during the 1950s. In 1957 she starred in a series pilot based on the 1951 film *The Model and the Marriage Broker*. Glenda seemed ideal in Thelma Ritter's screen role as the marriage broker, but the pilot didn't sell.

Glenda also made some sporadic film appearances during that decade, most notably as Joan Collins' mother in *The Girl in the Red Velvet Swing* (1956), a lackluster recreation of the Sanford White murder. The performances of both actresses were its sole virtues.

In March 1959 Glenda appeared onstage in New York as Cloris Leachman's mother in *Masquerade*, a flop which opened and closed the same night. Later that year Glenda had her best screen role in some time as Kim Novak's mother in *Middle of the Night* (1959), a depressing tale of a middle-aged man in love with a confused girl thirty years his junior. Although her screen time was minimal, Glenda turned in a heartfelt performance.

While her screen career was fading, Glenda continued to sparkle on television in the 1960s and gave several memorable performances. She co-starred as a nun, with Claudette Colbert and Robert Preston, in an adaptation of *Bells of St. Mary's*, and was also excellent in the television drama *A String of Beads* with Jane Fonda and George Grizzard. One of her favorite guests spots was in an episode of *Rawhide*, in which Frankie Avalon and her son Tommy also guest-starred. Ironically, it was Avalon who played her son in the entry.

Unlike many films stars, Glenda was not intimidated by the demanding schedule of preparing a television program in only a few days. "She enjoyed the variety of being able to do all kinds of different roles," Tommy said. "She didn't think it was that different from doing films, except that you had to do more in a shorter amount of time. She was used to that at Warners. It didn't take a hell of a lot of time to make some of those movies."

The peak of Glenda's career came in 1963. In January she gave a beautiful performance in "A Cardinal of Mercy," a two-part episode of *Ben Casey*. In May her performance was recognized with an Emmy Award as the Most Outstanding Supporting Actress in a drama.

In 1964 Glenda made two film appearances, but she was wasted in both. *Kissin' Cousins* was a piece of hillbilly hokum in which she played Elvis Presley's mother; and *The Disorderly Orderly* was an anemic Jerry Lewis farce. While making *Kissin' Cousins*, Glenda hurt her neck. Rather than bow out of the film, she wore a neck brace when not on camera and removed it when her scenes were filmed.

No doubt the main incentive for Glenda to make both films was the chance to co-star with Tommy, who recalls that his mother was always helpful to her fellow castmates during filming. "If she saw someone make a mistake, she would call them over to the side and tell them. She drew people like a moth to a flame. Everyone always came to her for advice," he said.

Glenda continued to make occasional television appearances over the next few years, and one last film, *Tiger by the Tail* (1968), before announcing her retirement. Glenda tried several hobbies to occupy her time, and often indulged in her favorite pastime—shopping.

"She loved to shop," recalled actress Nancy Coleman. "I met Glenda after I replaced her in a show one time and liked her very much. Years later we happened to run into each other one day in Manhattan. We got to talking and then spent the whole day together shopping. I remember she bought these two beautiful little pink ceramic jewelry boxes. After she died I dated Glenda's husband for a while. One time I saw the boxes at his apartment. I told him about the day we spent together and asked if I could have the boxes as a keepsake. I still have them."

Despite her best efforts to keep busy, Glenda seemed unfulfilled, and within a short time she became frustrated and irritable. At one point she even thought she was developing an ulcer. Dr. Ross came up with a different diagnosis—boredom had set in. "Call your agent. You need a job," was his prescription.

Her agent wasted no time in finding Glenda a dream role as Julie Harris' eccentric mother in the David Merrick comedy *Forty Carats*. Glenda was especially thrilled that after years of playing working women and, later, dowdy mothers she finally was given a glamorous role and stylish clothes to wear. Clive Barnes of *The New York Times* raved that Glenda's portrayal of a "mod grandmother" was "expertly done."

Glenda's run in *Forty Carats* also brought back memories of her Warners days and the good times she had working with Joan Blondell. "They used to call Joan and me 'the gimme girls.' We were always out to get a man with money. But those movies were risqué in the way that *Forty Carats* is risqué—sophisticated and fun."

While appearing in *Forty Carats*, the Rosses occupied a luxurious apartment in Manhattan as well as maintaining their home in Brewster. The one drawback Glenda found to being in New York was being separated from her pet cats, who remained in Brewster. To keep them from being lonely, Glenda arranged for each cat to have its own room with a color television.

Unfortunately, Glenda's run with the play was short-lived. She was forced to leave the cast after only two months because of poor health. She went to Florida to recuperate, but was eventually diagnosed with terminal lung cancer. "No one knows how she got it. She never smoked a day in her life," recounted Tommy.

Glenda eventually returned to New York and died in her Park Avenue apartment on May 1, 1971. She was buried at the United States

Military Academy at West Point, Dr. Ross' alma mater, and is the only actor to ever be placed in the Academy's cemetery.

Today Glenda's films are being rediscovered, and new generations are enjoying her snappy banter as the fast-talking reporter or the gold digger with a heart of gold. Ultimately, her greatest praise comes from her son Tommy, who remains her biggest fan. "She was marvelous. She never got a bad notice in her life."

FILMOGRAPHY

Lucky Boy (Tiffany, 1929) Directed by Norman Taurog. *Cast:* George Jessel, Rosa Rosanova, William K. Strauss, Margaret Quimby. (Glenda appeared unbilled.)

Little Caesar (Warner Bros., 1930) Directed by Mervyn LeRoy. *Cast:* Edward G. Robinson, Douglas Fairbanks, Jr., Glenda Farrell, William Collier, Jr., Ralph Ince, George E. Stone.

Life Begins (Warner Bros., 1932) Directed by James Flood. *Cast:* Loretta Young, Eric Linden, Aline MacMahon, Preston Foster, Glenda Farrell, Frank McHugh, Clara Blandick.

Three on a Match (Warner Bros., 1932) Directed by Mervyn LeRoy. *Cast:* Joan Blondell, Ann Dvorak, Bette Davis, Warren William, Lyle Talbot. (Glenda appeared unbilled.)

Scandal for Sale (Universal 1932) Directed by Russell Mack. *Cast:* Charles Bickford, Rose Hobart, Pat O'Brien, Claudia Dell, J. Farrell MacDonald, Harry Beresford, Glenda Farrell.

I Am a Fugitive from a Chain Gang (Warner Bros., 1932) Directed by Mervyn LeRoy. *Cast:* Paul Muni, Glenda Farrell, Helen Vinson, Preston Foster, Allen Jenkins, Edward J. Macnamara.

The Match King (Warner Bros., 1932) Directed by Howard Bretherton. *Cast:* Warren William, Lili Damita, Glenda Farrell, Harold Huber, Hardie Albright, Claire Dodd, Edmund Breese.

Mystery of the Wax Museum (Warner Bros., 1933) Directed by Michael Curtiz. *Cast:* Lionel Atwill, Fay Wray, Glenda Farrell, Frank McHugh, Gavin Gordon, Allen Vincent, Edwin Maxwell.

Grand Slam (Warner Bros., 1933) Directed by William Dieterle. *Cast:* Paul Lukas, Loretta Young, Frank McHugh, Glenda Farrell, Helen Vinson, Walter Byron, Ferdinand Gottschalk.

The Keyhole (Warner Bros., 1933) Directed by Michael Curtiz. *Cast:* Kay Francis, George Brent, Glenda Farrell, Allen Jenkins, Monroe Owsley, Helen Ware, Henry Kolker.

Central Airport (Warner Bros., 1933) Directed by William A. Wellman. *Cast:* Richard Barthelmess, Sally Eilers, Tom Brown, Glenda Farrell, Harold Huber, Grant Mitchell.

Girl Missing (Warner Bros., 1933) Directed by Robert Florey. *Cast:* Glenda Farrell, Mary Brian, Ben Lyon, Lyle Talbot, Guy Kibbee, Harold Huber, Edward Ellis, Ferdinand Gottschalk.

Gambling Ship (Paramount, 1933) Directed by Max Marcin. *Cast:* Cary Grant, Benita Hume, Roscoe Karns, Glenda Farrell, Jack La Rue, Edward Gargan, Edwin Maxwell, Spencer Charters.

Lady for a Day (Columbia, 1933) Directed by Frank Capra. *Cast:* May Robson, Warren William, Glenda Farrell, Guy Kibbee, Ned Sparks, Jean Parker, Walter Connolly, Nat Pendleton.

Mary Stevens, M.D. (Warner Bros., 1933) Directed by Lloyd Bacon. *Cast:* Kay Francis, Lyle Talbot, Glenda Farrell, Thelma Todd, Una O'Connor, Charles Wilson, Hobart Cavanaugh.

Bureau of Missing Persons (Warner Bros., 1933) Directed by Roy Del Ruth. *Cast:* Lewis Stone, Pat O'Brien, Glenda Farrell, Bette Davis, Allen Jenkins, Ruth Donnelly, Hugh Herbert.

Havana Widows (Warner Bros., 1933) Directed by Ray Enright. *Cast:* Joan Blondell, Glenda Farrell, Lyle Talbot, Allen Jenkins, Guy Kibbee, Ruth Donnelly, Mayo Methot, Frank McHugh.

A Man's Castle (Columbia, 1933) Directed by Frank Borzage. *Cast:* Spencer Tracy, Loretta Young, Glenda Farrell, Walter Connolly, Arthur Hohl, Marjorie Rambeau, Dickie Moore.

Hi Nellie! (Warner Bros., 1934) Directed by Mervyn LeRoy. *Cast:* Paul Muni, Glenda Farrell, Douglass Dumbrille, Robert Barrat, Ned Sparks, Hobasrt Cavanaugh.

I've Got Your Number (Warner Bros., 1934) Directed by Ray Enright. *Cast:* Joan Blondell, Pat O'Brien, Glenda Farrell, Allen Jenkins, Eugene Pallette, Gordon Westcott, Henry O'Neill.

The Big Shakedown (Warner Bros., 1934) Directed by John Francis Dillon. *Cast:* Charles Farrell, Bette Davis, Ricardo Cortez, Glenda Farrell, Allen Jenkins, Henry O'Neill.

The Dark Hazard (Warner Bros., 1934) Directed

by Alfred E. Green. *Cast:* Edward G. Robinson, Genevieve Tobin, Glenda Farrell, Robert Barrat, Gordon Westcott, Hobart Cavanaugh.

Heat Lightning (Warner Bros., 1934) Directed by Mervyn LeRoy. *Cast:* Aline MacMahon, Preston Foster, Lyle Talbot, Ann Dvorak, Glenda Farrell, Ruth Donnelly, Frank McHugh.

Merry Wives of Reno (Warner Bros., 1934) Directed by H. Bruce Humberstone. *Cast:* Margaret Lindsay, Donald Woods, Guy Kibbee, Glenda Farrell, Hugh Herbert, Ruth Donnelly, Frank McHugh.

The Personality Kid (Warner Bros., 1934) Directed by Alan Crosland. *Cast:* Pat O'Brien, Glenda Farrell, Claire Dodd, Henry O'Neill, Robert Gleckler, Thomas Jackson.

Kansas City Princess (Warner Bros., 1934) Directed by William Keighley. *Cast:* Joan Blondell, Glenda Farrell, Robert Armstrong, Hugh Herbert, Osgood Perkins, Hobart Cavanaugh.

The Secret Bride (Warner Bros., 1935) Directed by William Dieterle. *Cast:* Barbara Stanwyck, Warren William, Glenda Farrell, Grant Mitchell, Arthur Byron, Henry O'Neill.

Gold Diggers of 1935 (Warner Bros., 1935) Directed by Busby Berkeley. *Cast:* Dick Powell, Gloria Stuart, Adolphe Menjou, Alice Brady, Glenda Farrell, Hugh Herbert, Frank McHugh.

Traveling Saleslady (Warner Bros., 1935) Directed by Ray Enright. *Cast:* Joan Blondell, Glenda Farrell, William Gargan, Hugh Herbert, Grant Mitchell, Al Shean, Ruth Donnelly.

Go Into Your Dance (Warner Bros., 1935) Directed by Archie Mayo. *Cast:* Al Jolson, Ruby Keeler, Helen Morgan, Glenda Farrell, Barton MacLane, Sharon Lynne, Patsy Kelly.

In Caliente (Warner Bros., 1935) Directed by Lloyd Bacon. *Cast:* Pat O'Brien, Dolores Del Rio, Leo Carillo, Edward Everett Horton, Glenda Farrell, the de Marcos, the Canova Family.

We're in the Money (Warner Bros., 1935) Directed by Lloyd Bacon. *Cast:* Joan Blondell, Glenda Farrell, Hugh Herbert, Ross Alexander, Hobart Cavanaugh, Phil Regan, Henry O'Neill.

Little Big Shot (Warner Bros., 1935) Directed by Michael Curtiz. *Cast:* Sybil Jason, Glenda Farrell, Robert Armstrong, Edward Everett Horton, Jack La Rue, Arthur Vinton, J. Carrol Naish.

Miss Pacific Fleet (Warner Bros., 1935) Directed by Ray Enright. *Cast:* Joan Blondell, Glenda Farrell, Hugh Herbert, Allen Jenkins, Minna Gombell, Warren Hull, Marie Wilson, Mary Treen.

Snowed Under (Warner Bros., 1936) Directed by Ray Enright. *Cast:* George Brent, Genevieve Tobin, Glenda Farrell, Patricia Ellis, Frank McHugh, Porter Hall, Helen Lowell.

Nobody's Fool (Universal, 1936) Directed by Arthur Greville Collins. *Cast:* Glenda Farrell, Edward Everett Horton, Edward Gargan, Warren Hymer, Cesar Romero, Diana Gibson.

The Law in Her Hands (Warner Bros., 1936) Directed by William Clemens. *Cast:* Margaret Lindsay, Warren Hull, Glenda Farrell, Lyle Talbot, Eddie Acuff, Addison Richards, Dick Purcell.

High Tension (20th Century–Fox, 1936) Directed by Allan Dwan. *Cast:* Brian Donlevy, Norman Foster, Glenda Farrell, Helen Wood, Robert McWade.

Here Comes Carter (Warner Bros., 1936) Directed by William Clemens. *Cast:* Ross Alexander, Glenda Farrell, Anne Nagel, Hobart Cavanaugh, Craig Reynolds, George E. Stone.

Gold Diggers of 1937 (Warner Bros., 1936) Directed by Lloyd Bacon. *Cast:* Dick Powell, Joan Blondell, Victor Moore, Glenda Farrell, Lee Dixon, Osgood Perkins, Rosalind Marquis.

Smart Blonde (Warner Bros., 1937) Directed by Frank McDonald. *Cast:* Glenda Farrell, Barton MacLane, Winifred Shaw, Craig Reynolds, Addison Richards, Jane Wyman.

You Live and Learn (Warner Bros.-Teddington, 1937) Directed by Arthur Woods. *Cast:* Glenda Farrell, Claude Hulbert, Glen Alyn, John Carol, James Stephenson, George Galleon.

Fly-Away Baby (Warner Bros., 1937) Directed by Frank McDonald. *Cast:* Glenda Farrell, Barton MacLane, Gordon Oliver, Hugh O'Connell, Marcia Ralston, Tom Kennedy.

Dance, Charlie, Dance (Warner Bros., 1937) Directed by Frank McDonald. *Cast:* Stuart Erwin, Jean Muir, Glenda Farrell, Allen Jenkins, Addison Richards, Charles Foy, Chester Clute.

Breakfast for Two (RKO Radio, 1937) Directed by Alfred Santell. *Cast:* Barbara Stanwyck, Herbert Marshall, Eric Blore, Glenda Farrell, Donald Meek, Etienne Girardot.

The Adventurous Blonde (Warner Bros., 1937) Directed by Frank McDonald. *Cast:* Glenda Farrell, Barton MacLane, Anne Nagel, Tom Kennedy, George E. Stone, Natalie Moorehead.

Hollywood Hotel (Warner Bros., 1938) Directed by Busby Berkeley. *Cast:* Dick Powell, Rosemary Lane, Lola Lane, Ted Healy, Johnny Davis, Alan Mowbray, Glenda Farrell.

Blondes at Work (Warner Bros., 1938) Directed by Frank McDonald. *Cast:* Glenda Farrell, Barton MacLane, Tom Kennedy, Betty Compson, Rosella Towne, John Ridgeley.

Stolen Heaven (Paramount, 1938) Directed by Andrew L. Stone. *Cast:* Gene Raymond, Olympe Bradna, Lewis Stone, Glenda Farrell, Porter Hall, Douglass Dumbrille, Esther Dale.

Prison Break (Universal, 1938) Directed by Arthur Lubin. *Cast:* Barton MacLane, Glenda Farrell, Ward Bond, Constance Moore, Paul Hurst, Frank Darien, Victor Kilian.

The Road to Reno (Universal, 1938) Directed by S. Sylvan Simon. *Cast:* Randolph Scott, Hope Hampton, Glenda Farrell, Helen Broderick, Alan Marshal, Samuel S. Hinds.

Torchy Gets Her Man (Warner Bros., 1938) Directed by William Beaudine. *Cast:* Glenda Farrell, Barton MacLane, Willard Robertson, Tom Kennedy, George Guhl, John Ridgeley.

Exposed (Universal, 1938) Directed by Harold D. Schuster. *Cast:* Glenda Farrell, Charles D. Brown, Otto Kruger, Maurice Cass, Richard Lane, Eddie "Rochester" Anderson, Irving Bacon.

Torchy Blane in Chinatown (Warner Bros., 1939) Directed by William Beaudine. *Cast:* Glenda Farrell, Barton MacLane, Henry O'Neill, Tom Kennedy, Patric Knowles, James Stephenson.

Torchy Runs for Mayor (Warner Bros., 1939) Directed by Ray McCarey. *Cast:* Glenda Farrell, Barton MacLane, Tom Kennedy, Frank Shannon, Irving Bacon, John Miljan, Jack Mower.

Johnny Eager (MGM, 1942) Directed by Mervyn LeRoy. *Cast:* Robert Taylor, Lana Turner, Van Heflin, Edward Arnold, Robert Sterling, Patricia Dane, Glenda Farrell, Henry O'Neill.

Twin Beds (Edward Small-United Artists, 1942) Directed by Tim Whelan. *Cast:* George Brent, Joan Bennett, Mischa Auer, Una Merkel, Glenda Farrell, Ernest Truex, Margaret Hamilton.

Talk of the Town (Columbia, 1942) Directed by George Stevens. *Cast:* Cary Grant, Jean Arthur, Ronald Colman, Edgar Buchanan, Glenda Farrell, Charles Dingle, Emma Dunn.

A Night for Crime (PRC, 1942) Directed by Alexis Thurn-Taxis. *Cast:* Lyle Talbot, Glenda Farrell, Lina Basquette, Donald Kirke, Marjorie Manners, Ralph Sanford.

City Without Men (Columbia, 1943) Directed by Sidney Salkow. *Cast:* Linda Darnell, Michael Duane, Sara Allgood, Edgar Buchanan, Glenda Farrell, Leslie Brooks, Margaret Hamilton.

Klondike Kate (Columbia, 1944) Directed by William Castle. *Cast:* Ann Savage, Tom Neal, Glenda Farrell, Lester Allen, Constance Worth, Sheldon Leonard, George Cleveland.

Ever Since Venus (Columbia, 1944) Directed by Arthur Dreifuss. *Cast:* Hugh Herbert, Billy Gilbert, Ina Ray Hutton, Glenda Farrell, Ann Savage, Ross Hunter, Alan Mowbray, Fritz Feld.

Heading for Heaven (Eagle-Lion, 1947) Directed by Lewis D. Collins. *Cast:* Stuart Erwin, Glenda Farrell, Milburn Stone, Irene Ryan, George O'Hanlon, Selmar Jackson, Dick Elliott.

I Love Trouble (Columbia, 1947) Directed by S. Sylvan Simon. *Cast:* Franchot Tone, Janet Blair, Janis Carter, Adele Jergens, Glenda Farrell, Steve Geray, Tom Powers, Eduardo Ciannelli.

Lulu Belle (Columbia, 1948) Directed by Leslie Fenton. *Cast:* Dorothy Lamour, George Montgomery, Otto Kruger, Albert Dekker, Glenda Farrell, Greg McClure, Harry Morgan.

Apache War Smoke (MGM, 1952) Directed by Harold Kress. *Cast:* Gilbert Roland, Robert Horton, Glenda Farrell, Barbara Ruick, Harry Morgan, Gene Lockhart, Myron Healey.

Girls in the Night (Universal-International, 1953) Directed by Jack Arnold. *Cast:* Glenda Farrell, Harvey Lembeck, Joyce Holden, Glen Roberts, Don Gordon, Patricia Hardy, Susan Odin.

Secret of the Incas (Paramount, 1954) Directed by Jerry Hopper. *Cast:* Charlton Heston, Robert Young, Thomas Mitchell, Nicole Maurey, Yma Sumac, Glenda Farrell, Michael Pate.

Susan Slept Here (RKO Radio, 1954) Directed by Frank Tashlin. *Cast:* Dick Powell, Debbie Reynolds, Anne Francis, Glenda Farrell, Alvy Moore, Horace MacMahon, Rita Johnson.

The Girl in the Red Velvet Swing (20th Century–Fox, 1956) Directed by Richard Fleischer. *Cast:* Ray Milland, Joan Collins, Farley Granger, Glenda Farrell, Cornelia Otis Skinner.

Middle of the Night (Columbia, 1958) Directed by Delbert Mann. *Cast:* Fredric March, Kim Novak, Glenda Farrell, Jan Norris, Lee Grant, Lee Phillips, Albert Dekker, Edith Meiser.

Kissin' Cousins (MGM, 1964) Directed by Gene Nelson. *Cast:* Elvis Presley, Arthur O'Connell, Glenda Farrell, Jack Albertson, Tommy Farrell, Joan Staley, Yvonne Craig.

The Disorderly Orderly (Paramount, 1964) Directed by Frank Tashlin. *Cast:* Jerry Lewis, Susan Oliver, Glenda Farrell, Everett Sloane, Kathleen Freeman, Karen Sharpe, Alice Pearce.

Tiger by the Tail (Commonwealth United, 1968) Directed by Robert G. "Bud" Springsteen. *Cast:* Christopher George, Dean Jagger, Charo, Glenda Farrell, Lloyd Bochner, Skip Homeier.

Kay Francis: "Trouble in Paradise"

No one suffered on-screen like Kay Francis. Throughout a series of Warners weepers in the '30s, Kay played a string of unwed mothers, streetwalkers and terminally ill heroines. Despite their dilemmas, their suffering was made easier by being draped in assorted furs, silk and diamonds.

Kay's screen incarnations had nothing on the lady herself, who endured no end of indignities during her last few years at Warners. Jack Warner considered it a real coup when he lured Kay from Paramount in 1932. Once Kay's star had fallen a few years later, she crashed and burned in the worst films the studio could dig up in the hopes that she'd leave. But Kay wouldn't quit, especially if it meant giving up her well-padded paycheck.

Kay rebounded somewhat with the successful *Four Jills in a Jeep* tour during World War II, and a Broadway stint in *State of the Union*, but she lived out her last years bitter over her mistreatment in Hollywood. Few remembered she was once the epitome of Hollywood chic.

Although she probably didn't plan it that way, Kay followed in the footsteps of her mother, a renowned actress named Katharine Clinton. Unlike Kay, Katharine was primarily a stage actress who achieved success in such classical roles as Jessica in *The Merchant of Venice*. Her career slowed down when she married Joseph Sprague Gibbs, an Oklahoma City hotel manager, on December 7, 1903. The exact date of Kay's birth is unclear, since at various times she listed several dates between 1899 and 1910. Most sources list her birth date as either January 13, 1903 (in which case her mother would have been eight months pregnant when she got married), or July 13, 1905. One thing is certain — on the night Katherine Edwina Gibbs was born, her father got drunk and arrived home by horseback, riding the animal through the hotel lobby and up the long staircase to the room where his wife and new daughter were resting.

When Kay was a year old her family moved to Santa Barbara and then Denver. When Kay was three or four her mother, fed up with Gibbs' drinking, took Kay and went east to resume her stage career. Kay rarely saw her father after that, and was bitter toward him for the rest of her life.

Kay's childhood was a depressing one, steeped in poverty and hunger. She and her mother tramped from one dirty theatrical boarding house to another. They sometimes subsisted on salty popcorn and water when they couldn't afford a decent meal. Kay's difficult childhood accounted for her resentment toward her mother, as well as her willingness to later accept whatever dreadful roles Warners gave her if it meant having a large and steady income.

Kay claimed to have been educated at the Holy Angels Convent in Fort Lee, New Jersey, and Notre Dame School in Roxbury, Massachusetts; however, there is no record of her attendance at either school. Her elementary school education was spotty, although Kay did attend Miss Fuller's Girls Academy in Ossining,

New York, where she said it was "Katie did" when she did something well, and, more often, "Katie didn't" when she fared poorly.

She spent two years at Miss Fuller's and then transferred to the Cathedral School of St. Mary in Garden City, New York, for her junior year. It was around this time that Kay's first brush with acting occurred, but again there's ambiguity. One version is that at Miss Fuller's Kay wrote a three-act play, which was performed at the school, and she played the male lead.

More probable is that Kay appeared in the leading male role in the play *You Never Can Tell*, which was written by her fellow classmate Katty Stewart, while at the Cathedral School. Still, Kay at the time had no desire to be an actress, and instead wanted to be a trapeze artist.

Kay never graduated from high school. In September 1921, at her mother's request, she enrolled in the Katharine Gibbs Secretarial School. After successfully completing the course, she got a secretarial job, for which she received $30 a week. She then bounced from one job to another, including working as a publicist and a real estate agent. Her first important job was as an assistant to Julianna Cutting, who booked coming-out parties for debutantes. Fringe benefits of the job included joining her boss on a European tour and establishing important social contacts with some of the wealthy young men she met. Kay was briefly engaged to Allan Ryan, Jr., of the Thomas Fortune Ryan family, but they didn't marry. On the night before his marriage to socialite Eleanor Barry, Ryan caused a minor scandal by escorting Kay to Harlem's Cotton Club.

Kay also modeled for artist Leo Mielziner, who later became her father-in-law. His oil painting of Kay attracted much attention and was exhibited at the British Royal Academy in 1926.

In January 1922 Kay met James Dwight Francis, the handsome scion of a wealthy Pittsfield, Massachusetts, family. Francis had attended Harvard for three and a half years, but left the school in 1919 without earning his degree and had since become a playboy who drank excessively. Kay found him charming, and loved being seen with him at New York's hottest spots.

They were married on December 6, 1922, but immediately there were problems. Francis had been living well beyond his financial means, and out of financial need they moved from New York to Pittsfield. The change of locale didn't help matters. Even worse, Francis physically abused Kay, which caused emotional scars that made it difficult for her to establish a successful relationship with any of her other husbands. After being married slightly more than a year, Kay divorced Francis but retained his surname.

Kay returned to New York, where she met Bill Gaston, with whom she had a torrid affair. When she suspected she was pregnant, they were secretly wed. Two days after they were wed, she discovered she wasn't expecting, and Gaston asked for a divorce. A single woman again, Kay rented a flat with her friend Lois Long. The women became part of a clique that spent their nights frequenting one speakeasy after the other.

It was around this time that Kay began considering a stage career. Kay had two handicaps: She lacked experience and formal acting training, and she had a terrible lisp, which made all of her r's sound like w's. Her friend Dwight Deere Wiman, an up-and-coming theatrical producer, suggested that she take speech therapy, which, to some degree, took care of one problem.

Through her friend Charles Baskerville, Kay was introduced to producer Edgar Selwyn, who engaged her to understudy Katherine Cornell in *The Green Hat*. Obviously, a neophyte like Kay could never equal Cornell as an actress, but physically she was a good match. Fortunately for both Kay and Selwyn, Cornell never missed a performance.

In November 1925 Kay made her Broadway debut in Horace Liveright's modern dress production of *Hamlet* starring Basil Sydney as the Danish prince. The show opened to mixed reviews, and Kay, as the Player Queen, went unnoticed by critics. Years later, when Kay was asked how she was cast in the challenging play, she joked, "By lying a lot — to the right people."

Kay was anxious to gain experience on the stage, which led to a successful audition with Stuart Walker's stock company. She spent five months touring with the company in Indianapolis, Cincinnati and Dayton, playing bits, walk-ons and occasional second leads in *Candida*, *Polly Preferred* and *Puppy Love*. Kay regarded this experience as her real acting training.

Warners couldn't wait to steal Kay Francis from Paramount, then later on couldn't wait to lose her.

Kay's best opportunity came when she won a supporting role in the underworld drama *Crime*, starring Sylvia Sidney and Chester Morris. Though critics again ignored Kay when the show premiered on February 22, 1927, at Broadway's Eltinge Theater, audiences seemed to enjoy her work, and she stayed with *Crime* for its 133-performance run.

Following her appearance in the short-lived *Amateur Anne*, Kay had an unusual role in *Venus*, by Rachel Crothers. She played a woman who takes a pill that gives her masculine energy, in this case, the urge to become an aviator.

She attracted some attention in *Venus* and in *Elmer the Great*, a Ring Lardner baseball farce starring Walter Huston. *Elmer the Great* closed after just forty performances, but it was a fortuitous show for Kay. Huston had been signed by Paramount to star in *Gentlemen of the Press* (1929), a newspaper drama being filmed at Astoria, Long Island. Paramount had not yet cast anyone as the vamp who seduces a reporter (Huston) and gets him involved with crooked politicians. Kay had the right look, and director Millard Webb and producer Monta Bell offered her a test. Although the script originally called for a "blonde menace," Kay's test proved so successful that she soon became a "brunette menace."

Concerned about Kay's inexperience before the camera and, even more critical, the microphone, Paramount had her work extensively with dialogue director John Meehan. Their close time working together led to more amorous feelings, and they were married—briefly. The marriage was dissolved so quickly that some of Kay's friends didn't even know about it.

Kay's cool beauty and her poise when it came to wearing clothes balanced out any liabilities she had conveying great emotion. Still, Webb was impressed by her understanding of the part and expressed his feelings to Paramount execs. "Her snake-like study of this part is absolutely fascinating. She can become the first great vamp of the audible screen," he said.

Paramount took note and offered her a contract, starting at $500 a week. Her first role after signing was as another vamp in *The Cocoanuts* (1929) with The Four Marx Brothers, also filmed at Astoria. Though she got to ask Harpo Marx, "Did anyone ever tell you that you look like the Prince of Wales?" the funny stuff was all left to the Marxes, and the musical numbers to Mary Eaton. Kay seemed to get lost in the shuffle.

Kay's first film shot in Hollywood was *Dangerous Curves* (1929), in which she finally got to live out her earlier fantasy of being a trapeze artist. Kay vamped it up again as Zara, an aerialist who seduces her partner (Richard Arlen) and then abandons him. Arlen finds happiness with leading lady Clara Bow, as a circus waif.

Bow was most helpful to Kay during the making of *Dangerous Curves* and immediately sensed that Kay would become a major star. It was Bow who suggested that instead of Katherine Francis, she should be billed as Kay Francis, which would fit better on a marquee.

Judging by the roles Kay was getting, it didn't seem that Paramount shared Bow's assessment. She was wasted in minor roles in *Illusion* (1929), with Nancy Carroll, and *The Marriage Playground* (1929), a popular version of Edith Wharton's novel *The Children*, starring Fredric March and Mary Brian.

Then Paramount finally entrusted Kay with a juicy supporting role as a vixen who drives scheming magician William Powell to suicide in *Behind the Makeup* (1930). "Kay Francis does nicely as the adventuress," said Mordaunt Hall of *The New York Times*.

Response to the Powell-Francis teaming was enthusiastic, so Paramount planned a starring vehicle for their new romantic duo. *Street of Chance* (1930), directed by John Cromwell, featured Kay as the wife of a gambler (Powell) whose addiction is beyond any help she can offer. Stilted and melodramatic today, *Street of Chance* was considered strong drama when it was released and provided evidence of the lure of the Powell-Francis matchup. For Kay it was an enormous personal success that showed she was capable of displaying sincerity and compassion.

At the time, musical revues were in vogue on the screen. MGM hit the jackpot with *Hollywood Revue of 1929* (1929), Warners had *The Show of Shows* (1929) and Fox had *Happy Days* (1930). Paramount's entry was a star-studded affair called *Paramount on Parade* (1930), with Maurice Chevalier, Gary Cooper, Ruth Chatterton and Helen Kane topping the line-up of more than 20 headliners. Kay had little to do but look attractive in her two spots—one as a Spanish señorita and another as George Bancroft's stooge in a drawing room skit.

Kay was back to vamping in *A Notorious Affair* (1931), her first film at Warners, with Billie Dove. Kay played a titled nymphomaniac who seduces nobleman Basil Rathbone. *The New York Times* despised the film ("Offers no end of witticisms and alleged epigrammatic dialogue") but liked Kay, whom the reviewer said "puts Miss Dove somewhat in the shade."

For the Defense at her home studio was a well-made legal drama based on the career of criminal attorney William J. Fallon. William Powell was the alcoholic lawyer having a hard time holding onto both his career and the woman (Kay) who loves him.

Paramount then loaned Kay to producer Samuel Goldwyn for her first stab at sophisticated comedy (one can hardly count her work in *The Cocoanuts*) in *Raffles* (1930), opposite Ronald Colman. The film was a delightful story of a suave safecracker (Colman) who is just as adept at charming women as he is stealing. Colman was the epitome of the debonair Englishman, and Kay showed a surprising flair for witty dialogue.

Raffles netted a handsome $200,000, a considerable sum for that time. The film's success is amazing considering that director Harry d'Abaddie D'Arrast was fired by Goldwyn in mid-production for playing the scenes too fast. He was replaced by George Fitzmaurice. *Raffles* was released without a directorial credit.

Back at Paramount Kay was scheduled to make *The Virtuous Sin* (1930), with Walter Huston, but since the film wasn't ready to go into production, Kay was thrown into a king-sized turkey called *Let's Go Native* (1930). The outlandish plot had survivors of a shipwreck landing on a tropical isle run by a king (Skeets Gallagher) who hailed from Brooklyn! The incongruent talents of Jeanette MacDonald, Jack Oakie and Kay didn't blend well under Leo McCarey's misguided direction. It's notably strictly for the chance of seeing Kay sing a duet with Oakie.

By the time *Let's Go Native* was thankfully finished, Kay was set to start work on *The Virtuous Sin*, though it might not have been worth the wait — at least from an artistic standpoint. Kay suffered nobly in this one, as the wife of a scientist (Kenneth MacKenna) who is willing to sleep with a general (Walter Huston) to prevent her husband's court-martial. *Variety* felt there was no excuse for the picture "running 80 minutes when 70 would have been better."

The Virtuous Sin may not have been the high-water mark of Kay's screen career, but it was important as the film that really established Kay's on-screen persona. Throughout the '30s, especially in her Warners vehicles, Kay would forever be the epitome of tragic chic as she made one grand sacrifice after another.

It was *The Virtuous Sin* that also brought together Kay and MacKenna, the son of Leo Mielziner, who had painted Kay's portrait in 1922. The two tried to keep their romance a secret, but rumors of an engagement began making the rounds of gossip columnists. They were wed on January 17, 1931, at Avalon on Catalina Island. Indicative of Kay's lifelong fear of reliving her destitute childhood, prior to the ceremony she had her lawyer draw up a prenuptial agreement.

In less than two years Kay had blossomed from supporting player to one of the top female draws in Hollywood. Her face was often splashed on the covers of fan magazines, though she rarely granted interviews. When one magazine ran an article citing her as the best dressed woman in the movies, Kay responded, "I'm not well-dressed on the screen — I'm usually overdressed."

Kay was certainly handsomely attired in MGM's *Passion Flower* (1930), a typical "woman's" picture that pitted her against Kay Johnson for chauffeur Charles Bickford.

At Paramount Kay was given two strong scripts — the newspaper drama *Scandal Sheet* (1931) and the crime thriller *The Vice Squad* (1931), and acquitted herself nicely under John Cromwell's fast-moving direction in both.

Sandwiched between those two films was the racy *Ladies' Man* (1931), a drama fascinating more for its subject matter and casting than for its execution. William Powell, still playing heels, starred as a gigolo who enjoys letting women supply him with the niceties of life in exchange for sexual favors. He eventually sees the error of his ways when he nearly drives away the one woman (Kay) who loves him, and causes the suicide of another (Carole Lombard).

Though some critics reviled *Ladies' Man*, it holds up better than many of the more-revered films of the early sound era by presenting an unusually black portrait of life among New York high society. Kay is fine in *Ladies' Man*, but it's Powell's polished performance that carries the movie. While Kay won his heart in the movie, Lombard was the victor in real life, and they wed only a few weeks after *Ladies' Man* was released.

Kay went back to suffering in her next two films, *Transgression* (1931) at RKO and *Guilty Hands* (1931), an implausible courtroom drama at MGM. She returned to Paramount for *24 Hours* (1931), in which she and Clive Brook played a bored married couple who contemplate affairs (he with Miriam Hopkins and she with Regis Toomey) during a twenty-four hour period.

Girls About Town (1931), Kay's next, was released with little fanfare, an odd move since this was one of her best films. Inspired by Zoe Akins' play *The Greeks Had a Word for It*, the picture had Kay and Lilyan Tashman playing a pair of charming gold diggers. Kay sets her sights on handsome Joel McCrea, while Tashman digs her claws into the more generous — and married — Eugene Pallette.

Smart, sexy and sophisticated, *Girls About Town* gave Kay a break from the melodramas she had been appearing in of late, and judging by her performance, she welcomed the change. George Cukor, who had a way with actresses, worked well with Kay by bringing out a lighter, more carefree aspect of her personality than had been evidenced up to now. She seemed more relaxed and had a nice rapport with both McCrea and Tashman.

Kay was back to being noble — at least by the fadeout — in *The False Madonna* (1932), in which she played a cardsharp posing as a dead woman to steal a fortune. Having fared well in *Girls About Town*, Paramount put her in another romantic comedy, *Strangers in Love* (1932), with Fredric March, and again she was delightful.

At this time Kay seemed to have everything she could possibly want. Her films were consistent moneymakers and she was a favorite with audiences, especially women. Likewise, her marriage appeared to be a happy one. She and Kenneth had a mutual love of the theater, books and tennis. He taught Kay about sailing and it became another of her passions. Kenneth had also turned from acting to directing, which reduced any chance of career jealousy between them.

Kay had become so popular that she soon found herself in the middle of a battle of the studios for her services. With the exception of MGM, the major Hollywood studios were all having financial problems during the Depression and operating at a considerable loss. Paramount had been especially hard hit. Warner Bros. decided the best way to solve its own money problems was by luring stars from other studios. In a gutsy move, Warners went on a studio raid of Paramount and made offers to William Powell, Ruth Chatterton and Kay, all of whom accepted. In Kay's case, Warners promised her solo starring vehicles and three months vacation.

Paramount was furious and a court battle between the studios ensued. The judge ruled in favor of Warners, but it was decided that Paramount could ask for Kay's services as needed.

Warners trumpeted its acquisition of Kay with the following publicity statement: "Has very tender vocal chords and is unable to scream when called upon to do so; to save her throat has somebody else to scream for her."

Screaming was hardly called for in her first Warners film, *Man Wanted* (1932), a sophisticated affair with Kay as a bored wife and career woman who turns to her male secretary (David Manners) for some after-office-hours relief. Sprightly direction by William Dieterle helped Kay turn in a fresh, charming performance.

"Kay Francis radiates so much charm throughout *Man Wanted* ... that the familiar theme somehow does not matter," hailed Richard Nason of *The New York Times*.

Street of Women (1932) was more typical of Kay's Warners films. Inspired by the success of *Back Street* (1932), *Street of Women* was a standard triangle with Kay as the understanding mistress of a married man (Alan Dinehart) so besotted with love for him that she rejects a life of respectability with Roland Young. Complicating matters is her brother (Allan Vincent), who gets involved with her lover's daughter (Gloria Stuart). *Variety* found it "slow and choppy."

Much better was the sparkling comedy *Jewel Robbery* (1932), in which she was re-teamed with William Powell. Kay played a banker's bored wife who falls for a charming jewel thief (Powell) in William Dieterle's mostly successful attempt to make a film in the Lubitsch vein.

Kay then had her best weepie with *One Way Passage* (1932), a five–Kleenex winner and her last with Powell. What must have sounded rather mawkish on paper (a dying girl and a doomed prisoner meet aboard a ship and fall in love) was given an entertaining spin thanks to a tight screenplay by Wilson Mizner and Joseph Jackson, and crisp direction by Tay Garnett. The movie also benefited from superb performances by Frank McHugh as a pickpocket, Aline MacMahon as a phony countess and Warren Hymer as the policeman in charge of Powell. Garnett tried to weave as much humor into the film as possible, even with his two stars, whose roles were hardly a laughing matter. Robert Lord won an Academy Award for his original story.

One Way Passage was a difficult shoot for everyone involved. The studio hired a rickety iron boat for location shooting and to take the cast offshore. Uncomfortably hot temperatures, bad food, drunken behavior and Garnett's moodiness were prevalent throughout filming. Warners finally got fed up with the delays and ordered Garnett and company to finish the film at the studio.

Despite all of those problems, MacMahon recalled in interviews that Kay was completely professional the whole time, performing with dignity and never complaining at any time.

Kay sparkled once again in *Trouble in Paradise* (1932), an Ernst Lubitsch gem which was the director's favorite of his films. The "Lubitsch Touch" of sexual innuendo and sophistication was apparent all throughout this smart tale of two jewel thieves, Gaston Monescu/LaValle (Herbert Marshall) and Lily Vautier (Miriam Hopkins), who plan to fleece a perfume company executive, Mme. Mariette Colet (Kay Francis), of her fortune by posing as her secretary and maid. Their plan goes awry when Gaston falls for Mariette, and is recognized by a former victim.

Kay was at her most alluring in *Trouble in Paradise*, and also at her most intelligent. She performed the sharp, witty dialogue with a skill that resulted in her finest screen performance.

"A shimmering engaging piece of work ... in virtually every scene, a lively imagination shines forth," beamed *The New York Times*. "Kay Francis is attractive and able as Mariette, whose sins consist of being too credulous and in being very fond of romantic adventures."

Trouble in Paradise made nearly every critic's Ten Best list in 1932, but for Kay it was a disappointment because she was third-billed under Miriam Hopkins and Herbert Marshall. Only one year earlier Kay had been billed over Hopkins in *24 Hours*, but this seemed like Paramount's attempt at payback for her defection to Warners.

Trouble in Paradise also ran over schedule, which meant Kay could not play the lead in *42nd Street* at Warners as planned. The studio couldn't delay the start of *42nd Street*, and Bebe Daniels filled Kay's dancing shoes as the temperamental star of a Broadway musical.

Instead, Kay was loaned to the Goldwyn Studios after Goldwyn's latest discovery, socialite Dorothy Hale, proved unsuitable for the wronged wife in *Cynara* (1932). The movie was a well-carved piece of soap about a prominent London barrister (Ronald Colman) who becomes involved with a much younger woman (Phyllis Barry) while his wife is on vacation. Their affair turns into a scandal when the girl gets pregnant and then commits suicide. Under King Vidor's direction, Kay delivered one of her most sensitive performances and received excellent notices.

From this point on, though, the general quality of Kay's films and performances seemed to decline over the next few years. Instead of stylish romances like *One Way Passage*, or intelligent fare like *Girls About Town* and *Trouble in Paradise* (and, to a lesser extent, *Jewel Robbery*), she began getting scripts that can best be described as potboilers. *The Keyhole* (1933), directed by Michael Curtiz, had Kay as a glamorous wife whose jealous husband has her shadowed during a cruise. The obvious plot machination with the detective (George Brent) falling for his client's wife could be seen at first glance. The plot was used to more harmonious effect as the basis for Doris Day's first film, *Romance on the High Seas* (1948), also directed by Curtiz.

Kay then toiled at MGM in the visually stunning but artistically challenged *Storm at Daybreak* (1933) as a mayor's (Walter Huston) wife having an illicit affair with his best friend (Nils Asther). Back at Warners she was *Mary Stevens M.D.* (1933), sacrificing her infant son (illegitimate, of course) to save other children during a shipboard epidemic. Though Kay was the star, it was more typical of the cookie cutter, economical programmers made by Warners' second-string players, such as Joan Blondell and, at the time, Bette Davis.

I Loved a Woman (1933) was a more expensive and prestigious production, more so for the presence of Edward G. Robinson than for Kay. The period drama featured Kay as an opera star who is loved by a Chicago meat packer accused of sending U.S. troops tainted meat during the Spanish-American War. Kay was allotted surprisingly little screen time after three of her scenes were deleted from the film before it was released. Little wonder that in *The New York Times* review of the film Kay was cited as "part of the supporting cast."

Kay stayed in period garb for *The House on 56th Street* (1933), which had been rejected by Ruth Chatterton. Kay played a Floradora girl who leaves her lover (John Halliday) to marry into New York society. She later is charged with the murder of her lover and sent to prison for twenty years. She returns to her home, which has been turned into a speakeasy.

The House on 56th Street gave Kay her first opportunity to age on-screen, and she looks attractive as a silver-haired, middle-aged matron. Otherwise, the movie was unashamedly sentimental and dramatically overripe, adjectives that could easily be applied to many of her Warners films. Kay disregarded the movie and gave a frank assessment of its appeal: "If it does any better than my other films, it's because I parade thirty-six costumes instead of sixteen."

While Kay may have downplayed the quality of the film or her contribution to it, there's no denying the professionalism and diligence she brought to her work. She typically woke up about 6 a.m. each day, and was on the set in full costume and makeup by 9 a.m. She usually worked until 6:30 p.m., minus a short lunch break. She then went over her scenes for the next day, or viewed the rushes and was home between 7:30 and 8 p.m. Once home, she had a refreshing shower, then joined Kenneth for dinner, served on a tray. By 10:30 p.m. she was in bed, ready to follow the same rigorous routine the next day.

Chatterton had also rejected *Mandalay* (1934), a delirious piece of camp that could give Marlene Dietrich's *Blonde Venus* (1932) a good run as the most audacious pre–Code film. Kay played Tanya, yet another misguided heroine, this time being sold by her deserting lover (Ricardo Cortez) to a white slaver (Warner Oland). Within five years Tanya is transformed into a gaudily attired (especially for Kay) madam named Spot White, or as one patron says, "It ought to be Spot Cash." The remainder of the film deals with her attempts to go straight with a new identity, Marjorie Lang. As expected, her former lover returns, which leads to the movie's most famous scene, in which Kay poisons Cortez and then neatly disposes of his body through a ship's porthole. No one will ever accuse *Mandalay* of being artistic, but boring it isn't.

The New York Times found Kay "highly decorative."

Mandalay was released in February 1934, the same month that Kay was granted a divorce from Kenneth. Kay testified that her husband "nagged and harassed her ... ridiculed her selection of home, manner of dressing and even her acting did not suit him. [He] assumed an air of superiority and made slighting remarks in the presence of friends." Kay neglected to reveal her own problems, which included being argumentative after having a few too many drinks.

Wonder Bar (1934), Kay's next film, fueled her anger with Warner Bros. Kay was unhappy about playing yet another dissatisfied wife, this time married to a ruthless lawyer (Douglas Dumbrille). Matters got worse as Kay's part was continually trimmed to provide more scenes for Dolores Del Rio, who had just joined Warners after leaving RKO. As a result, the film is dominated by Al Jolson and the fiery Del Rio, with Kay reduced to a supporting role. The popularity of Jolson and the imaginatively staged musical numbers by Busby Berkeley (save the politically incorrect "Goin' to Heaven on a Mule") made *Wonder Bar* a wonder at the box office.

Doctor Monica (1934) was more women's magazine fare with Kay as the titled doc who finds herself in the unlikely position of delivering her friend's (Jean Muir) illegitimate child sired by the medic's husband (Warren William). Director William Keighley packed plenty of drama into this highly improbable but oddly compelling film's fifty-three minutes. "It moves apace and the acting is excellent," said Mordaunt Hall of *The New York Times*.

Warners then put her in a spy thriller, *British Agent* (1934), which was tightly knit and well-acted, though she had to take a back set to Leslie Howard.

Sooner or later it seemed like every Warner Bros. leading lady got teamed with George Brent. Actresses generally liked working with Brent—for two important reasons: He lent a sturdy, masculine presence to their films, and his performances were generally so bland there was little chance that he would steal the spotlight from them. Unfortunately, the films Kay made with Brent—*Living on Velvet* (1935), *Stranded* (1935) and *The Goose and the Gander* (1935)—all fared poorly, which gave Warners pause to think about the team's potency. Not everyone was disinterested in them. One reviewer of *The Goose and the Gander* noted, "the Francis-Brent team seems to be a happy combination. Mr. Brent's engaging comedy is an excellent antidote for Miss Francis' penchant for heavy tragedy, and he keeps her from taking her art too seriously."

After completing *Stranded* and *The Goose and the Gander*, Kay took a much-needed ocean voyage to France, leaving from New York on the Aquitania. Reporters flooded Kay's stateroom on the day of her departure. Basically, they got to take some nice photos of her modeling her latest outfit—something called a tailleur, which was a basic black dress with a big lace vest on it and equally large lacy cuffs. To round out the ensemble, she wore a hat that looked like the top of a black cat's head. When one reporter dared to ask her some personal questions, a flustered Kay clammed up, and then her cabin door was closed to the press.

When Kay returned she made *I Found Stella Parish*, a top-notch tale of mother love. Kay starred as Stella, a famous actress on the London stage who has refused dozens of offers to appear in New York because of her dark past, which she wants to keep hidden from her young daughter (Sybil Jason). An inquisitive reporter (Ian Hunter) affects a disguise to worm his way into Stella's confidence—and her heart—in hopes of getting an exclusive story.

Though Kay seemed awkward in her early scenes, appearing onstage as England's answer to Eleanora Duse, overall she gave a moving performance. It was a pleasure to see Kay in some lighter moments with Jason. The former child star developed an immediate bond with Kay, whom she said was the "spitting image" of her mother. "She treated the crew and the extras with no less attention than she would have given to any executive, and they adored her for it," she said.

Though *The New York Times* enjoyed the performances of Hunter and Jason, Kay didn't fare as well. "Francis' unfortunate lisp continues to plague this corner; it makes even more unbelievable the notion that London could regard Stella Parish as the Duse of the day." Audiences disagreed and the film was Kay's last hit for Warners.

It was around this time that Warners' option on Kay was about to expire. Dissatisfied with the sometimes tasteless and subordinate roles she had been getting, she was reluctant to renew her contract. "Even if it was me the public so kindly went to see, there was a limit to the number of times a certain type of story or motif could be repeated," she said.

Based on the strength of *I Found Stella Parish*, Jack Warner still considered Kay a bankable star and persuaded her to extend her contract with the promise of the lead in *Tovarich* (1937). Hopeful of a good part, Kay signed. She was also happy about getting to play her first biographical role in *The White Angel* (1936), which she saw as a welcome departure from the "True Confessions" type of movies she had been doing.

Unfortunately, this story of English nurse Florence Nightingale demonstrated Kay's limitations as an actress. Rather than being an enlightened look at Nightingale's life, it was a stilted, historically inaccurate production, that looked great, especially for its scenes at the Crimea Hospital, but failed to entertain. Try as Kay might, she was unable to come across as anything more than the great movie star in awe of the woman she was portraying. As the *Journal of the American Medical Association* put it, her performance was "antiseptic."

With comments like that, *The White Angel* was a financial disaster and marked the beginning of Kay's decline. Her next film, *Give Me Your Heart* (1936), playing her umpteenth self-sacrificing mother, was a less expensive film to mount, but still was responsible for red ink on Warners' ledgers. Throughout filming of *Give Me Your Heart*, Kay had a stormy relationship with director Archie Mayo, whom she felt did not have a good grip on the material. Much of her frustration, however, stemmed from her insecurity regarding her performance in *The White Angel*.

At the end of 1936 Kay was the highest paid employee on the Warners roster, with a salary of $227,500. A distant second was Joe E. Brown, who made $201,562. The difference, though, was that the budgets on Brown's movies were generally about one-quarter of what Kay's films cost, plus they had been consistent moneymakers.

Kay's position at the studio became even more precarious in 1937 with the release and subsequent failure of her next three movies—*Stolen Holiday*, *Confession* and *Another Dawn*. Of that trio, *Confession*, a remake of Pola Negri's German film *Mazurka*, was the most interesting. Kay played a washed-up cabaret singer who shoots her former lover (Basil Rathbone) when he attempts to seduce the mature daughter (Jane Bryan) she gave up as an infant. Director Joe May's creative use of flashbacks in structuring the story made *Confession* at least interesting for its novel film technique, even if the trite script was typical Francis fodder.

Kay did get one last good opportunity at Warners with *First Lady* (1937), based on the George S. Kaufman-Katherine Drayton play that had been a hit for Jane Cowl. Kay played the wife of the Secretary of State (Preston Foster), whom she hopes will be a candidate for the presidency. Kay's rival on-screen was Verree Teasdale as the wife of a Supreme Court Justice with her eye on the White House. By this point, Kay had become dispirited over her career and it showed in her performance, which lacked the cattiness her scenes with Teasdale demanded. Critics cited Kay as the film's weak link, and once again she had another flop.

Missing from Kay's 1937 roster was *Tovarich*, which Warners gave to Claudette Colbert, borrowed from Paramount. Kay was furious and brought suit against Warners to cancel her contract because the studio reneged on its promise about *Tovarich*. After considerable press from both Kay and Warners, it was announced that an "amicable" settlement had been reached.

For the second year in a row, Kay was the

highest paid employee on the Warners roster, though her salary had dropped to $209,100. Jack Warner, who only five years earlier promised Kay full star treatment when she left Paramount, felt Kay was no longer worth her hefty paycheck.

"Kay was making too much money, and her films were not bringing enough money back into the studio," said actor Jimmy Lydon, a friend of Kay's during her Hollywood years. "One thing should be cleared up. All actors in those days were always saying that Jack Warner hated actors. That's extremely untrue. He was a businessman and did what he felt was best to keep the studio running smoothly."

In Kay's case, she became a second-class citizen on the lot. On the premise that her plush dressing room suite was going to be redecorated, her belongings were moved from there to a single room in the Featured Players Dressing Room. Unfortunately, they weren't brought back. While it was true that her dressing room was being redecorated, no one told her that it was for a new occupant — John Garfield, who was on the brink of stardom in *Four Daughters* (1938).

Kay wasn't even being handed any new scripts. Instead, she was assigned to do screen tests of young hopefuls the studio was considering as contract players. She was usually given a 9 a.m. studio call, though she wasn't generally used until mid-afternoon. She'd be there sitting on the sidelines, knitting and getting in a nip of gin from a silver flask. Once Kay was needed, she was used merely to feed lines to the actor being tested. The whole time the camera would be focused on the unknown actor, shooting over Kay's shoulder. Though Kay felt humiliated by the demeaning way in which she was being treated, she refused to go on suspension and give up her $4,000 a week paycheck as Warner hoped.

Perhaps Kay's most denigrating experience during her downfall was when she brought two friends to the studio commissary for lunch and was denied two passes. No explanation was given. A rueful Kay just told the commissary worker, "I understand. Thank you anyway."

Most of the Warner Bros. employees were sympathetic toward Kay. Two of her greatest champions were Bette Davis and James Cagney, who were so appalled about the situation that they arranged to meet with Harry Warner, president of Warner Bros., to get him to do something. Though Harry appeared sympathetic, he said his brother was in charge of production and he didn't want to usurp Jack's authority. Afterwards, there was an unconfirmed rumor around the studio that the plot to destroy Kay was devised by Harry, and that Jack Warner was merely carrying out orders.

Kay wound up doing pictures for producer Bryan Foy's B unit — undoubtedly the only B performer in Hollywood earning a six-figure income. *Women Are Like That* (1938), with Pat O'Brien, was so bad that *Photoplay* remarked, "Poor Kay Francis certainly got a dirty deal in this. Unbelievably gauche and tiresome…. Maybe we'd better pretend we didn't know about it."

Her next two were no better received. The slushy *My Bill* (1938) had Kay as a widow with four of the most obnoxious children ever put on the screen, and *Secrets of an Actress* (1938) was a lame soap opera with stage star Kay falling for an architect (George Brent).

Kay's offscreen romantic exploits seemed just as bumpy as her professional life. She had just ended a long affair with up-and-coming producer Delmer Daves, whom it was rumored she would marry. Then in the summer of 1937 she met Baron Raven Erik Barnekow, a force in the aviation business, while staying at the Beverly Hills home of Countess di Frasso. In March of 1938 Kay announced that they would be married in the spring and she would retire from films.

It's easy to see why Kay would have been attracted to Barnekow. He was handsome, sophisticated, charming and wealthy. At the same time, she seemed to overlook his less attractive qualities, such as his jealous nature, a penchant for alcohol and an Old World European attitude toward women. He objected to Kay wearing makeup, as well as her questions about any last-minute trips he occasionally went on. Those secret trips led some of Kay's friends to suspect that he might be a German agent.

Kay's nerves weren't helped by the script for her next film, a dreary soap opera called *Comet Over Broadway* (1938), which had already caused a rift between Bette Davis and Warners. The Busby Berkeley–directed drama had Kay as an actress who implicates her husband (Ian Hunter) in a murder and then tries to get him paroled.

Berkeley had been warned by other directors on the lot that Kay could be difficult and tactless with co-workers, but he saw no evidence of it on this picture. "I do know she was unwilling to participate in the publicity game. That didn't interest her at all. And it seemed to me she lacked that driving ambition an actress needs in order to get the best parts in the best films," recalled Berkeley to author Tony Thomas. "I found her to be cooperative and humorous, perhaps because she knew this was one of her last films for Warners. She had been under contract since 1932 at the rate of four pictures a year, and I think she was rather glad the grind was coming to an end."

No one could blame her, based on the terrible films she was given in 1938. She had hoped that Jack Warner might consider her for Empress Carlotta in the studio's prestigious *Juarez* (1939), starring Paul Muni as the Mexican leader. Not surprisingly, Bette Davis, the new queen of the Warners lot, got the part.

In 1939, Davis also had outstanding roles in *Dark Victory*, *The Private Lives of Elizabeth and Essex* and *The Old Maid*. Kay, by contrast, was tossed into *King of the Underworld* (1939), a transgendered remake of *Doctor Socrates* (1935), in which she was the medic previously played by Paul Muni. As if further evidence of Kay's diminished stature was needed, she was billed below the title in letters about half the size of her co-star, Humphrey Bogart.

Vincent Sherman, who co-wrote the screenplay with George Bricker, saw no temperament from Kay, despite those circumstances. "I only got to know her briefly but liked her," he said. "She was a tall statuesque lady with a certain talent and was at one time one of the Warner Brothers big draws, but the films they gave her did not capitalize on her qualities and she fell into disfavor. The diffference between success and failure in Hollywood does not always depend on talent alone."

Kay finished her contract in a B called *Women in the Wind* (1939), an aviation drama directed by John Farrow, who previously worked with her on *My Bill*. This one, in which Kay was an aviatrix in a "power puff derby" race, was as dreary as their previous film together.

Though Kay's last two years at Warner Bros. had been hellish, she at least received one nice gesture on her last day: As she drove off the lot, the cop at the gate saluted her.

Most people figured Kay was washed up in Hollywood, but her friend Carole Lombard came to the rescue when she recommended Kay for the role of Cary Grant's bitchy wife in *In Name Only* (1939) at RKO. The combination of career troubles and her unstable relationship with Barnekow caused Kay to gain twenty pounds. Aghast at how she looked in her wardrobe tests, Kay succeeded in losing the excess weight.

In Name Only was directed by John Cromwell, who had helmed several of Kay's Paramount films, which made her feel at ease on the set. Lombard played an artist in love with a married man (Grant) whose wife refuses to give him a divorce. Though it was a supporting role, Kay was given above-the-title billing with Lombard and Grant, and all three gave outstanding performances. The film showed that when given a literate script and a role she cared about, Kay was capable of a fine performance. Bosley Crowther, never Kay's greatest fan, on this occasion cheered that she was "the model cat, suave, superior and relentless."

In Name Only was a tremendous hit, and for Kay its success and her favorable reviews were sweet revenge after her treatment at Warners. The three stars of *In Name Only* repeated their roles for *Lux Radio Theater* in December 1939.

Prior to the release of *In Name Only*, Kay broke her engagement to Barnekow. Their last few months together had been particularly ugly after the Baron instituted a slander suit against the Countess di Frasso, whom he claimed called him a Nazi spy. Di Frasso denied the charges, and the District Attorney dismissed the case. A vigilant Barnekow repeated the charges to the press, which only succeeded in putting an end to Kay's friendship with the countess.

Despite these recent troubles, Kay still wanted to marry Barnekow. Fearing he would be interned as an enemy alien, Kay proposed that they head off to Hawaii, where they could easily retire on her savings. The Baron refused and, against Kay's wishes, returned to Germany for the outset of World War II in September 1939.

Kay tried to pick up the pieces by concentrating on her career, which had been rejuvenated with the success of *In Name Only*. At

Universal, she made *It's a Date* (1940), a lighthearted musical starring the studio's top draw, Deanna Durbin. Kay played Durbin's glamorous mother, who falls for dashing Walter Pidgeon. Though *It's a Date* was clearly a star vehicle for Durbin, Kay was radiant. It proved a good follow-up to *In Name Only*, and made a ton of money.

By contrast, her other Universal effort, *When the Daltons Rode* (1940), was a step back. The whitewashed account of the Dalton gang featured Kay as Randolph Scott's sweetheart. But she seemed better suited to Central Park West than the Wild West.

Kay then played one of her favorite roles, the grown-up Jo March in *Little Men* (1940), Louisa May Alcott's sequel to *Little Women*. In the film, Jo, now married, runs a school with her husband (Carl Esmond). Her biggest problems are dealing with the school's finances and Danny (Jimmy Lydon), a troublesome youth put in her charge.

Kay enjoyed working with director Norman Z. McLeod, whom cast and crew referred to as "The Stick Man" because he would map out every scene for his actors using drawings of stick figures. McLeod had a hard time directing *Little Men* because of a large boil on his buttocks, and he had to sit on a rubber-inflated cushion. Despite his discomfort, he was pleasant to his actors.

Co-star Jack Oakie was also responsible for Kay's fondness for *Little Men*. According to Lydon, Oakie kept everyone amused with his antics on the set, planning out his laugh-getters the night before.

As for Kay, Lydon had only pleasant memories of working with her. Though he was only sixteen when they made the movie, Kay wasn't the least bit condescending. "Kay was a wonderful gal," he said. "She had been a big, big star at Warners, and I already had a long career from the stage. We worked together as two professionals. I still have a picture she gave me that's signed, 'To Danny, With Love from Kay,' and then another one that says 'To Jimmy, Love Kay.' She did a lot of heavies before *Little Men*. This was a tender part, which she liked."

Although everyone's heart was in the right place, *Little Men* suffered from low-budget production values and a makeshift script by Mark Kelly and Arthur Caesar. Most of the publicity went to Elsie the Cow, loaned for the film by the Borden company.

Far worse was *Play Girl* (1941), a supposed comedy in which gold digging Kay teaches a neophyte (Mildred Coles) the art of snagging a rich beau. The weak screenplay by Larry Cady and the arch performances of Kay and Coles made for a rather dull *Play Girl*.

Kay returned to Universal for *The Man Who Lost Himself* (1941), a comedy with Brian Aherne that bypassed New York. She fared better with the wonderful *Charley's Aunt* (1941) at Fox, co-starring with Jack Benny in one of his funniest films. Though Kay's role was subordinate to Benny's, she seemed to enjoy herself and gave one of her most spirited performances.

She followed with another good comedy role in *The Feminine Touch* (1941) at MGM, with Rosalind Russell, Don Ameche and Van Heflin. Her last few films demonstrated that she could be quite the farceur, and perhaps she had been wrongly cast in so many weepie roles.

Kay amazingly agreed to return to Warners when her friend Walter Huston insisted on her as his co-star in *Always in My Heart* (1942), a semi-musical designed to showcase Warners' answer to Deanna Durbin, the colorless Gloria Warren. The maudlin story had Kay about to remarry when her former husband (Huston), newly released from prison, shows up. Warren's endless singing and the weak script, which climaxed with its junior soprano at sea in the middle of a tempest, made for one soggy flop.

Kay played a mother again in *Between Us Girls* (1942), a Universal comedy that was meant to serve as a springboard for newcomer Diana Barrymore. Kay was at her most elegant as Barrymore's mother in this tale of mother-daughter romances. In Kay's case, her paramour was John Boles, while Barrymore was wooed by Robert Cummings. Critics decided that Barrymore lacked the acting gene of her more famous relatives, and the film had a poor box office take.

Lonely, and with no interesting film offers coming her way, Kay decided she could be of service in the war effort. She signed up for a USO tour, along with Martha Raye, Carole Landis and Mitzi Mayfair. The four women traveled to Bermuda, Northern Ireland, England and North Africa to entertain thousands of soldiers hungry for entertainment and news from home.

The troupe, which became known as Four

Jills in a Jeep, sang, jitterbugged and engaged in snappy bantering with the soldiers. Everywhere they went, all four women delighted their audiences. They generally only got about five hours sleep each night, and dined on the same food as the GIs. Kay considered the tour one of the real high points of her life.

The tour was chronicled in the book *Four Jills in a Jeep*, which became a bestseller in 1943, and was picked up by 20th Century–Fox. The film featured Kay, Raye, Landis and Mayfair recreating their exploits, and appearances by top Fox stars, such as Alice Faye and Betty Grable. Interspersed with the musical numbers was a love story involving Mayfair and Dick Haymes.

Kay's enjoyment of *Four Jills and a Jeep* prompted her to focus on jump-starting her film career once more. She signed a deal to produce three films for Poverty Row graveyard Monogram, whose work ethic was to get the film in the can quickly and cheaply. Kay took full control on *Divorce* (1945), *Allotment Wives* (1945) and *Wife Wanted* (1946). She not only convinced distinguished actors such as Bruce Cabot, Paul Kelly and Otto Kruger to work for less than usual, but she also worked with the screenwriters on fine-tuning the scripts.

The films were generally shot in about ten days, and, unfortunately, the haste and tight-fistedness in which they were made was evident. They had relatively little distribution, and ended up being a rather ignoble curtain call to Kay's film career.

Prior to shooting *Wife Wanted*, Kay agreed to appear in the play *Windy Hill*, a summer stock tryout directed by Ruth Chatterton and starring Patsy Ruth Miller, Roger Pryor and newcomer Eileen Heckart. The show, which went through excessive rewrites, was a difficult experience for Kay, who battled with the playwright, John Van Druten. Still, the strength of its stars' names helped *Windy Hill* do good business.

Midway in production of *Wife Wanted*, producer Leland Hayward asked Kay if she could replace Ruth Hussey in *State of the Union* on Broadway. An ecstatic Kay jumped at the offer.

In New York Kay was abetted by Howard "Hap" Graham, the stage manager who helped get her ready for rehearsals with director Howard Lindsay. As such, she was effective in the role. She also entered into a romance with Graham, which began well but was soon marked by arguments.

Their on-again, off-again affair continued when both went on tour with *State of the Union*. Kay hated touring, which brought back unpleasant memories of traveling with her mother, but the show played to packed houses. Kay was tired and depressed most of the time, reaching her worst state in Columbus, Ohio, when she took an overdose of sleeping pills. Graham phoned a doctor who told him to feed her plenty of coffee and make sure she got fresh air until he arrived.

Graham took Kay to the window and leaned her head outside. When he tried to force coffee into her, he accidentally scalded her neck, which caused her to faint against the burning radiator, which had been turned on the night before to heat her dinner. Graham soon noticed that her legs had been burned. Kay was immediately rushed to the hospital, where her stomach was pumped and she was treated for second-degree burns. Graham, meanwhile, was arrested on suspicion of intent to kill. When Kay regained consciousness five hours later and heard of the arrest, she immediately phoned the jail and had Graham released.

Arrangements were made for Kay to be transferred to New York's Cornell Medical Center where she underwent extensive and often painful treatments for her burns. She wasn't released from the hospital until five months later, in June of 1948.

That summer she joined a touring company of *The Last of Mrs. Cheyney*, the first of several companies she appeared with over the next few years. She later appeared in stock productions of *Let Us Be Gay*; *Goodbye, My Fancy*; *The Web and the Rock*; *Mirror, Mirror*; *Theater*; and *Portrait in Black*.

During the tour of *Theater*, Kay began a relationship with the show's director, Dennis Allen, which lasted nearly ten years. In addition to being her last great romance, Allen also was a strong source of support for Kay as she experienced many medical setbacks, including surgical removal of both a lung and a kidney; fracturing a bone in her ankle; and injuring her back after a fall in the bathtub. The last incident forced her to wear a brace.

By 1961, as Kay became more infirm, her quarrels with Allen became more frequent and intense, and they finally severed their relationship. Over the next few years Kay's health worsened. She developed breast cancer and underwent a mastectomy. She stayed in bed most of the time, spending her days reading, watching television, drinking and taking medication.

Kay died on August 26, 1968, leaving the bulk of her $2 million estate to Seeing Eye Inc., a Morristown, New Jersey, charity that trains seeing eye dogs. The bequest came as a surprise to Seeing Eye, which had no idea Kay was aware of the organization. A friend later revealed that Kay felt loss of sight was the worst ill that could happen to anyone.

Kay's story was more tragic than that of any of the cardboard heroines she played. She might have helped her cause during her decline by being cooperative with the press and getting them to rally behind her. Instead, Kay chose to go it alone, and sadly that was how she ended up.

FILMOGRAPHY

Gentlemen of the Press (Paramount, 1929) Directed by Millard Webb. *Cast:* Walter Huston, Charles Ruggles, Betty Lawford, Katherine (Kay) Francis. (Released in silent and talkie versions.)

The Cocoanuts (Paramount, 1929) Directed by Joseph Santley and Robert Florey. *Cast:* The Four Marx Bros., Mary Eaton, Oscar Shaw, Katherine (Kay) Francis, Margaret Dumont.

Dangerous Curves (Paramount, 1929) Directed by Lothar Mendes. *Cast:* Clara Bow, Richard Arlen, David Newell, Kay Francis, Anders Randolph. (Released in silent and talkie versions.)

Illusion (Paramount, 1929) Directed by Lothar Mendes. *Cast:* Charles "Buddy" Rogers, Nancy Carroll, Kay Francis, June Collyer, Regis Toomey. (Released in silent and talkie versions.)

The Marriage Playground (Paramount, 1929) Directed by Lothar Mendes. *Cast:* Mary Brian, Fredric March, Lilyan Tashman, Kay Francis, Huntley Gordon, William Austin, Seena Owen.

Behind the Makeup (Paramount, 1930) Directed by Robert Milton. *Cast:* Hal Skelly, William Powell, Kay Francis, Fay Wray, E.H. Calvert, Paul Lukas, Agostino Borgato.

Street of Chance (Paramount, 1930) Directed by John Cromwell. *Cast:* William Powell, Kay Francis, Jean Arthur, Regis Toomey, Stanley Fields, Brook Benedict, Betty Francisco.

Paramount, on Parade (Paramount, 1930) Eleven directors, supervised by Elsie Janis. *Cast:* Maurice Chevalier, Kay Francis, Helen Kane, Ruth Chatterton, Clive Brook, George Bancroft, Nino Martini, William Powell, Clara Bow, Richard Arlen, Charles "Buddy" Rogers, Gary Cooper, Jean Arthur, Fay Wray, Leon Errol, Jack Oakie, Mitzi Green, Nancy Carroll, Warner Oland.

A Notorious Affair (Warner Bros., 1930) Directed by Lloyd Bacon. *Cast:* Billie Dove, Basil Rathbone, Kay Francis, Montagu Love, Kenneth Thomson.

For the Defense (Paramount, 1930) Directed by John Cromwell. *Cast:* William Powell, Kay Francis, Scott Kolk, William B. Davidson, John Elliott, Thomas Jackson, James Finlayson.

Raffles (Goldwyn-United Artists, 1930) Directed by Harry d'Abbadie D'Arrast. *Cast:* Ronald Colman, Kay Francis, Bramwelll Fletcher, Frances Dade, David Torrance, Alison Skipworth.

Let's Go Native (Paramount, 1930) Directed by Leo McCarey. *Cast:* Jeanette MacDonald, Jack Oakie, Kay Francis, Skeets Gallagher, James Hall, William Austin, David Newell.

The Virtuous Sin (Paramount, 1930) Directed by George Cukor and Louis Gasnier. *Cast:* Walter Huston, Kay Francis, Kenneth MacKenna, Paul Cavanaugh, Jobyna Howland.

Passion Flower (MGM, 1930) Directed by William C. de Mille. *Cast:* Kay Francis, Charles Bickford, Zasu Pitts, Kay Johnson, Winter Hall, Lewis Stone, Dickie Moore.

Scandal Sheet (Paramount, 1931) Directed by John Cromwell. *Cast:* George Bancroft, Kay Francis, Clive Brook, Lucien Littlefield, Gilbert Emery, Regis Toomey.

Ladies Man (Paramount, 1931) Directed by Lothar Mendes. *Cast:* William Powell, Kay Francis, Carole Lombard, Gilbert Emery, Olive Tell, Martin Burton, John Holland.

The Vice Squad (Paramount, 1931) Directed by John Cromwell. *Cast:* Kay Francis, Paul Lukas,

Helen Johnson, William B. Davidson, Rockliffe Fellows, Esther Howard, Monte Carter.

Transgression (RKO Radio, 1931) Directed by Herbert Brenon. *Cast:* Kay Francis, Paul Cavanaugh, Ricardo Cortez, Nance O'Neil, John St. Polis, Adrienne d'Ambricourt.

Guilty Hands (MGM, 1931) Directed by W.S. Van Dyke. *Cast:* Lionel Barrymore, Kay Francis, Madge Evans, William Bakewell, C. Aubrey Smith, Polly Moran, Alan Mowbray.

24 Hours (Paramount, 1931) Directed by Marion Gering. *Cast:* Clive Brook, Kay Francis, Miriam Hopkins, Regis Toomey, George Barbier, Adrienne Ames, Charlotte Granville.

Girls About Town (Paramount, 1931) Directed by George Cukor. *Cast:* Kay Francis, Joel McCrea, Lilyan Tashman, Eugene Pallette, Alan Dinehart, Lucille Webster Gleason.

The False Madonna (Paramount, 1932) Directed by Stuart Walker. *Cast:* Kay Francis, William "Stage" Boyd, Conway Tearle, John Breeden, Marjorie Gateson.

Strangers in Love (Paramount, 1932) Directed by Lothar Mendes. *Cast:* Fredric March, Kay Francis, Stuart Erwin, Juliette Compton, George Barbier, Sidney Toler, Lucien Littlefield.

Man Wanted (Warner Bros., 1932) Directed by William Dieterle. *Cast:* Kay Francis, David Manners, Andy Devine, Una Merkel, Kenneth Thomson, Claire Dodd, Charlotte Merriam.

Street of Women (Warner Bros., 1932) Directed by Archie Mayo. *Cast:* Kay Francis, Alan Dinehart, Marjorie Gateson, Roland Young, Gloria Stuart, Allen Vincent, Louise Beavers.

Jewel Robbery (Warner Bros., 1932) Directed by William Dieterle. *Cast:* William Powell, Kay Francis, Hardie Albright, Andre Luguet, Henry Kolker, Lee Kohlmar, Spencer Charters.

One Way Passage (Warner Bros., 1932) Directed by Tay Garnett. *Cast:* William Powell, Kay Francis, Aline MacMahon, Frank McHugh, Warren Hymer, Frederick Burton, Douglas Gerrard.

Trouble in Paradise (Paramount, 1932) Directed by Ernst Lubitsch. *Cast:* Miriam Hopkins, Herbert Marshall, Kay Francis, Charles Ruggles, Edward Everett Horton, C. Aubrey Smith.

Cynara (Goldwyn-United Artists, 1932) Directed by King Vidor. *Cast:* Ronald Colman, Kay Francis, Phyllis Barry, Henry Stephenson, Viva Tattersall, Florine McKinney, Clarissa Selwyn.

The Keyhole (Warner Bros., 1933) Directed by Michael Curtiz. *Cast:* Kay Francis, George Brent, Glenda Farrell, Allen Jenkins, Monroe Owsley, Helen Ware, Henry Kolker.

Storm at Daybreak (MGM, 1933) Directed by Richard Boleslawski. *Cast:* Kay Francis, Nils Asther, Walter Huston, Phillips Holmes, Eugene Pallette, C. Henry Gordon, Louise Closser Hale.

Mary Stevens, M.D. (Warner Bros., 1933) Directed by Lloyd Bacon. *Cast:* Kay Francis, Lyle Talbot, Glenda Farrell, Thelma Todd, Una O'Connor, Charles Wilson, Hobart Cavanaugh.

I Loved a Woman (First National, 1933) Directed by Alfred E. Green. *Cast:* Edward G. Robinson, Kay Francis, Genevieve Tobin, J. Farrell MacDonald, Henry Kolker, Robert Barrat.

The House on 56th Street (Warner Bros., 1933) Directed by Robert Florey. *Cast:* Kay Francis, Ricardo Cortez, Gene Raymond, John Halliday, Margaret Lindsay, Frank McHugh, Sheila Terry.

Mandalay (First National, 1934) Directed by Michael Curtiz. *Cast:* Kay Francis, Ricardo Cortez, Warner Oland, Lyle Talbot, Ruth Donnelly, Reginald Owen, Hobart Cavanaugh.

Wonder Bar (First National, 1934) Directed by Lloyd Bacon. *Cast:* Al Jolson, Dolores Del Rio, Kay Francis, Ricardo Cortez, Dick Powell, Hal LeRoy, Guy Kibbee, Ruth Donnelly.

Dr. Monica (Warner Bros., 1934) Directed by William Keighley. *Cast:* Kay Francis, Warren William, Jean Muir, Verree Teasdale, Philip Reed, Emma Dunn, Herbert Bunston.

British Agent (First National, 1934) Directed by Michael Curtiz. *Cast:* Leslie Howard, Kay Francis, William Gargan, Philip Reed, Irving Pichel, Walter Byron, Ivan Simpson.

Living on Velvet (Warner Bros., 1935) Directed by Frank Borzage. *Cast:* Kay Francis, George Brent, Warren William, Helen Lowell, Henry O'Neill, Samuel S. Hinds, Russell Hicks.

Stranded (Warner Bros., 1935) Directed by Frank Borzage. *Cast:* Kay Francis, George Brent, Patricia Ellis, Donald Woods, Robert Barrat, Barton MacLane, Joseph Crehan, William Harrigan.

The Goose and the Gander (Warner Bros., 1935) Directed Alfred E. Green. *Cast:* Kay Francis, George Brent, Genevieve Tobin, John Eldredge, Claire Dodd, Ralph Forbes.

I Found Stella Parrish (First National, 1935) Directed by Mervyn LeRoy. *Cast:* Kay Francis, Ian Hunter, Paul Lukas, Sybil Jason, Jessie Ralph, Barton MacLane, Harry Beresford.

The White Angel (First National, 1936) Directed by William Dieterle. *Cast:* Kay Francis, Ian Hunter, Donald Woods, Nigel Bruce, Donald Crisp, Henry O'Neill, Billy Mauch.

Give Me Your Heart (Warner Bros., 1936) Directed by Archie L. Mayo. *Cast:* Kay Francis, George Brent, Roland Young, Patric Knowles, Henry Stephenson, Frieda Inescourt, Helen Flint.

Stolen Holiday (Warner Bros., 1937) Directed by Michael Curtiz. *Cast:* Kay Francis, Claude Rains, Ian Hunter, Alison Skipworth, Alexander D'Arcy, Betty Lawford, Walter Kingsford.

Another Dawn (Warner Bros., 1937) Directed by William Dieterle. *Cast:* Errol Flynn, Kay Francis, Ian Hunter, Frieda Inescourt, Herbert Mundin, G.P. Huntley, Jr., Billy Bevan.

Confession (First National, 1937) Directed by Joe May. *Cast:* Kay Francis, Ian Hunter, Basil Rathbone, Jane Bryan, Donald Crisp, Dorothy Peterson, Laura Hope Crews, Robert Barrat.

First Lady (Warner Bros., 1937) Directed by Stanley Logan. *Cast:* Kay Francis, Preston Foster, Anita Louise, Walter Connolly, Verree Teasdale, Victor Jory, Marjorie Rambeau.

Women Are Like That (Warner Bros., 1938) Directed by Stanley Logan. *Cast:* Kay Francis, Pat O'Brien, Ralph Forbes, Melville Cooper, Thurston Hall, Grant Mitchell, Gordon Oliver.

My Bill (Warner Bros., 1938) Directed by John Farrow. *Cast:* Kay Francis, Dickie Moore, Bonita Granville, John Litel, Anita Louise, Bobby Jordan, Maurice Murphy, Elisabeth Risdon.

Secrets of an Actress (Warner Bros., 1938) Directed by William Keighley. *Cast:* Kay Francis, George Brent, Ian Hunter, Gloria Dickson, Isabel Jeans, Penny Singleton, Dennie Moore.

Comet Over Broadway (Warner Bros., 1938) Directed by Busby Berkeley. *Cast:* Kay Francis, Ian Hunter, John Litel, Donald Crisp, Minna Gombell, Sybil Jason, Melville Cooper, Ian Keith.

King of the Underworld (Warner Bros., 1939) Directed by Lewis Seiler. *Cast:* Kay Francis, Humphrey Bogart, James Stephenson, John Eldredge, Jessie Busley, Arthur Aylesworth.

Women in the Wind (Warner Bros., 1939) Directed by John Farrow. *Cast:* Kay Francis, William Gargan, Victor Jory, Maxie Rosenbloom, Eddie Foy, Jr., Sheila Bromley, Eve Arden.

In Name Only (RKO-Radio, 1939) Directed by John Cromwell. *Cast:* Cary Grant, Carole Lombard, Kay Francis, Charles Coburn, Helen Vinson, Grady Sutton, Katherine Alexander.

It's a Date (Universal, 1940) Directed by William A. Seiter. *Cast:* Deanna Durbin, Kay Francis, Walter Pidgeon, Eugene Pallette, Lewis Howard, Samuel S. Hinds, Cecilia Loftus, Fritz Feld.

When the Daltons Rode (Universal, 1940) Directed by George Marshall. *Cast:* Randolph Scott, Kay Francis, Andy Devine, Frank Albertson, Mary Gordon, Harry Stephens.

Little Men (RKO-Radio, 1940) Directed by Norman Z. McLeod. *Cast:* Kay Francis, Jack Oakie, George Bancroft, Jimmy Lydon, Ann Gillis, Carl Esmond, Richard Nichols, Elsie the Cow.

Play Girl (RKO-Radio, 1941). Directed by Frank Woodruff. *Cast:* Kay Francis, James Ellison, Mildred Coles, Nigel Bruce, Margaret Hamilton, Katharine Alexander, George P. Huntley.

The Man Who Lost Himself (Universal, 1941) Directed by Edward Ludwig. *Cast:* Brian Aherne, Kay Francis, Henry Stephenson, S.Z. Sakall, Nils Asther, Sig Rumann.

Charley's Aunt (20th Century–Fox, 1941) Directed by Archie Mayo. *Cast:* Jack Benny, Kay Francis, James Ellison, Anne Baxter, Edmund Gwenn, Reginald Owen, Laird Cregar.

The Feminine Touch (MGM, 1941) Directed by W.S. Van Dyke. *Cast:* Rosalind Russell, Don Ameche, Kay Francis, Van Heflin, Donald Meek, Gordon Jones, Henry Daniell, Sidney Blackmer.

Always in My Heart (Warner Bros., 1942) Directed by Jo Graham. *Cast:* Walter Huston, Gloria Warren, Kay Francis, Patty Hale, Frankie Thomas, Una O'Connor, Sidney Blackmer.

Between Us Girls (Universal, 1942) Directed by Henry Koster. *Cast:* Diana Barrymore, Kay Francis, Robert Cummings, John Boles, Andy Devine, Guinn "Big Boy" Williams, Scotty Beckett.

Four Jills in a Jeep (20th Century–Fox, 1944) Directed by William A. Seiter. *Cast:* Kay Francis, Carole Landis, Martha Raye, Mitzi Mayfair, Alice Faye, Carmen Miranda, Betty Grable, George Jessel, John Harvey, Phil Silvers, Dick Haymes, Lester Matthews, Glenn Langan.

Divorce (Monogram, 1945) Directed by William Nigh. *Cast:* Kay Francis, Bruce Cabot, Helen Mack, Craig Reynolds, Jean Fenwick, Larry Olsen, Addison Richards, Jonathan Hale, Ruth Lee.

Allotment Wives (Monogram, 1945) Directed by William Nigh. *Cast:* Kay Francis, Paul Kelly, Otto Kruger, Gertrude Michael, Teala Loring, Bernard Nedell, Matty Fain, Anthony Ward.

Wife Wanted (Monogram, 1946) Directed by Phil Karlson. *Cast:* Kay Francis, Paul Cavanaugh, Robert Shayne, Veda Ann Borg, Teala Loring, Jonathan Hale, John Hamilton.

Ruby Keeler: "Those Dancing Feet"

Ruby Keeler always found it amazing that she became such a success in films. She once said, "I had a terrible singing voice, and I can see that I wasn't the greatest tap dancer in the world either."

In truth, that seems to be a fair assessment. As an actress, Ruby was the first to admit that she would never be a rival to Bette Davis, or even Kay Francis. Her singing lacked the emotion of contemporaries like Helen Morgan, or the softness of Alice Faye. And while Ruby's dancing was professional and thorough, she lacked the grace of Ginger Rogers or the panache of Ann Miller.

What Ruby did have was a girlish charm and down-to-earth manner that audiences responded to. Playing the chorus girl who gets her big break when the star conveniently breaks her leg in *42nd Street* (1933), Ruby, in her own way, served as a symbol of hope for poverty stricken moviegoers. She was the nice innocent triumphing over Bebe Daniels' bitchy diva. When Warner Baxter tells Ruby, "You're going out a youngster, but you've got to come back a star!" she does, and she remained so through her next eight films at Warners.

Ruby's own rags-to-riches story seems like it could easily be crafted into a Warner Bros. musical. Ethel Hilda Keeler was born on August 25, 1910, in Halifax, Nova Scotia, to hard-working, Irish-Canadian parents. Elnora and Ralph Keeler worked in a family-owned grocery store, hardly a lucrative means of supporting a family, which also included Ruby's older brother, Bill. A third child, Gertrude, was born in 1911. Ruby also had three other sisters: Helen (1913), Anna May (1915) and Margie (1917).

In 1912 the Keeler clan moved to New York City, a period which Ruby recalled vividly as a difficult but happy time in her life. Ruby had fond memories of roller skating from the family's flat on 70th Street up to 85th Street to buy a loaf of French bread for her mother. "We were poor," Ruby said in 1971. "My father was with the Knickerbocker Ice Company and we lived on the East Side in a tenement. But I had a fun childhood until I was 13. It was hard on my parents, but kids never realize the sacrifices that parents make."

As a child, Ruby was given a good Catholic education at St. Catherine of Siena's on East 69th Street. It was there that her aptitude for dancing first became known. An instructor, Helen Guest, used to come to the school once a week to teach the students "drill," which were classes in rhythmical exercises conducted to music. Ruby learned folk dances, such as the Highland Fling and the Irish jig, and, according to Ruby, Guest thought she had some talent and told Elnora. Ruby took lessons from Guest every Saturday at her studio. The classes only cost five cents per week, and Ruby learned some popular dances of the day, as well as ballet.

Ruby's parents then enrolled her in the Professional Children's School in New York. When she was 12 she attended the Jack Blue School of Rhythm and Taps. Ruby credited Blue, a former dancing master of George M.

Cohan, with teaching her all she knew about dancing.

In 1923 Ruby appeared in Blue's *Foolish Follies* at the Wilson Theater on New York's West Side. The *Follies* were shown in conjunction with a movie, and Ruby was in two numbers.

At Blue's school Ruby became friendly with fellow student Patsy Kelly, who would also go on to have a successful career on stage and screen, as a comedienne. She and Ruby would finally get to work together in 1971 in the Broadway revival of *No, No, Nanette*.

Ruby was 13 when a friend of Blue's told her about an opening in the chorus of Cohan's *The Rise of Rosie O'Reilly*. Lying about her age, Ruby tried out and got a job in the show at the princely sum of $45 per week.

It was during the run of *Rosie O'Reilly* that Ruby attracted the attention of stage director Earl Lindsay, who offered her a two-year contract at $75 a week to dance at the Strand Hotel Roof Garden. Ruby accepted, but she wasn't there long. Broadway impresario Nils Thor Granlund, who had noticed Ruby in a beauty and talent contest he had sponsored during the run of *Rosie O'Reilly*, offered her a job as a chorus girl at his new nightclub, The El Fey Club. The establishment, which was run by Larry Fey, had quickly become a hot night spot thanks to the boisterous presence of its hostess, Texas Guinan, the renowned "Queen of the Night Clubs." Guinan had a way of working an audience that attracted both the New York upper crust as well as underworld figures. On any night, tables would be filled by the likes of screen star Pola Negri, boxer Jack Dempsey, and Lord and Lady Mountbatten, as well as assorted thugs and gangsters.

At the time, Ruby was so naive that she didn't even realize the El Fey was a speakeasy or that gangsters were among its regular patrons. "We called it a nightclub. It was small, yet I guess anybody who was anybody went to

Ruby Keeler was Warners' musical sweetheart, but moviemaking never really interested her.

the Guinan club. All the stars," Ruby told the *New York Times* in 1970. "I remember Guinan as a very large and very wonderful woman, warm and kind to us and always singing."

The girls who worked there often earned most of their money from the generous tips that customers offered. One night, millionaire Crane Garts made a bet that no man in the club could out-buck-and-wing Ruby. Comics Joe Frisco and Franklyn Farnum were among the takers, but Ruby won hands-down and left the club that night $500 richer. Ruby also danced sometimes at The 300 Club, another night spot where Guinan worked.

In 1926 Ruby landed a spot in a musical called *Tip Toes*, which featured Jeanette MacDonald and Eddie Buzzell, but she dropped out during rehearsals because everyone was so unfriendly to her. Soon after, she received an offer to dance at the Silver Slipper nightclub.

Earl Lindsay, who hadn't seen Ruby since she left the Strand Roof, spotted her at the Silver Slipper one night and offered her a job in the upcoming Broadway revue *Bye, Bye, Bonnie*. The show opened in January of 1927 with Dorothy Burgess as Bonnie, and also featured William Frawley. Ruby's big number was the "Tampico Tap," which went over well with audiences. *The Herald-Tribune* was charmed by Ruby: "She pushes enough personality across the footlights to make her own personable self well worth the price of the entertainment."

Ruby wasn't with the show for long. Producer Charles Dillingham wanted her for his new show *Lucky*, which opened in March 1927. Mary Eaton, Walter Catlett and Richard "Skeets" Gallagher were the stars. *The New York Times* noted, "Ruby Keeler does some fast 'hoofing' specialties, heading a contingent which is highly proficient in that respect."

The show closed within a matter of weeks, to Ruby's disappointment. Dillingham, who had been pleased with Ruby's work in *Lucky*, quickly engaged her for *The Sidewalks of New York*, a musical homage to New York City that opened at the Knickerbocker Theater on October 10, 1927. Ruby played an orphan named Mamie and got to perform several dances staged by Lindsay, including one called the "Goldfish Glide." *Sidewalks of New York* was a tremendous hit and was one of Ruby's favorite show business experiences.

At the time Ruby was working at the El Fey, she became involved in a tacit romance with Johnny "Irish" Costello, a racketeer who was a regular among the Broadway scene. Costello kept a watchful eye on Ruby, taking special notice if anyone should make a pass at her while she was performing her dance specialty. For all of his shady business dealings, Costello was surprisingly quiet, and neither smoked nor drank. Most importantly, he was always a gentleman with Ruby.

Ruby's agent, Billy Grady, kept Costello well-informed regarding any business he conducted for her. One of the deals Grady arranged was to book Ruby in a show at Sid Grauman's Chinese Theater in Hollywood, with a six-week guarantee at $500 a week.

The train that Ruby took to California also had a far more famous passenger on board, Fanny Brice. When Ruby's train pulled into the station at Los Angeles, her West Coast rep from the William Morris Agency was there to meet her. Standing next to him was legendary entertainer Al Jolson, who was on hand to welcome Brice. Jolson, who had been infatuated with Ruby since he saw her in the Chicago run of *Sidewalks of New York*, asked her rep for an introduction. Charmed by Jolson, Ruby agreed to go with him to an opening that night, on the condition that she bring a friend with them. Jolson had a car pick them up at Ruby's aunt's home in Long Beach.

For eighteen-year-old Ruby, the worldly Jolson was exciting. She seemed oblivious to the fact that he was forty-six, the same age as her father. At the same time, she was afraid of getting into a deeper relationship with him, mainly because of Costello. According to Grady, Ruby was in California only a few days before she placed a frantic call to him at Dinty Moore's. She explained that Jolson had been sending her flowers and inviting her to dinner, and insisted that Costello wire the money for her return trip.

Five days later Ruby was back in New York. Grady immediately went about finding her bookings at theaters in Boston and Philadelphia. While she was in Philadelphia, Jack Warner called Grady to get Ruby for a show the studio was planning at its Hollywood theater. With the assurance from Warner that Ruby would be paid $1,500, and, more importantly, that Jolson, one of Warners' top stars, would be in Florida, Grady accepted the offer after getting an OK from Costello.

As it turned out, Jolson was still in Hollywood and he again pursued Ruby. There was a repeat of the frantic calls from Ruby and more wiring of money for her return back to New York. When Ruby arrived at Grand Central Station, Costello was there with a diamond engagement ring.

Grady secured several more picture house engagements for Ruby, but Jolson seemed to follow her no matter where she went. He finally won her over during an engagement in Washington, D.C. When Ruby's agent gave Costello the news that she was in love with Jolson, Costello remained silent for a long time, staring at his clenched fists. After banging them together, he got up from the table where they were seated and went outside to cry. Reportedly, Costello gave Ruby up after a conference with Jolson, with the racketeer warning him to be good to Ruby.

Al and Ruby made front-page headlines when they were married on September 21, 1928, in Port Chester, New York. Because he was Jewish and she was Catholic, they were wed in a civil ceremony performed by a Justice of the Peace. The following day they set sail for a brief honeymoon to Europe aboard the White Star liner Olympic, occupying the Prince of Wales suite. They originally hoped to be married on the ship by the captain, but discovered that under existing company regulations the practice of captains performing marriages had been discontinued.

The newlyweds returned to New York and settled into a spacious apartment at the Ritz Towers on Park Avenue and 57th Street. Ruby immediately went into rehearsals for the new show she was doing, *Whoopee*, starring Eddie Cantor and produced by Florenz Ziegfeld. Despite receiving good notices, Ruby quit the show after the out-of-town tryouts, at Jolson's request.

"Mr. Jolson," recalled Ruby in 1970, "who should have known better, said, 'Ruby, I want you to come to California with me.' 'But what will I do about the show?' I asked. 'Better come to California with me, Ruby,' he said. And so I did, which wasn't a very nice thing to do to Mr. Ziegfeld."

Ziegfeld had no ill will toward Ruby. He gave her the starring role of Dixie Dugan in the lavish *Show Girl* in 1929. Ruby was under much pressure, since the fate of the show rested on her. *Show Girl* had a five-week rehearsal period, and a supportive Al attended every rehearsal. Grady recalled that Ruby would often be edgy, which led to occasional differences between Al and her. During Ruby's tense moments, Grady would advise Al to leave her alone.

Show Girl was a genuine smash when it opened at the Colonial Theater for its Boston tryout. The audience enjoyed Ruby's numbers, which included the show-stopping "Liza" just before the first act finale. Midway in the verse Ruby forgot the lyrics. There was a moment of silence before Jolson stood up and went into the aisle, where he picked up the lyrics to "Liza" while Ruby danced onstage. The number met with thunderous applause.

When the show reached New York, Ziegfeld begged Jolson for a repeat of the "Liza" incident. Once again the routine was a sensation. Years later Ruby gave a simple explanation for Jolson's vocal accompaniment: "Al liked to sing, and when he felt like singing, he sang."

Ruby, whom her husband insisted be billed as Ruby Keeler Jolson, was delighted with her reviews. "It should not surprise us to find Ruby Keeler the next leading lady to gain the stellar position in musical comedy so long held by Marilyn Miller," said *Broadway Theater Guild*.

Even though *Show Girl* was one of the top draws of the Broadway season, Ruby gave her notice one month after its New York premiere so she could join Al in Los Angeles, where he was enjoying success in a series of sentimental musicals for Warner Bros., such as *Sonny Boy* (1928).

Although Ruby's name occasionally showed up in the press, for the most part she was Mrs. Al Jolson for the next few years. Ruby had always been close to her family, and she was thrilled when her parents and her sisters also headed west shortly after she moved to California. Her sisters Gertrude and Helen both had ambitions of working in motion pictures, and they were later featured as members of Busby Berkeley's chorus in some of Ruby's films.

Ruby relied on her family a great deal, especially since relatives were the only ones she got to socialize with at this time. In 1991 Ruby told Trudy Lee Brule, editor of the newsletter of The International Al Jolson Society, that although Jolson could be warm and generous at times, his possessive streak made life difficult for her. She said she wasn't allowed to go anywhere without him, not even out to dinner with a married couple. She and Al spent much of their free time out on the golf course, on fishing trips or at the racetrack.

Ruby used to visit the sets of Al's films frequently when they were first married, but after a while she stopped dropping by. "I found out that I made Al nervous," she told *Picturegoer* in 1935. "He's highly strung and upset enough during the making of a picture, and when I was on the set, it was just one more thing to worry him. So I didn't visit any more — ever."

Living in California and being married to one of the movies' most prominent performers, it was only a matter of time before film producers would begin looking at Ruby. She had already made one film appearance. During her trek to Hollywood in 1928 she was in a two-minute Fox Movietone short, which was a test to illustrate how the sound of tap dancing reproduced on film.

Joseph Schenck, head of Twentieth Century Pictures, wanted Ruby to co-star with Al in the Depression-era musical *Hallelujah, I'm a Bum* (1933). After deliberating over his offer, she decided it wouldn't be a good idea to make her feature-length film debut in one of Al's movies. "It just wouldn't do," she said in *Picturegoer*. "Al knows that I know nothing about pictures. He'd be worrying about my part as well as his own. It wouldn't be fair to either one of us."

A Warner Bros. executive viewed her screen test and liked what he saw. He approached Ruby and offered her a contract, along with a starring role in *42nd Street* (1933), a musical Warners was planning. This time Ruby readily accepted.

42nd Street was a tremendous risk for Warners. Since the inception of sound in 1927, the studios cranked out musicals by the dozens. At first the public flocked to see these tunefests, but as the films became increasingly familiar, audiences' appetite for musicals had pretty much been sated by 1933. *42nd Street*, however, was a musical with a twist. Rather than the standard boy meets girl, boy loses girls, boy dances with girl storyline, *42nd Street* was a realistic and witty look at the backstage goings-on behind a Broadway show.

With its multiple storylines, it seemed like a *Grand Hotel* with tap shoes. Director Julian Marsh (Warner Baxter) is banking on his new show, *Pretty Lady*, to be a success so he can retire and get the much-needed rest he needs. But he encounters many problems on the road to opening night, starting with his temperamental leading lady (Bebe Daniels), who is having an affair with one of the show's angels (Guy Kibbee). Further complicating matters is that she's two-timing her sugar daddy by renewing a romance with an old flame (George Brent).

The other stories concern chorus girl Peggy Sawyer (Ruby), the ultimate lamb in the big city, who is wooed by the show's juvenile lead (Dick Powell). When the star accidentally breaks her leg on the eve of opening night, Peggy is given her big chance to go on in her place.

What really made *42nd Street* stand out from previous musicals were the bold numbers choreographed by Busby Berkeley. "Shuffle Off to Buffalo" was a whimsical number set aboard a Pullman train carriage that featured Ruby and Clarence Nordstrom as newlyweds heading for Niagara Falls. It opens with the newlyweds crooning the song and then dancing through the car as they pass the more jaded passengers, including Ginger Rogers, Una Merkel and other Berkeley chorines, who offer their own snappy parody of "Shuffle Off to Buffalo."

Even better is "I'm Young and Healthy," sung by Dick Powell to Toby Wing. For this number, Berkeley outdid himself with the camera, shooting his chorines from every possible angle and arranging them in as many geometric patterns as he could think of.

The show stopper was the title song, a mini-musical melodrama, that had Ruby inviting everyone to the famed thoroughfare, "where the underworld can meet the elite," as she danced among cardboard skyscrapers and on top of taxis. Berkeley did a masterful job of depicting life in midtown Manhattan, with such shocking images as a girl plunging from a third-story window into the arms of her lover and then being stabbed by another jealous beau. As for Ruby, though at times her footing seemed clumsy, she carried off the number winningly.

Ruby joined a trainload of Warners stars traveling across country to promote the film as it opened in fourteen major cities. In New York the stars were greeted wildly by enthusiastic crowds. When *42nd Street* opened, it was received with the same excitement.

"It is a film which reveals the forward strides made in this medium since the first screen musical features came to Broadway," raved *The New York Times*. The reviewer found that Ruby's "ingratiating personality, coupled with her dances and songs, adds to the zest of this offering."

42nd Street received the ultimate honor when it received an Oscar nomination for Best Picture. It lost to Fox's more prestigious — but less enduring — *Cavalcade* (1933).

Warners wasted no time in trying to cash in on the success of *42nd Street* with a follow-up, *Gold Diggers of 1933* (1933). Joan Blondell, Aline MacMahon and Ruby played showgirls who go on the make for three rich men — a stuffy businessman (Warren William), his middle-aged partner (Guy Kibbee) and the composer/leading man (Dick Powell) of the show they're in.

Gold Diggers of 1933 was actually shot on two stages at the same time. Director Mervyn LeRoy filmed his non-musical scenes with one portion of the crew, while Berkeley worked on the production numbers with another crew.

Once again, there were sparks between Ruby and Powell on-screen, and their electricity together was put to good use in two Berkeley numbers— the smarmy "Pettin' in the Park" and the exquisite "Shadow Waltz." For "Pettin' in the Park," Berkeley pushed the limits of the Production Code — and good taste — by teasing the audience with revealing silhouettes of chorus girls changing out of their dresses after being caught in a downpour. The scene is given even more of a peep show feel when a leering dwarf (Billy Barty) tries to pull up the drawn shade over their dressing rooms. But the clincher is the ending, in which the young women emerge clad in aluminum outfits, all the better to keep their sex-hungry boyfriends at bay. Just before Powell can admit total defeat, Barty hands him a can opener, which Powell uses to undo Ruby's dress.

"Shadow Waltz," by contrast, is Berkeley at his most urbane and appealing. The haunting tune is first sung by Powell to Ruby and then performed by a bevy of blonde-wigged Berkeley girls, who are all dressed in white and playing the tune on neon-lit violins. The number is both hypnotic and romantic, and is still regarded as a Berkeley masterpiece.

Gold Diggers of 1933 was another triumph for Warners, and Ruby once again received fine reviews. "Ruby Keeler proves her hit in *42nd Street* was no accident," said *Modern Screen*.

The New York Times also liked Ruby, though its comment, "Ruby Keeler does quite well as the heroine," was considerably more toned-down.

Hoping for a third straight smash, Warners immediately brought back Ruby, Powell and Blondell for *Footlight Parade* (1933), the best of the Berkeley musicals. *Footlight Parade* greatly benefited from zippy direction by Lloyd Bacon, a sharp screenplay by Manuel Seff and James Seymour, two of Berkeley's most imaginative numbers, and an exuberant star performance by James Cagney. The film had more plot than usual for a Warners musical — in this case, dealing with producer Chester Kent (Cagney), who has to cope with a host of problems, including having his ideas for prologues stolen by a competitor, two crooked partners who are juggling the books, a money-grubbing ex-wife and a sexy man trap (Claire Dodd). Helping him keep his sanity is his faithful secretary Nan (Blondell), who is secretly in love with her boss.

Ruby was Bea Thorne, a plain-Jane office girl who wears horn-rimmed glasses and frumpy dresses that leave everything to the imagination. When the show's star, Scotty (Powell), makes a play for her, she sheds her mousy look to reveal a swan who yearns to be a dancer.

The film sported four Berkeley extravaganzas, all of which featured Ruby. "Sitting on a Backyard Fence," the least ambitious of these, had Ruby dressed as a cat, cavorting with some kittenish chorines before joining her favorite tomcat.

"Honeymoon Hotel" was a racy number that followed the exploits of newlyweds Dick and Ruby as they check into the title establishment. Apparently, they seem to be the only couple staying there that is really married. The humorous number, which also features Billy Barty as a voyeuristic midget, is pleasant, though the least memorable in the film.

"By a Waterfall," by comparison, was a Berkeley triumph. Berkeley claimed he got the idea for the gorgeous water ballet after the premiere of *Gold Diggers of 1933*. When theater owner Sid Grauman asked him how he'd top the numbers in *Gold Diggers*, the idea of a water number suddenly came to Berkeley's mind. He envisioned a big waterfall coming down through the rocks, with dozens of scantily clad girls sliding into an enormous pool with twenty-four gold springboards and a gold fountain telescoping into the air.

There was one thing Berkeley didn't count on. On the first day production began on "By a Waterfall," Berkeley announced, "Everyone into the pool to rehearse." Ruby piped up, "But Buzz, I can't swim." Ruby spent the rest of the day taking swimming lessons, or at least learning how to stay underwater for a few seconds. Luckily, she only had a small amount of time in the water and spent most of her time on dry land warbling the Al Warren–Harry Dubin tune with Powell.

Footlight Parade's grand finale was the exotic "Shanghai Lil," which took place in a combination gin joint and opium den in China.

Cagney played an American sailor looking for Lil (a slanty-eyed Ruby). When Lil, whom the prostitutes in the bar describe as "detrimental to our industry," sees Bill, she croons the song (with an embarrassing Chinese accent), and then she and Cagney engage in some hoofing on the bar. As the sailors leave for their ship, the dancers come together to form the NRA insignia and puzzles of Franklin Delano Roosevelt and Old Glory.

Once again Berkeley struck gold, and *Footlight Parade* did wonders to help keep Warners afloat during the Depression. Theater patrons at the film's premiere in New York gave "By a Waterfall" a standing ovation. Some theater patrons even threw their programs in the air.

One month after *Footlight Parade* was released, Twentieth Century Pictures came out with *Broadway Thru a Keyhole* (1933), a look at the dark side of Broadway from an original story written by columnist Walter Winchell. The plot about a dancer (Constance Cummings) at Texas Guinan's club who gets engaged to a racketeer (Paul Kelly) but really loves a bandleader (Russ Columbo) was practically a carbon copy of Ruby's relationship with Costello and Jolson. The movie gained some notoriety when Jolson, having read the script, knocked Winchell out when they met accidentally at the Hollywood American Legion stadium on July 21, 1933.

Dames (1934), directed by Ray Enright, was another delightful blending of daffy doings and musical splendor. Hugh Herbert was Ezra Ounce, a straitlaced millionaire who wants nothing to do with Jimmy (Powell), the black sheep of the family, who's staging a musical. Horace (Guy Kibbee) and Mathilda Ounce (ZaSu Pitts) are worried that cousin Ezra might disinherit them if he learns their daughter Barbara (Ruby) is dating Jimmy. Even worse for Horace is when a designing woman (Joan Blondell) blackmails him into backing Jimmy's show, which features Barbara.

The adept comic performances of Blondell, Kibbee, Herbert and Pitts kept *Dames* lively when no one was singing. *Dames* also featured two of Berkeley's finest routines—the title song, in which Berkeley goes to extremes for unique kaleidoscopes of his dancers, and "I Only Have Eyes for You," which is beautifully sung by Powell to Ruby on the subway, where they both soon fall asleep. A dream sequence follows, with dozens of chorus girls all wearing Benda masks of Ruby. The girls later fit together pieces of a puzzle of Ruby's face.

Brilliant as the staging of "I Only Have Eyes for You" may be, it also illustrates what Ruby always considered her greatest challenge in her Warners musicals. "The most difficult thing for me in those old films were the songs. I'd have to react to everything Dick Powell sang and of course the song would have eighty choruses. After a while, my mouth would get crooked," she said in a 1970 *Newsweek* interview.

Ruby ran into the same dilemma on *Flirtation Walk* (1934), which transported Powell and her from Broadway to West Point. Director Frank Borzage, who typically gravitated toward more socially minded fare, such as *Little Man, What Now?* (1934), was given the task of adding some layers to this lightweight romance about a cadet (Powell) and a general's daughter (Ruby).

Several of the scenes were filmed on location at West Point, and indeed, with its shots of Kissing Rock, fencing at Flirtation Walk and cadets marching in full dress parade, the film at times has the look of a recruiting poster. Borzage, however, did a creditable job of weaving the West Point locale with the pleasant story and lively musical numbers, with Powell's rendition of "Mr. and Mrs. Is the Name" the most notable.

Oddly, Ruby had no dance numbers in the film, and for the first time was showcased as an actress rather than a dancer. While her role was undemanding, she was sincere, if nothing else.

Flirtation Walk was diverting entertainment and another rousing feather in Warners' musical cap. Borzage, who had been the only director to date to win two Oscars, was an Academy favorite, which might explain *Flirtation Walk*'s unlikely nomination for Best Picture of 1934. It lost to that year's Cinderella champ *It Happened One Night*.

So far, each of Ruby's films had been hugely profitable for Warners. To Ruby, though, her career was secondary to her private life. In May of 1934 she and Al adopted a seven-week-old infant from a New York orphanage. The proud parents and their new son, Al Jolson, Jr., were flooded by reporters as they headed for their train to Los Angeles.

"The baby can't say mammy yet, but he

cries beautifully," Ruby said prior to boarding the train in New York. "Sonny Boy," as his parents later called him, helped make life with Jolson more bearable for Ruby.

Soon after the adoption of Al Jr., Ruby reported back to Warners for her next film. Even though *Flirtation Walk* was a huge hit, Ruby and Powell both made it clear to the front office that they didn't want to be paired again for a while. "We knew that there would be no escape for either of us, from that type of backstage romance, unless we were given fresh screen partners," Ruby told *Film Weekly*. "Mind you, Dick and I always got along swell together and never had a cross word, but we saw how being teamed meant more than ever being closely typed."

Thus, *Gold Diggers of 1935* (1935), originally intended for Powell and Ruby, was recast with Gloria Stuart as his leading lady. Warners decided that if Ruby wasn't going to be paired with her regular screen partner, she might as well team up with her partner in real life in *Go Into Your Dance* (1935). Ruby at first was reluctant about working with Al, as she had been two years earlier, but she eventually gave in.

"We know each other so much better now. I don't think my being on the set will worry Al as it once did, and I know he won't bother me. In fact, I think we'll help each other. I'm not worried," she told *Picturegoer*.

Certainly Al needn't have worried about Ruby stealing the picture from him, which was a Jolson showcase all the way. Al played an irresponsible entertainer who is about to be brought up on charges by Actors Equity for missing performances of a show. Along the way he becomes involved with a sweet nightclub performer (Ruby), gangsters and a budding singer (Helen Morgan), who is the mistress of a mob kingpin (Barton MacLane).

Director Archie Mayo kept the action moving at a reasonable pace, and choreographer Bobby Connolly made the musical numbers pleasant, even if he lacked Berkeley's imagination. The film's best numbers are Al's lively performance of "Latin from Manhattan" and Ruby's "Have a Good Old-Fashioned Cocktail."

Frank S. Nugent of *The New York Times* found the movie entertaining, though he was split on Ruby's performance: "Miss Keeler is not altogether successful in her attempt to do the Rhumba, the Tango and other Spanish dances. Her tap dancing is so much better."

The public was anxious to see Mr. and Mrs. Jolson and came out en masse. Warners considered a follow-up, although some reports claimed that Al feared comparisons with Ruby would be made and he didn't want to be part of a husband and wife screen team. Ruby was always quick to point out that any reports of Al's being envious of her success were ridiculous.

The Powell-Keeler separation wasn't a long one, and the two stars were reteamed for two more efforts. *Shipmates Forever* (1935), again with Borzage, was basically *Flirtation Walk* at sea, shifting the locale from West Point to the U.S. Naval Academy at Annapolis. For authenticity, much of the film was shot at the Academy, and a naval officer and two midshipmen served as technical advisors. They still couldn't fire up the formula story of a crooner (Powell) who'd rather sing than follow in his admiral father's (Lewis Stone) footsteps. With the help of a dance teacher (Ruby), he gradually does a turnaround.

Nugent noted that the performances of supporting players Stone, Ross Alexander and others "tend to make one overlook Mr. Powell's occasional attempts to be lachrymose and Miss Keeler's studied winsomeness."

Colleen (1936), Ruby's last film with Powell, fared worse. The nothing plot had Hugh Herbert playing an eccentric millionaire (was there any other kind in movies like this?) who entrusts his dress shop to a golddigging blonde (Joan Blondell). His nephew (Powell) unwittingly gives the job of running the store to the lady in his life (Ruby).

"If you happen to like the Keeler-Powell musicals, you probably will find this one entirely satisfying. Its resemblance to last year's and the year's before that is unquestionable," sniped Nugent.

Though *Colleen* was minor entertainment, Ruby thought it contained some of her best dancing. "[Choreographer] Paul Draper was such a perfectionist! I wasn't used to this kind of dancing and he made me do everything fifty-five times, but by gosh, I did it," she said.

Colleen, unfortunately, demonstrated how the Warners musical seemed to be on a decline since the great triple play of *42nd Street*, *Gold Diggers of 1933* and *Footlight Parade* three years earlier. At the same time, RKO was having a problem with the Fred Astaire-Ginger Rogers dancefests it was producing. The team's latest,

Shall We Dance (1937), was profitable, though far less so than their previous ventures. RKO decided on a temporary separation for Fred and Ginger, which meant a new partner for Astaire in his upcoming *A Damsel in Distress* (1937).

RKO approached Warners about borrowing Ruby, but apparently negotiations didn't pan out, much to Ruby's disappointment. Still, she didn't express any bitterness about it. "I am terribly thrilled to have been paid the compliment Astaire paid me when he even suggested me for the part," she told *Film Weekly*.

Instead, Warners placed Ruby in *Ready, Willing and Able* (1937), a musical trifle that had a wafer-thin story about an aspiring dancer named Jane Clark (Ruby) who pretends to be a London stage star (Winifred Shaw), also named Jane Clark, to secure the lead in a Broadway show. The movie was notable for introducing the Johnny Mercer standard "Just Too Marvelous for Words," which Warners reprised four times. For the big production number, Ruby and co-star Lee Dixon danced to the tune on the keys of a giant typewriter. This proved to be Ruby's favorite dance routine.

Ruby's romantic interest in *Ready, Willing and Able* was Ross Alexander, a promising leading man who committed suicide shortly before the picture's release. Ruby was saddened by his death, although she remembered how unhappy he seemed while they were making *Ready, Willing and Able*. "You know, after he'd gone, I remembered how nervous he was all through the picture," she said. "While he was waiting between shots, he'd sit on the set and pick holes in his hands—make them bleed. I don't think anybody knew what was going on in his mind."

More pleasant for Ruby was working with Winifred Shaw, one of her best friends during her Warners days. The two often shared breakfast or lunch in one or the other's dressing rooms. Shaw remembered Ruby as strong-willed and determined, as well as devoted to her family.

"She's not much of a one to talk about her triumphs or her career; it's her family that interests her most," Shaw told *Film Fan Monthly* in 1971. "The Keelers have always been close, and there were quite a few of them. At Warner Bros. you couldn't walk through the lot without tripping over a Keeler."

Critical response to the picture was generally poor. *Variety* called it "a rather weak-kneed total. Lightweight."

Frank S. Nugent of *The New York Times* was harsher, saying *Ready, Willing and Able*, "overestimates itself by two-thirds, possibly by three…. The picture has one moment of revelation: Miss Keeler, of the wee sma' voice, listens to a smaller one and admits she can't sing. We've been waiting a long time for that."

Ruby had been vocal about her disapproval with the recent scripts she had been handed by Warners. One project the studio considered as a follow-up to *Ready, Willing and Able* was something called *College Girl*, but Ruby balked at the title. "Do you think the public will accept me as a college girl?" she asked W.H. Mooring of *Film Weekly*.

Apparently Warners also decided no one would, and the project was abandoned. For the next seven months after completion of *Ready, Willing and Able*, Ruby rejected every script Warner Bros. tossed her away. Although Ruby was obligated to make two more films for Warners, she was released from her contract in May of 1937.

Immediately the rumors began to fly that RKO was once again courting her to co-star with Astaire, although by that time contract player Joan Fontaine had been cast in *A Damsel in Distress*. Ruby also was being wooed by Universal to star in *Merry-Go-Round of 1937*, which ultimately was released as *Merry-Go-Round of 1938* sans Ruby.

RKO won, with Ruby signing a contract for two pictures a year at $40,000 each. As it turned out, her first film wasn't with Astaire. The reaction to Astaire without Rogers in *A Damsel in Distress* was lukewarm at best. RKO decided to play it safe and reteam Fred and Ginger in *Carefree* (1938). Ruby was paired with Anne Shirley and Fay Bainter in the homespun comedy *Mother Carey's Chickens* (1938), based on the novel by Kate Douglas Wiggins. Set in turn of the century New England, the movie was a charming slice of Americana about the Carey clan's efforts to put down roots in a new home despite dwindling finances. Much of the movie dealt with the sisters' (Ruby and Shirley) attempts to settle the family's money matters and their romances.

As quaint as a Whitman sampler, *Mother Carey's Chickens* was whimsical and disarming. Though Ruby didn't perform any musical numbers, she seemed far more poised and relaxed than she did in most of her Warners outings, turning in a surprisingly endearing performance. Amazingly, Ruby's role was originally earmarked for Katharine Hepburn, who refused to do it. Instead, she bought out the remainder of her contract for $220,000.

The New York Times beamed over *Mother Carey's Chickens*, which it called "a rollicking, folksy comedy for all its vintage and as delightful an entertainment as one dare hope to meet in such unpleasant weather.... Ruby Keeler and Anne Shirley are splendid as the sisters."

Mother Carey's Chickens was a relatively inexpensive film, and as such turned out to be a tidy money-spinner for RKO. The story was dusted off again twenty-five years later for Walt Disney's *Summer Magic* (1963).

Despite the success of *Mother Carey's Chickens*, Ruby didn't do any more films for RKO. She objected to taking second billing to Shirley, whom the studio saw as a more promising commodity, and asked for her release.

Soon after completing *Mother Carey's Chickens*, Ruby took a trip by herself to Honolulu. It was a chance for her to sort out the issues in her marriage and her career. She agreed to appear in Al's new show, *Hold on to Your Hat*, prior to her Hawaiian trip, but walked out during the Chicago tryouts when Al kept making references to their marital problems during rehearsals.

The Chicago incident was just the latest in a series of difficulties that had put a strain on their marriage. The differences in their ages and religions, as well as their different slants on career and family, were other problems. Worst of all was Al's domineering nature. The final straw was when Al arrived home one night from doing his radio show at the same time Ruby came home from a card game with some friends. Al saw Ruby give a thank-you kiss on the cheek to her friend, comedian Bert Wheeler, after he drove her home. As soon as she came in the house, Al put her through the third degree, asking who she was kissing and why she was so late. Ruby, fed up with his possessiveness, began divorce proceedings the following morning.

Ruby was granted a divorce on December 26, 1939, in a Los Angeles court on grounds of mental cruelty. She said Al called her "stupid" and would keep her up all night calling her names.

In her divorce complaint Ruby stated: "He would sit at the table and refuse to talk and make me keep up the conversation. Then he would go upstairs to bed and leave me to entertain our friends. He would never agree with me on anything; when I said anything he would fly into a rage."

Ruby was awarded custody of Al Jr. and was granted $400 a month alimony for as long as she remained single, and a lump sum of $50,000 if she remarried.

Jolson, in New York, told the press he was "sorry" he gave Ruby an inferiority complex, and even gave intimations of a possible reconciliation: "Who knows? It takes a year out in California for a divorce to become final. You know, once those things are over you feel better, but Ruby's a wonderful girl."

Ruby kept a low profile after the divorce. She only made one more film during this period, a lame musical called *Sweetheart of the Campus* (1941) for Columbia. Ruby was cast against type as a cynical, wisecracking showgirl who runs a nightclub on a college campus. Also in the cast were Ozzie Nelson and his orchestra. *Sweetheart of the Campus* was thankfully the shortest of all of Ruby's films (a mere sixty-four minutes). Ruby served as her own critic on *Sweetheart of the Campus*: "It was so bad I had no regrets about quitting."

Not that she retired with any bitterness. "I wasn't disillusioned with show business," she said in 1970. "I just thought there was more to life. I was right."

In this case, the "more" was John Homer Lowe, a handsome bachelor whom Ruby met while having dinner with friends at a golf club. The two hit it off immediately. John, a prominent California real estate broker and builder, shared Ruby's desire for a home and family.

Ruby became Mrs. John Lowe on October 29, 1941, at St. Charles Borromeo Church in North Hollywood, California. Some cynics sneered about Ruby, who had been divorced, being able to get married in a Catholic church, but Ruby had her own way of looking at it. "People thought the church was showing favoritism, but they didn't understand. Al and I were married by a justice of the peace, even though Al's father was a cantor and one of the most truly religious men I ever met. So in the eyes of the church, my marriage to Al was not a blessed marriage," she told *The New York Times* in 1970.

The Lowes lived a quiet life in Orange County, and Ruby was never happier. Whereas Jolson made Ruby feel inferior, John was understanding and loving toward her. He was also a good father to Al Jr., who eventually took Lowe as his last name.

The greatest joy for Ruby was when she became pregnant for the first time. Their daughter, Theresa, was born in 1943, and over the next few years the couple had three more children — Christine, John Jr. and Kathleen. "My life was rewarding, exciting and fulfilling. I carted the children to school, athletic events, parties, proms and graduation ceremonies. I can't begin to tell you how wonderful it was," Ruby said.

In 1945 Columbia announced plans to film *The Jolson Story* (1946), starring Larry Parks as Jolson. The studio was anxious to get Ruby's permission to depict her marriage to Jolson. When Ruby politely refused, the studio said, "OK, we'll call you Pearl or Julie."

Columbia lived up to its word. Mrs. Al Jolson was called Julie Benson, though everyone knew she was modeled after Ruby. Evelyn Keyes turned in a beautiful performance as Julie and did a fine job of recreating some of Ruby's famous dance routines. Though the film was largely fictional, it was among the biggest money-makers of the year.

Ruby said she never saw *The Jolson Story* until nearly forty years later, and she said there was little truth in it. She also harbored ill feelings about its making for many years to come, as Keyes discovered when she finally got to meet Ruby in the early '70s. Keyes had recently recreated Ruby's Broadway role in the road company of *No, No, Nanette*, with Don Ameche, and had now retired to her home in northern Connecticut. One night she and some of her former cast members decided to drive to Springfield, Massachusetts, to see the theater-in-the-round production of *No, No Nanette* in which Ruby was now appearing with Ameche.

"We all had a ball, and after the show we went backstage to say hello," Keyes said. "I first went to see Don and he was a real doll. After that I knocked on Ruby Keeler's dressing room door. I said, 'Hello, Ms. Keeler. I'm Evelyn Keyes.' I then put my hand out, and she recoiled. She put her hand behind her back. I couldn't believe it. After that I just wanted to get the hell out of there. I was in *The Jolson Story*, which was a great hit and which was wonderful for my career, but I was just an actress having a career."

Once Ruby divorced herself from Jolson, she seemed to close the door on that chapter of her life. She preferred living in the present, which as Mrs. John Lowe allowed her ample time to indulge in her favorite pastime — golf. The Lowes were members of the celebrated Lakeside Golf Club in Toluca Lake, California, an establishment whose membership included Bob and Dolores Hope, Bing Crosby, and Howard Hughes. Ruby became an expert golfer with a 12 handicap.

It was there that Ruby met Nancy Marlow-Trump, a former RKO starlet who would become a friend for life. "Ruby was so marvelous," she said. "The qualities I liked about her were her humility and her spirituality. She was just a regular person. There was none of that Hollywood attitude."

Though Marlow-Trump was about twenty years younger than Ruby, they still had much in common. "We couldn't play golf together because I was so bad. We played poker afterward, and she had great fun doing that," Marlow-Trump joked.

While Ruby's professional days as a dancer may have been behind her, she still liked to kick up her heels every once in a while by performing in some of the productions at the Lakeside. "We did a takeoff on *Damn Yankees* called *Damn Golfers*, and we had fun doing it," recalled Marlow-Trump. "It was funny because I was the director and she was the chorus girl, and she didn't mind a bit."

The 1960s proved to be a difficult decade for Ruby. Her son John was drafted and fought in the Vietnam War. Ruby was happy that he came home safely, and proud that he was awarded a Bronze Star for his efforts.

The real blow to Ruby came when her beloved husband died in 1969. At that point her children were all grown, and suddenly she was no longer the wife and mother. Ruby decided that she wanted to give show business another whirl. She made a cameo appearance in *They Shoot Horses, Don't They?* (1969), a grim drama about a 1930s dance marathon, but for some reason her scene was deleted from the final print.

She then appeared in *The Phynx* (1970), a disastrous film that blended rock music with cameos of old film stars, such as Ruby and her friend from her Warners days, Joan Blondell.

Then Ruby was approached by producer Harry Rigby about a featured role in his revival of the 1925 musical *No, No, Nanette*. Ruby said she was terribly flattered but unsure whether she could do it. She explained her dilemma to Marlow-Trump, who convinced her to accept.

"She said, 'I have to ask you about something. They asked me to go to Broadway to do *No, No, Nanette*. I don't know what I should do.' I said to her, 'You're going to do it, aren't you? Because if you don't, I will,'" Marlow-Trump joked. "She was worried because she hadn't performed in so long. She thought she was out of shape, which was ridiculous because she was in great shape. Then when John Lowe, Jr., was hired as stage manager and her sister Gertrude got to be dresser, that cinched it for her."

When Ruby also learned that she'd have the chance to work once again with her good friend Busby Berkeley, who was the supervising producer, she knew it was too good an opportunity to pass up. She began rehearsals for the show on August 15, 1970. When she arrived she was greeted affectionately with applause from the dancers in the company. Though Ruby was now sixty and had silver hair, she still looked trim at 112 pounds, and her face was still lit up by her charming smile and big blue eyes.

No, No, Nanette had an impressive pedigree, which included a book by Frank Mandel and Otto Harbach, lyrics by Irving Caesar and a tuneful score that featured such standards as "Tea for Two" and "I Want to Be Happy," which was Ruby's big number. Charles Gaynor wrote the lyrics for some new songs and adapted the original book. The polished cast included Helen Gallagher, Bobby Van, Cyril Ritchard, Jack Gilford and Patsy Kelly. Kelly, who had known Ruby when they grew up together on New York's East Side, was in awe whenever Ruby rehearsed her number.

"This gives me duck bumps," she told *Look*. "One of the thrills of my life is doing a show with her. She's a real lady. Always has been, always will be."

Ruby was glad she had only one song, a patter number with Gilford. "I can talk a song, I just can't sing," she told *The New York Times*. "One thing that was difficult for me at first was learning lines again. I still walk up and down backstage thinking, 'Now what are my lines in this next scene?' I never really had a lot of lines to learn before, especially on stage. I'm not an actress. You certainly can't call what I did on the screen acting."

The show opened in Boston to rave reviews. Ruby's sister, Gertrude, was delighted about the way the critics rhapsodized over Ruby. "Isn't that beautiful? They've accepted her," she said.

No, No, Nanette premiered in New York on January 19, 1971, and the reception to both the show and Ruby was even more enthusiastic than it had been in Boston. "Her opening night was fantastic," Marlow-Trump said. "I remember after the show we went out to Sardi's and she was the toast of the town. It was the most spectacular comeback Broadway has seen to this day."

The critics were charmed. Charles Mac-Harry of *The Daily News* even wrote a column headed "Love Letter" in which he sang the praises of the *No, No, Nanette* cast and crew.

"Dear Busby Berkeley, Ruby Keeler, Jack Gilford, Patsy Kelly, Helen Gallagher, Bobby Van, the two pianos, the orchestra, etc.—whoever you are and everyone connected with Broadway's revival of 1925's *No, No, Nanette*. You, collectively, are darlings. I have never attended an opening night that generated more enthusiasm, and may I say I whooped, applauded and otherwise cheered with all the others. I could not have been happier if I had been a backer."

No, No, Nanette quickly became the hottest ticket on Broadway and enjoyed a successful 861-performance run. When the show closed on February 3, 1973, Ruby continued to appear in one of the road companies with Don Ameche.

As far as Ruby was concerned, *No, No, Nanette* was strictly a one-shot deal. She had no interest in doing any further shows, and in 1973 announced her official retirement. *No, No, Nanette* was a nice way to cap her career, and it also helped introduce a new generation to her work and renew interest in her films.

Sadly, Ruby was never quite as vital after *No, No, Nanette*. In 1974 she had an aneurysm attack during a visit to her grandchildren in Montana, which left her unconscious. She was rushed for emergency brain surgery, and although her chances of survival were iffy, she pulled through.

Following two months in the hospital, Ruby returned to her home in Newport Beach, where she began a long and painful physical therapy. She also drifted in and out of consciousness, remembering incidents from a long time earlier. Her daughter Kathleen had given up her job in New York to care for her mother.

The road to recovery was a long one, and it wasn't until 1979 that Ruby seemed able to get around well. In March of 1979 she was invited to present the Best Song Oscar at that year's Academy Awards telecast. Ruby's co-presenter, Kris Kristofferson, introduced a film clip from *42nd Street* and then introduced Ruby. Nervous about making her first public appearance since her stroke, she bravely walked out on stage with the use of a cane topped with a carved dog's head. Ruby was gratified by the standing ovation she received.

Later that year the family thought Ruby was well enough to attempt taking a trip. She and Kathleen boarded the cruise ship Rotterdam, with Kathleen as her companion. On board, Ruby was recognized by English entertainers Jackie and Roy Toaduff, who were performing on the ship. They introduced themselves to Ruby and Kathleen and invited them to their show that evening.

No one on ship was aware that Ruby was aboard. When she and Kathleen arrived for the show, the Toaduffs saluted Ruby and introduced her to the audience. Ruby stood up and waved as the other guests applauded loudly and then rose to give her a standing ovation. After the show, Kathleen thanked the Toaduffs for the happiness they brought to Ruby that evening.

Through the Toaduffs, Ruby began a new phase in her career by doing several cruises for the Cunard Line's Queen Elizabeth 2. She remained close friends with the Toaduffs, and visited them on six occasions over the next few years at the hotel they owned in Dronfield, England.

Ruby moved to Rancho Mirage, California, in the early '80s, where the desert climate did her a world of good. She also did much work for the Stroke Activity Center in Palm Desert. Ruby would visit with stroke victims and get them out of their wheelchairs to dance with her. She also offered words of encouragement: "Continue to do as much as you possibly can. Use the facilities you have and live life to its fullest."

Her last few years were spent enjoying visits with friends, her children and her fourteen grandchildren. In late 1992 Ruby was diagnosed with cancer and wasn't given much longer to live. "I was with her a week before she passed away. I remember the priest was there. She knew me and said 'Hi Nance,'" said Marlow-Trump. Ruby died on February 28, 1993.

Since then, Marlow-Trump has done her best to keep Ruby's spirit and talent alive. She learned some of Ruby's routines from *No, No, Nanette* and put on a couple of shows about her friend at the Lakeside Golf Club. "It was a nice tribute to her. She's my angel."

FILMOGRAPHY

Fox Movietone (Fox Film, 1928)
42nd Street (Warner Bros., 1933) Directed by Lloyd Bacon. *Cast:* Bebe Daniels, Warner Baxter, Dick Powell, Ruby Keeler, George Brent, Ginger Rogers, Una Merkel, Guy Kibbee.
Gold Diggers of 1933 (Warner Bros., 1933) Directed by Mervyn LeRoy. *Cast:* Joan Blondell, Warren William, Dick Powell, Ruby Keeler, Aline MacMahon, Ginger Rogers, Guy Kibbee.
Footlight Parade (Warner Bros., 1933) Directed by Lloyd Bacon. *Cast:* James Cagney, Joan Blondell, Dick Powell, Ruby Keeler, Guy Kibbee, Frank McHugh, Hugh Herbert, Ruth Donnelly.
Dames (Warner Bros., 1934) Directed by Ray Enright. *Cast:* Joan Blondell, Ruby Keeler, Dick Powell, Guy Kibbee, Hugh Herbert, ZaSu Pitts, Arthur Vinton, Lela Bennett, Berton Churchill.
Flirtation Walk (Warner Bros., 1934) Directed by Frank Borzage. *Cast:* Dick Powell, Ruby Keeler, Pat O'Brien, Ross Alexander, John Arledge, Henry O'Neill, Guinn "Big Boy" Williams.

Go Into Your Dance (Warner Bros., 1935) Directed by Archie Mayo. *Cast:* Al Jolson, Ruby Keeler, Helen Morgan, Glenda Farrell, Barton MacLane, Sharon Lynne, Patsy Kelly.

Shipmates Forever (Warner Bros., 1935) Directed by Frank Borzage. *Cast:* Dick Powell, Ruby Keeler, Lewis Stone, Ross Alexander, Eddie Acuff, Richard (Dick) Foran, John Arledge.

Colleen (Warner Bros., 1936) Directed by Alfred E. Green. *Cast:* Joan Blondell, Dick Powell, Ruby Keeler, Jack Oakie, Hugh Herbert, Louise Fazenda, Paul Draper, Marie Wilson.

Ready, Willing and Able (Warner Bros., 1937) Directed by Ray Enright. *Cast:* Ruby Keeler, Lee Dixon, Allen Jenkins, Louise Fazenda, Carol Hughes, Ross Alexander, Winifred Shaw.

Mother Carey's Chickens (RKO Radio, 1938) Directed by Rowland V. Lee. *Cast:* Ruby Keeler, Anne Shirley, James Ellison, Fay Bainter, Walter Brennan, Frank Albertson.

Sweetheart of the Campus (Columbia, 1941) Directed by Edward Dmytryk. *Cast:* Ruby Keeler, Ozzie Nelson, Harriet Hilliard, Gordon Oliver, Don Beddoe, Kathleen Howard.

The Phynx (Warner Bros., 1970) Directed by Lee H. Katzin. *Cast:* A. Michael Miller, Ray Chippeway, Dennis Larden, Lonny Stevens, Lou Antonio, Mike Kjellin, Michael Ansara, George Tobias, Joan Blondell. (Ruby made a cameo appearance.)

Andrea King: "The Femme Fatale"

Whenever one thinks of the great screen femme fatales, certain names automatically come to mind — Barbara Stanwyck in *Double Indemnity*, Jane Greer in *Out of the Past*, Joan Bennett in *Scarlet Street*. For some reason, no one immediately thinks of Andrea King in *Hotel Berlin*, which is a shame. Andrea's devious Nazi sympathizer Lisa Dorn can slink right along with the best screen villainesses, using her feminine wiles to lure her willing victim — in this case, underground hero Martin Richter (Helmut Dantine) — into a carefully constructed trap. And like all good bad girls, she eventually meets her well-deserved end.

During her all-too-brief period at Warner Bros., Andrea carved a niche playing such duplicitous females. Like her Warners colleague Alexis Smith, Andrea possessed a cool reserve that suggested a woman of social standing or a woman of danger. On several occasions it meant both. Even in lighter fare, such as *My Wild Irish Rose*, Andrea's Lillian Russell, with her Park Avenue airs and bedroom eyes, seemed as if she was corrupting the innocent Chauncey Olcott (Dennis Morgan). We all knew he would be better off with Arlene Dahl's doe-eyed innocent, but it was Andrea who supplied the fire and excitement. On those rare occasions when Andrea got to play a sympathetic role, such as Ida Lupino's hard-working sister in *The Man I Love*, she showed herself to be an actress of great sensitivity.

Andrea's career at Warners seemed to parallel that of Nancy Coleman's — both began their careers on the stage and both were cited by critics as potential stars in their first major screen roles. In Andrea's case, the studio had great plans to mold her into another Bette Davis by giving her important roles in *The Corn Is Green* and *Ethan Frome*. Intervention from Davis and the collapse of the studio system put an end to Andrea's career at Warner Bros. Though Andrea never achieved the stardom of Davis or Stanwyck, she did develop into a versatile and dependable supporting player who often left a more indelible impression than the leading players.

It seems unlikely that Andrea would have ever chosen any other career path, given the influence of her mother, Lovinia Belle Hart. Belle, as she was known, was born in Cleveland, Ohio, in 1885, and was the youngest daughter of George and Deborah Hart. George's claim to fame was that he was the inventor of the grain elevator.

From an early age, Belle yearned for a career on the stage, but her staid parents didn't consider acting a dignified profession and encouraged her to get an education. She later made her way to New York, where she found work as a teaching companion for the child of Alonso Robert Yates, a prominent American diplomat. After that job Belle became a disciple of dancer Isadora Duncan, then living in New York. When Duncan fled the United States for France in 1917, Belle decided to join her. Belle's parents were unaware of her dancing endeavors, so she couldn't ask them to pay for her trip. Instead, the resourceful Belle signed up with Ann Morgan, daughter of financier J.P.

Morgan, as a volunteer ambulance driver with the American Red Cross in Paris.

In Paris Belle once again encountered Yates, and the two of them spent a great deal of time together, despite the fact that he was married. Supposedly, Belle also became enamored of a handsome young pilot in the Lafayette Escadrille named George Andre Barry, the man who, as she later told her daughter, was Andrea's father. The facts surrounding Andrea's birth, though, are decidedly fuzzy. Belle maintained that she and Barry were married in 1918, and in the fall of that year he was killed when German fliers shot down his plane. Belle at the time was six months pregnant.

Belle gave birth on February 1, 1919, in Paris to Andrea nee Georgette Andre Barry, who was named for the father she never knew. Shortly after Andrea was born, Belle became gravely ill with Childbirth Fever and might surely have died if Yates had not obtained an experimental saline solution from Madame Marie-Louise Vallery-Radot, daughter of Louis Pasteur.

Andrea always found the circumstances of her birth to be somewhat nebulous. In later years her suspicions seemed grounded when she learned there were no birth or death records of George Barry, and, for that matter, no marriage certificate for her parents' union.

It seemed more likely that the attentive Yates might have been her actual father, a theory that was corroborated by Evelyn Yates Inman, Yates' daughter, who confessed to Andrea in 1980 that they were half-sisters. Belle, however, denied her claim and stuck to her original story about George Barry until her death in 1986 at 101. To this day, Andrea remains uncertain as to her actual birthright, although she seems certain that her mother's version was a pure fabrication.

Whatever the circumstances, Belle was faced with the difficulty of raising a child by herself. Financial necessity forced Belle to return to her family in Cleveland, Ohio. Belle had been notified prior to leaving Paris that her father was in deteriorating health. Sadly, he died while she and Andrea were en route to the States.

"We went to Cleveland to live with my grandmother. Mother came with sixteen canaries and a French nurse that didn't speak any English. Mother was wrapped up in fur to look very French. I'm sure my grandmother was horrified," Andrea said.

Belle had a difficult time getting reacclimated to Cleveland after the glitter and excitement of Paris. Belle again expressed interest in heading to New York to become an actress, and again met with the same opposition from her mother. She did get to go to New York, but it was as a student at Columbia University. For Andrea, those early childhood years of separation from her mother were difficult. She remained with her grandmother in Cleveland and then when Belle's mother moved to Palm Beach, Florida, a couple of years later.

Mother and daughter were finally reunited when Andrea was four. Belle married Douglas McKee, vice president of the Title Guarantee & Trust Company, and for the first time Andrea finally experienced some semblance of family life. Belle was relieved that the years of financial burden had at long last come to an end. The family settled into a large home in Forest Hills, New York, and welcomed another child, Anne Douglas McKee, who was born in 1926.

When Andrea was a little older, Belle sent her to an art camp in the Adirondacks, an establishment owned by another close friend of Isadora Duncan. At the camp, Andrea was exposed to theatrics, singing and dancing, and she loved every minute of it. Clearly her mother's daughter, Andrea's mind was already set on becoming an actress.

Belle did her best to make her daughters' home life as pleasant as possible, but McKee admittedly didn't understand or particularly like children. By the time she was eleven, Andrea became so unhappy with her home life that she attempted to run away, with Hollywood as her goal. She only made it as far as the Long Island freight yards and was returned home safely.

A few years later Andrea was enrolled in the renowned Edgewood School, a boarding school in Greenwich, Connecticut, and the first progressive school in the United States. The school proved to be a haven for Andrea, one in which she felt free to indulge her love of the arts. Lessons in drama, dance and most of the other art forms filled Andrea's curriculum.

Andrea pursued her love of drama passionately and showed a tremendous aptitude for her craft. She was especially delighted during the 1932 school year when she landed the dream role of Juliet in the Christmas production of

Warners had big plans for Andrea King until Bette Davis got in the way.

William Shakespeare's *Romeo and Juliet*. Andrea worked extra hard preparing for opening night, unaware of just how pivotal that performance would be to her career. Her hard work showed and the program met with cheers from the audience.

After the show, Andrea and Belle met the uncle of Andrea's roommate, who was introduced to both simply as Mr. Grenecker. They soon learned that C.P. Grenecker was the head of public relations for theatrical producer Lee Shubert and was looking for thirty teenagers to fill many roles in a new play he was preparing called *Growing Pains*. He approached Belle by telling her that he was impressed with Andrea's performance as Juliet and thought she might be right for one of the parts. Belle discussed the matter with Andrea, who was anxious to try out for the role.

Andrea's audition was a success, and she appeared with the *Growing Pains* company, in an ensemble role, billed as Georgette McKee. Junior Durkin starred as a teenager coming to terms with love for the first time. *Growing Pains* opened at Broadway's Ambassador Theater on November 23, 1933, to mixed notices, and closed after just six weeks.

Andrea had better luck in *Fly Away Home*, Dorothy Bennett and Irving White's seriocomic play with Thomas Mitchell as an errant father who returns home after a long absence to attend his ex-wife's wedding. During his visit he has a chance to get reacquainted with the five children he left behind. Mitchell also staged the play, which was produced by Theron Bamberger and, coincidentally, Warner Bros. Warners eventually filmed the play as *Daughters Courageous* (1939), with the Lane Sisters, John Garfield and Claude Rains.

Andrea portrayed Buff, the second-youngest of Mitchell's children. Also in the cast as her brother was a gifted newcomer named Montgomery Clift, who became a great friend. Clift and Andrea shared many enjoyable moments during the run of the play, as well as the same aspirations.

According to Bamberger, the lively Andrea captivated him so during her audition that she was hired on the spot. "She came in one day last June, deeply tanned from a visit in Florida and full of the same bubbling personality which comes over the footlights," he told *The New York Times*. "I felt so sure of her merely from talking with her in the office that I did not ask her to read, but told her she was engaged. She was a great success at Stockbridge and when rehearsals were called in New York, Thomas Mitchell was so pleased with her that he did a good deal to build up her role. Georgette is gay, irrepressible, high-spirited. Her personality on the stage is as free, simple and genuinely childlike as it is off."

Andrea has fond memories of *Fly Away Home*—in particular, the surprising turn of events when the play opened on January 20, 1935, at the Forty-Eighth Street Theater.

Mitchell appeared in the play every day except Wednesdays and Saturdays, when he was directing Tallulah Bankhead in *Reflected Glory*. When the curtain came up for the first time on *Fly Away Home*, Andrea and Clift were onstage, directing their lines to Trigger, a cat who was placed in a large bay window.

"Imagine our dismay when we rushed to enfold the cat, saying, 'Come on Trigger, we have a surprise for you,' to see in the window a glamorous head of hair and a graceful hand holding a glass of champagne and to hear it say, 'Oh my God, what a daahling kitty.' The body and voice tumbled over the bay window with a screeching cat, onto our stage," Andrea recalled.

The curtain fell immediately and Mitchell announced there was an electrical malfunction so that the audience would not know that Bankhead had wandered onto the wrong stage.

Fortunately, the incident didn't throw the actors and the play opened to rave reviews. "Excepting the midriff section, when the tale goes pretty much to pieces, *Fly Away Home* is hilarious stuff," wrote the estimable Brooks Atkinson of *The New York Times*. He added that, "it is acted with sufficient animal vigor to keep the play as racy as the dialogue," and found Andrea "artless enough to be charming."

The following year Andrea scored another hit in the Bella and Sam Spewack comedy *Boy Meets Girl*, in which she understudied the lead, a pregnant waitress. The farce, which nicely lampooned Hollywood, concerned two eccentric studio publicity men who turn the waitress' baby into a popular child star even before it is born.

After finishing with *Boy Meets Girl*, Andrea went on several auditions, including one for the Lillian Gish company of *Life with Father* in Chicago. Based on Clarence Day's humorous novel about his youth in turn of the century New York — in particular, growing up under the iron thumb of his Victorian-thinking father — the play had been a tremendous hit in New York. Andrea was assigned the role of Mary Skinner, young Clarence's first love.

Andrea remembered Gish as a quiet person who generally kept to herself. However, she was protective of the members of her company, often referring to them as her "flock of children."

Life with Father enjoyed a lengthy run, which was fortuitous for Andrea from both a professional and a personal standpoint. It was during the run of *Life with Father* that she met Nat Willis, a young lawyer who charmed Andrea with his tall good looks and outgoing personality. Just as impressive to Andrea was that Willis was a direct descendant of George Washington. It also helped that Willis respected Andrea's desires to pursue her theatrical career and thus had no qualms about asking her to become his wife. "Before we married I told him I couldn't possibly continue without acting. That was mentioned right up front and it was never a problem. He always understood," she said. They wed on October 6, 1940.

Prior to her marriage, Andrea made her film debut in a docudrama called *The Ramparts We Watch* (1940). RKO distributed the film, which was produced by Time Inc., and which combined newsreel footage with live action. The film focused on the inhabitants of a typical American town during World War I, with the intent to show how Americans on the brink of a second World War needed to understand the events of the past to protect their current freedom. Producer-director Louis de Rochemont used scenes from the *March of Time* newsreel *Baptism of Fire*, a Nazi propaganda film, to help illustrate how a mechanically trained Army could destroy an unprepared foe. Billed as Georgette McKee, Andrea had a pivotal role as one of the townspeople.

Flush from her success in *Life with Father*, Andrea was chosen to appear in the road company of the Victorian thriller *Angel Street* by Patrick Hamilton in 1941. The classic chiller about a murderous husband's plan to drive his wife insane had already been a hit on both the London and Broadway stages, as well as a popular British film in 1940. Andrea had her first bad girl role as Nancy, the Cockney maid who has a fling with her nefarious employer. Once again both she and the play were a success.

It was also around this time that Andrea had her first encounter with Errol Flynn, whom she would later get to know while working at Warner Bros. It was also her first taste of his wicked sense of humor. She was heading home to her husband in Chicago on the Twentieth Century Limited, which, coincidentally, had Flynn and his bodyguard, named Wiles, among the passenger list. Shortly after boarding, a porter handed her a note from Flynn which said, "Would you join Mr. Wiles and myself in compartment No. 12 for cocktails? I love your hat and would like to see what is under it."

Andrea clutched her purse and a copy of *Sister Carrie* and headed over to Flynn's quarters. Flynn apparently liked what was under her hat, since he then invited Andrea for dinner with Wiles and himself. After dinner, Wiles excused himself, saying that he was meeting a producer in the bar. Andrea, likewise, grabbed her purse and thanked Flynn for the evening before heading back to her cabin.

The next day, as Andrea was embracing Nat at the station, the same porter who had given her Flynn's note tapped her on the shoulder and handed her *Sister Carrie*. "You left this in Errol Flynn's compartment last night," he said. Andrea explained the incident to her husband and they both had a good laugh.

Andrea's happiness was temporarily interrupted when the United States entered World War II and Nat enlisted in the Coast Guard the day after the Japanese bombing of Pearl Harbor. Nat was stationed in New York in the Judge Advocate's department as an attorney handling court-martial cases. In 1943 Nat was notified that he was being sent overseas. He set sail from San Francisco as Andrea watched his ship leave the harbor. Although Andrea was unaware of where he was going at the time, she later learned that he was stationed at Guadalcanal.

It was Montgomery Clift who suggested to Andrea before she left for San Francisco that she should go to Hollywood and see if the Myron Selznick Agency, which was handling him at the time, could possibly help her find some work in motion pictures. Andrea followed his advice and impressed the Selznick agency enough so that they took her on as a client. She and her agent began making the studio rounds to see if any might be willing to offer her a screen test, starting at Paramount. "The casting man there was so nice," Andrea recalled. "He said, 'We have five young ladies the same age as you under contract right now.' And they did. They had Diana Lynn, Gail Russell and quite a few others. He told my agent to take me to Warner Bros."

To prepare for her test, Andrea worked with Warners acting coach Sophie Rosenstein, who had served as a sort of surrogate mother for most of the young contract players at the studio. It was Rosenstein's job to teach them all of the basics, from correct posture and speech to emoting for the camera. Like most of the Warners players, Andrea had great respect for Rosenstein, and she became a good friend to Andrea during her years at Warners. "For my test, Sophie had me pick one of three scenes. There was one called 'The Man,' which was a very emotional scene between a father and a daughter, that I really wanted to do, but Sophie said, 'No, Andrea, it's not right for you.' I picked it anyway and it went well. I also did another test, which was a scene from *The Philadelphia Story*. Warners liked both and they signed me." The first thing Jack Warner did was change her name from Georgette McKee to Georgia King, which she hated.

"It sounded like the name of a burlesque queen," Andrea joked.

The Selznick office also arranged for Andrea's lodgings during her first month in California, a small home in fashionable Brentwood. Andrea remembers her first night there, an evening that began uneventfully but which was sparked by an unexpected caller.

"The day I moved in there was an announcement about submarines being spotted off of Malibu," Andrea recalled. "At about 6:00 the doorbell rang. I opened the door and there was Gary Cooper. I almost fainted. He said, 'I'm an air raid warden and I wanted you to know that in about four minutes there's going to be an air raid test. I'm going to bring you to Frank Capra's house.' That was where we were supposed to meet in case of an air raid. The next night it was Fred MacMurray at my door, then after that it was Tyrone Power, then Cesar Romero. I thought to myself, 'Where am I living?' I was dumbfounded. I loved the whole thing."

At about 5:30 p.m. the second day she was in Brentwood, Andrea received a call from Warner Bros. She was told to report to wardrobe at 4:30 the next morning and get fitted for a nurse's uniform for a scene with Bette Davis in *Mr. Skeffington*. Andrea was elated about the prospect of appearing with Davis, an actress whom she held in high esteem. Understandably, she was also filled with tremendous anxiety.

Andrea arrived on time the following morning and was fitted for her costume. Once that was done, she headed to the set where her scene was to be shot. "I was very nervous. The whole place was like a beehive. I was only twenty-three and here I was working with one of my idols," Andrea said.

One important factor that helped ease Andrea's nerves was the congenial behavior of Davis. "Bette Davis was very nice. She asked me to join her in her trailer for a cup of tea. She understood I was new and she was very gracious."

Mr. Skeffington was a first-class Davis vehicle, with the star chewing up the scenery as shallow Fanny Skeffington, a socialite whose selfishness and vanity destroy her marriage to a kind-hearted Jewish banker (Claude Rains). In one of the film's most humorous scenes, Fanny pays a visit to a psychiatrist (George Coulouris), who quickly loses his patience with her and tells her exactly what's wrong with her. Andrea has a brief appearance as the doctor's nurse.

Despite Andrea's jitters about doing the scene, everything went beautifully. "I thank God I only had a few lines," she joked.

Vincent Sherman, who directed *Mr. Skeffington*, was quite impressed with Andrea. "Andrea King I recall as a nice-looking young actress who performed well," he said. "I never had a chance to get to know her well, but I thought she was most capable and would have a big career at Warner Bros."

Mr. Skeffington served as a good launching pad for Andrea's introduction to moviemaking. She had just enough screen time to get used to working before the camera without being overwhelmed. Thus she was far more relaxed for her next, far more substantial role in *The Very Thought of You* (1944), a bittersweet wartime romance starring Dennis Morgan and Eleanor Parker as a soldier and his girl, Janet, who want to get married. With the exception of Janet's father (Henry Travers) and a younger sister, no one in Janet's unlikable family approves of their relationship, which causes considerable conflict. Andrea had a juicy role as Janet's cold-hearted sister Molly, a war wife who goes out on the town every night while her husband is overseas.

The Very Thought of You was not only Andrea's first featured role at Warners, but it marked the first time she was billed as Andrea King. It was during filming that Andrea fought Jack Warner about getting her name changed from Georgia King. Warner next suggested adapting her middle name to Andrea, which she liked immediately. Her new name also proved to be a good luck charm. In a cast which boasted such impressive performers as Parker, Travers, Dane Clark and Beulah Bondi, it was newcomer Andrea that critics cited as the standout.

"Andrea King, whom the Warners could pass off for Ida Lupino in a pinch, gives a venomous portrait of Molly. Miss King is definitely a newcomer with a bright future," raved *The New York Times*.

Indeed, Andrea's scenes in *The Very Thought of You* gave the film some much-needed spark. Director Delmer Daves gave Andrea a great deal of guidance during the making of the film, and helped her make the unsavory Molly a wonderfully loathsome character.

Those hours when Andrea wasn't needed on the set were spent working with Rosenstein and other studio instructors, who gave Andrea lessons in fencing, dialects, ballet and film technique, among other things. "It was hard work, but we learned everything. And I loved it," recalled Andrea with affection.

Little of those lessons came in handy for Andrea's cameo in *Hollywood Canteen* (1944), Warners' flag-waving musical that boasted appearances by more than forty Hollywood stars. She then appeared in two equally patriotic documentary shorts: *Proudly We Serve* (1944), in which Sergeant Tex Gordon (Gordon Douglas) is shocked to learn that his aerial gunnery instructor is a female sergeant (Andrea); and *Navy Nurse* (1945), with Andrea in the title role.

Having been impressed with the response to Andrea's nasty turn in *The Very Thought of You*, Warners decided to take full advantage of her flair for playing scheming vixens. As such, Andrea played a femme fatale in *Hotel Berlin* (1945), a dramatization of the Vicki Baum novel. With its multiple plots and subplots, and an assortment of colorful characters, *Hotel Berlin* was obviously patterned after Baum's signature novel, *Grand Hotel*, which was transformed into the 1932 Best Picture winner. *Hotel Berlin* depicted a weary Germany on the brink of defeat as World War II nears an end. Unlike most Hollywood films at the time, several of the Germans are presented in a sympathetic manner, including a Nazi commandant (Raymond

Massey) being forced to commit suicide after a botched military objective. Other assorted hotel dwellers included Martin Richter (Helmut Dantine), a freedom fighter disguised as a hotel waiter; Tillie (Faye Emerson), the hotel's "hostess," who is willing to pay more than she should to get a pair of shoes; and Lisa Dorn (Andrea), Berlin's most celebrated actress, who is also the commandant's mistress. When Lisa discovers Martin hiding in her room, she agrees to help him, but only if he can help her flee Germany. Eventually, her deceitful ways jeopardize the lives of the commandant and Martin.

Although *Hotel Berlin* was an ensemble piece, and Faye Emerson, who had just married First Son Elliott Roosevelt, was top-billed, Andrea's performance was most definitely a star turn. She worked extra hard to hone her performance, which included studying with a German coach to affect a convincing accent The end result was an excellent portrait in evil, with Lisa depicted as a walking Venus flytrap, complete with beautifully coifed blonde hair, the nattiest finery and a velvet tongue. Andrea's flair for histrionics were especially effective during her final confrontation with Dantine after he discovers she has betrayed him to the Nazis. She was also able to display Lisa's tender side in her poignant scenes with Massey.

"I loved doing that film. It was a great part because it allowed me to do everything from A to Z," Andrea said fondly.

Andrea was also thrilled to be in the company of a distinguished group of character actors, including Alan Hale as a German sergeant, Steven Geray as the defeatist hotel clerk, Henry Daniell as a fleeing underground figure, Peter Lorre as a scientist and Helene Thimig, who was especially touching as the mother of Emerson's fiancé.

Hotel Berlin plays like a Wagnerian opera sans the arias, yet its ninety-eight minutes of melodrama move far more swiftly thanks to Peter Godfrey's brisk direction. Bosley Crowther of *The New York Times* enthused: "There's no question that Warner Brothers has got a sleek and suspenseful show." He found Andrea King "ultra-svelte" as Lisa.

The schedule for *Hotel Berlin* was a demanding one because the studio was anxious to get the picture released to coincide with the end of the war. As such, a typical day of filming lasted eighteen hours. In order to accurately depict the bustling activity in the hotel, as well as the turmoil going on in Berlin, hundreds of extras were required for many scenes. Despite the hectic pace, there was a period when Andrea found herself with two days in which she wasn't needed on the set. Since Warners never liked to have idle players on the lot, Andrea reported for a small role in *Roughly Speaking* (1945), directed by the studio's most important filmmaker, Michael Curtiz. That film, based on Louise Randall Pierson's bestselling autobiography, starred Rosalind Russell as the free-thinking Pierson, who longs for a place in the world of business. In the course of two hours she finds romance with a dull salesman (Donald Woods), raises a family of six children, divorces her husband, struggles to keep her family together and finds happiness with her second husband, a likable eccentric played with charm by Jack Carson.

Curtiz was unhappy with the actress playing one of Russell's grown daughters in the last quarter of the film, and asked for Andrea to replace her. Although Andrea's screen time was minimal and the role undemanding, she still appreciated the chance to work with Curtiz. "He was to the point, and very dramatic, but a brilliant director," she said.

Shortly after *Hotel Berlin* was released, Andrea went on her first studio tour, along with her friend and co-star Dantine. The stars were sent to New York to promote another Dantine release, *Escape in the Desert* (1945), a misguided remake of *The Petrified Forest* (1936) in which the diner patrons were held at gunpoint by Nazis, rather than gangsters. At the Strand Theater, where *Escape in the Desert* was showing, Andrea and Dantine displayed their comic gifts by appearing eight times a day in a stage show before each screening of the movie.

"I had a wonderful comedy skit with (comedian) Lew Parker," Andrea said. "We got to make fun of the love scenes in *Hotel Berlin*. The audiences loved it. That's when Helmut and I became good friends. Helmut had a great sense of humor. He was in his element on the stage."

In between shooting *Hotel Berlin* and making the tour, Andrea appeared as Dennis Morgan's wife in *God Is My Co-Pilot* (1945), a popular war drama based on Colonel Robert L. Scott, Jr.'s bestseller about his exploits in World War II. As the only female in the cast, Andrea supplied the romantic interest during the homefront scenes. Since most of the action took place in the combat zone, Andrea was able to shoot all of her scenes in one day. Despite mostly negative reviews, which dismissed the film as heavy-handed, *God Is My Co-Pilot* was Warners' biggest financial success of the year.

While *God Is My Co-Pilot* was Andrea's most notable on-screen war effort, she spent much of her free time visiting convalescing soldiers. Twice a week she organized a group of performers to go to a huge hospital in the valley and would visit paralyzed veterans. She often took time to talk with the soldiers and did her best to make them feel better.

Andrea's life as an Army wife also came to an end in 1945, just around the time *Hotel Berlin* was released. Nat returned from the service and the two picked up exactly where they had left off four years earlier. Andrea was at her most content having both her Warners family and able to finally begin establishing a home with her husband.

Not that she found her next film assignment especially rewarding. *Shadow of a Woman* (1946) reunited Andrea and Dantine in a bargain basement version of *Suspicion* (1941). The unconvincing screenplay by Whitman Chambers and C. Graham Baker found Andrea as the bride of the seemingly charming Dantine, a handsome dietician she marries after a whirlwind courtship. Shortly after their marriage she discovers that he's been divorced and has a young son who stands to claim a large inheritance. More devastating is that her husband is trying to starve the boy to death in order to take possession of the fortune. As she uncovers more hidden truths, she also places her own life in jeopardy.

Joseph Santley, best known for directing Ann Sothern B films at RKO, and Broadway musicals, failed to pack much suspense into the slight film, although Andrea and Dantine did the best they could with their roles. Andrea, in fact, was quite effective in many of her scenes and helped supply what little interest the film generated. *Variety* called it "a heavy melodrama that packs little dramatic weight."

Andrea agreed: "I was not pleased with it. It was a bad script."

Shadow of a Woman had to be even more distasteful for Andrea because it came after she lost out on two roles far more worthy of her abilities. Andrea initially won the role of the Cockney trollop whose unplanned pregnancy causes havoc for a Welsh miner with dreams of going to Oxford in *The Corn Is Green*, based on Emlyn Williams' celebrated play. The rights to the play were purchased as a vehicle for Bette Davis, who had been so helpful to Andrea in *Mr. Skeffington*. This time, however, Davis proved to be an adversary.

"I really wanted to play that part. But Bette Davis and Errol Flynn had star power, and they were the only ones at the studio who could always get what they wanted. She said I was too young and pretty, and I got removed from the film. I knew I could do it—I had played a Cockney before in *Angel Street*—but that didn't matter. That was one beautiful Academy Award nomination I never got," Andrea remarked with a tinge of bitterness.

Davis instead gave her consent when the studio auditioned Joan Lorring, a talented seventeen-year-old actress who lacked Andrea's glamour. To make matters worse for Andrea, Lorring did indeed earn a Supporting Actress Oscar nomination for her performance, losing to Anne Revere for *National Velvet*.

It was also no secret that part of the conflict stemmed from Davis' resentment when Andrea was chosen to play Lisa Dorn in *Hotel Berlin*, a part Davis had publicly campaigned for.

Soon after that incident Andrea was edged out of another dream role, again because of Davis. The studio wanted Andrea to play Mattie, the doomed heroine in Edith Wharton's classic *Ethan Frome*. "I was all set to play the ingenue. Then came word that Bette wanted to play the young girl. But the studio thought she was too old and that was that," Andrea said.

Considering that Bette was thirty-eight at the time and, because of stress related to her personal problems, looked several years older, the studio's refusal to let her play Mattie seems justified. The project was aborted, and the novel was not filmed until 1993, as an *American Playhouse* production with Patricia Arquette and Liam Neeson.

If nothing else, the one positive aspect of the situation was that the studio did at least recognize Andrea's potential. Even if *Shadow of a Woman* was a dubious effort, at least Andrea was given a lead role. All the more reason that she balked at her next assignment, an unlikely horror film entitled *The Beast with Five*

Fingers (1946), which curiously was released on Christmas Day. Robert Florey, who had directed Andrea previously in *God Is My Co-Pilot*, helmed *Beast*, a macabre tale of an Italian pianist (Victor Francen) who is mysteriously murdered. Since his death, the villagers have been afraid to go near his estate because they believe his spirit still lives on in the form of his severed hand, which is determined to seek revenge. Andrea was cast as Julie, the pianist's nurse to whom he bequeathed his estate.

After hearing the ludicrous title, Andrea had no desire at all to make this picture, but since the alternative was suspension, she reluctantly agreed. Her co-star, Robert Alda, was equally indignant about the project. Warners originally had high hopes for Alda when he was cast as George Gershwin in the composer's biopic *Rhapsody in Blue* (1945). But when neither Alda nor the film clicked, he was relegated to dismal supporting roles for the remainder of his Warners contract. The only one who didn't seem to mind being cast in *Beast* was Peter Lorre, for whom the film was reminiscent of his earlier *Mad Love* (1935). *Beast* proved to be a tour de force for Lorre, who had a scenery-chewing role as a demented astronomer in love with Julie.

The casting of Lorre turned out to be the smartest move Warners could have made. His wicked sense of humor made the film one of the most pleasurable of Andrea's Warners assignments. In particular, Lorre's animosity toward the far more sober Francen resulted in some unexpected hijinks that kept the rest of the cast entertained. "Victor Francen was a top character actor. He was very distinguished and took himself very seriously. Peter just didn't care for him, so he would purposely try to do things to upset him," Andrea remembered gleefully." We had this one huge dining room scene where there were about twelve of us sitting at the table. We were all supposed to be having dinner while Victor was talking about his will. Whenever Victor would start saying his lines, Peter would stick parsley out of his ear, or out of his nose. Well, that would break us all up. Victor would have none of this, but Peter would just say, 'Who cares?' Finally, Peter got a note from the front office to behave better to Victor. It took us two days to film that one scene."

Fortunately, Francen's character was killed off early in the film, or else *The Beast with Five Fingers* might have gone several months beyond schedule.

Critics, however, didn't seem to think the film was nearly as much fun to watch as it had been to make. "This Christmas package which was opened at the Victoria yesterday is hardly a thing of joy," carped *The New York Times*.

Time felt *Beast*, "Is for strong stomachs only…. Director Robert Florey plainly untroubled by considerations of taste, concentrated on peddling gooseflesh to cinema goers who dote on being frightened."

Seen today, *The Beast with Five Fingers* is rather tame compared to the gore of modern horror films. Lorre's wildly over-the-top performance, however, enlivened the Grand Guignol-ish proceedings, and elevated the movie from minor horror to first-rate camp. As such, it made a tidy profit for Warners and has since attained a devoted cult following. "Since then it's shown up a lot on television. Every Halloween it's playing somewhere," Andrea pointed out with pride.

Andrea followed *Beast* with one of her best performances as Ida Lupino's hard-working sister in Raoul Walsh's sudser *The Man I Love* (1946). Lupino starred as Petey, a sultry torch singer who comes to New York to visit her two sisters and soon finds herself caught up in the problems of everyone she encounters. Andrea portrayed her more stable, married sibling who struggles to raise her children while also coping with her war-weary husband, who's in the hospital for psychiatric treatment. Petey also tries to find a beau for her shy kid sister (Martha Vickers), and becomes involved in the amorous entanglements of a shady club owner (Robert Alda) having an affair with her sisters' married neighbor (Dolores Moran). Petey also has her own romantic difficulties in the form of a turbulent relationship with a brooding composer (Bruce Bennett). By the end of the film Petey manages to solve everyone's problems—except her own.

The Man I Love is the type of "woman's" picture that Warners excelled at in the 1940s, with Lupino smoldering seductively through a haze of cigarette smoke. Andrea, in the film's quieter moments, came through with a thoughtful portrait of a compassionate woman who deserved a better fate than she'd been handed. Andrea was pleased to play a normal person for a change, rather than the seductresses or women in danger she had played of late. She also had a wonderful time working with Lupino.

"Ida and I felt like sisters," Andrea said. "People often said we looked alike, which is probably why we were cast as sisters."

When filming began, Andrea was struck by the bond between Lupino and Walsh, old friends who had worked together on *They Drive by Night* (1940) and *High Sierra* (1941). Andrea was thrilled when she was taken into their inner circle. "They were like father and daughter. The two of them liked their cooking sherry and would often have a drink during shooting. I was so excited when one day I was invited into Ida's dressing room for some sherry," Andrea gleamed.

In spite of Andrea's excellent work in *The Man I Love*, Warner seemed to think that she was better suited to bitchy roles, and, as such, cast her as the woman determined to break up the romance of Alexis Smith and Ronald Reagan in the equine yarn *Stallion Road* (1947). Andrea was uninterested in another bitch role, especially one that wasn't even a lead, and went on suspension. Since she had only been at the studio eighteen months and was still not an established star, such a move was risky. Warner's wrath was piqued and Andrea was let go.

For Andrea, it was difficult to leave her many friends at Warners. "It was hard, hard work." she said. "You often worked sixteen to eighteen hours a day and worked on Saturdays. You only had Sundays off. But I couldn't wait to get to the studio. It was what I wanted all my life. We all got to know each other. If someone was giving a party, we were all invited. We all knew how to sing or dance or play piano. It really was like a family."

Andrea was fortunate to find work at other studios, and began a successful career as a freelancer. For her first project she was back to playing a dangerous woman in *Ride the Pink Horse* (1947), a brooding film noir directed by Robert Montgomery and released by Universal-International. Charles Lederer and Ben Hecht's complex screenplay takes place in the bordertown of San Pablo, Mexico, which is in the process of preparing for its annual Mexican Fiesta. A new arrival in town is Gagin (Montgomery), a tough, mysterious and laconic stranger who's out to find enigmatic crime boss Frank Hugo. Also after Hugo is an FBI agent. Meanwhile, trailing Gagin is a local peasant girl named Pila (Wanda Hendrix in her most memorable film role), who foresees danger and possibly death for the cynical stranger. Eventually we discover the real reasons behind Gagin's interest in Hugo, as well as a number of other secrets. Andrea had a showy role as Hugo's girlfriend, another in her gallery of femme fatales. Like the other characters in this film, she also has her own hidden objectives.

Of Montgomery's two attempts at directing film noir in the '40s (*Lady in the Lake*, made the previous year, is the other), *Ride the Pink Horse* is the more interesting one. Montgomery did a neat job of creating a dark and cynical atmosphere, and in bringing to life the complicated characters of the script, a motley lot enshrouded in layer upon layer of secrecy and deception.

Ride the Pink Horse is one of Andrea's favorites, even though she admits "people either liked it or they didn't understand it." She also remembered Montgomery as, "very, very hard working and a very quiet man. He never showed much emotion, but he knew what he was doing."

Apparently so, since the movie got glowing reviews. "Mr. Montgomery, as director and star, has contrived to make it look shockingly literal and keep it moving at an unrelenting pace," said *The New York Times*. Twenty-five years later, Pauline Kael described *Ride the Pink Horse* as, "One of a kind; no one in his right mind would imitate it."

The same could not be said of director David Butler and *My Wild Irish Rose* (1947), another of the many questionable musical biopics cranked out by Hollywood in the 1940s. This time the unlucky subject whose life story was distorted was Irish tenor Chauncey Olcott (Dennis Morgan). Peter Milne's free-wheeling screenplay (from a story provided by Rita Olcott) followed Chauncey's path to success in turn of the century New York, which was complicated by his affections for a beautiful colleen named Rose (the stunning Arlene Dahl in her film debut) and famed entertainer Lillian Russell (played with gusto by Andrea). Also mixed up in this mild Irish stew were Ben Blue as Olcott's best friend, George O'Brien as boxer Iron Duke Muldoon, William Frawley as singer William Scanlon and Sara Allgood as Olcott's mother.

Filmed in vibrant Technicolor, *My Wild Irish Rose* was stuffed with more than twenty Irish ditties, most of them sung pleasantly by Morgan. Andrea's musical numbers, however, were dubbed. "I had never sung professionally, so there was no question of my doing the numbers. It was just a matter of being able to breathe at the right times and singing to the music," she said.

Virginia Bruce was set to play Lillian Russell but dropped out. Physically, Andrea was a an ideal fit, and she relished the part. "My costumes were the most beautiful I'd ever seen, and the jewelry I wore was real. I had two armed guards with me at all times," she said.

My Wild Irish Rose also meant a return to Warners and the chance to again work with Dennis Morgan, whom she became friendly with during the making of *The Very Thought of You*.

Despite the fact that Warners opened *My Wild Irish Rose* during the Christmas season, the critics were not charitable. "To say that *My Wild Irish Rose* tells a story is a gross overstatement, and even in this season of benevolence, one cannot truthfully say that there is a recommendable spirit to the interminable song, dance and specialty interludes that fill out this picture," wrote *The New York Times* reviewer. He added that, "the Lillian Russell of Andrea King is garish."

Audiences didn't mind and *My Wild Irish Rose* was one of Warners' top grossers of 1948.

Having enjoyed the light touch of *My Wild Irish Rose*, Andrea was delighted to land a comedic role in the romantic fantasy *Mr. Peabody and the Mermaid* (1948) for Universal-International. Inspired by the English comedy *Miranda* (1947), *Mr. Peabody and the Mermaid* told of a New Englander (William Powell) who catches a lovely mermaid (Ann Blyth) during one of his fishing trips. The problem is that everyone believes he's crazy when he tells them what happened. Andrea had a showy role as a flirtatious actress with designs on Mr. Peabody. Once again she was playing a bitchy character, although one with more of a mischievous nature than a sadistic streak. She relished the more playful aspects of the part — in particular, an amusing scene where she was bitten by Ann Blyth underwater.

An extra perk was the chance to work with Powell, whom Andrea adored. "He was just incredible." she said. "He was very ill. He had a kidney disease and he had his male nurse by his side all the time. But he was just a delight to work with. Ann Blyth and I both adored him."

If there was one drawback to the movie, it was the cold temperatures the cast had to deal with, especially during any scenes involving water. "The water was cold." Andrea recalled. "The film was supposed to be made in August, but instead it got pushed to December. They had a huge water tank built on the back lot. It was horrendous."

The reception to *Mr. Peabody and the Mermaid* was, unfortunately, as chilly as the water. "The film swims along with gay urbanity until the novelty of the ichthyic lady has worn thin. Then, disastrously, the joke begins to dry up, leaving the mermaid flopping around in a scenario which doesn't know where to go," wrote *The New York Times*. The reviewer said that Andrea performed her role with "standard competence."

Andrea went to Paramount for the soapy *Song of Surrender* (1949), with Claude Rains and Wanda Hendrix, followed by a good turn in MGM's *Dial 1119* (1950). The nifty thriller marked the feature length directorial debut of Gerald Mayer, whose previous experience making short subjects shone through in his ability to keep the action moving at a fast clip. Andrea played one of six restaurant patrons held hostage by a demented gunman (Marshall Thompson).

"*Dial 1119* comes off with more suspense and conviction than is found in the average minor melodrama from the coast," raved *The New York Times*. "Andrea King lends competent support as a girl debating whether to try an illicit weekend with Leon Ames, an oily salesman."

Unfortunately, her other 1950 releases — *Southside 1-1000*, *Buccaneer's Girl* and *I Was a Shoplifter* — were less impressive. The last two were part of a picture deal for Universal-International, which became a frequent venue of employment for Andrea after leaving Warners. "I wasn't signed to Universal, although I did so many pictures there that they said they should have signed me since they paid me very well," Andrea said.

The Lemon Drop Kid (1951), with Bob Hope was, at least, a huge moneymaker, even though Marilyn Maxwell was the lead actress while Andrea had a supporting role. Following a routine adventure, *Mark of the Renegade* (1951), Andrea teamed up with Peter Graves for her first endeavor into science fiction, an odd concoction called *Red Planet Mars* (1952). Graves and Andrea played a married pair of scientists who believe they have made contact with Mars. They discover from the information they receive that the red planet is a Christian Utopia. The message from Mars is that Earth's people can be saved by reconnecting in worship to God. Instead of inspiring faith, the messages from Mars produce fear and revolution, as the messages spread to Russia. There's also uncertainty as to the validity of the messages, as an ex–Nazi (Marvin Miller) claims he was duping the Americans.

Red Planet Mars was imaginative, but its incredible theme of Mars as a Christian haven and its attempt to convert Earth was a difficult selling point for United Artists, which distributed the movie. "I thought it was a wonderful script and I adored Peter Graves," Andrea said. "The problem was that the studio didn't publicize it. So it didn't really go anywhere. Once it was shown on television, people began to see it and they loved it, and now it's become a cult movie."

As far as the performances, *The New York Times* noted that "Peter Graves and Andrea King are serious and competent if slightly callow in appearance as the indomitable scientists."

Andrea finished the year by appearing in the adventure yarn *The World in His Arms*, once again at Universal. The film about the exploits of a seagoing adventurer (Gregory Peck) was typical of the male-oriented fare Universal cranked out in the '50s. Andrea and leading lady Ann Blyth had little to do but look decorative.

In general, her roles in recent years had been far less interesting than the characters she played in most of her Warners movies. It probably didn't help that Andrea missed the kinship of her Warners colleagues. "As a freelance, I was like a fish out of water." she said. "You felt so protected at the studio. It was like home. You knew who you were working with. Working as a freelancer, I knew professionally what I had to do, but it was lonely."

With a lack of rewarding film roles, Andrea began accepting work on television, which at the time was still looked upon with resentment and uncertainty by many in the film community. Andrea, however, felt the fledgling medium held great promise. Her first small screen venture was opposite Charles Boyer in "The Officer and the Lady," an episode of *Four Star Theater*, in 1952.

The following year Andrea signed on for her first live television appearance in an adaptation of the Agatha Christie courtroom thriller *Witness for the Prosecution* for *Lux Video Theater*. Andrea played Romaine Vole, a cold-blooded wife whose husband is on trial for murdering a rich widow. Her distinguished co-star was Edward G. Robinson as the wily barrister defending her husband. Andrea recalled that she was extremely anxious about the live performance, but was put somewhat at ease when she discovered that the veteran Robinson was just as fearful as she was that something might go wrong.

"Eddie said, 'I'll break your leg and you break my leg.' Eddie was one of the quietest, gentlest men I knew," Andrea said. To everyone's relief, the program went off without a hitch.

After the minor suspense film *Silent Fear* (1954), Andrea took her first break from acting in 1955 with the birth of her daughter Deborah Ann. When she returned to work a year later, she found television to be conducive to her dual roles as mother and actress. "I did about 300 television shows. I never went back to the stage, however. My daughter was born and I didn't want to be away from her. The theater would have taken up too much of my time."

Andrea was lucky to find continued and varied work on television for the next two decades, landing guest spots on such popular series as *The Donna Reed Show*, *77 Sunset Strip*, *Bourbon Street Beat*, *Hawaiian Eye*, *Surfside Six*, *Family Affair* and *Dragnet*. She was also featured in numerous episodes of *Maverick*, *Perry Mason* and *Fireside Theater*, and had a small role in *Prescription Murder* (1967), the telefilm that led to the *Columbo* series with Peter Falk.

In between her television work Andrea made film appearances in *The Outlaw Queen* (1957); *Band of Angels* (1957), with Clark Gable and Yvonne De Carlo; and *Darby's Rangers* (1958), with James Garner. The last two brought

Andrea back to Warner Bros., but she wasn't waxing nostalgic. "It felt very different." she said. "Everything still looked the same, but there were all new people there, and I felt like I didn't belong. It was wonderful when I was under the studio system there, but now I just felt like a stranger."

Andrea later turned up in supporting roles in the melodrama *Daddy's Gone A-Hunting* (1969) and an oddity called *Blackenstein* (1973), an unintentionally comic horror flick that put a trendy racial spin on the legend of Frankenstein's Monster.

When Andrea wasn't working she could usually be found outdoors. Rarely a weekend would pass for Andrea without getting in a few sets of tennis. Another of her loves was swimming, and she enjoyed horseback riding as well. She also maintained a close relationship with her sister Ann, who was now happily married to professional golfer Richard Chapman.

Andrea was crushed in 1970 when her beloved husband, Nat, died after a bout with lung cancer. A few years later she was introduced by Chapman to her second husband, a Cuban golf champion. Andrea described the union as "a huge mistake," and they divorced within a year. She never married again.

These days Andrea leads a pleasant, active life in Los Angeles. Deborah Ann now lives in Connecticut with her husband Tim Callahan and her three children, Kate, Drew and Christopher, and Andrea tries to visit them several times a year.

Andrea also still enjoys acting and has remained in demand in recent years. Her last notable television appearance was in a 1990 episode of *Murder, She Wrote*. She was also a welcome presence in the 1992 comedy *The Linguine Incident*, with David Bowie and Roseanna Arquette, and supplied the film with its only enjoyable moment. Andrea's two most recent films—*The Color of Evening* (1994), with Martin Landau and Ellen Burstyn, and *Inevitable Grace* (1994), with Maxwell Caulfield and Tippi Hedren—have never been released.

Andrea spends much of her spare time writing. She has written a series of unpublished children's stories, as well as *More Than Tongue Can Tell*, a memoir of her relationship with her mother, co-authored with Paul Miles Schneider, which is awaiting publication.

For many fans, Andrea remains one of the most enduring members of the Warners' family during its golden age. Actor Rand Brooks summed up what made Andrea so appealing: "Andrea King is one of the loveliest and most unappreciated actresses in the world. Warner Brothers was an elegant studio. If you went to sit down, you'd find a chair right under you. Andrea fit in."

FILMOGRAPHY

The Ramparts We Watch (RKO Radio, 1940) Directed by Louis de Rochemont. *Cast:* John Adair, Andrea King (billed as Georgette McKee), Almira Sessions.

Mr. Skeffington (Warner Bros., 1944) Directed by Vincent Sherman. *Cast:* Bette Davis, Claude Rains, Walter Abel, Richard Waring, George Coulouris, Jerome Cowan. (Andrea was unbilled.)

The Very Thought of You (Warner Bros.,1944) Directed by Delmer Daves. *Cast:* Dennis Morgan, Eleanor Parker, Dane Clark, Faye Emerson, Beulah Bondi, William Prince, Andrea King.

Hollywood Canteen (Warner Bros., 1944) Directed by Delmer Daves. *Cast:* Joan Leslie, Robert Hutton, Janis Paige, Dane Clark, Richard Erdman. *Guest Stars:* The Andrews Sisters, Jack Benny, Joe E. Brown, Eddie Cantor, Kitty Carlisle, Jack Carson, Joan Crawford, Helmut Dantine, Bette Davis, Faye Emerson, John Garfield, Sydney Greenstreet, Alan Hale, Paul Henreid, Andrea King, Peter Lorre, Ida Lupino, Irene Manning, Joan McCracken, Dolores Moran, Dennis Morgan, Eleanor Parker, William Prince, Joyce Reynolds, Roy Rogers, Zachary Scott, Alexis Smith, Barbara Stanwyck, Craig Stevens, Jane Wyman.

Proudly We Serve (Warner Bros., 1944) Directed by Crane Wilbur. Screenplay by Crane Wilbur.

Documentary short starring Andrea and Gordon Douglas.

Navy Nurse (Warner Bros., 1944) Documentary short with Andrea as the title character.

God Is My Co-Pilot (Warner Bros., 1945) Directed by Robert Florey. *Cast:* Dennis Morgan, Raymond Massey, Andrea King, Dane Clark, Alan Hale, John Ridgeley, Stanley Ridges.

Hotel Berlin (Warner Bros., 1945) Directed by Peter Godfrey. *Cast:* Faye Emerson, Helmut Dantine, Raymond Massey, Andrea King, Peter Lorre, Henry Daniell, George Coulouris.

Roughly Speaking (Warner Bros., 1945) Directed by Michael Curtiz. *Cast:* Rosalind Russell, Jack Carson, Alan Hale, Robert Hutton, Andrea King, Jean Sullivan, Donald Woods, Ann Doran.

Shadow of a Woman (Warner Bros., 1946) Directed by Joseph Santley. *Cast:* Helmut Dantine, Andrea King, Don McGuire, Dick Erdman, William Prince, Elvira Curci.

The Beast with Five Fingers (Warner Bros., 1946) Directed by Robert Florey. *Cast:* Peter Lorre, Robert Alda, Andrea King, J. Carrol Naish, Victor Francen, Charles Dingle.

The Man I Love (Warner Bros., 1947) Directed by Raoul Walsh. *Cast:* Ida Lupino, Andrea King, Robert Alda, Bruce Bennett, Martha Vickers, Alan Hale, Dolores Moran, John Ridgeley.

Ride the Pink Horse (Universal-International, 1947) Directed by Robert Montgomery. *Cast:* Robert Montgomery, Wanda Hendrix, Andrea King, Fred Clark, Thomas Gomez, Art Smith.

My Wild Irish Rose (Warner Bros., 1947) Directed by David Butler. *Cast:* Dennis Morgan, Arlene Dahl, Andrea King, Ben Blue, George O'Brien, Sara Allgood, William Frawley.

Mr. Peabody and the Mermaid (Universal-International, 1948) Directed by Irving Pichel. *Cast:* William Powell, Ann Blyth, Irene Hervey, Andrea King, Clinton Sundberg.

Song of Surrender (Paramount, 1949) Directed by Mitchell Leisen. *Cast:* Wanda Hendrix, Claude Rains, Macdonald Carey, Andrea King, Henry Hull, Elizabeth Patterson, Art Smith.

Southside 1-1000 (Allied Artists, 1950) Directed by Boris Ingster. *Cast:* Don De Fore, Morris Ankrum, Andrea King, Barry Kelley, Charles Cane, George Tobias, Robert Osterloh.

I Was a Shoplifter (Universal-International, 1950) Directed by Charles W. Lamont. *Cast:* Mona Freeman, Scott Brady, Charles Drake, Andrea King, Nana Bryant, Tony Curtis.

Dial 1119 (MGM, 1950) Directed by Gerald Mayer. *Cast:* Marshall Thompson, Virginia Field, Andrea King, Leon Ames, Keefe Brasselle, Richard Rober, James Bell, William Conrad.

Buccaneer's Girl (Universal-International, 1950) Directed by Frederick de Cordova. *Cast:* Yvonne De Carlo, Philip Friend, Robert Douglas, Elsa Lanchester, Andrea King.

The Lemon Drop Kid (Paramount, 1951) Directed by Sidney Lanfield. *Cast:* Bob Hope, Marilyn Maxwell, Lloyd Nolan, Jane Darwell, Andrea King, Fred Clark, Jay C. Flippen.

Mark of the Renegade (Universal-International, 1951) Directed by Hugo Fregonese. *Cast:* Ricardo Montalban, Gilbert Roland, Cyd Charisse, J. Carrol Naish, Andrea King, George Tobias.

Red Planet Mars (United Artists, 1952) Directed by Harry Horner. *Cast:* Peter Graves, Andrea King, Walter Sande, Marvin Miller, Herbert Berghof, Willis B. Bouchey, Tom Keene.

The World in His Arms (Universal-International, 1952) Directed by Raoul Walsh. *Cast:* Gregory Peck, Ann Blyth, Anthony Quinn, John McIntire, Andrea King, Carl Esmond.

Silent Fear (Allied Artists, 1954) Directed by Edward L. Cahn. *Cast:* Andrea King, Peter Adams, Henry Brandon, Eduardo Alcaraz, Víctor Alcocer, Malcolm Atterbury.

Outlaw Queen (Globe Releasing, 1957) Directed by Herbert Greene. *Cast:* Andrea King, Harry James, Robert Clarke, Vince Barnett, Kenne Duncan, William Murphy, Harold Peary.

Band of Angels (Warner Bros., 1957) Directed by Raoul Walsh. *Cast:* Clark Gable, Yvonne De Carlo, Sidney Poitier, Patric Knowles, Torin Thatcher, Efrem Zimbalist, Jr., Andrea King.

Darby's Rangers (Warner Bros., 1958) Directed by William A. Wellman. *Cast:* James Garner, Jack Warden, Edd Byrnes, Torin Thatcher, Peter Brown, Murray Hamilton, Andrea King.

House of the Black Death (Medallion, 1965) Directed by Harold Daniels. *Cast:* Lon Chaney, Jr., John Carradine, Tom Drake, Dolores Faith, Andrea King, Sabrina, Jerome Thor.

Daddy's Gone A-Hunting (National General, 1969) Directed by Mark Robson. *Cast:* Carol White, Paul Burke, Scott Hylands, Mala Powers, Andrea King, Rachel Ames, Barry Cahill.

Blackenstein (Exclusive Productions, 1973) Directed by William A. Levey. *Cast:* Joe di Sue, John Hart, Roosevelt Jackson, Andrea King, James Cougar, Liz Renay, Ivory Stone.

The Linguini Incident (Rank/Solar, 1991) Directed by Richard Shepard. *Cast:* Rosanna Arquette, David Bowie, Buck Henry, Viveca Lindfors, Marlee Matlin, Andrea King.

Inevitable Grace (1994) Directed by Alex Monty Canawati. *Cast:* Maxwell Caulfield, Stephanie Knights, Jennifer Nicholson, Tippi Hedren, Samantha Eggar, Andrea King.

The Color of Evening (Christara, 1994) Directed by Stephen Stafford. *Cast:* Gretchen Becker, Kyle Chandler, Ione Skye, Bill Erwin, Martin Landau, Stuart Whitman, Andrea King.

Priscilla Lane: "Warners' Blonde Sweetheart"

Good things come in threes, and Warner Bros. was indeed fortunate in the late 1930s to have a trio of Lane Sisters—Priscilla, Rosemary and Lola—under contract at the same time. Together they made a potent attraction in films such as *Four Daughters* and *Daughters Courageous*. Separately, only Priscilla really commanded attention on the screen.

A bubbly personality, striking blonde hair and an uncanny resemblance to Ginger Rogers, to whom she was sometimes compared, proved to be the attractions that made Priscilla so popular with audiences. From her first film, she revealed a delightful flair for comedy and an appealing way with a song that helped give a lift to many of Warners' lighter screen entries. Too often, though, she was wasted in inferior films. She eventually lost interest in making movies, instead preferring to devote herself full-time to her husband and four children, and she never looked back.

Priscilla Mullican was born on June 12, 1915, in Indianola, Iowa, a small college town south of Des Moines. Pat, as she came to be called by her family and friends, was the fifth and youngest daughter of Lorenzo A. Mullican, a local dentist, and his wife, Cora Bell Hicks.

Prior to marrying Lorenzo, Cora had worked as a reporter with a local newspaper in Macy, Indiana. However, her real love was acting, and she always harbored a desire to perform on the stage. Unfortunately, her parents were strict Methodists who looked upon show business as an undignified profession.

When Lorenzo and Cora were first married they settled in Macy, which was the birthplace of their three eldest daughters, Leota, Martha and Dorothy, who were born, respectively, in 1904, 1905 and 1906. The family then moved into a sprawling twenty-two room home in Indianola in 1907. A fourth daughter, Rosemary, arrived in 1913.

Pat was always close to her sisters and recalled her childhood with delight. "It was always open house for our friends. And we used to go on wiener and marshmallow roasts. In winter, after sleigh rides, we'd have oyster stew at home," she said. "We had a big tree in our yard, and I used to climb up high in it, and tie notes and clues to branches. I'd hide clues all over the house, too. Each clue would give instructions for the next step in finding treasure—little trinkets I had buried."

For fun-loving Pat, it's no wonder that Indianola struck her as a quiet, straitlaced town back then. "It was against the law to dance anywhere in town. It was against the law to sell cigarettes there, too. And drinking—well, people didn't even talk about it," Pat recalled.

It was through Cora's influence that four of her daughters ended up pursuing show business careers. Cora saw to it that Pat and her sisters participated in cultural activities, and the girls all studied music, which included lessons in both singing and playing a musical instrument. Martha was the only one who steered away from the entertainment world and instead eloped with a college professor with whom she had one child. The couple later divorced and she went to work as a medical secretary.

Leota departed for New York in the mid-20s with theatrical ambitions. Dorothy moved in with her in 1928, as she embarked on her own stage career. After going on several auditions, they both obtained parts in *Greenwich Village Follies*, a musical revue produced by Gus Edwards. It was Edwards who changed their names to Lane; consequently, Dorothy became Lola Lane.

Pat's father was unhappy about his daughters' theatrical careers, an issue that caused much friction between Cora and him. The situation between them only worsened when Pat also announced her plans to follow in her sisters' footsteps. Pat graduated from high school in 1931 and spent that summer in New York with Leota, who was then appearing in a musical revue. Pat fell in love with New York, although many years later she admitted that New York was "a fascinating city, but because I'm not a city girl, I like leaving it."

At the time, though, Broadway was a glittering place featuring shows with the likes of Katherine Cornell, Helen Hayes and George M. Cohan. Pat was taken with the magic of the theater, and decided she wanted to take dramatic lessons. Leota agreed to pay for her tuition at the nearby Fagen School of Dramatics. Pat appeared in several of Fagen's productions, one of which was seen by Al Altman, a Hollywood talent scout. Impressed with Pat, he arranged for her to do a screen test for MGM, but it proved unsuccessful.

Meanwhile, the tension between Lorenzo and Cora became intolerable and she finally left him in 1932. Lorenzo then filed for divorce proceedings against his wife on the grounds of desertion. The divorce was granted the following year.

After leaving Indianola, Cora went to New York with Rosemary, now ready to try her luck on the stage. Cora acted as manager for Pat and Rosemary, but she had no luck landing an audition with Broadway producers. Instead, the girls got jobs as song pluggers with a music publishing company. It was there that Pat and Rosemary were discovered by bandleader Fred Waring in 1933. He heard the girls harmonizing and liked how they sounded. Their audition was a success and he offered them a contract. With Cora's approval, Pat and Rosemary, who had by now also adopted Lane as their surname, signed with Waring and boarded the bus

Pretty Priscilla Lane used to get more fan mail than any Warners actress, except for Bette Davis.

with him and his musicians, dubbed the Pennsylvanians. Cora also came along to act as her daughters' chaperone.

Pat and Waring developed an immediate rapport, which began with her first performance. Pat was understandably anxious about performing for the first time before an audience and started chewing gum to help calm her nerves prior to going on stage. When it was time for her to sing, she forgot to remove the gum and couldn't utter a note. Waring picked up on her predicament and began joking with her. Pat countered with a snappy ad lib. Waring was so taken with her spontaneity that the routine became a part of the act. As they toured, he worked in several other ad-libbed exchanges with Pat, which established her reputation as a sparkling comedienne.

Despite the hectic schedule of the band tours, not to mention the discomfort of traveling by bus and living out of a suitcase, Pat loved the excitement and unpredictability of life on the road. On one occasion the band traveled during a heavy snowstorm to reach the theater where they were scheduled to perform. When they arrived they learned that the show had been canceled because of the weather. The band then boarded the bus once again for their hotel, but on the way back stopped to help the occupants of a stranded car, who turned out to be members of a wedding party. Waring offered to take the group to the wedding via the bus. Since the band was now free for the evening, they stayed for the reception and performed for the guests.

In his spare time Waring was an inventor who had his greatest success with the Waring blender, from which he became quite wealthy. Pat, who shared Waring's love of new gadgets, supposedly helped him work out ideas for some of his inventions, said her son, Joe Howard.

When Waring and his band were signed by Warner Bros. in 1937 to appear in *Varsity Show*, a Dick Powell musical, Pat and Rosemary headed west with the rest of the Pennsylvanians. The film was a pleasant affair, with Powell as a down on his luck producer recruited by the students of Winfield College to stage their annual varsity show. The highlight was the Busby Berkeley–staged finale, which featured the choreographer's trademark overhead shots as hundreds of male and female dancers formed the insignias of various U.S. colleges and universities.

In the film, Rosemary played Powell's romantic interest, while Pat got to clown around and perform in several musical numbers. Pat's winning personality and photogenic features did not go unnoticed. Bosley Crowther of *The New York Times* remarked that *Varsity Show* "affords a long-delayed screen outlet for the Waring instrumentalists and vocalists, among whom is the attractive Priscilla Lane, a definite screen discovery."

Warners evidently was also impressed with the work of both Lane Sisters and offered both studio contracts. Pat was reluctant to accept, and instead wanted to remain with the Pennsylvanians. Rosemary eventually convinced her to give movies a try, and Warners purchased both of their contracts from Waring. Lola, a veteran of thirteen films since her screen debut in 1929, was already under contract to Warners and had just scored with a sensational performance in *Marked Woman* (1937), opposite Bette Davis and Humphrey Bogart. Pat and Rosemary settled into a rented ranch home in the San Fernando Valley, which they shared with their mother.

Pat had a bigger role in *Love, Honor and Behave* (1938), a romantic comedy about a competitive man (Wayne Morris) who discovers the meaning of sportsmanship following a series of misadventures. In the film's most amusing scene, Morris was required to give Pat a good spanking, for which she refused to have a double. "She insisted on taking that spanking in person. She's a real trouper," said Rosemary in an interview with *The New York Times*.

Warners' publicity department thought Pat and Morris made an attractive couple and suggested that they be seen together in the Hollywood night spots. The two became fond of one another and dated briefly, but it never developed into a serious romance.

Still, Warners took advantage of the relationship by pairing them up again in *Men Are Such Fools* (1938), a domestic drama which should have been better than it was considering it was directed by Busby Berkeley and had Humphrey Bogart in a supporting role. Instead, the movie was an undistinguished seventy-minute programmer that suffered from a trite screenplay. Pat played an ambitious account executive with an advertising agency who marries a hulking ex-football star (Morris) with the understanding that she can continue her career. She eventually resigns when her husband becomes jealous of the attention her boss (Bogart) is paying her, but she quickly becomes disenchanted with both life as a housewife and her unambitious husband. She returns to her job and begins a romance with her boss. Her husband then tries to establish himself in the business world to try and win her back.

A bored Crowther pulled no punches: "For the benefit of those who like to know what a picture is about, we can only say that *Men Are Such Fools* is about an hour too long."

Cowboy from Brooklyn (1938), her next venture, was somewhat better than its title indicated. In it, Dick Powell played a singing drifter who gets a job as a ranch hand and is discovered by a talent scout. Unfortunately, the plot seemed reminiscent of several recent Powell musicals, with only the western setting as a novelty. The film's chief attraction was the song "Ride, Tenderfoot, Ride," which became a staple of Warners Bros. Looney Tunes. Pat got to sing a few numbers in the film but otherwise had little to do.

Though the quality of Pat's films at Warners varied greatly, there was always one constant: a pair of brown leather shoes that she wore in every scene of every movie she made. The superstitious Pat always considered them her good luck charm. They certainly did the trick with her next film, *Four Daughters* (1938), based on *Sister Act*, a Fannie Hurst tearjerker about the romances of four musically inclined sisters. The studio envisioned *Because of a Man*, as the film was originally called, as a property for Bette Davis. When she turned it down, Lola Lane approached Jack Warner about developing it as a starring vehicle for Pat, Rosemary and herself. Warner liked the idea and even agreed to test Leota to round out the quartet. When Leota proved unsuitable, contract player Gale Page was given the assignment.

Warner also felt that casting Errol Flynn as Felix, the charming suitor whom all of the sisters find themselves falling for, would be box-office insurance. Flynn, however, wouldn't commit to the film until his part was expanded. Instead, he boarded his yacht and sailed as far away from the studio as possible. Van Heflin was next considered, but he was already committed to *The Philadelphia Story* in New York. The role finally went to dependable (if pallid) contract player Jeffrey Lynn, his first of many teamings with Pat.

Four Daughters was given all the best Warners trimmings, including the estimable Michael Curtiz as its director, a sensitive Lenore Coffee-Julius Epstein screenplay (adapted from Hurst's novel), an evocative Max Steiner score and a supporting cast consisting of Warners' most reliable character actors, including Claude Rains as the girls' father, May Robson as Grandma and Frank McHugh as one of their suitors.

Although the film was meant to be a showcase for the Lane trio, it was newcomer John Garfield as Mickey Borden, a brooding musician who believes the fates are all against him, who attracted the most attention. Garfield had approached everyone from Curtiz to producer Henry Blanke to give him the role, which was originally planned for another newcomer, Eddie Albert. Garfield stole the notices and earned a Supporting Actor Oscar nomination.

Pat, in the most dramatic of the film's female roles, was the standout among the sisters. As Ann Lemp, torn between her true feelings for the reliable Felix (Jeffrey Lynn) and her compassion for the cynical Mickey, Pat was sincere without being syrupy. She was particularly moving during her scene with Garfield as she tries to comfort him shortly before he dies.

Despite an occasional overdose of sentimentality, *Four Daughters* was one of Warners' most profitable films of 1938 and made several Ten Best lists. "One of the best pictures of anybody's career," raved Bosley Crowther of *The New York Times*. He also singled out Pat's performance: "*Four Daughters* is also a triumph for Priscilla Lane, who is much more attractive, animated and intelligent than the run of ingenues."

Equally successful was *Brother Rat* (1938), the amusing film version of the Broadway smash about three cadets at the Virginia Military Institute. Pat played Joyce, the visiting girlfriend of the mischievous "Brother Rat" (Wayne Morris), whose poorly calculated schemes always land him and his buddies (Ronald Reagan and Eddie Albert) in trouble. To give the film authenticity, Warners paid VMI $5,000 to shoot on location, and also drafted 700 cadets to work as extras.

In January 1939 Pat surprised everyone by eloping to Yuma, Arizona, with Oren Haglund, an assistant movie director. It was an impulsive decision that she soon regretted. Pat left Haglund the day after they were married and immediately filed for a divorce, though she didn't release any details regarding the breakup.

One month after her impromptu marriage, Pat was making news again with her next movie, *Yes, My Darling Daughter* (1939), a seemingly innocent yarn that stirred up a tempest of controversy. The frothy comedy was adapted by Casey Robinson from Mark Reed's Broadway hit about a free-thinker (Pat) who announces to her family that she plans to go away for a romantic weekend with her boyfriend (Jeffrey Lynn). While the premise would be considered tamer than an episode of *Friends* by today's standards, the film at the time was considered quite racy and caught plenty of fire from the New York State Board of Censors, which held up its release. "The example which this picture affords is a very dangerous one to follow," claimed Irwin Esmond, director of the State Education Department's motion picture division. "The picture teaches young people the freedom from recognized convention that would be morally disastrous if generally practiced."

The movie was further damned by the Catholic Legion of Decency, which branded it with a C rating, meaning they condemned the film for maintaining "an attitude contrary to the fundamental concepts of marriage, morality and parental authority."

Warners eventually made some edits to the movie prior to its screening for the New York Boards of Regents, which, on February, 24, 1939, approved the film now that the "weekend interlude" was subjugated to a "minor" role and was made "less attractive."

The following day, *Yes, My Darling Daughter* opened to packed houses at New York's Strand and Globe Theaters. The negative publicity turned what might have been a forgotten film into a box-office smash for Warners. Even better was that after all the hoopla the movie also garnered favorable reviews. "William Keighley's direction has paced it at a brisk farce tempo, except where the censors' blows have struck, and although the picture isn't at all naughty, it is rather nice," wrote Frank S. Nugent of *The New York Times*. "The film is most amiably played, with Priscilla Lane as the starry-eyed Ellen."

Up to that point, Pat's most successful film had been *Four Daughters* with her sisters. Warners, which had bought the rights to the 1935 play *Fly Away Home*, decided it might make a good follow-up vehicle for all three Lanes. As it turned out, nearly the entire cast of *Four Daughters* was used in the film, with the addition of Fay Bainter as the girls' mother. *Daughters Courageous* (1939), as the play was retitled for the screen, dealt with four sisters who meet the father (Claude Rains) who left their mother twenty years earlier and has now come home, as his former wife is about to be remarried. Also figuring into the proceedings is a moody drifter (John Garfield, who by now was specializing in this role) who romances Buff (Pat). Laced with more humor than *Four Daughters*, including one sweetly naughty moment when Buff's bathing suit comes undone on the beach, *Daughters Courageous* did booming business.

Warners liked the chemistry between Garfield and Pat in their films together. Her sunny manner brought a certain degree of tenderness to his brusque, mad-at-the-world disposition. As such, they were partnered once more for *Dust Be My Destiny* (1939), one of the weaker entries in Warners' series of society's losers films of the '30s.

Pat played Mabel, the stepdaughter of a drunken prison gang foreman (Stanley Ridges), who falls for Joe (Garfield), a falsely imprisoned inmate. When Joe is released, he and Mabel marry. Despite Joe's efforts to reform, he becomes implicated in the murder of Mabel's stepfather. Joe stands trial and is acquitted, paving the way for he and Mabel to begin a new life.

Neither Garfield nor Pat were particularly happy about doing *Dust Be My Destiny*, but they agreed to do it rather than take a suspension. Director Lewis Seiler did his best to give the film a realistic, gritty look. For the prison farm sequences the studio rented a nearby ranch for $125 a day. Nine cows and four horses were also rented for a daily fee of $5 per animal. Forty-five chickens were leased at 45 cents apiece each day. The studio also employed seven wranglers, at $8.25 a day, to look after the animals, and six extras who knew how to milk cows.

Despite the believable atmosphere on the set, the script veered away from the edginess of similar Warners entries, such as *I Am a Fugitive from a Chain Gang* (1932) and *The Life of Jimmy Dolan* (1933). Pat had little to do except stand by as Garfield tried to keep one step ahead of the law. She did shine in her one big scene as she offers a heartfelt plea before a jury to set Joe free.

"Although story is overlong and episodic, these deficiencies are partially overcome by excellent performances," *Variety* enthused.

By contrast, *The New York Times* labeled the film, "the latest of the Brothers' apparently interminable line of melodramas about the fate-dogged boys from the wrong side of the railroad tracks ... we detect signs in Mr. Garfield of taking even his cynicism cynically, and of weariness in Miss Lane at having to redeem Mr. Garfield all over again. It's no career for an actress."

The Roaring Twenties (1939), however, was one of the real high points of Pat's career at Warners, and the most versatile role the studio gave her. Raoul Walsh directed this tough gangster yarn about Eddie Bartlett (James Cagney), a World War I veteran who comes back home and finds that the only way he can make a decent living is as a bootlegger. He also becomes the owner of a speakeasy, whose employees include Jean (Pat), a sweet singer whom Eddie is in love with; Lloyd (Jeffrey Lynn), an honest lawyer and bookkeeper whom Jean loves; and Panama Smith (Gladys George), the speakeasy hostess wearing her heart on her sleeve for Eddie. Jean and Lloyd eventually break free and marry. When Prohibition is repealed, Eddie and Panama find themselves down on their luck. Lloyd, meanwhile, has become a district attorney out to prosecute some of the racketeers he had been involved with in his speakeasy days. When they threaten to kill him, Jean turns to Eddie for help, and he is shot in his effort to protect them.

Though *The Roaring Twenties* is more romanticized than Warners' earlier gangster epics, such as *Little Caesar* (1930) and *Public Enemy* (1931), it's still a solid indictment on the Prohibition Era. Cagney provides the film with much of its spark, and he and Pat play off each other quite nicely. Pat regarded Cagney as one of her favorite leading men, primarily because, like her, he was also a singer and dancer at heart. The bond between them brought believability to the relationship between Jean and Eddie, which was patterned loosely after that of torch singer Ruth Etting and gangster Moe "the Gimp" Snyder, a role Cagney played in *Love Me or Leave Me* (1955). As Jean, Pat was used to outstanding effect both dramatically and musically. Her renditions of the standards "It Had to Be You," "Melancholy Baby" and "I'm Just Wild About Harry" were among the film's many pleasures.

Pat was then back in more family-oriented fare with her siblings and Gale Page in *Four Wives* (1939), the first of two sequels to *Four Daughters*. In this outing, Ann Lemp (Pat) gets help from a budding psychologist (Eddie Albert) as she tries to get over the death of Mickey Borden (John Garfield seen in flashbacks from the previous film), for which she feels responsible. More heavy-handed and sluggish than *Four Daughters*, the sequel nonetheless proved popular.

After her recent string of successes, Pat had become so popular that her volume of fan mail was second only to Bette Davis. Pat was even considered for Melanie in *Gone with the Wind* but lost the part to Olivia de Havilland. She also felt that her $750 a week salary was insufficient in light of her growing stature at the studio, and demanded an increase. Warners, which had already been through a series of salary disputes with Edward G. Robinson, Cagney, Davis and a number of other contract players, was typically being tight fisted and refused Pat's demand. As punishment, the studio offered Pat *Money and the Woman* (1939), a B-grade cops and robbers flick. Pat refused to do the film and was replaced by Brenda Marshall.

She also took a suspension rather than star in *My Love Came Back* (1940), director Kurt (Curtis) Bernhardt's lively comedy about the romantic complications of a female violinist. This time she was replaced by Olivia de Havilland, whose relationship with Warners was also becoming strained. At one point Pat was also considered for Anne Shirley's role in *Saturday's Children* (1940). When that film's star, John Garfield, heard that Pat was up for the role, he remarked, "I like Pat, and she could do the role OK, but they'd probably find some way to work in all of her sisters."

Pat did finally get her raise, but in retaliation for what was considered difficult behavior, Warners began finding the worst possible scripts to assign her. *Brother Rat and a Baby* (1940) reunited the cast from *Brother Rat* in a lame effort in which the former cadets have to cope with life in the "real world."

Three Cheers for the Irish (1940) was lukewarm corned beef and cabbage, with Pat as the daughter of an Irish policeman (Thomas Mitchell) who is forced to retire. The old man really gets his Irish up when his daughter marries the Scotsman (Dennis Morgan) who takes over his old beat.

"The brogues are thick enough to cut with a knife and so is the plot," said Crowther. He added: "Miss Lane is the daughter who fixes everything as she has tended to do in her last two or three pictures, by being brought to child-bed. This time, by way of novelty, Miss Lane has twins."

The only interesting thing about Pat's next, *Ladies Must Live* (1940), was that audiences got to see her as a brunette. Otherwise, this adaptation of George M. Cohan's *The Hometowners* was lightweight entertainment.

Pat finally got to work with Curtis Bernhardt on *Million Dollar Baby* (1941), but the film was an undistinguished affair with the unoriginal theme that money doesn't necessarily buy happiness. Casey Robinson, Richard Macaulay and Jerry Wald prepared the screenplay from a story by Leonard Spigelgass; yet, for all that talent, the script lacked spark. Pat played a woman who is given a million dollars by a crotchety old biddy (May Robson). When her newfound riches end up driving away her boyfriend (Jeffrey Lynn), she tries to give away the money.

Crowther called *Million Dollar Baby* "one of the most formula-made pictures to ever come along." He was equally dour on the performance of its leading lady: "There is Priscilla Lane looking and acting as much as possible like Ginger Rogers in *Kitty Foyle*. (Notice we say 'as much as possible.')"

Even an impending lawsuit, which resulted in a settlement that smacked of the handiwork of Warners' publicity department, didn't generate much interest in the movie. When the studio decided to change the working title of *Miss Wheelwright Discovers America* to *Million Dollar Baby*, members of the Earl Carroll Vanities lodged a complaint against Warner Bros. with the Supreme Court. The showgirls had formed the "Million Dollar Baby" Club in December 1940 "with the purpose of bettering relations with prospective millionaire husbands." Club president Joy Barlow contended that she and her fellow members were "the sole and exclusive owners of the name 'Million Dollar Baby' Club," and demanded that Warners refrain from using it.

Shortly after the injunction was submitted, Pat and studio representatives met with Barlow. As a compromise, Pat asked if the studio could use the title if she became a member of the club. Barlow informed her that membership was restricted to Earl Carroll girls only. The resolution was that Pat would appear in the Vanities for one night and then become eligible to join the club. As a bonus, Pat received six dollars and forty cents, her pay for a good night's work, and a note from a customer inviting her to a late supper She declined and instead headed straight home to bed.

Pat's next assignment was the engrossing musical drama *Blues in the Night* (1941), directed by Anatole Litvak. Robert Rossen adapted Edwin Gilbert's play *Hot Nocturne* for his melodramatic screenplay about the problems that members of a jazz band encounter as they perform in one sleazy joint after another. In the midst of their musical performances they also become involved with a pair of gangsters (Howard da Silva and Lloyd Nolan) and their moll, Kay (Betty Field). Pat played Character, the band singer married to trumpeter Leo (Jack Carson), who develops feelings for Jigger (Richard Whorf), the band's leader.

Despite its often bleak depiction of life on the road, *Blues in the Night* was a mature, well-acted film that stood out from the escapist musicals of the period. Its dark, smoky atmosphere served as a forefather to later, though less effective, jazz-themed musicals like *Pete Kelly's Blues* (1955) and *Young Man with a Horn* (1950). A genuine asset was the movie's excellent collection of Johnny Mercer-Harold Arlen numbers, including the title song and "This Time the Dream's on Me."

Warners' working title for the film was *Hot Nocturne*, which was used on some of the pre-release publicity material. The studio then decided to call the movie *New Orleans Blues*, but during production, Jimmy Lunceford recorded "Blues in the Night," which became a massive hit. Anxious to capitalize on the song's popularity, Warners finally settled on the actual title. Wartime audiences were unprepared for this almost surreal film noir, which veered from the flashy, Technicolored song-and-dance confections they were used to, and the film fared poorly. Since then, it has attained cult status and is considered innovative for its time.

Pat's last film for Warners was *Arsenic and Old Lace* (1944), Frank Capra's uneven version of the stage hit about two adorable old ladies who think nothing of slipping some arsenic into the elderberry wine drunk by the old men who rent a room in their Brooklyn home. Cary Grant played their nephew Mortimer (a part assayed by Allyn Joslyn in the stage play), who is afraid to marry his fiancée (Pat) out of fear that his family is nuts. As he puts it, "Insanity runs in my family. It practically gallops!"

Capra originally planned to make the film at United Artists, but when that deal fell through he took the project to Warners, which jumped at the chance to film the black comedy. The macabre humor of the story seemed better suited to the talents of Hitchcock, as opposed to Capra, whose terrain was typically small-town Americana and films about the everyman. Capra's uneasiness with the dark elements of the story was apparent throughout. Even worse was that the film contained one of Grant's weakest performances, a hammy turn filled with enough yelps and squeals to make Robin Williams seem subdued. By contrast, Raymond Massey, in Boris Karloff's stage role as Mortimer's mentally unbalanced brother Jonathan, underplayed his part to the point of seeming somnambulant. Whatever zest the film has came from the delightful performances of the three members of the Broadway production: Josephine Hull and Jean Adair as Mortimer's aunts, and John Alexander as Cousin Teddy, who thinks he's Theodore Roosevelt.

Pat, in effect, played straight woman to the assortment of loonies, which gave her few colorful moments. Still, as the semblance of normalcy in the proceedings, her restrained performance was a welcome relief to balance out Grant's hyperactive behavior.

The film was further weakened by the Hays Office's demands that some of the original dialogue be rewritten. The play's famous tagline, "Darling, I'm a bastard!" which a gleeful Mortimer cries upon hearing that he's not related to the nutty Brewster clan, was the first thing to go. Instead, the line was changed to the far sillier, "Darling, I'm the son of a sea cook!"

Arsenic and Old Lace was completed in early 1942, but because of a stipulation by the play's producers that the film could not be released until the show had closed, the movie didn't hit theaters until 1944. Despite its flaws, wartime audiences found *Arsenic and Old Lace* to be good escapist fare and made it a tremendous success. Pat regarded it among her most enjoyable films.

By early 1942 Pat had reached an impasse with Warners. The studio was no longer providing her with interesting roles, and seemed to also be hindering her from tackling outside projects. In one instance she was invited to appear on Bing Crosby's radio program, but the studio refused to let her do the show. Things got worse that year when she became ill and was told by her doctor that she needed to rest a while to restore her health. Warners, which stipulated that she appear in a certain number of films each year, hounded her to return to work. The ensuing tension between Pat and the studio ended in a mutual agreement to terminate her contract.

She was fortunate to find herself in demand at other studios. Universal took advantage of her services and cast her in *Saboteur* (1942), a classic Alfred Hitchcock thriller that utilized one of the director's favorite themes, that of an innocent man (Robert Cummings) on the run. In this case, he's been accused of sabotaging the aircraft plant where he works and of killing his best friend in the process. His attempts to prove his innocence lead him on what Hitchcock called "a seven-reel chase" to uncover the Nazi spies behind the act of sabotage. Along the way he encounters a young woman (Pat) who at first doubts his innocence but eventually decides to help him. Borrowing from earlier Hitchcock films, most notably *The Thirty-Nine Steps* (1935) and *Foreign Correspondent* (1940), *Saboteur* was vintage Hitchcock suspense that culminated in a thrilling chase between the hero and the actual saboteur (Norman Lloyd) atop the Statue of Liberty.

Hitchcock made no secret of the fact that he did not want either Cummings or Pat in the leads. He approached Universal's front office about casting Gary Cooper and Barbara Stanwyck, both of whom were bigger box-office draws. Universal refused, much to Hitchcock's annoyance. As such, Pat remembered him as being stern and gruff throughout the entire filming. By contrast, Pat found Cummings friendly and amusing. Despite Hitchcock's behavior, *Saboteur* was one of Pat's favorites of her films, and it contains what is arguably her best screen performance.

Saboteur was completed a few months after Pat's divorce from Haglund had became final in May 1941. One month later she announced her engagement to John Barry, publisher of a weekly newspaper in Victorville, California. Since Barry was expected to be called for army training, no wedding date was set.

She surprised everyone when she broke the engagement in 1942. She instead became interested in Joseph Howard, a young Air Force lieutenant whom she met while vacationing at a dude ranch in the desert at Yucca-Loma, California. Following a brief courtship, they were married on May 22, 1942, by a justice of the peace in Las Vegas, at the home of the executive officer of an Army Air Force gunnery school. The newlyweds then settled in Victorville, although Pat traveled with her husband to various army bases, depending on his training assignment.

Pat made two films shortly after her marriage, both of which she had committed to months earlier. She appeared in her first western, *The Silver Queen* (1942), which producer Harry Sherman distributed through United Artists, as a devoted girl trying to raise money for her father, only to have it squandered by her husband on a worthless silver mine. The routine yarn resembled a Warner Bros. refugee camp, with former contract players Pat and George Brent in the leads, and director Lloyd Bacon at the helm.

She then appeared in one of her most enjoyable assignments, *The Meanest Man in the World* (1943), opposite Jack Benny at 20th Century–Fox. The frenetic farce had Benny as a kind-hearted lawyer who realizes that the only way he can become a success is by turning into an ogre. Although the movie was clearly a showcase for Benny, Pat, as his fiancée, earned her share of laughs as well. She found Benny to be just as amusing off the set and ranked him, along with Cagney, as one of her favorite co-stars.

The only ones who were not amused by *The Meanest Man in the World* were five lawyers in New Haven, Connecticut, who filed an injunction with the Superior Court to have the film barred from local screens on the grounds that it "debased, defamed and disgraced the legal profession." Superior Court Judge Patrick B. O'Sullivan admired their zeal but ruled that there was no standing "to obtain the relief they seek."

The Meanest Man in the World was the last movie Pat was to make for the next four years. Her new career as an army wife was now her top priority, and in no time at all she became popular among the citizens of Victorville. She was so beloved by the townsfolk there that she was appointed an Honorary Sheriff and even given a badge and a gun. Pat also accompanied Joe to various army bases over the next couple of years, depending on the assignment.

When the war ended, Joe, who had a degree in engineering, went to work as a building contractor. On December 31, 1945, Pat became a mother for the first time with the birth of her son Joseph Laurence Howard, whom she always called Larry. Motherhood was a new role for Pat, and as far as she was concerned, her most fulfilling one. "It's so strange," Pat said in 1948. "Babies ... you don't think about them, much. They're cute, of course. Everybody knows that. But then, after you have one of your own — you wonder what you ever did without one!"

In December 1946 the Howards settled into a beautiful, roomy house in Van Nuys, California. A selling point was the huge garden, which consisted of sixty-one different varieties of camellias. Pat did an expert job of tending to her garden, which became a source of pride for her.

Although she was content, Pat couldn't resist one last foray before the cameras. She accepted roles in two films — *Fun on a Weekend* (1947), a comedy for director Andrew Stone, and *Bodyguard* (1948), a gripping film noir at RKO opposite tough guy Lawrence Tierney.

"I didn't realize how much I had missed it until I came back," she said at the time. "I love this work, and I hope to make many, many more pictures."

As it turned out, *Bodyguard* was her screen swan song. Pat opted to spend more time with her family, which soon also included her daughter, Hannah, who was born on April 17, 1950.

A few years earlier Joe had accompanied Pat on a personal appearance tour that included a stopover in Boston. From there the couple traveled to New Hampshire where Joe showed her the lake front property he owned in Derry, New Hampshire. Pat fell in love with New England, and in 1951 the Howards moved into a custom-built home in Andover, Massachusetts.

By the early 1950s several national magazines printed stories claiming that Pat had given up show business. "That's not true. I never said it," Pat countered in a 1952 interview. "I love show business, but my first duty is to a wonderful husband and two lovely children."

Pat also had two more children — Judith, born on August 22, 1953, and James, who arrived on December 4, 1955. Her son Joe remembers Pat very much like the characters she often played on film — high-spirited and always in the mood for a good joke. One of his most vivid memories is when Pat staged a contest to see which family member could squirt the most whipped cream into someone else's mouth.

Pat also devoted much of her time to community projects, including serving as a Girl

Scout troop leader, directing school plays (as well as a production for Merrimack College in North Andover) and doing volunteer work at two local hospitals, the Parkland Medical Center and Holy Family Hospital. She was also an avid reader, with a special fondness for mysteries and westerns, and enjoyed listening to classical pieces.

In 1958 Pat starred in *The Priscilla Lane Show*, a morning television program in Boston, in which she interviewed guests and screened old movies. The program lasted just one season. She also filmed a few commercials in New York a few years later before officially retiring from show business. Although she did receive other offers for work, she turned them all down. She also continued to receive fan letters, but she only answered them selectively.

Throughout the years Pat also kept in close contact with her sisters, although she only made one return trip to California after moving to New England. Pat's father had died in 1938, and her mother passed away in January 1951 at her San Fernando Valley home.

In 1972 Pat and her husband left Andover and moved to the Howards' family farm in Derry, New Hampshire. On May 18, 1976, Pat's husband died at the age of sixty-one. He was buried with full military honors at the Arlington National Cemetery. For Pat, it was a crippling loss, one from which she never fully recovered. "I'm still trying to pull myself together," she said in a 1977 interview with *The Boston Herald American*.

One source of comfort for Pat was the close relationships she had with her children, all of whom had developed successful careers. Her son Joe became a computer Systems Engineer in the private sector and at the same time achieved the rank of lieutenant colonel in the Air Force Reserve. Hannah became a commercial artist, Judith became a doctor of family medicine and James started his own heavy construction business.

Pat continued to lead a busy, active life for many more years. In 1994 she was told that she had lung cancer. A strong-willed Pat refused radiation or chemotherapy treatments and instead chose to go on with her life as usual until February 1995. She then moved in with her son Joe and his family in Andover, but by the next month her cancer had advanced and she required hospitalization. Later that month she was discharged from the hospital and sent to the Wingate Nursing Home in Andover. She died one week later, on April 4, from cancer and chronic heart failure. She was buried at Arlington National Cemetery in Virginia next to her husband.

Even though Pat died six years ago, she still has not been forgotten. Her son Joe still receives about four to six letters each year from fans who have vivid memories of her performances. To Pat, though, her real legacy was her four children and six grandchildren she left behind. Joe's daughter, Jennifer, is the only one to follow in her grandmother's footsteps by entering the entertainment field. She is currently a modern dancer with Lucinda Childs in New York. Ironically, Pat had once said that her secret desire was to be "the greatest dancer in the world, dancing especially to symphonic accompaniment."

Pat's warmth and playful nature come through in each of her roles, and it's something that film buffs can still appreciate today. Her son Joe, more than anyone, understood the secret of her continued popularity: "Her greatest qualities as an actress and as a person were her great sense of humor and her ability to not take herself too seriously."

FILMOGRAPHY

Varsity Show (Warner Bros., 1937) Directed by William Keighley. *Cast:* Dick Powell, Rosemary Lane, Priscilla Lane, Fred Waring and His Pennsylvanians, Ted Healy, Walter Catlett.
Love Honor and Behave (Warner Bros., 1938) Directed by Stanley Logan. *Cast:* Wayne Morris, Priscilla Lane, John Litel, Thomas Mitchell, Barbara O'Neil, Mona Barrie, Dick Foran.
Men Are Such Fools (Warner Bros., 1938) Directed by Busby Berkeley. *Cast:* Wayne Morris,

Priscilla Lane, Humphrey Bogart, Hugh Herbert, Johnny Davis, Penny Singleton, Mona Barrie.

Cowboy from Brooklyn (Warner Bros., 1938) Directed by Lloyd Bacon. *Cast:* Dick Powell, Pat O'Brien, Priscilla Lane, Dick Foran, Ann Sheridan, Johnny Davis, Ronald Reagan, Emma Dunn.

Four Daughters (Warner Bros., 1938) Directed by Michael Curtiz. *Cast:* Priscilla Lane, Lola Lane, Rosemary Lane, Gale Page, Claude Rains, Jeffrey Lynn, John Garfield, May Robson.

Brother Rat (Warner Bros., 1938) Directed by William Keighley. *Cast:* Priscilla Lane, Wayne Morris, Johnny Davis, Jane Bryan, Eddie Albert, Henry O'Neill, Ronald Reagan, Jane Wyman.

Swingtime in the Movies (Warner Bros., 1938) Short subject directed by Crane Wilbur. *Cast:* Fritz Feld, Katherine Kane, John Carroll, Charlie Foy, Jerry Colonna, Helen Lynd, Irene Franklin, John Harron, Eddie Kane and Faye McKenzie. Guest appearances by George Brent, Marie Wilson, Pat O'Brien, Humphrey Bogart, Leo Gorcey, Priscilla Lane, Rosemary Lane, John Garfield, Huntz Hall, Gabriel Dell and Bobby Jordan.

Yes, My Darling Daughter (Warner Bros., 1939) Directed by William Keighley. *Cast:* Priscilla Lane, Jeffrey Lynn, Roland Young, Fay Bainter, May Robson, Genevieve Tobin, Ian Hunter.

Daughters Courageous (Warner Bros., 1939) Directed by Michael Curtiz. *Cast:* Priscilla Lane, Lola Lane, Rosemary Lane, Gale Page, John Garfield, Claude Rains, Jeffrey Lynn, Fay Bainter.

Dust Be My Destiny (Warner Bros., 1939) Directed by Lewis Seiler. *Cast:* John Garfield, Priscilla Lane, Alan Hale, Frank McHugh, Billy Halop, Bobby Jordan, Charley Grapewin.

The Roaring Twenties (Warner Bros., 1939) Directed by Raoul Walsh. *Cast:* James Cagney, Priscilla Lane, Humphrey Bogart, Gladys George, Jeffrey Lynn, Frank McHugh.

Four Wives (Warner Bros., 1939) Directed by Michael Curtiz. *Cast:* Priscilla Lane, Rosemary Lane, Lola Lane, Gale Page, Claude Rains, Jeffrey Lynn, Eddie Albert, May Robson, Dick Foran.

Brother Rat and a Baby (Warner Bros., 1940) Directed by Ray Enright. *Cast:* Priscilla Lane, Wayne Morris, Jane Bryan, Ronald Reagan, Jane Wyman, Eddie Albert, Peter B. Good.

Three Cheers for the Irish (Warner Bros., 1940) Directed by Lloyd Bacon. *Cast:* Priscilla Lane, Dennis Morgan, Thomas Mitchell, Alan Hale, Virginia Grey, Irene Hervey, Frank Jenks.

Four Mothers (Warner Bros., 1941) Directed by William Keighley. *Cast:* Priscilla Lane, Rosemary Lane, Lola Lane, Gale Page, Claude Rains, Jeffrey Lynn, Eddie Albert, May Robson.

Million Dollar Baby (Warner Bros., 1941). Directed by Curtis Bernhardt. *Cast:* Jeffrey Lynn, Ronald Reagan, May Robson, Lee Patrick, Helen Westley, George Barbier, Nan Wynn.

Blues in the Night (Warner Bros., 1941) Directed by Anatole Litvak. *Cast:* Priscilla Lane, Richard Whorf, Betty Field, Lloyd Nolan, Jack Carson, Elia Kazan, Wallace Ford, Peter Whitney.

Saboteur (Universal, 1942) Directed by Alfred Hitchcock. *Cast:* Priscilla Lane, Robert Cummings, Otto Kruger, Alma Kruger, Alan Baxter, Pedro de Cordoba, Vaughan Glaser.

The Silver Queen (United Artists, 1942) Directed by Lloyd Bacon. *Cast:* George Brent, Priscilla Lane, Bruce Cabot, Lynne Overman, Eugene Pallette, Janet Beecher, Guinn Williams.

The Meanest Man in the World (20th Century–Fox, 1943) Directed by Sidney Lanfield. *Cast:* Jack Benny, Priscilla Lane, Eddie "Rochester" Anderson, Edmund Gwenn, Anne Revere.

Arsenic and Old Lace (Warner Bros., 1944) Directed by Frank Capra. *Cast:* Cary Grant, Priscilla Lane, Raymond Massey, Josephine Hull, Jean Adair, Jack Carson, Peter Lorre.

Fun on a Weekend (United Artists, 1947) Directed by Andrew Stone. *Cast:* Eddie Bracken, Priscilla Lane, Tom Conway, Allen Jenkins, Arthur Treacher, Clarence Kolb, Alma Kruger.

Bodyguard (RKO-Radio, 1948) Directed by Richard O. Fleischer. *Cast:* Lawrence Tierney, Priscilla Lane, Philip Reed, June Clayworth, Elisabeth Risdon, Steve Brodie.

Joan Leslie: "The Girl Next Door"

Half a century ago every studio had at least one actress under contract who personified the wholesome, all-American girl next door, whether it was June Allyson at MGM, Jeanne Crain at Fox or Anne Shirley at RKO. Joan Leslie was Warners' ingenue in residence, a pretty and perky actress with a pleasant demeanor who photographed well, could sing and dance when called for, and could emote effectively against the likes of Ida Lupino and Humphrey Bogart.

As far as Jack Warner was concerned, he expected Joan's private life to be just as sweet and squeaky clean as her screen persona. He personally nurtured and guided her during her beginnings at the studio, much in the way of an overprotective — or, some might say, overbearing — father. And then when she had the nerve to defy him, he, in effect, grounded her — by making sure that no other studio would hire her. Joan ultimately got the last laugh by leaving show business in the 1950s and enjoying a successful marriage.

Joan Agnes Theresa Brodel was born in Detroit, Michigan, on January 26, 1925, the youngest of John and Agnes Brodel's three daughters. Agnes was a pianist and therefore encouraged Joan and her sisters, Mary and Betty, to pursue musical activities. Mary, who was six years older than Joan, learned the saxophone, while Betty, who was three years Joan's senior, took up the banjo. The two older girls also took up dancing to become more poised. As children, they sang and danced at local socials and events, accompanied by their mother on the piano. Joan made her debut at age two and a half when she toddled out onto a Detroit theater stage and sang "Let a Smile Be Your Umbrella." From then on, the sister act became a threesome. Within a few years, Joan likewise was given an instrument to study — the accordion.

When Joan's father lost his banking job during the Depression, the girls began to accept vaudeville bookings to help with the family finances. Joan and her siblings, billed as "The Three Brodels," hit the road and appeared in stage shows throughout Canada and the east coast. Mary and Betty would open the act, performing à la the Boswell Sisters. But it was nine-year-old Joan who proved to be the standout, with her impersonations of such popular film stars as Katharine Hepburn, Greta Garbo, ZaSu Pitts, Luise Rainer and even Jimmy Durante.

For a while the girls worked with a southern unit of a kiddie show, traveling by car and living in small hotels. In addition to the family members, Joan, always an animal lover, had two dogs who accompanied her.

"We were a very unorthodox group," Joan said. "We weren't a family with any theatrical tradition. To the contrary, we were just a close clan that sang and danced together for sheer enjoyment, and we were thrilled when someone paid us to perform. It was a crazy quilt kind of childhood, but thank goodness my parents were along to help keep us on an even keel."

One problem the family ran into was trying to adhere to the child labor laws. Technically,

Fresh-faced Joan Leslie longed for the glamour treatment, but Warners wouldn't think of it.

minors were not supposed to be performing in theaters. As a cover, ten-year-old Joan passed herself off as sixteen, and Mary, then fourteen, pretended to be twenty-one. The girls' education was spotty, and they only received lessons from an assigned tutor when the family stayed in any major city for a long stretch, such as Montreal, Detroit and New York.

At one point their finances were so low that the girls didn't have the two dollars they needed to pay for their dancing lesson. As security, Mary pawned her saxophone and Betty did the same with her banjo. "[The pawn broker] skipped town with them. We never let on to papa, but we used to get off by ourselves and cheer about it," Mary said in a 1941 *Collier's* interview.

The Brodels were playing at the Stanley Theater in Pittsburgh in 1936, and by then were feeling more than a little anxious to break out of the small-town circuit they had been playing. A family conference took place and it was decided that the girls should head to New York if they ever planned to get anywhere in show business.

When they arrived in New York the resourceful Mary approached the manager of the Paradise Club about booking the act into the new show he was preparing. Although the manager was reluctant about speaking with them because Joan was a minor, he auditioned the act anyway and liked what he saw. He was still worried that the Gerry Society, which enforced child labor laws, might find out about Joan and cause trouble.

"We'll go as long as we can and run when they get hot," Mary argued. It only took four weeks for the Gerry people to catch up with them. Finished at the Paradise, the Brodel sisters then got booked into the Park Central Hotel; this time it was two weeks before the Gerry Society found them, but luckily the girls were tipped off about their visit. On the night they showed up, Joan was pulled out of the act and Mary took over her spot. The ruse worked and the girls played at the hotel for eight weeks.

It was during the Brodels' next stint, at Ben Marden's Riviera, that Joan was discovered by MGM talent scout Al Altman, who offered her a screen test. Joan's test featured a script written by her mother, and co-starred her dog. MGM signed her at $200 a week and gave her a bit in *Camille* (1936) as Robert Taylor's sister, Marie Jeanette. Joan originally had two lines, which were cut. All that's left of her scene is a quick kiss on the forehead from Lionel Barrymore. Not knowing what else to do with her, MGM dropped Joan after six weeks.

A despondent Joan rejoined her sisters back east but returned to Hollywood shortly afterwards with her mother when Mary was signed by Universal. Mary told the bosses at her studio that they should take a look at her little sister. Universal wasn't interested, but other studios were, and Joan got bit parts in Paramount's *Men with Wings* (1938), Warner Bros.' *Nancy Drew, Reporter* (1938), RKO's *Love Affair* (1939) and Walter Wanger's *Winter Carnival* (1939).

Joan's first screen role of any significance was in a charming B at RKO called *Two Thoroughbreds* (1939), which starred Jimmy Lydon as an orphan trying to raise a stray colt against his greedy uncle's objections. Joan was cast as

Lydon's sweetheart, the first of many such wholesome roles she'd play over the next seven years. Shot on location by director Jack Hively in Malibu Lake, California, the film was gorgeous to look at. Hively, a former film cutter, elicited sensitive performances from his two human stars, as well as his equine players, all of which made *Two Thoroughbreds* a modest financial success.

Lydon has fond memories of Joan. "She was a real redhead and cute as a button," he said. "We spent twenty-one days together making that movie. Jack Hively was very easy with actors, so we had a good time. Joan, even then, was very professional. She arrived promptly with her mom on the set every day. Her sister was also in it as an extra, and they were all very sweet."

Despite the success of *Two Thoroughbreds*, the picture proved to be a one-shot deal with RKO and she was back to scouring the other studios for work. Joan next tried her luck at 20th Century–Fox, where she was put in *High School* (1940) with Jane Withers. Joan's role was a small one, but she attracted attention, especially since she had to wear glasses.

Withers found her delightful, both in the film and off the set, and they began a friendship that has lasted more than sixty years. Joan was a frequent visitor to Withers' home, which became known as Withers USO, a sort of junior Hollywood Canteen where GIs would gather on Sundays for barbecues, swimming, badminton and dancing with young stars from the various studios.

"I liked Joan right away," Withers said. "She had a great personality, and was beautiful both on the inside and outside. She and Ann Blyth and I still get together for lunch at least once a month and just have a great time together."

Joan stayed at Fox for small roles in *Young as You Feel* (1940) and *Star Dust* (1940) before she was dropped. Bits in *Military Academy* (1940), *Foreign Correspondent* (1940) for Alfred Hitchcock and *Laddie* (1940) at RKO followed, but she caused little stir in those.

Although Joan did not do a lot of dating during this period, there were occasions when she did attend special functions with a beau, such as Hollywood newcomer Rand Brooks, who had appeared with Joan in *Laddie*. "I took her out on her first date," said Brooks. "I asked if she would go to a sneak preview of the picture. We had a good time. We didn't go out again, but I have pleasant memories of her. She was very pretty and sweet and we laughed a lot."

In 1940 Joan's career took an upswing. Warner Bros. executives had been struck by Joan's small appearance as one of Bonita Granville's classmates in *Nancy Drew, Reporter* and offered her a screen test. For the test, Joan not only performed two dramatic scenes, but she sang, danced and did some of her impersonations. Warners' head acting coach, Sophie Rosenstein, took great care directing Joan's screen test, which took an entire workday to film.

Impressed by her abilities, Warners signed her to a contract. The first order of business was to change her last name to Brooks because Joan Brodel sounded too much like Joan Blondell. For whatever reasons, the studio soon after changed Joan Brooks to Joan Leslie.

The studio obviously had high expectations for Joan, since within two weeks of signing her contract she was tested for the second female lead in *High Sierra* (1941), a prestigious production with a top-flight director, Raoul Walsh. The movie would not only serve as a launching pad for Joan, but also to gauge the star power of Humphrey Bogart and Ida Lupino, both of whom had finally graduated to leads after years of supporting roles in 'B' films. Joan was fortunate to have Walsh direct her screen test and also to get Bogart to feed her the lines.

Bogart played tough ex-con Roy Earle, an aging gangster anxious to pull one last robbery, from which he expects to make enough money to retire. Joan played Velma, a lame girl whom Roy becomes smitten with. Although Velma does not have the same feelings for him, Roy hopes that by paying for her corrective surgery she will marry him out of gratitude. Instead, she bitterly rejects him and takes up with someone else. The dejected Roy finds comfort with Marie (Lupino), a moll who is devoted to him.

High Sierra gave a significant career boost to all three of its stars. Bogart established himself as Warners' premier tough guy, while Lupino became the heir apparent to Bette Davis' throne. Joan also acquitted herself quite nicely, and was especially touching in the scene when Roy asks Velma to marry him. More surprising was the venomous streak she displayed in her final screen moment when she tells Roy that she never cared for him at all. "A newcomer named Joan Leslie handles a lesser role effectively," said Bosley Crowther of *The New York Times*.

Joan's next appearance was in a rarely seen short subject called *Alice in Movieland* (1941), produced by Jack Warner, Jr., and directed by Jean Negulesco. Joan played a starry-eyed miss on her way to Hollywood and, she hopes, a career in movies. After arriving in Hollywood she gets a menial job and is immediately discovered by a talent scout, which leads to a screen test and a bit part. When an assistant director berates her, she gives him a solid tongue lashing, which the director sees as the emotional fire of a great actress. She then gets a starring role and wins an Academy Award before waking up from her dream. Joan remembered it as a delightful story that she had fun performing.

Impressed with the box-office take on *High Sierra* and the positive reaction to his new female star, studio head Jack Warner took a special interest in Joan. As part of his nurturing process, Warner gave Joan a strict set of guidelines that he felt befit her refined image. Prior to leaving for New York on a publicity tour, Warner advised her, "I don't want to see you smoking or drinking." When Joan told him she did neither one, he snapped back, "Well, see that you don't."

Warner also saw to it that Joan went to the best parties, but only with men who wouldn't sully her image. At a lavish studio party honoring visiting Army dignitaries, she was accidentally put next to Hollywood's leading womanizer, Errol Flynn. "How do you do, Joan?" he asked. "I'm afraid we never met." In the room, which was brimming with photographers, it was only a matter of time before someone took notice of Joan's encounter with Flynn.

"Cameras went off and flashed pictures of us smiling at each other in a most cordial, but rather formal way," Joan recalled. "And in no time at all, a publicity man, of which there were an enormous number at that time, came in and separated us, and pulled Flynn off one way and pulled me off another way as if I was urgently needed to take a picture with some important person. Then I heard that the pictures were killed."

Joan's off-camera hours were just as taxing as the time she spent filming. California law necessitated that sixteen-year-old Joan attend school for three hours each day. The rest of her time was devoted to costume fittings, rehearsals, diction and ballet lessons, color tests, dialogue tests, and posing for publicity stills.

Joan's hard work paid off with her first leading lady role in *The Great Mr. Nobody* (1941), an amusing B co-starring Eddie Albert as an accident-prone reporter. Joan played his girlfriend, and there was no denying they made a cute couple.

Warners thought they worked so well together that they were paired up two more times, in *The Wagons Roll at Night* (1941) and *Thieves Fall Out* (1941). The former was a remake of *Kid Galahad* (1937), with the locale shifted from the boxing ring to a circus ring. Albert played a wide-eyed innocent who becomes a successful lion tamer for a tough circus owner (Humphrey Bogart). Problems begin for the tamer when he falls for his boss' young sister (Joan). While not as powerful as the original, *The Wagons Roll at Night* has its share of exciting moments, particularly two chilling scenes in which Albert comes close to being mauled by one of the vicious cats.

The Wagons Roll at Night also is interesting for its subliminal incestuous themes that seem to be evident in Bogart's character. His jealousy over the relationship between his sister and the lion tamer smacks more of the spurned lover than the protective older sibling.

Thieves Fall Out was pretty lightweight stuff, with Jane Darwell as a feisty old biddy who outwits a gangster to protect her shy grandson (Albert). Granny also works her magic on getting Joan and Albert locked in each other's arms for a happy, if predictable, ending.

Then Warner finally saw to it that Joan appeared in a production of the level of *High Sierra*. She was chosen to appear opposite Gary Cooper in *Sergeant York* (1941), director Howard Hawks' stirring biography of World War I hero Alvin York. The movie, in which York served as technical advisor, began with a look at his early years as a Tennessee farm boy before moving on to his military service career. Joan played Gracie, the backwoods girl he romances and later marries.

According to Joan, the original depiction of Gracie, as penned by screenwriters Abem

Finkel, Harry Chandler, Howard Koch and John Huston, was hardly the typical Joan Leslie type of role. Their original script was penned with Hawks' original choice, Jane Russell, in mind, and depicted Gracie as something of a sexpot. When the York family refused to give permission to film unless the character was made more wholesome, the script was revised and Joan got the part.

During filming of the picture, Joan met Mrs. York, whom she remembered as the antithesis of the glamour girl Warners originally envisioned. "She was the kind of person who after she got her hair fixed to go out had a hairnet over it all, right down almost to her eyebrows," she said. "And she just didn't say anything more than 'How do?' to me."

For Joan, the greatest thrill was the chance to work with Cooper, an actor she had long admired. She had only one concern: how to address him. "I couldn't possibly call a co-star 'Mr. Cooper,' even though he was entitled to that, and I wouldn't dare call him 'Gary.' The first time he met me, he said, 'Well now, here she is, here's Gracie.' And I said, 'How do you do, Alvin?' and that was it. I called him Alvin at all times."

Cooper's easygoing manner and helpful attitude made for a pleasant working relationship with Joan. On several occasions when Joan asked Cooper if he wouldn't mind redoing a scene with her, he graciously replied, "Sure, Gracie."

Joan also had great respect for Hawks, whom she said was a master at directing gestures and getting actors to use their bodies to convey attitude. She also appreciated his leisurely approach to filming, which included ample rehearsal time. "He would not be rushed by anybody. If he came in and started to rehearse at nine, and didn't make a take until 11:30, no one said a word to him about that," Joan said.

Warners had no reason to complain — *Sergeant York* ended up being the top-grossing film of 1941, and Cooper's sincere performance earned him a Best Actor Oscar. Although Joan was not entirely successful at affecting a southern accent (Crowther said she played a mountain beauty "with little more than a bright smile, a phony accent and a tight dress"), she had a friendly demeanor that charmed audiences.

Also successful was *The Male Animal* (1942), the film version of James Thurber's topical stage comedy that used football and campus politics to parody government. Joan played Olivia de Havilland's kid sister whose biggest concern is keeping a hulking quarterback (Don DeFore) away from the campus vamp, nicknamed "Hot Garters." Whatever appeal the film had on stage got lost on-screen, although it was buoyed by the lively performances of Henry Fonda as an idealistic professor, Jack Carson as his former rival for his wife's affections and Eugene Pallette as the tyrannical college president. Joan's role was small and undemanding.

It was around this time that Joan asked for some time off to take a vacation with her family in New York. She hoped to catch up with old friends, do some shopping and just relax after her first exciting, but exhausting, year at Warners. The studio agreed, but once she was East, she discovered Warners had created its own itinerary for her. "They booked us into a nice hotel, but as soon as I got there they saw to it that I had interviews, and I got tickets for plays I otherwise never would have gone to see, and every moment was booked," Joan said. "I didn't have the wardrobe I wanted to have. I thought it would be a little time for myself. It was an exciting, glamorous, wonderful world, but there were limitations on your freedom that were hurtful at times. You had no say about that unless you wanted to be difficult, which was not in my nature. I went along with them, but I didn't feel good about it."

Joan felt better about being cast as Mrs. George M. Cohan in *Yankee Doodle Dandy* (1942). Warners' flag-waving musical, based on the life of the famous showman, was more to her liking. As Mary Cohan, Joan was required to age roughly thirty years over the course of one hundred and twenty-six minutes. Perc Westmore did an excellent job of applying Joan with the appropriate makeup and attractive wigs to make her look convincingly middle-aged.

Yankee Doodle Dandy was essentially the typical Hollywood musical biography of the '40s — that is, short on facts and long on elaborate musical numbers. The difference in this case was James Cagney's exuberant performance, the high point of his career. The movie opened with Cohan meeting with President Franklin D. Roosevelt, a device that opened the door for a flashback tour of Cohan's life, which covered his birth on July 4, 1878 (actually July 3), his childhood in the limelight, his romance and marriage to Mary, his success on Broadway, and his retirement and triumphant comeback.

The movie was Warners' first attempt to do a big-budget musical since its Busby Berkeley extravaganzas of the early to mid–1930s. Director Michael Curtiz, who was more at home directing Errol Flynn costume epics (*The Adventures of Robin Hood*) or gritty social dramas (*Angels with Dirty Faces*), tackled the musical numbers with style, and was greatly abetted by his leading man, as well as Walter Huston and Rosemary De Camp as Cohan's parents, and Jeanne Cagney as his sister, Josie. Joan was nicely spotlighted in several numbers, including "She's the Warmest Baby in the Bunch" and "Mary."

With its patriotic heart in the right time and place, *Yankee Doodle Dandy* was the wow Warner expected, grossing a whopping $4.8 million and earning an Academy Award for Cagney. Though *Yankee Doodle Dandy* was unquestionably Cagney's movie, it also did wonders for Joan's career. Crowther raved that Joan was "excellent as Mrs. George M. Cohan."

Joan has always expressed special affection for *Yankee Doodle Dandy* and considers it the real turning point in her career. "I was just a kid, taking things as they came, the good roles, the bad ones," Joan told *The New York Times* in 1944. "It was all new and a lot of fun. But in *Yankee Doodle Dandy*, the idea of the whole thing began opening up. I realized that, or was starting to realize, where it was I wanted to go and how hard it was going to be to get there."

Throughout filming of *Yankee Doodle Dandy* Joan received plenty of publicity, which included being the victim of one shabby, craftily engineered stunt. On her seventeenth birthday, Warner invited a slew of publicists and photographers to the set as he presented Joan with her gifts—a watch and a brand new automobile, which he had wheeled onto the lot. As flash bulbs went off and all the onlookers applauded, Warner handed Joan the keys and told her, "Enjoy it." As soon as everyone left, Warner took the keys away from her and had the car removed. It was the last Joan ever saw of her "present."

Publicists generally found Joan to be unusual among the crop of starlets and glamour girls that populated Hollywood at the time. For one thing, Joan was probably the only leading lady in Hollywood who still wore braces on her teeth. "Of course, I take them out when I'm working, but at all other times, here they are!" she said in a 1942 interview. "They're necessary, of course—the cameramen have to shoot around one side of my mouth on account of how this side has a very long tooth and a little baby tooth right next to it, showing, which looks very funny—and I can't expect cameramen to be crouching on all fours, shooting up at one side of my mouth forever!"

Joan still lived with her parents and her sisters in their Toluca Lake home, and as such seemed uncorrupted by the many temptations of Hollywood. Her off hours were spent palling around with Jeanne Cagney, whom she met on the set of *Yankee Doodle Dandy*, and Jane Withers. "We didn't work on Saturdays. There was a regular group of us, Ann (Blyth), Diana Lynn and Joan, who would get together and go to the movies," Withers recalled. "Since I had a convertible, I would drive everyone. We'd get some fast food and take it with us to the theater. We'd usually call the manager ahead of time to let him know we were coming. The balconies would be closed for other people, and when we would get there, they'd open it up for us and we could eat by ourselves. It was just a lot of fun."

In keeping with her wholesome image, Joan was not prone to hitting the night spots frequently or wearing a lot of makeup. Onscreen, though, she yearned for the glamour girl treatment her contemporaries, like Alexis Smith and Faye Emerson, were receiving. "Other ladies who had starring roles such as I did would come in at seven and have makeup and hair done carefully, and report to the set at nine. They couldn't do that with me because I was allowed to be on the lot only a certain number of hours," Joan explained. "So the two hours [for makeup] was shrunk to one hour, one hour had to be for lunch, or sometimes for rest, three hours for school, and I had to be off the lot by five or six, depending on when I came in. So I never had a glamour makeup. I never had false eyelashes. I laugh about it now, but at the time it meant a lot to me."

A certain amount of glamour did creep into Joan's characterization of Katie Blaine in

The Hard Way (1943), a juicy saga about the backbiting world of Broadway and sibling rivalry. Joan played a thinly veiled version of Ginger Rogers, who gets pushed by her older sister, Helen (Ida Lupino), into a career on Broadway. The manipulative Helen destroys Katie's marriage to a broken-down vaudevillian (Jack Carson) who eventually commits suicide. His death has a profound effect on the wholesome Katie, who then becomes a party girl dating a different man every night and nursing a hangover each morning. Helping her to piece her life back together is Paul (Dennis Morgan), her husband's former vaudeville partner. Helen tries to tear this relationship apart as well, because she's also in love with Paul.

Joan admitted *The Hard Way* was a tough film to make because she was constantly being handed new dialogue. At the core of the problem was Lupino's dissatisfaction with playing such an unsympathetic role. In a bid to soften her character she became demanding about changes to the script. She and director Vincent Sherman would then get into serious discussion, which usually prompted him to say, "Joan, you'd better go put in some school time."

When Joan would return from her lessons, she'd find several revised pages of the script. She had to learn the new dialogue quickly before heading to the set, which put her at a disadvantage. On the plus side, Joan admitted they were always changes for the better.

Unlike the virginal heroines she had previously played up to now, Katie called for a certain amount of worldliness. Sherman was uncertain whether Joan would be able to meet the challenge. "I felt she would be perfect in the early part of our story, when she was supposed to be sweet and innocent, but I questioned whether she would be able to convey the corruption and degradation called for in the latter part," he said. "She was too young and her life experience was limited. When I presented the problem to [Hal] Wallis, he dismissed me by saying it was up to me to get this quality out of her. Joan is a grand person and was a pleasure to work with. When I stop to think and realize that she did *The Hard Way* when she was only eighteen, I am amazed at how successful she was in the role. I tried to give her as much physical activity as possible in the latter part to add to her corruption."

The usually tough Crowther said, "Joan Leslie is just as deft and versatile as the character she is supposed to be."

Time, likewise, noted, "Joan Leslie romps attractively through a difficult part."

Having proved herself as the heroine in one patriotic musical (*Yankee Doodle Dandy*), Joan was tossed into another Michael Curtiz-directed wartime extravaganza, *This Is the Army* (1943), based on Irving Berlin's stage show. Unlike the stage version, which essentially was a pastiche of patriotic songs written by Berlin, the film included a storyline about a World War I veteran (George Murphy) and his son (Ronald Reagan), a soldier in the Second World War. Joan supplied the modern-day love interest for Reagan. In addition to the principals, who volunteered their services, the cast included the three hundred and fifty enlisted men from the show, who appeared in the film for their regular soldier's pay.

Filmed in vibrant Technicolor and featuring Kate Smith doing the definitive version of "God Bless America," as well as Berlin's endearingly awful rendition of "Oh How I Hate to Get Up in the Morning," audiences flocked to the theater. Warners accepted just enough of the gross to cover the film's initial costs, with the remaining $1,951,045.11 going to Army Emergency Relief.

Supposedly, when Joan first heard that she was being considered as Fred Astaire's partner in his next film, she sent him a telegram that said, "Heard a rumor and hope it's true. I'm paying daily visits to the wishing well." Joan's wish was granted and she was loaned to RKO for *The Sky's the Limit* (1943), a pleasant but minor Astaire outing that was buoyed by excellent Harold-Arlen Johnny Mercer tunes. The slight story of a flyer (Astaire) on leave who finds romance with a pretty photographer (Joan) was primarily an excuse for some flag waving and to see the dance master perform one of his best routines, a dramatic performance of "One for My Baby." While Joan was admittedly no match for Astaire on the dance floor, she proved to be a capable partner and was a pleasure to watch in the peppy "We've Got a Lot in Common" number.

Dancing with Astaire proved to be as magical for Joan as she had imagined ever since seeing her first Fred Astaire/Ginger Rogers musical as a child. "He was a very strong leader. It was very easy to follow him," Joan said. "Because of my long experience as a dancer, it was easy for me to learn the steps. It was not a big picture, where a lot of time was put into a lot of intricate steps. They were two fairly simple routines. I thought I did them all right, but I'm not Ginger Rogers and I'm certainly not equal to Fred Astaire, but I had a wonderful time."

Reviewers were split on the Astaire-Leslie pairing. Crowther took the offensive, carping that, "Mr. Astaire and Miss Leslie, in two dances, work hard for slight effect. For the simple fact is that Miss Leslie, while a gracious and neatly attractive miss, is not a Ginger Rogers when she tries to make with her feet."

Time was more gracious: "Joan Leslie imparts the double impression in their dance numbers that she is hanging onto [Astaire's] thumb and that she is doing remarkably well in view of the fact that she is not Fred Astaire. At less strenuous moments, Cinemactress Leslie is so nice to look at that her feet are the last thing anybody is likely to notice."

As an example of how important Joan had become, in order to acquire her services for *The Sky's the Limit*, as well as those of fellow Warners performer John Garfield in *The Fallen Sparrow* (1943), RKO agreed to give Warners the rights to both *Of Human Bondage* (1934) and *The Animal Kingdom* (1932). Both films were remade unsuccessfully by Warner Bros. in 1946.

Back at her home studio Joan was quickly becoming Warners' first musical sweetheart since Ruby Keeler a decade earlier. As such, she was next put into two all-star song-and-dance-fests—*Thank Your Lucky Stars* (1943) and *Hollywood Canteen* (1944). Of the two, Joan was better served by *Thank Your Lucky Stars*, despite a silly plot that had Eddie Cantor in a dual role as himself and a lookalike tour guide who can't break into movies because of his resemblance to Banjo Eyes. Joan played the daffy girlfriend of Dennis Morgan, an aspiring singer who thinks if he can appear in a benefit featuring Warner Bros.' biggest stars, it will be his ticket to a Hollywood career. Joan's spirited performance, especially her duet with Morgan of "Ridin' for a Fall," helped make *Thank Your Lucky Stars* a popular entertainment.

Hollywood Canteen worked on the assumption that servicemen might have popular pin-ups, such as Betty Grable and Rita Hayworth, splashed on their lockers, but it was nice girls like Joan that they all pined for back home. Audiences were asked to swallow the shallow plot that GI Robert Hutton dreamed of spending his leave at the Canteen so he could meet Joan and persuade her to wait for him to return from the service. The embarrassing scenario was barely noticed by filmgoers who instead relished cameos by nearly everyone on the Warners lot (sans Ann Sheridan, who hated the script and went on suspension), and musical performances by the likes of the Andrews Sisters, Eddie Cantor, Jane Wyman and dozens of others. With such a star-studded line-up, it was no surprise that the film was Warners' top moneymaker of 1944.

At the time it seemed that Joan could do no wrong. She had been in a string of box-office hits, and her popularity with both men and women had been continually on an upswing. Likewise, she had been a good girl, never giving Jack Warner cause for concern. She had not been temperamental like many of the actresses on the lot, and had never refused a role, even though she was anxious to tackle some heavier material than the fluff Warners often assigned her.

One part she was keen on playing was Tessa, a fourteen-year-old girl dying of consumption in *The Constant Nymph* (1943). "It seemed all set," Joan said in *Movies*. "When I went to see the director, Edmund Goulding, he hemmed and hawed and then said, 'Somehow, Joanie, I just can't see you in the part. Maybe it's because, so much of the time, I see you bicycling around the lot with an apple in your mouth.'" Joan Fontaine won the role and an Oscar nomination.

More surprisingly, Joan envisioned herself playing Bessie, the Cockney tramp whose illegitimate pregnancy threatens the future of a young Welshman in *The Corn Is Green* (1945). Although Joan seemed determined to play the role, Warners execs convinced her she was not quite right for the part. Newcomer Joan Lorring got the plum role.

Joan was loaned to 20th Century–Fox for a fanciful musical history lesson called *Where Do We Go from Here?* (1945), directed by Gregory Ratoff. Fred MacMurray played a civilian deemed unfit for World War II military service. In typical Aladdin style, he rubs a magic lamp and asks a genie (Gene Sheldon) to help him get in the army. The problem is that he's always sent to the wrong era in history. He ends up with George Washington's troops at Valley Forge and as a member of Columbus' crew. In each episode he meets the same two women: the one he thinks he's in love with (June Haver) and the faithful girl who loves him (Joan). By the end of the film MacMurray is back in 1945 as a marine marching off to war with Joan by his side.

The melodious Kurt Weill score and lyrics by Ira Gershwin added to the fun and originality of *Where Do We Go from Here?*, which was certainly a cut above the next batch at Warners. First was *Cinderella Jones* (1946), a wartime musical that marked director Busby Berkeley's first film at Warners since leaving the studio for MGM in 1939. Unfortunately, *Cinderella Jones* had none of the ingenuity or sophistication of his previous Warners efforts. Joan played a dim bulb named Judy Jones, who stands to inherit ten million dollars if she marries a man of extremely high intelligence by a certain date. In trying to find her brilliant mate, she falls for bandleader Tommy Coles (Robert Alda), a man with looks and, as she discovers just in time for the finale, brains as well. Along the way she ends up in a number of ridiculous escapades, such as slipping laundry soap in cheese sandwiches.

Cinderella Jones was actually completed in 1944, but Warners decided to keep it on the shelf for two years so it would follow the release of Joan's next film, *Rhapsody in Blue* (1945), a misguided attempt to dramatize the life of George Gershwin. Alda played the composer, and the studio believed it would be a more prestigious film debut than the flimsy *Cinderella Jones*. Unfortunately, *Rhapsody in Blue* suffered from a routine screenplay that shed little light on the troubled Gershwin's drive for success, which led to his untimely death. Joan played a fictitious character named Julie Adams who, along with Alexis Smith as a slick socialite, vied for Gershwin's affections. Joan was given a few Gershwin standards to perform, including "Somebody Loves Me" and "Delicious," which were dubbed by Sally Sweetland. Joan admittedly was always anxious about singing on-screen, and was especially pleased with Sweetland's interpretations. "She did a beautiful job of sounding lovely, but sounding like an actress singing, instead of like a singer singing. She didn't just sing in perfect voice, she sang the words like she meant the meaning of them, and I loved that," Joan said.

Joan enjoyed the challenge of *Too Young to Know* (1945), her first stab at domestic drama. As the wife of an Army captain (Robert Hutton), Joan dealt with serious issues, including giving away her child. Though Crowther labeled the film "a thoroughly amateurish job," Joan regards it as a breakout role. "I felt that I underwent a certain growth during that picture. I played a wife and a mother, and had some scenes that were wrenching, and I felt good about it," she said.

Finally, Warners released *Cinderella Jones*, which did more harm than good to Joan's career. Since the film had been gathering dust for two years, the studio decided to re-edit it to delete wartime-related scenes and references so that it wouldn't look dated. Instead, it just looked foolish and incomprehensible. The film dashed any hopes of ever building Robert Alda into a star, and Joan, likewise, was beginning to feel that Warners was losing interest in her.

Janie Gets Married (1946), the sequel to the hit *Janie* (1944), didn't ease her concerns. Joan took over as Janie, played in the first film by Joyce Reynolds, and was again paired with Robert Hutton as her new husband. Though Joan enjoyed her reunion with director Vincent Sherman, who helped her turn in an excellent performance in *The Hard Way*, *Janie Gets Married* was much thinner material. The light as a feather comedy concerned the problems the newlyweds confront during their first year of marriage. The supporting cast, which included Edward Arnold, Ann Harding and, in his last role, Robert Benchley, fared better than the two leads. "Her picture is as childish and bromidic as was her first reckless, juvenile farce," said *The New York Times*.

Considering the careful build-up and quality projects Joan had previously been accustomed to, she was understandably angered by the poor roles she was now being given. Joan's lawyer explained to her that a loophole in California law allowed anyone who signed a contract as a minor to reconsider the contract when they turned 21. She notified the studio through her lawyer that she disaffirmed her minority contract. Warners met her challenge by formally exercising its option on her services and suspending her salary. Thus, a series of lengthy legal proceedings began between both parties, with Warners even seeing to it that no other major studio would hire Joan. At one point Joan had announced that she would appear in *The Chase* (1946) and *Lured* (1947), two thrillers for United Artists. Warners obtained an injunction preventing her from making both films. When the injunction was voided, Warners appealed to the California Supreme Court. By that time, Michele Morgan had gotten *The Chase* and Lucille Ball was given *Lured*.

The case went to the District Court of Appeals, where there was a split decision, with Warners ultimately winning. Joan soon learned that the original loophole her lawyer discovered also had a loophole. The law stated that any minor can disaffirm a contract — unless the party in question is a jockey, prizefighter, actor or actress. Though the studio was the victor, Warners gave Joan her freedom and a settlement was reached. At the same time, a gentleman's agreement was declared, in which the other studios agreed not to use Joan, who was labeled "difficult."

Joan's final Warners release, completed before litigation began, was *Two Guys from Milwaukee* (1946), with Dennis Morgan and Jack Carson. Warners saw Morgan and Carson as its answer to Bob Hope and Bing Crosby. As such, the focus of this comedy was on Morgan as a prince and Carson as the cabbie he befriends during his stay in the United States. Joan was supposed to be the pair's version of Dorothy Lamour, who is wooed by both men. Though the movie was Joan's most entertaining feature since *Where Do We Go from Here?*, her male co-stars and vivacious Janis Paige seemed to be having all the fun.

Worst of all, Morgan and Carson got billing before the title, while Joan was third-billed after the title. She filed a second suit against the studio for $2.725 million with the Federal court and asked for a restraining order to prevent *Two Guys from Milwaukee* from being shown until she was also given top billing. Joan claimed the studio promised her star billing alongside Morgan and Carson, but that her previous lawsuit fueled her demotion because of "malice and ill will" on Warners' part. She added that Warners' action was "intended to implant in the minds of the theatrical profession that she had lost her position as a star actress by reason of inferior ability."

Joan lost the case and the film was released with her below-the-title billing still intact. The film ended up being one of Warners' top grossers of 1946.

Thanks to Warners' injunction, Joan remained offscreen for nearly two years. Most of her time was spent conferring with lawyers. Joan finally found work with Eagle-Lion Films, a low-budget studio that poured more money than usual into *Repeat Performance* (1947), its first venture with Joan. *Repeat Performance* had an interesting premise, even if the execution was not completely successful. Joan played Sheila, an actress who murders her scoundrel of a husband (Louis Hayward) after catching him with another woman (Virginia Field) one New Year's Eve. Feeling remorseful for her crime, she turns to her friend, producer John Friday (Tom Conway), a man who seems to have the power to let her relive the events of the past year. The rest of the film hinged on whether she could keep from committing her crime all over again.

Repeat Performance was an attempt for Joan to graduate from ingenue roles. Eagle-Lion even tried to promote the film by giving Joan a sexier image. Joan learned about the marketing ploy quite by accident. When she arrived in New York for the film's opening, she took a cab from the airport to Eagle-Lion's eastern office. On the way, she spotted a huge billboard ad for *Repeat Performance* that depicted her holding a gun with a rather revealing nightgown falling off of her bare shoulder. Joan was both embarrassed and furious by the ridiculous ad. When she arrived at Eagle-Lion, she immediately demanded that the studio have the billboard taken down.

Of course, it wasn't, not that it helped generate business anyway. Joan did her best with the Walter Bullock screenplay, but she seemed uncomfortable playing a New York sophisticate. The film also lacked the craftsmanship of her Warners vehicles, starting with director Alfred Werker's inability to develop the mystical feeling or brooding atmosphere that the story required. *Repeat Performance* did, at least, provide a boost to Richard Basehart, who was effective in his screen debut. Joan, however, was not as well served. Both she and the film received poor notices.

"Not only is dramatic credibility completely lacking in all this stew but the whole thing is done with such pretension that even the possible salve of ridicule is missed," Crowther said. "Joan Leslie plays the tortured female with childish anxiety."

Joan's only other film for Eagle-Lion was *Northwest Stampede* (1948), in which she played a rancher vying with James Craig for some prized horses and getting him in the bargain. Though the plot covered familiar turf, Joan loved the Canadian Northwest, where the film was shot, and the chance to do some horseback riding.

Joan was off the screen for nearly two years before appearing in the Joan Fontaine potboiler *Born to Be Bad* (1950) at RKO, which seemed to work better as campy fun than serious drama. Joan had a good supporting role as Zachary Scott's loyal fiancée whose engagement is destroyed by the manipulations of her conniving cousin, Cristabel (Fontaine). Joan, who was just shy of 25, enjoyed finally being allowed to portray a career woman, in this case, a book editor.

"I played a mature person," Joan said with pride. "So many of the other films I did were too useful, but not representative of any maturity on my part. Not only did they photograph me well, but Nicholas Ray worked on my voice a little. He was determined to make me a proper nemesis for Joan Fontaine."

Ray succeeded and guided Joan to a fine performance, particularly during the climactic scene when she confronts the seemingly sweet Cristabel, whom she now realizes is "as helpless as a wildcat."

Joan's appearance in *Born to Be Bad* also attracted the attention of RKO head Howard Hughes, who summoned her to his office to talk about her career. Sensing that Hughes wanted to offer Joan a contract, her lawyer and agent both advised her not to make a commitment. They feared he wanted to lock her into an agreement similar to the one he had with Jane Russell, in which she'd be under exclusive contract to Hughes at a flat salary and would be forced to appear in any role he decided on.

Hughes' proposal was exactly as Joan's representatives predicted. Though Joan found Hughes charming and gracious, she politely turned him down.

Still a free agent, Joan was happy to report to MGM to co-star opposite Robert Walker in *The Skipper Surprised His Wife* (1950), a mild comedy which was to be directed by Vincente Minnelli, who dropped out to do *Father of the Bride* (1950). Elliott Nugent instead helmed the domestic yarn about a sailor (Walker) who tries to run his home as tightly as he runs his ship.

Joan's only sad memory of making *The Skipper Surprised His Wife* (1950) was that her mother died during production. When she returned from the funeral, Walker offered his condolences. Joan appreciated his sympathy, and said, "This is difficult, but it was something we had to go through. I'm sure you've lost someone who was very dear to you." Walker responded, "No, Joan, I never have." Joan seemed surprised that he had forgotten losing his former wife, Jennifer Jones, to producer David O. Selznick five years earlier.

Joan was drawn to Walker and admitted, "we very easily could have become better than friends, but I was already interested in a very handsome young doctor." Joan's new love was Dr. William Caldwell, a Los Angeles physician she had begun dating in 1949. Following a seven-month courtship, they were married on March 17, 1950, in a quiet ceremony at Our Lady of Sorrows Church in Santa Barbara, California. Only immediate family members and a few close friends attended the ceremony.

Following *Man in the Saddle* (1951), a typical Randolph Scott horse opera at Columbia, and *Hellgate* (1952), a Sterling Hayden actioner, Joan signed a contract with Republic Pictures, the low-budget studio that specialized in popcorn fare, such as Roy Rogers westerns and Judy Canova hillbilly comedies. Republic had also become a stomping ground for many stars, such as MacDonald Carey and Ruth Hussey, that had been dropped by larger studios. While Republic was no match for Warner Bros. in terms of the quality of its films, Joan was treated well. She was given leading lady status and paid handsomely for her efforts. "I earned more on one picture at Republic than I did during five years at Warner Bros.," she said.

One of her favorite roles at Republic was the lead in *Flight Nurse* (1953), which was based on the real-life exploits of a Korean War nurse who worked with the injured both on the front line and on the aircraft that brought them home. Screenwriter Alan Le May also involved the nurse in a romantic triangle between two officers (Forrest Tucker and Arthur Franz).

Of the five films she did for Republic, *Jubilee Trail* (1954) was the most polished.

Though Republic chief of production Herbert J. Yates aimed to showcase his wife, Vera Ralston, as a flashy New Orleans belle named Florinda, it was Joan's restrained and affecting performance as a genteel widow whom she befriends that kept the movie afloat. In reviewing the performances of both women, *The New York Times* noted, "With these two to the fore throughout, Miss Leslie's performance, luckily, remains at least forthright."

Joan left Republic, which was suffering from financial difficulties, in 1955 and made only one more film. *The Revolt of Mamie Stover* (1956) was a sanitized version of William Bradford Huie's novel about a madam in Honolulu. In the film, Mamie (Jane Russell) was a dance hall girl rather than a member of the world's oldest profession. Joan played an heiress competing with Mamie for the love of an egotistic writer (Richard Egan). Considering the cast involved and the plot's potential, the movie seemed devoid of sex, which was the essence of the novel.

By this point Joan seemed less motivated to appear before the cameras. Her husband was a successful obstetrician and gynecologist with his own private practice. Joan also wanted to spend more time with her daughters, Patrice and Ellen, identical twins born on January 5, 1951. "My daughters were five years old. I felt that they had reached the age where they needed me, but I never retired officially," Joan said. "I didn't close any doors behind me. Bill has always said that as long as it wasn't too hard for me, and that it was something I enjoyed, I should work if and when I wanted to."

Joan did make occasional guest appearances on television, starting back in 1951 with a guest spot on *Bigelow-Sanford Theatre*. Throughout the 1950s she also showed up in several episodes of *Fireside Theater*, *Schlitz Playhouse of Stars*, *Lux Video Theater* and *Ford Theater*.

"Doing television was wonderful. I liked the acting, I liked the way they were shot, very rapidly, and the direction seemed more crisp than films," she said.

Throughout the next few decades Joan also devoted much of her time to charity work for the St. Anne Home for Unwed Mothers. Joan's husband had been doing volunteer work for St. Anne's prior to meeting Joan, and through him she became involved with the home. During her forty-plus years with St. Anne's, Joan has chaired many fund-raising committees and arranged numerous special events.

In recent years Joan has made sporadic television appearances, including guest spots on *Branded*, *Police Story*, *Charlie's Angels* and *Simon and Simon*. Joan's most recent television appearances were in an episode of *Murder, She Wrote*, still looking as charming and fresh-faced as she did forty years earlier, and a cameo in the made-for-television movie *Turn Back the Clock* (1989), a remake of *Repeat Performance*.

Joan continues to make personal appearances at various film screenings and festivals. When she and Vincent Sherman attended the film group Cinephile's 1994 screening of *The Hard Way*, the crowd went wild. Both were greeted by thunderous applause, and after the film spent well over an hour answering questions and signing autographs. And to fans' pleasure, the now mature woman had aged very little from the sprightly performer who cavorted through the musical number "Youth Must Have Its Fling" in that movie.

Joan resides in Los Angeles, and has retained her zest for living, even though she faced the most difficult moment in her life when her beloved husband died in May 2000. Joan treasured her life away from the film world and never looked back at what might have happened if she had opted for the stardom that Howard Hughes had once offered her: "I met this wonderful man and I spent fifty years of my life with him, and I have absolutely no regrets."

FILMOGRAPHY

Camille (MGM, 1937) Directed by George Cukor. *Cast:* Greta Garbo, Robert Taylor, Lionel Barrymore, Henry Daniell, Elizabeth Allen, Lenore Ulric, Laura Hope Crews. (Joan was unbilled.)

Men with Wings (Paramount, 1938) Directed by William A. Wellman. *Cast:* Fred MacMurray, Ray Milland, Louise Campbell, Andy Devine, Lynne Overman, Porter Hall. (Joan was unbilled.)

Nancy Drew, Reporter (Warner Bros., 1938) Directed by William Clemens. *Cast:* Bonita Granville, Frankie Thomas, John Litel, Frank Orth, Renie Riano. (Joan was unbilled.)

Love Affair (RKO Radio, 1939) Directed by Leo McCarey. *Cast:* Charles Boyer, Irene Dunne, Maria Ouspenskaya, Lee Bowman, Astrid Allwyn, Maurice Moscovitch. (Joan was unbilled.)

Winter Carnival (Wanger-United Artists, 1939) Directed by Charles F. Riesner. *Cast:* Ann Sheridan, Richard Carlson, Helen Parrish, James Corner, Robert Armstrong, Joan Brodel (Leslie).

Two Thoroughbreds (RKO Radio, 1939) Directed by Jack Hively. *Cast:* Jimmy Lydon, Arthur Hohl, Marjorie Main, Joan Brodel (Leslie), J.L. Kerrigan, Selmar Jackson, Spencer Charters.

High School (20th Century–Fox, 1940) Directed by George Nicholls, Jr. *Cast:* Jane Withers, Joe Brown, Jr., Paul Harvey, Lloyd Corrigan, Cliff Edwards, Claire Du Brey. (Joan was unbilled.)

Young as You Feel (20th Century–Fox, 1940) Directed by Malcolm St. Clair. *Cast:* Jed Prouty, Spring Byington, June Carlson, Billy Mahan, Florence Roberts. (Joan was unbilled.)

Star Dust (20th Century–Fox, 1940) Directed by Walter Lang. *Cast:* Linda Darnell, John Payne, Roland Young, William Gargan, Charlotte Greenwood, Mary Beth Hughes. (Joan was unbilled.)

Susan and God (MGM, 1940) Directed by George Cukor. *Cast:* Joan Crawford, Fredric March, Ruth Hussey, John Carroll, Rita Hayworth, Nigel Bruce, Bruce Cabot, Rita Quigley, Rose Hobart, Constance Collier, Gloria De Haven, Marjorie Main. (Joan was unbilled.)

Military Academy (Columbia, 1940) Directed by D. Ross Lederman. *Cast:* Bobby Jordan, Jimmy Butler, Tommy Kelly, Jackie Searl, David Holt, Walter Tetley, Joan Brodel (Leslie).

Foreign Correspondent (Wanger-United Artists, 1940) Directed by Alfred Hitchcock. *Cast:* Joel McCrea, Laraine Day, Herbert Marshall, George Sanders, Albert Basserman, Edmund Gwenn, Eduardo Ciannelli, Robert Benchley, Harry Davenport. (Joan was unbilled.)

Laddie (RKO Radio, 1940) Directed by Jack Hively. *Cast:* Tim Holt, Virginia Gilmore, Joan Carroll, Spring Byington, Robert Barrat, Miles Mander, Esther Dale, Joan Brodel (Leslie).

Alice in Movieland (Warner Bros., 1940) Directed by Jean Negulesco. *Cast:* Joan Leslie, David Bruce, Clarence Muse, Nana Bryant, Clara Blandick.

High Sierra (Warner Bros., 1941) Directed by Raoul Walsh. *Cast:* Ida Lupino, Humphrey Bogart, Joan Leslie, Henry Travers, Arthur Kennedy, Alan Curtis, Henry Hull, Elisabeth Risdon.

The Great Mr. Nobody (Warner Bros., 1941) Directed by Ben Stoloff. *Cast:* Eddie Albert, Joan Leslie, Alan Hale, John Litel, William Lundigan, Dickie Moore, Paul Hurst, Billy Benedict.

The Wagons Roll at Night (Warner Bros., 1941) Directed by Ray Enright. *Cast:* Humphrey Bogart, Sylvia Sidney, Eddie Albert, Joan Leslie, Cliff Clark, Charles Foy, Sig Rumann.

Thieves Fall Out (Warner Bros., 1941) Directed by Ray Enright. *Cast:* Eddie Albert, Joan Leslie, Jane Darwell, Alan Hale, William T. Orr, John Litel, Anthony Quinn, Edward Brophy.

Sergeant York (Warner Bros., 1941) Directed by Howard Hawks. *Cast:* Gary Cooper, Walter Brennan, Joan Leslie, Stanley Ridges, George Tobias, Ward Bond, Margaret Wycherley.

The Male Animal (Warner Bros., 1942) Directed by Elliott Nugent. *Cast:* Henry Fonda, Olivia de Havilland, Jack Carson, Joan Leslie, Eugene Pallette, Herbert Anderson, Don De Fore.

Yankee Doodle Dandy (Warner Bros., 1942) Directed by Michael Curtiz. *Cast:* James Cagney, Joan Leslie, Walter Huston, Rosemary De Camp, Jeanne Cagney, Richard Whorf, Irene Manning.

The Hard Way (Warner Bros., 1943) Directed by Vincent Sherman. *Cast:* Ida Lupino, Dennis Morgan, Joan Leslie, Jack Carson, Gladys George, Roman Bohnen, Faye Emerson.

This Is the Army (Warner Bros., 1943) Directed by Michael Curtiz. *Cast:* George Murphy, Ronald Reagan, Joan Leslie, Charles Butterworth, George Tobias, Stanley Ridges, Alan Hale, Dolores Costello, Frances Langford, Gertrude Niesen, Kate Smith, Sgt. Joe Louis, Irving Berlin.

The Sky's the Limit (RKO Radio, 1943) Directed by Edward H. Griffith. *Cast:* Fred Astaire, Joan Leslie, Robert Benchley, Elizabeth Patterson, Clarence Kolb, Robert Ryan, Richard Davies.

Thank Your Lucky Stars (Warner Bros., 1943) Directed by David Butler. *Cast:* Dennis Morgan, Joan Leslie, Edward Everett Horton, S.Z. Sakall. *Guest Stars:* Humphrey Bogart, Eddie Cantor, Jack Carson, Bette Davis, Olivia de Havilland, Errol Flynn, John Garfield, Alan Hale, Spike Jones and his orchestra, Ida Lupino, Hattie McDaniel, Ann Sheridan, Alexis Smith.

Hollywood Canteen (Warner Bros., 1944) Directed by Delmer Daves. *Cast:* Joan Leslie, Robert Hutton, Janis Paige, Dane Clark. *Guest*

Stars: The Andrews Sisters, Jack Benny, Joe E. Brown, Eddie Cantor, Kitty Carlisle, Jack Carson, Joan Crawford, Helmut Dantine, Bette Davis, Faye Emerson, John Garfield, Sydney Greenstreet, Alan Hale, Paul Henreid, Andrea King, Peter Lorre, Ida Lupino, Irene Manning, Dolores Moran, Dennis Morgan, Eleanor Parker, Roy Rogers, Zachary Scott, Alexis Smith, Barbara Stanwyck, Craig Stevens, Jane Wyman.

Where Do We Go from Here? (20th Century–Fox, 1945) Directed by Gregory Ratoff. *Cast:* Fred MacMurray, June Haver, Joan Leslie, Gene Sheldon, Anthony Quinn, Carlos Ramirez.

Rhapsody in Blue (Warner Bros., 1945) Directed by Irving Rapper. *Cast:* Robert Alda, Alexis Smith, Joan Leslie, Charles Coburn, Oscar Levant, Julie Bishop, Herbert Rudley, Albert Basserman, Morris Carnovsky, Rosemary De Camp, Darryl Hickman; with guest appearances by Al Jolson, Hazel Scott, Anne Brown, George White, and Paul Whiteman and his orchestra.

Too Young to Know (Warner Bros., 1945) Directed by Frederick De Cordova. *Cast:* Joan Leslie, Robert Hutton, Dolores Moran, Harry Davenport, Rosemary De Camp, Barbara Brown.

Cinderella Jones (Warner Bros., 1946) Directed by Busby Berkeley. *Cast:* Joan Leslie, Robert Alda, Julie Bishop, William Prince, S.Z. Sakall, Edward Everett Horton, Ruth Donnelly.

Janie Gets Married (Warner Bros., 1946) Directed by Vincent Sherman. *Cast:* Joan Leslie, Robert Hutton, Robert Benchley, Edward Arnold, Ann Harding, Dorothy Malone, Donald Meek.

Two Guys from Milwaukee (Warner Bros., 1946) Directed by David Butler. *Cast:* Dennis Morgan, Jack Carson, Joan Leslie, Janis Paige, S.Z. Sakall, Patti Brady, Rosemary De Camp, Franklin Pangborn; cameo appearances by Humphrey Bogart and Lauren Bacall.

Repeat Performance (Eagle-Lion, 1947) Directed by Alfred Werker. *Cast:* Joan Leslie, Louis Hayward, Tom Conway, Richard Basehart, Virginia Field, Natalie Schaefer, Benay Venuta.

Northwest Stampede (Eagle-Lion, 1948) Directed by Albert Rogell. *Cast:* James Craig, Joan Leslie, Jack Oakie, Chill Wills, Victor Kilian, Kermit Maynard, Stanley Andrews.

The Skipper Surprised His Wife (MGM, 1950) Directed by Elliott Nugent. *Cast:* Robert Walker, Joan Leslie, Edward Arnold, Spring Byington, Jan Sterling, Leon Ames, Paul Harvey.

Born to Be Bad (RKO Radio, 1950) Directed by Nicholas Ray. *Cast:* Joan Fontaine, Robert Ryan, Zachary Scott, Joan Leslie, Mel Ferrer, Virginia Farmer, Harold Vermilyea, Irving Bacon.

Man in the Saddle (Columbia, 1951) Directed by Andre de Toth. *Cast:* Randolph Scott, Alexander Knox, Joan Leslie, Ellen Drew, Richard Rober, Cameron Mitchell, John Russell.

Hellgate (Commander-Lippert, 1952) Directed by Charles Marquis Warren. *Cast:* Sterling Hayden, Ward Bond, Joan Leslie, James Arness, Peter Coe.

The Woman They Almost Lynched (Republic, 1952) Directed by Allan Dwan. *Cast:* Joan Leslie, Audrey Totter, John Lund, Brian Donlevy, Ben Cooper, Reed Hadley, Ann Savage.

Flight Nurse (Republic, 1953) Directed by Allan Dwan. *Cast:* Joan Leslie, Forrest Tucker, Arthur Franz, Jeff Donnell, Ben Cooper, Maria Palmer, James Brown, James Holden.

Jubilee Trail (Republic, 1954) Directed by Joseph Kane. *Cast:* Vera Ralston, Joan Leslie, Forrest Tucker, Pat O'Brien, John Russell, Ray Middleton, Glenn Strange, Grant Withers.

Hell's Outpost (Republic, 1955) Directed by Joseph Kane. *Cast:* Rod Cameron, Joan Leslie, Chill Wills, John Russell, Barton MacLane, Ben Cooper, Taylor Holmes, Kristine Miller.

The Revolt of Mamie Stover (20th Century–Fox, 1956) Directed by Raoul Walsh. *Cast:* Jane Russell, Richard Egan, Agnes Moorehead, Joan Leslie, Jorja Curtwright, Jean Willes.

TELEVISION FILM CREDITS

The Keegans (1976). *Cast:* Adam Roarke, Spencer Milligan, Heather Menzies, Joan Leslie.

Turn Back the Clock (1989) *Cast:* Connie Selleca, David Dukes, Gene Barry, Joan Leslie.

Fire in the Dark (1991) *Cast:* Olympia Dukakis, Lindsay Wagner, Jean Stapleton, Joan Leslie.

Ida Lupino: "Mum"

If Bette Davis was the reigning queen of the Warners lot in the early 1940s, Ida Lupino gave every indication of being her successor to the throne when she joined the studio in 1940. Her intense performances in *They Drive by Night* and *High Sierra* easily rank beside Davis' best work. Likewise, when Davis turned down *The Hard Way* in 1943, a reluctant Ida was cast as the scheming woman who exploits her younger sister to escape from a grungy mining town. The result was a tour de force performance that should have secured Ida's position at Warners.

For some reason, the studio never seemed to give Ida the proper push. Ida referred to herself as "the poor man's Bette Davis," but perhaps more accurate was *Picturegoer*'s assessment of her as "the Lady Macbeth of the slums."

Most of Ida's post–Warners career was spent behind the camera, where she showed a flair for swift, concise storytelling and a concern for doing socially relevant stories. It was the most creatively fulfilling period of her life.

Like Davis, Ida's birth took place on a stormy note. She was born in London on February 4, 1918, during the midst of a German zeppelin bombing on the city. From the start, Ida was destined to be an actress. Her family had a distinguished background in the English theater that stretched back to Renaissance Italy. A paternal ancestor, Giorgio Luppino, fled Italy as a political outcast and supported himself as a puppeteer. Ida's great-grandfather, George Hook Lupino, was a noted actor in Victorian England, and his son, George Jr., was born in a theater and also was a success on the London stage. His brothers, Arthur and Harry, had a popular musical-comedy act.

Ida's father, Stanley Lupino, was at the time of her birth regarded as one of England's best actor-comedians. Stanley had been performing since he was six, as part of his father's troupe in *King Klondyke*, playing a monkey. His difficult childhood memories were of living out of trunks, scrounging for food and looking for work.

When he was twenty Stanley landed a role in the touring company of *Go to Jericho*, in which a dancer named Connie O'Shea was the leading lady. During rehearsal, Stanley and Connie got into a terrible argument, which ended with Stanley storming out of the theater. They met accidentally at a tea shop later that day and made amends, and by that night were engaged.

Connie proved to be a good luck charm for Stanley. He soon began to find work in children's musicals and pantomimes. That experience with children was perhaps part of the reason Stanley was such a loving father to Ida and her sister Rita, who was born in 1921. Stanley, from the start, sensed Ida was going to be the most famous Lupino of all.

Ida loved accompanying her parents to the theater for rehearsals. Because of the odd hours that her parents worked, she and Rita were often left in the care of her grandfather, nicknamed "Old George," and Connie's mother, Granny O'Shea. By the time Ida was a child,

Old George was confined to a wheelchair because of a stroke. Although he could be stern and crotchety, Ida adored him and he remained an important influence in her life. It was Old George who taught Ida how to sing and compose music, and the fine points of oil painting.

As a child, Ida wrote short plays, including *Savoy Faire*, which she also performed for her parents and their friends. The skit, which centered around characters entering the Savoy after a theatrical premiere, showed off Ida's wit and gave an early sample of her flamboyant acting style.

At his daughters' request, Stanley built the fifty-seat Tom Thumb Theater in the family garden as their Christmas present. For their first production, Stanley wrote a musical revue consisting of thirty-two scenes and ten numbers, and agreed to direct. The cast members, aged five to thirteen, were even given contracts to sign. The show opened to an overcapacity crowd of eighty spectators, including Tallulah Bankhead, playwright Sidney Howard, reporters and photographers.

Shortly before the curtain went up, Ida got stage fright and refused to go on. Stanley gave her a sharp reprimand, and, after that, she stepped onstage in her clown costume and opened the program by greeting the audience. The rest of the show was greeted to thunderous applause.

The Lupinos staged many other productions as Ida and Rita continued to learn their craft. As Ida matured, she tackled more demanding roles, such as Camille, Juliet and even Hamlet.

In January 1932 Ida enrolled at the Royal Academy of Dramatic Arts, and by March was chosen to play Agathe in *Les Folies Amoureuses*, directed by Alice Gachet, who had previously taught Charles Laughton and Vivien Leigh. Gachet was impressed by Ida, and, as such, Ida landed roles in many other RADA productions, including *Julius Caesar* and *Heartbreak House*.

Ida stayed at the RADA for two terms. She then began making the rounds of the British film studios and answering casting calls, but producers told her she was "too plain" or "too thin." American director Allan Dwan, who was in England preparing *Her First Affaire* (1933), a Lolita-esque comedy, felt differently. He had seen Ida in *Heartbreak House* and thought she might be suitable for the female lead in his film. In the movie, peroxide blonde Ida played a flirtatious young mantrap who has a fling with a married romance novelist. The film was a hit, even making its way to the United States, and Ida's performance was well-received in both countries.

Ida's success in *Her First Affaire* led to further roles in the English cinema. In *Money for Speed* (1933) Ida enjoyed playing the sexy tart vying for cyclists Cyril McLaglen and John Loder.

Shortly after completing *Money for Speed* Ida was nearly killed when an automobile struck her. Her face was bandaged, and she waited for several emotional months for the bandages to be removed. Her scars all faded, except for a tiny one on her forehead which she covered with hair.

Ida's British film career continued with *Prince of Arcadia* (1933), *The Ghost Camera* (1933) and *I Lived with You* (1933). The last was interesting for its casting: Ida played an innocent seduced by Ivor Novello, a close friend of Stanley's who was also her godfather.

Paramount executives had been impressed with Ida in *Money for Speed*—in particular, a scene in which she feigned sweetness with one of her beaus. Based on the scene, Paramount thought she might be right for *Alice in Wonderland* (1933) and made Ida a tempting offer. Although Ida couldn't envision herself as the winsome Alice, she accepted.

In Hollywood, studio executives soon realized that Ida was far too sophisticated to play Alice and instead gave the role to Charlotte Henry. As it turned out, despite an all-star cast that included W.C. Fields as Humpty Dumpty, Cary Grant as the Mock Turtle and Gary Cooper as the White Knight, *Alice in Wonderland* was a total bore that cost Paramount millions.

Unfortunately, Ida's initial Paramount film was not much better. *Search for Beauty* (1934) was a silly comedy in which she and Larry "Buster" Crabbe played Olympic athletes involved with con men in a health spa scam. The movie attracted some attention as a result of a contest Paramount ran to find the perfect physical specimens from all over the world to appear in the film. One of the lucky winners was Texas-born Clara Lou Sheridan, who later became Ann Sheridan.

About the best that could be said of Ida and Crabbe is that both were seen to excellent

Though intense both on screen and off, Ida Lupino always felt more comfortable behind the camera.

physical advantage in their bathing suits. Some cast members were given even greater exposure: Censors let slip a snippet of some barebottomed athletes racing through a men's shower.

Ida was aghast when she read the script for her next film, a quickie called *Come on Marines!* (1934), in which she served as little more than set decoration as Richard Arlen's girlfriend. Ida made no secret to the press that she was upset about being given such a thankless role.

Ida also got some publicity when she was seen dancing at the Trocadero with Howard Hughes. According to Ida, it was all "very proper, of course," with Connie as their chaperone. Still, Hughes did his best to woo Ida with expensive presents. For her sixteenth birthday he asked her what she wanted. She told him she wanted a pair of binoculars, but Hughes, who always liked to go to extremes, instead got her a telescope and a large bottle of French perfume.

"I didn't want a telescope," she related to reporter Paul Gardner in 1972, "and I didn't give a damn about Chanel Cinq. Finally, he got the message. He told me 'Ida, you're not a phony.'" Then she got the binoculars.

Shortly after Ida was set to begin *Ready for Love* (1934), she was stricken with polio and feared that she might spend the rest of her life in a wheelchair. Connie's constant attention and reassurance of a full recovery helped a despondent Ida through the crisis. Ida was fortunate to regain full use of her legs within a week. She returned to work on *Ready for Love*, a smart comedy in which she had fun pretending to be the mistress of a deceased playboy.

Ida was less excited about her dull roles in *Paris in Spring* (1935) and *Smart Girl* (1935), and went on suspension rather than do a bit in Cecil B. De Mille's *Cleopatra* (1934). She fought for the role of the Cockney trollop in *Peter Ibbetson* (1935), and was singled out by *The New* as "excellent in a brief part." But *Peter Ibbetson* was considered artsy fare and flopped.

Ida was then plunked into *Anything Goes* (1936), a loose translation of the Cole Porter stage hit. Her dissatisfaction with Paramount was building, and she was quick to accept *One Rainy Afternoon* (1936), a saucy comedy for producers Mary Pickford and Jesse Lasky. *One Rainy Afternoon* was an adaptation of the French farce *Monsieur Sans Gene*, in which Ida played an heiress who achieves unexpected notoriety when a suave stranger (Francis Lederer) kisses her in a movie theater. Shocked by his behavior at first, she soon becomes drawn to him.

One Rainy Afternoon was a delight, thanks to a witty screenplay by Stephen Morehouse Avery and Maurice Hanline. *The New York Times* liked the performances of both stars but noted that Lederer ran a "definite second to the quieter and vastly more attractive Miss Lupino, who impressed us as having her tongue in her cheek even while registering love's sweet surrender."

Throughout filming, Lederer developed romantic feelings for Ida. Although she considered him a good friend, she didn't reciprocate his feelings. Up to this point Ida had been in love only once, with a fellow RADA classmate named Johnny. The two had spoken seriously of marriage, but Johnny died in a bicycling accident a few days before Ida left England in 1933.

In Hollywood, Paramount contract player Tom Brown was Ida's most frequent beau, but a full-blown romance never materialized. Her first great love affair didn't occur until she met Louis Hayward, who became a poor man's Errol Flynn in films like *The Man in the Iron Mask*.

Hayward, who, like Ida, began work in British films, had first met her on the set of *Money for Speed*. At the time, Ida found him boring, and he thought she was just another dizzy blonde. They were reintroduced in Hollywood by a mutual friend, Felix Tissot, but now their impressions of each other were different. Ida was taken with Hayward's tall good looks, polished manners and directness. Like Ida, he was also sensitive and emotional. They soon became a regular twosome.

Ida's personal high was matched professionally. Pickford and Lasky cast her in another of their productions, *The Gay Desperado* (1936), a picturesque operetta with the clever premise that a band of Mexican bandits learn how to be hoodlums by watching American gangster films. Their exploits soon involve recruiting a singer (opera star Nino Martini) and kidnapping a fiery heiress (Ida) and her wimpy boyfriend (Mischa Auer). Ida gave a boisterous performance, which was highlighted by a wickedly funny fight scene as she defends herself against the amorous Martini.

Ida then returned to Paramount, which still seemed clueless as to what to do with her. A loanout to RKO for the naval actioner *Sea Devils* (1937) hardly seemed like a good career move. Following another loanout, to Columbia for *Let's Get Married* (1937), and a bland role in *Artists and Models* (1937) with Jack Benny, she asked Paramount for her release, even though she was then making a none-too-shabby $1,750 a week.

After making the witless *Fight for Your Lady* (1937) with John Boles and Jack Oakie at RKO, Ida became disillusioned when no other film offers materialized. She even contacted her agent, Leland Hayward, about securing film work for her in England at half her salary, but to no avail. Louis had proposed to Ida, but with her career in limbo, she couldn't make a commitment.

Louis suggested that Ida let his agent, Arthur Lyons, handle her, which led to an interview with Harry Cohn at Columbia. Cohn thought Ida had "an interesting pan" and put her in *The Lone Wolf Spy Hunt* (1939) and *The Lady and the Mob* (1939), but she wasn't pleased about either.

Soon after starting *The Lone Wolf Spy Hunt*, Ida and Louis were married in a civil service ceremony on November 17, 1938, in the Santa Barbara courthouse. In attendance were a few close friends, Connie, and Ida's sister, Rita. Stanley was performing in England and couldn't attend, much to Ida's disappointment. Ida was back to work on *The Lone Wolf Spy Hunt* the following day, but she and Louis managed a brief honeymoon in Malibu the following weekend.

In May 1939 Ida appeared opposite Orson Welles in "The Bad Man" on his *Mercury Theater on the Air* radio program. Her performance captured the attention of 20th Century–Fox, which cast her in *The Adventures of Sherlock Holmes* (1939). Ida played a distressed heiress who turns to the master detective (Basil Rathbone) when she fears her brother's life is in danger.

Unlike her Columbia efforts, *The Adventures of Sherlock Holmes* had a tight screenplay by Edward Blum and William Drake, crisp direction by Alfred Werker and superb cinematography by Leon Shamroy. With her hair back to its natural brown, and clad in lush Victorian finery, Ida was radiant and self-confident. The film remains one of the best of the Holmes entries.

Flush from the success of *The Adventures of Sherlock Holmes*, Ida began scouting around for a worthy follow-up. She appropriated a copy of the script for *The Light That Failed* (1939), which director William Wellman was preparing for Paramount. Ida loved Robert Carson's adaptation of the Rudyard Kipling tale about an artist who is slowly going blind, and was intrigued by the main female character, a tempestuous Cockney prostitute named Bessie Broke.

Realizing Bessie could be "the" role that would establish her in Hollywood, Ida stormed into Wellman's office and in no uncertain terms demanded a reading. When Wellman told her the film's star, Ronald Colman, was not available, she insisted that the director read with her. Impressed by her bravado, and perhaps as a means to get rid of her, Wellman agreed to perform with Ida the flamboyant scene in which Bessie becomes hysterical when the artist torments her to get the right expression. Mesmerized by Ida's dramatic shrieks and hysteria, Wellman took her to see producer B.P. Schulberg. After that, the part was Ida's. At least she thought it was.

Colman began pushing Schulberg to cast his friend Vivien Leigh, but Wellman insisted on Ida and Schulberg relented. The director became Ida's greatest supporter and saw to it that she was given a lavish dressing room equipped with a shower and a bathtub.

The Light That Failed was a favorite of the 1939 holiday season. Critics loved the film — and Ida. "A little ingenue suddenly bursts forth as a great actress," raved *The New York Times*.

On the strength of Ida's work in *The Light That Failed*, Warner Bros. producer Mark Hellinger realized Ida would be ideal as a murderess in *They Drive by Night* (1940). Studio head Jack Warner was set to cast unknown Catherine Emery, so Hellinger quickly arranged for a screen test for Ida. After seeing it, Warner said he wanted to sign her to a seven-year contract.

When Ida met with Warner, he promised that she would be another Bette Davis. To Ida that meant she would be insurance for when Davis became temperamental or refused a role. Ida gave the offer careful consideration and finally agreed after her agent arranged an unusually sweet deal. Ida would make two films a year for Warners at a salary of $2,000 a week, plus she had the right to do three films off her home lot and make radio appearances without studio control.

They Drive by Night (1940) combined elements from A.I. Bezzerides' novel *The Long Haul* and Warners' film *Bordertown* (1935), with Ida in Bette Davis' role as a sexually frustrated housewife. The strange brew that resulted is arguably the best of Warners' blue-collar dramas.

In the picture's first half, director Raoul Walsh does an effective job of showing the rigors of life as a trucker, where lack of sleep can mean the difference between life and death. One of the most chilling scenes has truckers Joe (George Raft) and Paul Fabrini (Humphrey Bogart) doing their best to keep the driver (John Litel) of another rig from veering off a mountain road.

The second half is pure melodrama, with Ida the focal point as Lana, the wife of a boorish trucking magnate (Alan Hale), who is obsessed with desire for Joe. Realizing he'll never bother with her as long as she's married, Lana murders her husband by leaving him in their garage with the car motor running. From Ida's first sequence, in which she criticizes her husband for yelling out the window, to her mad scene on the witness stand, she is fascinating. Sitting in the witness chair, she seems like a frightened child as she clutches her handkerchief. As she descends further into madness, screaming "the doors made me do it," she becomes a frightening object of pity.

Jack Warner claimed that Ida at first boycotted the set of *They Drive by Night* because an astrologer told her the film would bring her bad luck. Ida finally showed up, most likely at the urging of her agent, after a half million dollars was spent and some crew members had disbanded.

As it turned out, the astrologer couldn't have been more incorrect. Among the cast of heavyweights in *They Drive by Night*, it was Ida who received the accolades from reviewers. "Miss Lupino goes crazy about as well as it can be done," said *The New York Times*.

"Raft and Bogart, honest men, but Lupino steals the picture," echoed *Newsweek*.

Another nice outcome from working on *They Drive by Night* was that Ida got to renew her friendship with co-star Ann Sheridan, whom she knew slightly at Paramount. Like Ida, Sheridan had a witty tongue and could be forceful when it came to dealing with the Warner brass. Both women used to joke about which one had been on suspension more times while at Warners. Ida noted that Sheridan was "honest, feminine and yet had masculine directness."

Ecstatic over her performance in *They Drive by Night*, Hellinger cast Ida in *High Sierra* (1941), again directed by Walsh. Compared to Warners' 1930s gangster epics, such as *Little Caesar* (1930) and *Public Enemy* (1931), *High Sierra* presented a more sympathetic portrait of its criminal. Forty-something Roy Earle (Humphrey Bogart) has just been released from prison and is intent on pulling one last job, from which he'll make enough money to retire comfortably. His plans are complicated by several factors, not the least of which are the two women he encounters: Velma (Joan Leslie), a sweet, club-footed teenager whom Roy tries to help in the hope that she will marry him; and Marie (Ida), a former dance hall girl who sticks by Roy up until he is captured and shot by the police. As Marie, Ida's hard shell belied her tenderness and vulnerability.

Because Ida had become a more established star than Bogart after her performance in *They Drive by Night*, she received top billing in *High Sierra*. Good as Ida was, the film ultimately belonged to Bogart, whose riveting portrayal of Roy was his ticket out of Warners' "B" hive.

Ida was again on the wrong side of the law, this time as a fugitive from justice in *The Sea Wolf* (1941), the most exciting of several film versions of the Jack London novel. As in the novel, the central focus of the film was the conflict between tyrannical captain Wolf Larsen (Edward G. Robinson), who is gradually going blind, and idealistic writer Humphrey Van Weyden (Alexander Knox). *The Sea Wolf* is ultimately a tale of good versus evil, which unfortunately left Ida and John Garfield, as newly created characters, to appear incidental to the film's center, which belonged to Robinson and Knox, who both deliver outstanding performances.

On several occasions Ida locked horns with her director, Michael Curtiz, who refused to listen to any of her suggestions. She finally got her revenge at the closing party when she and Garfield pushed Curtiz into a tank of cold water.

Ida's animosity towards Curtiz was countered by her friendship with Garfield, whom she regarded as a brother. Both shared a rebellious streak and a witty sense of humor. As such, they were happy to be reteamed for *Out of the Fog* (1941), a sanitized version of Irwin Shaw's play *The Gentle People*. The moody drama was about two fisherman (Thomas Mitchell and John Qualen) in Brooklyn's Sheepshead Bay who are being extorted by a crooked Howard Goff (Garfield). For Stella (Ida), the daughter of one of the fishermen, Goff represents the excitement that's been missing from her drab life, and she immediately is drawn by the sexual magnetism he exudes. When Barbara Stanwyck turned down the role of Stella, Ida was vocal about being cast instead. Humphrey Bogart was considered for Goff, but Ida insisted on Garfield.

Screenwriters Robert Rossen, Jerry Wald and Robert Macaulay were hampered by the limits of the Production Code and had to water down the play's street flavor. The ending, in which the fishermen get their revenge on Goff, was altered so that his death was an accident.

In spite of these changes, *Out of the Fog* was entertaining, and Ida and Garfield make an intense couple. Despite Goff's crooked nature, it's easy to see why Stella would prefer him over her nice but dull boyfriend (Eddie Albert). Director Anatole Litvak's realistic depiction of Sheepshead Bay, and the dank presentation of its fish-reeking inhabitants, helped compensate for the liabilities of the script.

While Ida's career with Warners was soaring, Louis had been stuck toiling in B-grade mysteries (*The Saint in New York*) or costume epics (*Son of Monte Cristo*). His best role had been as Brian Aherne's spoiled offspring in *My Son, My Son* (1940) for producer Edward Small.

Ida was somewhat old-fashioned in her views on marriage, believing that the man was the master of the house. She was unnerved that she had become the bigger star of the two. She was happy they shared billing in Columbia's *Ladies in Retirement* (1941), a gripping thriller with Ida as Ellen, a sinister housekeeper who murders her employer, Miss Fiske (Isobel Elsom), when the woman demands that Ellen's two mad sisters (Elsa Lanchester and Edith Barrett) leave her house.

Flora Robson, who played Ellen as a middle-aged frump on Broadway, had been hailed by critics, and Ida was worried about trying to equal her in the role. Ida refused to see the play because she didn't want to be intimidated by Robson's performance.

Producer Lester Cowan wanted Lillian Gish to play Ellen, but she was doing *Life with Father* in Chicago and couldn't get out of her contract. Cowan then cast twenty-three-year-old Ida, to which Harry Cohn ranted, "You are out of your mind choosing this child to play that role."

Despite Cohn's protests, director Charles Vidor did his best to make Ida look as close to forty as possible by having her wear prim clothes and little makeup. Cinematographer Charles Barnes' harsh lighting was also instrumental in giving Ida a steely, somewhat jaundiced look.

Ladies in Retirement plays like a Brothers Grimm fairy tale brought to life with dashes of Edgar Allan Poe eeriness. The interment of Miss Fiske in the oven seems like a fitful homage to *Hansel and Gretel*. But it's Ida's chilling performance that really lifts the film, especially during the pivotal strangulation of Miss Fiske, which Vidor shot with expert subtlety.

Critics were in rapture over Ida's performance. "Perhaps she is too slight to portray the stolid threat that lay in Flora Robson's original performance, but she is none the less the thin ribbon of intensity that makes the film hair-raising," praised *The New York Times*.

Ida later cited Ellen as her favorite role, although in a 1941 interview with Theodore Strauss of *The New York Times*, she joked, "Of course, the role I really want is one that will let me wear false eyelashes to here and glamorous clothes and let me lie on a haystack and have Charles Boyer whisper I'm wonderful. What happens? I wear a stiff pompadour, high collars, heavy eyebrows, no lipstick and I kill a nice old lady. But (deep sigh) I'm no raving beauty. In fact, I'm very skinny and nobody can say, 'Oh what a lovely girl!' So I have to do something."

Ida also gave her first intimation that she might consider giving up acting at some point. In her spare time she loved writing stories and composing music, such as her "Aladdin Suite," which had been performed by the Los Angeles Philharmonic. "I don't know, but when you write a piece of music, it's something you can play and listen to for years to come," she said. "When your film is carried away in cans to the storehouse, what do you have? A lot of cold press clippings?"

Ida was then announced for what she called "the small and secondary role of Cassie" in *King's Row* (1942), but she turned it down, claiming she "could not feel the part or see herself doing it." Far more damaging was the studio's decision to put Ida in the aviation flick *Captains of the Clouds* (1942) as the bland heroine torn between James Cagney and Dennis Morgan. Ida refused to even consider it and went on the first of many suspensions at Warners. Her suspension was extended when she soon after rejected *Juke Girl* (1942), which went to Ann Sheridan.

Rather than sit at home brooding, Ida used her time off constructively. "I used to go and sit on the set when I was on suspension, which was a great deal of the time," Ida said in an interview with *Box Office Magazine* in 1975. "I used to ask if I could sit in the cutting room and see how a film was put together. And ... you learn why a director asked you to do such and such."

Although Ida was still on suspension, Warner let her appear in *Forever and a Day* (1943), actor-director Cedric Hardwicke's episodic all-star tribute to England, if she worked for free. Ida and Brian Aherne played a maid and a coalman who plan to leave England for the United States at the turn of the century. *Forever and a Day* was made in 1941 but wasn't released until 1943.

Ida's professional difficulties seemed small compared to her personal problems. Her father was still in wartorn London, where he served as an Air Raid Precautions Warden. Ida feared for his safety, and cried when reading his letters. The war hit her even closer to home when Louis, who had become an American citizen on December 6, 1941, enlisted in the U.S. Marine Corps.

Ida forgot her troubles somewhat thanks to her friend Hellinger, now a producer at 20th Century–Fox, who recommended Ida to costar with French import Jean Gabin in *Moontide* (1942), a remake of *Quai des Brumes*. Ida was convincing as Ada, a potential suicide who is rescued and cared for by a rough seaman, but the film fared poorly.

Ida stayed at Fox for *Life Begins at 8:30* (1942), another grim film in which she played the lame daughter of a once-famous thespian (Monty Woolley) whose drinking has him reduced to dressing as Santa Claus in a department store. To make the limp she affected seem convincing, Ida wore an orthopedic boot during the month it took to shoot the movie. By the time the film wrapped, Ida's foot muscles were inflamed and aching, but her performance was letter-perfect.

Back on her home lot Ida had misgivings about *The Hard Way* (1943), director Vincent Sherman's powerful backstage drama which was supposedly inspired by the relationship between actress Ginger Rogers and her first husband, vaudevillian Jack Pepper.

Ida played Helen Chernen, a bitter housewife who's dissatisfied with life in Green Hills, the drab mining town where she lives with her apathetic husband Sam (Roman Bohnen) and her vibrant sister, Katharine (Joan Leslie), who dreams of being a successful dancer. Helen sees a chance to escape her dull existence when Katharine meets vaudevillians Paul Collins (Dennis Morgan) and Albert Runkel (Jack Carson). Within the next twenty-four-hours, Helen fixes it so that Katharine marries Albert and becomes a third member of the vaudevillian's act. Helen leaves Sam to accompany her sister, but her interference causes Paul to leave the act. The calculating Helen soon manages to get Katharine the lead in a Broadway show. Katharine becomes the toast of Broadway, but her success costs her the love of Albert, whose own career failure and his refusal to become "Mr. Katharine Blaine" leads to his suicide. Paul eventually helps Katharine reclaim the pieces of her life, but not before she and Helen have a revealing showdown.

The Hard Way was beset with problems from the start. Sherman was unhappy with Irwin Shaw's screenplay and did a major doctoring of it. By the time he was finished, the story was so far removed from Shaw's original that Shaw demanded his name be deleted. Bette Davis had already turned down the part of Helen, and Ida likewise didn't want to do it because she felt the character was a too unsympathetic. To assuage her fears, Sherman added a scene in which Helen softens and confesses her love to Paul. When he rebuffs her, she returns to her conniving ways.

"She was playing against her own nature, and that's hard to do. That's why she was so uncomfortable in it," Leslie said. "But God knows she played it to the hilt, and she was just marvelous. Really pushy, really aggressive and deserved all the credit that she got for it."

Ida was also difficult about playing the early scenes in the film sans makeup. While Sherman and producer Jerry Wald believed she'd look more in character as the unattractive hausfrau of a steel worker by not wearing makeup, Ida feared she'd look awful. In the end, Ida lost out; as Sherman suspected, her pallid complexion gave credibility to her Green Hills scenes.

As if Ida wasn't under enough pressure, during mid-production she learned that Stanley had died from cancer. With all of those setbacks, *The Hard Way* finished nineteen days behind schedule. A frustrated Ida never said good-bye to Sherman when the film ended.

No one was more surprised than Ida over the raves accorded her performance. *Time* enthused, "Top acting honors go to Ida Lupino, who plays the most hateful jade since Bette Davis in *The Little Foxes*." Pauline Kael agreed: "Ida Lupino's English accent comes through at times, but she gives one of the best of her intense, hyperaware, overcontrolled performances."

Buoyed by the wonderful reaction to her work in *The Hard Way*, an ecstatic Ida phoned Vincent Sherman. When he answered the phone, Ida blurted, "Oh darling, how are you?" without the slightest recollection of their disagreements on the set. From then on they were friends.

Ida's rich performance in *The Hard Way* earned her The New York Film Critics Award for Best Actress of 1943. Surprisingly, when the Oscar nominations were announced in January 1944, Ida's performance was forgotten. Her disappointment was capped when Warners wasted her in the literary lemon *Devotion* (1946), a botched biography on the Bronte sisters. *Devotion*'s release was held up until 1946, largely because of the studio's legal battles with co-star Olivia de Havilland. Unfortunately, the film had not improved with age and was savaged by critics. *The New York Times* felt that Ida played Emily Bronte "in a meek and poignant way."

Ida was under considerable strain during the making of *Devotion*. Louis had been stationed for active duty in Quantico, Virginia. He was allowed to come home for Christmas, and their days together became even more precious after Louis told Ida he was being sent overseas.

Ida followed *Devotion* with cameos in two all-star extravaganzas, *Thank Your Lucky Stars* (1943) and *Hollywood Canteen* (1944). In the former, Ida, de Havilland and George Tobias cut up as jitterbuggers; in the latter, Ida was one of many stars helping out at the Canteen. Her work in the second film was hardly a stretch, since she often spent much of her free time doing just that, as well as appearing at war relief benefits for the Red Cross.

The war served as the backdrop for the turgid *In Our Time* (1944), again with Sherman. Ida played Jennifer, the British secretary/companion of a cantankerous antique dealer (Mary Boland) visiting Poland. Jennifer meets and soon after marries Count Stephan Orvid (Paul Henreid), the member of a once-wealthy Polish family. Their marriage is jeopardized by the resentment of his selfish mother (Nazimova) and embittered sister (Nancy Coleman) toward Jennifer. Their family problems become dwarfed by the impending invasion of Nazi soldiers.

Sherman noted that Ida was far more pleasant and cooperative while making this film, primarily because she enjoyed playing a more likable character than Helen in *The Hard Way*. Being likable, however, did not necessarily make for a compelling performance.

The year 1943 ended on a bittersweet note for Ida when Louis returned home with an honorable discharge one week before Christmas. Ida had prayed for his safe return, but the man she welcomed back was a shell of his former self. Louis had been appointed captain of a special photographic unit which was sent to Tarawa to film the Japanese attack, which cost the lives of hundreds. Louis shot the carnage that ensued that November 20, 1943, one of the bloodiest episodes of the war. He was one of only seventeen U.S. servicemen who miraculously survived the atrocity after finding refuge in a foxhole next to a crater with fifteen dead Japanese soldiers.

Louis' footage formed the documentary *With the Marines at Tarawa* (1944), which won an Oscar as Best Documentary. He was also given a bronze star from Admiral Nimitz for "meritorious conduct in the performance of outstanding service." Neither honor was proper compensation for the hell that Louis endured. The film had been replayed in his mind thousands of times, which caused him to be moody and withdrawn. He couldn't sleep and found it difficult to communicate with others, especially Ida. He was treated for depression at three different hospitals, but his recovery was going to be a long, arduous process. Louis asked Ida for a separation. On May 11, 1945, they were divorced, but their friendship endured.

The light-hearted *Pillow to Post* (1945) was just what Ida needed to lift her spirits. Ida played a traveling saleswoman who poses as the wife of a soldier (William Prince) to share his room during the housing shortage. In addition to the obvious sexual innuendo, there were lots of amusing physical gags, including Ida's face to face encounter with a slimy bullfrog. Critics scoffed at *Pillow to Post*, but it turned a tidy profit. More surprisingly, Ida told the film's director, Vincent Sherman, that she received more fan mail about *Pillow to Post* than for any other movie she made.

Ida then delivered one of her most memorable performances in *The Man I Love* (1946), one of the great unsung "women's" pictures of the '40s. Ida played Petey, a torch singer who's had nothing but bad luck with men. Her luck doesn't get any better when she falls for a brooding pianist (Bruce Bennett) who's carrying the torch for a member of cafe society.

The Man I Love was vintage Lupino, one of those films where you can tell how serious the romantic complications are by how many cigarettes the characters light up. The bristling screenplay by Catherine Turney gave Ida plenty of sharp lines that she delivered in her trademark acerbic manner. Peg La Centra dubbed Ida's numbers, which included a sultry rendition of the title song and the torch standard "Why Was I Born?"

The New York Times called *The Man I Love* "silly and depressing, not to mention dull," but it was a favorite with female moviegoers. Ida's no-nonsense performance bore echoes of a vulnerable version of Helen from *The Hard Way*, and is cherished by her fans.

Offscreen, Ida had become a popular bachelor girl around Hollywood. For a while she was involved in a tempestuous affair with actor Helmut Dantine, whom she described as "full of enthusiasm, which I like because, as you know, that's the way I am." Their frequent battles, and Dantine's sometimes violent nature, made for many stormy moments. Ida's need for stability and her increasing irritation over Dantine's quixotic ways led her to break off the relationship.

Professionally, Ida's career reached an ebb with *Escape Me Never* (1947), in which she played an Italian waif whose love for a ne'er-do-well composer (Errol Flynn) is complicated by his brother's flirtatious fiancée (Eleanor Parker). Peter Godfrey's leaden direction and the miscasting of Ida and Flynn made *Escape Me Never* an excruciating bore.

Much better was *Deep Valley* (1947), in which Ida delivered a powerful performance as Libby, a shy mountain girl who harbors an escaped prisoner (Dane Clark). Libby was a far cry from the usual flamboyant Lupino heroine, but Ida's restrained performance ranks among her best.

Shortly after Ida's twenty-eighth birthday she was offered an extravagant seven-year contract by Warners. Despite a hefty salary increase, she said no. "I had decided that nothing lay ahead of me but the life of the neurotic star with no family and no home," Ida said in 1965. "It was not for me. I didn't like anything about it — the acting, the daily facials, the so-called glamour."

By the time of Ida's breakup with Warners she had become an American citizen and was dating Collier Young, an executive at Columbia. Ida and Collie, as she called him, shared similar interests, including sailing, reading and, above all, a desire to write and produce their own films.

Things were also looking up for Ida career-wise. Her new agent, Charles K. Feldman, had purchased the rights to the novel *Dark Love* for her and sold the project to 20th Century-Fox, which renamed it *Road House* (1948). Fox provided Ida with three fine co-stars — Cornel Wilde, Richard Widmark and recent Oscar winner Celeste Holm — and ace director Jean Negulesco, who had just been fired by Warners, which thought he had botched *Johnny Belinda* (1948). Instead, the movie earned many awards and was Warners' biggest grosser of the year.

Road House was a well-mounted film noir in which Ida played Lily, a sexy lounge singer hired by Widmark to work at the road house owned by him and his partner (Wilde). Widmark doesn't count on Lily and his partner falling in love, and seeks revenge when they plan to run off.

One of the delights of *Road House* was Ida's musical numbers, in which she did her own singing. Though it was apparent from Ida's throaty deliveries that she was no rival to Lena Horne, her raspy vocals had a raw quality that passed for sensuality. As Holm says of her rendition of "One for My Baby," "She can do more without a voice than anyone I've heard."

In August 1948 Ida and Collie were married at a Presbyterian church in La Jolla, California. Their honeymoon was spent sailing to Catalina's Toyon Bay on a yacht loaned to them by radio comic Ed Gardner. When they returned they settled into their New England farmhouse-style home in the Santa Monica Mountains.

Collie was so busy at Columbia that he and Ida rarely got to see each other. Ida agreed to star in Columbia's *Lust for Gold* (1949) so that she might at least have lunch with her husband. Instead, most of the movie was shot in Phoenix. S. Sylvan Simon, best known for his comedies with Red Skelton and Lucille Ball, directed the grade-A western in which Ida played a schemer who plays up to an outlaw (Glenn Ford), hoping to beat him to the claim on a lost gold mine.

Ida was in search of a follow-up film when she was given an original story by writer Malvin Wald about an unwed mother and how she copes with her situation. Ida loved it and urged Collie to get Harry Cohn to let him produce it for Columbia. When Cohn refused, Collie quit.

Ida and Collie then took the story to Anson Bond, president of independent Emerald Productions. Bond agreed to co-produce the film, called *Not Wanted* (1949), and Collie was made production supervisor. Ida and Paul Jarrico reworked Wald's original story.

For the unwed mother in *Not Wanted*, Ida selected Sally Forrest, a twenty-year-old dancer who had played a few bit parts in MGM musicals. "There were about 300 women at her house who came out for the audition," said Forrest. "Right there, she hired me. I was very young, and very innocent. I gave the appearance of a real girl next door, and I suppose that's why she chose me. It was most exciting. On the way home I stopped to call my mother to say, 'I got the part.' She said, 'That's nice. Now don't be late for dinner.'"

A few days before filming was to begin, director Elmer Clifton suffered a mild heart attack. Time and budget constraints necessitated that Ida direct the film, but she insisted that Clifton get screen credit. Ida's knowledge of technical details and her understanding of actors made it immediately apparent that she had the tools to be a good director.

"Ida was a brilliant woman," Forrest said. "On the set she knew everything. She knew about lighting. She could just look up and say, 'There's not enough light on Sally.' I think she also understood women well. That's why the roles she created were so good. She was also one of the first directors who did pre-rehearsal. We would rehearse our scenes for a week before filming. Then when we were ready to film, we usually got to do the scene in one take."

In addition to filmmaking techniques, Ida became an expert on the business matters behind her films. For example, to minimize wardrobe costs, Ida supplied her own clothes for Forrest to wear in *Not Wanted*. In one instance, sharing Ida's dress size had its fringe benefits for Forrest.

"She used to rehearse us at her home. I remember it must have been about the second or third day of rehearsal, and she and her husband were going to an elegant party. She had just bought some beautiful clothes. Well, she gave me a dress to wear and they took me along. I thought that was a dear thing to do," recalled Forrest.

Ida strove for believability in structuring *Not Wanted*. Key to the story were scenes filmed at a home for unwed mothers. "She understood that there were poor girls who would find themselves in these conditions. She was telling a lot of girls who didn't realize it that there were places like this where they could find help," said Forrest.

Also in those scenes Ida wanted to present a diverse ethnic population of Afro-American, Asian and Hispanic women, but one of the men financing the film sternly objected. A defiant Ida snuck in one Chinese woman, and, after the film's release, received an irate letter from the backer.

Reviewers praised *Not Wanted* for its straightforward narrative and honest atmosphere. "Much of the picture's force comes from its flat ... insistence on telling the story straight. Its dirty children, dilapidated porches and stuffy hall bedrooms are authentically grimy; its dialogue often catches the nagging overtones of everyday frustration and defeat," said *Time*.

The New York Times agreed that *Not Wanted* deserved credit for braving new frontiers, but found that "in their desire to avoid the trappings of cheap sensationalism, the producers have come up with a picture that is dramatically limp when it is not downright dull."

Not Wanted now plays better as a fascinating time capsule on post-war America's moral code than as a statement on the ills of an unplanned pregnancy, but Ida's artistry behind the camera can still be admired. The initial sequence in which a dazed Forrest wanders the streets of Los Angeles and walks off with a baby she believes is her own is immediately compelling.

Not Wanted was shot in ten days and only cost $153,000 to make. Within two weeks of its release date the movie earned enough for Ida and Collie to pay back their loan from the Chemical Bank of New York to finance the film. *Not Wanted* ended up grossing nearly $1 million.

Ida and Collie severed ties with Bond and Emerald Productions after *Not Wanted* because they couldn't agree on business arrangements. Instead, the couple and Malvin Wald formed their own independent company called Filmakers. Their biggest obstacle, though, was a lack of capital for their next film. The Youngs stripped much of their own bank accounts and asked friends for additional financing.

Ida also agreed to act in *Woman in Hiding* (1950), a thriller with Ronald Reagan, so her salary could be used for Filmakers. She was disappointed to learn that Reagan injured his thigh in a charity softball game and her new leading man would be Howard Duff.

Ida and Duff had met once before, but their initial encounter proved to be a tremendous letdown. "I thought he was stuck-up," Ida related to *TV Guide* in 1957.

"And Ida struck me as everything phony," Howard countered.

Her opinion changed on the first day of shooting *Woman in Hiding* when Duff handed her a box of white orchids. "It was a ballroom scene in white tie and evening gown," Ida recalled. "I was so staggered, I tripped backwards over a cable and sat right down with the orchids."

In *Woman in Hiding* Ida played a wealthy bride fleeing from her brutal husband (Stephen McNally), who wants to murder her for her money. Duff played a stranger she meets, who at first thinks she's crazy but gradually realizes she's in danger. Good performances and the fast-moving direction of Michael Gordon made up for the familiar screenplay and predictable ending.

Throughout the making of *Woman in Hiding* Ida immersed herself in preparing the script with Collie on their first Filmakers production, *Never Fear* (also known as *The Young Lovers*). Inspired by Ida's bout with polio in 1934, *Never Fear* starred Sally Forrest as a dancer whose dreams are cut short when she is stricken with the disease. Ida this time was the official director.

By the time *Woman in Hiding* was wrapped, Ida's marriage to Young also seemed finished. Ida's feelings for Howard was one obvious problem. Her bitter arguments with Collie while preparing the script for *Never Fear* didn't help matters. Worst of all, as filming was set to begin, Collie told Ida that some of their investors had pulled out and they might have to shut down production. Ida's agent Charles Feldman came to the rescue with a loan of $65,000.

Ida shot several scenes on location at the Kabat-Kaiser Rehabilitation Institute in Los Angeles, using footage of actual doctors and patients. In one innovative scene she staged a wheelchair dance. The scene was visually striking, as Ida had her camera tell the story.

Ida completed *Never Fear* in fifteen days for $150,000. Unfortunately, Collie was unable to find new investors, which put Filmakers heavily into the red. Ida had already depleted most of her savings, plus she had her debt to Feldman. The lack of funds and grim subject matter made it impossible for Collie to get *Never Fear* booked by large theater chains.

Despite limited bookings, *Never Fear* did hit a positive chord with those who saw it, especially polio victims. "I got a lot of fan mail from people who thought these things really happened to the actors involved," remembered Forrest. "I also got many letters from people stricken with the disease who wrote, 'What you did inspired me.' It was very touching."

In the summer of 1949 Ida and Collie separated. She rented a beach house at Malibu just a few doors away from Howard, whom she now turned to for support. "It was the tiniest thing ever. A living room, a kitchen, a bedroom — just big enough for me and a housekeeper," Ida said.

Despite their fragile marital state, Ida and Collie remained business partners. Shortly after a preview of *Never Fear* in December 1949, they acquired a new partner. Howard Hughes, who had recently purchased RKO, was impressed with the film — in particular, Ida's ability to make $150,000 look like $1 million. He made them a tempting offer: Filmakers would be established as an independent unit at RKO, and the studio would give Ida and Collie $750,000 to finance three films to be made over a nine-month period. In exchange, RKO would receive half the profits.

Collie negotiated the final deal, which gave RKO ownership of Filmakers' pictures and its new personalities, as well as approval on story ideas. Worst of all, Hughes could use Filmaker's profits to promote its films. Furious with Collie, Ida filed for divorce on December 28, 1949.

Ida now began being seen regularly with Duff. Rugged and masculine, Howard had a way with women, having been involved in well-publicized romances with Yvonne De Carlo and Ava Gardner. Howard was quiet and less outgoing than Ida, but he was the love of her life.

Despite the differences between Ida and Collie, they somehow managed to remain friends. They worked together with Malvin Wald on the screenplay for *Outrage* (1950), an unsparing look at the effects that a sexual assault has on a young woman.

"I just felt it was a good thing to do at the time without being too preachy," Ida said in *Showmen's Trade Review*. "After all, it was not the girl's fault. I just thought so many times the effect rape can leave on a girl isn't easily brought out. The girl won't talk about it or tell the police. She is afraid she won't be believed."

Ida auditioned about two hundred actresses for the lead in *Outrage* before choosing Mala Powers, a stunning eighteen-year-old brunette whose prior experience had mostly been on the stage and radio. RKO's publicity department released a story to the press that Ida had met Powers at a radio show, but it was pure fabrication: "I didn't meet Ida until I auditioned for *Outrage*," said Powers. "I read one scene and she jumped out of her seat and said, 'You're it! You're it!'"

Still, Hughes would have the final say on casting. To ensure his approval, Ida supervised Powers' portrait session. "First I had my hair cut and styled. Then Ida took me into the portrait gallery and directed the gallery sitting. She talked to me and got the expression she wanted. She selected the clothes that I wore. To this day, I have never seen anyone do that."

When Powers went with her mother to meet the eccentric Hughes, he was immediately impressed. "When I look at my life, I can't even imagine what my career would have been like without her. She was the one that gave it to me," said a grateful Powers.

Ida had said, "I'm not the kind of woman who can bark orders." Instead, she took a softer approach, which her colleagues appreciated, and had the cast and crew refer to her as "Mum."

"She would say 'Could you do this for mum?' She handled the crew in a feminine way, but I don't mean by batting her eyelashes or swishing her hips," said Powers. "She worked it so that everyone wanted to please her. If you did something and she didn't care for it, she'd suggest, 'Mum would really like to do this another way. Ida knew that one of the director's chief functions was to give confidence to an actor. She knew I was very good. She would tell me, in effect, what she wanted to see from a directorial standpoint through the camera. She wouldn't necessarily tell me how to act. Instead, she might say, 'We need it a little faster darling.' It was like you would speak to a colleague that you had cooperation with. I never heard her talk to anyone as a director. I always felt completely safe with her. I knew if it wasn't good, she wasn't going to print it."

Outrage was a well-meaning, if overwrought, melodrama that started off brilliantly. The centerpiece of the film is the attack, in which Ida made effective use of shadows and camera movement. Most striking is an overhead shot of Powers as she tries to flee from her attacker in the empty, open streets. With nowhere to hide, she is shown as being completely vulnerable. Equally effective are the scenes after the attack, when neighbors whisper behind Powers' back and her co-workers greet her with stony stares and silent disapproval.

The New York Times felt that *Outrage*'s "preachment is indeed honorable, but its execution lacks punch and conviction." Audiences, however, found *Outrage* engrossing and daring, and it was one of RKO's most successful films of the year.

Ida followed up *Outrage* with *Hard, Fast and Beautiful* (1951), a sort of *The Hard Way* set on a tennis court. With Hughes and RKO behind *Hard, Fast and Beautiful*, Ida had enough money to afford a name star (Claire Trevor) to portray a domineering mother who pushes her teenage daughter (Sally Forrest) into the cut-throat world of professional tennis.

Hughes did become involved in the production of *Hard, Fast and Beautiful*, only it wasn't casting or plot development that were his major concerns. "Mr. Hughes was an odd man who was intrigued with the sound of tennis balls," Forrest remembered. "He insisted that the tennis balls must sound just right. He would spend a lot of time in the editing room to get the right sound."

Hard, Fast and Beautiful was Ida's most mainstream film so far. Though it lacked the controversial nature of her three previous efforts, the film still made for entertaining drama, thanks largely to the excellent performance of Trevor and Ida's skillful direction of the tennis scenes. In an echo of Hitchcock, Ida and RKO player Robert Ryan made a cameo as onlookers in the stands.

Ida and Ryan were allotted more screen time in *On Dangerous Ground* (1951) for RKO, which she made to repay Feldman. Director Nicholas Ray's film noir featured Ida as a blind woman who works with a detective (Ryan) to solve a murder. The film was gripping, thanks to Ray's moody direction and one of Ida's finest performances, but RKO posted a $425,000 loss.

For their next Filmakers project, Ida and Collie chose to film *The Man*, which had been a Broadway play about a widow who is terrorized by an unbalanced handyman. Ida had hoped to cast her friend John Garfield as the handyman, but his difficulties with the House Un-American Activities Committee and his ensuing health problems made that impossible.

Ryan was finally selected for the male lead, and for the first time Ida starred in one of Filmaker's movies and left the direction to Mel Dinelli, the play's author and director. At Hughes' request, the film was called *Beware My Lovely*, and the result was a suspenseful drama that was marred by a weak ending. Screenwriter Harry Horner wanted it to end as the play did, with the woman murdered, but Collie objected. The revised ending had the unconscious handyman suddenly waking up, with no recollection of the terror he's inflicted on his victim, and just leaving. Whether or not the ending was the cause, *Beware My Lovely* was not a success.

On October 20, 1951, Ida's divorce from Collie became final. The following day she married Howard Duff. Although Ida had been anxious to marry Duff, he told Ida he didn't want to be tied down. When Ida told him she was pregnant, he had little choice but to marry her.

Their daughter, Bridget Mirella Duff, was born prematurely on April 23, 1952, weighing a mere four pounds. Bridget spent two months in an incubator before Ida and Howard were able to take her home. Her godparents were Collie and his new wife, Joan Fontaine.

Motherhood didn't keep Ida from working as hard as ever. Even during her pregnancy Ida worked with Collie on the production side of Filmakers' *On the Loose* (1952), a preachy drama about juvenile delinquency, with Melvyn Douglas and Joan Evans.

Ida said she used to get ideas for her movies from reading the newspaper. One story that intrigued her was the 1951 murder spree of Billy Cook. She used the incident as the framework for her best directorial effort, *The Hitch-Hiker* (1953), a relentless thriller about two buddies (Edmond O'Brien and Frank Lovejoy) whose fishing trip becomes a nightmare when they're held hostage by a hitch-hiker (William Talman) who turns out to be a serial killer.

Robert Joseph wrote the taut screenplay, and Ida kept the action moving at a fast clip. Unlike her previous female-driven efforts, Ida this time worked with a predominantly male cast. All three actors gave forceful performances, with Talman outstanding. *Time* called *The Hitch-Hiker* "a crisp little thriller." After *The Hitch-Hiker*, Filmakers and RKO parted company.

After appearing in the modest thriller *Jennifer* (1953), Ida became the first woman to direct herself on-screen, in *The Bigamist* (1953), an underrated gem about a businessman (Edmond O'Brien) with one wife (Joan Fontaine) in San Francisco and another (Ida) in Los Angeles. Collie penned the intelligent script, which avoided the pitfalls of making one wife the good one or showing Ida as the conniving other woman. Likewise, O'Brien is not depicted as a criminal, but as an average guy who marries his second wife when she becomes pregnant. His motivation for bigamy stems from his desire to not hurt either of his wives. In the end, he hurts both.

Some critics felt the finale was too open-ended, but it was the only logical conclusion for the story. In the end, O'Brien's sentence is suspended, and it's left to the audience to decide what will happen to him. Ida's careful use of close-ups suggests that she is likely to take him back.

The Bigamist was backed by investors, which meant production costs had to be trimmed to the bone. Because of the heavy costs of self-distribution and promotion, the film never reached a large audience and put Filmakers' ledgers in red ink.

Ida's business troubles were compounded a few weeks after *The Bigamist*'s release when Howard announced he wanted a separation. They soon reconciled, but it was the beginning of a recurring pattern of separations and reunions throughout their marriage.

Ida and Howard worked together on *Private Hell 36* (1954), a film noir for Filmakers about two detectives (Howard and Steve Cochran) trying to nail counterfeiters. Ida played a nightclub singer, and Don Siegel directed. Neither this film nor Filmakers' last effort, *Mad at the World* (1954), a drama about juvenile delinquents, were successful. Lacking the funding and the personnel to distribute its pictures, Filmakers went under.

How sad that, after striving to make innovative films, Ida should be dumped into *Women's Prison* (1955) at Columbia. She played the cruel warden in this campy exercise that recycled clichés from other women's prison movies. She fared a little better in her other '50s movies—*The Big Knife* (1955), *While the City Sleeps* (1956) and *The Strange Intruder* (1957).

Ida had become interested in television since her appearance on *Four Star Playhouse* in 1953. Ida was so impressed with Four Star Productions, which was created by Charles Boyer, Dick Powell, David Niven and agent Don Sharpe, that two years later she joined the series. "I was snobbish toward TV at first," Ida admitted in 1965. "But that changed fast. The pressure, the opportunities, the fantastic challenges—it's all fantastic, darling."

In one episode, *Face of Danger*, Ida played a one-hundred-year-old woman who reflects on her romance with a cowboy (Paul Picerni) more than half a century earlier. Picerni cited Ida as one of his favorite co-stars, and in one instance couldn't resist some innocent flirting with her.

"I had a love scene with her," he said. "which required some kissing between us. In the process of the love scene I got over-rambunctious. Ida then stepped back from our kiss, and in that voice of hers scolded, 'Howard wouldn't like it.' Then we both laughed about it. She was a great gal."

In 1956 Collie came up with the idea for a situation comedy about a husband and wife who happen to also be movie stars. CBS liked it and approached Howard and Ida about starring in it. Believing that working together might help their marriage, the Duffs accepted CBS' offer to star in *Mr. Adams and Eve*, as the show was titled. Ida insisted that Howard receive top billing.

Mr. Adams and Eve debuted to good ratings on January 4, 1957. Writer Sol Saks tried to use as many actual incidents as possible in the Duffs' life for inspiration. "Those scripts of Sol's are at least sixty percent true," Ida told *TV Guide*.

Ida's humorous efforts were rewarded with an Emmy nomination for Best Actress in a Comedy in 1958, but she lost to Jane Wyatt for *Father Knows Best*. More important to her was the lack of tension between Howard and her during the run of *Mr. Adams and Eve*. Ida considered this the happiest period of their marriage, but it was short-lived: *Mr. Adams and Eve* was canceled after sixty-six episodes.

Ida and Howard continued to find television work, including a guest appearance on *The Lucy-Desi Comedy Hour* in the 1959 episode "Lucy's Summer Vacation." Ida also made a memorable solo appearance in the classic *Twilight Zone* episode "The Sixteen-Millimeter Shrine," in which she played an old-time actress who becomes lost forever in her film clips.

The 1950s ended badly for Ida when her mother was involved in an automobile accident on Christmas Eve. She died two days later, and Ida's spirit went with her. Ida had been very close to Connie, and she never fully recovered from her death. Connie was buried next to Ida's friend, Errol Flynn, who had died only two months earlier, at Forest Lawn's Wee Kirk o' the Heather.

Ida was also depressed over her crumbling marriage. When Ida and Howard were together, there were frequent shoutings and plenty of alcohol consumed by both. "Once she was married to Howard Duff, she was so besotted with alcohol, that was it. They were like George and Martha in *Who's Afraid of Virginia Woolf?*" said her friend Robert Osborne.

Their rifts led to another separation in the fall of 1960, but they soon reconciled. Work kept Ida going, and she was lucky to begin a prolific career as a television director. Starting with *Have Gun, Will Travel* in April, 1960, Ida directed segments of *The Donna Reed Show*, *The Big Valley*, *Bewitched*, *The Twilight Zone*, *Alfred Hitchcock Presents* and dozens of other series.

One of Ida's favorite directorial assignments was "The Man in the Cooler" episode of *The Untouchables* in 1963. "She was a good director," said Paul Picerni, a regular on the series. "She let the actors have a free hand. Mike Curtiz would yell and scream to get what he wanted. Ida never did that. If she saw something she liked, she would leave it. It she wanted more, she would recommend doing it a certain way, or say, 'Do it this way for Mum.'"

In 1966 Ida directed her first feature film in thirteen years, *The Trouble with Angels*, a comedy based on *Life of Mother Superior*, a first novel by Jane Trahey. The raucous yarn about two incorrigible teenage girls (Hayley Mills and June Harding) and the havoc they wreak upon the stern Mother Superior (Rosalind Russell) of a Catholic boarding school was a far cry from *Outrage*, not to mention her recent television assignments, such as *Boris Karloff's Thriller*.

Ida often refused jobs that would take her away from home for long periods. Despite her image as an aggressive female pioneer in a male-dominated industry, Ida never viewed herself in that light. If anything, her views on marriage and women in the work force were almost Victorian.

"Any woman who wishes to smash into the world of men isn't very feminine," she told reporter Paul Gardner. "Baby, we can't go smashing. I believe women should be struck regularly—like a gong. Or is it bong? If a woman has a man who loves her, she better stick close to home. I've turned down jobs in Europe because I'd have to leave my husband and my daughter and my cats. I couldn't accept those jobs unless I was a guy."

Instead she accepted many television guest spots, including *Family Affair*, *Nanny and the Professor* and *The Mod Squad*. She and Howard appeared together as guest villains on *Batman*.

Ida still occasionally was sent film scripts, but she didn't like the new permissive direction Hollywood had taken. "I was sent a perfectly filthy script," Ida told *New York Times* reporter Judy Stone in 1969. "*I Am Curious Yellow* must be a virtuous film compared to this."

One she liked was *Junior Bonner* (1973), in which she played the mother of a rodeo star (Steve McQueen). Ida had given the film's director, Sam Peckinpah, his start when she hired him as an assistant director to Don Siegel on *Private Hell 36*. Peckinpah's direction sometimes confused Ida, and their collaboration was not a pleasant one. "I don't dig directors who want me to analyze my role. The only method I have goes, 'Dear God, I hope I make it today!'" Ida told Paul Gardner. "Sam Peckinpah's directions were, 'Surprise me, baby, but keep it clean.'"

No one was more surprised than Ida when she received most of the attention from critics. "The movie is made to order for both McQueen and (Robert) Preston, but the loveliest performance is that of Miss Lupino," said Vincent Canby of *The New York Times*.

"I don't know why the critics have been so nice to me. I can't judge my acting. I can't stand to see myself on the screen. Why? Because I don't care for myself," Ida told Gardner.

In the summer of 1972 Howard fell in love with Judy Jenkinson, a young woman in her twenties whom he met while appearing in *The Price* at the Ivorton Playhouse. Although Howard moved out of their home, he and Ida didn't file for divorce until 1983. Ida secretly hoped Howard would come back, but he didn't. From then on she began to retreat into her own private world.

Ida made sporadic television appearances, notably in *I Love a Mystery* (1973), based on the old radio series; and *The Letters* (1973), an anthology film that ABC envisioned as a possible series. Her last three film appearances were in *The Devil's Rain* (1975), *Food of the Gods* (1975) and *My Boys Are Good Boys* (1978), none of which were particularly enjoyable. If anything, it was sad to see Ida, who had lit up so many classy dramas, reduced to appearing in drive-in fare.

In October 1976 Ida was given the lead in *The Thoroughbreds*, a racing tale filmed in Kentucky, but she had a difficult time remembering her lines and was replaced by Vera Miles.

In 1977 Ida appeared on an episode of *Charlie's Angels* as a former actress who hires the trio of luscious detectives to find out who is trying to drive her insane. Again she had trouble remembering her lines, but she managed to complete the show. It was her last performance.

Ida then became more reclusive. The peace and solitude of her home was a refreshing change after her stormy marriage to Howard, and she wallowed in it. She spent much of her time tending to her garden, but rarely had guests in her home. She attended parties, but only if she knew old friends would also be there.

Although Ida had become wary of strangers, she did become friendly with Mary Ann Anderson, the daughter of actress Emily McLaughlin, who became Ida's companion. Anderson managed Ida's home and was later conservator of Ida's estate.

In 1988 Ida's health began to deteriorate and she was hospitalized. Worried that Ida could go at any minute, Anderson searched for someone from Ida's past to come see Ida before she died. Ironically, the person she contacted was Olivia de Havilland, with whom Ida had a less-than-loving relationship when they shot *Devotion*. De Havilland was in Hollywood for the Academy Awards, which she was planning to attend with Robert Osborne that evening.

"Instead we went to the hospital and Olivia took charge," Osborne recalled. "Ida had been drugged to keep her calm. She was given the last rites. Olivia noticed there was something wrong with Ida's mouth because it had sores on it. Olivia called a dentist and had him come in. This all happened over a two-day time period. Ida's system had been poisoned by her rotting mouth. Olivia made sure she got the medical attention she needed, and in a couple of months Ida was released. That was when their relationship started, and they remained friends until Ida died."

Another person from her past with whom Ida renewed a friendship was Mala Powers. "There weren't that many people who went to see her. She needed me ... she needed people," Powers said. "You had to have a certain amount of patience with her. She said exactly what she thought. Any tact that had been present in her earlier years was not there. Good heavens, if you were on the opposite side of any political fence of hers. She could become incensed over politicians she didn't like. She said what she wanted to say, strongly and dramatically."

Ida also became enraged whenever a reporter or columnist disparaged friends from the past. "If the name Errol Flynn came up in a negative way, she would go on a tirade. She would have practically killed them verbally. She didn't want anybody bad-mouthed," recalled Powers.

At the same time, Ida still retained her sharp wit and her wry sense of humor. Ida's favorite day of the year was Halloween, in which she enjoyed pretending that she, Powers and Anderson were the three witches from *Macbeth*.

The final blow for Ida was when Howard died of a massive heart attack on July 9, 1990. For all of their troubles, he remained the love of her life, and she felt more alone than ever.

Ida spent her last few years secluded in her home. Her health worsened from years of alcohol abuse, and she developed cerebral circulatory problems. Her medical ills developed into cancer and she had a stroke in 1995. On August 3, 1995, Ida died at the age of seventy-seven.

Rather than a memorial service, a celebration of Ida's life, consisting of remembrances of Ida by friends and family members, was held at Mala Powers' home. Among those who shared their memories were Powers, Roddy McDowall, Vincent Sherman, Bridget Duff and Rita Lupino.

Ironically, coinciding with Ida's death was a renewed interest in her films as a director. Ida would be proud to know that *The Hitch-Hiker*, *The Bigamist* and others are suddenly being studied for the unique social commentaries that they are. Equally proud would be Stanley Lupino, happy to know that his prediction that Ida would be the most famous Lupino of all came true.

FILMOGRAPHY

ACTRESS CREDITS

Her First Affaire (Sterling, 1932) Directed by Allan Dwan. *Cast:* Ida Lupino, Arnold Riches, George Curzon, Diana Napier.

Money for Speed (Hall Mark-United Artists, 1933) Directed by Bernard Vorhaus. *Cast:* Ida Lupino, Cyril McLaglen, John Loder, Moore Marriott.

High Finance (First National-British, 1933) Directed by George King. *Cast:* Gibb McLaughlin, Ida Lupino, John Batten, John Roberts.

The Ghost Camera (Julien Hagen-Twickenham, 1933) Directed by Bernard Vorhaus. *Cast:* Ida Lupino, Henry Kendall, John Mills.

I Lived with You (Gaumont-British, 1933) Directed by Maurice Elvey. *Cast:* Ivor Novello, Ursula Jeans, Ida Lupino, Minnie Raynor.

Prince of Arcadia (Gaumont-British, 1933) Directed by Hans Schwarz. *Cast:* Carl Brisson, Margot Grahame, Ida Lupino, Annie Esmond.

Search for Beauty (Paramount, 1934) Directed by Erle C. Kenton. *Cast:* Buster Crabbe, Ida Lupino, Robert Armstrong, James Gleason, Gertrude Michael, Roscoe Karns, Toby Wing.

Come on Marines (Paramount, 1934) Directed by Henry Hathaway. *Cast:* Richard Arlen, Ida Lupino, Roscoe Karns, Grace Bradley, Monte Blue, Lona Andre, Fuzzy Knight, Toby Wing.

Ready for Love (Paramount, 1934) Directed by Marion Gering. *Cast:* Richard Arlen, Ida Lupino, Marjorie Rambeau, Trent Durkin.

Paris in Spring (Paramount, 1935) Directed by Lewis Milestone. *Cast:* Mary Ellis, Tullio Carminati, Lynne Overman, Ida Lupino.

Smart Girl (Paramount, 1935) Directed by Aubrey Scotto. *Cast:* Ida Lupino, Kent Taylor, Gail Patrick, Joseph Cawthorn, Sidney Blackmer, Pinky Tomlin, Luise Brien, Theodore von Eltz.

Peter Ibbetson (Paramount, 1935) Directed by Henry Hathaway. *Cast:* Gary Cooper, Ann Harding, John Halliday, Ida Lupino, Douglass Dumbrille, Virginia Weidler, Dickie Moore.

Anything Goes (Paramount, 1936) Directed by Lewis Milestone. *Cast:* Bing Crosby, Ethel Merman, Charles Ruggles, Grace Bradley, Ida Lupino, Chill Wills, Arthur Treacher.

One Rainy Afternoon (Pickford Lasky-United Artists, 1936) Directed by Rowland V. Lee. *Cast:* Francis Lederer, Ida Lupino, Hugh Herbert, Roland Young, Erik Rhodes, Mischa Auer.

Yours for the Asking (Paramount, 1936) Directed by Alexander Hall. *Cast:* George Raft, Dolores Costello Barrymore, Ida Lupino, Reginald Owen, Charlie Ruggles, Lynne Overman.

The Gay Desperado (Pickford Lasky-United Artists, 1936) Directed by Rouben Mamoulian. *Cast:* Nino Martini, Ida Lupino, Leo Carillo, Harold Huber, Mischa Auer, Paul Hurst.

Sea Devils (RKO Radio, 1937) Directed by Ben Stoloff. *Cast:* Victor McLaglen, Preston Foster, Ida Lupino, Donald Woods, Helen Flint, Gordon Jones, Pierre Watkin, Murray Alper.

Let's Get Married (Columbia, 1937) Directed by Alfred E. Green. *Cast:* Ida Lupino, Walter Connolly, Ralph Bellamy, Raymond Walburn, Reginald Denny, Arthur Hoyt, Granville Bates.

Artists and Models (Paramount, 1937) Directed by Raoul Walsh. *Cast:* Jack Benny, Ida Lupino, Richard Arlen, Gail Patrick, Ben Blue, Judy Canova, Martha Raye, Donald Meek.

Fight for Your Lady (RKO Radio, 1937) Directed by Ben Stoloff. *Cast:* John Boles, Jack Oakie, Ida Lupino, Margot Grahame, Erik Rhodes, Billy Gilbert, Gordon Jones, Paul Guilfoyle.

The Lone Wolf Spy Hunt (Columbia, 1939) Directed by Peter Godfrey. *Cast:* Warren William, Ida Lupino, Rita Hayworth, Virginia Weidler, Tom Dugan, Don Beddoe.

The Lady and the Mob (Columbia, 1939) Directed by Ben Stoloff. *Cast:* Fay Bainter, Ida Lupino, Lee Bowman, Henry Armetta, Warren Hymer, Harold Huber, Tom Dugan.

The Adventures of Sherlock Holmes (20th Century-Fox, 1939) Directed by Alfred Werker. *Cast:* Basil Rathbone, Nigel Bruce, Ida Lupino, Alan Marshal, George Zucco, Terry Kilburn.

The Light That Failed (Paramount, 1939) Directed by William A. Wellman. *Cast:* Ronald Colman, Walter Huston, Muriel Angelus, Ida Lupino, Dudley Digges, Fay Helm.

They Drive by Night (Warner Bros., 1940) Directed by Raoul Walsh. *Cast:* George Raft, Ann Sheridan, Humphrey Bogart, Ida Lupino, Alan Hale, Roscoe Karns, Gale Page, John Litel.

High Sierra (Warner Bros., 1941) Directed by Raoul Walsh. *Cast:* Ida Lupino, Humphrey Bogart, Joan Leslie, Henry Travers, Arthur Kennedy, Alan Curtis, Henry Hull, Elisabeth Risdon.

The Sea Wolf (Warner Bros., 1941) Directed by Michael Curtiz. *Cast:* Edward G. Robinson, John Garfield, Ida Lupino, Alexander Knox, Barry Fitzgerald, Gene Lockhart, Stanley Ridges.

Out of the Fog (Warner Bros., 1941) Directed by

Anatole Litvak. *Cast:* Ida Lupino, John Garfield, Thomas Mitchell, Eddie Albert, Aline MacMahon, John Qualen, George Tobias.

Ladies in Retirement (Columbia, 1941) Directed by Charles Vidor. *Cast:* Ida Lupino, Louis Hayward, Evelyn Keyes, Elsa Lanchester, Isobel Elsom, Edith Barrett.

Moontide (20th Century–Fox, 1942) Directed by Archie Mayo. *Cast:* Jean Gabin, Ida Lupino, Claude Rains, Thomas Mitchell, Jerome Cowan, Sen Yung, Tully Marshall, Helene Reynolds.

Life Begins at 8:30 (20th Century–Fox, 1942) Directed by Irving Pichel. *Cast:* Monty Woolley, Ida Lupino, Cornel Wilde, Sara Allgood, Melville Cooper, J. Edward Bromberg.

The Hard Way (Warner Bros., 1943) Directed by Vincent Sherman. *Cast:* Ida Lupino, Dennis Morgan, Joan Leslie, Jack Carson, Gladys George, Roman Bohnen, Faye Emerson.

Forever and a Day (RKO Radio, 1943) Directed by Rene Clair, Edmund Goulding, Cedric Hardwicke, Frank Lloyd, Victor Saville, Robert Stevenson, Robert Wilcox. *Cast:* Brian Aherne, Gladys Cooper, Robert Cummings, Edmund Gwenn, Cedric Hardwicke, Buster Keaton, Charles Laughton, Ida Lupino, Herbert Marshall, Jessie Matthews, Ray Milland, Anna Neagle, Merle Oberon, Kent Smith, Arthur Treacher, Ruth Warrick, Dame May Whitty, Roland Young.

Thank Your Lucky Stars (Warner Bros., 1943) Directed by David Butler. *Cast:* Dennis Morgan, Joan Leslie, Edward Everett Horton, S.Z. Sakall, Ruth Donnelly, Joyce Reynolds. *Guest Stars:* Humphrey Bogart, Eddie Cantor, Jack Carson, Bette Davis, Olivia de Havilland, Errol Flynn, John Garfield, Alan Hale, Ida Lupino, Hattie McDaniel, Ann Sheridan, Alexis Smith.

Hollywood Canteen (Warner Bros., 1944) Directed by Delmer Daves. *Cast:* Joan Leslie, Robert Hutton, Janis Paige, Dane Clark. *Guest Stars:* Jack Benny, Joe E. Brown, Eddie Cantor, Joan Crawford, Bette Davis, John Garfield, Sydney Greenstreet, Paul Henreid, Ida Lupino, Dennis Morgan, Eleanor Parker, Roy Rogers, Alexis Smith, Barbara Stanwyck, Jane Wyman.

In Our Time (Warner Bros., 1944) Directed by Vincent Sherman. *Cast:* Ida Lupino, Paul Henreid, Nancy Coleman, Mary Boland, Victor Francen, Alla Nazimova, Michael Chekhov.

Pillow to Post (Warner Bros., 1945) Directed by Vincent Sherman. *Cast:* Ida Lupino, William Prince, Sydney Greenstreet, Stuart Erwin, Ruth Donnelly, Barbara Brown, Willie Best.

Devotion (Warner Bros., 1946) Directed by Curtis Bernhardt. *Cast:* Ida Lupino, Paul Henreid, Olivia de Havilland, Sydney Greenstreet, Nancy Coleman, Arthur Kennedy, Dame May Whitty.

The Man I Love (Warner Bros., 1947) Directed by Raoul Walsh. *Cast:* Ida Lupino, Andrea King, Robert Alda, Bruce Bennett, Martha Vickers, Alan Hale, Dolores Moran, John Ridgeley.

Escape Me Never (Warner Bros., 1947) Directed by Peter Godfrey. *Cast:* Errol Flynn, Ida Lupino, Eleanor Parker, Gig Young, Reginald Denny, Isobel Elsom, Albert Basserman.

Deep Valley (Warner Bros., 1947) Directed by Jean Negulesco. *Cast:* Ida Lupino, Dane Clark, Wayne Morris, Fay Bainter, Henry Hull, Willard Robertson.

Road House (20th Century–Fox, 1948) Directed by Jean Negulesco. *Cast:* Ida Lupino, Cornel Wilde, Richard Widmark, Celeste Holm, O.Z. Whitehead, Robert Karnes, Douglas Gerrard.

Lust for Gold (Columbia, 1949) Directed by S. Sylvan Simon. *Cast:* Ida Lupino, Glenn Ford, Gig Young, William Prince, Edgar Buchanan, Paul Ford, Will Geer.

Woman in Hiding (Universal-International, 1950) Directed by Michael Gordon. *Cast:* Ida Lupino, Howard Duff, Stephen McNally, Peggy Dow, John Litel, Taylor Holmes, Irving Bacon.

On Dangerous Ground (RKO Radio, 1951) Directed by Nicholas Ray. *Cast:* Ida Lupino, Robert Ryan, Ward Bond, Charles Kemper, Sumner Williams, Anthony Ross, Ed Begley.

Beware My Lovely (RKO Radio, 1952) Directed by Harry Horner. *Cast:* Ida Lupino, Robert Ryan, Taylor Holmes, Barbara Whiting, O.Z. Whitehead, James Willmas, Dee Pollack.

Jennifer (Allied Artists, 1953) Directed by Joel Newton. *Cast:* Ida Lupino, Howard Duff, Robert Nichols, Mary Shipp.

The Bigamist (Filmakers, 1953) Directed by Ida Lupino. *Cast:* Joan Fontaine, Edmond O'Brien, Ida Lupino, Edmund Gwenn, Jane Darwell, Kenneth Tobey.

Private Hell 36 (Filmakers, 1954) Directed by Don Siegel. *Cast:* Ida Lupino, Steve Cochran, Howard Duff, Dean Jagger, Dorothy Malone.

Women's Prison (Columbia, 1955) Directed by Lewis Seiler. *Cast:* Ida Lupino, Howard Duff, Audrey Totter, Jan Sterling, Cleo Moore, Phyllis Thaxter, Ross Elliott, Mae Clarke.

The Big Knife (United Artists, 1955) Directed by Robert Aldrich. *Cast:* Jack Palance, Ida Lupino, Rod Steiger, Everett Sloane, Wendell Corey, Shelley Winters, Jean Hagen, Ilka Chase.

While the City Sleeps (RKO Radio, 1956) Directed by Fritz Lang. *Cast:* Dana Andrews, Ida Lupino, Rhonda Fleming, Thomas Mitchell, George Sanders, Howard Duff, Sally Forrest.

Strange Intruder (Allied Artists, 1957) Directed by Irving Rapper. *Cast:* Edmund Purdom, Ida Lupino, Ann Harding, Jacques Bergerac, Carl Benton Reid, Gloria Talbott, Marjorie Bennett.

Deadhead Miles (Paramount, 1972) Directed by

Vernon Zimmerman. *Cast:* Alan Arkin, Paul Benedict, Hector Elizondo, Oliver Clark, Charles Durning, Larry Wolf, Barnard Hughes, Loretta Swit, Allen Garfield, Bruce Bennett, John Milius, Ida Lupino, George Raft.

Junior Bonner (Cinerama, 1972) Directed by Sam Peckinpah. *Cast:* Steve McQueen, Robert Preston, Ida Lupino, Ben Johnson, Joe Don Baker, Barbara Leigh, Mary Murphy.

The Devil's Rain (Bryanston, 1975) Directed by Robert Fuest. *Cast:* Ernest Borgnine, Eddie Albert, Ida Lupino, William Shatner, Keenan Wynn, Tom Skerrit, John Travolta.

Food of the Gods (American International, 1976) Directed by Bert I. Gordon. *Cast:* Marjoe Gortner, Pamela Franklin, Ralph Meeker, Ida Lupino, John McLiam, Jon Cypher.

My Boys Are Good Boys (Lone Star, 1978) Directed by Bethel Buckalew. *Cast:* Ralph Meeker, Ida Lupino, Lloyd Nolan, David F. Doyle, Sean T. Roche.

TELEVISION FILM CREDITS

Backtrack (1969) *Cast:* Neville Brand, James Drury, Doug McClure, Ida Lupino.

Women in Chains (1972) *Cast:* Ida Lupino, Lois Nettleton, Jessica Walter.

The Strangers in 7A (1972) *Cast:* Andy Griffith, Ida Lupino, Michael Brandon, James Watson.

Female Artillery (1973) *Cast:* Dennis Weaver, Ida Lupino, Sally Ann Howes, Linda Evans.

I Love a Mystery (1973) *Cast:* Ida Lupino, Les Crane, David Hartman, Jack Weston.

The Letters (1973) *Cast:* Barbara Stanwyck, John Forsythe, Ida Lupino, Ben Murphy.

DIRECTOR CREDITS

Not Wanted (Emerald–Film Classics, 1949) Directed by Elmer Clifton (Ida took over direction when he became ill, but he received screen credit). *Cast:* Sally Forrest, Keefe Brasselle, Leo Penn.

Never Fear (Filmakers–Eagle Lion, 1950) *Cast:* Sally Forrest, Keefe Brasselle, Hugh O'Brian, Eve Miller, Lawrence Dobkin. (Also known as *The Young Lovers.*)

Outrage (Filmakers–RKO Radio, 1950) *Cast:* Mala Powers, Tod Andrews, Robert Clarke.

Hard, Fast and Beautiful (Filmakers–RKO Radio, 1952) *Cast:* Sally Forrest, Claire Trevor, Robert Clarke, Kenneth Patterson, Joseph Kearns, William Hudson.

The Hitch-Hiker (Filmakers–RKO Radio, 1953) *Cast:* Edmond O'Brien, Frank Lovejoy, William Talman, Jose Torvay, Sam Hayes, Wendel Niles, Jean Del Val.

The Bigamist (see Actress filmography)

The Trouble with Angels (Columbia, 1966) *Cast:* Rosalind Russell, Hayley Mills, June Harding, Binnie Barnes, Mary Wickes, Camilla Sparv, Gypsy Rose Lee.

Eleanor Parker: "Woman of a Thousand Faces"

Gorgeous Eleanor Parker was one of Warners' rare commodities—a delicate, blue-eyed beauty with a chameleon-like ability to transform herself into any character the studio assigned her to play. Equally adept at romantic comedy (*Voice of the Turtle*) and tense melodrama (*Caged*), Eleanor was labeled by publicists as "the Woman of a Thousand Faces."

Yet for all her skills, Eleanor never attained the superstardom that critics and even her colleagues anticipated. Part of the fault lies with Warners, which often assigned her poor vehicles. It also didn't help Eleanor's cause that she didn't play the Hollywood game: She preferred spending an evening at home with her family to being photographed in a nightclub. Neither was she one for doing cheesecake shots or giving out endless interviews to the fan magazines. With such a publicity-shy nature, she wasn't likely to get the same sort of build-up by Warners that someone like Ann Sheridan received. But when she was given a good role, as in *Interrupted Melody*, in which she poignantly portrayed soprano Marjorie Lawrence, she was unforgettable.

Eleanor was born on June 26, 1922, in Cedarville, Ohio, where her father, Lester K. Parker, taught mathematics at the local high school. Eleanor was movie struck from the time she was five. Blessed with a vivid imagination, she did imitations of her favorite stars in the family living room and the backyard, and as she got older, wrote, staged, directed and starred in short plays. She also cast all the parts, always reserving the lead for herself.

"The other kids weren't much interested, but that was all right with me. I just wanted to hear my own voice anyway," she said.

By the time the Parkers moved to Cleveland in the mid–1930s, Eleanor was intent on being an actress. She was fortunate to have the support of her parents, who sent her to the Tucker School of Expression in Cleveland. When she was fifteen they let her go to Martha's Vineyard in Massachusetts, where she spent two summers with the stock company of Tucker's sister school, the prestigious Rice School of Expression. To support herself, Eleanor waited on tables.

"That's where you learn about human nature," Eleanor said in a 1955 interview. "Even though you're one of a group, working toward a common goal, put on a uniform and you're a waitress. It used to hurt me a little to be treated in such an offhand manner by boys and girls I knew by their first names in school, but luckily I had sense enough not to let it bother me. I accepted it as part of the price I had to pay."

Eleanor's hard work paid off with a bit in *What a Life*, before she decided to go back to Cleveland and finish her high school education. Upon graduating in 1940, Eleanor headed west and began studying at the Pasadena Playhouse, which is where she was discovered by a Warner Bros. talent scout. There are several accounts as to how she caught his attention. The first, and more probable, version is that she was appearing in a play and the talent scout was taken with her rich, throaty voice. A second version is that he spotted her in the audience

Ravishing Eleanor Parker might have become a bigger star if she was willing to play the publicity game.

and was struck by her green eyes, luscious reddish-brown hair and delicate skin.

However it happened, Eleanor made a successful screen test and was signed by Warners three days later on her nineteenth birthday. Things began poorly when her bit in *They Died with Their Boots On* (1941), a loosely detailed biography of George Armstrong Custer, was deleted.

"I had to kiss my sweetheart off to battle," she said later, "and the director said I was fine. But the picture — almost two and a half hours when finished — was too long for those days, and my whole part was cut out."

Eleanor's film debut instead was in a two-reel Technicolor short on the Army's Medical Corps entitled *Soldiers in White* (1942), which was filmed at Fort Sam Houston in Texas.

Eleanor spent much of her first months at Warners under the tutelage of acting coach Sophie Rosenstein and her associates before making *Busses Roar* (1942), sort of a quickie version of *Speed* (1994). More ludicrous was *The Mysterious Doctor* (1943), about a Nazi disguised as a headless ghost who terrorizes a mining village and sabotages British war efforts. As laughable as it sounds, Eleanor suffered valiantly, no doubt wishing she was back in Army films.

Despite the inferior material Eleanor had been handed so far, she acquitted herself well, both from a dramatic and a photographic standpoint. As a reward, Warners at last put her in an 'A' film, *Mission to Moscow* (1943), the controversial drama based on Ambassador Joseph Davies' book about his experiences in Russia. Walter Huston was cast as Davies, with Ann Harding as his wife and Eleanor as their daughter. Michael Curtiz was given directing chores.

According to Jack Warner, *Mission to Moscow* was made at the request of Franklin D. Roosevelt, who wanted support for the Russian war effort. What emerged on-screen, however, was unabashed propaganda that opened none-too-subtly with a prologue by the real Davies proclaiming the events in the film were "the truth as I saw it." The rest of the movie chronicled his meetings with Russian leaders, a recreation of the purge trials and visits to Russian factories.

Although some critics praised the movie as a brave and important achievement, others called it one of the biggest blunders in the studio's history. Not only was *Mission to Moscow* a bust at the box office, but in 1947 Jack Warner and the film came under fire when he was forced to defend it before a congressional committee investigating Communism in the film industry.

Politics aside, the movie is well-crafted, with excellent reproductions of Russian settings and uniformly good performances. Huston was properly dignified and forceful as Davies, and Eleanor lbrought elegance to her role.

It was during the making of *Mission to Moscow* that Eleanor met Lieutenant Fred L. Losee, a Navy dentist who was a visitor on the set. Following a brief courtship, they were married on March 21, 1943. Unfortunately, the marriage didn't last long, and they were divorced in December of 1944. During their divorce proceedings, Eleanor testified that Losee embarrassed her in front of their friends by stating that he couldn't care less about her film career.

Eleanor's next film should have been the Bette Davis–Miriam Hopkins clawfest *Old Acquaintance* (1943). Director Vincent Sherman wanted Eleanor to play Hopkins' daughter in the latter half of the movie, but he was shot down by Warner, who explained that Dolores Moran had been cast in pre-production when Edmund Goulding was set to direct. Eleanor visited the set of *Old Acquaintance* frequently, and she and Sherman became good friends. Sherman once more attempted to work with Eleanor when he was making the telefilm *The Last Hurrah* (1979), but its star, Carroll O'Connor, did not think she was right for the part of his wife.

Instead of *Old Acquaintance*, Eleanor made *Between Two Worlds* (1944), an absorbing remake of *Outward Bound* (1930). The prestigious cast also included John Garfield, Paul Henreid, Faye Emerson, Sydney Greenstreet and Edmund Gwenn. The story concerns a group of dead passengers on a fog-enshrouded boat as they await their final judgment. Paul Henreid and Eleanor teamed up as two of the ship's inhabitants, lovers who committed suicide.

The theatrical roots of *Between Two Worlds* are evident in its claustrophobic setting. Most of the action occurs on the ship, which makes the movie static and talky. A saving grace were the fine performances, notably Greenstreet as the judge and Gwenn as his assistant. Eleanor was touching, especially in her early scenes as she tries to stop Henreid from killing himself. More of an artistic endeavor than escapist fare, *Between Two Worlds* was a flop.

After toiling in the inconsequential Bs *Crime by Night* (1944) and *The Last Ride* (1944), Eleanor had her first leading role in *The Very Thought of You* (1944), a well-made wartime romance directed by Delmer Daves. Eleanor starred as Janet, a war factory worker who meets marine Dennis Morgan on a bus. She invites him home to meet her family, who, for the most part, give him a frosty reception. Despite her familial problems, the couple elopes and enjoys a brief honeymoon before he returns to active duty. While he is away, Janet becomes pregnant. Her child's birth coincides with the news that her husband has been wounded in action. The movie ends awash in tears as the couple is reunited and Janet's selfish family asks for her forgiveness.

The Very Thought of You struck a chord with wartime audiences. Though less effective than Vincente Minnelli's *The Clock* (1945), which covered similar ground in greater depth, *The Very Thought of You* is an interesting timepiece depicting wartime marriage on the run. Eleanor's sincerity helped the slight material stretch further than it would have in lesser hands. *The New York Times* called it a "distasteful and irritating picture" but thought, "Eleanor Parker is just the kind of sight any GI would be grateful for, even without spending two years in the Aleutians."

Although Eleanor was treated pretty shabbily on-screen by Andrea King, who played her sister, the two became close friends when the cameras weren't rolling. "Eleanor Parker was a dear to work with," King said. "At the time I was doing *The Very Thought of You* I had found a new house, but it was about an hour and a half from the studio. Eleanor only lived about five minutes from the studio, so she asked if I'd like to stay with her while we were making the movie. It took about five weeks to shoot the movie. She was just wonderful."

Eleanor's cameo appearance in *Hollywood Canteen* (1944) was followed by one of her best roles—in *Pride of the Marines* (1945), a powerful, thought-provoking drama about a returning veteran. The movie was inspired by Roger Butterfield's *Life* magazine article on Al Schmid, a marine who machine-gunned roughly two hundred Japanese soldiers during a fierce night attack on Guadalcanal. The price of Schmid's heroism was the loss of his eyesight from an incoming grenade. Even after he was struck blind, Schmid refused to give up his position and continued to gun down the enemy by having a wounded buddy tell him where to point his gun.

To play Schmid, Warners chose John Garfield, in what may be his best role while under contract to the studio. Alexis Smith was the original choice to play his fiancée, Ruth, but Garfield took a shine to Eleanor during *Between Two Worlds* and requested her.

Pride of the Marines served as a warm-up for *The Best Years of Our Lives* (1946), but it is just as gritty in its depiction of the plight of returning war veterans. Albert Maltz's hard-hitting script dealt believably with Schmidt's difficult adjustment to his handicap — in particular, his fears that Ruth would now only see him as an object of pity. Maltz also deserves credit for his multi-dimensional treatment of the faithful Ruth, which Eleanor played beautifully. She is especially moving in the climactic scene when she pleads with Al not to leave her, and then rushes to his aid when he falls into a Christmas tree. "Eleanor Parker, given full opportunity, puts the beauty of a strong girl's spirit into the role of Ruth Harley," wrote reviewer Bosley Crowther.

After her sensitive performances in *The Very Thought of You* and *Pride of the Marines*, Eleanor seemed like an odd choice for Mildred, the shrewish Cockney waitress in director Edmund Goulding's remake of W. Somerset Maugham's *Of Human Bondage* (1946). To publicize the film, the April 30, 1945, issue of *Life* ran a two-page photo spread showing Eleanor in her Mildred characterization displaying various emotions, ranging from anger to pity.

Maugham's portrait of obsession concerns lame medical student Phillip Carey (Paul Henreid), who becomes emotionally bound to Mildred Rogers, a Cockney waitress who is indifferent to him. Phillip gives up his chance at happiness with a successful novelist (Alexis Smith) who adores him because he is bound to Mildred. He is deeply hurt when Mildred runs off with his roguish friend (Patric Knowles), whose illegitimate baby she bears. Phillip takes mother and daughter into his home when they are deserted. He gradually begins to see Mildred for the pathetic wretch that she is, and feels little remorse for her when she finally dies. Phillip eventually finds happiness with Sally (Janis Paige), the daughter of his professor friend (Edmund Gwenn).

Catherine Turney adapted the novel for her screenplay but was only partially successful. Part of the problem lies with the novel itself. While in print, the attraction that Phillip has for Mildred seems more apparent; onscreen, in both the 1934 Bette Davis version and this one, it's never clear why Phillip is so willing to submit to Mildred's boorish and degrading behavior. Turney also went for a sunny ending, as opposed to the more somber and ambiguous finale of the first version.

Several critics were unimpressed with both the production and the stars' performances. "Most of the reviews contrasted me unfavorably with Bette Davis in the original," Eleanor told reporter Howard Thompson. "Some of them even accused me of imitating her walk. I really slaved to get a cockney accent of my own. I even wrote out phonetically and memorized it that way."

Comparisons to Davis' Mildred were inevitable, but at least Eleanor had one reviewer in her corner. "Miss Parker seemed to me a lot more plausible than Miss Davis as Mildred, possibly because she indulges less frequently in hyperthyroid hysterics," said *The New Yorker*.

In fairness to both women, it seems ridiculous to compare their performances, since each offered her own unique interpretation. Though bitch roles were not Eleanor's forte, her Mildred is surprisingly commanding. Sans makeup, and with tightly curled hair and dressed in tatters from the studio's "rag bag," Goulding stripped Eleanor of her usual glamour and refined manners. Eleanor has always ranked him among her favorite directors.

"Eddie usually acts out every part, even a baby's, but I was the only one in the cast he just — well, suggested to that time," Eleanor told *The New York Times* in 1953. "And I added what I got from [Maugham's] book. Not that earlier picture. Then I hadn't even seen it."

Eleanor's Mildred is appropriately exasperating and vulgar, but it is far from a one-note performance. She is equally effective in the film's quieter moments, such as when she pleads with Philip to let her and her baby move in with him. And in one dynamic scene Eleanor is downright frightening as she destroys Philip's apartment and slashes his artwork. *Of Human Bondage* only really seems to catch fire when Eleanor appears on-screen. Like the 1934 version, this remake was also a commercial disappointment.

Eleanor at this point was becoming disenchanted with the scripts she was being offered. She turned down the lead in *Stallion Road* (1947), a dreary romance among the horsey set, and was replaced by Alexis Smith. Then in August of 1945 she was once again on suspension when she refused to play a debutante masquerading as a dance hall girl in *Love and Learn* (1946). This time, newcomer Martha Vickers was Eleanor's substitute. Such assignments clearly show that Warners just didn't know how to cast Eleanor. After showing her ability to play fragile heroines, Warners should have been grooming her for deeper roles in that vein, such as the deaf mute heroine of *Johnny Belinda* (1948) or the shy mountain girl in *Deep Valley* (1947).

It was also during this lull when Eleanor married for a second time. On January 5, 1946, she eloped to Las Vegas with Bert Friedlob, who later produced *The Fireball* (1950), with Mickey Rooney, and *The Star* (1952), with Bette Davis. Eleanor, who yearned to start a family of her own, had three children during this union: daughters Susan and Sharon, born, respectively, in 1948 and 1950, and a son named Richard who arrived in 1952.

When Eleanor's suspension was over she was thrown into *Never Say Goodbye* (1946), a sugary comedy about an artist (Errol Flynn) anxious to win back his ex-wife from the arms of a brawny soldier (Forrest Tucker). It took five screenwriters to pen the script, which relied on every cliché imaginable, including the old standby of having the couple's too-cute-for-words daughter (Patti Brady) pretend to run away from home to reunite her parents.

Eleanor was back with Flynn in *Escape Me Never* (1947), an antiquated soap opera based on the novel by Margaret Kennedy. Eleanor played Fenella, an aristocratic beauty engaged to a reliable young man (Gig Young) but in love with his rakish brother (Flynn). Directed with a shaky hand by Peter Godfrey, *Escape Me Never* was unsure if it was supposed to be a comedy or a soap opera, and it failed in both respects. *The New York Times* tore the film to shreds, but said, "Eleanor Parker has our deepest sympathy."

After the less-than-stellar triple play of *Of Human Bondage*, *Never Say Goodbye* and *Escape Me Never*, Eleanor was in desperate need of another film of the caliber of *Pride of the Marines*. When Warners purchased the rights to John Van Druten's stage hit *The Voice of the Turtle* (1947), speculation immediately began over who would assume the starring role that won critical raves for Margaret Sullavan.

Ronald Reagan, who had the male lead, had appeared in two box-office duds—*Stallion Road* and *That Hagen Girl* (1947)—since his return from the service in 1945. In need of a hit, he tried to persuade Warners to borrow his friend June Allyson from MGM to play opposite him. Warner saw no reason to do MGM a favor and, to Reagan's initial displeasure, cast Eleanor instead.

Alfred de Liagre, who had produced *The Voice of the Turtle* on Broadway, was also not happy about that decision. De Liagre had come to the West Coast to produce the film version but returned to New York after only a few weeks, claiming that the casting of the principals was not what he hoped for. While he did not "disparage the ability of Warner Bros.' players," he then added that Sullavan was the ideal choice for Sally. De Liagre was replaced by Charles Hoffman.

Then Van Druten, who wrote the screenplay and was to direct, also departed because of casting. His replacement, Irving Rapper, likewise voiced concern about Eleanor and was ready to go on suspension until Warner persuaded him to stay.

"I got me a shingle bob and a nervous stomach from the first two weeks' shooting," Eleanor told Howard Thompson. "Irving Rapper, the director, and I had a head-on blowup. Then we were good friends." Rapper later told the press that he was grateful to his boss for making him do the picture, "since Miss Parker more than met the challenge."

Reagan also revised his opinion about Eleanor. "It took only one scene with Eleanor for me to realize I'd be lucky if I could stay even," he wrote in his autobiography.

Despite all the gloom-and-doom speculation, *The Voice of the Turtle* was a delightful romance between Sally, a starry-eyed budding actress, and Bill (Reagan), a soldier on a three-day pass. The two are thrown together when Sally's flirtatious friend Olive (Eve Arden in a side-splitting performance) dumps Bill for another man (Wayne Morris). When Bill can't get a hotel room, he ends up spending the weekend at Sally's apartment. It all begins innocently, but as the two grow fonder of one another, they find it increasingly hard to resist temptation.

Sally Middleton was one of the highlights of Eleanor's screen career. She displayed impeccable timing and also showed a knack for physical humor with her unusual way of turning down a bed, and in her frantic attempts to hide Bill from Olive.

In general, critics pointed out the freshness of Eleanor's performance. "Eleanor Parker brings a delightful spontaneity to the role of Sally Middleton," raved *Newsweek*.

The New York Times' Thomas M. Pryor paid Eleanor the ultimate compliment: "Miss Parker brings to [the role] the innocence and bewilderment of youth that is so essential, and in this respect she is even more successful than Miss Sullavan."

The Voice of the Turtle proved to be the shot in the arm Eleanor's career needed. The film was one of Warners' most profitable for that year, and Eleanor gained new respect as an actress.

Eleanor went from the sophistication of modern-day New York to Victorian England for *The Woman in White* (1948), based on Wilkie Collins' nineteenth-century mystery novel. Eleanor was given the challenge of playing a dual role: Laura Fairlie, the heiress to a handsome fortune, and Ann Catherick, her lookalike cousin who has escaped from a sanatorium. Plotting against both women is evil Count Fosco (a ghoulish Sydney Greenstreet). He has kept Ann hidden so that it will not be revealed that she is his wife's illegitimate daughter, and now he has arranged for Laura to marry sinister Sir Percival Clyde (John Emery). Ann wants to warn Laura that Sir Percival plans to kill her so that he and Fosco can then claim her fortune.

The Woman in White was perhaps director Peter Godfrey's best film. That is not to say it is a great film, but it is good fun, thanks to the performances of Greenstreet and Emery as the villains. Eleanor was fetching as Laura but seemed less secure as the frightened Ann, sometimes reduced to such mannerisms as pressing her hand to her mouth in fear at the sight of Count Fosco. *The New York Times* commented that, "Eleanor Parker is old-fashioned, too, going crazy and hearing the birdies singing in about as quaint a way as our grandmothers would allow."

Eleanor was off the screen for nearly two years after the birth of her first two children. She had a cameo in *It's a Great Feeling* (1949), a breezy Doris Day musical, then wasn't seen again until *Chain Lightning* (1950), opposite Humphrey Bogart. The airborne drama about a former World War II flier who test pilots a new jet that its manufacturer is trying to sell to the Air Force was a good aerial show but hardly stimulating drama, with its tired romantic subplot. Eleanor gamely played Bogart's wife, but the part hardly mustered excitement.

Far superior was *Caged* (1950), a gripping women's prison drama that provided Eleanor with the type of multi-faceted role she excelled at. Eleanor, then twenty-seven, played nineteen-year-old Marie Allen, a doe-eyed innocent who is sent to prison for being an accomplice in an armed robbery in which only forty dollars was netted and her husband was killed. As an indifferent prison clerk tells Marie, "Five dollars less and it wouldn't be a crime." During the medical exam Marie learns she is pregnant. The compassion of Mrs. Benton (Agnes Moorehead), the crusading warden, is small consolation for the cruelty Marie receives from a sadistic matron (Hope Emerson). Marie's life in prison becomes even more hellish when she goes into premature labor after witnessing the hanging suicide of a fellow inmate (Olive Deering), and sees her baby put in an institution. Worst of all is when Marie gets turned down for parole and makes a failed escape attempt. The embittered Marie eventually gets released when a vice queen (Lee Patrick) sets her up with a job on the outside, which in reality is a front for a shoplifting gang.

Screenwriter Virginia Kellogg visited four state jails and soaked up plenty of atmosphere to get the proper mood for *Caged*. Despite her efforts, the screenplay she co-wrote with Bernard C. Schoenfeld occasionally lapses into women's prison movie clichés. The obligatory cell riot scene was included, along with such trite dialogue as, "In this cage you get tough or you get killed." Marie's fellow inmates at times seem like members of a slumber party, sharing humorous anecdotes about their criminal pasts.

In general, *Caged* is a hard-hitting indictment on the penal system, thanks to John Cromwell's no-nonsense direction, especially the harrowing scene in which Marie's hair is shaved. The humming of the razor is the only sound effect as the camera zooms in for a devastating close-up of Marie's eyes as she watches her hair fall.

Eleanor's gutsy performance is surely one of her finest. She manages Marie's difficult transformation with credulity, beautifully conveying her loneliness and despair in the first half of the film, and equally, if not more effectively, showing her anger and frustration in the latter portion. *The New York Times* found *Caged* to be "awfully hollow," but, "Miss Parker gives a creditable and expressive performance as the unfortunate heroine."

Eleanor earned her first Best Actress Oscar nomination for *Caged*. Unfortunately, the race was one of the toughest in Oscar history as she faced off against Gloria Swanson in *Sunset Boulevard*, Bette Davis and Anne Baxter in *All About Eve*, and Judy Holliday in *Born Yesterday*. Although Swanson and Davis were sentimental favorites, columnist Bob Thomas insisted even on the eve of the Oscars, "It's still a wide-open race, particularly among the fillies." In the end, Holliday was the victor. Still, Eleanor was chosen Best Actress in the World at the Venice Film Festival for *Caged*.

Eleanor then teamed up with two other Warners hopefuls—Patricia Neal and Ruth Roman—in the underrated *Three Secrets* (1950), a compelling drama directed by Robert Wise. The movie was inspired by the plight of three-year-old Kathy Fiscus of Los Angeles, who fell down a well in 1949. Rescue efforts were recorded live by a local news team, as millions of concerned viewers waited for the outcome. Sadly, the little girl did not survive.

The child victim in *Three Secrets* is a five-year-old boy who is the sole survivor of a plane crash in which his adopted parents were killed. Eleanor, Neal and Roman play the three women who each believe he is the son they gave up for adoption exactly five years earlier. Through flashbacks we learn the circumstances that led to their decision to give away their babies: Susan (Eleanor), who was in love with a soldier engaged to someone else, was goaded into the adoption by her domineering mother; Phyllis (Neal) was an ambitious, globe-trotting reporter whose lack of domestic skills drove away her husband (Frank Lovejoy); and Anne (Roman) was sent to prison after she shot her child's father, a racketeer who was no longer interested in her.

Three Secrets seems patterned after Joseph L. Manckiewicz's *A Letter to Three Wives* (1949), with its opening present-day segment, its three flashbacks and the answer to the film's burning question—in this case, who is the real mother? Unlike Manckiewicz's film, which was a witty dissection of three marriages, *Three Secrets* doesn't probe into character analysis. Instead, it relies more heavily on soap opera manipulations for its revelations, but Wise's careful grip on the material, and a smart script by Martin Rackin and Gina Kaus, helped make *Three Secrets* several cuts above the typical woman's picture. Wise also tried to underscore what even he considered "soap opera" by injecting as much realism as possible into the rescue effort, which plays almost like a news story. "Wise's favorite part of the film was the rescue effort, which included using actual climbers from the Sierra Club, and veteran interviewer Bill Welsh to play the newsman."

Also key to the success of *Three Secrets* were the superlative performances of the three leading ladies. Though Eleanor had the least interesting role, her understated performance is among her best. Critics have on occasion accused Eleanor of overplaying or resorting to hysterics for dramatic effect. Wise kept her in check and helped her deliver an honest, thoughtful performance that made her character sympathetic and endearing.

After *Three Secrets* Eleanor chose not to renew her contract with Warners. She was anxious for diverse roles, though her first effort as a freelancer seemed a few notches below many of her Warners films. *Valentino* (1951), for Columbia, claimed to be the life story of silent screen legend Rudolph Valentino, but was merely a fictionalized Hollywood hack-job that suffered from limp direction by Lewis Allen, a terrible screenplay by George Bruce and a flat performance by newcomer Anthony Dexter as Valentino. Eleanor suffered bravely as Joan Carlyle, a fictional silent star who supposedly had a great romance with the Sheik and, as this tale implies, was probably the woman in black who visited Valentino's grave.

As Richard Mallett so aptly wrote in *Punch*: "The dialogue is unbelievably ham, the 'entirely imaginary' story commonplace; the players deserve sympathy."

Despite the negative reviews, *Valentino* was more popular than it should have been. At least in her first full-length Technicolor film Eleanor looked breathtaking.

Valentino was so bad it bordered on comedy. *A Millionaire for Christy* (1951) was supposed to be amusing, and for the most part, it was. Produced by her husband Bert for 20th Century-Fox, Eleanor was engaging as a gold-digging secretary on the make for her millionaire boss (Fred MacMurray). Hardly a novel plot, the stars made the slight tale click.

Eleanor then worked with director William Wyler on *The Detective Story* (1951), Paramount's filmization of Sidney Kingsley's hard-hitting drama about the events that transpire during one day in a New York City police precinct. Central to the day's activities is callous detective Jim McLeod (Kirk Douglas), whose career and marriage come under fire because of his own misguided code of justice. With an attitude that everyone is guilty until proven innocent, he thinks nothing of beating those he arrests, in particular, Dr. Schneider, a suspected abortionist. Later McLeod's wife Mary (Eleanor) becomes the target of her husband's warped sense of justice when he learns she went to Schneider when she was in her teens for an abortion.

"*Detective Story* is the kind of part I just love. Drama. Tragedy done the tasteful Wyler way," Eleanor told the *New York Times*.

Along with Goulding, Wyler was a director for whom Eleanor had nothing but praise: "Willie will say, 'Now let's exaggerate it.' Then, 'Now we'll underplay. Then he has you do it down the middle and shade from both sides."

Wyler also deserves credit for tackling the difficult subject matter in an adult manner. Though the Hays Office would not allow the word abortion to be uttered on-screen in 1951, the message is made clear, and the scene between Douglas and Parker when her secret is revealed is high drama. *The Detective Story* grossed a whopping $2.8 million.

Though *The New York Times* called it a "brisk, absorbing film," Crowther felt, "Kirk Douglas is so forceful and aggressive as the detective with a kink in his brain that the sweet and conventional distractions of Miss Parker as his wife appear quite tame."

Although Eleanor was second-billed after Douglas, her minimal screen time made her role seem like a supporting one. Surprisingly, when Oscar nominations were announced, Douglas was absent from the Best Actor lineup, while Eleanor was a Best Actress contender. She lost to odds-on favorite Vivien Leigh for *A Streetcar Named Desire*, but with back-to-back Oscar nominations, Eleanor was becoming a bankable star.

Hoping to cash in was MGM, which signed Eleanor to a contact that allowed her one outside film each year. Her initial MGM venture was Rafael Sabatini's colorful swashbuckler *Scaramouche* (1952). The movie was originally intended as a vehicle for Gene Kelly until Stewart Granger proved himself a popular adventure star in *King Solomon's Mines* (1950). Ava Gardner was originally slated for Eleanor's role. Sabatini's actioner, which takes place in pre-Revolutionary France, deals with dashing Andre Moreau (Granger) and his plan to avenge the death of his friend who was killed by the nefarious Marquis de Maynes (Mel Ferrer) in a duel. To perfect his fencing skills, Andre joins up with the Commedia del'Arte and romances Lenore (Eleanor), an old flame whom he once deserted. Their pairing has shades of Petruchio and Kate in *Taming of the Shrew*, and their comic performances together give the appearance of a flesh-and-blood Punch and Judy. Moreau eventually conquers his adversary, but once again rejects the tempestuous Lenore in favor of the delicate Aline (Janet Leigh), a member of the French aristocracy. In one of the wildest stretches of historical accuracy, Lenore finds comfort with a new lover — Napoleon!

Director George Sidney wisely focused on the comic elements of Sabatini's novel so that *Scaramouche* moves along at a spirited pace. Granger, in his first swashbuckling role, made a dashing hero in the best Errol Flynn tradition. As Lenore, Eleanor had the juicier female role, which afforded her the opportunity to engage in physical comedy and even wield a sword, both of which she did with great vigor. With radiant, shoulder-length red tresses, and dressed in both period gowns and tight-fitting eighteenth-century leotards, Eleanor was at her most seductive.

MGM up to that time had not dallied

much with tales of derring-do, but *Scaramouche* was such a big hit that it paved the way for a series of MGM adventure flicks in the '50s, including *Ivanhoe* (1952) and *Knights of the Round Table* (1954).

Eleanor next appeared in her first of three screen teamings with Robert Taylor, *Above and Beyond* (1953), a solid drama about Col. Paul Tibbets, the man who piloted the Enola Gay and dropped the atomic bomb over Hiroshima in 1945. Taylor played the troubled Tibbets and Eleanor was his patient wife, Lucy. Obviously, in such a film the more exciting sequences took place in the air, especially the climactic bombing, but Eleanor and Taylor brought great strength to the domestic scenes.

"I'd call it an important drama, basically a love story seen through the eyes of a woman," was how Eleanor described the film in a rare interview with *The New York Times*.

Devotion to her family drove her to turn down the female lead in *Tea and Sympathy*, a new play by Robert Anderson. Although she was intrigued by the role of a prep school housemaster's wife who awakens the sexual desires of a sensitive young student, she refused to leave her family or have her children uprooted. Deborah Kerr played the role instead.

"I'm afraid I'm not as ambitious as I might be—say, as ambitious as my husband is for me," she told *The New York Times*. "Now—I have Bert, the children and our friends, mostly in the business end of the industry. When we're not busy, we just lie around the house in slacks. That's the kind of people we are."

Eleanor then added: "Things have a way of working out right for me. I've had no real hard knocks, career-wise. I never did any starving in an attic. I come from a money-less background of schoolteachers and farmers in and around Cleveland. Doors opened, though. I maintain that if you work, believe in yourself and do what is right for you, without stepping all over others, the way opens up."

Despite Eleanor's somewhat idyllic description of life with Friedlob, there were obviously problems. On July 2, 1953, she filed suit for divorce, claiming that he caused her "grievous mental suffering." They divorced four months later.

Even though she was now single, Eleanor stayed close to home with her family. "I never go to night clubs and skip parties—the big ones, that is—when I can do it gracefully," she said. "I don't like them. It seems to me that most of the people at these affairs are unhappy. They must have some escape from themselves, I suppose, and find it in crowds. For me there's too much good music to hear, too many books waiting to read and, thank heavens, so much work."

Ironically, it was her next film that would serve as a stepping stone to her third marriage. *Escape from Fort Bravo* (1953) was a well-mounted, if familiar, western with the popular William Holden. The film was standard cavalry versus the Indians fare, but director John Sturges kept the action moving, and the on-location shooting at Death Valley made it look realistic.

At the time, Eleanor was looking for an artist to paint her portrait, and Holden recommended Paul Clemens, a painter who specialized in portraits. Eleanor was impressed with both the artist and his work, and he likewise became fascinated with his subject.

"It was one of the most exciting sittings I ever had," Clemens told reporter Hyatt Downing. "The portrait was to be small—just the head and shoulders—and while I was doing the preliminary sketch, we talked. I found that she possessed a lively and intelligent curiosity about my work; had none of the usual easy but superficial patter which a great many people employ to cover their abysmal ignorance about art. What she said made sense."

They soon discovered they had similar tastes in literature, classical music and art. What began as a friendship soon blossomed into romance, and they were married on November 24, 1954. During the time they were married, Clemens did fourteen portraits of Eleanor.

Shortly before her marriage, Eleanor completed *The Naked Jungle* (1954) for Paramount, an adventure yarn in which she played the mail-order bride of a South American plantation owner (Charlton Heston). The movie was an odd mixture of sexual tension and George Pal special effects, as armies of deadly ants approached Heston's estate. Though the scene in which the swarms of insects attack was especially gripping, Eleanor and Heston made attractive sparring partners in the rest of the film.

Following a double play with Taylor—in the visually appealing but boring *Valley of the*

Kings (1954) and the amusing frontier romp *Many Rivers to Cross* (1954), Eleanor starred in what she called "just about the best picture I ever made." The film was *Interrupted Melody* (1955), the honest and inspiring story of Australian soprano Marjorie Lawrence, who was stricken with polio at the height of her success.

The project had actually been kicking around at MGM since 1952 when it was envisioned as a vehicle for Greer Garson. The advent of new gimmicks such as 3D, Cinemascope and Cinerama caused MGM to hesitate on the Lawrence project. Realizing *Interrupted Melody* would be an expensive film to mount, the studio feared audiences might not be eager to see a story about opera and polio over trendier films such as *House of Wax* (1953).

Once the 3D fad ran its course in 1954, MGM's interest in *Interrupted Melody* was piqued once more. By that point Garson had left the studio, and producer Jack Cummings had to begin a search for a new leading lady. According to gossip maven Louella Parsons, when Eleanor arrived for her audition with Cummings, she flamed into his office and immediately took on the role of prima donna. She took the offensive and accused Cummings of disliking her, and then told Cummings exactly how she would play the role if she got it, and proceeded to show him. Cummings replied by telling her if she got the part she would do as she was told. "Then Cummings, one of our smartest producers ... realized the girl had deliberately pricked him into seeing how temperamental she could be," wrote Parsons. "And that's how Eleanor got the part."

Curtis Bernhardt, who left Warners for MGM in 1947, was chosen to direct. Several top male stars were approached to co-star as Dr. King, and all turned it down, fearing they would be stuck playing second fiddle. Glenn Ford, however, welcomed the chance to do a tender drama after a string of westerns and crime yarns. He later said how much he liked working with Eleanor, whom he described as "the most un-temperamental girl in Hollywood."

The movie opened with Lawrence rushing to catch a train so that she can compete in a talent competition in Sydney. She wins and heads to Paris to study with a renowned voice teacher (Francoise Rosay). Marjorie studies hard and eventually gets to play Carmen. She is well-received and soon becomes a leading opera star. At a party one night she meets Thomas King, who is studying to be an obstetrician. Although Marjorie and King like each other, they regard their encounter as a case of "two ships that pass in the night." King, now a successful doctor, encounters Marjorie in New York a few years later. This time they realize they cannot live without each other and get married. Their love for each other is tested when Marjorie develops polio. She gives up her career and at one point even attempts suicide. It is only after she is asked to sing at an army hospital, and she sees others in worse physical condition than herself—but with a spirit to live—that she at last accepts her illness and finally returns to the stage.

Eleanor's performance in *Interrupted Melody* may well be the apex of her career. Although she obviously could not handle the arias the story required, she did an effective job of mouthing while Eileen Farrell sang.

"I had to be letter perfect, because while I didn't actually sing the songs—I couldn't, of course—the movements of my lips in forming the words had to sync exactly with those of the great soprano's as they came off the soundtrack," Eleanor said. "I learned three operas in three languages during two weeks. I drove to work in the morning with the score propped up on the steering wheel of my car, and I woke up at night to find I'd been repeating the songs in my sleep."

Dramatically, Eleanor captured all of the nuances and personality changes the role called for. From her jubilation at winning the talent contest to her despair as she loses the will to live, she is mesmerizing. In the film's pivotal scene Eleanor is outstanding as Marjorie's husband forces her to turn off the phonograph that is playing her record. Both the physical and emotional hurt Eleanor expresses in this scene make it almost painful to watch.

Eleanor won accolades for her performance. Parsons boasted that, "Eleanor Parker catches the full scope of a great operatic personality: the bounce and vitality of the young farm girl, the arrogance of the young star, the tyranny of the invalid, the full-heartedness of a woman who can give and receive love."

The New York Times raved, "No one can take from Miss Parker the full credit for the emotional power she brings to the scenes of agonizing self-torment that come later in the film."

MGM took some liberties with Lawrence's repertoire. The music department relied on more popular arias from the likes of *Carmen* and *Madame Butterfly* rather than some of the heavier items that Lawrence was known for, to ensure theater patrons would not be turned off by the operatic numbers. The blend of culture and high drama helped the film do brisk business.

Interrupted Melody earned Eleanor a third Oscar nomination, but she lost to Anna Magnani for *The Rose Tattoo* (1955). William Ludwig and Sonya Levien won for their story and screenplay. Eleanor, however, took her Oscar loss in stride.

"I think it's possible for a performer to set too high a value on the Academy Award. I'd like to win it, of course — who wouldn't? — but it will never become an obsession with me. It's fine to hitch your wagon to a distant star, but failure to reach that shining goal could end in bitterness and frustration. I'm never going to let that happen to me."

Director Otto Preminger was so impressed with Eleanor's movements as an invalid in *Interrupted Melody*, that he specifically asked for her to play Frank Sinatra's wheelchair-bound wife in *The Man with the Golden Arm* (1955). The film was the first penetrating look at drug addiction, with Sinatra as Frankie, a down-and-out drummer who had been institutionalized to try and kick his heroin habit. He returns home to his wife Zosch (Eleanor), who blames him for the accident that crippled her. In reality, Zosch has regained the use of her legs, but she fears that if Frankie finds out the truth he will leave her. She is not the only one clinging to Frankie: His drug pusher (Darren McGavin) continues to hound him, making it impossible for Frankie to break free of his demons. He turns to Molly (Kim Novak) to help cure him of his addiction. Frankie eventually becomes drug free and strong enough to finally leave Zosch, especially when he discovers her secret. When she tries to stop him from leaving her, she has a fatal accident.

Preminger, who was never afraid to push cinema boundaries, whether it was with frank sexual discussion (*Anatomy of a Murder*), racial themes (*Carmen Jones*) or homosexuality (*Advise and Consent*), was unsparing in his depiction of drug addiction in *The Man with the Golden Arm*. Sinatra's withdrawal scenes are frighteningly real, and both he and the usually stoic Novak bring great conviction to those moments. Although critics thought Eleanor was too beautiful to be convincing as Sinatra's harpy of a wife, she still had her moments, most notably her confrontation with Novak in which she shouts, "He put me in this chair, and as long as I sit here he'll never leave me. He knows he belongs to me. I wouldn't want to live if he left me, and I'd rather see him dead, too, than have him go with you."

Much publicity and the controversial subject matter made *The Man with the Golden Arm* an enormous success. By contrast, the best that could be said of her next two films were that they were interesting failures. Eleanor made *The King and Four Queens* (1956) for the chance to work with Clark Gable, but it was a terrible western that even a soupcon of sex couldn't liven up. Gable played a cowboy after gold and the hand of one of Jo Van Fleet's four daughters. It was no surprise as to whose hand he got. A rare Raoul Walsh misfire, *The King and Four Queens* was sabotaged by poor editing, which included the deletion of several of Eleanor's key scenes.

Eleanor was not served much better by *Lizzie* (1957), a psychological drama based on *The Bird's Nest* by Shirley Jackson, in which she played a woman with three different personalities. A psychiatrist (Richard Boone), sounding more like a plumber than a doctor, offers his assessment of her condition: "She's stopped up the main pipeline of her mind with some disturbing obstruction." The obstruction, not surprisingly, harkens back to her unhappy childhood.

Though released shortly before the similarly themed *The Three Faces of Eve* (1957), *Lizzie* suffered from an overripe script by Mel Dinelli and uninspired direction by Hugo Haas. Likewise, Eleanor's performance paled in comparison to Joanne Woodward's dynamic Oscar-winning turn in *Eve*.

Neither it nor *The Seventh Sin* (1957) fared well with audiences. The latter, directed by Ronald Neame, was a remake of *The Painted Veil* (1934), with Eleanor taking on Greta Garbo's old role as the adulterous wife of a bacteriologist (Bill Travers). When her married lover (Jean-Pierre Aumont) refuses to leave his wife, Carol (Eleanor) has no choice but to travel with her husband from Hong Kong to a Chinese village with a cholera epidemic. The shallow Carol eventually begins to see her husband's good qualities—his love of children, his concern for others—and also takes a look at herself. She finds comfort by volunteering at a local convent, and also learns about love through the relationship between her friend Tim (George Sanders) and his Asian wife. She even begins to feel affection for her husband and begs his forgiveness for her sin. Her pleas lead to one passionate night between them, but he still cannot forgive her, especially when she tells him she's pregnant and is unsure whether he or her lover is the father.

The Painted Veil was an odd choice for a remake, since it was one of Garbo's few flops. Still, this version benefits from beautiful cinematography and a fine performance by Eleanor. "Exquisitely gowned, Miss Parker makes a sincere, often moving heroine, in spite of ... her almost blinding beauty. It's a tough part and Miss Parker tackles it like a professional," said Howard Thompson of *The New York Times*.

Eleanor took some time off from filmmaking to give birth to her fourth child, Paul Clemens, Jr. Paul Sr. had earlier adopted Eleanor's three children from her previous marriage. "It's better that way. Now they'll all have the same last name," Eleanor said at the time.

She made a welcome return to the screen in *A Hole in the Head* (1959), a Frank Capra–directed comedy about a Florida widower (Frank Sinatra) whose irresponsible behavior, especially when it comes to raising his son (Eddie Hodges), is a bone of contention with his older brother and his wife (Edward G. Robinson and Thelma Ritter). Eleanor was a knockout as an attractive widow whom the ne'er-do-well gets fixed up with. Packed with plenty of laughs and an Oscar-winning song ("High Hopes"), the movie was one of the year's big hits.

Eleanor also had a good supporting role as the wife of philandering Texas rancher Robert Mitchum in *Home from the Hill* (1960), her last for MGM. Though the movie did more for newcomers George Peppard and George Hamilton than it did for Eleanor, she turned in a lovely performance under Vincente Minnelli's direction.

Eleanor had been curtailing her film work in favor of spending more time with her children. In the summer of 1960 she and her family moved from their Bel Air mansion to a seven-bedroom beach house at Lido Isle, which was about fifty-five miles away from Los Angeles. She dismissed all of the servants except for Paul Jr.'s nurse. Instead, she assigned household chores to each of the older children.

Eleanor loved peaceful Lido Isle, which also attracted such neighbors as Jane Wyman, Claire Trevor and Rock Hudson. "It's like living in a small town. We all bicycle back and forth to the markets, and the children all go to school together on a bus," Eleanor said. "There's never any fear for the children because there are not many automobiles cruising past the houses."

She did make the trek back to Hollywood the next year for two movies released by 20th Century–Fox. In *Return to Peyton Place* (1961), a sequel to the 1957 smash, *Peyton Place*, Eleanor took over Lana Turner's role as Constance Mackenzie, one of the New England Babylon's citizens who is furious over the salacious tell-all book her daughter Alison (Carol Lynley) has written about her hometown. Less steamy and more talky than the first film, *Return to Peyton Place* was dominated by Mary Astor's scenery-chewing performance as a domineering matron leading the campaign to have the book banned from the school library.

Her other Fox film was *Madison Avenue* (1962), a poor drama about the advertising industry, in which Eleanor was transformed from a struggling failure to a power-hungry executive thanks to the help of Dana Andrews. The movie may not have been heralded by critics, but Andrews remarked that Eleanor is "the least heralded great actress." Director Bruce Humberstone was even more flattering: "It's one-take pros like Eleanor who make directors look good."

In the early '60s Eleanor began dabbling in television, with appearances as Sister Cecelia in a 90-minute adaptation of Ernest Hemingway's *The Gambler, the Nun and the Radio*, and as a stripper in an episode of *Checkmate*. She also received an Emmy nomination in 1963 for her work in "Why Am I Grown So Cold?" an episode of *The Eleventh Hour*.

In 1962 several interesting proposals were announced as possible projects for Eleanor: *I Was a Spy*, the true story of an American housewife who becomes part of a Communist organization to help the FBI; *Mother Cabrini*, a biography of the American saint, which also had director Curtis Bernhardt attached to it; *Away from Home*, based on Rona Jaffe's novel about Americans in Brazil; *The Park Avenue Story*, a romantic comedy that would have teamed her with James Cagney; and *Madeleine*, a modern version of *Medea* for Federico Fellini.

For whatever reasons, none of these projects ever materialized, either with or without Eleanor. In fact, she stayed offscreen until 1964, when she surfaced for a small role in *Panic Button*, a sort of low-grade version of *The Producers* (1968) made in Italy. Maurice Chevalier and Akim Tamiroff also appeared in the film, but it had few bookings.

Director Robert Wise had fond memories of working with Eleanor on *Three Secrets*. When he began work on the film version of Rodgers and Hammerstein's *The Sound of Music* (1965) he immediately thought of Eleanor to play the Baroness who falls in love with Captain von Trapp. "I thought she had the right quality to play the baroness. She was so elegant and had a regal way about her," said Wise.

Though most of the movie's focus was on the romance between Maria, governess to the von Trapp children, and the stern captain, Eleanor provided some extra zest as "the other woman" who hopes to become the next Madame von Trapp. Although Eleanor's role is brief, she's both amusing in her awkward attempt to mingle with the children in a lawn game, and touching in the scene with Julie Andrews when she advises Maria to forget about von Trapp.

"I just thought she was wonderful in that scene," said Wise. "She played it beautifully and gave me exactly what I wanted. She was just a total joy to work with. A complete professional. She's still an absolute delight."

The Sound of Music was the most successful film Eleanor ever appeared in, and for several years it was the second highest all-time moneymaker, right behind *Gone with the Wind* (1939). It is also the only film Eleanor appeared in to ever win a Best Picture Oscar.

Sadly, it was also her last good feature film. Her movies over the next few years—*The Oscar* (1966), *An American Dream* (1966), *Warning Shot* (1967) and *The Tiger and the Pussycat* (1967)—were all dreadful and unworthy of her talent. Although Eleanor looked much younger than her forty-four years, she was no longer being offered the romantic leads that she used to get.

Eleanor became even less driven about her career. She had divorced Clemens on March 9, 1965, and shortly afterward met prominent businessman Raymond N. Hirsch. They wed on April 17, 1966, and have been happily married ever since.

She did make one more feature during this period, *Eye of the Cat* (1969), an inconsequential thriller in the *Psycho* vein but without the Hitchcock touch. Still, its premise about a young man (Michael Sarrazin) with a fear of cats who moves into the home of his rich aunt (Eleanor) with a passion for felines had its scary moments.

With few interesting movie offers coming her way, Eleanor accepted a starring role in the television series *Bracken's World*, a look at the complicated lives of the people who work at a motion picture studio. Eleanor played Sylvia Chase, girl Friday to studio head Bracken, who was mentioned but never seen. Looking far more radiant than most of the young starlets who graced the show, Eleanor brought her usual skill and dignity to the series.

Critics, however, panned it. "Attractive people, led by Eleanor Parker, brave the confusion on the movie lot, but it is Bracken, the ostensible tycoon of the studio, who is the wisest character. He does not put in an appearance, a decision to be heartily supported by the set owner," said *The New York Times*.

Eleanor left the series during the middle of its first season, and without her the show lost whatever spark it had and was canceled early in its second year. Her performance was recognized with a Golden Globe nomination. Still, she never did another regular series.

Eleanor did pop up in several well-made television movies: *Hans Brinker* (1969), as the title character's mother; *Maybe I'll Come Home in the Spring* (1971), a generation-gap drama with Eleanor as the ultra-conservative mother of hippie Sally Field; *Vanished* (1972), a gripping political miniseries based on Fletcher Knebel's novel; *Home for the Holidays* (1972), a Yuletide-themed thriller that allowed Eleanor to have a highly emotional breakdown at the climax; and *The Great American Beauty Contest* (1974), in which she stole the show as a former pageant winner harboring guilt over how she won the contest.

In the 1970s Eleanor undertook her first venture on the stage since appearing at the Pasadena Playhouse. She starred in the Los Angeles production of *Forty Carats* in 1971, and was a popular draw with both audiences and critics. Five years later she appeared in a revival of *Pal Joey* at the Circle In The Square Theatre in New York, glamorous as ever playing Vera, the wealthy patroness of the arts who romances and supports the title character (Edward Villella).

In 1979 Eleanor returned to the big screen after a ten-year absence in the comedy-mystery *Sunburn*, another of several failed attempts to turn former *Charlie's Angel* Farrah Fawcett into a movie star. Eleanor appeared briefly alongside several other veteran actors, such as Art Carney, Joan Collins and Keenan Wynn. It remains her last feature film to date.

The remainder of Eleanor's credits have been in television. She appeared in two more telefilms, *She's Dressed to Kill* (1979) and *Madame X* (1981), and did the obligatory veteran star guest appearances in the likes of *Fantasy Island*, *The Love Boat* and *Murder, She Wrote*.

In 1991 she made her final appearance to date in the made-for-cable movie *Dead on the Money* as Corbin Bernsen's grasping mother. The film was so-so, but Eleanor's reviews were glowing. "Eleanor Parker as a matriarch flashes so much style with just a cold calculating smile that it's a shame the veteran actress hasn't found more regular work," said *The New York Post*.

In truth, Eleanor didn't seem concerned about finding more work. She was content being with her family and living a happy, quiet life at her home in Palm Springs, California. Eleanor always felt fortunate about having her chance in the limelight.

"I even got my three wishes granted," she said in a 1953 interview. "To be an actress, to give mother a mink coat and to buy the folks a house."

FILMOGRAPHY

They Died with Their Boots On (Warner Bros., 1941) Directed by Raoul Walsh. *Cast:* Errol Flynn, Olivia de Havilland, Arthur Kennedy, Sydney Greenstreet, Walter Hampden. (Eleanor's scenes ended up on the cutting room floor.)

Soldiers in White (Warner Bros., 1942) Directed by B. Reeses Eason. A two-reel color short on the Medical Corps., with Eleanor as a nurse.

Busses Roar (Warner Bros., 1942) Directed by D. Ross Lederman. *Cast:* Richard Travis, Julie Bishop, Charles Drake, Eleanor Parker, Elisabeth Fraser, Richard Fraser, Peter Whitney.

The Mysterious Doctor (Warner Bros., 1943) Directed by Ben Stoloff. *Cast:* John Loder, Eleanor Parker, Bruce Lester, Lester Matthews, Forrester Harvey, Matt Willis, Creighton Hale.

Mission to Moscow (Warner Bros., 1943) Directed by Michael Curtiz. *Cast:* Walter Huston, Ann Harding, Oscar Homolka, Eleanor Parker, George Tobias, Gene Lockhart, Richard Travis.

Between Two Worlds (Warner Bros., 1944) Directed by Edward A. Blatt. *Cast:* Paul Henreid, John Garfield, Faye Emerson, Eleanor Parker, Sydney Greenstreet, Edmund Gwenn.

Crime by Night (Warner Bros., 1944) Directed by William Clemens. *Cast:* Jerome Cowan, Jane Wyman, Faye Emerson, Eleanor Parker, Charles Lang, Stuart Crawford, Cy Kendall.

The Last Ride (Warner Bros., 1944) Directed by D. Ross Lederman. *Cast:* Richard Travis, Charles Lang, Eleanor Parker, Jack La Rue, Cy Kendall, Mary Gordon, Wade Boteler.

The Very Thought of You (Warner Bros., 1944) Directed by Delmer Daves. *Cast:* Dennis Morgan, Eleanor Parker, Dane Clark, Faye Emerson, Beulah Bondi, William Prince, Andrea King, Henry Travers.

Hollywood Canteen (Warner Bros., 1944) Directed by Delmer Daves. *Cast:* Joan Leslie, Robert Hutton, Janis Paige, Dane Clark. *Guest Stars:* The Andrews Sisters, Jack Benny, Joe E. Brown, Eddie Cantor, Jack Carson, Joan Crawford, Bette Davis, Faye Emerson, John Garfield, Sydney Greenstreet, Paul Henreid, Andrea King, Peter Lorre, Ida Lupino, Dennis Morgan, Eleanor Parker, Roy Rogers, Zachary Scott, Alexis Smith, Barbara Stanwyck, Jane Wyman.

Pride of the Marines (Warner Bros., 1945) Directed by Delmer Daves. *Cast:* John Garfield,

Eleanor Parker, Dane Clark, Rosemary De Camp, John Ridgeley, Ann Doran, Ann Todd.

Of Human Bondage (Warner Bros., 1946) Directed by Edmund Goulding. *Cast:* Paul Henreid, Eleanor Parker, Alexis Smith, Janis Paige, Edmund Gwenn, Patric Knowles, Henry Stephenson.

Never Say Goodbye (Warner Bros., 1946) Directed by James V. Kern. *Cast:* Errol Flynn, Eleanor Parker, Forrest Tucker, Lucile Watson, S.Z. Sakall, Donald Woods, Peggy Knudsen.

Escape Me Never (Warner Bros., 1947) Directed by Peter Godfrey. *Cast:* Errol Flynn, Ida Lupino, Eleanor Parker, Gig Young, Reginald Denny, Isobel Elsom, Albert Basserman.

The Voice of the Turtle (Warner Bros., 1947) Directed by Irving Rapper. *Cast:* Ronald Reagan, Eleanor Parker, Eve Arden, Wayne Morris, Kent Smith, John Emery, Erskine Sanford.

The Woman in White (Warner Bros., 1948) Directed by Peter Godfrey. *Cast:* Alexis Smith, Eleanor Parker, Sydney Greenstreet, Gig Young, Agnes Moorehead, John Emery, John Abbott.

It's a Great Feeling (Warner Bros., 1949) Directed by David Butler. *Cast:* Doris Day, Dennis Morgan, Jack Carson, Bill Goodwin. *Guest Stars:* Gary Cooper, Joan Crawford, Errol Flynn, Danny Kaye, Patricia Neal, Eleanor Parker, Edward G. Robinson, Ronald Reagan, Jane Wyman.

Chain Lightning (Warner Bros., 1950) Directed by Stuart Heisler. *Cast:* Humphrey Bogart, Eleanor Parker, Raymond Massey, Richard Whorf, James Brown.

Caged (Warner Bros., 1950) Directed by John Cromwell. *Cast:* Eleanor Parker, Agnes Moorehead, Hope Emerson, Ellen Corby, Jan Sterling, Betty Garde, Gertrude Michael.

Three Secrets (Warner Bros., 1950) Directed by Robert Wise. *Cast:* Eleanor Parker, Patricia Neal, Ruth Roman, Frank Lovejoy, Leif Erickson, Ted de Corsia, Katherine Emery, Arthur Franz.

Valentino (Columbia, 1951) Directed by Lewis Allen. *Cast:* Anthony Dexter, Eleanor Parker, Patricia Medina, Richard Carlson, Dona Drake, Otto Kruger, Lloyd Gough.

A Millionaire for Christy (20th Century–Fox, 1951) Directed by George Marshall. *Cast:* Eleanor Parker, Fred MacMurray, Richard Carlson, Kay Buckley, Una Merkel, Douglas Dumbrille.

The Detective Story (Paramount, 1951) Directed by William Wyler. *Cast:* Kirk Douglas, Eleanor Parker, William Bendix, George Macready, Lee Grant, Cathy O'Donnell.

Scaramouche (MGM, 1952) Directed by George Sidney. *Cast:* Stewart Granger, Eleanor Parker, Janet Leigh, Mel Ferrer, Nina Foch, Lewis Stone, Henry Wilcoxon, Robert Coote.

Above and Beyond (MGM, 1952) Directed by Melvin Frank and Norman Panama. *Cast:* Robert Taylor, Eleanor Parker, James Whitmore, Larry Keating, Larry Gates, Marilyn Erskine.

Escape from Fort Bravo (MGM, 1953) Directed by John Sturges. *Cast:* William Holden, Eleanor Parker, John Forsythe, William Demarest, William Campbell, John Lupton, Polly Bergen.

The Naked Jungle (Paramount, 1954) Directed by Byron Haskin. *Cast:* Charlton Heston, Eleanor Parker, William Conrad, Abraham Sofaer, Romo Vincent, Douglas Fowley.

Valley of the Kings (MGM, 1954) Directed by Robert Pirosh. *Cast:* Robert Taylor, Eleanor Parker, Carlos Thompson, Kurt Kasznar, Victor Jory, Samia Gamal.

Many Rivers to Cross (MGM, 1955) Directed by Roy Rowland. *Cast:* Robert Taylor, Eleanor Parker, Victor McLaglen, Jeff Richards, Russ Tamblyn, James Arness, Rosemary De Camp.

Interrupted Melody (MGM, 1955) Directed by Curtis Bernhardt. *Cast:* Eleanor Parker, Glenn Ford, Roger Moore, Cecil Kellaway, Francoise Rosay, Peter Leeds.

The Man with the Golden Arm (United Artists, 1955) Directed by Otto Preminger. *Cast:* Frank Sinatra, Kim Novak, Eleanor Parker, Arnold Stang, Darren McGavin, Robert Strauss.

The King and Four Queens (United Artists, 1956) Directed by Raoul Walsh. *Cast:* Clark Gable, Eleanor Parker, Jo Van Fleet, Barbara Nichols, Sara Shane, Jean Willes, Roy Roberts.

Lizzie (MGM, 1957) Directed by Hugo Haas. *Cast:* Eleanor Parker, Richard Boone, Joan Blondell, Hugo Haas, Ric Roman, Johnny Mathis, Dorothy Arnold, Marion Ross.

The Seventh Sin (MGM, 1957) Directed by Ronald Neame. *Cast:* Eleanor Parker, Bill Travers, Jean-Pierre Aumont, George Sanders, Francoise Rosay, Ellen Corby.

A Hole in the Head (United Artists, 1959) Directed by Frank Capra. *Cast:* Frank Sinatra, Edward G. Robinson, Eleanor Parker, Thelma Ritter, Carolyn Jones, Eddie Hodges.

Home from the Hill (MGM, 1960) Directed by Vincente Minnelli. *Cast:* Robert Mitchum, George Peppard, George Hamilton, Eleanor Parker, Luana Patten, Constance Ford.

Return to Peyton Place (20th Century–Fox, 1961) Directed by Jose Ferrer. *Cast:* Eleanor Parker, Carol Lynley, Jeff Chandler, Robert Sterling, Mary Astor, Tuesday Weld, Brett Halsey.

Madison Avenue (20th Century–Fox, 1962) Directed by Bruce Humberstone. *Cast:* Dana Andrews, Eleanor Parker, Jeanne Crain, Eddie Albert, Howard St. John, Kathleen Freeman.

Panic Button (Gorton Associates, 1964) Directed by George Sherman. *Cast:* Maurice Chevalier,

Akim Tamiroff, Jayne Mansfield, Eleanor Parker, Michael Connors.

The Sound of Music (20th Century–Fox, 1965) Directed by Robert Wise. *Cast:* Julie Andrews, Christopher Plummer, Eleanor Parker, Richard Haydn, Peggy Wood, Anna Lee, Marni Nixon.

An American Dream (Warner Bros., 1966) Directed by Robert Gist. *Cast:* Stuart Whitman, Janet Leigh, Eleanor Parker, Barry Sullivan, Lloyd Nolan, Murray Hamilton, J.D. Cannon.

The Oscar (Paramount, 1966) Directed by Russell Rouse. *Cast:* Stephen Boyd, Elke Sommer, Tony Bennett, Eleanor Parker, Milton Berle, Joseph Cotten, Jill St. John.

The Tiger and the Pussycat (Il Tigre) (Embassy, 1967) Directed by Dino Risi. *Cast:* Vittorio Gassman, Ann-Margret, Eleanor Parker, Antonella Stani, Fiorenzo Fiorentini, Caterina Boratto.

Warning Shot (Paramount, 1967) Directed by Buzz Kulik. *Cast:* David Janssen, Lillian Gish, Ed Begley, Keenan Wynn, Sam Wanamaker, Eleanor Parker, Stephanie Powers, Walter Pidgeon, George Sanders, George Grizzard, Steve Allen, Carroll O'Connor, Joan Collins.

Eye of the Cat (Universal, 1969) Directed by David Lowell Rich. *Cast:* Eleanor Parker, Michael Sarrazin, Gayle Hunnicutt, Tim Henry, Laurence Naismith.

Sunburn (Hemdale/Bind Films, 1979) Directed by Richard C. Sarafian. *Cast:* Charles Grodin, Farrah Fawcett, Art Carney, Joan Collins, William Daniels, Eleanor Parker, John Hillerman.

Television Film Credits

Hans Brinker (1969) *Cast:* Robin Askwith, John Gregson, Richard Basehart, Eleanor Parker.

Maybe I'll Come Home in the Spring (1970) *Cast:* Sally Field, Eleanor Parker, Jackie Cooper.

Vanished (1970) *Cast:* Richard Widmark, James Farentino, Robert Young, Eleanor Parker.

Home for the Holidays (1972) *Cast:* Sally Field, Eleanor Parker, Walter Brennan, Julie Harris.

The Great American Beauty Contest (1972) *Cast:* Eleanor Parker, Louis Jourdan.

Fantasy Island (1977) *Cast:* Ricardo Montalban, Herve Villechaize, Bill Bixby, Eleanor Parker.

The Bastard (1978) *Cast:* Andrew Stevens, Patricia Neal, Buddy Ebsen, Barry Sullivan, Harry Morgan, Lorne Greene, Donald Pleasence, Tom Bosley, William Shatner, Eleanor Parker.

She's Dressed to Kill (1979) *Cast:* Joanna Cassidy, Gretchen Corbett, Cassandra Gava, Peter Horton, John Rubinstein, Connie Selleca, Jessica Walter, Eleanor Parker, Clive Revill.

Once Upon a Spy (1980) *Cast:* Ted Danson, Mary Louise Weller, Eleanor Parker.

Madame X (1981) *Cast:* Tuesday Weld, Len Cariou, Eleanor Parker, Robert Hooks.

Dead on the Money (1991) *Cast:* Corbin Bernsen, John Glover, Eleanor Parker.

Ann Sheridan: "The Oomph Girl"

Ann Sheridan is a prime example of the power of the Hollywood publicity machine. She got her start by winning a studio-sponsored beauty contest in 1933. Six years later her star rose, thanks to another contest in which she was crowned with the ridiculously immodest title of "Oomph" Girl.

The Sheridan screen persona was akin to that of a hash-house version of Carole Lombard, displaying a flair for brittle comedy laced with sex appeal. Like Lombard, the off-camera Ann Sheridan could swear as well as any truck driver and reveled in off-color jokes with cast and crew, who loved her congenial and down-to-earth manner.

Despite fine performances in such films as *They Drive by Night* (1940) and *King's Row* (1942), Ann never developed into the icon of new generations the way that Bette Davis or Olivia de Havilland did. Yet, Ann's parboiled heroines seem more in tune with modern times than those of many of her contemporaries. Her performances hold up remarkably well, thanks to the strength and intelligence Ann brought to her roles, and the independent spirit of the characters she played.

Ann's body of work is especially remarkable considering she had no formal acting training as she was growing up in Denton, Texas, a small town outside of Dallas. Clara Lou Sheridan was born in Denton on February 21, 1915, to George W. Sheridan and his wife Lula Stewart Warren. George, who boasted of being a direct descendant of Civil War General Philip Sheridan, worked as a garage mechanic. Lula had a full-time job caring for her large brood, which included Clara Lou's older siblings Kitty, Pauline, Mabel and George. Another child died while still an infant.

Clara Lou attended Robert E. Lee Grade School and later Denton Junior High School. During those formative years the carrot-topped youngster began to develop the fun-loving spirit that would later come across in her screen comedies. As a child, Clara Lou was something of a tomboy, preferring football and basketball to playing with dolls. She also developed a fondness for horses and became an excellent rider, a skill that would later serve her well in several westerns.

In school Clara Lou was always among the first to sign up for an audition whenever a new school play was planned, but usually was picked as an understudy rather than a principal.

In the fall of 1932 Clara Lou attended North Texas State Teachers College, planning to be an art teacher. Neither the art program nor her instructor were as lively as Clara Lou hoped, so she switched to drama. Myrtle Hardy, the enthusiastic head of the drama department, served as a mentor who inspired Clara Lou to perfect her readings and use her body to express emotion.

Music, another of Clara Lou's passions, became an important part of her college years. Though Clara Lou was not a trained vocalist, her warm contralto conveyed enough sincerity and heart for the school bandleader to offer her a regular gig as the band's singer.

Ann Sheridan came to Warners at just the right time, when the studio needed a glamour girl.

In early 1933 *The Dallas News* printed an announcement about a local beauty contest it was representing in conjunction with Paramount Pictures for its upcoming film, appropriately titled *Search for Beauty*. The winner would be given a Paramount contract, including a bit part in the movie. Kitty Sheridan submitted a photo of Clara Lou in a bathing suit, without telling her sister. Clara Lou found out when the newspaper's editor, John Rosenfield, called to tell her she had made the finals. Years later Ann described herself during this period as "pudgy fat with kinky hair and a space between my teeth," but at the time she went along with it, figuring her chances of winning were slim. Instead, Clara Lou was the regional winner, and a few days later was off to Hollywood, along with 29 other contest winners from the United States and the British Empire.

"In those days, they held all sorts of beauty contests, just for publicity purposes," she told *Screen Facts* in 1966. "And they're dreadful. They're horrible on kids, because they break so many hearts. I think every kid who wins a beauty contest thinks, 'Well, now I've got a chance.' Well, it may be a vague chance, but that's when your hardest work begins."

Clara Lou's prize was a six-month contract with Paramount at fifty dollars a week. Since the extent of Clara Lou's work experience had consisted of helping her mother take care of the house, she felt fortunate to be making what she considered good money.

Her inauspicious film debut was *Search for Beauty*, a frivolous comedy starring Ida Lupino and former Olympic swimmer Larry "Buster" Crabbe as Olympic athletes duped into becoming editors of a health and beauty magazine run by two con men (Robert Armstrong and James Gleason). Clara Lou appeared briefly as the "Dallas contest winner" during a pageant.

Clara Lou spent the remainder of 1934 as an extra in roughly one dozen movies, including *Bolero*, *Murder at the Vanities*, *The Notorious Sophie Lang* and *Mrs. Wiggs of the Cabbage Patch*, but one has to have an extremely keen eye to spot her in any of them.

At Paramount, Clara Lou studied with a drama coach, Nina Mousie, whose job was to take new contract players and put them in a stock company that performed plays for the studio executives. Since most of these players had little or no previous stage training, the stern and exacting Mousie was usually unimpressed with their work.

Clara Lou appeared in *The Pursuit of Happiness* and *The Milky Way* with the Paramount players. The latter was done shortly after Paramount took up Clara Lou's second option in early 1935. Paramount thought Clara Lou Sheridan was too long for a marquee, so they asked her to come up with a shorter name. She suggested Lou, which the studio felt was too masculine. A fellow actor suggested that she call herself Ann, which was the name of her character in *The Milky Way*. From then on, Clara Lou would forever be known as Ann Sheridan.

Ann's penchant for fun didn't gel with Mousie, who at one point told Ann to head back to Texas because she wasn't serious about her craft. When Ann told Mousie what she thought of her suggestion, the drama coach recommended that the studio release Ann. Ann then made a heartfelt plea to one of Paramount's executives to convince him she was a dedicated professional.

Ann later said that her plea, and, more importantly, the support of director Mitchell Leisen, prolonged her stay at Paramount. Leisen requested Ann for a bit in *Behold My Wife* (1935), with Sylvia Sidney and Gene Raymond. In it, Ann got to commit a highly dramatic suicide. When Leisen showed the rushes of the scene to the front office, the studio renewed Ann's option.

Her roles were getting bigger, even if the films were still inconsequential. She had her first lead in the police yarn *Car 99* (1935), opposite Fred MacMurray, and then teamed with Randolph Scott in *The Rocky Mountain Mystery* (1935), a combination western and whodunit. Poverty Row studio Ambassador borrowed her for a dog called *Red Blood of Courage* (1935), with Kermit Maynard and fallen star Charles King. Ann's main purpose in all three was to look pretty.

At her home lot Ann had bit parts in *The Glass Key* (1935) and Cecil B. De Mille's *The Crusades* (1935), a sure sign that Paramount was again losing interest in her. In the first, she had a brief appearance as George Raft's nurse. In the second, Ann was clad in a ridiculous black wig and got to utter the immortal line, "The cross, the cross, let me kiss the cross."

Ann was making one hundred dollars a week, but Paramount didn't think she was worth another $25 a week when her option came up for renewal. As Ann put it: "They had other people at fifty dollars they could use for the same things, so why bother with me?"

She found work playing a wealthy Communist in *Fighting Youth* (1935) at Universal with Charles Farrell. While Ann had no love for the script of *Fighting Youth*, she was grateful for the three hundred and seventy-five dollars she earned for her three weeks on the picture. Her salary from that film pretty much was her sole income — by choice — through August of 1936. Ann's agent, Bill Miklejohn, promised to find her extra work after *Fighting Youth*, but Ann wisely refused. She dropped Miklejohn and signed with Dick Pollimer, whose clients included Anita Louise.

During this professional lull Ann began dating actor Edward Norris. The handsome Norris began his screen career at MGM with a bit part in *Queen Christina* (1933), but he was dropped by the studio in 1935. When he met Ann, Norris, who had been married twice before, was ready to settle down. "I wanted marriage. I liked the idea of a home, a place to put down roots as it were. I met Ann Sheridan and fell madly in love with her," Morris told *Movies* in 1939.

Ann liked Norris' adventurous spirit, and delighted in hearing tales of his youth, which included purchasing some fake seaman's papers for $1.50 when he was fifteen and joining the crew of a four-masted schooner bound for Seattle via the Horn. The two also supported each other as they struggled with the temporary setbacks in their careers.

"After seven months, during which I gave the matter a lot of serious thought, I decided that here at last was a girl with whom I could always be happy," Norris said. "To me, Ann was the loveliest thing in the world." They were married in July 1936.

Things began looking up. Pollimer showed Ann's photos to Max Arno, casting director at Warners, who arranged for her to test for the upcoming *Always Leave Them Laughing*. Ann did a scene from the movie well enough to get the part and a six-month contract at $75 a week. The film, released as *Sing Me a Love Song* (1936), was meant to spotlight opera singer James Melton, but he failed to click. Ann was seen sparingly and to little effect.

Her next three films were vastly superior. In the powerful social drama *Black Legion* (1937) Ann had a small but well-played role as the girlfriend of Dick Foran, a factory worker who is lynched by a racist group patterned after the Ku Klux Klan. In *The Great O'Malley* (1937) she had several good scenes as Humphrey Bogart's schoolteacher girlfriend. And in the prison drama *San Quentin* (1937) Ann was torn between her love for Pat O'Brien, a law enforcement official, and Bogart, her no-good brother whom O'Brien sends to the title place. The last was a routine prison drama highlighted by Ann's throaty warbling of "How Could You?"

Like Bette Davis, Joan Blondell and Glenda Farrell, Warners made sure it got its money's worth from Ann. As such, between 1937 and 1938 Ann appeared in an incredible thirteen films, most of them Bs with such bizarre titles as *Wine, Women and Horses* (1937), *The Footlight Heiress* (1937), *She Loved a Fireman* (1938) and *The Cowboy from Brooklyn* (1938), an odd musical with Dick Powell and Priscilla Lane. Warners also gave Ann the lead in *The Patient in Room 138* (1938) and *Mystery House* (1938), two efficient whodunits.

Ann's bustling career was also putting a strain on her marriage, especially since her star was rising much faster than that of her husband. "I believe our marriage would have succeeded had it not been for our careers," Norris told *Movies*. "What I had not counted on was that Ann would become so involved in her own career that she might lose sight of my own struggles and successes. What Ann had not expected was that my career was not all a jolly road to stardom."

These marriage woes were exacerbated by Ann winning a supporting role in *A Letter of Introduction* (1938) at Universal. The strong plot centered on a brilliant actor (Adolphe Menjou) whose career has been destroyed by alcohol. He attempts to sober up after he meets his long-lost daughter (Andrea Leeds), an aspiring actress who hopes her father can help her. Director John M. Stahl hoped to borrow Lucille Ball from RKO to play Menjou's bitchy girlfriend, but when RKO refused, he interviewed Ann. She borrowed a fox fur and a fancy hat from Warners' wardrobe department for her meeting. The dressy outfit and her intelligent reading won her the part.

Ann was given about five short scenes in *A Letter of Introduction*, but she made a distinct impression. Karl Freund did an expert job of photographing Ann, who looked far more attractive in this film than any she had made so far. In addition, she also showed a flair for tart dialogue.

Back at Warners Ann made *Broadway Musketeers* (1938), a loose remake of *Three on a Match* (1932), in Joan Blondell's old role as a bad girl who reforms from her evil ways. It paled in comparison to the original and was tagged by *Variety* as "a programmer of little distinction."

The reaction to Ann in *A Letter of Introduction* spurred Warners to consider Ann's star potential. The studio assigned noted photographer George Hurrell to take some stills of Ann for publication in the national fan magazines. The most famous of these shots depicted a sultry Ann clad in a lounging suit and posing seductively on a leather couch. The photos created a sensation and formed the beginnings of the studio's massive "Oomph" campaign, which was engineered by West Coast publicity chief Charles Einfeld and his East Coast counterpart, Mitch Rawson.

At the same time the studio cast Ann in an 'A' film, *Angels with Dirty Faces* (1938). Headlining the film was James Cagney, the studio's top male star after Errol Flynn, and directing was Michael Curtiz, Warners' most distinguished craftsman.

Angels with Dirty Faces was the old standby about childhood friends who grow up on opposite sides of the law. Rocky Sullivan (Cagney) is a criminal who becomes the idol of a street gang (the Dead End Kids), much to the disappointment of his childhood pal, Father Jerry (Pat O'Brien). Ann supplied the love interest as Rocky's girlfriend, Laury.

Angels with Dirty Faces was distinguished by Cagney's bravura performance, which earned him an Oscar nomination. Likewise, the grittiness of Curtiz's direction and his faithful reincarnation of tenement life added to the film's realism. Ann's role was secondary, but she had some good moments, especially her dramatic plea to O'Brien to call off his anti-vice campaign aimed at Rocky. As Warners hoped, *Angels with Dirty Faces* did sensational business.

It was during the making of *Angels with Dirty Faces* that Ann's marriage was reaching an impasse. "I went out to the studio to see her rushes. That night I told her that I knew I had married a very beautiful woman, but never before did I realize that I had also married a fine actress," Norris told *Movies*. "That seems to have been a mistake, for after that Ann felt that she no longer needed advice nor encouragement from me."

In August 1938 Ann and Norris came to an amicable separation. The failure of her marriage took a toll on Ann's health. She had lost considerable weight and was smoking up to three packs of cigarettes a day. She moved to North Hollywood where she shared an apartment with Gwen Woodford, a friend from high school. The divorce became final in early 1939.

Perhaps if Ann had still been married the studio might have been less likely to build her up as Hollywood's "Oomph" Girl. The fact that Warners began pushing Ann in that direction came as a surprise to the industry. Whereas MGM had such glamour girls as Lana Turner and Hedy Lamarr, and Columbia was grooming Rita Hayworth, Warners had been a male-oriented studio, with Cagney, Edward G. Robinson and Errol Flynn as its top stars. Warners' only true female star at this point was Bette Davis, who never fit Hollywood's definition of a glamour queen.

Ann, on the other hand, seemed to have the necessary requirements to meet Warners' glamour criteria. Standing at five feet, five inches, and weighing one hundred and twenty-two pounds, she had a lithe figure. Her fiery red tresses also helped paint the illusion of a seductress. For the "Oomph" campaign, Warners sent Ann's photo to a panel of thirteen judges, including Rudy Vallee, the Earl of Warwick, David Niven, Busby Berkeley, designer Orry-Kelly and nightclub owner Earl Carroll. The judges were also given photos of the other "Oomph" candidates, including Carole Lombard, Alice Faye and Hedy Lamarr. On March 16, 1939, the judges gathered at the Los Angeles Town House for a sumptuous dinner of lobster supreme, Columbia salmon and roasted squab. After that feast Ann was officially crowned the Oomph Girl.

Each judge had his own definition of "oomph." The Earl of Warwick called it "a feminine desirability which can be observed with pleasure, but cannot be discussed with respectability," while C. Graham Baker said, "Oomph is to a girl what a pearl is to an oyster."

As far as Ann was concerned, "Oomph is what a fat man says when he leans over to tie his shoelace in a telephone booth."

If Ann was the unanimous choice of the judges, that was exactly what Warners had intended. The studio had engineered the contest so that Ann would be a cinch to win over the other choices. "They took the back of Hedy Lamarr's head and the back of whoever else's heads they entered in the contest ... to these guys to find out who was the most glamorous," Ann recalled in 1966. "Of course, it was all a set-up to pick me. They could never have had a good picture of Hedy Lamarr and said I was more glamorous than she was."

Ann ended up eclipsing Lamarr when it came to both star appeal and box-office longevity. The "Oomph" campaign snowballed to a magnitude far beyond Warners' expectations. Ann's photo graced just about every newspaper and magazine over the next two years. In a five-page spread in the July 23, 1939, issue of *Life*, Ann was dubbed "a second Jean Harlow."

Equally prolific in 1939 was Ann's film output, which included six releases. The year started out with small but telling parts as a drunken floozy in *They Made Me a Criminal* and a saloon singer in *Dodge City*, her first in Technicolor. Ann was featured prominently with Errol Flynn and Olivia de Havilland in the ads for *Dodge City*, a strong sign of her rising popularity.

Ann's musical numbers in *Dodge City* convinced Warners that she could handle the lead in *Naughty But Nice* (1939). She received top billing over Dick Powell, and was even given more songs than him. No one seemed to care, though. Bosley Crowther of *The New York Times* called it "pretty flat ... even down to the borrowed music."

Producer Walter Wanger, who had turned the gorgeous Lamarr into a star a year earlier in *Algiers*, thought Ann had a similar appeal and requested her for *Winter Carnival* (1939). Ann played a duchess who returns to her alma mater for homecoming and rekindles a romance with an old flame (Richard Carlson). Ann looked stunning and displayed a comedic flair, thus proving she could carry an "A" picture.

Whereas at Warners Ann was called Annie by everyone on the set and treated like one of the family, Wanger saw to it that Ann got the star treatment. He appeared on the set every day and told everyone on the lot to address her as Miss Sheridan. He also arranged for Ann to have an elegant portable bungalow. While Ann appreciated Wanger's hospitality, she preferred being "Annie" with her friends at Warners and didn't go for the Hollywood treatment.

"I only met her a few times, but she was like one of the boys. Just a regular person," said actor Rand Brooks.

Ann finished the year in *Indianapolis Speedway* (1939), a serviceable remake of *The Crowd Roars* (1932), with Pat O'Brien, and was reunited with the Dead End Kids in *Angels Wash Their Faces* (1939), a hollow attempt to recapture the magic of *Angels with Dirty Faces*. Cagney was not on hand for this film, and his presence was sorely missed.

By February 1940 Ann had become the

most publicized actress in Hollywood. Her fan mail at the studio was topped only by that of Bette Davis and Priscilla Lane. It's no surprise that 1940 was such a busy year for Ann, with five releases— starting with *Castle on the Hudson*, a remake of *20,000 Years in Sing Sing* (1933), with John Garfield and Ann generating much heat in the roles originally played by Spencer Tracy and Bette Davis.

Warners then paid the handsome sum of $50,000 for the rights to *And It All Came True* by Louis Bromfield. By the time filming began, the title had been shortened to *It All Came True* (1940), and it was an amusing concoction about a gangster who hides out in a theatrical boarding house in New York run by the mother (Una O'Connor) of an old friend (Ann). The film got its share of laughs from the stars' efforts to turn the boarding house into a nightclub. Less interesting was the romantic subplot between Ann and Jeffrey Lynn. *Variety* felt *It All Came True* was "a missed opportunity ... a 'B' film that might have been a superb 'A.'"

Critical reaction was better for Ann's follow-up, the lusty *Torrid Zone* (1940), in which she and Cagney again ignited sparks. *Torrid Zone* bore a resemblance to MGM's *Red Dust* (1932), though lacking its steaminess. Ann was a nightclub singer stranded in Panama who becomes the object of desire of the manager of a banana plantation (Pat O'Brien) and his best worker (Cagney). The film benefited from fast-paced direction by William Keighley, crackling dialogue and the sharp playing of the stars, especially Ann, who captivated critics.

"Ann Sheridan steps up a notch or two in our estimation as the femme fatale of the piece," raved *The New York Times*. "If the males are two-fisted, Miss Sheridan meets them blow for blow, line for line."

Ann had a similar role in *They Drive by Night* (1940), as a smart-talking waitress who gets involved with a two-fisted truck driver (George Raft). Ann's ability to wring every bit of tartness from her lines was evident throughout *They Drive by Night*. When a diner patron comments on her "classy chassis," she neatly snaps back, "You couldn't even pay for the headlights!" Like *Torrid Zone*, *They Drive by Night* was a huge money spinner for Warner Bros.

Ann was now a red-hot commodity. The publicity department felt it was vital that she be seen with someone of equal stature at the top nightspots. One such beau was actor George Brent, a husky, sophisticated gentleman with a keen sense of humor. Brent was also quite the ladies man, with two failed marriages and a string of affairs to his reputation.

The romance with Brent began as a studio-engineered ploy, but within six months of their first date, he and Ann were seeing each other exclusively. Ann was fascinated by Brent's previous exploits. Born in Ireland in 1904, Brent came to the United States in 1915 to live with relatives after his parents died. A few years later he returned to Ireland, where he played some bit parts with the Abbey Theater. He also became involved in some subversive activities during the Irish Rebellion and fled Ireland by stowing away on a freighter bound for Canada. He stayed in Canada for two years as part of a stock company and then followed them to the Bronx. He landed bit roles on Broadway, and then made his film debut in 1931. The next year he was signed by Warners, where he found a comfortable niche as a romantic lead for the likes of Kay Francis and Bette Davis.

As their romance intensified, the publicity department had a field day. When Brent gave Ann a French poodle, whom she named Amos, Warners began issuing statements that the two were planning an elopement. A few months later, when Ann began sporting a square-cut diamond on the third finger of her left hand, Ann denied rumors of an engagement.

"It's just a gift. The ring fits THAT finger, so that's where I'm going to wear it. But it doesn't mean I'm engaged," Ann stated emphatically to *Movie Radio Guide*. "I like the boys in the publicity department, they're all swell fellows, but that was just their work again. Every time George gives me anything, they have us married."

When asked if the pair were considering a Christmas 1940 wedding, Ann remarked, "You are wrong again, honey. Do you think I would spoil Christmas that way?"

Ann rounded out the year in *City for Conquest* (1940), a sentimental drama based on the novel by Aben Kandel. Both Ginger Rogers and Sylvia Sidney had passed on the role of Peggy, the ambitious dancer who dumps her happy-go-lucky boyfriend (James Cagney) after literally getting swept off her feet by a slick new partner (Anthony Quinn) who promises her stardom. It turned out to be a break for Ann, who ranked *City for Conquest* as one of her favorites.

Much of the film centers on Cagney, who turns from truck driver to prizefighter to pay for the musical education of his composer brother (Arthur Kennedy). He also hopes that his success in the ring will help win back Peggy. His moving performance and an excellent re-creation of the teeming streets of New York were compensations for the cloying ending in which Danny, now blind and running a newsstand, is reunited with the now washed-up Peggy.

For Ann, *City for Conquest* was a chance to prove herself as a dramatic actress. She could identify with Peggy, who was ambitious yet vulnerable. As such, she was excellent — in particular, as she tearfully listens to the radio broadcast as Danny gets pummeled in his last fight.

Ironically, in spite of having five successful films in 1940, the Harvard Lampoon voted Ann as the actress of the year who was "most unlikely to succeed." In her typical no-nonsense manner, Ann replied, "Harvard is the home of the unadulterated heel — and you may quote me."

Ann also made headlines in 1940 when she engaged in the first of several salary disputes with her bosses at Warners. Jack Warner had agreed to up her salary to $600 a week, but Ann felt all of the "Oomph" publicity had made millions for the studio, and she deserved more. "It will take $2,000 a week to get her to oomph anymore," was her agent's reported ultimatum to Warner. He refused and Ann went on suspension, thus losing *The Strawberry Blonde* to Rita Hayworth.

Ann remained on suspension for six months before she and the studio settled. Although she didn't get the salary she wanted, she did get a hefty raise and retroactive pay. Best of all, the studio gave her the plum role of Randy Monaghan in the ambitious *King's Row* (1942). Typical of Warners' negotiations, Ann also had to agree to do a pair of films she positively loathed.

Honeymoon for Three (1941) was an obvious bid to capitalize on the Brent-Sheridan romance, but whatever flames the two generated in their private lives failed to ignite this remake of *Goodbye Again* (1933). Ann played the adoring secretary to a novelist (Brent) who renews an old romance with a former classmate (Osa Massen). At the same time, he tries to fend off the advances of just about every other female in the film.

"Ann Sheridan plays the secretary in one key of bored tolerance, which is not surprising in view of her employer's juvenile behavior," carped *The Times*' Bosley Crowther.

Worse was *Navy Blues* (1941), an abysmal nautical musical in which Ann and other talented performers, including Martha Raye, Jack Oakie, Jack Haley and Jackie Gleason, were all left at sea under Lloyd Bacon's direction. The laugh-free story of two dim-witted sailors (Oakie and Haley) trying to keep an ace "gun pointer" (Herbert Anderson) on ship until after the gunnery trials showed how the Warners musicals had deteriorated since the Busby Berkeley heyday.

In spite of everything, *The New York Times* had kind words for Ann: "Miss Sheridan is on hand to sing a couple of songs and wear a grass skirt (which ain't hay)."

With those turkeys out of the way, Ann began *King's Row*, a dark and disturbing portrait of small-town America at the turn of the century. The film's protagonist is Parris Mitchell (Robert Cummings), an idealistic youth who thinks King's Row is the ideal town where he can fulfill his dream of becoming a great doctor. Influencing him in his future endeavors are his beloved grandmother (Maria Ouspenskaya); his best friend Drake McHugh (Ronald Reagan), the town lothario; his mentor Dr. Tower (Claude Rains); the doctor's daughter Cassie (Betty Field), Parris' first love; and Randy Monaghan, a sensible and dependable girl who eventually marries Drake.

As the story unfolds, Parris' illusions about medicine and his home town are shattered by several incidents: Cassie's death and her father's consequent suicide; the loss of his grandmother; and a botched operation that results in the unnecessary amputation of Drake's legs.

Ann often said Randy Monaghan was her favorite role, one which gave her a chance to display a warm side to her acting that had hitherto only surfaced on occasion, as in *City for Conquest*. Interestingly, Warners had not even thought about Ann for Randy at first. She found out through Humphrey Bogart that Warners had bought the rights to the novel, and it was he who urged Ann to do whatever she could to get the part. She remained grateful to him until her death.

Randy is probably the most reasonable and least complicated of the inhabitants of King's Row, and as such is the easiest character for the audience to identify with. Ann's sincerity and compassion are more apparent in her scene following Drake's surgery, in which she must console him when he asks, "Where's the rest of me?" Ann is equally effective in her confrontation with Parris when she convinces him to practice medicine in King's Row.

In general, critics praised the film and remarked on what a revelation Ann's performance was. *Time* enthused, "Director Sam Wood's cineversion of *King's Row* is potent, artful cinema.... The surprise of *King's Row* is beauteous, lazy Ann Sheridan, who manages her shanty Irish role with credible facility. Somebody (probably Mr. Wood) has very nearly 'de-Oomphed' her."

At the same time Ann made *King's Row*, she also played Lorraine Sheldon, a pampered stage diva modeled after Gertrude Lawrence, in the film version of the Broadway smash *The Man Who Came to Dinner* (1942). William Keighley was assigned to direct the film, which boasted a brilliant cast headed by Monty Woolley hilariously re-creating his stage role as Sheridan Whiteside, Bette Davis as his secretary, Jimmy Durante as a Harpo Marx knockoff, Reginald Gardiner doing a Noel Coward impersonation, and Mary Wickes as Whiteside's harried nurse.

As the flashy Lorraine, Ann was a sensation, deliciously vamping as Davis' rival for the affections of a budding playwright (Richard Travis). Even though she was razor sharp, Ann hated making two films at once, not to mention getting only one salary for both films.

"My only love was Randy Monaghan. I didn't care about playing Lorraine Sheldon," Ann said in 1966. "I used to work, say, one day on *King's Row* and the next on *The Man Who Came to Dinner*, or one morning I'd work as Lorraine Sheldon and that afternoon I was Randy Monaghan." As she moved from set to set, she also had to have her makeup and hair redone for each role. Despite her objections, Ann once again received raves for her performance.

By now Ann was the studio's top female draw after Davis. But while her career had progressed, her relationship with Brent was at a standstill. Brent had confided to friends that he didn't believe an actor and actress on the same lot should be married, a mistake he made once before. He was also disillusioned from his marriage to actress Constance Worth, which lasted only a few months.

Ann, too, had misgivings, since her first marriage barely lasted past the first anniversary. And while Brent had a successful career, Ann was unquestionably the bigger star, a factor that did much to destroy her first marriage. After months of speculation the two kicked off the New Year with a wedding on January 5, 1942, followed by a honeymoon in Palm Springs.

Juke Girl (1942), directed by Curtis Bernhardt, hardly seemed like much of a wedding present from Warners. The studio usually excelled at working-class dramas, but not this time. A.I. Bezzerides' screenplay dealt with Florida crop pickers who become involved in a marketing war and murder. For fun they spend their evenings with juke girls, whom we learn are dance-joint girls looking for men with enough nickels to feed the jukebox and enough dollars to buy them drinks. As expected, the film contained a great many fist fights and chase scenes, with an assortment of fruits and vegetables turning into roadkill. Some none-too-interesting romance was provided by tough trucker Ronald Reagan and juke girl Ann.

Ann complained to the front office, but at the risk of another suspension she had no choice but to report to the set. As expected, the reviews were dreadful. "As grade B as its title would indicate," said *Variety*. *The New York Times*' Bosley Crowther was a little kinder, saying, "There are some good individual scenes in the picture, but consistency it has not."

In the midst of making *Juke Girl*, Ann learned that Warners had secured the rights to Edna Ferber's sprawling novel *Saratoga Trunk*. She desperately wanted to play the heroine, a sort of Creole version of Scarlett O'Hara. In between takes on *Juke Girl*, Ann worked with a French teacher to master the accent the role demanded. For her screen test Ann donned a blonde wig. Although Ann never saw the test after it was made, she commented that her Franco-Texan accent sounded horrible, and she knew the part would never be hers. Instead, it went to Ingrid Bergman, who also had problems wrestling between her natural Swedish accent and the Creole dialect.

Ann felt more at home in the flag-waving *Wings for the Eagle* (1942), her first of many teamings with Dennis Morgan and Jack Carson. The film was a tribute to aircraft factory workers, and, like many wartime dramas, its intentions were more honorable than its execution. Plenty of screen time was devoted to the day-to-day challenges faced by the workers, but the film's chief selling point was the romantic triangle involving shiftless drifter Morgan, his unemployed friend (Carson) and his friend's frustrated wife (Ann). A timely subplot revolved around the dismissal of a Greek superintendent (George Tobias) who never obtained his American citizenship.

Variety found the movie "inspirational without ever being preachy." The obvious camaraderie and engaging performances of the three stars helped *Wings for the Eagle* fly high at the box office. Ann became great friends with her two male co-stars. The three actors took time off from filming to sell war bonds at Lockheed.

Ann had even more fun working with Jack Benny in the zany domestic farce *George Washington Slept Here* (1942), the George S. Kaufman-Moss Hart warhorse about city slickers who buy a dilapidated farmhouse in the country and encounter all sorts of problems. In the play it was the husband who bought the house before showing it to his dismayed wife. For the film the roles were reversed to allow Benny plenty of his famous double takes as he fell through ceilings, dealt with a leaky roof and even plummeted down a well. Though sometimes the laughs were forced, most of the gags worked beautifully. The original script called for a dream sequence with Benny and Ann as George and Martha Washington, but it never made it to the final print.

In addition to delightful performances by the two stars, there was fine support by Charles Coburn as her cantankerous uncle and Percy Kilbride as a caretaker. The latter's deadpan rendition of "I'll Never Smile Again" nearly stole the film from the principals.

Ann admitted that her role in *George Washington Slept Here* was hardly a challenge, but working with Benny was a treat. "If the script's bad, I can put up with that. I won't like it and I may beef, but I've got to have fun working with the people on the set. I don't like dissention at all," she told *Screen Facts*. "Everybody should get in there and pull their load as far as I'm concerned. I could fight with the front office, but I never wanted to do that either. I didn't beef about *George Washington Slept Here* because it was Jack Benny. I certainly beefed about *Juke Girl*. There were many things that I fought not to do. And there were many times, too, that I went on suspension and then came back and did the picture to get a salary raise."

Edge of Darkness (1943) teamed Ann with Errol Flynn, and again she found a co-star who made the set lively. The powerful drama featured a cast of heavy-hitters, which also included Walter Huston, Ruth Gordon, Judith Anderson, Helmut Dantine and Nancy Coleman. Ann and Flynn played the leaders of a local group of Norwegian freedom fighters determined to save their fishing village after it's taken over by Nazis.

The film was made in the midst of Flynn's infamous trial in which he was accused of the statutory rape of a minor. Ann recalled that he would go to the courtroom in the morning and then report to the set of *Edge of Darkness* in the afternoon, where cast and crew would gather around each day anxiously awaiting Flynn's latest updates on the case.

Ann was anxious to wrap up work on *Edge of Darkness* because she wanted to head to Mexico to obtain her divorce from Brent. As Brent had feared, the pressures of two stars working at the same studio took its toll on their marriage. The studio didn't know about her plans and asked her to report for work on *Thank Your Lucky Stars* (1943), its all-star musical revue. Ann agreed to do her number in the film, but only if it could be shot as quickly as possible.

Director David Butler filmed Ann's sequence in only three days, and the end result was one of the highlights of the film. Bedecked in a white gown and lacy matching snood, Ann was dazzling as she performed a husky rendition of "Love Isn't Born, It's Made." Once it was shot, Ann dashed off to Mexico, where her divorce was granted on January 5, 1943, on what would have been the couple's first anniversary.

Ann returned from Mexico to begin *Shine*

on, Harvest Moon (1944), a highly fictionalized biography of vaudeville entertainers Nora Bayes (Ann) and Jack Norworth (Dennis Morgan), peppered with plenty of old songs and comic turns by Jack Carson and Marie Wilson. Though Ann made a stunning Bayes and sang pleasantly, the weak story was a severe liability.

"What is done in the name of biography in Warner Brothers' *Shine on, Harvest Moon* is something that shouldn't be done to a burglar—let alone to the memory of Nora Bayes," wrote Crowther. "As for the performances of Ann Sheridan and Dennis Morgan in the pseudo-biographical roles, we can only say that history does not repeat itself."

Despite the pans, *Shine on Harvest Moon* was one of Ann's most successful films.

One of Ann's biggest rows with Warners occurred in 1944 when she was assigned to play herself in the wartime musical *Hollywood Canteen* (1944). As a patriotic gesture, Warners produced the all-star extravaganza and asked every star on the lot to waive their salaries, which instead would be given to the canteen. The ridiculous story, directed by Delmer Daves, was supposed to be about a GI (Robert Hutton) who arrives in Hollywood and heads straight to the canteen to meet the love of his life—Ann Sheridan. By the end of the film Ann was supposed to promise to marry him when he returns from the war. Ann despised the whole thing.

"I said [to the producers], 'What a horrible thing to do to a GI. You're going to get every guy in the army all upset, thinking he can marry a movie queen. He doesn't even know what he's getting into,'" Ann said in *Screen Facts*. "Honey, you should have seen that script. I'm sorry, I like the man who did it, Delmer Daves, but this was dreadful!"

So Ann was back on suspension, and Joan Leslie took her place. The story Warners released was that Ann had planned a much-needed vacation to Mexico. Even after her refusal Warners still had hopes that Ann would change her mind. The optimistic producers even filmed street shots of Ann's stand-in to start the movie. "They would not believe that I wouldn't do it. They'd say, 'It's your patriotic duty!' Well, that had nothing to do with patriotism," Ann said.

Ann's take on *Hollywood Canteen* was on target. Although the film's undeniable star power helped make it a box-office bonanza for Warners, critics universally panned it. Sadly, Ann's judgment was less keen with the other script she turned down at the time—*Mildred Pierce* (1945), which won Joan Crawford an Academy Award and revived her career.

There was more dissention from Ann when she was assigned to *The Doughgirls* (1944). At the time, the Joseph Fields comedy was still on Broadway, where it was enjoying a long run. The racy story concerned the marital complications of three former showgirls who are unexpectedly reunited when they end up sharing the same hotel room in crowded wartime Washington, D.C. Ann didn't like the play, and told the studio she didn't want any part of the film version. "I figured that unless you could use the dirt of the play, which they certainly couldn't do on the screen with the Johnston Office, that it would lose all its color," Ann told *Screen Facts*. "Which it did. But oh, there was a big knock-down, drag-out fight over that, threatening me with suspension."

The battle got even bloodier when Warners arranged to have Ann pulled from a scheduled appearance on Bing Crosby's radio show. "Warner, who'd given his OK three weeks before, said that if I didn't do *Doughgirls*, I couldn't do the Crosby show," Ann related. "And I said that I was sorry, but I was going to go down and try to do it. I drove down to the station, but they wouldn't take me. He'd already called and cancelled it."

At the urging of her good friend Mark Hellinger, Ann agreed to do *The Doughgirls* only if Warner would allow her to do a USO tour once the film was completed. Ann had been begging the studio for nine months to let her make the tour. Permission had been granted on many occasions, but then Ann would find a new script at her door and be back to work on a another film.

With the studio's OK for the tour, Ann reported for work on *The Doughgirls*. Directed by James V. Kern, *The Doughgirls*, which featured such talented performers as Alexis Smith, Jane Wyman, Jack Carson, Eve Arden, Charlie Ruggles and Craig Stevens, emerged as a noisy farce disguised as a topical comedy. The actors were all delightful, with one surprising exception: Ann's performance seemed unusually forced, relying on mugging and shrieks to get laughs.

With *The Doughgirls* behind her, Ann boarded the USO plane that June for a tour through China, Burma and India. Also on board were comic-dancer Ben Blue, master of ceremonies Jackie Miles, dancer Mary Landa and accordionist Ruth Denas. The tour received a warm welcome from the weary servicemen upon their arrival in Yankai, China. One soldier who remembered their arrival particularly well was John A. Johns, who painted Ann's image on the nose of a B-25 plane that then became known as the Sheridan Express.

"I was contacted the morning the Sheridan group was to arrive and was asked to 'do something.'" recalled Johns. "I luckily found some housepaint, but no brushes. I fashioned a brush out of a piece of rope, flaired an edge and attached it to a piece of wood. I had no photograph of Ms. Sheridan, but I knew she was a red-haired beauty. The paint was still wet when the troupe arrived. I was shocked when I saw she had dyed her hair blonde!"

The "Oomph" Girl serenades GIs during her USO tour in China in 1944. (Courtesy of Ken Easdon.)

Edith Nash, Ann and Mary Landa in front of the Sheridan Express. (Courtesy of Ken Easdon.)

Ann's role in the show consisted of singing a few songs and playing straight woman to Blue during one of his routines. Although Ann loved performing for the GIs, she didn't appreciate the oppressive conditions she and the other cast members had to endure. Thermometers hardly ever dipped below the 95 degree mark, and perspiration was her typical body makeup. Desert sand continually flew into the eyes and teeth of the actors as they performed onstage.

Even worse than the weather were the distasteful meals the troupe was served. The more appetizing menus consisted of K-rations, but frequently the actors had to dine on far more stomach-churning fare. "I was starving to death for milk," Ann recalled in *Screen Facts*. "We had boiled milk in one place. I can't bear boiled milk. And also, we had ice cream full of bugs. Night bugs that flew, little gnats. You know I got so I didn't mind? It was ice cream. Didn't taste like ice cream, but it was cold. They froze it by sticking it into a well. Not really frozen, just crispy enough to stand up for two minutes."

Sleeping quarters were typically bucket seats or airplane floors. By the end of the trip Ann had lost sixteen pounds and was exhausted. It also didn't help that Jack Warner was constantly sending telegrams asking Ann when she would be returning for work on her next picture.

Ann's irritability didn't show in her performance. Bob Neese, a member of the 159th AACS Squadron, had fond memories of Ann when the tour arrived in Chengdu, China. "I thought that she was a good looking girl," he recalled. "and I still remember the good hug she gave me. No wet kisses, damn it! At the time I was in what was supposed to be a hospital in Chengdu. This is why a half dozen or so of us got special treatment and front row seats."

Johns, likewise, recalled that Ann seemed to be having a good time while she was performing: "All I remember of Ann Sheridan is that she just broke up with loud laughter on whatever Ben Blue did. The men enjoyed what they presented to us."

When Ann returned to New York in late September 1944, the first thing she did was buy two quarts of milk and an ice cream cone. Satiated from her dairy fix, Ann headed to a friend's apartment, said hello to the maid and went to bed. She had become so used to sleeping on hard surfaces that she couldn't fall asleep on the soft mattress. She took a sheet, a pillow and a blanket, which she laid out on the bedroom floor, and fell into a glorious eighteen-hour sleep.

Warners meanwhile was furious because the tour lasted one month longer than scheduled. One of the special service men in Casablanca sent the tour on the wrong route, which resulted in a one-month delay getting into India. When Ann finally returned to the studio, she was rushed into *The Animal Kingdom*, a remake of the 1932 film that had starred Leslie Howard and Ann Harding. The previous film, based on Phillip Barry's play, was an oversexed drama about a playboy torn between two women — an idealistic writer and a conniving socialite. He marries the latter and soon realizes his mistake. Ann had actually begun work on the film in late 1943, with Irving Rapper directing. Five weeks into production Jack Warner shut down the project when he learned that the producer had never sent the script to the Johnston Office for approval.

Production now resumed, but it had undergone numerous changes. For starters, the film had been retitled *One More Tomorrow* (1946), and Peter Godfrey had taken over the directing duties. Dennis Morgan was the playboy, Alexis Smith was "the other woman" who steals Morgan from Ann, and Jack Carson, Jane Wyman and Reginald Gardiner had supporting roles. The script had also been toned down to appease the Johnston Office. There was less emphasis on sex than in the original version, and more of an accent on social consciousness. Since some of Rapper's footage was retained in the final print, the whole affair came across as decidedly uneven.

"You can tell the difference in the scenes between the things Rapper had done and what Godfrey did," Ann recalled. "It was one of the most horrible things I'd ever seen in my life."

One More Tomorrow languished on the studio's shelf until May 1946, and was a huge failure. To make matters worse, Warners kept handing Ann one poor script after the other, which finally caused her to go on strike. Her option was coming up and she was in an enviable position. Her demands were for better scripts, a pay raise and a picture deal. It took eighteen months before an agreement was reached. Both parties benefited, but Ann was the unofficial winner, landing a six-picture deal over a three-year period, with a flat fee for each and script approval.

Her first film under the new deal was *Nora Prentiss* (1947), a taut drama directed by Vincent Sherman about a gentle doctor (Kent Smith) living in San Francisco with a domineering wife (Rosemary De Camp) and his two children. His longing for excitement leads to an affair with Nora (Ann), a sexy nightclub singer. When Nora realizes that Richard can't divorce his wife, she accepts a job offer in New York. The distraught doctor finds a way out of his predicament by assuming the identity of a patient who dies in his office. He and Nora attempt to begin a new life in New York, but fear of discovery leads him to a life of secrecy, seclusion and jealousy.

Sherman envisioned the doctor as the main focus of the film, but when Warners told him they needed a new vehicle for Ann, he retooled the screenplay and made Nora its center. The rewrite pleased Ann, who took an immediate liking to Sherman. He likewise had nothing but affection for Ann, and regarded her as among the best and most underrated actresses he worked with.

Even though the reviews at the time for *Nora Prentiss* were hardly raves (*The New York Times* called it "motion picture making at its worst"), the film holds up surprisingly well. Ann's performance as Nora is one of her most diverse. The part called for equal parts comedienne, sex symbol and dramatic actress, and she blended them together nicely. She also performed two songs ("Would You Like a Souvenir?" and "Who Cares What People Say?") with relish.

Nora Prentiss was one of Warners' biggies of 1947, thus reassuring the studio that its recent negotiations with Ann were worth every penny. Warner pitched James M. Cain's *Serenade* to both Ann and Sherman as a follow-up, but both realized the homosexual aspects of the story made it unfilmable. Sherman and screenwriters David Goodis and James Gunn instead came up with *The Unfaithful* (1947), a well-mounted revamping of *The Letter* (1940). Ann played a California socialite who stabs an intruder in what seems to be self-defense. Later it's revealed that she had been romantically involved with her victim while her husband (Zachary Scott) was in the service, and she had posed for an incriminating statue that the dead man had sculpted.

The chief difference between *The Letter* and *The Unfaithful* is that Chris Hunter (Ann) is hardly the villainess played so brilliantly by Bette Davis in 1940. Ann's character feels remorse for what she's done and therefore doesn't meet the same fate as Davis' Leslie Crosbie. As expected, Ann's performance lacked the power and the nuances of Davis', but because of the gentler nature of her character she added more warmth. The result was an emotionally charged performance.

Ann was also fortunate to have an excellent supporting cast, which included Scott, Lew Ayres as her lawyer and, best of all, Eve Arden as Scott's bitchy cousin. *The New York Times* said, "Ann Sheridan deserves great credit for making Chris Hunter a credible character, even though hers is not a penetrating study of a shamed woman."

As a good luck gesture for John Huston, she did a cameo as a Mexican prostitute in *The Treasure of the Sierra Madre* (1948). No doubt Ann had more fun doing that quick scene than she did filming all 104 minutes of *Silver River* (1948), with Errol Flynn as a cashiered Army officer hungry for power. Ann made *Silver River* because she wanted to work with Flynn once again, and she liked the rare chance to appear in a western. But she admitted it was a dud.

It was also around this time that Ann became involved in what was literally a pet project. Ann had always been a dog fancier, and she especially adored Amos, the French poodle given to her by Brent. She combined her love of animals with her knowledge of poodles, and joined forces with a veterinarian friend in a business venture to raise poodles. Each partner held a fifty percent stake in the business, which lasted until the vet's death in 1959.

Ann also continued to be seen in the Hollywood night spots several times a week with publicity agent Steve Hannagan. Columnists for a long time intimated that the two would tie the knot, but it never happened. Hannagan and Ann remained good friends after they stopped dating. As a sign of his devotion, when Hannagan died in 1953, he left Ann nearly $250,000.

Her dealings with Warners, meanwhile, were still tenuous. The studio couldn't come up with a suitable script for her after *Silver River*, so she went to RKO for *Good Sam* (1948), Leo McCarey's well-meaning attempt at Capraesque whimsy that never seemed to find the right chord. Gary Cooper played a soft-hearted (and soft-headed) family man who can't say no to anyone, much to the frustration of his patient wife (Ann). The film lacked the punch that someone like Preston Sturges could have given it and relied too often on sentiment for its big moments. Ann felt that the lack of chemistry between Cooper and her was the film's biggest flaw.

Even after *Good Sam*, Warners could not come up with a suitable property for Ann. Her desire to break ties with Warners was hastened when Howard Hawks sent her the script for *I Was a Male War Bride*. "I would have taken anything of Howard Hawks'—and with Cary Grant in it—sight unseen," Ann said.

On January 8, 1949, Ann bought out her Warners contract for $35,000. Though anxious to be her own boss, Ann hated leaving the many other contract players and crew members that she had become friendly with during her twelve years at the studio. Ann had once said that her life at the studio was excellent socially but difficult professionally.

Whatever misgivings Ann had about leaving Warners were pushed aside as she headed to London to begin *I Was a Male War Bride* (1949) for 20th Century–Fox. The amusing farce was based on the actual adventures of French captain Henri Rochard during World War II. In the film, Rochard (Cary Grant) is assigned to work with American lieutenant Catherine Gates (Ann Sheridan), an old girlfriend to whom he was unfaithful. Despite their bitter parting, the two still have feelings for each other. After spending time together in Germany, their flame is reignited and they attempt to get married. The military red tape they have to cut through to get permission to marry is nothing compared to the obstacles that keep them from consummating their marriage. Matters are further complicated when Catherine's army unit gets recalled to the United States. To keep from being separated, Catherine has Henri dress up as a war bride so he can sail with her.

Although it was hard to believe Grant could be French, it was of little importance to the enjoyment of the film. The obvious rapport between Ann and Grant on-screen was just as real off the set. Ann enjoyed many nights socializing with Grant and his wife, Betsy Drake, while they were in London. It was fortunate that both stars liked each other so much, since *I Was a Male War Bride* was a film beset with problems. For starters, the continual rain and wind in London seemed more fitting for a horror film than a comedy.

When the production company moved to Heidelberg, Germany, to shoot the exteriors, Ann encountered a nasty situation with customs officials. While traveling on the train from France to Germany, Ann's luggage was taken from her compartment at the French-German border while she was taking a nap. Customs had mistaken her for another passenger suspected of smuggling. It took a great deal of effort on Fox's part to convince officials that they had made an error.

In Heidelberg cast and crew found weather conditions even worse than those of London. On one of the first days of filming in Germany Ann was asked to drive a motorcycle with a sidecar in the midst of a torrential rain, even though she had never handled such a contraption in her life. A German paratrooper gave her some basic training, but her first rehearsal drive, with Grant in the sidecar, was a disaster. The sharp vibrations of the motorcycle jolted her nerves, which were shaken even further when she accidentally ran over a goose. Reluctantly, Ann did it again. In time she became more relaxed and capable. Grant's encouragement and joking helped lift her spirits.

The dismal weather and poor living conditions in Heidelberg took their toll on the key figures involved in *I Was a Male War Bride*. Ann contracted pneumonia, and it took several weeks before she was back to normal. Shortly after she returned, Grant came down with a case of infectious hepatitis. Grant asked to be sent back to London where he could get the best medical care, which meant shutting down production for several more weeks. In the midst of Grant's illness, Hawks broke out in hives, no doubt in reaction to the turmoil that had befallen his film.

The remaining scenes that had been set to be filmed in Germany, as well as retakes of some of the London scenes, were eventually completed in California. In all, *I Was a Male War Bride* took ten months to complete, but it was worth all the trouble. Though much of the humor is obviously dated, the film is still a raucous and racy precursor to the bedroom farces that became so popular during the 1950s and 1960s, but it is laced with far more sophistication than its many imitations.

I Was a Male War Bride was a tremendous hit, grossing $4.1 million. Thrilled with its brisk box office and critical reception, Ann seemed happier in her career than at any other point so far. "There have been three phases in my career — and the present one, playing comedy and to hell with the 'Oomph' — is by far the most satisfying," she said at the time.

Ann was next supposed to play a New Orleans belle in *My Forbidden Past*, a turn of the century drama based on *Carriage Entrance* by Polan Banks, for RKO. Ann's contract with Banks, who was co-producing with Howard Hughes, head of RKO, guaranteed her both script and leading man approval. The problem was that she and Hughes couldn't agree on an actor to play the lead: She wanted Robert Mitchum, while Hughes was pushing for newcomer Mel Ferrer. Then Hughes came up with three other choices, none of which suited Ann. She came back with three more actors, but Hughes disapproved of all three. Hughes finally abrogated the contract and tried to stall the movie. Banks, in turn, filed suit. Ann was understandably angry over the turn of events and also sued RKO. She ended up winning a settlement from RKO, as well as employment on another project pending her approval.

Ann's real victory may have been losing out on *My Forbidden Past*, which eventually did get filmed, with Mitchum and Ava Gardner, in 1951. The film was a critical and commercial disaster that resulted in a $700,000 loss for the studio.

Instead, she wound up in the equally dire *Stella* (1950) for Fox. The black comedy about a family who attempts to dispose of an uncle who dies at a family picnic may have seemed funny on paper, but the laughs never materialized on-screen.

In 1952 Ann signed a three-picture deal with Universal, which specialized in drive-in fare such as westerns and B-grade comedies. Ann's films—*Steel Town* (1952), *Just Across the Street* (1952) and *Take Me to Town* (1953)—were typical Universal fodder. *Take Me to Town*, a folksy western directed by Douglas Sirk, was unquestionably the best of the trio. Ann played Vermillion O'Toole, a sexy saloon singer who hides out at the home of a minister (Sterling Hayden) and his three sons to avoid testifying against her murderous boyfriend (Philip Reed). Ann said Vermillion O'Toole was "the silliest name I'd ever heard in my life," and she may have been right. Still, she brought exuberance to her role and helped liven up otherwise maudlin material.

Like Vincent Sherman, Sirk found her a joy to work with. "She had real presence, a wonderful glow," Sirk told author Jon Halliday in *Sirk on Sirk*. "And there was some sadness about her, underlying the gaiety of the part, which I think enhanced her performance to a discriminating eye. At any rate, I thought in this little picture she was at the same time less and more than she had been before. She maybe had lost in sex-appeal, and gained in a human one. This movie was something of a farewell to cinema for her."

Unfortunately, Ann agreed to a percentage deal in exchange for a salary on her three Universal films, but only *Steel Town* turned a profit, albeit a small one. From then on Ann demanded a flat fee for any film commitments.

That decision was a wise one, especially considering her next film, a dog called *Appointment in Honduras* (1953), which she did for RKO, which still owed her a movie after the *My Forbidden Past* fiasco. The film turned out so bad that Ann said she never even saw it.

Ann didn't make another film until the charming rural drama *Come Next Spring* in 1956. Steve Cochran (in a rare sympathetic role) starred as an ex-convict who returns to his wife (Ann) and children, a son (Richard Eyer) and a mute daughter (Sherry Jackson). He finds them indifferent to him at first, but in time they are able to rebuild their lives and become a family once again.

Though sentimental, *Come Next Spring* was buoyed by lovely performances from Ann and Cochran, who also served as producer. The film was shot in the summer of 1955 in Sacramento, which made it hard for the actors to pretend they were enjoying the spring of the title.

Come Next Spring ended up being distributed by lowly Republic Studios, which did little to promote the picture. Republic boss Herbert J. Yates sold the film as a second feature and basically took whatever bookings he could get for it, which were scant.

Ann's next project marked her first time working at MGM, in a lavish, all-star musical remake of Clare Booth Luce's *The Women* (1939). *The Opposite Sex* (1956), as the new film was called, starred June Allyson in Norma Shearer's old role as a devoted wife who finds out that her producer husband (Leslie Nielsen) is having a fling with a vixenish showgirl (Joan Collins). Ann was the epitome of Manhattan chic as Amanda, Allyson's novelist friend and confidante.

The Opposite Sex was Ann's last grade-A production. Her final film was a disastrous African melodrama called *The Woman and the Hunter* (1957), in which she played a murderess who makes her victim's son and a white hunter her prey. The film was shot on location in Kenya, but even the authentic locales couldn't bring a touch of realism to the film.

With no good film roles on the horizon, Ann turned to the stage. She appeared with Dan Dailey and Franchot Tone in *The Time of Your Life* in Brussels as part of the Exposition in 1958. Buoyed by her initial theatrical venture, she sold her Hollywood home and took an apartment in New York. Her first U.S. theatrical foray was a summer stock production of *Kind Sir*, a pleasant farce by Norman Krasna that opened in June 1958 at East Hampton on Long Island. The show did solid business and received good reviews during its fifteen-week run.

Another happy outcome of *Kind Sir* was that Ann fell in love with her leading man, Scott McKay. He was a delightful companion for Ann and helped her feel at ease in her new venue.

The following year Ann accepted the female lead in playwright Robin Long's *Odd Man In*, which was adapted from a popular French farce. The American version had promise, but suffered in its translation across the Atlantic. Ann accepted the part with the understanding that the troubled scenes would be rewritten and that the show would be brought to Broadway. She soon realized she had been duped. The play opened in Philadelphia without a single word being rewritten. Reviewers commented that the highlight of the evening was Ann's coughing fit, caused by an infected sinus, which forced her to leave the stage.

Odd Man In ran five months, with a grueling tour that covered sixty-nine U.S. cities. Ann eventually learned that the producers never intended to bring the show to New York, and they were only interested in making as much money as they could by playing the show in one-night stands. "That was the hard way to learn about theater," she said a few years later.

Surprisingly, Ann spent a great deal of her time in the 1960s as a regular fixture on daytime television. She made a number of guest appearances on game shows, including *Match Game, Missing Links, The Price Is Right* and *To Tell the Truth*. In 1964 she landed a spot on the soap opera *Another World*, a job which lasted for about one year.

Ann's life took a dramatic upswing in 1966, sparked by two events. In June she and McKay finally married. Then in September CBS premiered Ann's first prime-time series, *Pistols and Petticoats*, which spoofed traditional TV westerns such as *Gunsmoke* and *The Big Valley*. Ann played a widow who was as quick with a gun as she was with a kiss. In support were veteran actors Douglas Fowley and Ruth McDevitt as her sharp-shooting parents, former *McHale's Navy* crew member Gary Vinson as the bumbling sheriff, and pretty newcomer Carole Wells as Ann's daughter. Despite mixed reviews from critics, the show caught on quickly with audiences.

Unfortunately, Ann's newfound happiness was cut short. Her years of chain smoking had taken their toll on her health, and in the fall of 1966 she was diagnosed with advanced lung cancer. She died on January 21, 1967, just one month short of her fifty-second birthday. Ironically, the news was broadcast in New York the following day, just minutes before local station WNEW was set to air its Sunday afternoon movie—*Angels Wash Their Faces*.

Only a few months before her death Ann looked back on her career, which she saw as rather unexciting: "Some people have such interesting things happen to them during the knock-down, drag-out try for a career. Others, it just seems to drag along, and mine sounds so boring. If something exciting had happened I could understand, but it was just hard work, that's all."

FILMOGRAPHY

(Ann was unbilled in the first 15 films listed below, as well as *Mississippi*)

Search for Beauty (Paramount, 1934) Directed by Erle C. Kenton. *Cast:* Buster Crabbe, Ida Lupino, Robert Armstrong, James Gleason, Gertrude Michael, Roscoe Karns, Toby Wing. (Ann appears as the Search for Beauty Texas winner.)

Bolero (Paramount, 1934) Directed by Wesley Ruggles. *Cast:* George Raft, Carole Lombard, Sally Rand, Frances Drake, William Frawley, Raymond Milland, Gertrude Michael.

Come on Marines (Paramount, 1934) Directed by Henry Hathaway. *Cast:* Richard Arlen, Ida Lupino, Roscoe Karns, Grace Bradley, Monte Blue, Lona Andre, Toby Wing.

Murder at the Vanities (Paramount, 1934) Directed by Mitchell Leisen. *Cast:* Carl Brisson, Victor McLaglen, Kitty Carlisle, Dorothy Stickney, Gertrude Michael, Toby Wing.

Kiss and Make Up (Paramount, 1934) Directed by Harlan Thompson. *Cast:* Cary Grant, Helen Mack, Genevieve Tobin, Edward Everett Horton, Lucien Littlefield.

Shoot the Works (Paramount, 1934) Directed by Wesley Ruggles. *Cast:* Jack Oakie, Ben Bernie, Dorothy Dell, Arline Judge, Alison Skipworth, Roscoe Karns, William Frawley.

The Notorious Sophie Lang (Paramount, 1934) Directed by Ralph Murphy. *Cast:* Gertrude Michael, Paul Cavanaugh, Arthur Byron, Alison Skipworth, Leon Errol.

Ladies Should Listen (Paramount, 1934) Directed by Frank Tuttle. *Cast:* Cary Grant, Frances Drake, Edward Everett Horton, Rosita Moreno, George Barbier.

Wagon Wheels (Paramount, 1934) Directed by Charles Barton. *Cast:* Randolph Scott, Gail Patrick, Billy Lee, Jan Duggan, Leila Bennett, Monte Blue.

Mrs. Wiggs of the Cabbage Patch (Paramount, 1934) Directed by Norman Taurog. *Cast:* Pauline Lord, W.C. Fields, Zasu Pitts, Evelyn Venable, Kent Taylor, Donald Meek.

College Rhythm (Paramount, 1934) Directed by Norman Taurog. *Cast:* Jack Oakie, Joe Penner, Mary Brian, Lanny Ross, Helen Mack, Lyda Roberti, George Barbier, Franklin Pangborn.

Limehouse Blues (Paramount, 1934) Directed by Alexander Hall. *Cast:* George Raft, Anna May Wong, Jean Parker, Kent Taylor, Montagu Love, Billy Bevan, Eric Blore, Colin Tapley.

Enter Madame (Paramount, 1935) Directed by Elliott Nugent. *Cast:* Elissa Landi, Cary Grant, Lynne Overman, Sharon Lynne, Frank Albertson, Cecelia Parker, Wilfred Hari, Paul Porcasi.

Home on the Range (Paramount, 1935) Directed by Arthur Jacobson. *Cast:* Jackie Coogan, Randolph Scott, Evelyn Brent, Dean Jagger, Addison Richards, Fuzzy Knight, Philip Morris.

Rumba (Paramount, 1935) Directed by Marion Gering. *Cast:* Carole Lombard, George Raft, Margo, Lynne Overman, Monroe Owsley, Iris Adrian, Gail Patrick, Samuel S. Hinds.

Behold My Wife (Paramount, 1935) Directed by Mitchell Leisen. *Cast:* Sylvia Sidney, Gene Raymond, Juliette Compton, Laura Hope Crews, H.B. Warner, Monroe Owsley, Ann Sheridan.

Car 99 (Paramount, 1935) Directed by Charles Barton. *Cast:* Fred MacMurray, Ann Sheridan, Sir Guy Standing, Frank Craven, William Frawley, Marina Schubert, Dean Jagger.

Rocky Mountain Mystery (Paramount, 1935) Directed by Charles Barton. *Cast:* Randolph Scott, Charles "Chic" Sale, Ann Sheridan, Mrs. Leslie Carter, Kathleen Burke, George Marion.

Mississippi (Paramount, 1935) Directed by Edward A. Sutherland. *Cast:* Bing Crosby, W.C. Fields, Joan Bennett, Queenie Smith, Gail Patrick, Claude Gillingwater, John Miljan.

Red Blood of Courage (Ambassador, 1935) Directed by Jack English. *Cast:* Kermit Maynard, Reginald Barlow, Ann Sheridan, Ben Hendricks, Jr., Charles King, George Regis, Nat Carr.

The Glass Key (Paramount, 1935) Directed by Frank Tuttle. *Cast:* Edward Arnold, George Raft, Claire Dodd, Rosalind Keith, Ray Milland, Ronald Glecker, Guinn Williams, Ann Sheridan.

The Crusades (Paramount, 1935) Directed by Cecil B. De Mille. *Cast:* Henry Wilcoxon, Loretta Young, Ian Keith, Katherine De Mille, C. Aubrey Smith, George Barbier, Joseph Schildkraut, Alan Hale, William Farnum, Hobart Bosworth, Montagu Love, Ann Sheridan.

Fighting Youth (Universal, 1935) Directed by Hamilton MacFadden. *Cast:* Charles Farrell, June Martel, Andy Devine, Ann Sheridan, J. Farrell MacDonald, Edward Nugent, Jean Rogers.

Sing Me a Love Song (Warner Bros., 1936) Directed by Ray Enright. *Cast:* James Melton, Patricia Ellis, Hugh Herbert, Zasu Pitts, Allen Jenkins, Nat Pendleton, Ann Sheridan.

Black Legion (Warner Bros., 1937) Directed by Archie Mayo. *Cast:* Humphrey Bogart, Erin O'Brien-Moore, Dick Foran, Robert Barrat, Ann Sheridan, Helen Flint, Paul Harvey.

The Great O'Malley (Warner Bros., 1937) Directed by William Dieterle. *Cast:* Pat O'Brien, Sybil Jason, Humphrey Bogart, Ann Sheridan, Frieda Inescourt, Donald Crisp, Henry O'Neill.

San Quentin (Warner Bros., 1937) Directed by Lloyd Bacon. *Cast:* Pat O'Brien, Humphrey Bogart, Ann Sheridan, Barton MacLane, Joseph Sawyer, Veda Ann Borg, James Robbins.

Wine, Women and Horses (Warner Bros., 1937) Directed by Louis King. *Cast:* Barton MacLane, Dick Purcell, Ann Sheridan, Peggy Bates, Walter Cassel, Lottie Williams.

Footloose Heiress (Warner Bros., 1937) Directed by William Clemens. *Cast:* Craig Reynolds, Anne Nagel, William Hopper, Ann Sheridan, Hugh O'Connell, Teddy Hart, Hal Neiman.

Alcatraz Island (Warner Bros., 1938) Directed by William McGann. *Cast:* John Litel, Ann Sheridan, Mary Maguire, Gordon Oliver, Dick Purcell, Addison Richards, George E. Stone.

She Loved a Fireman (Warner Bros., 1938) Directed by John Farrow. *Cast:* Ann Sheridan, Dick Foran, Robert Armstrong, Eddie Acuff, Veda Ann Borg, May Beatty, Eddie Chandler.

The Patient in Room 18 (Warner Bros., 1938) Directed by Bobby Connolly and Crane Wilbur. *Cast:* Ann Sheridan, Patric Knowles, Eric Stanley, John Ridgeley, Rosella Towne, Vicki Lester.

Mystery House (Warner Bros., 1938) Directed by Noel Smith. *Cast:* Ann Sheridan, Dick Purcell, Anne Nagel, William Hopper, Anthony Averill, Dennie Moore, Hugh O'Connell.

Cowboy from Brooklyn (Warner Bros., 1938) Directed by Lloyd Bacon. *Cast:* Dick Powell, Pat O'Brien, Priscilla Lane, Dick Foran, Ann Sheridan, Johnny Davis, Ronald Reagan.

Little Miss Thoroughbred (Warner Bros., 1938) Directed by John Farrow. *Cast:* Ann Sheridan, John Litel, Frank McHugh, Janet Chapman, Eric Stanley, Robert Homans.

A Letter of Introduction (Universal, 1938) Directed by John M. Stahl. *Cast:* Adolphe Menjou, Andrea Leeds, Edgar Bergen and Charlie McCarthy, George Murphy, Eve Arden, Ann Sheridan.

Broadway Musketeers (Warner Bros., 1938) Directed by John Farrow. *Cast:* Ann Sheridan, Margaret Lindsay, Marie Wilson, John Litel, Janet Chapman, Dick Purcell, Richard Bond.

Angels with Dirty Faces (Warner Bros., 1938) Directed by Michael Curtiz. *Cast:* James Cagney, Pat O'Brien, Ann Sheridan, The Dead End Kids, Humphrey Bogart, George Bancroft.

They Made Me a Criminal (Warner Bros., 1939) Directed by Busby Berkeley. *Cast:* John Garfield, Claude Rains, Gloria Dickson, The Dead End Kids, May Robson, Ann Sheridan.

Dodge City (Warner Bros., 1939) Directed by Michael Curtiz. *Cast:* Errol Flynn, Olivia de Havilland, Ann Sheridan, Bruce Cabot, Frank McHugh, Alan Hale, John Litel, Henry Travers.

Naughty but Nice (Warner Bros., 1939) Directed by Ray Enright. *Cast:* Ann Sheridan, Dick Powell, Gale Page, Helen Broderick, Ronald Reagan, Allen Jenkins, Zasu Pitts, Jerry Colonna.

Winter Carnival (Wanger–United Artists, 1939) Directed by Charles F. Riesner. *Cast:* Ann Sheridan, Richard Carlson, Helen Parrish, James Corner, Robert Armstrong, Joan Brodel (Joan Leslie).

Indianapolis Speedway (Warner Bros., 1939) Directed by Lloyd Bacon. *Cast:* Pat O'Brien, Ann Sheridan, John Payne, Gale Page, Frank McHugh, Grace Stafford, Granville Bates.

Angels Wash Their Faces (Warner Bros., 1939) Directed by Ray Enright. *Cast:* Ann Sheridan, Ronald Reagan, The Dead End Kids, Frankie Thomas, Henry O'Neill, Eduardo Ciannelli.

Castle on the Hudson (Warner Bros., 1940) Directed by Anatole Litvak. *Cast:* John Garfield, Ann Sheridan, Pat O'Brien, Burgess Meredith, Jerome Cowan, Henry O'Neill, Guinn Williams.

It All Came True (Warner Bros., 1940) Directed by Lewis Seiler. *Cast:* Ann Sheridan, Humphrey Bogart, Jeffrey Lynn, Zasu Pitts, Jessie Busley, Felix Bressart, Una O'Connor.

Torrid Zone (Warner Bros., 1940) Directed by William Keighley. *Cast:* James Cagney, Ann Sheridan, Pat O'Brien, Andy Devine, Helen Vinson, Jerome Cowan, George Tobias.

They Drive by Night (Warner Bros., 1940) Directed by Raoul Walsh. *Cast:* George Raft, Ann Sheridan, Humphrey Bogart, Ida Lupino, Alan Hale, Roscoe Karns, Gale Page, John Litel.

City for Conquest (Warner Bros., 1940) Directed by Anatole Litvak. *Cast:* James Cagney, Ann Sheridan, Frank Craven, Arthur Kennedy, Donald Crisp, Frank McHugh, George Tobias.

Honeymoon for Three (Warner Bros., 1941) Directed by Lloyd Bacon. *Cast:* George Brent, Ann Sheridan, Osa Massen, Charles Ruggles, Jane Wyman, Lee Patrick.

Navy Blues (Warner Bros., 1941) Directed by Lloyd Bacon. *Cast:* Ann Sheridan, Jack Oakie, Jack Haley, Martha Raye, Herbert Anderson, Jack Carson, Jackie Gleason, John Ridgeley.

King's Row (Warner Bros., 1942) Directed by Sam Wood. *Cast:* Ann Sheridan, Robert Cummings, Ronald Reagan, Betty Field, Charles Coburn, Claude Rains, Judith Anderson.

The Man Who Came to Dinner (Warner Bros., 1942) Directed by William Keighley. *Cast:* Bette Davis, Ann Sheridan, Monty Woolley, Richard Travis, Jimmy Durante, Reginald Gardiner.

Juke Girl (Warner Bros., 1942) Directed by Curtis Bernhardt. *Cast:* Ann Sheridan, Ronald Reagan, Richard Whorf, Gene Lockhart, Faye Emerson, Betty Brewer, George Tobias.

Wings for the Eagle (Warner Bros., 1942) Directed by Lloyd Bacon. *Cast:* Ann Sheridan, Dennis Morgan, Jack Carson, George Tobias, Russell Arms, Don De Fore, Tom Fadden.

George Washington Slept Here (Warner Bros., 1942) Directed by William Keighley. *Cast:* Jack Benny, Ann Sheridan, Charles Coburn, Percy Kilbride, Hattie McDaniel, William Tracy.

Edge of Darkness (Warner Bros., 1943) Directed by Lewis Milestone. *Cast:* Errol Flynn, Ann Sheridan, Walter Huston, Nancy Coleman, Helmut Dantine, Judith Anderson, Ruth Gordon.

Thank Your Lucky Stars (Warner Bros., 1943) Directed by David Butler. *Cast:* Dennis Morgan, Joan Leslie. Guest stars: Humphrey Bogart, Eddie Cantor, Jack Carson, Bette Davis, Olivia de Havilland, Errol Flynn, John Garfield, Ida Lupino, Ann Sheridan, Alexis Smith.

Shine on, Harvest Moon (Warner Bros., 1944) Directed by David Butler. *Cast:* Ann Sheridan, Dennis Morgan, Jack Carson, Irene Manning, S.Z. Sakall, Marie Wilson, Robert Shayne.

The Doughgirls (Warner Bros., 1944) Directed by James V. Kern. *Cast:* Ann Sheridan, Alexis Smith, Jane Wyman, Irene Manning, Jack Carson, Eve Arden, Charles Ruggles, Barbara Brown.

One More Tomorrow (Warner Bros., 1946) Directed by Peter Godfrey. *Cast:* Ann Sheridan, Dennis Morgan, Alexis Smith, Jack Carson, Jane Wyman, Reginald Gardiner, John Loder.

Nora Prentiss (Warner Bros., 1947) Directed by Vincent Sherman. *Cast:* Ann Sheridan, Kent Smith, Robert Alda, Bruce Bennett, Rosemary De Camp, Wanda Hendrix, John Ridgeley.

The Unfaithful (Warner Bros., 1947) Directed by Vincent Sherman. *Cast:* Ann Sheridan, Lew Ayres, Zachary Scott, Eve Arden, Steven Geray, John Hoyt, Peggy Knudsen, Douglas Kennedy.

Treasure of the Sierra Madre (Warner Bros., 1948) Directed by John Huston. *Cast:* Humphrey Bogart, Walter Huston, Tim Holt, Bruce Bennett. (Ann has a cameo as a prostitute.)

Silver River (Warner Bros., 1948) Directed by Raoul Walsh. *Cast:* Errol Flynn, Ann Sheridan, Thomas Mitchell, Bruce Bennett, Tom D'Andrea, Barton MacLane, Monte Blue, Jonathan Hale.

Good Sam (RKO Radio, 1948) Directed by Leo McCarey. *Cast:* Gary Cooper, Ann Sheridan, Ray Collins, Edmund Lowe, Joan Lorring, Louise Beavers, Clinton Sundberg, Ruth Roman.

I Was a Male War Bride (20th Century–Fox, 1949) Directed by Howard Hawks. *Cast:* Cary Grant, Ann Sheridan, Marion Marshall, Randy Stuart, William Neff, Eugene Gericke.

Stella (20th Century–Fox, 1950) Directed by Claude Binyon. *Cast:* Ann Sheridan, Victor Mature, David Wayne, Frank Fontaine, Randy Stuart, Marion Marshall, Leif Erickson.

Woman on the Run (Universal-International, 1950) Directed by Norman Foster. *Cast:* Ann Sheridan, Dennis O'Keefe, Robert Keith, Ross Elliott, Frank Jenks, John Qualen.

Steel Town (Universal-International, 1952) Directed by George Sherman. *Cast:* Ann Sheridan, John Lund, Howard Duff, James Best, Eileen Crowe, Chick Chandler, Nancy Kulp.

Just Across the Street (Universal-International, 1952) Directed by Joseph Pevney. *Cast:* Ann Sheridan, John Lund, Robert Keith, Cecil Kellaway, Natalie Schaefer, Harvey Lembeck.

Take Me to Town (Universal-International, 1953) Directed by Douglas Sirk. *Cast:* Ann Sheridan, Sterling Hayden, Philip Reed, Lee Patrick, Lee Aaker, Harvey Grant, Dusty Henley.

Appointment in Honduras (RKO Radio, 1953) Directed by Jacques Tourneur. *Cast:* Ann Sheridan, Glenn Ford, Zachary Scott, Rodolfo Acosta, Jack Elam, Ric Roman, Rico Alaniz.

Come Next Spring (Republic, 1956) Directed by R.G. Springsteen. *Cast:* Ann Sheridan, Steve Cochran, Walter Brennan, Sherry Jackson, Richard Eyer, Edgar Buchanan, Sonny Tufts.

The Opposite Sex (MGM, 1956) Directed by David Miller. *Cast:* June Allyson, Ann Sheridan, Joan Collins, Dolores Gray, Ann Miller, Leslie Nielsen, Agnes Moorehead, Joan Blondell.

The Woman and the Hunter (Gross-Krasne-Phoenix, 1957) Directed by George Breakston. *Cast:* Ann Sheridan, David Farrar, John Loder, Jan Merlin.

Alexis Smith: "The Ice Princess"

A regal beauty and a patrician manner helped Alexis Smith carve a place in film history as the screen's ultimate ice princess. In her Warners films she was often cast as a cool socialite (*The Constant Nymph*, *Rhapsody in Blue*) or the calculating "other" woman (*The Two Mrs. Carrolls*), a persona that she didn't necessarily aspire to, as well as one that clashed with her offscreen personality. On rare occasions Warners allowed her to frolic with the likes of Errol Flynn and Jack Benny, and she clearly enjoyed the change of pace.

Unlike the more rebellious Bette Davis and Olivia de Havilland, Alexis never refused a role nor was she ever placed on suspension. She was a team player who gave her all to every role, many of which were unworthy of her talents. When Alexis left Warners she did find more diverse parts, though she never found that signature screen role which should have elevated her to the stardom level of her friend Jane Wyman. It's to Alexis' credit that she was able to establish a far more interesting second phase of her career as a celebrated star of the stage.

The fact that Alexis was able to change the direction of her career fits in with her healthy philosophy toward living. "I have an insatiable curiosity about everything," she said. "It leads me into paths I wouldn't ordinarily pursue, and makes for a life that is rich — you find yourself in all sorts of situations and experiences."

Rarely was there a period in her life when Alexis wasn't taking lessons or tackling a new challenge. Certainly Alexis' upbringing and, in particular, the strong influence of her mother pinpoints the roots of her thirst for knowledge and upbeat attitude. Margaret Alexis Fitzsimmons Smith was born on June 8, 1921, in Penticton, British Columbia, to a family steeped in the traditions of its Scottish heritage. Her father, Alexander Smith, was born in the Shetland Islands. At fifteen, Alexander and his father moved to Colorado, but soon afterward his father returned to Scotland and Alexander was sent to live with a family in British Columbia. Alexander was sent to work for a hardware retailer, where he studied the ways of the business world. He used his business knowledge and the money he had saved to eventually open his own grocery store.

Alexis' mother, Gladys, was a secretary, but her first love was the arts. Her father had been a painter who also had many other talents, including a flair for architectural design. Gladys grew up with a love for literature and music, two passions that she shared with Alexis.

When Alexis was about a year old, Alexander was offered a job in Los Angeles as a manager for the West Stockeley Company, a seller of canned foods. Gladys was pleased because Alexis would be better served by the climate and educational opportunities in California. From an early age Alexis was encouraged by her mother to pursue as many art forms as possible.

"Alexis loved to study," said Frances Rafferty, Alexis' friend from childhood. "Mrs. Smith established that as a child. Alexis was naturally bright and studying kept her mind

Stunning Alexis Smith begged Warners to put her in musicals, but the studio saw her as a serious actress.

occupied. Her mother believed that if you kept girls busy studying, they wouldn't get into trouble."

Gladys saw to it that, in addition to her school lessons, Alexis was given an introduction to literature. As a daily ritual, Gladys read from the classics, which Alexis loved. Gladys also bought books that contained reproductions of famous paintings, and had Alexis play a game called "Who Painted This One?" As Alexis got older she was given regular instruction in dance and piano, two areas in which she became proficient. In 1931 Alexis won a dance scholarship to the prestigious Edith Jane Studio in Los Angeles. Alexis took her studies, which included tap, ballet and modern dance, very seriously and quickly became one of the prize students in the class.

For the first few years Alexis attended classes at the Edith Jane Studio she was accompanied by her mother, who was always her greatest supporter. By the time Alexis was twelve, Gladys felt her daughter was responsible enough to travel by herself on the Red Car, a public streetcar that ran through Los Angeles. On one of those trips Alexis noticed a fellow classmate who got on a few stops later. She and the other girl, Frances Rafferty, started talking and discovered they had much in common. The girls' spirited sense of humor and their mutual love of dance and music served as the foundation for a friendship that lasted until Alexis' death.

"We always went to the ballet together as girls," Rafferty said. "We were together all the time. It was a sharing relationship always. People took us for sisters. In fact, Alexis gave me a photograph with the inscription, 'May we be happy sisters for many years to come.' I still have it. We would share books. When we were going on interviews, we would share clothes. We both loved music and we would go to the Hollywood Bowl all the time. It was a sharing relationship."

Alexis and Gladys maintained a similar relationship. Gladys had shared with Alexis a love of music, as well as the importance of good health and nutrition. Gladys also taught Alexis to maintain a steady diet consisting of ample portions of fruits and vegetables, coupled with regular exercise and daily vitamins. Alexis remained an avid nutritionist and exercise buff throughout her life, although as a child there were times she resented her mother's nutritional bent.

"I always took my lunch to school because of my mother's idea about diet, and the lunch always included a raw carrot. As you could guess, my nickname became 'Rabbit.' How I hated it!" Alexis recalled in a 1970 interview with *Films in Review*.

As the Depression waged on, the Smiths' financial situation was not especially healthy. Gladys was a gifted seamstress, and to help reduce clothing expenses she designed all of Alexis' outfits. Gladys was unaware, though, that Alexis' peers looked down on her because she didn't wear expensive, frilly dresses from the May Company or Sears. Alexis never told her parents about the humiliations she suffered at school.

"I was a well-behaved child. I respected and loved both of my parents," she said.

If Gladys was rigid about nutrition and money matters, she was equally fervent about taking care of her home. Everything was kept in its proper place, and her home always looked meticulous—more traits passed on from mother to daughter. "Alexis was very neat. Everything had to be just so. I, on the other hand, was a slob. We were like the odd couple," Rafferty laughed.

By the time she was thirteen, Alexis had developed from a promising student into an accomplished dancer. When she auditioned for a role as a dancer in the Hollywood Bowl's production of *Carmen* in 1934, the producers were impressed and she was signed. "She got in at thirteen, which was ghastly," joked Rafferty. The following year, both Alexis and Rafferty danced in the Hollywood Bowl's production of *Prince Igor*.

In her sophomore year at Hollywood High Alexis choreographed and danced in *The Red Mill*. The next year she began dabbling in dramatics and entered a city-wide acting contest, which she won. She then moved on to the state-wide competition, where she performed a scene from *Elizabeth the Queen*, playing both Queen Elizabeth and Lord Essex. She came in second, losing to Jack Edwards, also from Los Angeles. Alexis and Edwards returned home on the same train. When they arrived they found a brass band and a welcoming crowd at the station to honor the winner. A dejected Alexis didn't even want to get off the train.

"My father came looking for me and gave me a lecture about never quitting that I've never forgotten. I got off the train," Alexis said.

In her senior year a nervous Alexis auditioned for the plum role of Lady Macbeth. She trembled during her entire reading and her hands never stopped shaking, but her high school teacher mistook her jangled nerves for emotion and she won the part.

It was no surprise to Alexis' family when she told them she planned to major in drama when she entered City College in Los Angeles in 1939. Although Alexis continued with her dance studies, she also wisely realized the importance of having a well-rounded theatrical background of both musical and dramatic training. "Acting incorporates all the arts, all of life," she said.

By this time Alexis had developed into a desirable young woman. Standing at five feet, nine inches, and with a well-toned figure and shapely legs from all her years of dance training, she was the epitome of elegance. Her honey-blonde hair and soft green eyes added to her allure, which was not lost on her male classmates. Alexis had not been allowed to date until she was sixteen, and even then it was under the watchful eye of her father. Prior to Alexis turning eighteen, her father always picked her up and brought her home from her dates. She was given a little more freedom in college, but anyone she went out with still had to pass inspection by her parents. Alexis often dated boys she knew from the campus, but did not become seriously involved with anyone at the time. City College was challenging, and Alexis' top priority was academics.

"It was a strict school. Over a hundred of us went in at the same time, and by the end of the second year twelve were left. The only excuse for missing classes was death — our own," Alexis quipped in *Films in Review*.

In 1940 the theater group at City College presented *The Night of January Sixteenth*, a popular mystery of the time, with Alexis in the lead. On opening night Vic Orsatti, a Warner Bros. talent scout, was in the audience, and he took notice of Alexis. Impressed by her commanding stage presence and stunning features, he went backstage and approached her about making a screen test at Warners. Alexis was ecstatic.

Solly Bianco of Warners' casting department arranged for Alexis to work with drama coach Sophie Rosenstein to prepare for her test. When the test was run, Jack Warner and Steve Trilling, Warner's assistant, expressed concern about Alexis' height. With the exceptions of Errol Flynn and George Brent, most of Warners' leading men were less than six feet tall and tended to be self-conscious when working with a statuesque actress. Rosenstein convinced them that Alexis photographed well and had a regal, sophisticated quality lacking in most of the studio's leading ladies. At her urging, Alexis was signed to a seven-year contract.

Prior to signing, Alexis consulted Jerry Blunt, her drama advisor at City College. His response: "The opportunity may never come again." She then put her name on the contract.

Alexis' first year at the studio was something of a blur. She did little except appear in tests with potential contract players and pose for some cheesecake publicity shots. She eventually graduated to bit parts, making a barely noticeable screen debut as one of the guests in a wedding scene in *The Lady with Red Hair* (1940), a period piece starring Miriam Hopkins as Mrs. Leslie Carter and Claude Rains as famed producer David Belasco.

The beginning of 1941 was looking just as grim for Alexis as she bounced from one insubstantial film to another in uncredited bits. Her most substantial assignment was as a member of the Navy Blues Sextet to promote *Navy Blues* (1941), a brassy musical starring Ann Sheridan. Essentially, the six starlets (Kay Aldridge, Georgia Carroll, Marguerite Chapman, Peggy Diggins and Lorraine Gettman were the others) toured theaters to drum up interest in the movie. Although she never appeared in the film, Alexis attracted enough attention during the tour to land a screen test for *Dive Bomber* (1941), a rousing airborne epic starring Warners' top male action star Errol Flynn, Fred MacMurray (borrowed from Paramount), Ralph Bellamy and a handsome newcomer named Craig Stevens.

"The picture was all completed and then it was decided that they needed a girl," recalled Stevens. "They looked at I don't know how many girls before Alexis got the part."

Though the part only consisted of about three scenes, Alexis was given the full glamour treatment. It helped that *Dive Bomber* was being lensed in Technicolor, so Alexis' natural physical attributes would be seen to full advantage. *The New York Times*' reviewer clearly took notice of the luscious newcomer. "In the few glimpses we have of her, Alexis Smith looks good; can't tell you yet how she acts," wrote Bosley Crowther.

As expected, *Dive Bomber* cleaned up at the box office. Warner Bros. gave Alexis the star build-up, which included the silly tag of the Dynamite Girl, which she detested. Even more ridiculous was the publicity stunt that followed. A Warners publicist arranged for the "president of the Dynamite Guild of America" to present Alexis with the Guild's pseudo-Oscar—five sticks of phony dynamite. As Alexis was presented her "award," the "president" said: "To Alexis Smith, who is full of tremendous energy and is likely to explode on the slightest impulse, like dynamite."

Alexis' first film after the ridiculous stunt hardly caused an explosion at the box office. *The Smiling Ghost* (1941) was a B mystery obviously modeled after Paramount's Bob Hope hit *The Cat and the Canary* (1939). Like the Hope film, *The Smiling Ghost* involved murder and other strange goings-on in an eerie mansion. Alexis' co-star was Wayne Morris, a beefy actor who showed promise as a boxer in *Kid Galahad* (1937) but had since been relegated to programmers.

Crowther tagged it "a fair B-guiler," but he was again taken with Alexis. "Alexis Smith, a Warner newcomer, makes a decorative kiss of death girl," he wrote.

Her next assignment, *Steel Against the Sky* (1941), would prove to be a pivotal film, though more as a personal milestone than as cinematic art. *Steel Against the Sky* was essentially a retread of earlier blue-collar dramas, such as *Slim* (1937), *They Drive by Night* (1940) and *Manpower* (1941), that Warners specialized in. Like those other films, rough-and-tumble humor about men doing dangerous jobs was intertwined with a romantic triangle. This time the laborers were bridge builders. Alexis was top-billed as Helen Powers, a beautiful socialite who comes between two brothers—rough-around-the-edges Rocky (Lloyd Nolan), who heads up the bridge crew, and his shiftless brother Chuck (Craig Stevens), who takes a job with the crew to impress Helen. The film's ominous fadeout has Alexis marrying the reformed Stevens.

Alexis and Stevens knew each other slightly during the making of *Dive Bomber*, but their relationship reached a new plateau while shooting *Steel Against the Sky*. The climax involved Nolan and Stevens fighting for their lives on a bridge under construction during a dangerous ice storm at night, while Alexis waited on the ground for them to come down safely. The difficult scene took a long time to shoot, with filming often running into the evening hours. Although Alexis had made it a firm policy not to date men from the studio, she accepted Stevens' invitations to get a bite at the end of the long day.

"That's when we got to know each other," recounted Stevens. "She was a lot of fun. It was then that she told me that she didn't want me in the picture. She thought [her friend] Charles Drake should play the role. Of course, she didn't really have any say in casting, but I thought it was kind of amusing." Alexis likewise found her dinner companion charming.

Alexis' career was moving as swiftly as her new romance. In *Gentleman Jim* (1942) she was again paired with Flynn, this time in an enjoyable, light-hearted biography of champion boxer James J. Corbett. The rollicking screenplay by Vincent Lawrence and Horace McCoy was supposedly based on Corbett's autobiography, *The Roar of the Crowd*, but because of legal problems with Corbett's estate, many of the details were fictitious, including the romance between Corbett and high-toned blue-blood Victoria Ware (Alexis). What ultimately emerged was a lively yarn following the brash Corbett from a young man in turn of the century San Francisco up to winning the boxing crown from John L. Sullivan (Ward Bond in a touching performance).

Despite the inaccuracies, Raoul Walsh's spirited direction, and the polished performances of Flynn and a supporting cast of old pros (Jack Carson, Alan Hale, S.Z. Sakall) made *Gentleman Jim* a knockout among boxing films. Alexis received encouraging reviews for her performance. "Alexis Smith carries the romantic interest very entertainingly," said *The New York Times*.

Flynn often remarked that he hated acting, but *Gentleman Jim* was one of the few movies he admittedly enjoyed making. His immediate rapport with Alexis was no doubt a factor. The two shared many jokes on the set and became close friends. When Alexis asked Flynn if he wanted to live to be an old man, he replied, "No, I like this half of life best and I want to live it to the hilt."

Although Flynn was renowned for having affairs with many of his leading ladies, his relationship with Alexis was strictly platonic. "He had feelings for her, but he also had great respect for her," Stevens said. "He treated her with dignity, respect and humor. He never made a pass at her."

It wasn't until sixteen years later, only a few months before his death, that Flynn finally confessed his true feelings to Alexis. "When he was making *Too Much, Too Soon* he called one day," Stevens said. "I answered the phone and he said, 'Hey Old Boy, is your lady there?' When Alexis got on the phone he asked if she would meet him at Warners for lunch. She said 'Of course.' The next day when she came home from that lunch, there were tears in her eyes. She said, 'He told her he knew he didn't have much longer to live. He wanted to tell me how much he enjoyed working with me and also that he loved me.' She never forgot it."

It's doubtful that Alexis would have plunged into an affair with Flynn anyway. At that point she and Stevens were inseparable. Tall and lean, with wavy black hair and an all–American handsomeness, Stevens seemed a perfect match for Alexis. Born Gail Shikles, Jr., on July 8, 1921, Stevens grew up in Liberty, Missouri, and since his father was a schoolteacher, education was an integral part of his childhood. While attending the University of Kansas, where he was majoring in dentistry, Stevens got the acting bug after taking a few drama classes. He studied further, receiving necessary training at Paramount's acting school and the Pasadena Playhouse. Following some brief appearances in summer stock, he was signed by Warner Bros. in 1941.

When Alexis wasn't seeing Stevens, she occupied her spare time with friends, as well as reading and attending the ballet. Rafferty recalled one memorable night at the ballet shortly after she and Alexis began their screen careers. "We decided to splurge. The Ballet Russe de Monte Carlo was appearing. We got orchestra seats. That night we got all dressed up and we looked beautiful. We drove to the theater and parked at the Biltmore Garage. We watched the ballet and had a great time. It was one of the most wonderful evenings in our lives. Then we discovered that neither one of us had money for the garage. Luckily the guys at the garage recognized us, so we got home, but it was pretty embarrassing. We paid them back the next day."

Alexis' stock rose with her next prestigious assignment: *The Constant Nymph* (1943), a romantic drama based on the novel by Margaret Kennedy and directed by Edmund Goulding, who had helmed two of Bette Davis' best vehicles, *Dark Victory* (1939) and *The Old Maid* (1939). The book had already been filmed in 1927, with Mabel Poulton in the lead, and again in England in 1933, with Elisabeth Bergner. For the third version Joan Fontaine was top billed as Tessa, a teenage girl stricken with consumption and an undying love for charming Lewis Dodd (Charles Boyer), a musician trapped in a loveless marriage to Tessa's haughty cousin, Florence (Alexis).

"It was Edmund Goulding who really gave her her big break when he cast her in *The Constant Nymph*," Stevens said. "He was very fond of her and wanted her for that role. She was a very young girl and she had to play an older woman, but he knew she could do it. She got wonderful notices and that was really when she finally got recognized as an actress."

Alexis was initially anxious about playing such a demanding role, and even more so about the fact that she towered over her leading man. "She was so excited about the chance to work with Boyer, but she was also concerned because she was quite statuesque and was about two inches taller than him," said her friend, actress Audrey Totter. "For her test she went about on bended knees the whole time so that she would appear shorter than him. He was very nice and stood on a box during their scenes together. She just adored him."

Goulding took great care helping Alexis shape her character and to add the necessary shadings that make for a multidimensional interpretation. She remained forever grateful to him. "There are two or three directors I've learned from and been challenged by; Edmund Goulding was the first," Alexis said. Frank Capra and Martin Ritt were the others she acknowledged.

Goulding gave her several shining moments—in particular, a touching scene when she reveals Florence's vulnerability as she confesses to her father (Charles Coburn) that she fears she's lost her husband to Tessa. She also sparkles in the climactic showdown with Tessa.

The Constant Nymph was a Warners weepie par excellence, in which Goulding masterfully drained every possible tear from Kathryn Scola's sentimental script. Although Fontaine received the lion's share of hosannas from the critics—and a Best Actress Oscar nomination—Alexis also enjoyed some of the best notices of her career. "Alexis Smith, launched in her first role of full stature, comes through with an intelligent rendition of the ill-starred wife. Her dramatic scene with Tessa, in which she fights for Dodd, is especially ably done," raved Crowther.

The Constant Nymph was an artistic success if not a commercial one, but it proved dramatically that Alexis could pose a threat to Ann Sheridan, Jane Wyman and up-and-comer Eleanor Parker. The downside was that *The Constant Nymph* may have been the cornerstone for Alexis' eventual typecasting as an aloof society woman. Sadly, *The Constant Nymph* is now probably the least accessible of Alexis' films. Legal complications over the copyright to this film have since prevented it from being shown commercially.

In a 1943 *Life* interview Alexis stated, "I'm a disappointed ballerina." As such, she was thrilled when she got to dance in Warners' all-star extravaganza *Thank Your Lucky Stars*. Alexis sparkled as she displayed her Terpsichorean abilities while Dennis Morgan sang "Goodnight, Good Neighbor." To Alexis' frustration, it was the only time she would ever dance onscreen.

Thirty-five years later, when she was in *Platinum* on Broadway, Alexis was more effusive about the studio's reluctance to cast her in a musical. "I was always one of those people you saw sitting in the audience applauding someone else who was little and cute. I'd run around the studio begging them, 'Please, put me in a musical. I know how to sing and dance!' But no one paid any attention to me. Hollywood liked cuddly little girls in its musicals. The trouble was, I wasn't cute. At five feet nine inches, I was also too big. Unlike Betty Grable and June Haver and Vera-Ellen, I was the one they always referred to as 'cold and statuesque.' Well, it all worked out very nicely. I have no complaints."

So while her pal Ann Sheridan was selected to play entertainer Nora Bayes in *Shine on Harvest Moon*, Alexis was instead seen in *The Adventures of Mark Twain* (1944), director Irving Rapper's earnest attempt to dramatize the life of one of the geniuses of American literature. Though Fredric March was persuasive in the title role, Alexis, as his wife Olivia, was given little to do but fawn over *Huckleberry Finn* and be supportive during Twain's legal and financial woes.

By contrast, *The Doughgirls* (1944) was a raucous farce that afforded Alexis a rare chance to play broad comedy. Based on the Broadway hit by Joseph Fields, *The Doughgirls* concerned the complex marital mishaps of three former showgirls (Ann Sheridan, Jane Wyman and Alexis) who are reunited in wartime Washington, D.C. Much of the humor revolved around the circumstances that prevent Wyman and husband Jack Carson from consummating their marriage. Seen today, the film is badly dated, with jokes about the wartime housing shortage and "meatless Tuesday" that will zip right past the heads of modern audiences.

Whatever pleasure *The Doughgirls* still provides stems from the delightful performances of Wyman, Jack Carson and, best of all, Eve Arden as a visiting Russian who likes to shoot pigeons from the hotel room terrace. Alexis, too, gave a sharp performance, obviously relishing the chance to indulge in some amusing on-screen sparring with Stevens, and hoofing a few dance steps with Sheridan and Wyman.

Both *The Doughgirls* and *Hollywood Canteen*, in which Alexis had a cameo as herself, were released just before Alexis and Craig were married on June 18, 1944. The wedding was held at their new home and attended by family members and a select group of close friends, including Rosalind Russell, Errol Flynn and Frances Rafferty.

Shortly afterwards, a fan magazine ran a story on the happy bride, in which writer Michael Sheridan noted, "Alexis Smith believes in good luck. When she was a little girl, she decided just how she wanted her life to be — and it all came true ... being a motion picture star ... finding her Prince Charming, handsome Craig Stevens. Even her lovely wedding was exactly as she had dreamed it." Indeed, their forty-nine year marriage ranks as one of the great romances in Hollywood history, though neither Alexis nor Craig could agree on the secret of its success.

"He doesn't believe in arguing," Alexis said in 1971. "He thinks it's a waste of time, and he's right. I go on and on and in about twenty minutes I run out, and there's no retaliation, and pretty soon I start to think the whole thing is funny."

Craig, on the other hand, took a more romantic stance. "We were apart a lot. Either she was on location, or I was doing a play in New York. So we would go and see each other. We always got to know each other all over again. It was never a drudge," he said.

While Alexis enjoyed being Mrs. Craig Stevens, motherhood was a role that she didn't envision for herself. "When I was first pregnant with my son," said Rafferty. "she told me 'I don't think that it's time for me right now to have a child.' She was right in the middle of being a big star. It wasn't until she died when I learned she had done an interview in which she was asked about not having any children and she said, 'I would like to have had that experience.'"

Alexis soon entered her most prolific period during her Warners years, appearing in seven releases between 1945 and 1946. First up was *The Horn Blows at Midnight* (1945), a clever send-up of the *Here Comes Mr. Jordan* school of fantasies that were popular in the early '40s. Jack Benny played a trumpet player who falls asleep during a radio broadcast and imagines he's an angel sent to Earth to destroy it by blowing his horn at the stroke of midnight. Naturally, he botches the whole thing up, so his heavenly girlfriend Elizabeth (Alexis) has to help him straighten things out. The crazy climax involves Benny getting stuck in a huge coffee pot that's part of an electric sign.

Whether it was the film's surreal elements or the studio's lack of interest, *The Horn Blows at Midnight* hit a sour note at the box office and killed Benny's film career. Benny could never resist taking a potshot at the movie during his monologues or in interviews. His kidding seemed to pique the curiosity of his admirers, thus creating a cult following for the film. *The Horn Blows at Midnight* greatly benefits from breezy direction by Raoul Walsh and a brilliant performance by Benny. Alexis was basically a straight woman for Benny's antics, but she looked lovely and displayed great charm. She adored working with Benny and they became great friends.

Conflict (1945), her next assignment, was a minor but interesting mystery with Humphrey Bogart as an architect who murders his indifferent wife (Rose Hobart in the ice princess role usually reserved for Alexis) so he can take up with her pretty and sweet younger sister Evelyn (Alexis). Bogart's plan soon comes unraveled, thanks to the police and a suspicious family friend (Sydney Greenstreet). While *Conflict* deviated little from such similar offerings as *The Suspect* (1944), it had its share of suspenseful moments. Crowther was unmoved by Alexis, whom he called a "blonde and placid iceberg."

Unfortunately, a similar review could have been written of her work in *Rhapsody in Blue* (1945), a less-than-rhapsodic biography of composer George Gershwin. The plot seemed more concerned with the dull fictional triangle involving Gershwin (Robert Alda) and the two women in his life: sweet singer Julie Adams (Joan Leslie) and worldly Christine Gilbert (Alexis), a socialite who wants to serve as Gershwin's patroness. Sadly, little time is devoted to Gershwin's own inner demons or the drive to succeed that led to his untimely death.

Warners had hoped *Rhapsody in Blue* would be a stepping stone to stardom for Alda, but its poor box office returns made the studio lose interest in him and he was soon relegated to second leads. Alexis likewise seemed bored throughout her few scenes.

"The director would yell 'Action' and I'd raise my eyebrows and act — it was another of those superficial, so-called sophisticated parts that were fun to do at first, dressing up to kill, etc., but after a while, ugh!" Alexis told *Films in Review*.

Alexis was happier in *San Antonio* (1945), which reteamed her with Flynn and was her first western. "She did several westerns and she liked doing them," Craig said. "Many of them were on the light side and had humor to them, and that appealed to her."

She was back in evening gowns and sipping champagne for *One More Tomorrow* (1946), a tame remake of Phillip Barry's play *The Animal Kingdom*, previously filmed by RKO in 1932. Alexis was again a frosty member of the upper crust, this time stealing reformed playboy Dennis Morgan from idealistic photographer Ann Sheridan. Neither the stars nor reliable supporting players Jack Carson and Jane Wyman could enliven the material, limply directed by Peter Godfrey.

As if enough damage to the history of popular music hadn't already been committed with *Rhapsody in Blue*, Warner Bros., in late 1945, announced plans to film a musical biography of Cole Porter. Reportedly, the studio paid Porter $300,000 for the rights to his life story and gave the songsmith considerable creative control over the production. Porter's desire to suppress the seamier portions of his life was the reason that *Night and Day* (1946) emerged as little more than a colorful cornucopia of more than 30 Porter hits, with a fictionalized love story woven through it.

The film followed Porter (Cary Grant) from his days at Yale through his army career in World War I, his triumphs on Broadway, his rocky marriage and the horseback riding accident that paralyzed him. Missing from the film were any intimations of Porter's drug abuse or his homosexuality, both of which were taboo subjects for 1940s Hollywood. Likewise, the businesslike marriage between Cole and Linda Porter (Alexis) was also ignored.

Alexis was once again playing the millionaire's daughter, although this one had a heart as golden as the spoon she was born with. What pleasure Alexis got from making *Night and Day* came from working with Grant. Stevens recalled Grant's graciousness when Alexis introduced the two men. "I was in the army and visited the set on leave. Alexis took me to meet Cary Grant. He said to me, 'You've got a great girl. Stay married and don't split up.' I took his advice," he said.

Stevens added that during the making of the film Grant was known to be difficult at times, but never with Alexis. In fact, she admired Grant's professionalism over even the smallest detail, which often resulted in constant rewrites of scenes. It got to the point where the cast had to memorize different-colored versions of the script every day and finally shoot the one that worked best for Grant. Even with all those rewrites, *Night and Day* still seemed quite silly.

Originally the studio planned to spotlight

many top-flight performers, including Fred Astaire and Sophie Tucker, in the musical numbers. Realizing that hiring such talent would send the film's budget skyrocketing, Warners instead had most of the numbers performed by such unlikely contract players as Eve Arden and Jane Wyman, and band singer Ginny Simms. Mary Martin's zippy striptease to "My Heart Belongs to Daddy" was the standout among the numbers.

Reviewers dismissed the biographical aspects of the film for the pure fiction that they were, and were entertained by the rest of the proceedings. "A generally pleasant and musically exciting show," was how *The New York Times* described it, adding that, "Alexis Smith's role as Mrs. Porter is largely fictional, but the actress performs it with great charm." *Night and Day* played to packed houses and became the biggest moneymaker of Alexis' Warners films.

Looking back on those roles she was given by Warners, Alexis in 1971 remarked how she admired her Warners colleagues, such as Bette Davis and Olivia de Havilland, who often turned down inferior roles and resisted typecasting. "People frequently said it was a shame Warner Brothers typecast me, but I believe I typecast myself," she said. "I ended up being the wife of Cole Porter sitting in the audience applauding the composer."

Alexis' other 1946 film, released the same month as *Night and Day*, was the ill-fated remake of *Of Human Bondage*, with Eleanor Parker and Paul Henreid in the roles made famous by Bette Davis and Leslie Howard twelve years earlier. Alexis had a minor role as the refined Nora, whom doctor Phillip Carey (Henreid) rejects for the boorish Mildred Rogers (Parker). Although it was essentially a supporting role, Alexis welcomed the chance to once again be directed by Edmund Goulding. Unfortunately, the film was poorly received.

As a reflection of the poor quality of the vehicles Alexis had been thrown into, she was voted the Worst Actress of the Year by the Harvard Lampoon, a dubious achievement she shared with Joan Crawford and June Allyson.

Alexis was the first to admit that many of her Warners films and performances didn't hold up. "When my friends call and tell me one of my old movies is on TV, I don't look at it. Those films weren't very good at the time, and they haven't improved with age," she said in 1971.

On her screen persona, Alexis confessed, "I simply don't identify with the woman I see. I don't ever believe it's me. I'd much rather read a good book."

Alexis' first 1947 release, *Stallion Road*, is a case in point. She played the owner of a horse farm who becomes involved in a romantic triangle with a veterinarian (Ronald Reagan) and a playboy (Zachary Scott). *Stallion Road* was a no-show at the box office, due largely to the film's pedestrian script and leaden direction by James V. Kern.

Alexis fared better with her next film, the moody thriller *The Two Mrs. Carrolls* (1947), which reunited her with Bogart and director Peter Godfrey. Most of the action took place at the Scottish countryside home of mysterious Geoffrey Carroll (Bogart), an artist with shades of Bluebeard. His new bride (Barbara Stanwyck) suspects that he may have murdered his first wife to marry her. She now fears that he has similar plans for her, so that he can run off with a beautiful heiress (Alexis). Although the film borrows heavily from superior thrillers, such as *Suspicion* (1941) and *Gaslight* (1944), *The Two Mrs. Carrolls* has some goosebump-inducing moments, especially when the menacing Bogart (made up to look almost as horrific as he did in *The Return of Dr. X*) surprises Stanwyck from behind a curtain. If Bogart seemed ill at ease as a Bluebeard, his co-stars compensated. Stanwyck was, as usual, excellent as the second Mrs. Carroll, and Alexis once again played the ice princess with just the right degree of frostiness.

"She had this quality of being dignified, formal and aloof in the parts she played. That was not the Alexis I knew," said Rafferty. "She had a face for playing that role. She looked aristocratic and she was beautifully sculptured. She did those parts well and they were easy for her."

Alexis worked with Godfrey again on the moody Victorian thriller *The Woman in White* (1948), the best of their five collaborations together. Based on the seminal mystery novel by Wilkie Collins, the complex plot dealt with diabolical Count Fosco (Sydney Greenstreet) and his plans to kill heiress Laura Fairlie and her mysterious sister Anne (both played by Eleanor Parker), who's been hidden in a sanatorium for many years. With both women dead, Fosco hopes to claim their family fortune. The film's many subplots include the romance between Laura's art teacher (Gig Young) and her cousin Marian (Alexis), Fosco's attempt to trick Marian into becoming his mistress, and the Count's bizarre marriage to his fragile wife (Agnes Moorehead).

While the plot is at times confusing, there's much to admire in *The Woman in White*. The fog-laden atmosphere of Victorian England provides just the right chills, and Max Steiner's haunting score adds to the eeriness of the proceedings. Both Alexis and Parker gave competent performances but were overshadowed by the showy supporting cast, which included John Abbott as Parker's hypochondriac uncle, John Emery as her nefarious fiancée and Moorehead as the daft Countess Fosco. Without question, though, Greenstreet dominates every frame with his towering performance as the villainous Fosco, and he's great fun to watch.

"Alexis was mesmerized by Sydney Greenstreet," said Stevens. "He memorized the entire script. He knew everyone's role. She just thought he was fascinating to be around."

Unfortunately, *The Woman in White* was Alexis' last grade-A production at Warners. Like most of her recent films, it fared poorly at the box office. Alexis' contract still had two years to run, but the potential she displayed earlier in *The Constant Nymph* was now being wasted on inferior scripts like *Whiplash* (1948), *The Decision of Christopher Blake* (1948) and *One Last Fling* (1949). Only *South of St. Louis* (1949), a western with Joel McCrea in which Alexis had the uncharacteristic role of a saloon gal, generated any interest.

"We were contract players," explained Craig. "We had no selection of roles. You went to work or else you went on suspension."

Alexis had always been a team player. She was a favorite among the casts and crew at Warners, and never prone to temperamental outbursts on the set. Alexis was the first to admit that if she had fought harder, she might have gotten juicier parts. "I always got the roles I didn't want, the ones everyone else turned down," Alexis recalled in *Films in Review* in 1970. "They would start at the top of the list— first Davis, then Lupino, then Sheridan. If they didn't want it, I got it. I got the dreck."

Alexis did have her eye on playing Dominique, the heroine in *The Fountainhead* (1949),

the studio's highly anticipated film of the Ayn Rand bestseller. Instead, the role went to newcomer Patricia Neal, who, like Alexis, was poorly cast while at Warners. As it turned out, *The Fountainhead* proved unfilmable and was a critical and financial disappointment.

In 1949 Alexis was loaned out, for the first time, to the Tiffany of studios, MGM, for *Any Number Can Play* (1949), with Clark Gable. Like Alexis, Gable was at a difficult point in his career. Since returning to the screen in 1945 following his Army discharge, most of Gable's films had been box-office disappointments. Adding to his concerns was that *Any Number Can Play* was his first film at Metro under the regime of producer Dore Schary, who was interested in making message films, as opposed to Gable's brand of hairy-chested action yarns.

In *Any Number Can Play* Gable played the owner of a casino who's ready to cash in his chips because of failing health. Equally weak are the strained relationships with his wife (Alexis) and teenage son (Darryl Hickman). The stars worked well together and were ably supported by Barry Sullivan, Wendell Corey, Frank Morgan and Audrey Totter, but it was only a modest hit.

Still, Alexis considered it a pleasant experience. In contrast to the hurried atmosphere at Warners, she appreciated the more leisurely pace and painstaking efforts everyone at MGM took in making their films. "MGM treated her so beautifully, and she told me what a great studio it was to work at," said Totter. "She and Clark Gable got along as any actor and actress would. She loved working with him, but then who wouldn't love working with Clark Gable."

Back at Warners Alexis was thrown into *Montana* (1950), a routine western with Flynn. It was her last film for Warners, an inauspicious exit after a decade of hard work. "They didn't want to pay the gain in her contract," recalled Stevens. "And she had been offered several things which were different, like *Here Comes the Groom*, which she wanted to do. She didn't leave with any ill feelings." Still, she never signed exclusively with another studio again.

As a free agent, Alexis made three pictures at Universal, but *Wyoming Mail* (1950), *Undercover Girl* (1950) and *Cave of Outlaws* (1951) were no better than her final Warners films.

It was director Frank Capra who came to

her rescue. He thought Alexis would be perfect as Boston blueblood Winifred Stanley in *Here Comes the Groom* (1951), a breezy musical at Paramount starring Bing Crosby, Franchot Tone and Alexis' good friend Jane Wyman. The result was a dexterous performance in which Alexis relished the chance to shed her ladylike image and engage in some outrageous physical comedy, including a riotous catfight with the genteel Wyman.

The picture, which became one of Paramount's biggest hits that year, also got a boost from its hit song "In the Cool, Cool, Cool of the Evening," which won the Best Song Oscar. For Alexis it provided her with one of her favorite roles and her first box-office smash since *Night and Day*.

Alexis followed up that triumph with superb performances in a pair of meaty dramas: Paramount's hard-hitting newspaper tale *The Turning Point* (1952), with William Holden and Edmond O'Brien, and the taut *Split Second* (1953) for director Dick Powell at RKO.

Following *The Sleeping Tiger* (1954), a psychological drama made in England with Dirk Bogarde, and *The Eternal Sea* (1955), a naval drama with Sterling Hayden, Alexis went on tour with Craig in *Plain and Fancy*, a lively stage musical that was both a critical and personal success.

She then returned to the screen in three interesting roles—as Mrs. Jimmy Walker in *Beau James* (1957), with Bob Hope; as an actress vying with Debbie Reynolds for the affection of Curt Jurgens in the lighthearted *This Happy Feeling* (1958); and as the sexually frustrated wife of an older lawyer who falls for ambitious attorney Paul Newman in *The Young Philadelphians* (1959). The last marked Alexis' return to Warners, which proved to be an eerie experience. "Most of the people I had worked with years before were still there—all except the actors," she joked in 1970.

Still, she and director Vincent Sherman had great respect for one another. "She was grand to work with." said Sherman. "She was a much better actress than most people gave her credit for, because for a long time all she did was play the love interest in Errol Flynn's films, and they were dedicated to action rather than serious love stories. While it doesn't make for news, she was never involved in a scandal, always behaved in a dignified manner and was charming to be around."

The one jarring note for Alexis during the making of *The Young Philadelphians* was a frightening horseback riding sequence. When Sherman yelled "Action!" Alexis took off, but her horse bolted and threw her to the ground. She fractured several vertebrae and was out of commission for seven weeks. Although Sherman was able to shoot some scenes around her, production was delayed and the film ran over budget. Luckily, the film netted a handsome profit and fared well with the critics. Alexis considered it her best screen performance. "I was more mature then, both as a person and as an actress," she said.

Despite the success of her last film, Alexis no longer seemed interested in making movies, especially after Craig scored a hit with the detective series *Peter Gunn*. "I was doing *Gunn* and that was taking up all my time. If she was working, we would never get to see one another. So she ran the house and she was happy not working," Craig contended.

Minus the demands of a 6 a.m. makeup call at the studio, Alexis was free to do all of the seemingly mundane chores that she had previously missed out on—grocery shopping, taking care of her home and, most of all, cooking. "When we were first married, Alexis literally couldn't boil water," Craig joked. "I was never demanding about it. I knew that wasn't the way to handle her. If I had been demanding, she would have done just the opposite. As time went on she would fiddle around in the kitchen and experiment. She was also constantly working and didn't have a lot of time to cook, so we hired someone. Later on, when she did have time to learn, she became a gourmet cook. After she died I got rid of 680 cookbooks."

"She would go through recipes and then pick one. The more exotic, the better," remembers Rafferty. "She'd make it once, and then she'd move on to something new. She'd already done that bit. And, in a way, that was her nature. Once she mastered something, she either wanted to know something more about it or else move on to something new."

When *Peter Gunn* was canceled in 1961 Craig got an offer to appear in a musical in London. Since Alexis was still in the midst of a well-earned retirement, she accompanied him and remained during his two years with the show. While Craig spent his days at rehearsals, Alexis had a grand time touring the country.

She also found time to indulge in her favorite pastime — studying. Alexis took lessons in both Italian and French, and, as usual, mastered each subject with ease.

"Once I studied to get a realtor's license," Alexis said. "If things didn't go well, I thought, I could sell real estate."

In 1964 Alexis and Craig moved to New York where he starred in *Here's Love*, a musical by Meredith Willson. Alexis enjoyed being part of the theater crowd and was excited by the cultural climate of New York. When *Here's Love* closed, Alexis decided she was ready to return to work. She and Craig spent the next few years on tour co-starring in several shows, including *Mary, Mary* and *Cactus Flower*.

Alexis enjoyed the diversity of the roles she was given and felt energized by the new direction her career was now taking. Following the end of their run with *Cactus Flower*, the couple returned to California. Anxious to keep working onstage, and still dreaming of performing in a musical, Alexis began studying with vocal coach David Craig.

Alexis' diligence soon paid off. She received word from her agent that producer Harold Prince was preparing *Follies*, a new musical about three former showgirls who reunite twenty-five years later at the theater where they appeared. The theater, which is being torn down, also served as a symbol for the crumbling marriages and unfulfilled dreams of the three women. Veteran choreographer Michael Bennett had been assigned to stage the show's many dance numbers, and Stephen Sondheim was the composer. Everyone from Yvonne De Carlo to Roberta Peters had already auditioned for the role of Phyllis, one of the former showgirls who is now an unhappily married society matron. The role seemed tailor-made for Alexis, who expressed interest as soon as her agent informed her that Prince was holding tryouts. Alexis auditioned for Prince three times before she won the coveted role. Others in the cast included Dorothy Collins and De Carlo as the other two Follies girls, John McMartin as Alexis' husband, and Gene Nelson.

David Craig knew everyone connected with the show and was instrumental in helping Alexis prepare for *Follies*' demanding vocal routines. Work on *Follies* proceeded quickly. Alexis had auditioned in the fall of 1970 and was signed and in rehearsal by December. By February 1971 the show had its Boston tryout, where it opened to less than glowing reviews. The consensus was that *Follies* was fine musically, but talky and morose the rest of the time.

The book was revamped, and certain numbers were thrown out and replaced by new ones. Among the changes were the addition of the show's biggest song, "I'm Still Here," which was given to De Carlo. Alexis, though, was given two spotlight numbers, "Could I Leave You?" and "Lucy and Jessie," which she performed winningly.

When the retooled *Follies* opened on Broadway in April 1971, the reviews were fantastic Of the seasoned cast, Alexis was the unanimous favorite of critics. "Miss Smith is one of those creatures who, after a respectable, but less than world-shaking career in films, emerges on stage as not only more animated and charming than she'd ever seemed before, but also more beautiful," raved Walter Kerr of *The New York Times*. "She sings winningly, dances with a wink and takes charge of her dialogue scenes with a lacquered authority that has crisp intelligence inside it."

Like Angela Lansbury five years earlier in *Mame*, Alexis conquered Broadway in a way that eluded her in Hollywood. Alexis was showered with awards for her performance, including the Drama Desk Award and a Tony Award. No one was happier for Alexis than Craig Stevens. "It was a big thrill for her," he said. "She had never won anything before. Later I said to her, 'The luckiest thing they ever did was get you.'"

Although Alexis was not one to dwell on the past, in 1972 Ralph Edwards devoted an episode of *This Is Your Life* to her. On hand to salute her were her *Follies* co-stars, old friends Nanette Fabray and Lloyd Nolan, and Craig. The loveliest honor came from Helen Hayes, the First Lady of the American Theater, who offered a warm and sincere tribute.

Alexis returned to Broadway in 1973 in a revival of Clare Booth Luce's catfest *The Women*, which boasted a high-caliber cast that included Kim Hunter, Rhonda Fleming and Myrna Loy. Alexis was the waspish Sylvia, a role Rosalind Russell made famous in the 1939 film version. Critics complained that the play had lost its sting, and it closed after only a few months.

Following her touching performance as a spinster in William Inge's drama *Summer Brave* in 1975, Alexis made a welcome return to the screen. Unfortunately, the smarmy *Jacqueline Susann's Once Is Not Enough* (1975) was hardly a cause celebre. Trapped in the sordid tale of musical beds among Manhattan's elite were Kirk Douglas (as the husband who married Alexis for her money), George Hamilton, Deborah Raffin, David Janssen, Brenda Vaccaro and Melina Mercouri (as a thinly veiled version of Greta Garbo). Alexis had the unlikely role of a bisexual society matron who has an adulterous affair with Mercouri.

Like the film version of Susann's other novels, *Valley of the Dolls* and *The Love Machine*, *Once Is Not Enough* was annihilated by the critics. According to Craig, Alexis' sole inducement for taking part in this sleazefest was the opportunity to work with Mercouri.

She fared much better with her next two roles—a deliciously sinister performance in the eerie *The Little Girl Who Lives Down the Lane* (1977), and a touching portrayal in *Casey's Shadow* (1978), one of her personal favorites.

After completing *Casey's Shadow*, Alexis returned to New York for a rest. One day, while shopping at Bloomingdale's, she heard someone yelling her name. It turned out to be James Coco, who was anxious to speak with her about a new musical he was directing called *Sunset*. Coco wanted Alexis to play Lila Halliday, a fading film star who attempts to rejuvenate her singing career by crossing over to rock and disco. When Alexis learned that she'd be given a diversity of songs, ranging from Big Band ballads to contemporary tunes, she leapt at the opportunity.

By the time rehearsals began, Coco had to bow out because of a film commitment, and Tommy Tune took over. The change of directors was the first of many alterations *Sunset* was to undergo before reaching Broadway. The show had its first performance in September 1977 at the Studio Arena Theater in Buffalo. In the audience were Barry Diller and Michael Eisner, then chairman and president, respectively, of Paramount Pictures. Both agreed the show had potential but needed retooling. They agreed to invest $300,000 and help with costumes, scenery and staging.

While it's unclear how significantly Paramount was involved in the show's revisions, there's no question that from that point on it was heading in a different direction. While revisions were being made, Tune left the show to work on *The Best Little Whorehouse in Texas*. His departure left the company in limbo until a replacement could be found. The producers decided on veteran director/choreographer Joe Layton. By the time the rewrite was done, the original story was completely unrecognizable and the show had been retitled *Platinum*, in reference to the fact that when a record sells more than one million copies it goes platinum.

Despite all of the chaos surrounding *Platinum*, Alexis remained optimistic and still relished this opportunity to do everything she never had the chance to do in films. At the same time, she was realistic about the possibility that the show might flop. "Acting isn't the be-all and end-all of my life," she told an interviewer. "There are so many other things in the world. I get into studying things—languages, seminars. I'd love to go back to school. When I want to learn to do anything—like singing, for example—I go and take lessons. I could be a nuclear physicist, if I wanted to. Isn't that wonderful? I'd start by going to the library and looking under N."

After much retooling, *Platinum* opened on November 12, 1978, at the Mark Hellinger Theater to mostly negative reviews. Richard Eder of *The New York Times* felt that it "takes an idea that is limp to the point of formlessness, pours it into an ill-written book, decks it out with inferior rock music, stages it shoddily and performs it with a widespread lack of skill."

Despite critics' panning of the show, Alexis' star power shone through and she received some of the most impressive notices of her career. Eder said, "she brings a cheerful dignity to it," while Douglas Wolf of *The Daily News* raved, "Alexis Smith turns gold into *Platinum*."

But it was Joel Siegel of WABC-TV who offered the ultimate valentine to Alexis: "Her name is Alexis Smith and she is a star. And she does what only stars can do. She grabs an audience, holds an audience, astounds and astonishes an audience. She is platinum as in rare and precious."

Platinum closed after a mere thirty-three performances, but Alexis' brilliant performance stayed in the memory of the theatrical community, who nominated her for a Tony Award for Best Performance by an Actress in a Musical.

Despite the disappointment of *Platinum*,

Alexis was not one to mope. She appeared in a fashion layout for *Harper's Bazaar*, looking just as stunning as she did in *The Constant Nymph*. Unlike many of her contemporaries, Alexis had maintained a youthful appearance without benefit of cosmetic surgery. Her figure was still fitfully trim, and her fashion sense hadn't wavered an iota. Likewise, her outlook on her life and career matched her physical well-being.

"I enjoy my work so much more now than I did ten years ago because it's in the proper perspective," she told *Harpers*. "I'm not occupied with a burning desire for star billing, and now my energy is going in the right direction."

Her energy served her well as Miss Mona in a touring company of *The Best Little Whorehouse in Texas*. Alexis was on the road for fourteen months, and the show played to sellout crowds in every city.

At the completion of the tour Alexis headed home to California, although she and Craig did make a return trip to New York in 1982 to appear in the *Night of 1,000 Stars* spectacular. Alexis was fortunate at this point in her career to be able to pick and choose her roles, most of which were for television. In 1984 she began a recurring role as the scheming Lady Jessica Montford on *Dallas*, and also made an impression with her performances in the miniseries *Dress Gray* (1985) and *A Death in California* (1986). Also in 1986 she appeared opposite Burt Lancaster and Kirk Douglas in the delightful comedy *Tough Guys*. As a widow romanced by former train robber Lancaster, Alexis looked radiant and gave a charming performance.

Following a short-lived series, *Hothouses* (1988), Alexis made few appearances. One exceptional turn was in an episode of *Cheers* as Kirstie Alley's former professor who has a fling with Sam (Ted Danson). For her work, Alexis received a well-deserved Emmy nomination.

Alexis' final appearance was in Martin Scorsese's handsome production of *The Age of Innocence* (1993), filmed on location in New York. As a member of Manhattan society at the turn of the century, Alexis looked positively regal in her few scenes.

Several months after she completed her last film, Alexis was admitted to a hospital near her home in California for minor female-related surgery in what was meant to be just an overnight stay. The day after the operation her doctor inquired as to how she was feeling. When she complained of having double vision, she was asked to remain for tests. It was then that a brain tumor was discovered. Doctors were able to successfully remove the tumor.

"I went to see her after the first operation on her brain tumor. She just wanted me to look at all the cards she received," remembers Frances Rafferty.

Following the operation, doctors reported a healthy prognosis, and Alexis was soon released from the hospital. "She was doing great. She was eating and looked fine. We went for radiation and we thought we had it under control," Craig recalled. "Then on Sunday of Memorial Day weekend she fell apart. She couldn't handle herself and neither could I. I had a hard time getting the doctor. When I finally did, I explained the situation. I told him we had to get her to a hospital. We discovered then that the cancer had gone through her whole system. I was with her when the doctor told her and I was amazed at how well she took it. She lasted about another week. She was on oxygen. I was told she wouldn't suffer and she didn't. That was the one thing I was grateful for."

Alexis died on June 9, 1993, just one day after her seventy-second birthday. By her side at the time were Craig, Rafferty and Rafferty's daughter.

In the end, Alexis can be remembered as a dedicated professional who never took herself too seriously. Unlike Bette Davis, Alexis' career wasn't the epicenter of her life. If Alexis never reached the apex of stardom that Davis fought so hard to achieve, Alexis instead found an inner happiness and a loving, stable relationship that Davis ultimately sacrificed for her art.

Alexis approached her career in much the same way that she lived her life: "As for my own work, whether it's films or theater, I want everything I do to be really good or else, well, it's over and out and on to something else."

FILMOGRAPHY

(Alexis appeared unbilled in the first 7 films listed below)

The Lady with Red Hair (Warner Bros., 1940) Directed by Kurt Bernhardt. Cast: Miriam Hopkins, Claude Rains, Laura Hope Crews, Richard Ainley, John Litel, Victor Jory.

She Couldn't Say No (Warner Bros., 1941) Directed by William Clements. Cast: Eve Arden, Roger Pryor, Cliff Edwards, Clem Bevans, Vera Lewis, Irving Bacon.

Flight from Destiny (Warner Bros., 1941) Directed by Vincent Sherman. Cast: Thomas Mitchell, Geraldine Fitzgerald, Jeffrey Lynn, James Stephenson, Mona Maris, Jonathan Hale.

Passage from Hong Kong (Warner Bros., 1941) Directed by D. Ross Lederman. Cast: Lucille Fairbanks, Keith Douglas, Paul Cavanaugh, Gloria Holden, Richard Ainley, Marjorie Gateson.

Three Sons o' Guns (Warner Bros., 1941) Directed by Ben Stoloff. Cast: Wayne Morris, Marjorie Rambeau, Irene Rich, Susan Peters, Tom Brown, William T. Orr, Moroni Olsen.

Singapore Woman (Warner Bros., 1941) Directed by Jean Negulesco. Cast: Brenda Marshall, David Bruce, Virginia Field, Jerome Cowan, Rose Hobart, Heather Angel, Richard Ainley.

Affectionately Yours (Warner Bros., 1941) Directed by Lloyd Bacon. Cast: Merle Oberon, Dennis Morgan, Rita Hayworth, Ralph Bellamy, George Tobias, James Gleason, Jerome Cowan.

Dive Bomber (Warner Bros., 1941) Directed by Michael Curtiz. Cast: Errol Flynn, Fred MacMurray, Ralph Bellamy, Alexis Smith, Robert Armstrong, Regis Toomey, Allen Jenkins.

The Smiling Ghost (Warner Bros., 1941) Directed by Lewis Seiler. Cast: Wayne Morris, Brenda Marshall, Alexis Smith, Alan Hale, Lee Patrick, David Bruce, Helen Westley.

Steel Against the Sky (Warner Bros., 1941) Directed by A. Edward Sutherland. Cast: Alexis Smith, Lloyd Nolan, Craig Stevens, Gene Lockhart, Edward Ellis, Walter Catlett, Julie Bishop.

Gentleman Jim (Warner Bros., 1942) Directed by Raoul Walsh. Cast: Errol Flynn, Alexis Smith, Jack Carson, Alan Hale, John Loder, William Frawley, Dorothy Vaughan, Ward Bond.

The Constant Nymph (Warner Bros., 1943) Directed by Edmund Goulding. Cast: Joan Fontaine, Charles Boyer, Alexis Smith, Charles Coburn, Dame May Whitty, Peter Lorre.

Thank Your Lucky Stars (Warner Bros., 1943) Directed by David Butler. Cast: Dennis Morgan, Joan Leslie, Edward Everett Horton, S.Z. Sakall. Guest Stars: Humphrey Bogart, Eddie Cantor, Jack Carson, Bette Davis, Olivia de Havilland, Errol Flynn, John Garfield, Alan Hale, Spike Jones and his orchestra, Ida Lupino, Hattie McDaniel, Ann Sheridan, Alexis Smith.

The Adventures of Mark Twain (Warner Bros., 1944) Directed by Irving Rapper. Cast: Fredric March, Alexis Smith, Donald Crisp, Alan Hale, C. Aubrey Smith, John Carradine.

The Doughgirls (Warner Bros., 1944) Directed by James V. Kern. Cast: Ann Sheridan, Alexis Smith, Jane Wyman, Irene Manning, Jack Carson, Eve Arden, Charles Ruggles, Barbara Brown.

Hollywood Canteen (Warner Bros., 1944) Directed by Delmer Daves. Cast: Joan Leslie, Robert Hutton, Janis Paige, Dane Clark, Richard Erdman. Guest Stars: The Andrews Sisters, Jack Benny, Joe E. Brown, Eddie Cantor, Kitty Carlisle, Jack Carson, Joan Crawford, Helmut Dantine, Bette Davis, Faye Emerson, John Garfield, Sydney Greenstreet, Alan Hale, Paul Henreid, Andrea King, Peter Lorre, Ida Lupino, Irene Manning, Joan McCracken, Dolores Moran, Dennis Morgan, Eleanor Parker, William Prince, Joyce Reynolds, Roy Rogers, Zachary Scott, Alexis Smith, Barbara Stanwyck, Craig Stevens, Jane Wyman.

The Horn Blows at Midnight (Warner Bros., 1945) Directed by Raoul Walsh. Cast: Jack Benny, Alexis Smith, Allyn Joslyn, Reginald Gardiner, Guy Kibbee, Dolores Moran.

Conflict (Warner Bros., 1945) Directed by Curtis Bernhardt. Cast: Humphrey Bogart, Alexis Smith, Sydney Greenstreet, Rose Hobart, Charles Drake, Grant Mitchell, Pat O'Moore.

Rhapsody in Blue (Warner Bros., 1945) Directed by Irving Rapper. Cast: Robert Alda, Alexis Smith, Joan Leslie, Charles Coburn, Oscar Levant, Julie Bishop, Herbert Rudley; with appearances by Al Jolson, Hazel Scott, Anne Brown, George White, and Paul Whiteman and his orchestra.

San Antonio (Warner Bros., 1945) Directed by David Butler. Cast: Errol Flynn, Alexis Smith, S.Z. Sakall, Victor Francen, Paul Kelly, Florence Bates, John Litel, Robert Shayne, Monte Blue.

One More Tomorrow (Warner Bros., 1946) Directed by Peter Godfrey. Cast: Ann Sheridan, Dennis Morgan, Alexis Smith, Jack Carson, Jane Wyman, Reginald Gardiner, John Loder.

Of Human Bondage (Warner Bros., 1946) Directed by Edmund Goulding. *Cast:* Paul Henreid, Eleanor Parker, Alexis Smith, Janis Paige, Edmund Gwenn, Patric Knowles, Henry Stephenson.

Night and Day (Warner Bros., 1946) Directed by Michael Curtiz. *Cast:* Cary Grant, Alexis Smith, Monty Woolley, Mary Martin, Ginny Simms, Jane Wyman, Eve Arden, Victor Francen.

Stallion Road (Warner Bros., 1947) Directed by James V. Kern. *Cast:* Ronald Reagan, Alexis Smith, Zachary Scott, Peggy Knudsen, Ralph Byrd, Angela Greene, Monte Blue.

The Two Mrs. Carrolls (Warner Bros., 1947) Directed by Peter Godfrey. *Cast:* Humphrey Bogart, Barbara Stanwyck, Alexis Smith, Nigel Bruce, Isobel Elsom, Ann Carter, Pat O'Moore.

Always Together (Warner Bros., 1947) Directed by Frederick De Cordova. *Cast:* Robert Hutton, Joyce Reynolds, Cecil Kellaway; with cameos by Humphrey Bogart, Jack Carson, Dennis Morgan, Janis Paige, Alexis Smith.

The Woman in White (Warner Bros., 1948) Directed by Peter Godfrey. *Cast:* Alexis Smith, Eleanor Parker, Sydney Greenstreet, Gig Young, Agnes Moorehead, John Emery, John Abbott.

The Decision of Christopher Blake (Warner Bros., 1948) Directed by Peter Godfrey. *Cast:* Alexis Smith, Robert Douglas, Cecil Kellaway, Ted Donaldson, John Hoyt, Harry Davenport.

Whiplash (Warner Bros., 1948) Directed by Lewis Seiler. *Cast:* Dane Clark, Alexis Smith, Zachary Scott, Eve Arden, Jeffrey Lynn, S.Z. Sakall, Alan Hale, Douglas Kennedy.

South of St. Louis (Warner Bros., 1949) Directed by Ray Enright. *Cast:* Joel McCrea, Alexis Smith, Zachary Scott, Dorothy Malone, Alan Hale, Victor Jory, Douglas Kennedy, Bob Steele.

One Last Fling (Warner Bros., 1949) Directed by Peter Godfrey. *Cast:* Alexis Smith, Zachary Scott, Helen Westcott, Jim Backus, Douglas Kennedy, Barbara Bates, Veda Ann Borg.

Any Number Can Play (MGM, 1949) Directed by Mervyn LeRoy. *Cast:* Clark Gable, Alexis Smith, Wendell Corey, Audrey Totter, Barry Sullivan, Mary Astor, Frank Morgan, Lewis Stone.

Montana (Warner Bros., 1950) Directed by Ray Enright. *Cast:* Errol Flynn, Alexis Smith, S.Z. Sakall, James Brown, Douglas Kennedy, Ian McDonald, Tudor Owen, Charles Irwin.

Wyoming Mail (Universal-International, 1950) Directed by Reginald Le Borg. *Cast:* Stephen McNally, Alexis Smith, Howard da Silva, Ed Begley, Dan Riss, Whit Bissell, Roy Roberts.

Undercover Girl (Universal-International, 1950) Directed by Joseph Pevney. *Cast:* Alexis Smith, Scott Brady, Richard Egan, Gladys George, Edmond Ryan, Gerlad Mohr, Royal Dano.

Here Comes the Groom (Paramount, 1951) Directed by Frank Capra. *Cast:* Bing Crosby, Jane Wyman, Franchot Tone, Alexis Smith, James Barton, Connie Gilchrist, Anna Maria Alberghetti.

Cave of Outlaws (Universal-International, 1951) Directed by William Castle. *Cast:* MacDonald Carey, Alexis Smith, Edgar Buchanan, Victor Jory, Hugh O'Brian, Houseley Stevenson.

The Turning Point (Paramount, 1952) Directed by William Dieterle. *Cast:* William Holden, Alexis Smith, Edmond O'Brien, Tom Tully, Ed Begley, Neville Brand, Dan Dayton, Ray Teal.

Split Second (RKO Radio, 1953) Directed by Dick Powell. *Cast:* Alexis Smith, Stephen McNally, Jan Sterling, Keith Andes, Paul Kelly, Arthur Hunnicutt, Richard Egan, Robert Paige.

The Sleeping Tiger (Anglo-Amalgamated/Insignia, 1954) Directed by Victor Hanbury. *Cast:* Dirk Bogarde, Alexis Smith, Alexander Knox, Hugh Griffith, Maxine Audley, Billie Whitelaw.

The Eternal Sea (Republic, 1955) Directed by John H. Auer. *Cast:* Sterling Hayden, Alexis Smith, Dean Jagger, Ben Cooper, Virginia Grey, Hayden Rorke, Douglas Kennedy.

Beau James (Paramount, 1957) Directed by Melville Shavelson. *Cast:* Bob Hope, Vera Miles, Alexis Smith, Paul Douglas, Darren McGavin, Joe Mantell, Walter Catlett.

This Happy Feeling (Universal-International, 1958) Directed by Blake Edwards. *Cast:* Debbie Reynolds, Curt Jurgens, Alexis Smith, John Saxon, Mary Astor, Estelle Winwood, Hayden Rorke.

The Young Philadelphians (Warner Bros., 1959) Directed by Vincent Sherman. *Cast:* Paul Newman, Barbara Rush, Alexis Smith, Brian Keith, Diane Brewster, Robert Vaughn.

Jacqueline Susann's Once Is Not Enough (Paramount, 1975) Directed by Guy Green. *Cast:* Kirk Douglas, Deborah Raffin, David Janssen, Alexis Smith, George Hamilton, Melina Mercouri.

The Little Girl Who Lives Down the Lane (ICL/Filmedis-Filmel, 1977) Directed by Nicolas Gessner. *Cast:* Jodie Foster, Alexis Smith, Martin Sheen, Scott Jacoby, Mort Shuman.

Casey's Shadow (Columbia, 1978) Directed by Martin Ritt. *Cast:* Walter Matthau, Alexis Smith, Robert Webber, Murray Hamilton, Andrew A. Rubin, Stephan Burns, Michael Hershewe.

The Trout (La Truite) (Gaumont/SFPC/TF1, 1982) Directed by Joseph Losey. *Cast:* Isabelle Huppert, Jeanne Moreau, Jean-Pierre Cassel, Daniel Olbrychski, Alexis Smith, Craig Stevens.

Tough Guys (Touchstone, 1986) Directed by Jeff Kanew. *Cast:* Burt Lancaster, Kirk Douglas,

Charles Durning, Alexis Smith, Eli Wallach, Dana Carvey, Darlanne Fluegel, Billy Barty.

The Age of Innocence (Columbia, 1993) Directed by Martin Scosese. *Cast:* Daniel Day-Lewis, Michelle Pfeiffer, Winona Ryder, Richard E. Grant, Alec McGowen, Geraldine Chaplin, Mary Beth Hurt, Stuart Wilson, Miriam Margolyes, Sian Phillips, Michael Gough, Alexis Smith.

TELEVISION FILM CREDITS

A Death in California (1985) *Cast:* Sam Elliott, Cheryl Ladd, Alexis Smith, Fritz Weaver.

Dress Gray (1986) *Cast:* Alec Baldwin, Patrick Cassidy, Eddie Albert, Alexis Smith.

Marcus Welby, M.D.: A Holiday Affair (1988) *Cast:* Robert Young, Alexis Smith.

Jane Wyman: "The Late Bloomer"

No one can accuse Jane Wyman of being an overnight success. She was in films for more than thirteen years before her breakthrough in *The Lost Weekend* (1945). Prior to that, Jane had made a steady progression up the Hollywood ladder, starting as a chorus girl, bit player and supporting player in the Glenda Farrell vein before proving herself as a capable dramatic actress.

Jane's lack of self-confidence and shy nature were part of the reason stardom eluded her for so long. Eventually she developed more of an assurance about her abilities, as evidenced in *The Lost Weekend* at Paramount and MGM's *The Yearling* (1946). Those loanouts convinced Warner Bros. that she was ready to tackle the demanding role of a deaf mute in *Johnny Belinda* (1948). Jane won an Academy Award, and Warners realized what a prize it had.

Since then, Jane has rarely been out of the public eye, whether it's been for her success on television, her charity work with the Arthritis Foundation, or to conjecture about what kind of First Lady she might have made had she remained married to former President Ronald Reagan.

Speculation also exists regarding Jane's birth. Recent accounts have suggested that Jane was an adopted child, a fact that she has neither confirmed nor denied. Jane maintains that her given name was Sarah Jane Fulks and that she was born in St. Joseph, Missouri, on January 5, 1917, not 1914 as most sources claim. Richard Fulks, Jane's father, at one time or another held several offices, including county collector and chief of detectives of St. Joseph. Although some sources have also claimed that he was mayor of St. Joseph, Jane said that was not the case.

Jane's mother, Emme Riese, was born in Germany and came to the United States as a girl. Both parents were already middle-aged when Jane was born, and were firm believers in Old World discipline when it came to raising Jane and her two siblings, a brother and sister who were already teenagers when Jane arrived. For Jane, her parents' strict rules meant not being able to attend school football games, being home at a certain time each day — with no excuses for tardiness — and no dating. The rigid atmosphere contributed to Jane's shyness and insecurity for much of her youth.

The one privilege Jane did enjoy was accompanying her mother regularly to downtown St. Joseph to see the local theater company. Jane also found refuge in the world of dance, which became one of the great joys of her life. As a child, Jane attended a dance school run by "Dad" Prinz, as she called him. Jane claimed that she "took to the swing and sway from the beginning," but her innate shyness made it hard for her to perform before an audience.

"I haunted the corners of the room, hoping the dancing master would not see me," Jane wrote in *Guideposts*. "The very thought of performing in front of someone made me wilt with fear, quite literally. The saddest part of it was that I idolized Dad Prinz, the dancing master. He was the most understanding man I had ever met and I longed to tell him so. I never did."

In spite of her problem, Jane demonstrated an amazing aptitude for dancing, which did not go unnoticed by her mother. In 1922, on the pretext of visiting relatives, Emme whisked eight-year-old Jane off to Los Angeles to make the rounds of the studios. Emme was told that Jane showed promise but needed more training. Discouraged, mother and daughter returned home.

Life for Jane in St. Joseph went on as usual until 1929 when her father died. With Jane's brother now practicing medicine in Los Angeles, and with her sister settled there as well, Jane and her mother took what little money they had and moved out west.

In Los Angeles Jane and her mother managed their household on their meager savings and the insurance money they received. Jane was overwhelmed by the busy streets of Los Angeles, which was a sharp contrast to rural St. Joseph. The adjustment to being the new girl at Los Angeles High School was also difficult, especially as far as dealing with the opposite sex was concerned. "It seemed to me that on some prearranged signal, every boy and girl in school paired off," Jane wrote in *Guideposts*. "Every girl, that is, except me. I don't know whether I could have had dates or not; it simply never occurred to me to try. Hadn't I been told many times that I was not pretty? I lugged home piles of books every night and disappeared into them."

Some sources have noted that upon graduation from high school Jane attended the University of Missouri, but such claims are false. There have also been reports that Jane was married briefly at age sixteen to Ernest Wyman, but Jane has never spoken of such a marriage.

Jane stated that the dwindling family finances made it imperative for her to find a job quickly, which she did at a local coffee shop. Jane reported for work at five in the morning for the daily grind of cutting pies and serving coffee. "Well, it didn't last long. I wasted more pie than I sold. So I was fired," Jane said in a 1982 *McCall's* interview.

Jane then took stock of her abilities and discovered the only thing she really knew how to do well — and also enjoyed — was dancing.

Jane Wyman languished in B films for more than 10 years before finally getting a star-making role.

Several accounts of Jane's life have intimated that her mother pushed her into show business, but Jane has been quick to deny that. "The Depression had started and my family was flat broke. I mean, we lost everything except the little roof over our heads. My mother wanted me to continue my education, but I didn't have the grades to get into college because I had goofed off in high school. Besides, we needed the money," she said.

Jane turned to LeRoy Prinz, the son of her old dance teacher, for help. The younger Prinz, now a successful Hollywood dance coach, gave Jane a tryout and was pleased to find that she had a sense of rhythm. "Dad had written me several times, describing her progress as a dancer, but even so, I was unprepared for the strong initial impression she made on me," Prinz recalled in 1953. " She wasn't beautiful, but very attractive and pretty in a pert way. She struck me then as a pixie."

Under Prinz' tutelage Jane landed a role in the chorus of *The Kid from Spain* (1932), a lavish musical produced by Samuel Goldwyn. It starred Eddie Cantor and featured elephantine production numbers staged by Busby Berkeley. One would be hard pressed to find Jane in the film, although Goldwyn Girls Betty Grable and Paulette Goddard are noticeable.

"It was work when the family badly needed the money, but for a girl who had grown up in terror of being looked at, it was also agony," Jane recounted in *Guideposts*.

As a mask to cover up her shyness, Jane became the cockiest chorus girl on the set. She talked the loudest and laughed the longest, and also sportest the longest and curliest pair of false eyelashes she could find. Jane kept wearing the ridiculous looking lashes until one day when a fellow chorus girl advised her: "Jane, you'd improve your looks about a thousand percent if you'd peel off those trimmings and wash your face." A crushed Jane wept uncontrollably afterwards.

The next day, though, Jane showed up sans eyelashes, yet feeling more insecure than ever. Within half an hour of arriving at rehearsal, a relative stranger saw her and remarked, "Gee Jane, you look great." For the first time she came to believe that maybe she was attractive after all.

As a chorus girl, Jane had bit parts in several films, including *Elmer the Great* (1933), with Joe E. Brown, *All the King's Horses* (1934), and *King of Burlesque* (1936), with Alice Faye. She might have gone on hoofing if William Demarest, then an agent, hadn't spotted her at Sardi's one day. "As I watched her," Demarest recalled, "I thought, 'This girl has everything that God could have given her for success on the screen.' I didn't even know then that she had any training or experience. I just knew there was something about her that I hadn't noticed in other girls."

Jane was content working as a dancer, but Demarest convinced her to consider acting. "I thought he was crazy!" Jane told *New Liberty* magazine in 1953. "Besides, my time step was getting better every day. I said 'Bill, I don't know how to act.' He answered, 'So you'll learn.'"

Demarest first took Jane to Paramount, where executives called her a capable singer and dancer, but saw no great star potential. She next tested at Universal and was put in *My Man Godfrey* (1936), but most of her scene ended up on the cutting room floor. "I'm still in the picture next to the monkey and the organ grinder, but you have to look fast to see me. And that monkey bit me, too," Jane said.

On May 6, 1936, Demarest took Jane to Warner Bros., which signed her to a standard contract with six-month options. Jane's Warners career began in *Stage Struck* (1936), in which she had one line, but it was a pip: "My name is Bessie Fumfnick. I can swim, ride, dive, imitate wild birds and play the trombone." Jane wrang the line for its full comic effect, which caused the film's star, Dick Powell, to break up so much that the scene resulted in $2,000 worth of retakes.

Soon after, Jane had a featured role (seventh-billed) in *Smart Blonde* (1936), the first of the Torchy Blane mysteries starring Glenda Farrell as the fast-talking reporter. The one interesting aspect of the film is that Jane would take on the role of Torchy three years later.

Jane's roles in *Gold Diggers of 1937* (1936), *The King and the Chorus Girl* (1937), *Ready, Willing and Able* (1937) and *The Singing Marine* (1937) consisted of only one or two scenes, though she did get a fair amount of screen time in *Slim* (1937) as Stuart Erwin's girl.

Jane finally got her first female lead in *Mr. Dodds Takes the Air* (1937), a remake of *The Crooner* (1932), with Kenny Baker as a small-town electrician who lands a radio spot in New York. His career is in danger of ending quickly when he develops bronchitis, which changes his voice from that of a tenor to a baritone. Jane played it straight as Baker's girlfriend.

Warners next assigned Jane another lead, in the B comedy *Public Wedding* (1937), an incredible tale about a group of itinerant show folk who stage a fake public wedding inside the mouth of a whale to drum up interest in their sideshow. Jane and William Hopper played the dismayed bride and groom who later discover that the marriage was actually legitimate. Hardly a whale of a film, *Public Wedding* did allow Jane to show the first glimmer of her flair for comedy.

In early 1937 Jane married Myron Futterman, a dress manufacturer from New Orleans who was married once before and had a teenage daughter. Jane's friends couldn't imagine what the twenty-three-year-old starlet and the middle-aged Futterman could have in common, and were hardly surprised when the couple separated after only a few months. "I thought I was doing the right thing at the time," Jane told *McCall's* in 1982. "Myron was a lovely, charming man, but it just didn't work out. I guess I married too young." Within two years of their wedding date they were divorced.

Jane's career became her chief concern, although *Spy Ring* (1938) at Universal, *Wide-Open Faces* (1938) at Columbia, and *Fools for Scandal* (1938) and *He Couldn't Say No* (1938) at Warners attracted little attention. A solid supporting role in *The Crowd Roars* (1938), an above-average boxing yarn at MGM, however, piqued some interest. Jane, who had dyed her hair from brown to blonde, gave a peppy performance as the dizzy girlfriend of punch-drunk boxer Robert Taylor who gets thrown over for Maureen O'Sullivan.

When Jane wasn't filming, she was often with fellow Warners newcomers, such as Priscilla Lane and Eddie Albert, on a tennis court or by a swimming pool posing for publicity shots. It was during one of those photo sessions that Jane met a handsome newcomer named Ronald Reagan.

"I didn't really get to know him until we did *Brother Rat* (1938). That's when we started dating. It wasn't love at first sight. It was a gradual friendship that grew," Jane told *McCall's*.

Brother Rat was a pivotal film for Jane. Not only did it spark romance with Reagan, but it also was a polished comedy that provided Jane with her first good role at Warners. The academic and romantic misadventures of three cadets had been a huge hit on Broadway. Jerry Wald and Richard Macaulay adapted the John Monks, Jr.-Fred Finkelhoffe play for the screen, and the result was a merry affair. Eddie Albert, from the original Broadway company, made a sensational debut as Bing, a hapless cadet trying to hide the fact that he's married and that his wife (Jane Bryan) is pregnant. Wayne Morris played a fast-talker whose schemes always get him and his roommates (Albert and Reagan) into trouble. Jane played the general's bookworm daughter who catches the eye of cadet Reagan once she removes her horn-rimmed glasses.

Director William Keighley succeeded in capturing the flavor of VMI. Background footage was photographed on the VMI campus, and the school requested — and was granted — final approval of the script. Keighley's brisk direction and the enthusiastic performances of the young cast made *Brother Rat* a profitable entry for Warners.

At 20th Century–Fox Jane made *Tail Spin* (1939), a romantic triangle pitting air pilots Constance Bennett and Alice Faye against each other for the affections of their captain (Kane Richmond). As Alabama, another flier, Jane spent most of her screen time exchanging wisecracks with Joan Davis. Back at Warners, Jane had the title role of *Private Detective* (1939), a mediocre B in the *Torchy Blane* mold, and *The Kid from Kokomo* (1939), an inane boxing comedy with Wayne Morris.

With both Joan Blondell and Glenda Farrell leaving Warners in 1939, pretty and pert Jane seemed the logical successor to fill their shoes in the snappy blonde reporter/detective/gold digger department. As such, Jane replaced Farrell as sleuthing reporter Torchy Blane in *Torchy Plays with Dynamite* (1939), which had the brassy blonde deliberately going to prison to get the goods on an escaped bandit. Perhaps because audiences had so identified Farrell with the role, *Torchy Plays with Dynamite* was the last entry in the popular series.

Jane finished out the year with yet another boxing farce, the amusing *Kid Nightingale* (1939), featuring John Payne as a singing waiter who takes to the ring after he loses his job. The gimmick: After he knocks out his opponent, he sings. Better than it sounds, the comedy was good fun, with Jane looking lovely as a music teacher who falls for the singing boxer. Walter Catlett, however, stole the film from both stars with his funny performance as Payne's manager.

At the end of 1939 Jane and Reagan appeared in a vaudeville show hosted by gossip queen Louella Parsons, a friend of both. The twelve-city tour played to packed houses, bolstered by interest in the Wyman-Reagan romance. By the end of the tour the couple were engaged.

Jane became Mrs. Ronald Reagan on January 26, 1940, in a ceremony at Wee Kirk o' the Heather in Forest Lawn Memorial Park in Glendale, California. The newlyweds then settled into their West Hollywood home, in a neighborhood Jane referred to as "*almost* Beverly Hills."

Publicity-savvy Warners teamed the newlyweds in *Brother Rat and a Baby* (1940) and *An Angel from Texas* (1940), which were released shortly after their marriage. Jane then went solo in *Flight Angels* (1940), a maudlin film that dwelt on the problems of stewardesses in the air and in love. The only time the movie soared was during a humorous hair-tugging fight between Jane and Margot Stevenson. More enjoyable was *My Love Came Back* (1940), an entertaining romance with Jane in fine form as the best friend of female violinist Olivia de Havilland.

Jane then hit the water for her next pair of films. She and Reagan played young lovers in *Tugboat Annie Sails Again* (1940), a soggy follow-up to *Tugboat Annie* (1933), with Marjorie Rambeau and Alan Hale receating the characters played by Marie Dressler and Wallace Beery. Much better was *Gambling on the High Seas* (1940), a fast-moving actioner about a reporter (Wayne Morris) who is anxious to nail a gambling czar (Gilbert Roland) for his crooked dealings and a murder. Morris makes a play for Roland's secretary (Jane) and corrals her into his plan.

Soon after completing *Gambling on the High Seas* in the spring of 1940, Jane learned she was pregnant. Jane was overjoyed after giving birth to her daughter, Maureen Elizabeth, on January 4, 1941. The happy Reagans had a new, larger home built in Beverly Hills.

Jane recalled in *McCall's* that it was an extremely happy period in her life: "I had such a lovely pregnancy with Maureen. There were no problems. In fact, I did two or three pictures while I was pregnant." *Honeymoon for Three* (1941), a fair comedy about an author and the women in his life, with Ann Sheridan and George Brent, and *Bad Men of Missouri* (1941), director Ray Enright's whitewashed account of the Younger brothers, were the films.

When Jane returned to work after Maureen was born, she appeared in two comedies of varying degrees. Following on the heels of Universal's smash *Buck Privates* (1941), which propelled Bud Abbott and Lou Costello to stardom, Warners released *You're in the Army Now* (1941), a service comedy that seemed funnier than it was, thanks to the wacky performances of its two stars, Jimmy Durante and Phil Silvers, as bumbling vacuum cleaner salesmen who accidentally enlist in the army, where they wreak nothing but havoc. Jane played it straight as an officer's daughter, but she was given two musical numbers and a lengthy screen kiss with Regis Toomey.

Her other comedy was *The Body Disappears* (1941), a surprisingly spirited invisible man tale with Jeffrey Lynn and Edward Everett Horton.

Larceny Inc. (1942) was an enjoyable bit of flim-flam that starred Edward G. Robinson as an ex-con who just can't go straight. He and his dim-witted cohorts (Edward Brophy and Broderick Crawford) buy a luggage shop so that they can drill a hole in the wall and rob the bank next door. But thanks to some meddling by Robinson's daughter (Jane), the cons are pushed into becoming legitimate businessmen and are dismayed to learn that they can earn more money legally than they ever did as crooks.

Everett Freeman and Edwin Gilbert based their slight script on Laura and S.J. Perelman's 1941 farce *The Night Before Christmas*. What the story lacked in originality was compensated for by Lloyd Bacon's smart direction and the ingratiating performance of Robinson and a stellar supporting cast, including Jackie Gleason in a bit as a soda jerk. For Jane, *Larceny Inc.* marked the first of many pairings with Jack Carson, who played her boyfriend. Though one doesn't think of them as a classic screen team, Carson's animal charm and Jane's brashness were a potent blend.

The good impression Jane made in *Larceny Inc.* was somewhat offset by a loanout to RKO for *My Favorite Spy* (1942), with Kay Kyser. While *My Favorite Spy* was wrapping up, Darryl F. Zanuck began shaping Betty Grable's latest Fox musical, the Broadway-themed *Footlight Serenade* (1942). The star suggested her pal Lucille Ball to play Grable's best friend Flo La Verne. Surprised when Ball turned down the role, Grable then suggested Jane, who jumped at the chance. As with nearly all Grable films of this period, *Footlight Serenade* made a bundle, and Jane's performance was well-received.

Jane was even better in Warners' charming *Princess O'Rourke* (1943), a royal romance that starred Olivia de Havilland as a princess traveling incognito in the United States who falls for a pilot (Robert Cummings). Jane and Jack Carson played Cummings' best friends, a married couple who occasionally bicker but are obviously still devoted to one another.

Princess O'Rourke, in effect, marked the beginning of a new Jane Wyman on the screen. For one thing, she changed her hair color back to her natural brunette. The brassy blonde was history and a softer, less caustic Jane emerged. As such, Jane's character in the film seemed less abrasive than the Torchy Blane clones she had been portraying, as exemplified by the moving scene wherein she learns Carson has been drafted. *The New York Times* observed that, "Jane Wyman and Jack Carson draw rich humor and honest sentiment from the roles of two friends."

Jane and Carson were reteamed in *Make Your Own Bed* (1944), which had them disguised as a butler and maid to get the goods on racketeer Ricardo Cortez. She was also undercover in *Crime by Night* (1944), with character actor Jerome Cowan, and then crooned "What Are You Doing the Rest of Your Life?" with Carson in *Hollywood Canteen* (1944). She and Carson also played newlyweds in *The Doughgirls* (1944).

Ever since Maureen was born, the Reagans had been anxious to have another child. However, with Jane's busy schedule she didn't want to take time off because of pregnancy. Instead, the Reagans adopted a son, Michael Edward, in 1945. "Michael was only twelve hours old when Ronnie and I got him," Jane said in *McCall's*. "I've never thought of him as an adoptive child, and he's never thought of me as an adoptive mother. As far as we're concerned, we're blood. What else can I say? He's my baby boy."

Career-wise, big changes were also ahead for Jane. Since Jane had been at Warners, she had been totally cooperative about working on even the most lackluster script. "In those days, I thought that as long as I was in front of the camera, I was doing okay. I took whatever parts were assigned to me, including the title role in the Torchy Blane B-grade epics," Jane recalled. "I thought that being one hundred percent cooperative would bring me better opportunities. Instead I was sadly neglected for some time. It wasn't until I started kicking over the traces and was loaned out to other studios that I began to go places."

Director Billy Wilder had been impressed with Jane's performance in *Princess O'Rourke* and thought she had the right qualities to play the faithful heroine in *The Lost Weekend*, his hard-hitting study of alcoholism. Ray Milland starred as Don, a down-and-out writer left alone in New York City on Labor Day Weekend. His addiction to alcohol has taken its toll on everyone in his life, especially his long-suffering brother (Philip Terry) and his girlfriend Helen (Jane). Don's weekend odyssey leads to several harrowing adventures, including a trip to a psychiatric ward and a frightening climax in which he imagines himself being attacked by a rat and a bat.

The Lost Weekend was at the forefront of the post-war cinema's attempt to tackle social problems. Wilder made no attempt to sugarcoat the devastating affects of alcoholism on both the person afflicted with the disease and his loved ones. Wilder's decision to film around Bellevue Hospital and grungy bars along Third Avenue was the antithesis of Hollywood's usual sanitized depiction of New York. His city is littered with refuse and populated by social misfits.

The one jarring note to *The Lost Weekend* is the pat ending, in which Don too easily overcomes his problem after a simple speech from Helen. It weakens the impact of the previous scenes, which packed quite a wallop. The unlikely casting of Milland as Don was a revelation. Wilder originally wanted then-unknown Broadway actor Jose Ferrer, but Paramount felt a more attractive — and well-known — star, such as Milland, would be more bankable. Jane, likewise, shed her cute and sassy image and gave a sensitive performance. Milland called his co-star "the most beautiful model of efficiency I've ever encountered."

Despite Jane's triumph in *The Lost Weekend*, she was relegated to supporting roles in her next two Warners releases. In the big-budgeted and highly fanciful *Night and Day* (1946), a misguided attempt to dramatize the life of Cole Porter, Jane played a gold digging song and dance girl, which allowed her to deliver her trademark wisecracks. She also gave the film some zing by performing the Porter standards "You Do Something to Me" and "Let's Do It."

One More Tomorrow (1946), which followed, had been on the Warners shelf for two years. Jane got to work with her Warners pals Dennis Morgan, Ann Sheridan, Alexis Smith and Jack Carson in Peter Godfrey's lifeless reworking of *The Animal Kingdom* (1932). Of the stars, Jane and Carson fared best.

Although Jane hadn't complained about the often innocuous roles she was given, she yearned for another meaty role like Helen in *The Lost Weekend*. "For ten years I portrayed the brassy dame who stormed the city desk snapping, 'Stop the presses! I've got a story that will break this town wide open!' And when I wasn't playing the Torchy Blane type, I was the crass chorine whose greatest achievement in dialogue was a curly-lipped 'Oh yeah?'" she wrote in *The New York Times* in 1954. "But I did not have to stay with it, and at least while I was a wise-cracking blonde on the screen I became knowledgeable about both the camera and my craft. Then, luckier than most actresses who get typed in one-dimensional characters, I was pulled out of this depressing circumstance by the role of Ma Baxter in *The Yearling*."

If *The Lost Weekend* had been a glimmer of the dramatic ability Jane had to offer, *The Yearling* (1946) was concrete evidence. MGM wanted Jane to play the embittered farmer's wife in its film version of Marjorie Kinnan Rawlings' Pulitzer Prize–winning novel about a young boy and his pet deer in the Florida wetlands. In her audition Jane confessed that she hadn't read the book, and, for that matter, had never even heard of it, but she got the part anyway.

The Yearling had been a pet project of producer Sidney Franklin's for eight years, and filming was even begun on a version starring Spencer Tracy and Anne Revere (in Jane's role) in 1941, with Victor Fleming directing. What started out as a labor of love for Franklin soon turned into a monumental headache. Tracy and Fleming had endless rows, which resulted in Fleming being replaced by King Vidor. By the time production resumed, the fawn chosen to play Flag had matured and was deemed unsuitable. Finally, when the location was plagued by an infestation of mosquitoes, production was finally halted, resulting in a $500,000 loss for MGM.

Franklin's persistence led MGM to once more try to film *The Yearling*. This time, all of the elements came together. Director Clarence Brown captured the beauty of the novel in all its splendor, and was ably abetted by cinematographers Charles Rosher, Leonard Smith and Arthur Arling, who brilliantly detailed the lushness of the Florida Everglades. The story chronicled the Baxter family: Pa (Gregory Peck), a poor, hard-working farmer with a kind heart for his family; the embittered Ma (Jane), who has difficulty showing her emotions; and Jody (Claude Jarman, Jr.), their dreamy-eyed youngster who yearns for a pet. Jody finds the animal he wants in Flag, a sweet but spirited fawn whom Jody aims to tame. Despite fierce objections from Ma, Pa lets Jody keep Flag, provided the animal can be kept from destroying the family's crops. Although Jody does his best to train Flag, all of his efforts fail, thus straining his relationship with his parents. The situation intensifies when Ma accidentally shoots Flag, and Jody runs away.

The Yearling got its power from the nicely drawn characterizations of its cast. Although Peck was too well-scrubbed to play the rough-hewn Pa, he did a credible job. For Jody, MGM investigated 19,863 aspirants before settling on Jarman, whom Brown discovered in a Nashville, Tennessee, grade school. Despite his inexperience, he was a natural in the part.

As for Jane, Ma Baxter was as far away from Torchy Blane as she could get. Heavily made up, clad in dowdy tattered dresses and with her hair pulled back, Jane personified the country woman she was playing, both inside and outside. Though Ma possessed a harsh exterior, Jane was able to bring the character's inner strength and unspoken warmth to the surface. Jane is especially moving when she receives a new shawl and tries to hold back her tears of joy.

Critics fawned over *The Yearling* and the performance of its leading lady. "Jane Wyman, hitherto a cute and wide-eyed comedienne in the Warner Brothers' books, takes on stature as a dramatic actress with a fine characterization of Baxter's wife," raved *Newsweek*.

Fred Majdalany of *The Daily Mail* (London) was equally enthusiastic: "She most subtly conveys the impression that love, not shrewishness, is behind her discipline."

Jane hoped for another challenging role when she returned to Warners. Instead, she was wasted in *Cheyenne* (1947), with Dennis Morgan. Jane played the wife of baddie Bruce Bennett, a.k.a. "The Poet," a bank robber whom gambler-turned-bounty-hunter Morgan is out to capture.

Jane fared better in *Magic Town* (1947) for RKO, a Capraesque slice of middle America about a pollster (James Stewart) who discovers a small town that mirrors the opinions of the United States at large. Jane played a cynical schoolteacher torn between stuffy Kent Smith and Stewart. From the beginning, though, it was obvious who she would choose.

Though *Magic Town* attempted to be somewhat eccentric, and paraded a series of colorful characters who were supposed to be endearing, the film was sluggishly paced and suffered from a case of being too cute for its own good. Still, Jane was more at ease than in her previous outing.

In February 1947 Jane was recognized by her peers with a Best Actress Oscar nomination for *The Yearling*. Though she lost to Olivia de Havilland for *To Each His Own*, Jane was hardly upset. She at last started to gain leveraging power at Warners.

Jane was even more jubilant when she soon afterwards learned that she was expecting another child. Her joy was shortly replaced by depression. In the fifth month of her pregnancy Ronnie was stricken with a life-threatening case of viral pneumonia and had to be rushed to the hospital. A distraught Jane went into premature labor and was rushed to another hospital. She gave birth to a girl on June 26, 1947. Despite doctors' efforts, the child died within a few hours.

Jane was despondent after the miscarriage, and despite Ronnie's efforts to cheer her up by taking her out dancing, she remained unhappy. She began to distance herself from her husband, and retreated in work.

Jane immersed herself in her next role, which would be the crowning achievement of her career. *Johnny Belinda* (1948), directed by Jean Negulesco, was a moving adaptation of Elmer Harris' play about a sweet deaf mute named Belinda (Jane) who leads a lonely existence in a Nova Scotia fishing village. Robert (Lew Ayres), a young doctor who has recently moved to the village, takes an interest in her. Unlike Belinda's indifferent father (Charles Bickford), her crotchety aunt (Agnes Moorehead) and the locals, who call her "The Dummy," Robert recognizes Belinda's intelligence and teaches her sign language and lip reading. Through him, Belinda for the first time experiences love. His good work is nearly undone when she is raped by Lochy, a local bully (Stephen McNally) who gets her pregnant. The village gossips suspect Robert is the father, which causes Belinda and her family to be ostracized. Despite the resulting problems, which include the murder of Belinda's father by Lochy, Belinda is a loving mother, shooting Lochy when he and his bride try to take her baby. Belinda is then put on trial and turns to Robert for help.

To prepare for her role, Jane studied for six months with a teacher at the Mary E. Bennett School for the Deaf in Los Angeles, where she learned the proper facial and manual requisites, and she wore plastic ear plugs. Negulesco was quoted as saying, "You could have shot a gun off behind her and even in close-up it wouldn't have registered on her face."

Jane also spent hours screening 16-mm movies of a deaf girl so she could become fluent in sign language, and she had to learn the lines of the rest of the cast. Normally right-handed, Jane instead used her left hand throughout the movie to capture Belinda's uncertainty of motion.

Though *Johnny Belinda* is now regarded as a classic, it was something of a hot potato at the time. Warner was aghast when he saw the daily rushes, complaining that Negulesco was spending too much time showing scenery. He was also horrified that Jane was devoid of glamour, and ordered Negulesco to have her wear makeup. Warner also wanted narration added to Jane's close-ups so that the audience would know what Belinda was thinking. Negulesco ignored all of his suggestions and was fired after the film was completed.

Warner couldn't have been more in error on every point. Though *Johnny Belinda* came close to bordering on the mawkish, it successfully veered away to become a tender and lyrical drama. *Johnny Belinda* was filmed in Mendicino, a lumber village just north of San Francisco, which cinematographer Ted McCord lovingly shot to recreate the bleak and rocky atmosphere of Nova Scotia. McCord's effective use of shadows and high beams was another plus in depicting the barren ambiance of Belinda's farmhouse. Heightening the atmosphere was one of Max Steiner's best film scores, which evoked both the sea and the tenderness of its heroine.

Negulesco also deserves commendation for his subtle and tasteful handling of the rape scene. His use of shadows and a close-up of Belinda's face, so that we can only see the fear in her eyes, were far more effective than any amount of graphic detail that would be allowed today.

The film's greatest asset, though, was Jane. It's ironic that after years of playing wise-cracking cuties, Jane gave her most penetrating performance without uttering a single word. Her childlike innocence over the birth of a new calf, and her vulnerability in the rape scene are conveyed without the least bit of caricature. Her finest moment is her poignant delivery of "The Lord's Prayer" in sign language during her father's funeral.

Warner was both flabbergasted and relieved when *Johnny Belinda* opened in October 1948 to magnificent reviews. "Miss Wyman brings superior insight and tenderness to the role. Not once does she speak throughout the picture. Her face is the mirror of her thoughts. Yet she makes this pathetic young woman glow with emotional warmth," raved Bosley Crowther.

Otis L. Guernsey, Jr., of *The New York Herald Tribune* echoed those sentiments, noting Jane's performance was "full of emotion ... as genuine as pure gold."

Johnny Belinda became Warners' top moneymaker for the year. Jane even had Warner take out a trade ad apologizing to the cast and crew for his previous statements about the movie.

Jane also felt that the movie gave her a completely different outlook on her career. "For the first time, I realized the value of sincerity and honesty in a film — of not only entertaining people, but making them aware of how other, less fortunate, people live," she said in *New Liberty*.

While making *Johnny Belinda* Jane developed an interest in painting. "Jean Negulesco is a wonderful painter and he got all of us — his wife, Dusty Anderson, Lew Ayres, Aggie Moorehead and myself — started on it," Jane said. "I'm not what you'd call an orthodox painter. For one thing, I prefer to paint only at night. For another, I don't use a brush. I put it on canvas with a knife, and some of the results I get are, to say the least, surprising!"

One of those surprises was a self-portrait that was displayed in the Philadelphia Museum of Art. Jane proved talented enough to receive a three-year art scholarship. She declined because she wanted to keep her art endeavors on a strictly recreational level.

Soon after the completion of *Johnny Belinda*, Jane's marriage came to an end. Though over the years neither she nor Reagan has discussed what led to the breakup, each has made statements that pinpoint certain problems. Reagan, in a 1948 interview with Louella Parsons, said Jane was taking her work too seriously, was "nervous and despondent" and that their lives together had become "humdrum." On another occasion he again alluded to Jane's commitment to her craft, and joked that *Johnny Belinda* should have been named co-respondent in their divorce.

Jane claimed Reagan buried himself in his activities serving the Screen Actors Guild, as well as his interest in government affairs. In 1975 *Time* reported that Jane was "so turned off by his pedantic political analyses at the breakfast table that she walked out with their two children."

Thanks to the success of *Johnny Belinda*, Jane had become the new queen of the Warners lot. Jane's position was solidified on March 24, 1949, when, to her surprise, she won an Academy Award for *Johnny Belinda*. "I was so sure I wouldn't win that when I heard my name called out, I didn't recognize it. I didn't get up, so Jerry Wald poked me, and my handbag dropped from my lap. My lipstick and everything went rolling on the floor," Jane said in *McCall's*.

She then delivered what may be the shortest acceptance speech in Academy history: "I won this award for keeping my mouth shut. So I think I'll do it again now."

Perhaps figuring that Jane had become so popular that the public would now see her in anything, Warners hastily shoved her into *A Kiss in the Dark* (1949), an amiable comedy with David Niven, and *The Lady Takes a Sailor* (1949), directed by Michael Curtiz. The latter, in which she was teamed with Dennis Morgan, featured plenty of slapstick, and was hugely popular.

Following a cameo with daughter Maureen in *It's a Great Feeling* (1949), Jane set sail for England to co-star with Marlene Dietrich, Richard Todd and several veteran British character actors in *Stage Fright* (1950), directed by Alfred Hitchcock. The complex story had Jane as Eve Gill, a student at the Royal Academy of Dramatic Arts trying to help her friend Jonathan (Todd) prove his innocence in a murder.

Her plan leads her to pose as the dowdy dresser for an exotic stage star (Dietrich) with whom Jonathan was having an affair when the star's husband was murdered.

Hitchcock, who had been in a slump after the poorly received trio of *The Paradine Case* (1947), *Rope* (1948) and *Under Capricorn* (1949), was not given a reprieve with *Stage Fright*. The *New York Times* said, "*Stage Fright* is dazzlingly stagey, but far from frightening."

Stage Fright's reputation was not enhanced by its director, who over the years expressed little affection for it. He also was not pleased about having to work with Jane, but because this was a Warners production—and she was the studio's top star—he had little choice in the matter. In truth, Jane didn't seem to jell as the daughter of the very British Alistair Sim and Dame Sybil Thorndyke, nor did she do her best to look as unattractive as her role demanded. Instead, between scenes Jane would often check her makeup and reapply more.

Jane at the time was also still distressed over the dissolution of her marriage. The heavy time demands of her career necessitated putting Maureen and Michael in boarding school, and she only saw them on weekends. Being in a foreign city where she knew no one other than the cast and crew of *Stage Fright* did not help matters. She found peace by walking around London and examining the changes in her life. On one of those occasions she wandered into Westminster Abbey, where she encountered a priest with whom she became engaged in deep conversation.

Eventually Jane spoke to him about her shyness and feelings of insecurity. His words proved insightful and offered Jane a revelation about herself. "Shyness, Miss Wyman, is a little matter of self-centeredness," he told her. "That's all. Just a little tendency to think of the whole world as terribly interested in oneself. You know, the feeling that every eye in the room is focused on one—whereas most of the other people there are pretty much involved in their own problems."

Jane subsequently had many interviews with the priest, and said that his words helped her to look at the world around her and develop more of an interest in others, as well as to understand her own shyness. Several years later Jane converted to Catholicism.

She was able to draw upon her natural shyness to play Laura, the lame girl who awaits her gentleman caller in Warners' adaptation of Tennessee Williams' *The Glass Menagerie* (1950). Director Irving Rapper placed most of the focus on Gertrude Lawrence as Amanda Wingfield, the domineering mother of Laura and her brother (Arthur Kennedy), who yearns to explore the world. Kirk Douglas played Jim, the gentleman caller.

While Lawrence seemed too studied and theatrical as Amanda, Rapper did help Jane, Kennedy and Douglas to turn in heartfelt performances, which made up for some of the liabilities the play suffered in its translation to the screen. Among these were a silly flashback sequence showing Amanda in her younger days surrounded by a slew of gentlemen callers. The scene was added at the request of the vain Lawrence, who feared audiences would believe she really looked like the middle-aged Amanda. Far worse was a tacked-on happy ending showing Kennedy at sea envisioning Laura as she watches her new gentleman caller coming to see her. These new elements weakened Williams' storyline and altered his interpretations of the characters.

At MGM Jane paired up with Van Johnson, Howard Keel and Barry Sullivan, who were *Three Guys Named Mike* (1951). The sprightly comedy of an airline stewardess (Jane) who juggles all three men was a hearty laugh getter, which Jane had great fun shooting.

Jane loved doing musicals and was excited about working with Bing Crosby in *Here Comes the Groom* (1951). The Frank Capra musical had Jane as Crosby's ex-girlfriend, who's tired of waiting for her irresponsible beau to settle down. She instead opts for marriage to a member of Boston's Back Bay society (Franchot Tone). Most of the film followed Crosby's efforts to stop the wedding, with the help of the girl (Alexis Smith) who's in love with Tone.

Here Comes the Groom was one of Jane's favorite assignments, and it shows in her energetic performance. Although she had proven herself as a deft light comedienne in previous screen outings, she also demonstrated a flair for physical comedy in the film's funniest scene, a knockdown fight with Smith. *Variety* called Jane's performance "a wow!"

For Jane, the biggest thrill was the chance to duet with Crosby on "In the Cool, Cool, Cool of the Evening," which won the Best Song

Oscar. Though Jane was self-effacing about her singing, her sassy rendition of the song was a nice complement to Crosby's crooning. Their duet led to a Decca recording contract.

"When Bing called and asked me to do a couple of discs with him, I thought he was kidding," said Jane in *New Liberty*. "I'm still not ready to take my singing seriously. In the first place, my top recordings were with Bing, and when you do a duet with him, you can't miss."

Jane had a far less cavalier attitude when it came to her film assignments. Gone was the Jane of a few years before who felt grateful just to be in front of a camera. She balked when Warners assigned her to co-star with Kirk Douglas in the grade B western *Along the Great Divide* (1951). Instead she went on suspension and was replaced by Virginia Mayo.

When she finally returned to work, it was for producer Jerry Wald's American remake of *La Voile Bleu*, a French drama based on an earlier film, *La Maternelle* (1932). The new film, called *The Blue Veil* (1951), referred to the traditional symbol associated with governesses. When Wald failed to interest Greta Garbo in starring as a governess who sacrifices her own chance for happiness for the love of the children in her care, he considered Ingrid Bergman. But by then she had gone off to Italy with director Roberto Rossellini.

Jane loved the part of Louise Mason and accepted when it was next offered to her. The episodic film begins with Louise as a widow during World War I. After the death of her only child in 1918, she devotes the next thirty years of her life to the care of other people's children. She first is employed by a corset manufacturer (Charles Laughton) to care for his son. When her employer proposes to her, Louise rejects him. When he marries his secretary (Vivian Vance), Louise is forced to leave. She then comes close to marrying an attractive tutor (Richard Carlson), but he changes his mind as they are about to elope. She then takes on a new charge, the neglected child (Natalie Wood) of a Broadway star (Joan Blondell). After helping mother and daughter rebuild their relationship, Louise becomes nanny to Tony, a young lad abandoned by his mother (Audrey Totter). When the mother, now remarried, returns to reclaim her son, Louise fights her for custody but loses. As she grows older, Louise finds it hard to get work as a nursemaid and ends up as a janitress in a public school. One day she meets one of her old charges (Don Taylor), now a doctor. Their encounter leads to the Kleenex-heavy finale as Louise is reunited with all of the children she used to care for.

Director Curtis Bernhardt, an old hand at making women's pictures, made sure that every teardrop was wrung from Norman Corwin's sentimental screenplay. The result was a wrenching tale of motherly love that ranks with *Stella Dallas* (1937) and *To Each His Own* (1946). Jane is superb as Louise, with the emotional custody sequence, in which the aged Louise pleads to become Tony's legal mother, featuring one of her best screen moments. Jane received her third Best Actress nomination, but lost to Vivien Leigh for *A Streetcar Named Desire*. Jane did win her second Picturegoer Gold Medal for her performance, having won previously for *Johnny Belinda*.

Jane attended the premiere of *The Blue Veil* with ten-year-old Maureen and with Greg Bautzer, a renowned Hollywood attorney who had dated many film stars, including Joan Crawford and Ginger Rogers. Also at the premiere was Ronald Reagan, with the new woman in his life, MGM contract player Nancy Davis. It was not known to the press that both couples were contemplating marriage, and that Jane and Bautzer had even gone so far as to have blood tests.

The planned nuptials between Jane and Bautzer never materialized, and their relationship came to an abrupt halt. Bautzer supposedly decided that he preferred to maintain his status as Hollywood's "elusive bachelor."

Jane's follow-up to *The Blue Veil* was an appearance as herself in *Starlift* (1951) at Warners. She then reteamed with Crosby, who requested Jane for his co-star in *Just for You* (1952), and again they scored a solid gold hit.

Jane admitted that the glamour treatment she received while making *Here Comes the Groom* and *Just for You* was a nice contrast to playing the unfashionable Eve Gill and Louise Mason. "One of the reasons that I'm so keen about doing musicals is that they give me a chance to doll up. I'm inclined to count the 'changes' when I read a script before deciding to do the role," Jane said in *New Liberty*. "I know very well that drab dowdy creatures win awards, but I'm like most women—the right clothes can send me real high."

Though her return film at Warners was another show business story, it wasn't a musical. *The Story of Will Rogers* (1952) was a simple, straightforward biopic on the beloved American humorist who died in a plane crash in 1935. The movie was something of a Rogers family affair, since it was based on stories by Rogers' widow, Betty (played by Jane), and starred Will Rogers, Jr., as his famous father. Director Michael Curtiz's affection for the subject was evident, but the film suffered from a slow-moving screenplay and the inexperience of its leading man. Jane was affecting as Mrs. Rogers, but her performance wasn't enough to satisfy audiences.

Soon after completion of *The Story of Will Rogers*, Louella Parsons reported in her March 13, 1952, column that Jane was engaged to Travis Kleefeld, a building contractor and the son of a socially prominent Beverly Hills family. Louella made a point of emphasizing that Kleefeld was twelve years younger than Jane. She also noted that the engagement happened to occur just nine days after Reagan and Nancy Davis announced plans to wed. Whether it was the age difference or the supposed disapproval of Kleefeld's family, the engagement was broken three weeks later.

Jane returned to the screen for *Let's Do It Again* (1953), an ill-advised musical remake of *The Awful Truth* (1937) for Columbia, in Irene Dunne's old role. Director Alexander Hall had only raves for his leading lady: "With Miss Wyman, there could only be one cause for complaint, and that's her attention to detail, which might make some directors feel slightly inadequate."

Let's Do It Again proved to be an ominous title for Jane. While at Columbia she met Fred Karger, a composer and orchestra leader who was working in the music department. Like Jane, he was also divorced and had a daughter, Terry. Jane and Karger began dating, although they kept it a secret. Most of Hollywood was shocked when it was announced that Jane and Karger had eloped to Santa Barbara on Saturday, November 1, 1952, and were married in El Montecito Presbyterian Church. They returned to Hollywood the next day, had a small dinner party that evening and reported to Columbia on schedule the following Monday morning. "I guess it surprised a lot of people," Jane said at the time. "Maybe, even me."

From the outset it was decided that the Kargers would try to manage on Fred's salary, even though Jane earned considerably more money. Jane moved from her Beverly Hills mansion into a more modest home. Michael and Maureen were taken out of their private schools so they could attend classes with Terry. Karger, at the time, seemed optimistic about the marriage: "Besides the children, we have music in common. While we both have film careers, in a sense our work isn't competitive enough to cause friction. I think it will have an opposite effect."

It didn't work out that way. The erratic schedules of Karger and Jane, the difficulties of merging two families, and the fact that Jane was a bigger show business personality doomed the marriage. Over the next two years, Jane and Karger separated, reconciled and separated once again. On November 9, 1954, Jane filed suit for divorce on grounds of mental cruelty.

Throughout her marriage Jane continued to be as driven about her career as she had ever been. With Jane having done such a grand job in *The Blue Veil*, Warners decided that *So Big* (1953), Edna Ferber's Pulitzer Prize–winning tale of maternal devotion, might be an excellent Wyman vehicle. Jane played Selena, a teacher in a Midwest farming community who takes a great interest in some of her pupils. Two special cases are an adolescent (Richard Beymer) with a gift for the piano, and a rugged farmer (Sterling Hayden), whom she later marries. Selena faces both joy and tragedy — the birth of her son is overshadowed by the tragic death of her husband in a farming accident. The widowed Selena devotes all of her love and affection to her son, but is disappointed when as a young man (Steve Forrest) he seems to care more for money and success than following his heart.

So Big had already been filmed twice before — with Colleen Moore in 1925 and with Barbara Stanwyck in 1932 — so it was hardly anything novel for 1953 audiences. Director Robert Wise, however, managed to breathe considerable life into the tearjerker by creating a realistic rural atmosphere and by fully developing the relationships between Selena and each of the people she encounters throughout the film. The latter portion of the film, which concentrates less on Selena and more on her son, is less riveting, but still well-handled by Wise.

Wise admitted that working with Jane was what sold him on doing the film. "I had always wanted to work with her," he said, "so I was glad when *So Big* came along. As soon as I heard she was in it, I said I'd do it. She was just a lovely person and a delight to work with. She was totally professional and she did a marvelous job in the film."

So Big was Jane's last film under contract to Warners. She did not sign another exclusivity contract with the studio, but instead chose to work on a per-picture basis. For her initial venture as a free agent, Jane was approached by an up-and-coming producer at Universal named Ross Hunter, who was planning a remake of the Irene Dunne hit *Magnificent Obsession* (1935). Jane, who had already proved adept at playing suffering types, seemed an ideal choice for the blind heroine of Lloyd C. Douglas' morality tale. For her co-star, Universal contract player Rock Hudson was given his first important assignment after five years in B roles.

Jane played Helen Phillips, the widow of a philanthropic doctor who believed in giving of himself in order to help others. Although she has tried her best to deal with her husband's death, she remains resentful of selfish playboy Bob Merrick (Hudson), who had a boating accident and needed the only life-support machine at the same time her husband needed it. Merrick later tries to make amends to Helen, and at the same time makes a play for her. When she tries to escape from him, she is hit by an oncoming car, which results in her blindness. A remorseful Bob reevaluates his life with the help of the man (Otto Kruger) who taught Dr. Phillips his philosophy. Bob decides to pursue a career in medicine in the hope of restoring Helen's sight. He takes a great interest in her but does not reveal his identity to her, even after they fall in love with each other.

Magnificent Obsession is as slick a package of soap bubbles as has ever been lathered across the screen. The film is practically a word-for-word duplicate of the original version, though this one has a glossier finish, thanks to rich Technicolor and Frank Skinner's lush score, which was heavily accented by an endless strain of violins, pianos and heavenly choirs.

To say that *Magnificent Obsession* taxes logic goes without saying. Even its director, Douglas Sirk, described it as "a combination of kitsch, and craziness, and trashiness." The movie has heavy doses of all three elements, but the fourth ingredient — professionalism — is what made it work surprisingly well. Although Hudson was eleven years younger than Jane, the stars brought great conviction to their love scenes. For Hudson, *Magnificent Obsession* was the breakout film that established him as a romantic leading man, as well as Universal's top male star.

To prepare for her difficult role, Jane had a blind companion, who served as a sort of technical advisor, to help her achieve the two main objectives of her performance: simplicity and authenticity. "The blind do not careen around rooms knocking over vases and lamps, nor do they grope wildly at the air in front of them," Jane stated in *The New York Times*. "With this type of handicap, as with all the others, I learned the importance of knowing how blind persons feel inside. In transmitting that sense of blindness and capped emotion, the problem, as with all acting, is to make the audience emote for you."

In general, *Magnificent Obsession* earned favorable reviews. "The same inspirational appeal which marked the 1935 making of Lloyd C. Douglas' bestseller is again caught in this version of *Magnificent Obsession*," said *Variety*. "It is a sensitive treatment of faith told in terms of moving, human drama which packs emotional impact."

Magnificent Obsession was Universal's biggest moneymaker in 1954 after *The Glenn Miller Story*. Its success also helped Jane place ninth on the list of Top Ten Box-Office Draws for 1954. The only other actress to make the list was Marilyn Monroe.

Magnificent Obsession earned Jane a third Picturegoer Gold Medal in addition to a fourth Best Actress Oscar nomination. She lost the latter to Hollywood's then-favorite, Grace Kelly, for Paramount's *The Country Girl* (1954). Ironically, *The Country Girl* had been considered by Warners as a possible vehicle for Jane, Humphrey Bogart and Kirk Douglas, but the studio's paltry $25,000 bid on the property paled in comparison to Paramount's final price of $100,000.

Universal was so pleased with the response to *Magnificent Obsession* that the golden team of Hunter, Jane, Hudson and Sirk were reunited immediately for *All That Heaven Allows*

(1955), another sudser. Jane once again played a widow, this time falling for her handsome gardener (Hudson). It doesn't take long before the nasty tongues in her small town begin wagging. Even her grown children are appalled at what they consider a shameful relationship.

As in *Magnificent Obsession*, *All That Heaven Allows* was given all the lush trimmings, and Frank Skinner again composed the evocative musical score. Jane was beautifully gowned by Bill Thomas. Despite all the polish, it was hard to disguise the triteness of Peg Fenwick's sentimental screenplay. The story covered similar ground as Warners' *My Reputation* (1946), although with more vitriol. *All That Heaven Allows* was buoyed by the still red-hot star power of Jane and Hudson; Universal boasted in its ad campaign that the two were "Together again... Surpassing their performances in *Magnificent Obsession*." The ads worked and the stars had another hit.

Since its release, *All That Heaven Allows* has developed an immense cult following and has become regarded as one of the best films of the romantic genre. Several film critics regard it as a biting portrait of small-town America and the mores and puritanicalism that have crept into our society, and it is among the Library of Congress' Film Registry of the greatest American films ever made. But to 1955 audiences it was merely another grandiose woman's picture.

The same could be said of Paramount's *Lucy Gallant* (1955), in which Jane played the title role, a character she could easily identify with — enterprising, career-bent, fashion-conscious and unlucky in romance. Based on Margaret Cousins' novel *The Life of Lucy Gallant*, the film focuses on Lucy, a sophisticated New Yorker who has been recently jilted and is now stranded in a Texas town gearing up for an oil boom. The enterprising Lucy smells money after she sells off her trousseau to the frumpily clad women of the town. She soon opens a popular dress salon, but her businesslike ways do not sit well with Casey (Charlton Heston), a Texas rancher who wants to marry her.

Lucy Gallant plays like a *Cosmopolitan* short story about the trials and tribulations of a woman trying to make it in a man's world. Like Jane's other films of this period, it played well with women age 25 and up, who were her core audience. Jane felt she was someone they could relate to. "I'm out to kill the dames like me in the audience," Jane told *Coronet* in 1956. "I know there are millions of them. If they understand me, I know I'm all right on ticket sales. I want them to say, 'There but for the grace of Central Casting, go I.'"

Jane at the time also offered her own definition of acting: "You don't need to go to school. Acting is instinct and watching people. It's trial and error."

Jane was commanding $200,000 per film when she made *Miracle in the Rain* (1956), her last Warner Bros. movie. Rudolph Maté directed the four-hankie weepie about the tragic romance between a plain New York girl (Jane) and a soldier (Van Johnson) who's killed in action. It was unadulterated schmaltz, but Jane's fans ate it up, and it has since become a favorite of romantics.

Jane's co-star Paul Picerni remembered Jane's playful side coming to the fore during their climactic scene at St. Patrick's Cathedral in New York: "We shot the final sequences where she was standing out in the rain and very sick. She meets the ghost of Van Johnson in front of St. Patrick's Cathedral and he gives her a gold Roman coin. Then he disappears and she collapses in the rain. I played the young priest who sees her lying there and takes her inside. Rudy Maté was getting a close shot of myself holding Jane, who was supposed to be unconscious. I looked down at that angelic face of Jane Wyman and gave her a very passionate kiss. Rudy started screaming in his German accent, 'Paul, vat are you doing?' Jane and I were both laughing hysterically. I thought Rudy was going to have a stroke."

Miracle in the Rain was Jane's last film for a while. Later that year she signed on to host *The Jane Wyman Theater* (also known as *Jane Wyman Presents* and *Jane Wyman Presents The Fireside Theater*) for NBC. Each week Jane would introduce — and occasionally star in — a different original half hour drama. According to Jane's contract, she could set her own salary — which was never less than $1,000 per performance — and she was allowed to produce, direct and write, as well as act. Jane's long list of duties on the show included reading scripts, choosing wardrobes, decorating sets and signing all the checks. The show ran for three exhausting seasons.

By 1959 Jane was past forty, the turning

point for most leading ladies, which meant being cast in more mature roles. Thus, in *Holiday for Lovers* (1959) Jane was the wife of Clifton Webb and mother to teenage daughters Jill St. John and Carol Lynley. She then played the crusty Aunt Polly in *Pollyanna* (1960), the Disney smash that made a star of Hayley Mills.

Her last screen role for a while was another Disney venture, *Bon Voyage* (1963), a wholesome comedy about an American family who become involved with diamond smugglers during their European vacation. Fred MacMurray played Dad to Jane's mom, and helped keep the film afloat even as it turned toward sitcom-level situations.

In between her two Disney films Jane surprised her friends and family by remarrying Fred Karger in 1961, but this reunion also ended in divorce four years later.

By the mid–'60s Jane became less interested in films, preferring to devote her energies to working as national campaign chairman for the Arthritis Foundation, an organization she became interested in when a close friend was crippled by the disease. "I didn't even know how to spell arthritis before I became involved with the foundation," she told *McCall's* in 1982. "But it turned out to be rewarding and exhilarating because I was doing something that was contributive."

Jane also continued painting, and sold more than one hundred of her small scenes done in oil. Painting began to consume so much of her time that she finally put down her brush in 1978. "I really enjoyed it at first. Then it became a trap. I was painting eight hours a day, sometimes into the night. Finally, I just packed up my paints and put them away," she said.

Jane did make one last screen appearance, in the dreadful Bob Hope comedy *How to Commit Marriage* (1970), which, fortunately, disappeared quickly from theaters. She fared better on television, appearing with Dean Stockwell and Dana Andrews in *The Failing of Raymond* (1971), an above average thriller for ABC. She also made guest appearances on several series, including *My Three Sons* and *The Love Boat*, in which she played a nun. Billed as Miss Jane Wyman, she played Granny Arrowroot in *The Incredible Journey of Doctor Meg Laurel* (1979), a CBS television movie, and in 1980 guest starred as a clairvoyant on *Charlie's Angels*.

Jane was then introduced to a whole new generation when she took on the role of tough-as-nails Angela Channing in the prime-time soap *Falcon Crest*. The show was originally titled *The Vintage Years*, but was changed by CBS, which feared that title would be a turn-off for younger viewers. Jane played the strong-willed matriarch who ran both the family winery and the lives of her children. Though she was in her mid-sixties when the show debuted in September 1981, Jane's lovely, wrinkle-free face belied her age by at least fifteen years.

After years of playing heartfelt heroines, the nasty Angela was a real about-face for Jane, who reveled in the role. "I love playing Angela," she related in *Ladies Home Journal* in 1985. "In most of my films, I've done very sympathetic characters, the 'four-handkerchief bits,' you know. But in a way, Angela *is* sympathetic. I even feel sorry for her sometimes."

"There is a little of Jane Wyman in Angela," she added. "Just a little. She's a flirt. She's hard. She runs everything and she goes straight through everything like a Mack truck."

Jane was well-paid for her weekly steamroller routine, earning $60,000 per episode. But her professionalism was worth it, and she had no tolerance for anyone who didn't meet her standards. When guest Lana Turner arrived on the set five hours late, an infuriated Jane bellowed, "I'm sick and tired of movie queen, prima donna antics. I will not tolerate any more of it."

Falcon Crest was a consistent winner in its time slot during its first seven seasons. It also earned Jane a Golden Globe Award in 1984 for Best Actress in a Television Dramatic Series. An elated Jane accepted her award by telling the audience, "I am really grateful for this. I'm having the best time of my life. I'm a little too old to be happy, but just old enough to be grateful."

As the "ex–Mrs. Ronald Reagan," Jane was also thrust into the limelight when her former husband moved into the White House on January 20, 1981. Jane, however, tired quickly of anyone who asked her if she ever pictured herself as First Lady, and refused to answer questions regarding her marriage to Reagan.

She was also firm about not getting married again. "I still think marriage is a marvelous thing," she told *McCalls* in 1982. "But for me — at my age, my stage in life — I don't want to get involved again. I just have too much fun being single. I enjoy coming and going as I please."

By the time *Falcon Crest* ended its eighth season it had fallen from the Top Ten to number forty-seven in the ratings. When *Falcon Crest* was renewed, it was announced that Jane would be seen in only two episodes. The storyline called for Angela to be injured and lapse into a coma, a device designed to leave the door open for Jane's possible return later in the season.

Executive producer Jerry Thorpe told *TV Guide* that the decision to curtail Jane's role was a mutual one to take the show in a new direction and also lighten her load. Translated, it meant the producers wanted to pursue a younger audience. Without Jane's electricity, the ratings tumbled even further and the show was canceled in 1990.

Jane did return to television one more time for a recurring role as Jane Seymour's strong-willed mother in *Dr. Quinn, Medicine Woman*, and was warmly received by fans.

Now retired, Jane lives in Rancho Mirage, California, where she continues to lead an active life. Although she no longer plays golf, which had been one of her passions, she has not given up her duties with the Arthritis Foundation, which include traveling throughout the country for fund-raisers and the opening of new chapters, and working on the group's telethon. Her approach to those projects has pretty much mirrored her approach to life in general.

"I don't sit still long and I like to do things. I get a project, and then once it's finished, I forget about it and go to the next one."

FILMOGRAPHY

(Jane appeared in unbilled bits in the first 14 films listed below)

The Kid from Spain (Goldwyn–United Artists, 1932) Directed by Leo McCarey. *Cast:* Eddie Cantor, Lyda Roberti, Robert Young, Ruth Hall, John Miljan, Noah Beery, J. Carrol Naish.

Elmer the Great (Warner Bros., 1933) Directed by Mervyn LeRoy. *Cast:* Joe E. Brown, Patricia Ellis, Frank McHugh, Claire Dodd, Sterling Holloway, Emma Dunn, Douglas Dumbrille.

All the King's Horses (Paramount, 1934) Directed by Frank Tuttle. *Cast:* Carl Brisson, Mary Ellis, Edward Everett Horton, Eugene Pallette, Katherine De Mille.

College Rhythm (Paramount, 1934) Directed by Norman Taurog. *Cast:* Jack Oakie, Joe Penner, Mary Brian, Lanny Ross, Helen Mack, Lyda Roberti, George Barbier, Franklin Pangborn.

Stolen Harmony (Paramount, 1935) Directed by Alfred Werker. *Cast:* George Raft, Ben Bernie, Grace Bradley, Iris Adrian, Lloyd Nolan, Rolf Harolde.

Rumba (Paramount, 1935) Directed by Marion Gering. *Cast:* Carole Lombard, George Raft, Margo, Lynne Overman, Monroe Owsley, Iris Adrian, Gail Patrick, Samuel S. Hinds.

King of Burlesque (20th Century–Fox, 1935) Directed by Sidney Lanfield. *Cast:* Warner Baxter, Alice Faye, Jack Oakie, Mona Barrie, Arline Judge, Dixie Dunbar, Gergory Ratoff.

Anything Goes (Paramount, 1936) Directed by Lewis Milestone. *Cast:* Bing Crosby, Ethel Merman, Charles Ruggles, Grace Bradley, Ida Lupino, Chill Wills, Arthur Treacher.

My Man Godfrey (Universal, 1936) Directed by Gregory La Cava. *Cast:* William Powell, Carole Lombard, Alice Brady, Eugene Pallette, Mischa Auer, Gail Patrick, Jean Dixon, Alan Mowbray.

Stage Struck (Warner Bros., 1936) Directed by Busby Berkeley. *Cast:* Dick Powell, Joan Blondell, Warren William, Frank McHugh, Jeanne Madden, Carol Hughes, Craig Reynolds.

Cain and Mabel (Warner Bros., 1936) Directed by Lloyd Bacon. *Cast:* Clark Gable, Marion Davies, Allen Jenkins, Roscoe Karns, Walter Catlett, Hobart Cavanaugh, Pert Kelton, E.E. Clive.

Polo Joe (Warner Bros., 1936) Directed by William McGann. *Cast:* Joe E. Brown, Carol Hughes, Richard "Skeets" Gallagher, Joseph King, Gordon Elliott, Fay Holden, George E. Stone.

Here Comes Carter (Warner Bros., 1936) Directed by William Clemens. *Cast:* Ross Alexander, Glenda Farrell, Anne Nagel, Hobart Cavanaugh, Craig Reynolds, George E. Stone.

Gold Diggers of 1937 (Warner Bros., 1936) Directed by Lloyd Bacon. *Cast:* Dick Powell, Joan Blondell, Victor Moore, Glenda Farrell, Lee Dixon, Osgood Perkins, Rosalind Marquis, Charles D. Brown.

Smart Blonde (Warner Bros., 1937) Directed by Frank McDonald. *Cast:* Glenda Farrell, Barton MacLane, Winifred Shaw, Craig Reynolds, Addison Richards, Jane Wyman.

The King and the Chorus Girl (Warner Bros., 1937) Directed by Mervyn LeRoy. *Cast:* Joan Blondell, Fernand Gravet, Edward Everett Horton, Jane Wyman, Alan Mowbray, Mary Nash.

Ready, Willing and Able (Warner Bros., 1937) Directed by Ray Enright. *Cast:* Ruby Keeler, Lee Dixon, Allen Jenkins, Louise Fazenda, Carol Hughes, Ross Alexander, Jane Wyman.

Slim (Warner Bros., 1937) Directed by Ray Enright. *Cast:* Pat O'Brien, Margaret Lindsay, Henry Fonda, Stuart Erwin, J. Farrell MacDonald, Jane Wyman.

The Singing Marine (Warner Bros., 1937) Directed by Ray Enright. *Cast:* Dick Powell, Doris Weston, Lee Dixon, Hugh Herbert, Jane Darwell, Allen Jenkins, Veda Ann Borg, Jane Wyman.

Mr. Dodds Takes the Air (Warner Bros., 1937) Directed by Alfred E. Green. *Cast:* Kenny Baker, Jane Wyman, Alice Brady, Gertrude Michael, Frank McHugh, Luis Alberni.

Public Wedding (Warner Bros., 1937) Directed by Nick Grinde. *Cast:* William Hopper, Jane Wyman, Dick Purcell, Berton Churchill, James Robbins, Marie Wilson, Veda Ann Borg.

The Spy Ring (Universal, 1938) Directed by Joseph H. Lewis. *Cast:* William Hall, Jane Wyman, Esther Ralston, Ben Alexander, Ray Mason, Jack Mulhall, Leon Ames, Don Barclay.

Fools for Scandal (Warner Bros., 1938) Directed by Mervyn LeRoy. *Cast:* Carole Lombard, Fernand Gravet, Ralph Bellamy, Allen Jenkins, Isaebel Jeans, Marcia Ralston, Jane Wyman.

He Couldn't Say No (Warner Bros., 1938) Directed by Lewis Seiler. *Cast:* Frank McHugh, Cora Witherspoon, Jane Wyman, Berton Churchill, Diana Lewis.

Wide Open Faces (Columbia, 1938) Directed by Kurt Neumann. *Cast:* Joe E. Brown, Jane Wyman, Alison Skipworth, Lyda Roberti, Alan Baxter, Lucien Littlefield, Sidney Toler.

The Crowd Roars (MGM, 1938) Directed by Richard Thorpe. *Cast:* Robert Taylor, Frank Morgan, Edward Arnold, Maureen O'Sullivan, William Gargan, Frank Craven, Jane Wyman.

Brother Rat (Warner Bros., 1938) Directed by William Keighley. *Cast:* Priscilla Lane, Wayne Morris, Johnny Davis, Jane Bryan, Eddie Albert, Henry O'Neill, Ronald Reagan, Jane Wyman.

Tail Spin (20th Century–Fox, 1939) Directed by Roy Del Ruth. *Cast:* Alice Faye, Constance Bennett, Joan Davis, Nancy Kelly, Charles Farrell, Jane Wyman, Kane Richmond, Wally Vernon.

The Kid from Kokomo (Warner Bros., 1939) Directed by Lewis Seiler. *Cast:* Pat O'Brien, Joan Blondell, Wayne Morris, May Robson, Jane Wyman, Stanley Fields, Maxie Rosenbloom.

Torchy Plays with Dynamite (Warner Bros., 1939) Directed by Noel Smith. *Cast:* Jane Wyman, Allen Jenkins, Tom Kennedy, Sheila Bromley, Joe Cunningham.

Kid Nightingale (Warner Bros., 1939) Directed by George Amy. *Cast:* John Payne, Jane Wyman, Walter Catlett, Edward Brophy, Harry Burns, John Ridgeley, Charles D. Brown.

Private Detective (Warner Bros., 1939) Directed by Noel Smith. *Cast:* Jane Wyman, Dick Foran, Gloria Dickson, Maxie Rosenbloom, John Ridgeley, Morgan Conway.

Brother Rat and a Baby (Warner Bros., 1940) Directed by Ray Enright. *Cast:* Priscilla Lane, Wayne Morris, Jane Bryan, Ronald Reagan, Jane Wyman, Eddie Albert, Peter B. Good.

An Angel from Texas (Warner Bros., 1940) Directed by Ray Enright. *Cast:* Eddie Albert, Rosemary Lane, Wayne Morris, Ronald Reagan, Jane Wyman, Ruth Terry, John Litel.

Flight Angels (Warner Bros., 1940) Directed by Lewis Seiler. *Cast:* Virginia Bruce, Dennis Morgan, Wayne Morris, Ralph Bellamy, Jane Wyman, John Litel, Nell O'Day, Jan Clayton.

My Love Came Back (Warner Bros., 1940) Directed by Kurt (Curtis) Bernhardt. *Cast:* Olivia de Havilland, Jeffrey Lynn, Charles Winninger, Eddie Albert, Spring Byington, Jane Wyman.

Gambling on the High Seas (Warner Bros., 1940) Directed by George Amy. *Cast:* Wayne Morris, Jane Wyman, Gilbert Roland, William Pawley, Murray Alper, Frank Wilcox, John Litel.

Tugboat Annie Sails Again (Warner Bros., 1940) Directed by Lewis Seiler. *Cast:* Marjorie Rambeau, Alan Hale, Jane Wyman, Ronald Reagan, Clarence Kolb, Charles Halton, Victor Kilian.

Honeymoon for Three (Warner Bros., 1941) Directed by Lloyd Bacon. *Cast:* George Brent, Ann Sheridan, Osa Massen, Charles Ruggles, Jane Wyman, Lee Patrick.

Bad Men of Missouri (Warner Bros., 1941) Directed by Ray Enright. *Cast:* Dennis Morgan, Arthur Kennedy, Wayne Morris, Jane Wyman, Victor Jory, Walter Catlett.

You're in the Army Now (Warner Bros., 1941) Directed by Lewis Seiler. *Cast:* Jimmy Durante, Phil Silvers, Donald MacBride, Jane Wyman, Regis Toomey.

The Body Disappears (Warner Bros., 1941) Directed by D. Ross Lederman. *Cast:* Edward Everett Horton, Jeffrey Lynn, Jane Wyman, Herbert Anderson, Marguerite Chapman.

Larceny Inc. (Warner Bros., 1942) Directed by Lloyd Bacon. *Cast:* Edward G. Robinson, Jane Wyman, Broderick Crawford, Anthony Quinn, Jack Carson, Edward Brophy, Harry Davenport, Jackie Gleason.

My Favorite Spy (RKO Radio, 1942) Directed by Tay Garnett. *Cast:* Kay Kyser, Ginny Simms, Ish Kabibble, Ellen Drew, Jane Wyman, Robert Armstrong, Helen Westley.

Footlight Serenade (20th Century–Fox, 1942) Directed by Gregory Ratoff. *Cast:* Betty Grable, John Payne, Victor Mature, James Gleason, Phil Silvers, Jane Wyman, Cobina Wright, Jr., June Lang.

Princess O'Rourke (Warner Bros., 1943) Directed by Norman Krasna. *Cast:* Olivia de Havilland, Robert Cummings, Charles Coburn, Jack Carson, Jane Wyman, Harry Davenport.

Make Your Own Bed (Warner Bros., 1944) Directed by Peter Godfrey. *Cast:* Jack Carson, Jane Wyman, Irene Manning, Ricardo Cortez, Alan Hale, George Tobias.

Crime by Night (Warner Bros., 1944) Directed by William Clemens. *Cast:* Jerome Cowan, Jane Wyman, Faye Emerson, Eleanor Parker, Charles Lang, Stuart Crawford, Cy Kendall.

The Doughgirls (Warner Bros., 1944) Directed by James V. Kern. *Cast:* Ann Sheridan, Alexis Smith, Jane Wyman, Irene Manning, Jack Carson, Eve Arden, Charles Ruggles, Barbara Brown, Craig Stevens.

Hollywood Canteen (Warner Bros., 1944) Directed by Delmer Daves. *Cast:* Joan Leslie, Robert Hutton, Janis Paige, Dane Clark. *Guest Stars:* Jack Benny, Joe E. Brown, Eddie Cantor, Jack Carson, Joan Crawford, Bette Davis, John Garfield, Sydney Greenstreet, Paul Henreid, Ida Lupino, Dennis Morgan, Eleanor Parker, Zachary Scott, Barbara Stanwyck, Jane Wyman.

The Lost Weekend (Paramount, 1945) Directed by Billy Wilder. *Cast:* Ray Milland, Jane Wyman, Philip Terry, Doris Dowling, Howard da Silva, Frank Faylen.

One More Tomorrow (Warner Bros., 1946) Directed by Peter Godfrey. *Cast:* Ann Sheridan, Dennis Morgan, Alexis Smith, Jack Carson, Jane Wyman, Reginald Gardiner, John Loder.

Night and Day (Warner Bros., 1946) Directed by Michael Curtiz. *Cast:* Cary Grant, Alexis Smith, Monty Woolley, Mary Martin, Ginny Simms, Jane Wyman, Eve Arden, Victor Francen.

The Yearling (MGM, 1946) Directed by Clarence Brown. *Cast:* Gregory Peck, Jane Wyman, Claude Jarman, Jr., Chill Wills, Clem Bevans, Margaret Wycherley, Henry Travers.

Cheyenne (Warner Bros., 1947) Directed by Raoul Walsh. *Cast:* Dennis Morgan, Jane Wyman, Bruce Bennett, Janis Paige, Arthur Kennedy, Alan Hale, Barton MacLane, Tom Tyler.

Magic Town (RKO Radio, 1947) Directed by William A. Wellman. *Cast:* James Stewart, Jane Wyman, Kent Smith, Regis Toomey, Donald Meek, Ned Sparks, Wallace Ford.

Johnny Belinda (Warner Bros., 1948) Directed by Jean Negulesco. *Cast:* Jane Wyman, Lew Ayres, Charles Bickford, Agnes Moorehead, Stephen McNally, Jan Sterling, Rosalind Ivan.

A Kiss in the Dark (Warner Bros., 1949) Directed by Delmer Daves. *Cast:* David Niven, Jane Wyman, Victor Moore, Broderick Crawford, Maria Ouspenskaya, Wayne Morris, Joseph Buloff.

The Lady Takes a Sailor (Warner Bros., 1949) Directed by Michael Curtiz. *Cast:* Jane Wyman, Dennis Morgan, Eve Arden, Allyn Joslyn, Robert Douglas, William Frawley, Tom Tully.

It's a Great Feeling (Warner Bros., 1949) Directed by David Butler. *Cast:* Doris Day, Dennis Morgan, Jack Carson, Bill Goodwin. *Guest Stars:* Gary Cooper, Joan Crawford, Errol Flynn, Danny Kaye, Patricia Neal, Eleanor Parker, Edward G. Robinson, Ronald Reagan, Jane Wyman.

Stage Fright (Warner Bros., 1950) Directed by Alfred Hitchcock. *Cast:* Jane Wyman, Marlene Dietrich, Richard Todd, Michael Wilding, Alistair Sim, Dame Sybil Thorndyke, Joyce Grenfell, Kay Walsh.

The Glass Menagerie (Warner Bros., 1950) Directed by Irving Rapper. *Cast:* Jane Wyman, Kirk Douglas, Arthur Kennedy, Gertrude Lawrence, Ann Tyrrell, John Compton.

Three Guys Named Mike (MGM, 1951) Directed by Charles Walters. *Cast:* Jane Wyman, Van Johnson, Howard Keel, Barry Sullivan, Phyllis Kirk, Jeff Donnell, Barbara Billingsley.

Here Comes the Groom (Paramount, 1951) Directed by Frank Capra. *Cast:* Bing Crosby, Jane Wyman, Franchot Tone, Alexis Smith, James Barton, Connie Gilchrist, Anna Maria Alberghetti.

The Blue Veil (RKO Radio, 1951) Directed by Curtis Bernhardt. *Cast:* Jane Wyman, Charles Laughton, Richard Carlson, Joan Blondell, Agnes Moorehead, Don Taylor, Audrey Totter.

Starlift (Warner Bros., 1951) Directed by Roy Del Ruth. *Cast:* Janice Rule, Ron Haggerty, James Cagney, Gary Cooper, Doris Day, Virginia Gibson, Phil Harris, Frank Lovejoy, Gordon MacRae, Virginia Mayo, Gene Nelson, Ruth Roman, Randolph Scott, Jane Wyman.

Just for You (Paramount, 1952) Directed by Elliott Nugent. *Cast:* Bing Crosby, Jane Wyman, Robert Arthur, Ethel Barrymore, Natalie Wood, Cora Witherspoon, Regis Toomey.

The Story of Will Rogers (Warner Bros., 1952) Directed by Michael Curtiz. *Cast:* Will Rogers Jr., Jane Wyman, Carl Benton Reid, Eve Miller, James Gleason, Slim Pickens, Noah Beery, Jr.

Let's Do It Again (Columbia, 1953) Directed by Alexander Hall. *Cast:* Jane Wyman, Ray Milland, Aldo Ray, Leon Ames, Karin Booth, Kathryn Givney, Tom Helmore, Valerie Bettis.

So Big (Warner Bros., 1953) Directed by Robert Wise. *Cast:* Jane Wyman, Sterling Hayden, Nancy Olson, Steve Forrest, Richard Beymer, Walter Coy, Elisabeth Fraser, Martha Hyer.

Magnificent Obsession (Universal-International, 1954) Directed by Douglas Sirk. *Cast:* Jane Wyman, Rock Hudson, Barbara Rush, Agnes Moorehead, Otto Kruger, Gregg Palmer.

All That Heaven Allows (Universal-International, 1955) Directed by Douglas Sirk. *Cast:* Jane Wyman, Rock Hudson, Agnes Moorehead, Conrad Nagel, Charles Drake, Virginia Grey.

Lucy Gallant (Paramount, 1955) Directed by Robert Parrish. *Cast:* Jane Wyman, Charlton Heston, Thelma Ritter, William Demarest, Claire Trevor, Wallace Ford, Tom Helmore.

Miracle in the Rain (Warner Bros., 1956) Directed by Rudolph Maté. *Cast:* Jane Wyman, Van Johnson, Peggie Castle, Fred Clark, Eileen Heckart, Paul Picerni, Josephine Hutchinson.

Holiday for Lovers (20th Century–Fox, 1959) Directed by Henry Levin. *Cast:* Clifton Webb, Jane Wyman, Jill St. John, Carol Lynley, Paul Henreid, Gary Crosby, Jose Greco, Nico Minardos.

Pollyanna (Disney, 1960) Directed by David Swift. *Cast:* Hayley Mills, Jane Wyman, Karl Malden, Richard Egan, Nancy Olson, Adolphe Menjou, Donald Crisp, Agnes Moorehead.

Bon Voyage (Disney, 1963) Directed by James Neilson. *Cast:* Fred MacMurray, Jane Wyman, Michael Callan, Deborah Walley, Jessie Royce Landis, Tommy Kirk, Ivan Desny.

How to Commit Marriage (Cinerama, 1970) Directed by Norman Panama. *Cast:* Bob Hope, Jackie Gleason, Jane Wyman, Leslie Nielsen, Maureen Arthur, Paul Stewart, Tina Louise.

TELEVISION FILM CREDITS

The Failing of Raymond (1971) *Cast:* Jane Wyman, Dean Stockwell, Dana Andrews.

The Incredible Journey of Doctor Meg Laurel (1979) *Cast:* Lindsay Wagner, Miss Jane Wyman, Andrew Duggan, Gary Lockwood, Brock Peters, John Reilly, Dorothy McGuire.

Bibliography

Arliss, George, *My Ten Years in the Studios* (Boston: Little, Brown, 1940).

Astor, Mary, *A Life on Film* (New York: Delacorte Press, 1971).

Cagney, James, *Cagney by Cagney* (New York: Doubleday, 1976).

Davis, Bette, *The Lonely Life* (New York: G.P. Putnam's Sons, 1962).

Davis, Bette, with Michael Herskowitz, *This 'n' That* (New York: G.P. Putnam's Sons, 1987).

de Havilland, Olivia, *Every Frenchman Has One* (New York: Random House, 1961).

Donati, William, *Ida Lupino: A Biography* (Lexington: University Press of Kentucky, 1996).

Eells, George, *Ginger, Loretta and Irene Who?* (New York: G.P. Putnam's Sons, 1976).

Flynn, Errol, *My Wicked, Wicked Ways* (New York: Berkley, 1959).

Fontaine, Joan, *No Bed of Roses* (New York: Berkley, 1978).

Freedland, Michael, *The Warner Brothers* (New York: St. Martin's Press, 1983).

Grady, Billy, *The Irish Peacock: Confessions of a Legendary Talent Agent* (New York: Arlington House, 1971).

Halliwell's Film and Video Guide, edited by John Walker (New York: HarperCollins, 1999).

Hirschhorn, Clive, *The Warner Bros. Story* (New York: Crown, 1979).

Inside Warner Brothers (1935–1951), selected, edited and annotated by Rudy Behlmer (New York: Viking Press, 1985).

Jerome, Stuart, *Those Crazy Wonderful Years: When We Ran Warner Brothers* (New York: Carol, 1983).

Jewell, Richard B., with Vernon Harbin, *The RKO Story* (New Rochelle, N.Y.: Arlington House, 1982).

Kass, Judith M., *Pyramid Illustrated History of the Movies: Olivia de Havilland* (New York: Pyramid, 1976).

Katz, Ephraim, *The Film Encyclopedia* (New York: Putnam, 1979).

Marlow-Trump, Nancy, *Ruby Keeler: A Photographic Biography* (Jefferson, N.C.: McFarland, 1998).

Meyer, William R., *The Warner Brothers Directors: The Hard-Boiled, the Comic, and the Weepers* (New Rochelle, N.Y.: Arlington House, 1978).

Morella, Joe, and Edward Z. Epstein, *Jane Wyman: A Biography* (New York: Delacorte Press, 1985).

Parish, James Robert, and William T. Leonard, *Hollywood Players: The Thirties* (New Rochelle, N.Y.: Arlington House, 1976).

Reagan, Ronald, *Where's the Rest of Me?* (New York: Duell, Sloane and Pearce, 1965).

Sennett, Ted, *Warner Brothers Presents* (New York: Castle Books, 1971).

Sherman, Vincent, *Studio Affairs* (Lexington: University Press of Kentucky, 1995).

Shipman, David, *The Great Movie Stars: The Golden Years* (New York: Crown, 1970).

Shipman, David, *The Great Movie Stars: The International Years* (New York: St. Martin's Press, 1972).

Spada, James, *More Than a Woman: An Intimate Biography of Bette Davis* (New York: Bantam, 1993).

Stewart, Lucy Ann Liggett, *Ida Lupino as a Film Director 1949–1953: An Auteur Approach* (New York: Arno Press, 1980).

Swindell, Larry, *Body and Soul: The Story of John Garfield* (New York: William Morrow, 1975).

Thomas, Tony, and Jim Terry, with Busby Berkeley, *The Busby Berkeley Book* (A & W Visual Library: 1973).

Vermilye, Jerry, *Pyramid Illustrated History of the Movies: Bette Davis* (New York: Pyramid, 1973).

Warner, Jack L., with Dean Jennings, *My First Hundred Years in Hollywood* (New York: Random House, 1965).

Wiley, Mason and Damien Bona, *Inside Oscar: The Unofficial History of the Academy Awards* (New York: Ballantine, 1986).

ADDITIONAL MATERIALS

Bowers, Ronald L., "Joan Blondell," in *Films in Review*, April 1972.

Chierichetti, David, "Olivia in London," in *Film Fan Monthly*, Issue 124, October 1971.

Davis, Bette, with Bill Davidson, "All About Me," in *Colliers*, November 25, 1955.

Davis, Bette, with Bill Davidson, "All About Me, Part 2," in *Colliers*, December 9, 1955.

DeCarl, Lennard, "Alexis Smith," in *Films in Review*, June-July 1970.

Hagen, Ray, "A Screen Facts Interview with Ann Sheridan," in *Screen Facts*, No. 14, 1966.

Maltin, Leonard, "FFM Interviews Joan Blondell," in *Film Fan Monthly*, No. 99, September 1969.

Parish, James R., and Gene Ringgold, "Kay Francis," in *Films in Review*, February 1964.

Wyman, Jane, "A Case of Shyness," in *Guideposts*, June 1964.

Index

Abbott, Bud 232
Abbott, George 7
Abbott, John 220
Above and Beyond 183
Adair, Jean 137
The Adams Chronicles 29
Adolfi, John 5
Advance to the Rear 13
Adventure 11
The Adventurers 70
The Adventures of Mark Twain 26, 217
The Adventures of Robin Hood 58, 59, 146
The Adventures of Sherlock Holmes 159
Advise and Consent 185
Affectionately Yours 40
Agatha Christie's Murder Is Easy 70
The Age of Innocence 224
Aherne, Brian 38, 58, 97, 161, 162
Airport 77 70
Akins, Zoe 5, 57, 90
Albert, Eddie 133, 135, 144, 161, 231
Alda, Robert 124, 149, 218
Aldrich, Robert 47, 70
Aldridge, Kay 214
Alexander, John 137
Alexander, Ross 109, 110
Alfred Hitchcock Presents 46, 170
Algiers 195
Alibi Ike 57
Alice in Movieland 144
Alice in Wonderland 156
All About Eve 37, 44, 181
All Quiet on the Western Front 25
All the King's Horses 230
All That Heaven Allows 240, 241
All This and Heaven, Too 39
Allen, Dennis 98
Allen, Hervey 58
Allen, Irwin 70
Allen, Lewis 181
Alley, Kirstie 224
Allgood, Sara 125
Allotment Wives 98
Allyson, June 10, 12, 49, 141, 206, 219

Along the Great Divide 238
Altman, Al 131, 142
Always in My Heart 97
Amateur Anne 88
The Amazing Mr. Williams 8
The Ambassador's Daughter 68
Ameche, Don 97, 112, 113
An American Dream 187
Ames, Leon 126
Anastasia: The Mystery of Anna 71
Anatomy of a Murder 185
Anderson, Dusty 236
Anderson, Ernest 41
Anderson, Herbert 197
Anderson, John Murray 45
Anderson, Judith 23, 25, 76, 199
Anderson, Mary Ann 171
Anderson, Maxwell 39
Anderson, Michael 70
Anderson, Robert 183
Andrews, Anthony 71
Andrews, Dana 29, 186, 242
The Andrews Sisters 148
Angel Baby 13
An Angel from Texas 232
Angel Street 119, 123
Angels Wash Their Faces 195, 207
Angels with Dirty Faces 146, 194, 195
The Animal Kingdom 148, 203, 218, 233
Ann-Margret 46, 48
Anna Christie 80
The Anniversary 48
Another Dawn 94
Another Man's Poison 44
Another World 207
Anthony Adverse 58
Any Number Can Play 220
Anything Goes 158
Appointment in Honduras 206
Arden, Eve 180, 200, 204, 217, 219
Arquette, Patricia 123
Arquette, Roseanna 128
Arlen, Harold 136, 147
Arlen, Richard 89, 157
Arling, Arthur 234
Arliss, George 34, 35, 37

Armstrong, Robert 192
Arno, Max 193
Arnold, Edward 149
Arsenic and Old Lace 136, 137
Arthur, Jean 81
Artists and Models 158
Astaire, Fred 109, 110, 147, 148, 219
Asther, Nils 92
Astor, Mary 186
Atwill, Lionel 77
Auer, Mischa 158
Aumont, Jean-Pierre 185
Avalon, Frankie 82
Avery, Stephen Morehouse 158
Away from Home 187
The Awful Truth 239
Ayres, Lew 64, 204, 235, 236

Bacall, Lauren 2
Back in Circulation 7
Back Street 91
Bacon, Lloyd 5, 6, 37, 107, 138, 197, 232
Bad Men of Missouri 232
The Bad Sister 33, 34
Bainter, Fay 9, 110, 134
Baker, C. Graham 123, 195
Baker, Kenny 230
Ball, Lucille 150, 165, 194, 232
Ballard, Karny 81
Bamberger, Theron 118
Bancroft, George 89
Band of Angels 127
Bankhead, Tallulah 13, 40, 44, 119, 156
Banks, Polan 205
Banyon 14
Barefoot in the Park 14
Barnekow, Baron Raven Erik 95, 96
Barnes, George 5, 7, 12
Barlow, Joy 136
Barnes, Charles 161
Barrett, Edith 161
Barrie, James M. 20, 65
Barry, Eleanor 87
Barry, George Andre 117
Barry, John 137

Barry, Phillip 203, 218
Barry, Phyllis 92
Barrymore, Diana 97
Barrymore, Ethel 42
Barrymore, John 40
Barrymore, Lionel 142
Barthelmess, Richard 34
Barty, Billy 107
Basehart, Richard 150
Baskerville, Charles 87
Batman 170
Baum, Vicki 121
Bautzer, Greg 238
Baxter, Anne 44, 181
Baxter, Warner 102, 106
The Beast with Five Fingers 123, 124
Beau James 221
Beckman, Henry 13, 14
Beery, Wallace 232
Behind the Makeup 89
Behold My Wife 193
Behrman, S.N. 80
Bell, Monta 88
Bellamann, Henry 23
Bellamy, Ralph 214
The Bells of St. Mary's (TV production) 81, 82
Ben Casey ("A Cardinal of Mercy" episode) 82
Benchley, Robert 149
Bendix, William 11
Bennett, Bruce 43, 124, 164, 234
Bennett, Constance 231
Bennett, Dorothy 118
Bennett, Joan 12, 81, 116
Bennett, Michael 222
Benny, Jack 97, 138, 158, 199, 211, 217, 218
Bergman, Ingrid 27, 42, 199, 238
Bergner, Elisabeth 216
Berkeley, Busby 3, 6, 7, 35, 78, 93, 95, 96, 105–109, 113, 132, 146, 149, 195, 197, 230
Berlin, Irving 147
The Berlin Wall 69
Bernhardt, Curtis 25, 44, 61, 135, 184, 187, 198, 238
Bernsen, Corbin 188
The Best Little Whorehouse in Texas 223, 224
The Best Years of Our Lives 178
"Bette Davis Eyes" 49
Between Two Worlds 177, 178
Between Us Girls 97
Beware My Lovely 168
Bewitched 170
Beymer, Richard 239
Beyond the Forest 43
Bezzerides, A.I. 159, 198
Bianco, Solly 214
Biberman, Herbert 29
Bickford, Charles 90, 235
Big Business Girl 4
Big City Blues 5
The Big Knife 169
The Big Shakedown 35, 78
The Big Valley 170, 207

The Bigamist 168, 169, 171
Bigelow-Sanford Theatre 152
Billingsley, Jennifer 69
The Bird's Nest 185
Black Legion 193
Blackenstein 128
Blaine, Vivian 10
Blanke, Henry 57, 133
Blonde Crazy 5
Blonde Venus 93
Blondell Ed, Jr. 3
Blondell Ed, Sr. 3
Blondell, Gloria 3, 7
Blondell, Joan 1–18, 74, 78–80, 82, 92, 106–109, 113, 143, 193, 194, 231, 238
Blondell, Kathryn Cain 3
Blondie Johnson 6
Blue, Ben 125, 201, 202, 203
Blue, Jack 102
The Blue Veil 12, 238, 239
Blues in the Night 136
Blum, Edward 159
Blunt, Jerry 214
Blyth, Ann 126, 127, 143, 146
The Body Disappears 232
Bodyguard 138
Bogarde, Dirk 68, 221
Bogart, Humphrey 1, 7, 8, 36, 37, 79, 96, 132, 141, 143, 144, 160, 161, 180, 193, 197, 218, 219, 240
Bohnen, Roman 162
Boland, Mary 27, 163
Bolero 192
Boles, John 97, 159
Bolton, Charla 27, 28
Bolton, Grania 27–29
Bolton, Whitney 19, 26–29
Bolton, Whitney French 27
Bon Voyage 242
Bonanza 13
Bond, Anson 165
Bond, Ward 215
Bondi, Beulah 121
Boone, Richard 185
Booth, Shirley 45
Bordertown 35, 159
Borgnine, Ernest 48
Boris Karloff's Thriller 170
Born to Be Bad 151
Born Yesterday 44, 181
Borzage, Frank 78, 108
The Boswell Sisters 141
Bourbon Street Beat 127
Bow, Clara 89
Bowie, David 128
Boy Meets Girl 119
Boyd, Stephen 29
Boyer, Charles 39, 61, 127, 161, 169, 216
Bracken's World 187
Brackett, Charles 45, 61, 64
Brady, Patti 179
Branded 152
Brent, George 7, 11, 24, 37–40, 58, 76, 81, 92, 93, 95, 106, 138, 196–199, 204, 214, 232

Brian, David 43
Brian, Mary 77, 78, 80, 89
Brice, Fanny 104
Bricker, George 96
The Bride Came C.O.D. 40
Brief Moment 80
British Agent 93
Broadway 33
Broadway Bad 6
Broadway Gondolier 7
The Broadway Melody 8
Broadway Musketeers 194
Broadway Through a Keyhole 108
Brodel, Agnes 141–143
Brodel, Betty 141, 142
Brodel, John 141, 142
Brodel, Mary 141, 142
Broken Dishes 33
Brolin, James 49
Bromfield, Louis 196
Brook, Clive 90
Brooks, Rand 39, 128, 143, 195
Brophy, Edward 232
Brother Rat 133, 135
Brother Rat and a Baby 135, 232
Brown, Clarence 234
Brown, Joe E. 7, 57, 78, 94, 230
Brown, Tom 158
Bruce, George 181
Bruce, Virginia 8, 126
Bryan, Jane 38–40, 94, 231
Buccaneer's Girl 126
Buchholz, Horst 47
Buck Privates 232
Bullets or Ballots 7
Bullock, Walter 150
Bunny O'Hare 48
Bureau of Missing Persons 35, 78
Burgess, Dorothy 104
Burke's Law 13
Burns, Robert E. 76
Burnt Offerings 48
Burstyn, Ellen 128
Burton, Richard 67
Busses Roar 176
Butler, David 125, 199
Butterfield, Roger 177
Buzzell, Eddie 103
Bye, Bye Birdie 47
Bye, Bye Bonnie 104
Byington, Spring 61

Caan, James 69
Cabin in the Cotton 34, 35
Cabot, Bruce 98
Cactus Flower 222
Cady, Larry 97
Caesar, Arthur 97
Caesar, Irving 113
Caged 175, 180, 181
Cagney, James 1, 4–6, 57, 61, 80, 95, 107, 108, 134, 135, 145, 146, 162, 187, 194–196
Cagney, Jeanne 146
Cain, James M. 204
Caldwell, Ellen 152
Caldwell, Patrice 152

Caldwell, Dr. William 151, 152
Calhern, Louis 33
Call Me Madam 12
Call It a Day 58
Callahan, Christopher 128
Callahan, Deborah Ann Willis 127, 128
Callahan, Drew 128
Callahan, Kate 128
Callahan, Tim 128
Camille 142
Campos, Rafael 69
Candida (1926 Stuart Walker production) 87
Candida (1952 Broadway production) 67
Canova, Judy 151
Cantor, Eddie 105, 148, 230
Capra, Frank 46, 77, 120, 136, 186, 216, 220, 221, 237
Captain Blood 57, 58
Captain from Castile 11
Captains of the Clouds 162
Car 99 193
Carefree 110
Carey, Harry, Jr. 49
Carey, Macdonald 151
Carlson, Richard 195, 238
Carmen 213
Carmen Jones 185
Carnes, Kim 49
Carney, Art 13, 188
Carriage Entrance 205
Carroll, Earl 195
Carroll, Georgia 214
Carroll, Nancy 89
Carson, Jack 122, 136, 145, 147, 150, 162, 199, 200, 203, 215, 217, 218, 232, 233
Carson, Robert 159
The Case of the Howling Dog 35
Casey's Shadow 223
Castle on the Hudson 196
The Cat and the Canary 214
The Catered Affair 46
Catlett, Walter 104, 231
Caulfield, Maxwell 128
Cavalcade 106
Cave of Outlaws 220
Center Door Fancy 14
Central Airport 77
Central Park 6
Chain Lightning 180
Chambers, Whitman 123
The Champ 14
Chandler, Harry 145
Chapman, Anne Douglas McKee 117, 128
Chapman, Marguerite 214
Chapman, Richard 128
The Charge of the Light Brigade 58
Charley's Aunt 97
Charlie's Angels 152, 171, 188, 242
The Chase 150
Chatterton, Ruth 34, 89, 91–93, 98
Chayefsky, Paddy 46
Checkmate 186

Cheers 224
Chevalier, Maurice 89, 187
Cheyenne 234
The Children 89
Christmas Eve 11
Ciannelli, Eduardo 37
The Cincinnati Kid 13
Cinderella Jones 149
City for Conquest 196, 197
City Without Men 81
Claire, Ina 5
Clark, Dane 43, 121, 164
Clarke, Mae 34
Clemens, Paul 183, 186, 187
Clemens, Paul, Jr. 186
Clemens, Richard 179
Clemens, Sharon 179
Clemens, Susan 179
Cleopatra 158
Clift, Montgomery 66, 118–120
Clifton, Elmer 165
The Clock 177
Cobra 76
Coburn, Charles 23, 41, 199, 216
Cochran, Steve 169, 206
Coco, James 223
The Cocoanuts 89
Coffee, Lenore 24, 133
Cohan, George M. 103, 131, 135, 145, 146
Cohan, Mary 145, 146
Cohn, Harry 81, 159, 161, 165
Colbert, Claudette 35, 81, 94
Coleman, Barbara 19, 21
Coleman, Charles 19, 20
Coleman, Grace (Sharplass) 19, 21
Coleman, Nancy 2, 19–30, 63, 82, 116, 163, 199
Coles, Mildred
Colleen 7, 109
Collins, Dorothy 222
Collins, Joan 81, 188, 206
Collins, Wilkie 180, 219
Colman, Ronald 60, 81, 89, 159
The Color of Evening 128
Columbo 127
Columbo, Russ 108
Come Back Little Sheba (film) 45
Come Back Little Sheba (play) 12
Come On Marines 157
Comet Over Broadway 38, 95, 96
Confession 94
Conflict 218
Connecting Rooms 48
Connolly, Bobby 109
Conroy, Frank 33
The Constant Nymph 148, 211, 216, 220, 224
Convention City 6
Conway, Tom 150
Cook, Donald 34
Cooper, Gary 40, 89, 120, 144, 145, 156, 204
Cooper, Gladys 41
Copper and Brass 13
Corey, Jeff 69
Corey, Wendell 220

The Corn Is Green 42, 48, 116, 123, 148
Cornell, Katherine 67, 87, 131
The Corpse Came C.O.D. 11
Cortez, Ricardo 93, 233
Corwin, Norman 238
Costello, Johnny "Irish" 104, 108
Costello, Lou 232
Cotten, Joseph 43, 70
Coulouris, George 121
The Count of Monte Cristo 57
The Country Girl 240
Cousins, Margaret 241
Cowan, Jerome 233
Cowan, Lester 161
The Cowboy from Brooklyn 132, 194
Cowl, Jane 94
Crabbe, Larry "Buster" 156, 192
Craig, David 222
Craig, James 151
Crain, Jeanne 141
Crane, Cheryl 48
Crawford, Broderick 232
Crawford, Joan 2, 31, 47, 48, 69, 70, 200, 219, 238
Crazy October 13
Crews, Laura Hope 33
Crime 88
Crime by Night 177, 233
Cromwell, John 35, 89, 90, 96, 181
The Crooner 230
Crosby, Bing 8, 79, 112, 137, 150, 200, 221, 237, 238
The Cross of Lorraine 25
Crothers, Rachel 22, 88
Crouse, Russell 81
The Crowd Roars (1932) 5, 195
The Crowd Roars (1938) 231
The Crusades 193
Cry Havoc 9
Cukor, George 33, 59–61, 67, 90
Culver, Roland 64
Cummings, Constance 108
Cummings, Jack 184
Cummings, Robert 12, 23, 63, 97, 137, 197, 232
Curtiz, Michael 6, 34, 35, 58, 59, 77, 92, 122, 133, 146, 147, 160, 170, 176, 194, 236, 239
Cutting, Julianna 87
Cynara 92

Daddy's Gone A-Hunting 128
Dahl, Arlene 116, 125
Dailey, Dan 206
Dall, John 42
Dallas 224
Dames 7, 108
A Damsel in Distress 110
Dangerous 36, 44
Dangerous Curves 89
Dangerously They Live 20, 23, 24
Daniell, Henry 122
Daniels, Bebe 92, 102, 106
Danson, Ted 224
Dantine, Helmut 19, 25, 116, 122, 123, 164, 199

Darby's Rangers 127
The Dark at the Top of the Stairs 12
Dark Hazard 78
Dark Love 164
The Dark Mirror 54, 64, 65, 69
The Dark Secret of Harvest Home 48
Dark Victory 37, 38, 96, 216
D'Arrast, Harry d'Abbadie 89
Darwell, Jane 144
da Silva, Howard 136
Dassin, Jules 45
Daughters Courageous 118, 130, 134
Daves, Delmer 95, 121, 177, 200
Davies, Joseph 176
Davis, Barbara (Bobbie) 31, 33, 36, 46
Davis, Bette 1–3, 5, 6, 31–54, 58, 60, 62, 63, 69, 70, 78, 80, 92, 95, 96, 102, 116, 120, 121, 123, 132, 133, 135, 143, 155, 159, 162, 163, 177–179, 191, 193, 195, 196, 198, 204, 211, 216, 219, 220, 224
Davis, Harlow Morrell 31, 36
Davis, Joan 231
Davis, Ossie 29
Davis, Ruth Favor 31–33, 35, 36, 43, 45, 46
Day, Clarence 119
Day, Doris 2, 92, 180
The Dead End Kids 194, 195
Dead on the Money 188
Dead Ringer 47
Dear Brutus 20
A Death in California 224
Death of a Man 68
Death on the Nile 48
De Camp, Rosemary 146, 203
De Carlo, Yvonne 127, 167, 222
Deception 43
The Decision of Christopher Blake 220
Deep Valley 164, 179
Deering, Olive 180
DeFore, Don 145
de Havilland, Olivia 1, 2, 25–27, 31, 40, 48, 54–73, 135, 145, 163, 171, 191, 195, 211, 219, 232, 235
de Havilland, Walter 54, 55
de Liagre, Alfred 179
Delilah 65
Del Rio, Dolores 93
Demarest, William 230
De Mille, Cecil B. 158, 193
Dempsey, Jack 103
Denas, Ruth 201
Dern, Bruce 69
de Rochemont, Louis 119
Desk Set 12
The Desperate Hours 28
Desperate Journey 25
The Detective Story 182
The Devil's Rain 170
Devotion 25–27, 63, 64, 163, 171
Dexter, Anthony 181
Dial 1119 126
Dieterle, William 38, 57, 91
Dietrich, Marlene 1, 93, 236, 237

di Frasso, Countess 95, 96
Diggins, Peggy 214
Diller, Barry 223
Dillingham, Charles 104
Dinehart, Alan 80, 91
Dinelli, Mel 168, 185
The Disappearance of Aimee 48
The Disorderly Orderly 82
Dive Bomber 61, 214, 215
Divided Honors 76
Divorce 98
Dixon, Lee 110
Doctor Monica 93
Dr. Quinn, Medicine Woman 243
Doctor Socrates 96
Dodd, Claire 107
Dodge City 59, 195
Doll Face 10
Don Juan Quilligan 11
Donat, Robert 57
The Donna Reed Show 127, 170
Donnelly, Ruth 5
Double Indemnity 116
The Doughgirls 200, 217, 233
Douglas, Gordon 121
Douglas, Kirk 28, 182, 223, 224, 237, 238, 240
Douglas, Lloyd C. 240
Douglas, Melvyn 8, 76, 168
Dove, Billie 89
Doyle, Laird 36
Dragnet 127
Drake, Betsy 205
Drake, Charles 215
Drake, William 159
Draper, Paul 109
Drayton, Katherine 94
Dress Gray 224
Dressler, Marie 232
Dubin, Al 107
Duel in the Sun 43
Duff, Bridget Mirella 168, 171
Duff, Howard 166–171
Duke, Vernon 45
du Maurier, Daphne 67
Dumbrille, Douglas 93
Dunaway, Faye 48
Duncan, Isadora 116, 117
Dunn, James 10
Dunne, Irene 239, 240
Durante, Jimmy 141, 198, 232
Durbin, Deanna 97
Durkin, Junior 118
Dust Be My Destiny 134
Dvorak, Ann 5
Dwan, Allan 156

Eagels, Jeanne 36
"Earl Carroll Vanities" 136
The Earl of Warwick 195
The Earth Between 33
East Side of Heaven 8
Eaton, Mary 89, 104
Edge of Darkness 19, 25, 199
The Edge of Night 28
Edwards, Gus 131
Edwards, Jack 213

Edwards, Ralph 222
The Effect of Gamma Rays on Man-in-the-Moon Marigolds 14
Egan, Richard 152
Einfeld, Charles 26, 194
Eisner, Michael 223
Eldredge, John 36
The Eleventh Hour 186
Elizabeth the Queen 39
Elmer the Great (film) 230
Elmer the Great (play) 88
Elsie the Cow 97
Elsom, Isobel 161
Emerson, Faye 2, 122, 146, 177
Emerson, Hope 180
Emery, Catherine 159
Emery, John 180, 220
The Empty Canvas 47
Enright, Ray 5, 108, 232
Epstein, Julius 133
Erickson, Leif 46, 65
Erwin, Stuart 5, 230
Escape from Fort Bravo 183
Escape in the Desert 122
Escape Me Never 164, 179
Esmond, Carl 97
Esmond, Irwin 133
The Eternal Sea 221
Ethan Frome 116, 123
Etting, Ruth 135
Evans, Joan 168
Evans, Madge 5
Ever Since Venus 81
Every Frenchman Has One 69
Ex-Lady 35
Eye of the Cat 187
Eyer, Richard 206

Fabray, Nanette 222
The Failing of Raymond 242
Fairbanks, Douglas, Jr. 5
Falcon Crest 242, 243
Falk, Peter 127
The Fallen Sparrow 148
The False Madonna 90
Family Affair 13, 127, 170
Family Reunion 48
The Famous Ferguson Case 5
The Famous Mrs. Fair 33
Fantasy Island 14, 188
Farmer, Frances 20
Farnsworth, Arthur 40, 42
Farnum, Franklyn 103
Farrell, Charles (actor) 193
Farrell, Charles (father of Glenda) 74, 75
Farrell, Dick 74, 81
Farrell, Eileen 184
Farrell, Gene 74, 81
Farrell, Glenda 1, 2, 5–7, 29, 74–85, 193, 228, 230, 231
Farrell, Tommy 6, 75–78, 80–83
Farrell, Wilhelmina "Minnie" 74–76
Farrow, John 96
Fashions of 1934 35
Father Knows Best 169

Father of the Bride 151
Favor, Dr. Paul 31
Fawcett, Farrah 188
Faye, Alice 49, 98, 102, 195, 230, 231
Fehmiu, Bekhim 70
Feldman, Charles K. 164, 166, 168
Fellini, Federico 187
The Feminine Touch 97
Fenwick, Peg 241
Ferber, Edna 34, 198, 239
Ferrer, Jose 233
Ferrer, Mel 182, 205
Fey, Larry 103
Field, Betty 23, 40, 136, 197
Field, Rachel 39
Field, Sally 187
Field, Virginia 150
Fields, Joseph 200, 217
Fields, W.C. 156
The Fifth Musketeer 70
Fight for Your Lady 159
Fighting Youth 193
Finkel, Abem 145
Finkelhoffe, Fred 231
The Fireball 179
Fireside Theater 127, 152, 241
First Lady 94
Fiscus, Kathy 181
Fitzgerald, Geraldine 2, 24
Fitzmaurice, George 89
Fleming, Rhonda 222
Fleming, Victor 60, 234
Flight Angels 61, 232
Flight Nurse 151
Flirtation Walk 108, 109
Florey, Robert 23, 24, 123
Fly Away Home 118, 119, 134
Flynn, Errol 1, 7, 8, 22, 25, 38, 39, 54, 58–62, 119, 120, 123, 133, 144, 146, 158, 164, 169, 171, 179, 182, 194, 195, 199, 204, 211, 214, 215, 217, 218, 220, 221
Fog Over Frisco 35
Follies 222
Fonda, Henry 37, 62, 68, 69, 145
Fonda, Jane 82
Fontaine, George M. 55
Fontaine, Joan 40, 55, 59, 62, 65, 70, 110, 148, 151, 168, 216
Fontaine, Lilian Ruse de Havilland 54–55, 70
Food of the Gods 170
Foolish Follies 103
Fools for Scandal 231
Footlight Parade 6, 107–109
Footlight Serenade 232
The Footloose Heiress 194
For Heaven's Sake 12
Foran, Dick 193
Ford, Glenn 43, 165, 184
Ford, Wallace 6
Ford Theater 152
Foreign Correspondent 137, 143
Forever and a Day 162
Forrest, Sally 165, 166, 168
Forrest, Steve 239

Forster, Robert 14
Forty Carats (Broadway production) 82
Forty Carats (Los Angeles production) 188
42nd Street 6, 7, 26, 34, 78, 92, 102, 106, 109, 114
Foster, Preston 94
The Fountainhead 220
Four Daughters 95, 130, 133–135
Four for Texas 47
Four Jills in a Jeep (book) 98
Four Jills in a Jeep (film) 98
Four Jills in a Jeep (USO tour) 86, 97, 98
Four Star Playhouse 169
Four Star Theater 127
Four Wives 135
Four's a Crowd 59
Fowler, Gene 26
Fowley, Douglas 207
Fox, Sidney 33
Foy, Bryan 95
Francen, Victor 124
Frances 20
Francis, Arlene 81
Francis, James Dwight 87
Francis, Kay 1, 2, 33, 80, 86–102, 196
Frankenstein 34
Franklin, Sidney 234
Franz, Arthur 151
Frawley, William 104, 125
Freeman, Edward 232
Freund, Karl 194
Friedlob, Bert 44, 179, 182, 183
Frings, Ketti 61
Frisco, Joe 103
Front Page Woman 36
Fulks, Emme Riese 228, 229
Fulks, Richard 228, 229
Fun on a Weekend 138
Furthman, Jules 11
Futterman, Myron 230, 231

Gabin, Jean 162
Gable, Clark 11, 60, 61, 76, 127, 185, 220
Gachet, Alice 156
Galante, Gisele 68, 71
Galante, Pierre 68, 69, 71
Gallagher, Helen 113
Gallagher, Skeets 89, 104
The Gambler, the Nun and the Radio 186
Gambling on the High Seas 232
Gambling Ship 77
Gang, Martin 63
Garbo, Greta 80, 141, 185, 186, 223, 238
Gardiner, Reginald 198, 203
Gardner, Ava 167, 182, 205
Gardner, Ed 165
Garfield, John 23, 24, 40, 95, 118, 133–135, 148, 160, 161, 168, 177, 178, 196
Garner, James 127
Garner, Peggy Ann 10

Garnett, Tay 8, 91
Garson, Greer 11, 41, 184
Garts, Crane 103
Gaslight 42, 219
Gaston, Bill 87
Gaudio, Tony 59
The Gay Desperado 158
The Gay Sisters 19, 24
Gaynor, Charles 113
Genn, Leo 28, 65
The Gentle People 160
Gentleman Jim 215
Gentlemen of the Press 88
George, Gladys 135
George Washington Slept Here 199
Geray, Steven 122
Gershwin, George 149
Gershwin, Ira 149
Gettman, Lorraine 214
The Ghost Camera 156
Gibbs, Joseph Sprague 86
Gibbs, Katharine Clinton 86
A Gift of Time 68–70
Gilbert, Edwin 136, 232
Gilford, Jack 113
The Girl from Tenth Avenue 36
The Girl in the Red Velvet Swing 81
Girl Missing 77
Girls About Town 90, 92
Gish, Lillian 49, 119, 161
Give Me Your Heart 94
Glasgow, Ellen 40, 62
The Glass Key 193
The Glass Menagerie 237
Gleason, Jackie 197, 232
Gleason, James 192
The Glenn Miller Story 240
Go Into Your Dance 79, 109
Go to Jericho 155
God Is My Co-Pilot 122–124
Goddard, Paulette 61, 230
Godfrey, Peter 122, 164, 179, 180, 203, 218, 219, 233
God's Country and the Woman 36
God's Gift to Women 4
Gold Diggers of 1933 6, 106, 107, 109
Gold Diggers of 1935 78, 79, 109
Gold Diggers of 1937 7, 79, 230
Gold Is Where You Find It 58
Golden, John 22
The Golden Arrow 36
Goldwyn, Samuel 5, 33, 40, 60, 89, 92, 230
Gone with the Wind 36–38, 59–61, 71, 135, 187
Good Girls Go to Paris 8
Good Sam 204
Goodbye Again 6, 197
Goodbye My Fancy 98
Goodis, David 204
Goodrich, Benjamin 66–68, 71
Goodrich, Marcus 65, 67, 68
The Goose and the Gander 93
Gordon, Michael 166
Gordon, Ruth 25, 199
Goulding, Edmund 11, 38, 39, 148, 177, 178, 182, 216, 219

Government Girl 63
Grable, Betty 98, 148, 216, 230, 232
Grady, Billy 104, 105
Graham, Howard "Hap" 98
Graham, Martha 33
Grahame, Gloria 68
Grand Hotel 5, 106, 121
Grand Slam 77
Granger, Stewart 182
Granlund, Nils Thor 103
Grant, Cary 81, 96, 136, 137, 156, 204, 205, 218, 219
Granville, Bonita 41
Grauman, Sid 107
Graves, Peter 127
Gravet, Fernand 7
Gray, Coleen 11
Grease 14
The Great American Beauty Contest 187
The Great Garrick 58
The Great Lie 40
The Great Mr. Nobody 144
The Great O'Malley 193
The Greatest Love 3
The Greeks Had a Word for It 90
The Greeks Had a Word for Them 5
Green, Guy 68
The Green Hat 87
Greenstreet, Sydney 25, 177, 180, 218–220
Greenwich Village Follies 131
Greer, Jane 116
Grenecker, C.P. 118
Grizzard, George 82
Growing Pains 118
Guest, Helen 102
Guilty Hands 90
Guinan, Texas 26, 103, 108
Guinness, Alec 46
Gunn, James 204
Gunsmoke 46, 207
Gwenn, Edmund 12, 177, 178

Haas, Hugo 185
Haglund, Oren 133, 137
Hailey, Arthur 49
Hale, Alan 59, 122, 160, 215, 232
Hale, Dorothy 92
Haley, Jack 197
Hall, Alexander 239
Hallelujah, I'm a Bum 106
Haller, Ernest 37
Halliday, John 92
Hamilton, George 68, 186, 223
Hamilton, Patrick 119
Hamlet (Horace Liveright's modern dress production) 87
Hammond, Thomas 67
Hanline, Maurice 158
Hannagan, Steve 204
Hans Brinker 187
Happy Birthday 12
Happy Days 89
Harbach, Otto 113
Hard, Fast and Beautiful 167
Hard to Get 59

The Hard Way 146, 147, 149, 152, 155, 162–164, 167
Harding, Ann 4, 149, 176, 203
Harding, June 170
Hardwicke, Cedric 162
Hardy, Myrtle 191
Harlow, Jean 195
Harriman, Averill 11
Harris, Elmer 235
Harris, Julie 82
Hart, Deborah 116, 117
Hart, George 116, 117
Hart, Lovinia Belle 116–118
Hart, Moss 40, 199
Havana Widows 6, 78
Have Gun, Will Travel 170
Haver, June 149, 216
Hawaiian Eye 127
Hawks, Howard 5, 144, 145, 204, 205
Hayden, Sterling 44, 151, 206, 221, 239
Hayes, Gabby 81
Hayes, Helen 131, 222
Haymes, Dick 98
Hayward, Leland 98, 159
Hayward, Louis 14, 150, 158, 159, 161–163
Hayworth, Rita 148, 195, 197
He Couldn't Say No 231
He Was Her Man 7
Heading for Heaven 81
Heat Lightning 78
Heath, Edward 70
Hecht, Ben 125
Heckart, Eileen 98
Hedren, Tippi 128
Heflin, Van 97, 133
The Heiress 54, 66, 67
Hellgate 151
Hellinger, Mark 159, 160, 162, 200
Hellman, Lillian 40, 41
Hell's House 34
Hemingway, Ernest 186
Hendrix, Wanda 125, 126
Henreid, Paul 25, 27, 41, 43, 48, 163, 177, 178, 219
Hepburn, Katharine 12, 111, 141
Her First Affaire 156
Her Sister's Secret 27
Herbert, Hugh 5, 7, 74, 79, 80, 108, 109
Here Come the Brides 13
Here Comes Mr. Jordan 217
Here Comes the Groom 220, 221, 237, 238
Here's Love 222
Heston, Charlton 183, 241
Hi Nellie! 78
Hickman, Darryl 220
Hicks, Cora Bell 130–132, 139
High School 143
High Sierra 125, 143, 144, 155, 160
High Tension 79
Hirsch, Raymond N. 187
Hitchcock, Alfred 64, 136, 137, 143, 168, 236, 237
The Hitch-Hiker 168, 171

Hively, Jack 143
Hobart, Rose 218
Hodges, Eddie 186
Hoffman, Charles 179
Hold Back the Dawn 61, 62, 64
Hold On to Your Hat 111
Holden, William 183, 221
A Hole in the Head 186
Holiday for Lovers 242
Holliday, Judy 44, 181
Hollywood Canteen 42, 121, 148, 163, 177, 200, 217, 233
Hollywood Hotel 79
The Hollywood Palace 70
Hollywood Playhouse 79
The Hollywood Revue of 1929 89
Holm, Celeste 44, 48, 164
Holm, John Cecil 7
Home for the Holidays 187
Home from the Hill 186
The Hometowners 135
Honeymoon for Three 197, 232
Hope, Bob 112, 126, 150, 214, 221, 242
Hope, Dolores 112
Hopkins, Arthur 76
Hopkins, Miriam 31, 37, 39, 41, 62, 66, 90–92, 177, 214
Hopper, Jerry 81
Hopper, William 230
The Horn Blows at Midnight 217, 218
Hornblow, Arthur 65
Horne, Lena 164
Horner, Harry 168
Horton, Edward Everett 232
Hot Nocturne 136
Hotel 49
Hotel Berlin 116, 121–123
Hothouses 224
A House Divided 37
House of Wax 184
The House on 56th Street 92
Housewife 35
How to Commit Marriage 242
Howard, Hannah 138, 139
Howard, James 138, 139
Howard, Jennifer 139
Howard, Joe 132, 138, 139
Howard, Joseph 137–139
Howard, Judith 138, 139
Howard, Leslie 8, 35–37, 58, 60, 93, 203, 219
Howard, Sidney 5, 156
Howe, James Wong 23
Hubbard, Lucien 5
Hudson, Rock 186, 240, 241
Hughes, Glenn 20
Hughes, Howard 38, 60, 112, 151, 152, 158, 166–168, 205
Huie, William Bradford 152
Hull, Henry 28
Hull, Josephine 137
Humberstone, Bruce 186
Hunt, J. Roy 34
Hunt, Marsha 9
Hunter, Ian 58, 93–95
Hunter, Kim 12, 45, 46, 222

Hunter, Ross 240
Hurrell, George 194
Hurst, Fannie 133
Hush ... Hush Sweet Charlotte 48, 69, 70
Hussey, Ruth 98, 151
Huston, John 40, 54, 62, 145, 204
Huston, Walter 25, 88–90, 92, 97, 146, 176, 177, 199
Hutton, Robert 148, 149, 200
Hyman, Ashley 48
Hyman, Barbara Davis (B.D.) Sherry 43, 45, 48, 49
Hyman, Jeremy 48
Hymer, Warren 91

I Am a Fugitive from a Chain Gang 76, 134
I Found Stella Parish 93, 94
I Lived with You 156
I Love a Mystery 170
I Love Trouble 81
I Want a Divorce (film) 8
I Want a Divorce (radio program) 8, 9
I Was a Male War Bride 204, 205
I Was a Shoplifter 126
I Was a Spy 186
Illicit 4
Illusion 89
In Caliente 79
In Name Only 96
In Our Time 27, 163
In This Our Life 40, 41, 62
The Incredible Journey of Dr. Meg Laurel 242
Indianapolis Speedway 195
Inevitable Grace 128
An Informal Evening with Bette Davis 48
Inge, William 222
Inman, Evelyn Yates 117
Intermezzo 27
Interrupted Melody 175, 184, 185
The Irish in Us 57
Irving, Amy 71
It All Came True 196
It Happened One Night 35, 36, 40, 108
It's a Date 97
It's a Great Feeling 180, 236
It's Love I'm After 37, 58
Ivanhoe 183
I've Got Your Number 7, 78

Jackson, Joseph 91
Jackson, Sherry 206
Jackson, Shirley 185
Jacqueline Susann's Once Is Not Enough 223
Jaffe, Rona 187
Jane Wyman Presents see *Fireside Theater*
The Jane Wyman Theater see *Fireside Theater*
Janie 149
Janie Gets Married 149

Janssen, David 223
Jarman, Claude, Jr. 234
Jarrico, Paul 165
Jason, Sybil 93, 94
Jealousy 43
Jenkins, Allen 5
Jenkinson, Judy 170
Jennifer 168
Jewel Robbery 91, 92
Jewison, Norman 13
Jezebel 37–39
Jimmy the Gent 35
John Paul Jones 46
Johnny Belinda 66, 164, 179, 228, 235, 236
Johnny Eager 81
Johns, John A. 201, 203
Johnson, Kay 90
Johnson, Van 237, 241
Jolson, Al 4, 79, 93, 104–106, 108, 109, 111, 112
Jolson, Al, Jr. 108, 109, 111, 112
The Jolson Story 112
Jones, Henry 12
Jones, Jennifer 151
Joseph, Robert 168
Joslyn, Allyn 136
Jowitt, Sir William 36, 37
Juarez 38, 96
Jubilee Trail 152
Juke Girl 162, 198, 199
June Bride 43
Junior Bonner 170
Jurgens, Curt 221
Just Across the Street 206
Just for You 238

Kandel, Aben 196
Kane, Helen 89
Kanin, Garson 68
Kansas City Princess 7, 78
Karger, Fred 239, 242
Karger, Terry 239
Karloff, Boris 137
Kaufman, George S. 9, 40, 94, 199
Kaus, Gina 181
Kazan, Elia 10, 67
Keel, Howard 237
Keeler, Anna May 102
Keeler, Bill 102
Keeler, Elnora 102, 105
Keeler, Gertrude 102, 105, 113
Keeler, Helen 102, 105
Keeler, Margie 102
Keeler, Ralph 102, 105
Keeler, Ruby 2, 6, 7, 14, 79, 102–115, 148
Keighley, William 93, 134, 196, 231
Keith, Brian 45
Kellogg, Virginia 180
Kelly, Gene 182
Kelly, George 4
Kelly, Grace 240
Kelly, Mark 97
Kelly, Nancy 22
Kelly, Patsy 103, 114
Kelly, Paul 45, 98, 108

Kennedy, Arthur 25, 197, 237
Kennedy, Margaret 179, 216
Kern, James V. 200, 219
Keyes, Evelyn 62, 112
The Keyhole 77, 92
Kibbee, Guy 5–7, 74, 77, 80, 106, 108
The Kid from Kokomo 8, 231
The Kid from Spain 230
Kid Galahad 37, 144, 214
Kid Nightingale 231
Kilbride, Percy 199
The Killing of Sister George 48
Kind Sir 206
King, Andrea 1, 2, 116–129, 177
King, Charles 193
The King and Four Queens 185
The King and the Chorus Girl 7, 230
King Klondyke 155
King of Burlesque 230
King of the Underworld 96
King Solomon's Mines 182
Kings Row 19, 22–24, 40, 161, 162, 191, 197, 198
Kingsley, Sidney 182
Kinnell, Murray 34
Kipling, Rudyard 159
A Kiss in the Dark 236
Kissin' Cousins 82
Kitty Foyle 39, 136
Kleefeld, Travis 239
Klondike Kate 81
Knapp, Evelyn 4
Knebel, Fletcher 187
Knights of the Round Table 183
Knowles, Patric 58, 178
Knox, Alexander 160
Koch, Howard 145
Kona Coast 13
Korngold, Erich Wolfgang 23, 59
Koster, Henry 67
Kramer, Stanley 68
Krasna, Norman 63, 68, 206
Kristofferson, Kris 114
Kruger, Otto 98, 240
Krupa, Gene 81
Kyser, Kay 232

La Centra, Peg 164
Ladd, Alan 68
Ladd, David 68
Laddie 143
Ladies in Retirement 161
Ladies Man 90
Ladies Must Live 135
Ladies They Talk About 78
The Lady and the Mob 159
Lady for a Day 46, 77
Lady for a Night 9
Lady in a Cage 69
Lady in the Lake 125
The Lady Takes a Sailor 236
The Lady with Red Hair 214
Laemmle, Carl, Jr. 33, 34
Lamarr, Hedy 1, 195
Lamour, Dorothy 14, 81, 150
Lancaster, Burt 224
Lanchester, Elsa 161

Index

Landa, Mary 201, 202
Landau, Martin 128
Landis, Carole 97, 98
Lane, Leota 130, 131, 133
Lane, Lola (Dorothy) 79, 118, 130–133
Lane, Martha 130
Lane, Priscilla 1, 2, 61, 118, 130–140, 194, 196, 231
Lane, Rosemary 118, 130–133
Lang, Walter 12
Langner, Armina 65
Langner, Lawrence 65
Lansbury, Angela 222
Larceny Inc. 232
Lardner, Ring 88
Lasky, Jesse 158
The Last Hurrah 177
The Last of Mrs. Cheyney 98
The Last Ride 177
Laughton, Charles 156, 238
Lauritz, Sarah 22
The Law in Her Hands 79
Lawrence, Gertrude 22, 198, 237
Lawrence, Marjorie 175, 184, 185
Lawrence, Vincent 215
Lawyer Man 6
Layton, Joe 224
Leachman, Cloris 81
Lederer, Charles 125
Lederer, Francis 158
Lee, Gypsy Rose 9, 10
Leeds, Andrea 194
Le Gallienne, Eva 33
Leigh, Janet 182
Leigh, Vivien 38, 60, 61, 67, 69, 156, 159, 182, 238
Leighton, Margaret 46, 47
Leisen, Mitchell 61, 64, 193
LeMay, Alan 151
The Lemon Drop Kid 126, 127
LeRoy, Mervyn 5, 76, 107
Leslie, Joan 1, 2, 141–154, 160, 162, 200, 218
Let Us Be Gay 98
Let's Do It Again 239
Let's Get Married 158
Let's Go Native 89, 90
The Letter 39, 40, 204
A Letter of Introduction 194
A Letter to Three Wives 181
The Letters 170
Levien, Sonya 185
Lewis, David 23
Lewis, Jerry 82
Libel 68
The Light That Failed 159
Life Begins (film) 76
Life Begins (play) 76
Life Begins at 8:30 162
The Life of Jimmy Dolan 134
The Life of Lucy Gallant 241
Life of Mother Superior 170
The Life of Reilly 81
Life with Father 119, 161
Light in the Piazza 68
Linden, Eric 5

Lindsay, Earl 103, 104
Lindsay, Howard 81, 98
Lindsay, Margaret 2, 27, 35
Lindsay, William 11
The Linguine Incident 128
Litel, John 160
Little Big Shot 79
Little Caesar 76, 135, 160
The Little Foxes 40, 163
The Little Girl Who Lives Down the Lane 223
Little Gloria, Happy at Last 49
Little Man, What Now? 108
Little Men 97
Little Women 74
Litvak, Anatole 38, 39, 65, 66, 136, 161
Living on Velvet 93
Lizzie 12, 185
Loder, John 156
Loftus, Claire 70
Logan, Joshua 48
Lombard, Carole 90, 96, 191, 195
London, Jack 160
The Lone Wolf Spy Hunt 159
The Lonely Life 46
Long, Lois 87
Long, Robert 206
The Long Haul 159
Lord, Robert 91
Lorre, Peter 122, 124,
Lorring, Joan 123, 148
Losee, Fred L. 177
The Lost Weekend 228, 233, 234
Loughton, Phyllis 65
Louise, Anita 2, 38, 193
Love Affair 142
Love and Learn 179
The Love Boat 14, 188, 242
Love, Honor and Behave 132
Love, Honor and Betray 76
The Love Machine 223
Love Me or Leave Me 135
Lovejoy, Frank 168, 181
Lowe, Christine 112
Lowe, John Homer 111, 112
Lowe, John, Jr. 112, 113
Lowe, Kathleen 112, 114
Lowe, Theresa 112
Loy, Myrna 65, 222
Lubitsch, Ernst 91
Luce, Clare Booth 206, 222
Lucky 104
Lucky Boy 76
The Lucy-Desi Comedy Hour 169
Lucy Gallant 241
The Lucy Show 13
Ludwig, William 185
Lulu Belle 81
Lunceford, Jimmy 136
Lund, John 64
Lupino, Arthur 155
Lupino, Connie O'Shea 155, 158, 159, 169
Lupino, George Hook 155
Lupino, George Hook, Jr. ("Old George") 155, 156

Lupino, Harry 155
Lupino, Ida 2, 25–27, 63, 116, 121, 124, 125, 141, 143, 147, 155–174, 192, 220
Lupino, Rita 155, 156, 159, 171
Lupino, Stanley 155, 156, 159, 162, 163, 171
Luppino, Giorgio 155
Lured 150
Lust for Gold 165
Lux Radio Theatre 96
Lux Video Theatre 12, 63, 127, 152
Lydon, Jimmy 95, 97, 142, 142
Lynley, Carol 186, 242
Lynn, Diana 120, 146
Lynn, Jeffrey 61, 133, 135, 136, 196, 232
Lyons, Arthur 159

Macaulay, Richard 136, 161, 231
MacDonald, Jeanette 89, 103
Mackaill, Dorothy 4
MacKenna, Kenneth 90–93
MacLane, Barton 79, 109
MacMahon, Aline 2, 6, 80, 91, 106
MacMurray, Fred 61, 120, 148, 149, 182, 193, 214, 242
Mad at the World 169
Mad Love 124
Madame X 188
Madeleine 187
Madison Avenue 186
Maggie the Magnificent 4
Magic Town 234, 235
Magnani, Anna 185
Magnificent Obsession 240, 241
Make Me a Star 5
Make Your Own Bed 233
Malden, Karl 28
The Male Animal 62, 145
Malone, Dorothy 2
The Maltese Falcon 36
Maltin, Leonard 6, 8, 10
Maltz, Albert 178
Mame 222
The Man 168
The Man from U.N.C.L.E. 13
The Man I Love 116, 124, 164
The Man in the Iron Mask 158
Man in the Saddle 151
Man Wanted 91
The Man Who Came to Dinner 40, 198
The Man Who Lost Himself 97
The Man Who Played God 34
The Man with the Golden Arm 185
Manckiewicz, Joseph L. 44, 181
Mandalay 93
Mandel, Frank 113
Manhattan Latin 79
Manners, David 91
Manning, Bruce 44
Manon, Gloria 14
Manpower 214
A Man's Castle 78
Mansfield, Jayne 12
Many Rivers to Cross 184

Index

March, Fredric 58, 65, 89, 90, 217
Mark of the Renegade 127
Marked Woman 37, 132
Marlow-Trump, Nancy 112–114
Marlowe, Hugh 44
The Marriage Playground 89
Marshall, Brenda 135
Marshall, Herbert 39, 40, 91, 92
Martin, Mary 219
Martini, Nino 158
The Marx Brothers 89
Mary, Mary 222
Mary of Scotland 36
Mary Stevens M.D. 78, 92
Masquerade 81
Massen, Osa 197
Massey, Raymond 28, 122, 137
Match Game 207
Mate, Rudolph 241
La Maternelle 238
Maugham, W. Somerset 35, 39, 178
Maverick 127
Maxwell, Marilyn 127
May, Joe 94
Maybe I'll Come Home in the Spring 187
Mayer, Gerald 126
Mayfair, Mitzi 97, 98
Maynard, Kermit 193
Mayo, Archie 35, 94, 109
Mayo, Virginia 2, 238
Mazurka 94
McCarey, Leo 89, 204
McCord, Ted 235
McCoy, Horace 215
McCrea, Joel 90
McDaniel, Hattie 41
McDevitt, Ruth 207
McDowall, Roddy 171
McGavin, Darren 185
McGuire, Dorothy 10
McHugh, Frank 5, 7, 91, 133
McKay, Scott 206, 207
McKee, Douglas 117
McKenna, Siobbhan 13
McLaglen, Cyril 156
McLaughlin, Emily 171
McLeod, Norman Z. 97
McMartin, John 222
McNally, Stephen 166, 235
McQueen, Steve 170
The Meanest Man in the World 138
Meehan, John 88
Meek, Donald 33
Meet the People 10
Melton, James 193
Men Are Such Fools 132
Men with Wings 142
The Menace 34
Mendelssohn, Felix 57
Menjou, Adolphe 194
Mercer, Johnny 110, 136, 147
The Merchant of Venice 86
Mercouri, Melina 223
Mercury Theater on the Air 159
Meredith, Burgess 54
Merkel, Una 106

Merman, Ethel 9
Merrick, David 82
Merrill, Gary 44–46
Merrill, Margot 45
Merrill, Michael 45
Merry-Go-Round of 1938 110
The Merry Wives of Reno 78
Middle of the Night 81
A Midsummer Night's Dream (film) 56, 57
A Midsummer Night's Dream (Hollywood Bowl production) 56, 57, 67
A Midsummer Night's Dream (Saratoga Community Players production) 56
Mielziner, Leo 87
Miklejohn, Bill 193
Mildred Pierce 200
Miles, Jackie 201
Miles, Vera 170
Milestone, Lewis 25
Military Academy 143
The Milky Way 192
Milland, Ray 64, 233, 239
Miller, Ann 102
Miller, Marilyn 105
Miller, Marvin 127
Miller, Patsy Ruth 98
Millie 4
Million Dollar Baby 135, 136
A Millionaire for Christy 182
Mills, Hayley 170, 242
Milne, Peter 125
Mimieux, Yvette 68
Minnelli, Vincente 151, 177, 186
Miracle in the Rain 241
Miranda 126
Mirror, Mirror 98
Miss Moffat 48
Miss Pacific Fleet 7, 79
Miss Pinkerton 5
Miss Pinkerton Inc. 9
Missing Links 207
Mission to Moscow 176
Mr. Adams and Eve 169
Mr. Dodds Takes the Air 230
Mr. Peabody and the Mermaid 126
Mr. Pim Passes By 33
Mr. Skeffington 42, 120, 121, 123
Mitchell, Margaret 59, 61
Mitchell, Millard 9
Mitchell, Thomas 64, 118, 119, 135, 161
Mitchum, Robert 68, 186, 205
Mizner, Wilson 91
The Mod Squad 170
The Model and the Marriage Broker (TV pilot) 81
Model Wife 9
Moen, Etta 6
Mohr, Hal 57
Money and the Woman 135
Money for Speed 156, 158
Monks, John, Jr. 231
Monroe, Marilyn 240
Montana 220
Montgomery, George 81

Montgomery, Robert 28, 125
The Moon Is Down 25
Moontide 162
Moore, Colleen 239
Moore, Erin O'Brien 75
Moore, Victor 79
Moorehead, Agnes 180, 220, 235, 236
Moran, Dolores 124, 177
More Than Tongue Can Tell 128
Morgan, Ann 116
Morgan, Dennis 41, 116, 121, 122, 125, 126, 135, 147, 148, 150, 162, 177, 199, 200, 203, 216, 218, 233, 234, 236
Morgan, Helen 102, 109
Morgan, J.P. 117
Morgan, Michele 150
Morgan, Ralph 76
Morning's at Seven 29
Morris, Chester 88
Morris, Wayne 8, 37, 132, 133, 180, 214, 231, 232
Mother Cabrini 187
Mother Carey's Chickens 110, 111
Mountbatten, Lord and Lady 103
Mourning Becomes Electra 27, 28
Mousie, Nina 192
Mrs. Bumpstead-Leigh 55
Mrs. Gibbons' Boys 81
Mrs. Miniver 24, 41
Mrs. Wiggs of the Cabbage Patch 192
Muir, Jean 93
Mullican, Lorenzo A. 130, 131, 139
Muni, Paul 35, 38, 76, 78, 96
Murder at the Vanities 192
Murder on the Orient Express 48
Murder, She Wrote 128, 152, 188
Murphy, George 8, 147
My Bill 95, 96
My Boys Are Good Boys 170
My Cousin Rachel 67
My Favorite Spy 232
My Forbidden Past 205, 206
My Girl Friday 4
My Love Came Back 61, 135, 232
My Man Godfrey 230
My Mother's Keeper 49
My Past 4
My Reputation 241
My Three Sons 242
My Wild Irish Rose 116, 125, 126
The Mysterious Doctor 176
Mystery House 194
Mystery of the Wax Museum 77

Nagel, Conrad 33, 34
Naish Airflyte Theater 12
The Naked Genius 9, 10
The Naked Jungle 183
Nancy Drew, Reporter 142, 143
The Nanny 48
Nanny and the Professor 170
Nash, Edith 202
Nash, Ogden 45
National Velvet 123
Naughty But Nice 195

Navy, Blue and Gold 8
Navy Blues 197, 214
Navy Nurse 121
Nazimova, Alla 27, 163
Neal, Patricia 181, 220
Neame, Ronald 185
Neese, Bob 202
Neeson, Liam 123
Negri, Pola 94, 103
Negulesco, Jean 144, 164, 235, 236
Nelson, Gene 222
Nelson, Harmon O. 33–35, 37, 38
Nelson, Ozzie 111
Never Fear (aka *The Young Lovers*) 166
Never Say Goodbye 179
Newman, Paul 28, 221
Nichols, Dudley 28
Nielsen, Leslie 206
Night and Day 218, 219, 221, 233
The Night Before Christmas 232
A Night for Crime 81
Night Nurse 4
The Night of January Sixteenth 213
The Night of 1,000 Stars 224
Night of the Iguana 46, 47
Nightmare Alley 11, 14
Nimitz, Adm. Chester 163
Niven, David 169, 195, 236
No, No, Nanette (1970 Broadway revival) 103, 113
No, No, Nanette (road company) 112, 113
Nobody's Fool 79
Nolan, Lloyd 136, 214, 222
Noon Wine 70
Nora Prentiss 203
Nordstrom, Clarence 106
Norris, Edward 193, 194
North and South Book II 70
Northwest Stampede 151
Not as a Stranger 68
Not Wanted 165, 166
A Notorious Affair 89
The Notorious Sophie Lang 192
Novak, Kim 81, 185
Novello, Ivor 156
Now, Voyager 41, 43
Nugent, Elliott 151

Oakie, Jack 89, 97, 159, 197
Ober, Philip 9
Oberon, Merle 40
O'Brien, Edmond 168, 169, 221
O'Brien, George 125
O'Brien, Pat 8, 57, 80, 95, 193–196
O'Connell, Patricia 29
O'Connor, Carroll 177
O'Connor, Una 59, 196
O'Donnell, Spike 78
Odd Man In 206, 207
Odets, Clifford 62
Of Human Bondage (1934) 35–37, 43, 148, 178, 179, 219
Of Human Bondage (1946) 178, 179, 219
Off the Record 8

The Office Wife 4
Oland, Warner 93
Olcott, Rita 125
Old Acquaintance 41, 42, 62, 177
The Old Maid (film) 38, 39, 41, 62, 96, 216
The Old Maid (play) 57
Olsen, Moroni 19, 20
On Dangerous Ground 168
On the Loose 168
On the Spot 76
One Last Fling 220
One More Tomorrow 203, 218, 233
One Rainy Afternoon 158
One Way Passage 91, 92
O'Neal, Patrick 46
O'Neill, Barbara 39
O'Neill, Eugene 27, 80
The Opposite Sex 12
Orry-Kelly 37, 195
Orsatti, Vic 213
Osborn, Paul 29
Osborne, Robert 31, 49, 54, 62, 68, 71, 170, 171
The Oscar 187
O'Shea, Granny 155
O'Sullivan, Maureen 14, 231
Other Men's Women 4
Ouspenskaya, Maria 23, 197
Out of the Fog 160
Out of the Past 116
Outrage 167, 170
The Outlaw Queen 127
Outward Bound 177
The Overtons 81

Page, Gale 133, 135
Paige, Janis 2, 150, 178
The Painted Veil 185, 186
Pal, George 183
Pal Joey 188
Pallette, Eugene 35, 59, 90, 145
Panic Button 187
Parachute Jumper 34
The Paradine Case 237
Paramount on Parade 89
Paris in Spring 158
The Park Avenue Story 187
Parker, Eleanor 1, 2, 121, 164, 175–190, 216, 219, 220
Parker, Jean 77
Parker, Lester K. 175
Parker, Lew 122
Parks, Larry 112
Parsons, Louella 11, 184, 231, 236, 239
Passion Flower 90
Pasteur, Louis 117
The Patient in Room 18 194
Patrick, Lee 180
Paxinou, Katina 28
Payment on Demand 44
Payne, John 231
Peck, Gregory 127, 234
Peckinpah, Sam 170
Penny Arcade 4
Peppard, George 186

Pepper, Jack 162
Perelman, Laura 232
Perelman, S.J. 232
The Perfect Specimen 7
Perry Mason 127
The Personality Kid 78
Pete Kelly's Blues 136
Peter Gunn 221
Peter Ibbetson 158
Peters, Roberta 222
The Petrified Forest 36, 122
Petticoat Junction 13
Peyton Place 186
The Philadelphia Story 120, 133
Phone Call from a Stranger 44
The Phynx 14, 112, 113
A Piano for Mrs. Cimino 49
Picerni, Paul 13, 169, 170, 241
Pickford, Mary 158
Pidgeon, Walter 97
Pierson, Louise Randall 122
Pillow to Post 164
Pistols and Petticoats 207
Pittney, Richard 22
Pitts, ZaSu 5, 108, 141
Plain and Fancy 221
Platinum 216, 223
Play Girl 97
Playhouse 90 12
A Pocketful of Miracles 46
Police Story 152
Polito, Sol 59
Pollimer, Dick 193
Polly Preferred 87
Pollyanna 242
Pope Joan 14
Porter, Cole 158, 218
Porter, Katharine Anne 70
Porter, Dr. Langley 55
Portrait in Black 98
Poulton, Mabel 216
Powell, Dick 6–10, 12, 13, 57, 80, 106–109, 132, 169, 195, 221, 230
Powell, Ellen 8, 12, 14
Powell, Norman Scott (Barnes) 7, 8, 12–14
Powell, William 6, 35, 89–91, 126
Power, Tyrone 11, 79, 120
Powers, Mala 167, 171
Preminger, Otto 185
Prescription Murder 127
Presley, Elvis 82
Preston, Robert 82, 170
The Price 170
Price, Vincent 49
The Price Is Right 207
Pride of the Marines 177–179
Prince, Harold 222
Prince, William 164
Prince Igor 213
Prince of Arcadia 156
Princess O'Rourke 63, 232, 233
Prinz, "Dad" 228, 229
Prinz, LeRoy 229, 230
The Priscilla Lane Show 139
Private Detective 231
Private Hell 36 169, 170

The Private Lives of Elizabeth and Essex 39, 60, 96
The Producers 187
Proudly We Serve 121
Prouvost, Jean 68
Pryor, Roger 98
Public Enemy 5, 135, 160
Public Wedding 230
Puppy Love 87
The Pursuit of Happiness 192

Quai des Brumes 162
Qualen, John 161
Queen Christina 193
Quinn, Anthony 197

Rackin, Martin 181
Rafferty, Frances 211–213, 215, 217, 219, 221, 224
Raffin, Deborah 223
Raffles (1930 film) 33, 89
Raffles (1940 film) 60
Raft, George 160, 196
Rainer, Luise 141
Rains, Claude 23, 41–43, 58, 118, 121, 126, 133, 134, 197, 214
Ralston, Vera 152
Rambeau, Marjorie 232
The Ramparts We Watch 119
Rand, Ayn 220
Rapper, Irving 24, 42–44, 179, 203, 217, 237
Rathbone, Basil 59, 89, 94
Ratoff, Gregory 148
Rawhide 82
Rawlings, Marjorie Kinnan 234
Rawson, Mitch 194
Ray, Nicholas 151, 168
Raye, Martha 97, 98, 197
Raymond, Gene 3, 193
Ready for Love 158
Ready, Willing and Able 110, 230
Reagan, Maureen Elizabeth 232, 233, 236–239
Reagan, Michael Edward 233, 237, 239
Reagan, Nancy Davis 238, 239
Reagan, Ronald 19, 23, 125, 147, 166, 179, 197, 198, 219, 228, 231–233, 235, 236, 238, 239, 242
Recaptured 76
The Reckless Hour 4
Red Blood of Courage 193
Red Dust 196
Red Planet Mars 127
Redgrave, Michael 28
Reed, Mark 133
Reed, Philip 206
Reflected Glory 119
Reid, Beryl 48
Reinhardt, Max 56, 57, 67
Repeat Performance 150, 152
The Return of Dr. X 219
Return to Peyton Place 186
Return to Witch Mountain 48
Revere, Anne 123, 234
The Revolt of Mamie Stover 152

Reynolds, Debbie 46, 221
Reynolds, Joyce 149
Rhapsody in Blue 124, 149, 211, 218
Rich, Buddy 81
Richards, Thomas 74, 75
The Rich Are Always with Us 34
Richardson, Ralph 66
Richmond, Kane 231
Ride Beyond Vengeance 13
Ride the Pink Horse 125
Ridges, Stanley 134
Rigby, Harry 113
Right of Way 49
The Rise of Rosie O'Reilly 103
Riskin, Robert 77
Ritchard, Cyril 113
Ritt, Martin 216
Ritter, Thelma 44, 46, 81, 186
Road House 164
The Roar of the Crowd 215
The Roaring Twenties 134, 135
Robbins, Harold 48, 70
Robbins, Jerome 45
Robinson, Casey 23, 41, 133, 136
Robinson, Edward G. 1, 7, 37, 76, 92, 127, 135, 160, 186, 195, 232
Robson, Flora 161
Robson, May 77, 133, 136
The Rocky Mountain Mystery 193
Rogers, Betty 239
Rogers, Ginger 6, 39, 62, 102, 106, 109, 110, 130, 136, 147, 148, 162, 196
Rogers, Henry 65
Rogers, Roy 151
Rogers, Will, Jr. 239
Roland, Gilbert 68, 232
Roman, Ruth 181
Roman Holiday 63
Romance on the High Seas 92
Romeo and Juliet 67
Romero, Cesar 76, 120
Rooney, Mickey 179
Roosevelt, Elliott 122
Roosevelt, Franklin D. 108, 176
Roots II: The Next Generation 70
Rope 237
The Rope Dancers 13
Rosay, Francoise 184
The Rose Tattoo 185
Rosenfield, John 192
Rosenstein, Sophie 120, 121, 143, 176, 214
Roshanara 33
Rosher, Charles 234
Ross, Dr. Henry 29, 81–83
Rossellini, Roberto 238
Rossen, Robert 136, 161
Roughly Speaking 122
Rouverol, Aurania 57
Rouverol, Jean 57
Rowlands, Gena 48
The Royal Romance of Charles and Diana 70
Ruggles, Charlie 200
Runyon, Damon 46
Ruse, Ernest Percy 54

Russell, Gail 120
Russell, Jane 145, 151, 152
Russell, Rosalind 28, 97, 122, 170, 217, 222
Ryan, Alan, Jr. 87
Ryan, Robert 168
Ryan, Thomas Fortune 87
Ryan's Hope 29

Sabatini, Rafael 57, 182
Saboteur 137
The Saint in New York 161
St. John, Jill 242
Sakall, S.Z. 215
Saks, Sol 169
San Antonio 218
San Quentin 193
Sanders, George 44, 186
Santa Fe Trail 61
Santley, Joseph 123
Saratoga Trunk 198
Sarrazin, Michael 187
Satan Met a Lady 36
Saturday's Children 61, 135
Savoy Faire 156
Saxe, Dr. and Mrs. Irving H. 80
Scandal for Sale 76
Scandal Sheet 90
The Scapegoat 46
Scaramouche 182, 183
Scarlet Street 116
Schary, Dore 220
Schenck, Joseph M. 106
Schlitz Playhouse of Stars 152
Schmid, Al 177, 178
Schneider, Paul Miles 128
Schoenfeld, Bernard C. 180
Schulberg, B.P. 159
Scofield, Paul 68
Scola, Kathryn 216
Scorsese, Martin 224
Scott, Randolph 97, 151, 193
Scott, Col. Robert L., Jr. 122
Scott, Zachary 151, 204, 219
The Screaming Woman 70
Sea Devils 158
The Sea Wolf 160
Search for Beauty 156, 192
The Secret Bride 78
Secrets of an Actress 95
Seff, Manuel 107
Seiler, Lewis 134
Selwyn, Edgar 87
Selznick, David O. 22, 43, 59–62, 151
Selznick, Irene 62
Separate Rooms 80, 81
Serenade 204
Sergeant York 40, 144, 145
Sermak, Kathryn 49
Seven Brides for Seven Brothers 13
Seventeen 32
The Seventh Sin 185, 186
77 Sunset Strip 127
Seymour, James 107
Seymour, Jane 71, 243
Shadow of a Woman 123

Shall We Dance 110
Shamroy, Leon 159
Sharpe, Don 169
Shaw, George Bernard 67
Shaw, Irwin 160, 162
Shaw, Winifred 110
She Loved a Fireman 194
Shearer, Norma 41, 206
Sheldon, Gene 148
Sheridan, Ann 1, 2, 23, 25, 148, 156, 160, 162, 175, 191–210, 214, 216–218, 220, 232, 233
Sheridan, George, Jr. 191
Sheridan, George W. 191
Sheridan, Kitty 191, 192
Sheridan, Lulu Stewart Warren 191
Sheridan, Mabel 191
Sheridan, Pauline 191
Sheridan, Gen. Philip 191
Sherman, Harry 138
Sherman, Vincent 27, 41, 42, 96, 121, 147, 149, 152, 162–164, 171, 177, 203, 204, 206, 221
Sherry, William Grant 42–44
Sherwood, Robert E. 36
She's Dressed to Kill 188
Shine On Harvest Moon 200, 217
Shipmates Forever 109
Shirley, Anne 61, 110, 111, 135, 141
Show Girl 105
The Show of Shows 89
Shubert, Lee 118
Shuster, Joe 79
The Sidewalks of New York 104
Sidney, George 182
Sidney, Sylvia 29, 88, 193, 196
Siegel, Don 169, 170
Siegel, Joe 79
Silent Fear 127
The Silver Queen 138
Silver River 204
Silver Theater 81
Silvers, Phil 232
Sim, Alistair 237
Simms, Ginny 219
Simms, Larry 24
Simon, Neil 14
Simon, S. Sylvan 165
Simon and Simon 152
Sinatra, Frank 185, 186
Sing Me a Love Song 193
Singin' in the Rain 81
The Singing Marine 230
Sinners Holiday 4
Sirk, Douglas 206, 240
Sister Act 133
Sister Carrie 120
The Sisters 38
Skelton, Red 165
Skidding 75
Skinner, Frank 240, 241
The Skipper Surprised His Wife 151
The Sky's the Limit 147, 148
Skyward 49
Slaves 29
The Sleeping Tiger 221
Slim 214, 230

Small, Edward 161
Smart Blonde 79, 230
Smart Girl 158
Smarty 7
The Smiling Ghost 214
Smith, Alexander 211, 213
Smith, Alexis 1, 2, 26, 116, 125, 146, 149, 178, 179, 200, 203, 211–227, 233, 237
Smith, Betty 10
Smith, Dodie 58
Smith, Gladys 211–213
Smith, Kate 147
Smith, Kent 203, 235
Smith, Leonard 234
The Snake Pit 54, 65, 66
Snowed Under 79
So Big (1932) 34
So Big (1953) 239, 240
Soldiers in White 176
Solid South 33
Something for the Boys 9, 12
The Son of Monte Cristo 161
Sondheim, Stephen 222
Song of Surrender 126
Sonny Boy 105
Sons 'o Guns 7
Sothern, Ann 9, 49, 69, 123
The Sound of Music 187
South of St. Louis 220
Southside 1-1000 126
Spaak, Catherine 47
Sparks, Ned 6, 77
Special Agent 36
Speed 176
Spellbound 64
Spelling, Aaron 49
Spewack, Bella 119
Spewack, Sam 119
Spigelgass, Leonard 136
Split Second 221
Spy Ring 231
Stack, Robert 46
Stage Door 21
Stage Fright 236, 237
Stage Struck 7, 230
Stahl, John M. 194
Stallion Road 125, 179, 219
Stander, Lionel 49
The Stand-In 8
Stanwyck, Barbara 4, 24, 116, 161, 219, 239
The Star 44, 45, 179
Star Dust 143
Starlift 238
State of the Union 86, 98
Stay Away, Joe 13
Steel Against the Sky 214, 215
Steel Town 206
Steiner, Max 37, 133, 220, 235
Stella 205, 206
Stella Dallas 238
Stephenson, James 39
Stevens, Craig 200, 214–218, 220–224
Stevens, George 81
Stevens, Mark 65

Stevenson, Margot 232
Stewart, James 8, 49, 54, 60, 62, 235
Stewart, Katty 87
Stockwell, Dean 242
Stolen Holiday 94
A Stolen Life 43
Stompanato, Johnny 48
Stone, Andrew 138
Stone, Lewis 4, 79, 109
Storm at Daybreak 92
Storm Center 45, 46
The Story of Will Rogers 239
Stranded 93
The Strange Intruder 169
Strangers in Love 90
Strangers: The Story of a Mother and a Daughter 48
The Strawberry Blonde 61, 197
Street of Chance 89
A Streetcar Named Desire 12, 67, 182, 238
Strictly Dishonorable 33, 76
A String of Beads 82
Stuart, Gloria 57, 91, 109
Studio One 12
Sturges, John 183
Sturges, Preston 204
Sullavan, Margaret 9, 179
Sullivan, Barry 44, 68, 220, 237
Summer Brave 222, 223
Summer Magic 111
Summerville, Slim 34
Sunburn 188
Sunset Boulevard 44, 181
Support Your Local Gunfighter 14
Support Your Local Sheriff 14
Surfside Six 127
Susan and God 22
The Suspect 218
Suspicion 40, 61, 123, 219
Swanson, Gloria 181
The Swarm 70
Sweetheart of the Campus 111
Sweetland, Sally 149
Sydney, Basil 87

Tail Spin 231
Take Me to Town 206
Talbot, Lyle 78, 80
Talbot, Stephen 78
Talk of the Town 81
Tallichet, Margaret 38
Talman, William 168
Tamiroff, Akim 187
Taradash, Daniel 45, 46
Tarkington, Booth 32
Tarnish 4
Tashlin, Frank 12
Tashman, Lilyan 90
Taylor, Don 238
Taylor, Robert 81, 142, 183, 231
Tea and Sympathy 183
Teasdale, Verree 94
Tennyson, Lord Alfred 58
Terry, Philip 233
Thank Your Lucky Stars 41, 63, 148, 163, 199, 216

That Certain Woman 37
That Girl 13
That Hagen Girl 179
That Lady 68
That Man from Tangier 28
Theater 98
There's Always a Woman 8
There's That Woman Again 8
They Died With Their Boots On 22, 62, 176
They Drive by Night 125, 159, 160, 191, 196, 214
They Made Me a Criminal 195
They Shoot Horses, Don't They? 112
Thieves Fall Out 144
Thimig, Helene 122
The Third Day 75
The 39 Steps 137
This Could Be the Night 12
This Happy Feeling 221
This Is the Army 147
This Is Your Life 222
This Land is Mine 25
This 'n That 49
This Thing Called Love 4
Thomas, Bill 241
Thompson, Marshall 126
Thorndyke, Dame Sybil 237
The Thoroughbreds 170
Thorpe, Jerry 243
Three Cheers for the Irish 135
The Three Faces of Eve 12, 185
Three Girls About Town 9
Three Guys Named Mike 237
Three Men on a Horse 7
Three on a Match 5, 76, 194
Three Secrets 181, 187
Thurber, James 145
Tierney, Lawrence 138
The Tiger and the Pussycat 187
Tiger by the Tail 82
The Time of the Cuckoo 12
The Time of Your Life 206
Tip Toes 103
Tissot, Felix 158
To Each His Own 54, 64, 65, 67, 68, 235, 238
To Tell the Truth 207
Toaduff, Jackie 114
Toaduff, Roy 114
Tobias, George 63, 163, 199
Todd, Mike, Jr. 11
Todd, Mike, Sr. 9–12
Todd, Richard 236
Toeplitz, Ludovico 36
Tone, Franchot 36, 62, 206, 221, 237
Too Much, Too Soon 215
Too Young to Know 149
Toomey, Regis 7, 90, 232
Topper 9
Topper Returns 9
Torchy Blane in Chinatown 80
Torchy Gets Her Man 79
Torchy Plays with Dynamite 231
Torchy Runs for Mayor 80
Torrid Zone 196

Totter, Audrey 216, 220, 238
Tough Guys 224
Tovarich 94
Tover, Leo 66
Tracy, Spencer 12, 78, 196, 234
Trahey, Jane 170
Transgression 90
The Traveling Saleslady 7, 79
Travers, Bill 185
Travers, Henry 121
Travis, Richard 198
The Treasure of the Sierra Madre 204
A Tree Grows in Brooklyn (film) 10, 11
A Tree Grows in Brooklyn (musical play) 12
The Trespasser 37
Trevor, Claire 167, 168, 186
The Trial of Mary Dugan 4
Trilling, Steve 214
Trouble in Paradise 91, 92
The Trouble with Angels 170
Tucker, Forrest 151, 179
Tucker, Sophie 219
Tugboat Annie 232
Tugboat Annie Sails Again 232
Tune, Tommy 223
Turn Back the Clock 152
Turner, Lana 8, 48, 49, 81, 186, 195, 242
Turney, Catherine 43, 164, 178
The Turning Point 221
Turpin, Ben 5
Twelvetrees, Helen 4
24 Hours 90, 92
20,000 Years in Sing Sing 34, 196
The Twilight Zone 13, 169, 170
Twin Beds 81
Two Girls on Broadway 8
Two Guys from Milwaukee 150
The Two Mrs. Carrolls 211, 219
Two Thoroughbreds 142, 143
Two's Company 45

Uncle Tom's Cabin 74
Under Capricorn 237
Undercover Girl 220
The Unfaithful 204
Union Depot 5
The U.S. Steel Hour 12, 28
The Untouchables 13, 170

Vaccaro, Brenda 223
Valentino 181, 182
Valentino, Rudolph 26, 181
Valiant Lady 28
Vallee, Rudy 195
Vallery-Radot, Madame Marie-Louise 117
Valley of the Dolls 223
Valley of the Kings 184
Van, Bobby 113
Van Druten, John 41, 75, 98, 179
Van Fleet, Jo 185
Vance, Vivian 238
Vanished 187

Varsity Show 132
Venus 88
Vera-Ellen 216
The Very Thought of You 121, 126, 177, 178
Vice Squad 90
Vickers, Martha 124, 179
Vidor, Charles 161
Vidor, King 43, 92, 234
Villella, Edward 188
Vincent, Allan 91
Vinson, Gary 207
Violence 27
The Virgin Queen 45
The Virginian 13
The Virtuous Sin 89, 90
The Voice of the Turtle 175, 179, 180

Wagon Train 46
The Wagons Roll at Night 144
Wald, Jerry 136, 161, 162, 231, 236, 238
Wald, Malvin 165–167
Walker, Nancy 13
Walker, Robert 151
Walker, Stuart 87
Wallace, Edgar 76
Wallis, Hal 147
Walsh, Raoul 62, 124, 125, 134, 143, 160, 185, 215, 217
Wanger, Walter 8, 40, 142, 195
Ward, Mary Jane 65
Waring, Fred 131, 132
Warner, Ann 60
Warner, Harry 95
Warner, Jack L. 1, 4, 6, 23, 26, 31, 35–38, 43, 60, 62, 63, 77, 80, 86, 94–96, 104, 120, 121, 125, 133, 141, 144, 146, 148, 159, 160, 162, 176, 177, 179, 197, 200, 202–204, 214, 235, 236
Warner, Jack, Jr. 144
Warning Shot 187
Warren, Gloria 97
Warren, Harry 107
Washington, George 119
Washington Square 66
Wasserman, Lew 27
Watch on the Rhine 41
Watcher in the Woods 48
Waterhole No. 3 13
Way Back Home 34
The Web and the Rock 98
Webb, Clifton 12, 242
Webb, Millard 88
Weill, Kurt 149
The Well-Groomed Bride 64
Welles, Carole 207
Welles, Orson 159
Wellman, William 159
Welsh, Bill 181
We're in the Money 7, 79
Werker, Alfred 150, 159
Wertenbaker, Lael Tucker 68
Westmore, Perc 42, 145
Whale, James 58
The Whales of August 49

Wharton, Edith 89, 123
What a Life 175
What Every Woman Knows 65
Whatever Happened to Baby Jane? 34, 47, 69
Wheeler, Bert 111
When the Daltons Rode 97
Where Do We Go from Here? 148–150
Where Love Has Gone 48
While the City Sleeps 169
Whiplash 220
White, Irving 118
The White Angel 94
White Mama 49
Whiting, Jack 81
Whoopee 105
Whorf, Richard 136
Who's Afraid of Virginia Woolf? 48
Wicked Stepmother 49, 50
Wickes, Mary 198
Wide-Open Faces 231
Widmark, Richard 164
Wife Wanted 98
Wiggins, Kate Douglas 110
Wilde, Cornel 164
Wilder, Billy 233
Will Success Spoil Rock Hunter? 12
William, Warren 5, 6, 77, 78, 93, 106
Williams, Emlyn 42, 123
Williams, Robin 137
Williams, Tennessee 46, 237
Willis, Nat 119, 120, 128
Willson, Meredith 222
Wilson, Marie 200
Wiman, Dwight Deere 87

Winchell, Walter 45, 108
Windy Hill 98
Wine, Women and Horses 194
Wing, Toby 78, 106
Wings for the Eagle 199
Wings of the Navy 59
Winninger, Charles 61
Winter Carnival 142, 195
Winter Meeting 43
Winters, Shelley 47
Wise, Robert 12, 181, 187, 239, 240
With the Marines at Tarawa 163
Withers, Grant 4
Withers, Jane 143, 146
The Woman and the Hunter 206
The Woman He Loved 71
Woman in Hiding 166
The Woman in White 180, 219, 220
The Woman Inside 14
The Women (1939 film) 12, 206, 222
The Women (1973 Broadway production) 222
Women Are Like That 95
Women in the Wind 96
Women's Prison 169
Wonder Bar 93
The Working Man 35
Worth, Constance 198
Wood, Natalie 12, 238
Wood, Sam 23, 60, 198
Woodford, Gwen 194
Woods, Donald 122
Woods, William 25
Woodward, Joanne 185
Woolley, Monty 40, 162, 198
The World in His Arms 127

The World of Carl Sandburg 46
Wray, Fay 77
Wright, Teresa 40
Wyatt, Jane 169
Wyler, William 37–40, 66, 182
Wyman, Ernest 229
Wyman, Jane 2, 12, 66, 79, 148, 186, 200, 203, 211, 216–219, 221, 228–246
Wynn, Keenan 44, 188
Wyoming Mail 220

Yankee Doodle Dandy 145–147
Yates, Alonso Robert 116, 117
Yates, Herbert J. 152, 206
The Yearling 228, 234, 235
Yellow 33
Yes, My Darling Daughter 133, 134
York, Alvin 144, 145
York, Gracie 144, 145
You Never Can Tell 87
Young, Collier 164–169
Young, Gig 24, 179, 220
Young, Loretta 4, 69, 78
Young, Robert 8
Young, Roland 9, 91
Young, Terence 68
Young as You Feel 143
Young Man with a Horn 136
The Young Philadelphians 221
You're in the Army Now 232

Zanuck, Darryl F. 11, 65, 232
Zefferelli, Franco 14
Ziegfeld, Florenz 105
Zindel, Paul 14

www.ingramcontent.com/pod-product-compliance
Lightning Source LLC
Chambersburg PA
CBHW081546300426
44116CB00015B/2780